Frequently Used Notations
Foundations of Finance, Sixth Edition

APR = annual percentage rate

APY = annual percentage yield

β = beta

DFN_t = discretionary financing needs for period t

$EBIT$ = earnings before interest and taxes

$EVA^{\circledR}$ = Economic Value Added

FCF_t = the annual free cash flow in time period t

FV_i = the future value of $1 at the end of year i

$FVIFA_{i,n}$ = the future value interest factor of a $1 annuity at i percent for n years

$FVIF_{i,n}$ = the future value interest factor of $1 at i percent in n years

IO = the initial outlay

IRR = internal rate of return

K_{wacc} = weighted average cost of capital

K_{cs} = cost of common stock financing

K_d = cost of debt financing

$MIRR$ = the modified internal rate of return

n = the number of years until payment will be received or during which compounding occurs

NPV = net present value

$OROA$ = operating return on assets

P = current selling price of a security

PI = profitability index

PMT = the annuity payment deposited or received at the end of each year

PV = the present value of a future sum of money

$PVIF_{i,n}$ = the present value interest factor of $1 received in year n at i percent

$PVIFA_{i,n}$ = the present value interest factor of a $1 annuity at i percent for n years

ROA = return on assets

σ = standard deviation

SIXTH EDITION

Foundations of Finance

THE LOGIC AND PRACTICE OF FINANCIAL MANAGEMENT

Sixth Edition

Foundations of Finance

THE LOGIC AND PRACTICE OF FINANCIAL MANAGEMENT

ARTHUR J. KEOWN

Virginia Polytechnic Institute and State University
R. B. Pamplin Professor of Finance

JOHN D. MARTIN

Baylor University
Professor of Finance
Carr P. Collins Chair in Finance

J. WILLIAM PETTY

Baylor University
Professor of Finance
W. W. Caruth Chair in Entrepreneurship

DAVID F. SCOTT, JR.

University of Central Florida
Holder, Phillips-Schenck Chair in American
Private Enterprise and Professor of Finance

PEARSON

Prentice
Hall

Upper Saddle River, New Jersey 07458

Library of Congress Cataloging-in-Publication Data

Keown, Arthur J.
    Foundations of finance : the logic and practice of financial management / Arthur J.
Keown, John D. Martin, J. William Petty.—6th ed.
        p. cm.
    Prev. ed. entered under title: Foundations of finance.
    Includes bibliographical references and index.
    ISBN–13: 978–0–13–233922–3
    1. Corporations—Finance. I. Martin, John D., 1945- II. Petty, J. William, 1942- III.
Title
    HG4026.F67 2007
    658.15—dc22   2007017551

AVP/Executive Editor: Mark Pfaltzgraff
Developmental Manager: Ashley Santora
Project Manager: Kerri Tomasso
Editorial Assistant: Kelly Loftus
Development Editor: Amy Ray
Media Project Manager: Ashley Lulling
Marketing Manager: Jodi Bassett
Marketing Assistant: Ian Gold
Associate Director, Production Editorial: Judy Leale
Managing Editor: Cynthia Zonneveld
Production Editor: Melissa Feimer
Permissions Coordinator: Charles Morris
Associate Director, Manufacturing: Vinnie Scelta
Manufacturing Buyer: Michelle Klein
Design/Composition Manager: Christy Mahon
Senior Art Director: Janet Slowik

Cover Design: Liz Harasymczuk
Interior Design: Liz Harasymczuk
Cover Photo: Richard Nowitz/National
  Geographic/Getty Images, Inc.
Director, Image Resource Center:
  Melinda Patelli
Manager, Rights and Permission: Zina Arabia
Manager, Visual Research: Beth Brenzel
**Manager, Cover Visual Research &
  Permissions:** Karen Sanatar
Image Permission Coordinator: Ang'john Ferreri
Photo Researcher: Melinda Alexander
Full-Service Project Management: Carlisle
  Communications, LTD
Printer/Binder: Quebecor World Dubuque
Typeface: 9.75/12 Janson Text

Credits and acknowledgments borrowed from other sources and reproduced, with permission, in this textbook appear on appropriate page within text.

Photo Credits

p. 4, Bill Aron/PhotoEdit Inc.; p. 30, Ethan Miller/Getty Images, Inc.; p. 60, Michel Porro/Getty Images Inc.; p. 94, Robert Henry Lendrum; p. 130, Jerry Driendl/Getty Images, Inc.; p. 170, Alison Parks/Whitfield Photography; p. 202, Chuck Nacke/Woodfin Camp & Associates; p. 228, R. Magunia/Joker/SV-Bilderdienst/The Image Works; p. 258, David Young-Wolff/PhotoEdit Inc.; p. 296, Andy Rain/Bloomberg News/Landov LLC; p. 332, Peter Morgan/REUTERS/Landov LLC; p. 374, Pascal/Redux Pictures; p. 414, Pete McArthur/Veer Inc.; p. 438, Bill Hogan/Chicago Tribune/NewsCom; p. 460, Dell Computer Corp./Bloomberg News/Landov LLC; p. 486, Lourens Smak/Alamy Images Royalty Free; p. 518, Mark Richards/PhotoEdit Inc.

Microsoft® and Windows® are registered trademarks of the Microsoft Corporation in the U.S.A. and other countries. Screen shots and icons reprinted with permission from the Microsoft Corporation. This book is not sponsored or endorsed by or affiliated with the Microsoft Corporation.

Pearson Education LTD.
Pearson Education Singapore, Pte. Ltd
Pearson Education, Canada, Ltd
Pearson Education–Japan

Pearson Education Australia PTY, Limited
Pearson Education North Asia Ltd
Pearson Educación de Mexico, S.A. de C.V.
Pearson Education Malaysia, Pte. Ltd

10 9 8 7 6 5 4 3

ISBN-13: 978-0-13-233922-3
ISBN-10: 0-13-233922-6

ABOUT THE AUTHORS

ARTHUR J. KEOWN is the R. B. Pamplin Professor of Finance at Virginia Polytechnic Institute and State University. He received his bachelor's degree from Ohio Wesleyan University, his M.B.A. from the University of Michigan, and his doctorate from Indiana University. An award-winning teacher, he is a member of the Academy of Teaching Excellence; has received five Certificates of Teaching Excellence at Virginia Tech, the W. E. Wine Award for Teaching Excellence, and the Alumni Teaching Excellence Award; and in 1999 received the Outstanding Faculty Award from the State of Virginia. Professor Keown is widely published in academic journals. His work has appeared in *The Journal of Finance*, the *Journal of Financial Economics*, the *Journal of Financial and Quantitative Analysis*, *The Journal of Financial Research*, the *Journal of Banking and Finance*, *Financial Management*, the *Journal of Portfolio Management*, and many others. In addition to *Foundations of Finance*, two other of his books are widely used in college finance classes all over the country—*Basic Financial Management* and *Personal Finance: Turning Money into Wealth*. Professor Keown is a Fellow of the Decision Sciences Institute, a member of the Board of Directors of the Financial Management Association, and former head of the finance department at Virginia Tech. In addition, he recently served as the co-editor of *The Journal of Financial Research* for six and a half years and as the co-editor of the Financial Management Association's *Survey and Synthesis* series for six years. He lives with his wife and two children in Blacksburg, Virginia, where he collects original art from *Mad Magazine*.

JOHN D. MARTIN is Professor of Finance and the holder of the Carr P. Collins Chair of Finance at Baylor University. Dr. Martin came to Baylor University in 1998 from the University of Texas at Austin where he taught for nineteen years and was the Margaret and Eugene McDermott Centennial Professor of Finance. He teaches corporate finance and his research interests are in corporate governance, the evaluation of firm performance, and the design of incentive compensation plans. Dr. Martin has published widely in academic journals including the *Journal of Financial Economics*, *The Journal of Finance*, *Journal of Monetary Economics*, *Journal of Financial and Quantitative Analysis*, *Journal of Corporate Finance*, *Financial Management*, and *Management Science*. His work has also appeared in a number of professional publications including *Directors and Boards*, the *Financial Analysts' Journal*, the *Journal of Portfolio Management*, and the *Journal of Applied Corporate Finance*. In addition to this book Dr. Martin is co-author of nine books including *Financial Management* (9th ed., Prentice Hall), *The Theory of Finance* (Dryden Press), *Financial Analysis* (2nd ed., McGraw Hill), and *Value Based Management* (Harvard Business School Press), and he is currently writing a book on interest rate modeling. He serves on the editorial boards of eight journals and has delivered executive education programs for a number of firms including Shell Chemical, Shell E&P, Texas Instruments, and The Associates.

J. WILLIAM PETTY is Professor of Finance and the W. W. Caruth Chairholder of Entrepreneurship at Baylor University. He holds a Ph.D. and M.B.A. from the University of Texas at Austin, and a B.S. from Abilene Christian University. He has taught at Virginia Tech University and Texas Tech University, and served as the dean of the business school at Abilene Christian University. His research interests include the creation and financing of high-potential entrepreneurial firms and shareholder value-based management. He is also the Director of the Entrepreneurship Program at Baylor University. He has served as the co-editor for the *Journal of Financial Research* and the editor of the *Journal of Entrepreneurial and Small Business Finance*. He has published in a number of finance journals and is the co-author of two leading corporate finance textbooks, *Basic Financial Management* and *Foundations of Finance*, and co-author of a widely used text, *Small Business Management*. Dr. Petty serves on the board of a publicly traded oil and gas firm. He has also served as a subject matter expert on a best-practices study by the American Productivity and Quality Center on the topic of shareholder value-based management. He recently served on a research team for the Australian Department of Industry to study the feasibility of establishing a public equity market for small and medium-sized enterprises in Australia.

DAVID F. SCOTT JR. received his Ph.D. from the University of Florida, an M.B.A. from the University of Detroit, and a B.S.B.A. from the University of Akron. He holds the Phillips-Schenck Chair in American Private Enterprise, is Executive Director of the Dr. Phillips Institute for the Study of American Business Activity, and is Professor of Finance at the University of Central Florida. From 1977 to 1982 he was Area Coordinator, then Head, Department of Finance, Insurance, and Business Law at Virginia Polytechnic Institute and State University. During 1985–1986 he was President of the Financial Management Association, an international group with 9,000 members. He was a member of the Board of Trustees of FMA from 1986 to 1993.

Dr. Scott is a member of the Board of Directors of CompBenefits Corporation, head-quartered in Atlanta, Georgia. He is a past member of the local Board of Directors of BankFIRST-Goldenrod (Florida), that specializes in commercial banking services for small businesses. He served on the Investment Policy Committee of the University of Central Florida Foundation for over 10 years. Dr. Scott is also past founding co-editor of the *Journal of Financial Research*, past associate editor for the *Akron Business and Economic Review*, and past associate editor for *Financial Management*. He is past president of the Southern Finance Association. In addition to *Foundations of Finance*, Dr. Scott is co-author of *Basic Financial Management, Cases in Finance*, and *Guide to Financial Analysis*. He is widely published in academic journals including *Financial Management, Engineering Economist, Journal of Financial and Quantitative Analysis, Business Economics*, and many others.

Dr. Scott's op-ed and research pieces have appeared in several leading outlets intended for consumer and practitioner audiences. These include *USA Today, The Miami Herald, The St. Petersburg Times, Florida Today, Orlando Sentinel*, and *Florida Trend*.

BRIEF CONTENTS

CONTENTS

CHAPTER 3

Understanding Financial Statements and Cash Flows   61

PART 2: THE VALUATION OF FINANCIAL ASSETS   128

Chapter 8

The Valuation and Characteristics of Stock 229

CHAPTER 11
The Cost of Capital   333

PART 4: CAPITAL STRUCTURE AND DIVIDEND POLICY   372

PART 5: WORKING-CAPITAL MANAGEMENT AND INTERNATIONAL BUSINESS FINANCE 436

PREFACE

In finance, our goal is to create wealth. This is done by providing customers with the best product and service possible, and it is the market response that determines whether we reach our goal. We are very proud of the market reaction to *Foundations of Finance*; the market's response has been overwhelming. With its success comes an even greater responsibility to deliver the finest possible textbook and supplementary package possible. We have done this with a two-pronged approach of refinement, based on users' comments, and of remaining the innovative leaders in the field, focusing on value-added innovations.

Foundations of Finance has gained the reputation for being "intuitive"—allowing the reader "to see the forest through the trees"—and "lively and easy to read." In the Sixth Edition of *Foundations of Finance*, we have tried to build on these strengths, introducing the latest concepts and developments in finance in a practical and intuitive manner.

PEDAGOGY THAT WORKS

This book provides students with a conceptual understanding of the financial decision-making process, rather than just an introduction to the tools and techniques of finance. For the student, it is all too easy to lose sight of the logic that drives finance and focus instead on memorizing formulas and procedures. As a result, students have a difficult time understanding the interrelationships among the topics covered. Moreover, later in life when the problems encountered do not match the textbook presentation, students may find themselves unprepared to abstract from what they learned. To overcome this problem, the opening chapter presents 10 underlying principles of finance, which serve as a springboard for the chapters and topics that follow. In essence, the student is presented with a cohesive, interrelated perspective from which future problems can be approached.

With a focus on the big picture, we provide an introduction to financial decision making rooted in current financial theory and in the current state of world economic conditions. This focus is perhaps most apparent in the attention given to the capital markets and their influence on corporate financial decisions. What results is an introductory treatment of a discipline rather than the treatment of a series of isolated problems that face the financial manager. The goal of this text is not merely to tech the tools of a discipline or trade but also to enable students to abstract what is learned to new and yet unforeseen problems—in short, to educate the student in finance.

TEN PRINCIPLES THAT FORM THE FOUNDATIONS OF FINANCIAL MANAGEMENT

Objective **4**

Explain the 10 principles that form the foundations of financial management.

To the first-time student of finance, the subject matter may seem like a collection of unrelated decision rules. This could not be further from the truth. In fact, our decision rules, and the logic that underlies them, spring from 10 simple principles that do not require knowledge of finance to understand. However, although it is not necessary to understand finance in order to understand these principles, it is necessary to understand these principles in order to understand finance. Keep in mind that although these principles may at first appear simple or even trivial, they provide the driving force behind all that follows. These principles weave together concepts and techniques presented in this text, thereby allowing us to focus on the logic underlying the practice of financial management.

Principle 1

The Risk–Return Trade-Off—We Won't Take On Additional Risk Unless We Expect to Be Compensated with Additional Return

At some point we have all saved some money. Why have we done this? The answer is simple: to expand our future consumption opportunities. We are able to invest those savings and earn a return on our dollars because some people would rather borrow money and forgo future consumption opportunities to consume more now. Maybe they're borrowing money to open a new business, or a company is borrowing money to build a new plant. Assuming there are a lot of different people who would like to use our savings, how do we decide where to put our money?

INNOVATIONS AND DISTINCTIVE FEATURES IN THE SIXTH EDITION

Part-opening Interviews with Business Professionals

These give students in-the-trenches insights into the application of theory to practice in the real world and provide perspective for *anyone* who is planning a career in business.

Real-World Opening Vignettes

Each chapter begins with a story about a current, real-world company faced with a financial decision related to the chapter material that follows. These vignettes have been carefully prepared to stimulate student interest in the topic to come and can be used as a lecture tool to provoke class discussion.

New and Improved Problem Sets

The end-of-chapter study problem sets have been improved and expanded to allow for a wider range of student problems.

New "Web Works" Internet Problems

Internet problems have been introduced at the end of each chapter. These problems direct the student to Internet sites that allow them to explore financial issues and solve financial problems using the Web.

Across the Hall

MANAGEMENT AND SELECTION CRITERIA FOR AN INVESTMENT BANKER

Comments and Procedure by David R. Klock, Ph.D.
Dr. David R. Klock is past CEO and currently chairman of the board of directors of CompBenefits Corporation, headquartered in Atlanta, Georgia. Dr. Klock holds a Ph.D. in finance from the University of Illinois and is a nationally known insurance economist. CompBenefits is a privately held national leader in providing a wide range of dental and vision insurance products. The firm's annual revenues are approximately $310 million. The firm continually works with venture capitalists who provide equity capital and access to debt capital in the nation's financial market system. Dr. Klock authored the following checklist that deals with selecting an investment banker within the context of seeking what are called "strategic buyers" by venture capital firms. Dr. Klock is highly familiar with the field, having spent time at the investment-banking firm of Goldman Sachs earlier in his career.

1. Competency
   - Technical skills/resources of total team
   - People skills/resources of total team
   - Knowledge of the firm
   - Knowledge of key potential buyers and their needs/ability to pay
2. Connections
   - Recent firm history of working with potential buyers
   - Individual banker's recent history of working with key potential buyers
   - Reputation of investment-banking firm with potential buyers
   - Intangibles
3. Conviction on Enterprise Value of the Firm
   - Valuation range and strength of valuation methods/matrix
   - Ability to strongly tell the firm's story and to be heard/understood by key individuals at potential buyers
   - Level of commitment to this transaction within the banking firm

"Across the Hall" Boxes

This box draws on professionals and their experiences from marketing, management, and accounting to illustrate how the material being presented pertains to what they do.

Use of an Integrated Learning System

The text is organized around the learning objectives that appear at the beginning of each chapter to provide the instructor and student with an easy-to-use integrated learning system. Numbered icons identifying each objective appear next to the related material throughout the text and in the summary, allowing easy location of material related to each objective.

"Can You Do It?" and "How Did You Do?"

The text provides examples for the students to work at the conclusion of each major section of a chapter, which we call, "Can You Do It?" followed by "How Did You Do?" several pages later in the text. This tool provides an essential ingredient to the building-block approach to the material that we use.

Can You Do It?

SOLVING FOR THE REAL RATE OF INTEREST

Your banker just called you up and has offered you the chance to invest your savings for one year at a quoted rate of 10 percent. You also saw on the news that the inflation rate is 6 percent. What is the real rate of interest you would be earning if you made the investment? (The solution can be found on page xxx.)

How Did You Do?

SOLVING FOR THE REAL RATE OF INTEREST

Nominal or quoted = rate of interest		real rate of interest	+	inflation rate	+	product of the real rate of interest and the rate inflation
k	=	k^*	+	IRP	+	$(k^* \times IRP)$
.10	=	k^*	+	.06	+	$.06k^*$
.04	=	$1.06k^*$				
k^*	=	.0377	=	3.77%		

"Did You Get It?"

At the end of most major sections, this too highlights the key ideas just presented and allows students to test their understanding of the material.

Integrated Examples

These provide students with real-world examples to help them apply the concepts presented in each chapter.

Did You Get It? ....

1. Explain the difference between (a) public offerings and private placements, (b) primary markets and secondary markets, (c) the money market and the capital market, and (d) organized security exchanges and over-the-counter markets.
2. Name the benefits derived from the existence of stock exchanges.
3. Briefly describe what is meant by the "NASDAQ system."

➤ EXAMPLE

If we place $1,000 in a savings account paying 5 percent interest compounded annually, how much will our account accrue to in 10 years? Substituting $PV = \$1,000$, $i = 5$ percent, and $n = 10$ years into equation (5-6), we get

$$FV_n = PV(1 + i)^n$$
$$= \$1,000(1 + .05)^{10}$$
$$= \$1,000(1.62889)$$
$$= \$1,628.89$$

Thus, at the end of 10 years we will have $1,628.89 in our savings account.

Ethics in Financial Management

THE TYCO SCANDAL. WHEN IT COMES TO ETHICS, LEADERSHIP MATTERS

Tyco International is a multinational conglomerate with business units selling products in the electronic-component, health care, fire safety, security, and fluid-control industries. In 1992, Dennis Kozlowski became CEO of Tyco, and for the next 10 years, the company went on an aggressive acquisitions spree. By some accounts, the firm acquired over 1,000 companies under Kozlowski's leadership, including businesses such as ADT Security and Curad and divisions of Siemens, Raytheon, and AT&T.

Throughout the 1990s, Tyco's earnings improved steadily each year, and Kozlowski was touted as one of the best managers in the country. Most investors considered Tyco's stock to be a blue chip, in fact. However, after it came to light in 2002 that Tyco's success was an illusion generated by the way in which the firm reported its financial earnings, the company's shares plummeted: At one point the shares had been trading for $60 apiece. After the scandal broke, the trading price dropped to just $8.

Kozlowski and Tyco's chief financial officer at the time, Mark Swartz, were later charged with stealing $170 million from the company and pocketing $430 million from fraudulent sales of Tyco's stock. Although both men were ultimately convicted, neither admitted wrongdoing.

Fortunately for its investors and employees, Tyco recovered from the scandal. In late 2006, its shares sold for $30—still only half of what they had once sold for, but definitely up from their all-time low. Tyco's current managers have vowed, via a new company mission statement, to base their leadership on integrity and ensure accountability at levels within the organization. Unfortunately, almost all managers embroiled in scandals have crafted missions statements such as these for their companies. Obviously, what counts is what you do, not what you say.

So what can we learn from the Tyco debacle? Much can be said for having good managerial controls and processes in to place to reduce the chances of fraud and unethical behavior. But if a company's leaders are determined to act unethically, no controls will prevent this from happening. Thus, it's paramount for the firm's current managers genuinely commit to ethical standards, which will, ultimately, permeate down through the entire organization.

Extensive Coverage of Ethics

Ethics is covered as a core principle and "Ethics in Financial Management" boxes appear throughout. These show students that ethical behavior is doing the right thing and that ethical dilemmas are everywhere in finance.

Remember Your Principles

These in-text inserts appear throughout to allow the student to take time out and reflect on the meaning of the material just presented. The use of these inserts, coupled with the use of the 10 principles, keeps the student focused on the interrelationships and motivating factors behind the concepts.

▓ *Remember your Principles*

Our first principle, **Principle 1: The Risk–Return Trade-Off—We Won't Take On Additional Risk Unless We Expect to Be Compensated with Additional Return**, established the fundamental risk–return trade-offs that govern the financial markets. We are now trying to provide you with an understanding of the kinds of risks that are rewarded in the risk–return trade-off presented in **Principle 1**.

Comprehensive
End-of-Chapter Problems

A comprehensive problem appears at the end of almost every chapter, covering all the major topics included in that chapter. This comprehensive problem can be used as a lecture or review tool by the professor. For the students, it provides an opportunity to apply all the concepts presented within the chapter in a realistic setting, thereby strengthening their understanding of the material.

Mini Case

The final stage in the interview process for an assistant financial analyst at Caledonia Products involves a test of your understanding of basic financial concepts and of the corporate tax code. You are given the following memorandum and asked to respond to the questions. Whether you are offered a position at Caledonia will depend on the accuracy of your response.

To: Applicants for the position of Financial Analyst
From: Mr. V. Morrison, CEO, Caledonia Products
Re: A test of your understanding of basic financial concepts and of the corporate tax code

Please respond to the following questions:

a. What are the differences between the goals of profit maximization and the maximization of shareholder wealth? Which goal do you think is more appropriate?

b. What does the risk–return trade-off mean?

c. Why are we interested in cash flows rather than accounting profits in determining the value of an asset?

d. What is an efficient market and what are the implications of efficient markets for us?

e. What is the cause of the agency problem and how do we try to solve it?

f. What do ethics and ethical behavior have to do with finance?

g. Define (1) sole proprietorship, (2) partnership, and (3) corporation.

h. The Carrickfergus Corporation has sales of $4 million this past year. Its cost of goods sold was $2.4 million, and its operating expenses were $600,000. Interest expenses on outstanding debts were $300,000, and the company paid $60,000 in preferred stock dividends. The corporation received $30,000 in preferred stock dividends and interest income of $22,000. The firm sold stock that had been owned for 2 years for $100,000; the original cost of the stock was $60,000. Determine the corporation's taxable income and its tax liability.

Financial Calculators

The use of financial calculators has been integrated throughout this text, especially with respect to the presentation of the time value of money. Where appropriate, calculator solutions appear in the margin.

Content Updating

In response to both the continued development of financial thought and reviewer comments, changes have been made in the text. Some of these changes include:

Chapter 1
AN INTRODUCTION TO THE FOUNDATIONS OF FINANCIAL MANAGEMENT

- Updated and revised to make the coverage of taxes as intuitive as possible, emphasizing the fact that while the corporate tax code appears to be progressive, the surtaxes take away the benefits of the lower marginal tax rates for large companies effectively making it a flat tax rate.

- New examples were added.

Chapter 2
THE FINANCIAL MARKETS AND INTEREST RATES

- This chapter was significantly revised, shortened, and simplified to make it livelier and more relevant to students. For example, the discussion of the U.S. Financial Market System was significantly shortened with emphasis place on providing the students with an intuitive understanding of how the markets work, examining the difference between public offerings and private placements, the primary and secondary markets, the money and capital markets, the spot and futures markets, and the organized security exchanges and over-the-counter markets.

- The discussion of interest rates was also simplified and made more intuitive in nature. This chapter was rewritten with an eye toward providing the student with need to know information that is used as building blocks to understand and introduce material in subsequent chapters.

Chapter 3

UNDERSTANDING FINANCIAL STATEMENTS AND CASH FLOWS

- Streamlined the presentation of the financial statements without losing content, making the presentation easier for the student to follow and understand.
- Tied the computation of free cash flows more closely to what is presented later in the text.
- Added the statement of cash flows in an appendix so that a student can compare the free cash flow presentation with the statement of cash flows provided in a firm's annual reports.
- Added a section on interpreting free cash flows so that the student can not only compute free cash flows, but can also answer the question, "So what?"
- Increased the number of real-world examples in "Finance at Work."

Chapter 4

EVALUATING FINANCIAL PERFORMANCE

- Added references by non-finance people as to the relevance of evaluating financial performance regardless of the department where a student will be working in a company. Simplified the presentation
- Make available a presentation of the DuPont analysis on the text's web site.

Chapter 5

THE TIME VALUE OF MONEY

- This chapter was revised with an eye toward making it more accessible to math-phobic students.
- More examples were added and the use of the time value of money tables, while still available, was deemphasized.
- Alternative approaches to solving time value of money problems were provided.
- An increased emphasis on the intuition behind the time value of money was provided stressing visualizing and setting up the problem.

Chapter 6

THE MEANING AND MEASUREMENT OF RISK AND RETURN

- Extensive updates of the chapter examples using Barnes & Noble and new examples of actual companies in the end-of-chapter problems.
- Enhanced the graphs to be more understandable as stand-alone presentations.

Chapter 7

VALUATION AND CHARACTERISTICS OF BONDS

- Added a section on convertible bonds.
- Enhanced the graphs to be more understandable as stand-alone presentations.

Chapter 8

VALUATION AND CHARACTERISTICS OF STOCK

- Updated all numerical examples.

Chapter 9

CAPITAL BUDGETING TECHNIQUES AND PRACTICE

- Increased the number of worked out examples in this chapter since this is one of the key chapters in the book and one that traditionally provides students with a great deal of difficulty.

- Rewrote the sections on capital rationing and mutual exclusive projects were rewritten to make these topics more accessible.

Chapter 10
CASH FLOWS AND OTHER TOPICS IN CAPITAL BUDGETING

- The discussion of the calculation of a project's free cash flows was simplified and made more intuitive in nature, while additional worked out problems were added to the chapter.

Chapter 11
COST OF CAPITAL

- The chapter opening was re-written to describe the cost of capital issue facing ExxonMobil.
- The chapter presentation was "opened up" through the use of explicit lists rather than using lengthy paragraphs. This technique highlights the key concepts for student readers.
- Every major problem concept contains a "Can you do it?" example with an accompanying "How did you do?" This resulted in the addition of eight new worked out examples.

Chapter 12
CAPITAL STRUCTURE AND DIVIDEND POLICY

- Chapter opening was replaced with a discussion of the growing role of private equity capital markets that now rival the public markets as a funding source for many firms.
- Discussion of business and financial risk completely re-written to focus on managerial decisions that drive these attributes of the firm including: the choice of a line of business, the choice of an operating cost structure (operating leverage) and the choice of a capital structure (financial leverage).
- New discussion of business risk that focuses on the key drivers including: stability of the domestic economy; exposure to, and stability of, foreign economies; sensitivity to the business cycle; and competitive pressures in the firm's industry.
- Discussion of break-even analysis re-written to focus on key results and to eliminate proofs.
- Elimination of the analytics of "degrees of" operating, financial, and total leverage. These metrics are not fixed for any given firm but change with the firm's sales level; consequently they are not useful operating metrics for the firm's management although the concepts are useful as motivators for the discussion of operating and financial risk. Consequently, the new discussion focuses on concepts, not calculations.
- Graphics used to discuss capital structure theory redone. Labels now write out the variables rather than use acronyms that make interpretation difficult and time consuming.
- Discussion of the survey of CFOs with regard to factors that influence the capital structure decision (done by Graham and Harvey are reported) has been added. This focuses student attention on "what matters" to executives.
- Every major problem concept contains a "Can you do it?" example with an accompanying "How did you do?" This resulted in the addition of five new worked out examples.

Chapter 13
DIVIDEND POLICY AND INTERNAL FINANCING

- Chapter opening re-written to focus on Microsoft's initiation of dividends.
- Empirical evidence regarding tests of the relevance of dividend policy eliminated. This is a topic significant interest in the halls of the academy but of little significance to

first time students of finance. Moreover, the evidence finds little relevance for a topic that is of obvious concern to corporate executives. This is often confusing to students who then wonder about the relevance of the chapter.

- Technical discussions of accounting for stock dividends versus a stock split were edited out of the chapter. Both topics are still compared and contrasted but no calculations are involved.

Chapter 14
SHORT-TERM FINANCIAL PLANNING

- Every major problem concept contains a "Can you do it?" example with an accompanying "How did you do?"
- This chapter (and this section of the book) is one that users increasingly avoid. So my revision to the Chapter was primarily focused on shortening and simplifying.

Chapter 15
WORKING CAPITAL MANAGEMENT

- Chapter opening was re-written to focus on how Dell manages its working capital.
- Cash conversion cycle discussion updated to emphasize the fact that Dell and Apple both do this quite well now.

Chapter 16
CURRENT ASSET MANAGEMENT

- Discussion of cash collection and disbursement procedures dramatically shortened. We continue to discuss each important tool for speeding up collections and managing disbursements. However, many of the details have been eliminated in an effort to make the material more interesting and less tedious.
- Detailed discussions of alternative forms of investments for marketable securities portfolio were eliminated. The focus is now on managing the portfolio not alternative security details.

Chapter 17
INTERNATIONAL BUSINESS FINANCE

- This chapter was revised and updated to reflect changes in exchange rates and in the global financial markets in general.

THE SUPPORT PACKAGE

PRINT SUPPLEMENTS:

For the Instrutor

Test Item File

This Test Bank, prepared by Alan D. Eastman of Indiana University of Pennsylvania, provides more than 1,600 multiple-choice, true/false, and short-answer questions with complete and detailed answers. The print Test Bank is designed for use with the new TestGen-EQ test generating software.

Instructor's Manual with Solutions

Prepared by J. William Petty, the Instructor's Manual follows the textbook's organization and represents a continued effort to serve the teacher in his or her goal of being effective in the classroom. Each chapter contains a chapter orientation, an outline of each chapter (also suitable for lecture notes), answers to end-of-chapter questions, and an extensive problem set for each chapter, including a large number of alternative problems along with answers.

The Instructor's Manual is also available electronically and instructors can download this file from the Instructor's Resource Center by visiting **www.prenhall.com/keown**.

For the Student

Study Guide

The Study Guide to accompany *Foundations of Finance: The Logic and Practice of Financial Management*, 6th Edition, was written by J. William Petty with the objective of providing a student-oriented supplement to the text. Each chapter of the Study Guide contains an orientation of each chapter along with a chapter outline of key topics, problems (with detailed solutions) and self-tests, which can be used to aid in the preparation of outside assignments and in studying for exams, a tutorial on capital budgeting, a set of tables that not only gives compound sum and present value interest factors but also shows how to compute the interest using a financial calculator.

TECHNOLOGY SUPPLEMENTS:

Companion Website

(**www.prenhall.com/keown**) The Website contains various activities related specifically to the Sixth Edition of *Foundations of Finance: The Logic and Practice of Financial Management*.

For the Student

EXCEL SPREADSHEETS

Created by J. William Petty, these spreadsheets correspond with the end-of-chapter problems from the text.

ONLINE STUDY GUIDE

The Online Study Guide, prepared by Philip Samuel Russel of Philadelphia University, offers students another opportunity to sharpen their problem-solving skills and to assess their understanding of the text material. The Online Study Guide is a truly comprehensive set of questions with exceptional coverage of the material in the textbook and written by the authors. The Online Study Guide grades each question submitted by the students and provides immediate feedback for correct and incorrect answers.

For the Instructor

Instructors may find *downloadable resources* from the link for the Instructor's Resource Center described here.

Instructor's Resource Center

This password-protected site is accessible at **www.prenhall.com/keown** and hosts all of the resources that follow. Instructors should click on the "Help Downloading Instructor Resources" link for easy-to-follow instructions on getting access or may contact their sales representative for further information.

Instructor's Manual

THE POWERPOINT LECTURE PRESENTATION

This lecture presentation tool, prepared by Philip Samuel Russel of Philadelphia University, provides the instructor with individual lecture outlines to accompany the text. The slides include many of the figures and tables from the text. These lecture notes can be used as is or professors can easily modify them to reflect specific presentation needs.

TESTGEN-EQ SOFTWARE

The print Test Item File is designed for use with the TestGen-EQ test generating software. This computerized package allows instructors to custom design, save, and generate classroom tests. The test program permits instructors to edit, add, or delete questions from the test bank; edit existing graphics and create new graphics; analyze test results; and organize a database of tests and student results. This new software allows for greater flexibility and ease of use. It provides many options for organizing and displaying tests, along with a search and sort feature.

SUBSCRIPTIONS:

Analyzing current events is an important skill for economic students to develop. To sharpen this skill and further support the book's theme of exploration and application, Prentice Hall offers you and your student's three news subscription offers:

THE *WALL STREET JOURNAL* PRINT AND INTERACTIVE EDITIONS SUBSCRIPTION

Prentice Hall has formed a strategic alliance with the *Wall Street Journal*, the most respected and trusted daily source for information on business and economics. For a small additional charge, Prentice Hall offers students a 15-week subscription to the *Wall Street Journal* Interactive Edition (wsj.com) and a 15-week complimentary print edition subscription. Upon receipt of 10 student registrations from an adopting institution, a professor can receive a one-year subscription of the print and interactive versions as well as weekly subject-specific *Wall Street Journal* educators' lesson plans.

THE *FINANCIAL TIMES*

We are pleased to announce a special partnership with the *Financial Times*. For a small additional charge, Prentice Hall offers your students a 15-week subscription to the *Financial Times*. Upon adoption of a special package containing the book and the subscription booklet, professors will receive a free one-year subscription. Please contact your Prentice Hall representative for details and ordering information.

ECONOMIST.COM

Through a special arrangement with Economist.com, Prentice Hall offers your students a 12-week subscription to Economist.com for a small additional charge. Upon adoption of a special package containing the book and the subscription booklet, professors will receive a free six-month subscription. Please contact your Prentice Hall representative for further details and ordering information.

ACKNOWLEDGMENTS

We gratefully acknowledge the assistance, support, and encouragement of those individuals who have contributed to the Sixth Edition of *Foundations of Finance*. Specifically, we wish to recognize the very helpful insights provided by many of our colleagues. For their careful comments and helpful reviews of the text, we are indebted to:

Haseeb Ahmed
Johnson C. Smith University

Joan Anderssen
Arapahoe Community College

Chris Armstrong
Draughons Junior College

Curtis Bacon
Southern Oregon University

Deb Bauer
University of Oregon

Pat Bernson
County College of Morris

Ed Boyer
Temple University

Joe Brocato
Tarleton State University

Joseph Brum
Fayetteville Technical Community College

Lawrence Byerly
Thomas More College

Janice Caudill
Auburn University

David Daglio
Newbury College

Julie Dahlquist
University of Texas at San Antonio

David Darst
Central Ohio Technical College

Maria de Boyrie
New Mexico State University

Kate Demarest
Carroll Community College

Cheri Etling
University of Tampa

Cheryl Fetterman
Cape Fear Community College

David R. Fewings
Western Washington University

Dr. Charles Gahala
Benedictine University

Deborah Giarusso
University of Northern Iowa

Gregory Goussak
University of Nevada, Las Vegas

Lori Grady
Bucks County Community College

Ed Graham
University of North Carolina Wilmington

Barry Greenberg
Webster University

Bruce Hadburg
University of Tampa

Marlin Jensen
Auburn University

John Kachurick
College Misericordia

Okan Kavuncu
University of California at Santa Cruz

Gary Kayakachoian
Rhode Island College

Mary LaPann
Adirondack Community College

Carlos Liard-Muriente
Central Connecticut State University

Christopher Liberty
College of St Rose, Empire State College

Edmund Mantell
Pace University

Peter Marks
Rhode Island College

Mario Mastrandrea
Cleveland State University

Anna McAleer
Arcadia University

Robert Meyer
Parkland College

Ronald Moy
St. John's University

Elisa Muresan
Long Island University

Anthony Pondillo
Siena College

Walter Purvis
Coastal Carolina Community College

Emil Radosevich
Central New Mexico Community College

Deana Ray
Forsyth Technical Community College

Ahmad Salam
Widener University

Jeffrey Schultz
Christian Brothers University

Ken Shakoori
California State University, Bakersfield

Suresh Srivastava
University of Alaska Anchorage

Maurry Tamarkin
Clark University

Fang Wang
West Virginia University

Paul Warrick
Westwood College

Jill Wetmore
Saginaw Valley State University

Jingxue Yuan
Texas Tech University

Me ngxin Zhao
Bentley College

We also thank our friends at Prentice Hall. They are a great group of folks. To Mark Pfaltzgraff, our executive editor, we owe an immeasurable debt of gratitude. He continued to push us to make sure that we delivered the finest textbook and supplementary package possible. His efforts go well beyond what one might expect from the best of editors. On top of this, Mark is just a great person—thanks, Mark. We would also like to thank Kerri Tomasso for her administrative deftness. Not only is she bright, insightful, and attentive to detail—in short, a gifted Project Manager—but she also made the revision a fun experience. She is a true friend. With Kerri watching over us, there was no way the ball could be dropped. Our thanks also go to Jodi Bassett for her marketing prowess. Jodi has an amazing understanding of the market, coupled with an intuitive understanding of what the market is looking for. We also thank Ashley Lulling, our media manager, who did a great job of making sure we are on the cutting edge in terms of Web applications and offerings. To Melissa Feimer, the production editor, we express a very special thank-you for seeing the book through a very complex production process and keeping it all on schedule while maintaining extremely high quality.

As a final word, we express our sincere thanks to those using *Foundations of Finance* in the classroom. We thank you for making us a part of your team. Always feel free to give any of us a call or contact us through the Internet when you have questions or needs.

—A.J.K. / J.D.M. / J.W.P.

PART 1

The Scope and Environment of Financial Management

➤ G. Bennett Stewart III is a senior partner with Stern Stewart & Co. (NY). Before cofounding Stern Stewart in 1982 with Joel Stern, he was a vice president with the financial advisory arm of the Chase Manhattan Bank. Stern Stewart & Co. is a global consulting firm that specializes in helping client companies in the measurement and creation of shareholder wealth through the application of tools based on modern financial theory. We interviewed Bennett to get his thoughts on how managers should think about finance. This is what he had to say:

To be honest, I think managers should think as little about finance as possible and as much about running their business as possible. That is, finance should really be the servant of the business and not the other way around. If there is one concept that should drive what managers do, it is this: As long as managers can raise money from investors and invest it in their business [while] providing a return on the investment that is higher than what the investors could earn from an equally risky portfolio of stocks and bonds, then value is created.

I like to think of finance with an analogy of a savings account. When I worked at Chase Manhattan Bank from 1976 until 1982, Chase Bank was offering a 5% rate of interest when Merrill Lynch came out with a money market account that paid as much as 15%. It didn't take a genius to figure out that getting 15% from Merrill Lynch was a lot better than getting 5% from Chase, so people stormed the bank and took their money down the street in search of the higher rate of return. I claim that the stock market works in exactly the same way. If the rate of return a company is earning inside its business isn't up to the return that the investors could earn elsewhere, they're going to withdraw their investment from the company, and its stock price will be depressed.

A sure sign that a firm has misallocated the money entrusted to it by the firm's investors is when the market value of the company is less than its underlying book value, which is the amount that investors have put into the business. The difference in the market value of the firm and the amount of money invested in the firm is known in finance as net present value or what we at Stern Stewart like to call the *MVA* or *market value added*. The essence of finance then is taking resources of all kinds and combining them in ways such that the value of the output is worth more than the cost of the input. It's like a chef who takes a menu of ingredients, stirs them, and cooks them to make a cake. If the value of the cake is more than the value of the ingredients, value has been created. This is the concept of *net present value*—a basic premise in finance.

I think that managers often forget these very basic ideas and begin to focus on accounting measures exclusively. Frequently, people on Wall Street become focused on reported earnings, earnings per share, earnings growth, profit margins, and such. In fact, there is kind of a bewildering array of these financial metrics and ratios and it's very easy for managers to lose sight of the forest for the trees and get away from the very simple, common-sense propositions that should guide them.

Back in the 1960s, my partner, Joel Stern, suggested that the mom and pop running the corner grocery store often know more about value creation than many senior executives. For example, mom and pop know that the key to their success is in the cigar box that holds their cash. As long as the lid on the cigar box was rising, they were doing okay for themselves. In finance, we say that as long as the "free cash flow" from the operations is increasing, all is well. But it's no different from the cigar box.

Enron is a good example of what I am describing. In its 2000 annual report, Enron reported that management was "laser-focused on earnings per share" and indeed it appears that it was. You have to conclude that the company aimed for increased earnings per share by investing too much money in unrewarding projects. In addition, it avoided issuing stock so it could maintain high earnings per share. This required Enron to use too much debt. In fact, I contend that every company that worships at the EPS altar will be tempted to either overinvest or use too much debt.

I have concluded that earnings per share is the opium of the executive suites and the Don Giovanni of corporate finance. We need to blackball this entire earnings management game!

After reading this chapter, you should be able to:

1. Identify the goal of the firm.

2. Compare the various legal forms of business organization and explain why the corporate form of business is the most logical choice for a firm that is large or growing.

3. Describe the corporate tax features that affect business decisions.

4. Explain the 10 principles that form the foundations of financial management.

5. Explain what has led to the era of the multinational corporation.

CHAPTER 1

An Introduction to the Foundations of Financial Management— The Ties That Bind

Apple Computer ignited the personal computer revolution in the 1970s with the Apple II and reinvented the personal computer in the 1980s with the Macintosh. But by 1997, it looked like it might be nearing the end for Apple. Mac users were on the decline, and the company didn't seem to be headed in any real direction. It was at that point that Steve Jobs reappeared, taking back his old job as CEO of Apple, the company he cofounded in 1976. To say the least, things began to change thereafter. In fact, between then and the end of 2006, the price of Apple's common stock climbed by over sixteenfold!

How did Apple accomplish all this? The company did it by going back to what it does best, which is producing products that make the optimal trade-off between ease of use, complexity, and special features. Apple then used its expertise to introduce new products such as the iPod, a digital music player; iTunes, an easy-to-use, legal way to purchase music on the Web; Xserve, a server; Airport, wireless networking equipment; and publishing and multimedia software. In addition, Apple improved its computer offerings with the sleek iMac and iBook, aimed at the consumer and education markets, and with the more powerful Power Mac and PowerBook, aimed at high-end consumers and professionals involved in design and publishing.

Although all these products have done well, the success of the iPod, introduced in 2001, has been truly amazing. Then, in 2004, Apple came out with the iPod mini, which is about the length and width of a business card. The iPod mini has also been a huge success, particularly among women. How successful have these new products been? By 2006, Apple was selling more iPods than its sig-nature Macintosh desktop and notebook computers, and iTunes now sells more than 3 million songs a day and has an 83 percent market share in the downloadable music industry.

But Apple didn't stop there. It was determined to keep improving its products and developing and introducing new products that consumers wanted. With this in mind, in September 2005, Apple unveiled its latest version of the iPod, the iPod Nano, which is thinner than a pencil and can hold over 1,000 songs.

How did Apple make the decision to introduce the original iPod, followed by the iPod Nano? The answer is through sound financial management. Financial management involves creating economic value by focusing on decision making with an eye toward creating wealth. As such, this text deals with financial decisions such as when to introduce new products, when to invest in new assets, when to replace existing assets, when to borrow from banks, when to sell stocks or bonds, when to extend credit to a customer, and how much cash and inventory to maintain. All of these aspects of financial management were factors in Apple's decision to introduce the iPod, iPod Nano, and the other iPod products, and the end result is having a major financial impact on Apple.

In this chapter, we lay a foundation for the entire book by discussing what finance is and then explaining the key goal that guides financial decision making: the maximization of share-holder wealth. We then discuss the legal and tax environment of financial decisions and describe the golden thread that ties everything together: the 10 basic principles of finance. Finally, we briefly look at what has led to the rise in multinational corporations.

Objective **1**

Identify the goal of the firm.

THE GOAL OF THE FIRM

In this text we emphasize that the goal of the firm and its financial managers should be the *maximization of shareholder wealth*, by which we mean maximization of the price of the existing common stock. Not only does this goal directly benefit the shareholders of the company, but also it provides benefits to society as scarce resources are directed to their most productive use by businesses competing to create wealth. To better understand this goal, we first discuss profit maximization as a possible goal for the firm. Then we compare it to maximization of shareholder wealth to see why, in financial management, the latter is the more appropriate goal for the firm.

Profit Maximization

In microeconomics courses, profit maximization is frequently cited as the goal of the firm. Profit maximization stresses the efficient use of capital resources, but it is not specific with respect to the time frame over which profits are to be measured. Do we maximize profits over the current year, or do we maximize profits over some longer period? A financial manager could easily increase current profits by eliminating the firm's research and development expenditures and cutting down on routine maintenance. In the short run, this might result in increased profits, but this clearly is not in the best long-run interests of the firm. If we are to base our financial decisions on a goal, that goal must be precise, not allow for misinterpretation, and deal with all the complexities of the real world.

In microeconomics, profit maximization functions largely as a theoretical goal, with economists using it to prove how firms behave rationally to increase profit. Unfortunately, it ignores many real-world complexities that financial managers must address in their decision making. In the more applied discipline of financial management, firms must deal every day with two major factors not considered by the goal of profit maximization: uncertainty and timing.

Microeconomics courses often ignore uncertainty and risk to present theory more easily. Projects and investment alternatives are compared by examining their expected values or weighted average profits. Whether one project is riskier than another does not always enter into these calculations; economists do discuss risk, but only tangentially.[1] In reality, projects differ a great deal with respect to their risk characteristics, and to disregard these differences in the practice of financial management can result in incorrect decisions. As we discover later in this chapter, there is a very definite relationship between risk and expected return—that is, investors demand a higher expected return for taking on added risk—and to ignore this relationship leads to improper decision making.

Another problem with the goal of profit maximization is that it ignores the timing of the project's returns. If this goal is concerned only with this year's profits, we know it inappropriately ignores profits in future years. If we interpret it to maximize the average of future profits, it is also incorrect. Inasmuch as investment opportunities are available for money in hand, we are not indifferent to the timing of the returns. Given equivalent cash flows from profits, we want those cash flows sooner rather than later. Thus, the real-world factors of uncertainty and timing force us to look beyond a simple goal of profit maximization as a decision criterion. We now turn to an examination of a more robust goal for the firm: the maximization of shareholder wealth.

The Maximization of Shareholder Wealth

In formulating the goal of maximization of shareholder wealth we are doing nothing more than modifying the goal of profit maximization to deal with the complexities of the operating environment. We have chosen maximization of shareholder wealth—that is, maximization of the market value of the existing shareholders' common stock—because the effects of

---

[1] See, for example, Robert S. Pindyck and Daniel Rubenfield, *Microeconomics*, 6th ed. (Upper Saddle River, NJ: Prentice Hall, 2005).

all financial decisions are thereby included. Investors react to poor investment and dividend decisions by causing the total value of the firm's stock to fall, and they react to good decisions by pushing up the price of the stock. In effect, under this goal, good decisions are those that create wealth for the shareholder.

Obviously, there are some serious practical problems involved with using changes in the firm's stock to evaluate financial decisions. After all, many things affect stock prices, including changes in the economy as a whole. To attempt to identify a reaction to a particular financial decision would simply be impossible and unnecessary. What we do focus on is the effect that our decision *should* have on the stock price if everything else were held constant. The market price of the firm's stock reflects the value of the firm as seen by its owners and takes into account the complexities and complications of the real-world risk. As we follow this goal throughout our discussions, we must keep in mind one more question: Who exactly are the shareholders? The answer: Shareholders are the legal owners of the firm.

Did You Get It?

1. What are the problems with the goal of profit maximization?
2. What is the goal of the firm?

THE LEGAL FORMS OF BUSINESS ORGANIZATION

Objective 2

Compare the various legal forms of business organization and explain why the corporate form of business is the most logical choice for a firm that is large or growing.

In the chapters ahead we focus on financial decisions for corporations because, although the corporation is not the only legal form of business available, it is the most logical choice for a firm that is large or growing. It is also the dominant business form in terms of sales in this country. In this section we explain why this is so. Focusing on corporations allows us to simplify the remainder of the text by following the corporate tax code, rather than examining different tax codes for different legal forms of businesses. Keep in mind that our primary purpose is to develop an understanding of the logic of financial decision making and that taxes become important only when they affect our decisions.

Although numerous and diverse, the legal forms of business organization fall into three categories: the sole proprietorship, the partnership, and the corporation. To understand the basic differences between each form, we need to define each one and understand its advantages and disadvantages. As the firm grows, the advantages of the corporation begin to dominate. As a result, most large firms take on the corporate form.

Sole Proprietorships

A **sole proprietorship** is *a business owned by an individual.* The owner retains the title to the business's assets and is responsible, generally without limitation, for the liabilities incurred. The proprietor is entitled to the profits from the business but must also absorb any losses. This form of business is initiated by the mere act of beginning the business operations. Typically, no legal requirement must be met in starting the operation, particularly if the proprietor is conducting the business in his or her own name. If a special name is used, an assumed-name certificate should be filed, requiring a small registration fee. Termination of the sole proprietorship occurs on the owner's death or by the owner's choice. Briefly stated, the sole proprietorship is for all practical purposes the absence of any formal *legal* business structure.

sole proprietorship a business owned by a single individual.

Partnerships

The primary difference between a partnership and a sole proprietorship is that the partnership has more than one owner. A **partnership** is *an association of two or more persons coming together as co-owners for the purpose of operating a business for profit.* Partnerships fall into two types: (1) general partnerships and (2) limited partnerships.

partnership an association of two or more individuals joining together as co-owners to operate a business for profit.

General Partnerships

general partnership a partnership in which all partners are fully liable for the indebtedness incurred by the partnership.

In a **general partnership** *each partner is fully responsible for the liabilities incurred by the partnership*. Thus, any partner's faulty conduct, even having the appearance of relating to the firm's business, renders the remaining partners liable as well. The relationship among partners is dictated entirely by the partnership agreement, which may be an oral commitment or a formal document.

Limited Partnerships

limited partnership a partnership in which one or more of the partners has limited liability, restricted to the amount of capital he or she invests in the partnership.

In addition to the general partnership, in which all partners are jointly liable without limitation, many states provide for **limited partnerships**. The state statutes permit *one or more of the partners to have limited liability, restricted to the amount of capital invested in the partnership*. Several conditions must be met to qualify as a limited partner. First, at least one general partner must have unlimited liability. Second, the names of the limited partners may not appear in the name of the firm. Third, the limited partners may not participate in the management of the business. Thus, a limited partnership provides limited liability for a partner who is purely an investor.

Corporations

corporation an entity that legally functions separate and apart from its owners.

The **corporation** has been a significant factor in the economic development of the United States. As early as 1819, U.S. Supreme Court Chief Justice John Marshall set forth the legal definition of a corporation as "an artificial being, invisible, intangible, and existing only in the contemplation of law."[2] This entity *legally functions separate and apart from its owners*. As such, the corporation can individually sue and be sued and purchase, sell, or own property, and its personnel are subject to criminal punishment for crimes. However, despite this legal separation, the corporation is composed of owners who dictate its direction and policies. The owners elect a board of directors, whose members in turn select individuals to serve as corporate officers, including the company's president, vice president, secretary, and treasurer. Ownership is reflected in common stock certificates, each designating the number of shares owned by its holder. The number of shares owned relative to the total number of shares outstanding determines the stockholder's proportionate ownership in the business. Because the shares are transferable, ownership in a corporation may be changed by a shareholder simply remitting the shares to a new shareholder. The shareholder's liability is confined to the amount of the investment in the company, thereby preventing creditors from confiscating stockholders' personal assets in settlement of unresolved claims. This is an extremely important advantage of a corporation. After all, would you be willing to invest in USAir if you would be held liable if one of its planes crashed? Finally, the life of a corporation is not dependent on the status of the investors. The death or withdrawal of an investor does not affect the continuity of the corporation. Its managers continue to run the corporation when stock is sold or when it is passed on through inheritance.

Which Organizational Form Should Be Chosen?

Owners of new businesses have some important decisions to make in choosing an organizational form. Whereas each business form seems to have some advantages over the others, the advantages of the corporation begin to dominate as the firm grows and needs access to the capital markets to raise funds.

Because of the limited liability, the ease of transferring ownership through the sale of common shares, and the flexibility in dividing the shares, the corporation is the ideal business entity in terms of attracting new capital. In contrast, the unlimited liabilities of the sole proprietorship and the general partnership are deterrents to raising equity capital. Between the extremes, the limited partnership does provide limited liability for limited partners, which has a tendency to attract wealthy investors. However, the impracticality of having a

---

[2] *The Trustees of Dartmouth College v. Woodard*, 4 Wheaton 636 (1819).

large number of partners and the restricted marketability of an interest in a partnership prevent this form of organization from competing effectively with the corporation. Therefore, when developing our decision models we assume we are dealing with the corporate form and corporate tax codes. Because our goal is to develop an understanding of the management, measurement, and creation of wealth, and not to become tax experts, we focus only on those characteristics of the corporate tax code that affect our financial decisions.

Organizational Form and Taxes: The Double Taxation on Dividends

In this chapter we will focus on taxes that the corporation pays. But for a moment we will set that aside and look at the taxes that a corporation's owners pay on dividends that they receive from the corporation. Historically, one of the drawbacks of the corporate form was the double taxation of dividends. This occurs when a corporation earns a profit, pays taxes on those profits (the first taxation of earnings), and pays some of those profits back to the shareholders in the form of dividends, and then the shareholders pay personal income taxes on those dividends (the second taxation of those earnings). This double taxation of earnings does not take place with proprietorships and partnerships. Needless to say, that had been a major disadvantage of corporations. However, in an attempt to stimulate the economy, the tax rate on dividends was cut with the passage of the Tax Act of 2003.

Before the 2003 tax changes, you paid your regular, personal income tax rate on your dividend income, which could be as high as 35 percent. However, with the new law, qualified dividends from domestic corporations and qualified foreign corporations are now taxed at a maximum rate of 15 percent. Moreover, if your personal income puts you in the 10 percent or 15 percent income rate bracket, your dividends will be taxed at only 5 percent, and in 2008, this rate drops to 0 percent. Unless Congress takes further action, this tax break on dividends will end after 2011 and individuals will once again be taxed at their regular personal tax rate.

S-Type Corporations and Limited Liability Companies (LLC)

One of the problems that entrepreneurs and small business owners face is that they need the benefits of the corporate form to expand, but the double taxation of earnings that comes with the corporate form makes it difficult to accumulate the necessary wealth for expansion. Fortunately, the government recognizes this problem and has provided two business forms that are, in effect, crosses between a partnership and a corporation with the tax benefits of partnerships (no double taxation of earnings) and the limited liability benefit of corporations (your liability is limited to what you invest).

The first is the **S-type corporation**, which provides limited liability while allowing the business's owners to be taxed as if they were a partnership—that is, distributions back to the owners are not taxed twice as is the case with dividends distributed by regular corporations. Unfortunately, a number of restrictions accompany the S-type corporation that detract from the desirability of this business form. For example, with an S-type corporation all the owners must be people. Thus, an S-type corporation cannot be used for a joint venture between two corporations. As a result, this business form has been losing ground in recent years in favor of the limited liability company.

S-type corporation a corporation that, because of specific qualifications, is taxed as though it were a partnership.

The **limited liability company (LLC)** is also a cross between a partnership and a corporation. Just as with the S-type corporation, the LLC retains limited liability for its owners but runs and is taxed like a partnership. In general, it provides more flexibility than the S-type corporation. For example, corporations can be owners in an LLC. However, because LLCs operate under state laws, both states and the IRS have rules for what qualifies as an LLC, and different states have different rules. But the bottom line in all this is that the LLC must not look too much like a corporation or it will be taxed as one.

limited liability company (LLC) a cross between a partnership and a corporation under which the owners retain limited liability but the company is run and is taxed like a partnership.

The Role the Financial Manager Plays in a Corporation

A firm can assume many different organizational structures. Figure 1-1 shows a typical presentation of how the finance area fits into a corporation. The vice president for finance, also called the chief financial officer (CFO), serves under the corporation's chief

FIGURE 1-1 How the Finance Area Fits into a Corporation

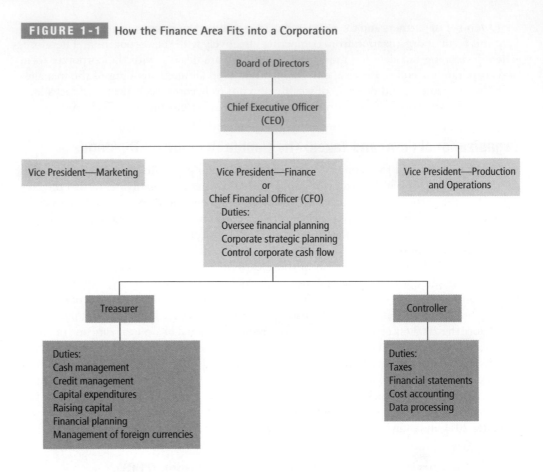

executive officer (CEO) and is responsible for overseeing financial planning, corporate strategic planning, and controlling the firm's cash flow. Typically, a treasurer and controller serve under the CFO. In a smaller firm, the same person may fill both roles, with just one office handling all the duties. The treasurer generally handles the firm's financial activities, including cash and credit management, making capital expenditure decisions, raising funds, financial planning, and managing any foreign currency received by the firm. The controller is responsible for managing the firm's accounting duties, including producing financial statements, cost accounting, paying taxes, and gathering and monitoring the data necessary to oversee the firm's financial well-being. In this textbook, we focus on the duties generally associated with the treasurer and on how investment decisions are made.

Did You Get It?

1. What are the primary differences between a sole proprietorship, a partnership, and a corporation?
2. Explain why large and growing firms tend to choose the corporate form.
3. What are the duties of a corporate treasurer? Of a corporate controller?

Objective **3**

Describe the corporate tax features that affect business decisions.

FEDERAL INCOME TAXATION

As the nation's politics change, so does the tax system. As we have explained, the purpose of looking at a country's tax structure is not to become tax experts, but rather to gain an understanding of taxes and how they affect business decisions. There is a good chance that corporate tax rates will change significantly before you enter the workforce. However, although rates may change, taxes will continue to remain a cash outflow and, therefore, something to avoid. Thus, we pay close attention to which expenses are and are not deductible for tax purposes and, in doing so, focus on how taxes affect business decisions.

The Objectives of Income Taxation

Originally, the sole objective of the federal government in taxing income was to generate financing for government expenditures. Although this purpose continues to be important, social and economic objectives have been added. For instance, a company may receive possible reductions in taxes if (1) it undertakes certain technological research, (2) it pays wages to certain economically disadvantaged groups, or (3) it locates its facilities in certain economically depressed areas. Other socially oriented stipulations in the tax laws include exemptions for dependents, old age, and blindness and a reduction in taxes on one's retirement income. In addition, the government uses tax legislation to stabilize the economy. In recessionary periods corporate taxes may be lowered to generate job growth. In short, three objectives may be given for the taxation of revenues: (1) the provision of revenues for government expenditures, (2) the achievement of socially desirable goals, and (3) economic stabilization.

Types of Taxpayers

To understand the tax system, we must first ask, "Who is the taxpayer?" For the most part, there are three basic types of taxable entities: individuals, corporations, and fiduciaries. Individuals include company employees, self-employed persons owning their own businesses, and members of a partnership or LLC: Income is reported by these individuals in their personal tax returns.[3] The corporation, as a separate legal entity, reports its income and pays any taxes related to these profits. The owners (stockholders) of the corporation need not report these earnings in their personal tax returns, except when all or a part of the profits are distributed in the form of dividends. Finally, fiduciaries, such as estates and trusts, file a tax return and pay taxes on the income generated by the estate or trust that isn't distributed to (and included in the taxable income of) a beneficiary.

Although taxation of individual and fiduciary income is an important source of income to the government, neither is especially relevant to the financial manager. Because most firms of any size are corporations, again, we restrict our discussion to the corporation. A caveat is necessary, however. Tax legislation can be quite complex, with numerous exceptions to most general rules. The laws can also change quickly, and certain details discussed here may no longer apply in the near future. However, the general approach should remain the same, regardless of changes.

Computing Taxable Income

The **taxable income** for a corporation is based on *the gross income from all sources, except for allowable exclusions, less any tax-deductible expenses*. **Gross income** equals *the firm's dollar sales from its products or services less the cost of producing or acquiring them*. Tax-deductible expenses include any operating expenses, such as marketing expenses, and administrative expenses and so forth. Also, the *interest expense* paid on the firm's outstanding debt is a tax-deductible expense. However, dividends paid to the firm's stockholders are *not* deductible expenses, but rather distributions of income. Other taxable income includes the interest income and dividend income that the corporation receives.

taxable income gross income from all sources, except for allowable exclusions, less any tax-deductible expenses.

gross income a firm's dollar sales from its product or services less the cost of producing or acquiring them.

To demonstrate how to compute a corporation's taxable income, consider the J and S Corporation, a manufacturer of home accessories. The firm, originally established by Kelly Stites, had sales of $50 million for the year. The cost of producing the accessories totaled $23 million. Operating expenses were $10 million. The corporation has $12.5 million in debt outstanding, with an 8 percent interest rate, which resulted in $1 million interest expense ($12,500,000 × .08 = $1,000,000). Management paid $1 million in dividends to the firm's common stockholders. No other income, such as interest or dividend income, was received. The taxable income for the J and S Corporation would be $16 million, as shown in Table 1-1.

Once we know J and S Corporation's taxable income, we can next determine the amount of taxes the firm owes.

---

[3] Partnerships report only the income from the partnership, but they do not pay taxes. The income is then reported again by each partner, who pays any taxes owed.

TABLE 1-1   J and S Corporation Taxable Income

Sales		$50,000,000
Cost of goods sold		23,000,000
Gross profit		$27,000,000
Operating expenses		
Administrative expenses	$4,000,000	
Depreciation expenses	1,500,000	
Marketing expenses	4,500,000	
Total operating expenses		$10,000,000
Operating income		
(earnings before interest and taxes)		$17,000,000
Other income		0
Interest expense		1,000,000
Taxable income		$16,000,000

Dividends paid to common stockholders ($1,000,000) are not tax-deductible expenses.

Computing the Taxes Owed

marginal tax rate the tax rate that would be applied to the next dollar of income.

The taxes to be paid by the corporation on its taxable income are based on the corporate tax rate structure. The specific rates for corporations, as of early 2007, are given in Table 1-2.

The tax rates shown in Table 1-2 are defined as the **marginal tax rates**, or *rates applicable to the next dollar of income*. For instance, if a firm has earnings of $60,000 and is contemplating an investment that would yield $10,000 in additional profits, the tax rate to be used in calculating the taxes on this added income is 25 percent; that is, the marginal tax rate is 25 percent.

The rates in Table 1-2 go up to a top marginal corporate tax rate of 35 percent for taxable income in excess of $10 million, and a surtax of 3 percent on taxable income between $15 million and $18,333,333. This means the corporation's marginal tax rate on income between $15 million and $18,333,333 is 38 percent (the 35 percent rate plus the 3 percent surtax). There is also a 5 percent surtax on taxable income between $100,000 and $335,000, which means the marginal rate on income between $100,000 and $335,000 is 39 percent (the 34 percent rate plus the 5 percent surtax). For example, the tax liability for J and S Corporation, which had $16 million in taxable earnings, would be $5,530,000, calculated as follows:

EARNINGS	×	MARGINAL TAX RATE	=	TAXES
$ 50,000	×	15%	=	$ 7,500
25,000	×	25%	=	6,250
9,925,000	×	34%	=	3,374,500
6,000,000	×	35%	=	2,100,000
				$5,488,250

Additional surtaxes:

- Add 5% surtax on income between $100,000 and $335,000
  (5% × [$335,000 − $100,000])   11,750
- Add 3% surtax on income between $15,000,000 and $18,333,333
  (3% × [$16,000,000 − $15,000,000])   30,000

Total tax liability	$5,530,000

J and S Corporation's marginal tax rate is 38 percent (this is because $16 million falls into the 35% tax bracket *with* a 3% surtax); that is, any additional income will be taxed at a rate of 38 percent. However, after taxable income exceeds $18,333,333, the marginal tax rate declines to 35 percent, and the 3 percent surtax no longer applies.

For financial decision making, it's the *marginal tax rate* rather than the average tax rate that we are concerned with. Why? Because, generally speaking, the marginal rate is the rate that corporation pays on the next dollar that is earned. We always want to consider the tax consequences of any financial decision. The marginal tax rate is the rate that will be appli-

TABLE 1-2 Corporate Tax Rates	
15%	$0–$50,000
25%	$50,001–$75,000
34%	$75,001–$10,000,000
35%	over $10,000,000

Additional surtax:
- 5% on income between $100,000 and $335,000
- 3% on income between $15,000,000 and $18,333,333

cable for any changes in earnings that occur as a result of the decision being made. Thus, when making financial decisions involving taxes, always use the marginal tax rate in your calculations.[4]

The tax rate structure used to compute J and S Corporation's taxes assumes that the income occurs in the United States. Given the globalization of the economy, it may well be that some of the income originates in a foreign country. If so, the tax rates, and the method of taxing the firm, frequently vary. As financial manager, you would try to minimize the firm's taxes by reporting as much income as possible in the low-tax-rate countries and as little as possible in the high-tax-rate countries.

Other Tax Considerations

In addition to the fundamental computation of taxes, several other aspects of the U.S. tax code are relevant to the financial manager. These are (1) the dividend-income exclusion on dividends received by corporations, (2) the effects of depreciation on the firm's taxes, and (3) the recognition of capital gains and losses. Let's look at each of these tax provisions in turn.

The Dividend Exclusion

A corporation can normally exclude 70 percent of any dividends it receives from another corporation. For instance, if corporation A owns common stock in corporation B and receives dividends of $1,000 in a given year, only $300 is subject to tax, and the remaining $700 (70 percent of $1,000) is tax exempt. If the corporation receiving the dividend income is in a 34 percent tax bracket, only $102 in taxes (34 percent of $300) will result.[5]

Depreciation

Depreciation is *the means by which an asset's value is expensed over its useful life for federal tax purposes*. Essentially, there are three methods for computing depreciation expenses: (1) straight-line depreciation, (2) the double-declining balance method, and (3) the modified accelerated cost recovery system. Any one of the three methods results in the same depreciation expense over the life of the asset; however, the last two approaches allow the firm to take the depreciation earlier as opposed to later, which in turn defers taxes until later. Because there is a "time value" associated with money, there is an advantage to using the accelerated techniques. (Chapter 5 fully explains the time value of money.) Also, manages can simultaneously use straight-line depreciation for reporting income to the firm's shareholders while still using an accelerated method for calculating taxable income.

depreciation the means by which an asset's value is expensed over its useful life for federal income tax purposes.

Capital Gains and Losses

An important tax consideration before 1987 was the preferential tax treatment for **capital gains (or losses)**; that is, *gains (or losses) from the sale of assets not bought or sold in the ordinary*

capital gain (or loss) as defined by the revenue code, a gain or loss resulting from the sale or exchange of a capital asset.

[4] On taxable income between $335,000 and $10 million, both the marginal and average tax rates equal 34 percent because of the imposition of the 5 percent surtax that applies to taxable income between $100,000 and $335,000. After the company's taxable income exceeds $18,333,333, both the marginal and average tax rates equal 35 percent because the 3 percent surtax on income between $15 million and $18,333,333 eliminates the benefits of having the first $10 million of income taxed at 34 percent rather than 35 percent.
[5] If corporation A owns at least 20 but less than 80 percent of corporation B, 80 percent of any dividend A receives from B can be excluded from its taxable income. If 80 percent or more is owned, all the dividends received can be excluded.

course of business. The Tax Reform Act of 1986 repealed any special treatment of capital gains and, although the Revenue Reconciliation Act of 1993 reinstituted preferential treatment in certain unique circumstances, in general, capital gains are taxed at the same rates as ordinary income. However, if a corporation has capital losses that exceed capital gains in any year, these net capital losses may not be deducted from ordinary income. The net capital losses may, however, be carried back and applied against net capital gains in each of the 3 years before the current year. If the capital loss is not completely deducted in the 3 prior years, any remaining capital loss can be carried forward and applied against any net capital gains in each of the next 5 years. For example, if a corporation has an $80,000 net capital loss in 2008, it may apply this loss against any net capital gains in 2005, 2006, and 2007. That, of course, would require a refiling of taxes; if any capital loss remains, it may be carried forward and applied against any capital gains through 2013.

Other Tax Concerns

As we mentioned, taxes are used not only to raise money but also to promote socially desirable goals and to maintain economic stability. One way in which both of these goals are met is through the creation and retention of jobs. As a result, to keep struggling firms afloat, there is a tax provision that allows a corporation with an operating loss (which is simply a loss from operating a business) to apply this loss against income in other years. This is commonly referred to as a **net operating loss carryback and carryforward**. *This tax feature allows firms that lose money to recapture taxes they had previously paid, carrying losses back up to 2 years or forward up to 20 years to offset their profits.* Hopefully this allows them to deal with the problems that resulted in the loss. The bottom line is that the government wants to keep as many people employed as possible and to keep the markets as competitive as possible, and to do this it has set up a tax code that helps those in trouble stay afloat.

net operating loss carryback and carryforward a tax provision that permits the taxpayer first to apply a loss against the profits earned in the 2 prior years (carryback). If the loss has not been completely absorbed by the profits in these 2 years, it may be applied to taxable profits in each of the 20 following years (carryforward).

Putting It Together: An Example

To illustrate certain portions of the tax laws for a corporation, assume that the Griggs Corporation had sales during the past year of $5 million; its cost of goods sold was $3 million; and it incurred operating expenses of $1 million. In addition, it received $185,000 in inter-

TABLE 1-3	Griggs Corporation's Tax Computations			
Sales				$ 5,000,000
Cost of goods sold				(3,000,000)
Gross profit				$ 2,000,000
Operating expenses				(1,000,000)
Operating income				$ 1,000,000
Other taxable income and expenses:				
Interest income		$185,000		
Dividend income	$ 100,000			
Less 70% exclusion	70,000	30,000		
Interest expense		(40,000)	$ 175,000	
Gain on land sale:				
Selling price		$100,000		
Cost		(50,000)	$ 50,000	
Total taxable income			$ 1,225,000	
Tax computation:				
15% × $ 50,000 = $ 7,500				
25% × 25,000 = 6,250				
34% × 1,150,000 = 391,000				
$ 1,225,000				
Add 5% surtax for income between $100,000 and $335,000		$ 11,750		
Tax liability		$ 416,500		

est income and $100,000 in dividend income from another corporation. In turn, it paid $40,000 in interest and $75,000 in dividends. Finally, the company sold a piece of land for $100,000 that had cost $50,000 six years ago. Given this information, the firm's taxable income is $1,225,000, as computed in the top part of Table 1-3.

Based on the tax rates from Table 1-2, Griggs's tax liability is $416,500, as shown at the bottom of Table 1-3. Note that the $75,000 Griggs paid in dividends is not tax deductible. Also, because the firm's taxable income exceeds $335,000 and the 5 percent surtax no longer applies, the marginal tax rate and the average tax rate both equal 34 percent; that is, we could have computed Griggs's tax liability as 34 percent of $1,225,000, or $416,500.

Did You Get It?

1. What is the difference between the average and marginal tax rates?
2. Do the largest corporations get a tax break on the first dollars they earn?
3. Because all depreciation methods result in the same depreciation expense over the life of the asset, why would a firm want to use an accelerated depreciation method rather than a straight-line method?

TEN PRINCIPLES THAT FORM THE FOUNDATIONS OF FINANCIAL MANAGEMENT

Objective **4**

Explain the 10 principles that form the foundations of financial management.

To the first-time student of finance, the subject matter may seem like a collection of unrelated decision rules. This could not be further from the truth. In fact, our decision rules, and the logic that underlies them, spring from 10 simple principles that do not require knowledge of finance to understand. However, although it is not necessary to understand finance in order to understand these principles, it is necessary to understand these principles in order to understand finance. Keep in mind that although these principles may at first appear simple or even trivial, they provide the driving force behind all that follows. These principles weave together concepts and techniques presented in this text, thereby allowing us to focus on the logic underlying the practice of financial management.

Principle 1

The Risk–Return Trade-Off—We Won't Take On Additional Risk Unless We Expect to Be Compensated with Additional Return

At some point we have all saved some money. Why have we done this? The answer is simple: to expand our future consumption opportunities. We are able to invest those savings and earn a return on our dollars because some people would rather borrow money and forgo future consumption opportunities to consume more now. Maybe they're borrowing money to open a new business, or a company is borrowing money to build a new plant. Assuming there are a lot of different people who would like to use our savings, how do we decide where to put our money?

First, for delaying their consumption investors demand a minimum return that must be greater than the anticipated rate of inflation. If they didn't receive enough to compensate for anticipated inflation, investors would purchase whatever goods they desired ahead of time or invest in assets that were subject to inflation and earn the rate of inflation on those assets. There isn't much incentive to postpone consumption if your savings are going to decline in terms of their purchasing power, due to inflation.

Investment alternatives have different amounts of risk and expected returns. Investors sometimes choose to put their money in risky investments because these investments offer higher expected returns over and above inflation. The more risk an investment has, the higher will be its expected return. This relationship between risk and expected return is shown in Figure 1-2.

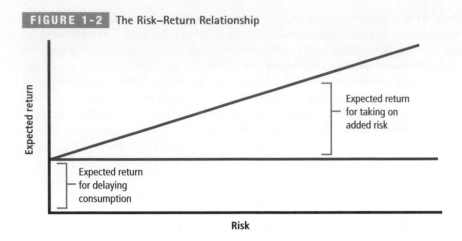

FIGURE 1-2 The Risk–Return Relationship

Notice that we keep referring to expected return rather than actual return. We may have expectations of what the returns from investing will be, but we can't know for certain.

This risk–return relationship is a key concept as we value stocks, bonds, and proposed new projects throughout this text. We also spend some time determining how to measure risk. Interestingly, much of the work for which the 1990 Nobel Prize for Economics was awarded centered on the graph in Figure 1-2 and how to measure risk. Both the graph and the risk–return relationship it depicts reappear often in this text.

Principle 2

The Time Value of Money—A Dollar Received Today Is Worth More Than a Dollar Received in the Future

As we mentioned, money has a time value associated with it: A dollar received today is worth more than a dollar received a year from now. Because we can earn interest on money received today, it is better to receive money earlier rather than later. In your economics courses, this concept of the time value of money is referred to as the opportunity cost of passing up the earning potential of a dollar today.

In this text, we focus on the creation and measurement of wealth. To measure wealth or value, we use the concept of the time value of money to bring the future benefits and costs of a project back to the present. Then, if the benefits outweigh the costs, the project creates wealth and should be accepted; if the costs outweigh the benefits, the project does not create wealth and should be rejected. Without recognizing the existence of the time value of money, it is impossible to evaluate projects with future benefits and costs in a meaningful way.

To bring future benefits and costs of a project back to the present, we must assume a specific opportunity cost of money, or interest rate. Exactly what interest rate to use is determined by **Principle 1: The Risk–Return Trade-Off**, which states that investors demand higher returns for taking on more risky projects. Thus, when we determine the present value of future benefits and costs, we take into account that investors demand a higher return for taking on added risk.

Principle 3

Cash—Not Profits—Is King

In measuring wealth or value we use cash flows, not accounting profits, as our measurement tool. That is, we are concerned with when we have money in hand, when we can invest it and start earning interest on it, and when we can give it back to the shareholders in the form of dividends. Remember, it is cash flows, not profits, that are actually received by the firm and can be reinvested. Accounting profits, on the other hand, are shown when they are earned rather than when the money is actually in hand. As a result, a firm's cash flows and accounting profits may not occur together. For example, capital expenses, such as the purchase of new equipment or a building, are depreciated over several years. Consequently, the annual depreciation subtracted from the firm's profits occurs only gradually. However, the cash flow associated with this expense generally occurs immediately. Therefore, cash outflows involving paying money out and cash inflows that can be reinvested correctly reflect the timing of the benefits and costs.

Principle 4

Incremental Cash Flows—It's Only What Changes That Counts

In making business decisions, we are concerned with the results of those decisions: What happens if we say yes versus what happens if we say no? **Principle 3** states that we should use cash flows to measure the benefits that accrue from taking on a new project. We are now fine-tuning our evaluation process so that we consider only incremental cash flows. The **incremental cash flow** is *the difference between the cash flows if the project is taken on versus what they will be if the project is not taken on.*

In 2006, when General Mills, the maker of Cheerios, Honey Nut Cheerios, Frosted Cheerios, Apple Cinnamon Cheerios, Berry Burst Cheerios, and Team Cheerios, introduced Yogurt Burst Cheerios—"the lightly sweet flavor of yogurt with the whole grain goodness of Cheerios"—it introduced a product that competed directly with General Mills' other cereals and, in particular, its Cheerios products. In fact, the Strawberry Yogurt Blast Cheerios, with its strawberry flavor sweetened with yogurt, tastes very much like Berry Burst Strawberry Cheerios. Certainly some of the sales dollars that ended up with Yogurt Burst Cheerios would have been spent on other Cheerios and General Mills' products if Yogurt Burst Cheerios had not been available. Although General Mills was targeting health conscious consumers with this sweetened cereal, there is no question that Yogurt Burst Cheerios sales bit into—actually cannibalized—sales from Cheerios and other General Mills lines. Realistically, there's only so much cereal anyone can eat. The difference between revenues General Mills generated after introducing Yogurt Burst Cheerios versus simply maintaining its existing line of cereals is the incremental cash flow. This difference reflects the true impact of the decision.

What is important is that we *think* incrementally. Our guiding rule in deciding whether a cash flow is incremental is to look at the company with and without the new product. In fact, let's take this incremental concept beyond cash flows and look at all consequences from all decisions on an incremental basis.

incremental cash flow the cash flows that result from the acceptance of a project the firm takes on.

Principle 5

The Curse of Competitive Markets—Why It's Hard to Find Exceptionally Profitable Projects

Our job as financial managers is to create wealth. Therefore, we look closely at the mechanics of valuation and decision making. We focus on estimating cash flows, determining what an investment earns, and valuing assets and new projects. However, it is easy to get caught up in the mechanics of valuation and lose sight of the process of creating wealth. Why is it so hard to find projects and investments that are exceptionally profitable? Where do profitable projects come from? The answers to these questions tell us a lot about how competitive markets operate and where to look for profitable projects.

In reality, it is much easier to evaluate profitable projects than find them. If an industry is generating large profits, new entrants are usually attracted. The additional competition is likely to drive profits down to the rate of return investors require. Conversely, if an industry is returning profits below the "required" rate of return, then some participants in the market drop out, reducing supply and competition. In return, prices are driven back up. This is precisely what happened in the VCR video rental market in the mid-1980s. This market developed suddenly with the opportunity for extremely large profits. Because there were no barriers to entry, the market quickly was flooded with new entries. By 1987 the competition and price cutting produced losses for many firms in the industry, forcing them to flee the market. As the competition lessened and firms moved out of the video rental industry, profits again rose to the point at which the required rate of return could be earned on invested capital.

In competitive markets, extremely large profits simply cannot exist for very long. Given that somewhat bleak scenario, how can we find good projects—that is, projects that return more than their expected rate of return given their risk level (remember Principle 1)? Although competition makes them difficult to find, we have to invest in markets that are not perfectly competitive. The two most common ways of making markets less competitive are to differentiate the product in some key way and to achieve a cost advantage over one's competitors.

If products are differentiated, the consumer's choice is no longer made on the basis of price alone. For example, many people are willing to pay a premium for Starbucks coffee. They simply want Starbucks and price is not important. In the pharmaceutical industry, patents create competitive barriers. For example, Hoffman–La Roche's Valium, a tranquilizer, is protected from direct competition by patents.

Service and quality are also used to differentiate products. For example, Levi's has long prided itself on the quality of its jeans. As a result, it has been able to maintain its market share. Similarly, much of Toyota's and Honda's brand loyalty is based on quality. Service can also create product differentiation, as shown by McDonald's fast service, cleanliness, and consistency of product, which bring customers back. Whether product differentiation occurs because of advertising, patents, service, or quality, the more the product is differentiated from competing products, the less competition it will face and the greater the possibility of large profits.

Economies of scale and the ability to produce at a cost below competition can effectively deter new entrants to the market and thereby reduce competition. Wal-Mart is one such case. For Wal-Mart, the fixed costs are largely independent of the store's size. For example, inventory costs, advertising expenses, and managerial salaries are essentially the same regardless of annual sales. Therefore, the more sales that can be built up, the lower the per-sale dollar cost of inventory, advertising, and management. Restocking from warehouses also becomes more efficient because delivery trucks can be used to full potential.

Regardless of how the cost advantage is created—by economies of scale, proprietary technology, or monopolistic control of raw materials—it deters new market entrants while allowing production at below industry cost. This cost advantage has the potential of creating large profits.

The key to locating profitable investment projects is to first understand how and where they exist in competitive markets. Then the corporate philosophy must be aimed at creating or taking advantage of some imperfection in these markets, through either product differentiation or creation of a cost advantage, rather than looking to new markets or industries that appear to provide large profits. Any perfectly competitive industry that looks too good to be true won't be for long. It is necessary to understand this to know where to look for good projects and to accurately measure the project's cash flows. We can do this better if we recognize how wealth is created and how difficult it is to create.

Principle 6

Efficient Capital Markets—The Markets Are Quick and the Prices Are Right

efficient market a market in which the prices of securities at any instant in time fully reflect all publicly available information about the securities and their actual public values.

As we have said, our goal as financial managers is the maximization of shareholder wealth. But how do we measure shareholder wealth? It is the value of all the shares that the shareholders own. To understand what causes stocks to change in price, as well as how securities such as bonds and stocks are valued or priced in the financial markets, it is necessary to have an understanding of the concept of **efficient markets**. *These are markets in which the values of all assets and securities at any instant in time fully reflect all available information.*

Whether a market is efficient has to do with the speed with which information is impounded into security prices. An efficient market is characterized by a large number of profit-driven individuals who act independently. In addition, new information regarding securities arrives in the market in a random manner. Given this setting, investors adjust to new information immediately and buy and sell a security until they feel the market price correctly reflects the new information. In efficient markets information is reflected in security prices with such speed that there are no opportunities for investors to profit from publicly available information. Investors competing for profits ensure that security prices appropriately reflect the expected earnings and risks involved and, thus, the true value of the firm.

What are the implications of efficient markets for us? First, the price is right. Stock prices reflect all publicly available information regarding the value of the company. This means we can implement our goal of maximization of shareholder wealth by focusing on the effect each decision *should* have on the stock price if everything else is held constant. That is, over time good decisions result in higher stock prices and bad ones in lower stock prices. Accounting changes, for example, do not result in price changes because they do not affect cash flows. Rather, market prices reflect the expected cash flows available to shareholders. Thus, our preoccupation with cash flows to measure the timing of the benefits is justified.

As we will see, it is indeed reassuring that prices reflect value. It allows us to look at prices and see value reflected in them. Although it may make investing a bit less exciting, it makes corporate finance much less uncertain.

Principle 7

The Agency Problem—Managers Won't Work for the Firm's Owners Unless It's in Their Best Interest

Although the goal of the firm is the maximization of shareholder wealth, in reality the agency problem may interfere with the implementation of this goal. The **agency problem** *results from the separation of the management and the ownership of the firm.*

To begin with, an agent is someone who is given the authority to act on behalf of another, who is referred to as the principal. In the corporate setting, the shareholders are the principals, because they are the actual owners of the firm. The board of directors, the CEO, the corporate executives, and all others with decision-making power are agents of the shareholders. Because of this separation of the decision makers and owners, managers may make decisions that are not in line with the goal of maximizing shareholder wealth. They may approach work less energetically and attempt to benefit themselves in terms of their salaries and "perks" at the expense of shareholders. The firm's top managers might also avoid any projects that have risk associated with them—even if they're great projects with huge potential returns and a small chance of failure. Why is this so? Because if the project doesn't turn out, these agents of the shareholders may lose their jobs.

The costs associated with the agency problem are difficult to measure, but occasionally we see the problem's effect in the marketplace. For example, if the market feels the management of a firm is damaging shareholder wealth, we might see a positive reaction in the stock price following the removal of that management. In 2005, on the announcement of the death of Roy Farmer, the CEO of Farmer Brothers, a seller of coffee-related products, Farmer Brothers' stock price rose about 28 percent. Generally, the tragic loss of a company's top executive raises concerns over a leadership void, causing the share price to drop, but in the case of Farmer Brothers, investors thought a change in management would have a positive impact on the company.

If the managers of the firm work for the owners, who are the shareholders, why don't the managers get fired if they don't act in the shareholders' best interest? *In theory*, the shareholders pick the corporate board of directors and the board of directors in turn picks the managers. Unfortunately, *in reality* the system frequently works the other way around. Managers select the board of director nominees and then distribute the ballots. In effect, shareholders are offered a slate of nominees selected by the management. The end result is that

agency problem problems and conflicts resulting from the separation of the management and ownership of the firm.

the directors may have more allegiance to the managers than to shareholders. This in turn sets up the potential for agency problems, with the board of directors not monitoring managers on behalf of the shareholders as they should.

We spend considerable time discussing monitoring managers and trying to align their interests with shareholders. The interests of managers and shareholders can be aligned by establishing management stock options, bonuses, and perquisites that are directly tied to how closely their decisions coincide with the interest of shareholders. The agency problem will persist unless an incentive structure is set up that aligns the interests of managers and shareholders. In other words, what is good for shareholders must also be good for managers. If that is not the case, managers will make decisions in their own best interest rather than maximizing shareholder wealth.

Principle 8

Taxes Bias Business Decisions

Hardly any decision is made by the financial manager without considering the impact of taxes. When we introduced **Principle 4**, we said that only incremental cash flows should be considered in the evaluation process. More specifically, the cash flows we consider are the *after-tax incremental cash flows to the firm as a whole.*

When we evaluate new projects, we will see income taxes play a significant role. For example, when the company is analyzing the possible acquisition of a plant or equipment, the returns from the investment should be measured on an after-tax basis. Otherwise, the company is not evaluating the true incremental cash flows generated by the project.

The government also realizes taxes can bias business decisions and uses taxes to encourage spending in certain ways. If the government wants to encourage spending on research and development projects, it might offer an *investment tax credit* for such investments. This would have the effect of reducing taxes on research and development projects, which would in turn increase the after-tax cash flows from those projects. The increased cash flow would turn some otherwise unprofitable research and development projects into profitable projects. In effect, the government can use taxes as a tool to direct business investment to research and development projects, to the inner cities, and to projects that create jobs.

Principle 9

All Risk Is Not Equal—Some Risk Can Be Diversified Away, and Some Can Not

Much of finance centers around **Principle 1, the Risk–Return Trade-Off**. But before we can fully use **Principle 1**, we must decide how to measure risk. As we will see, risk is difficult to measure. **Principle 9** introduces you to the process of diversification and demonstrates how it can reduce risk. We also provide you with an understanding of how diversification makes it difficult to measure a project's or an asset's risk.

You are probably already familiar with the concept of diversification. There is an old saying, "don't put all your eggs in one basket." Diversification allows good and bad events to cancel each other out, thereby reducing the total variability of a project, or investment, without affecting its expected return.

To see how diversification complicates the measurement of risk, let's look at the difficulty Louisiana Gas has in determining the level of risk associated with a new natural gas well-drilling project. Each year Louisiana Gas might drill several hundred wells, with each well having only a 1 in 10 chance of success. If the well produces, the profits are quite large, but if it comes up dry, the investment is lost. Thus, with a 90 percent chance of losing everything, we would view the project as being extremely risky. However, if each year Louisiana Gas drills 2,000 wells, all with a 10 percent, independent chance of success, then it would typically have 200 successful wells. Moreover, a bad year may result in only 190 successful

wells, whereas a good year may result in 210 successful wells. If we look at all the wells together, the extreme good and the bad results tend to cancel each other out and the well-
drilling projects taken together do not appear to have much risk or variability of possible
outcome.

The amount of risk in a gas well project depends on our perspective. Looking at the well
standing alone, it looks like a lot of risk. However, if we consider the risk that each well contributes to the overall firm risk, it is quite small. This occurs because much of the risk associated with each individual well is diversified away within the firm. The point is we can't look
at a project in isolation. Later, we will see that some of this risk can be further diversified
away within the shareholder's portfolio.

Perhaps the easiest way to understand the concept of diversification is to look at it graphically. Consider what happens when we combine two projects, as depicted in Figure 1-3. In
this case, the cash flows from these projects move in opposite directions, but when they are
combined, the variability of their combination is totally eliminated. Notice that the return has
not changed—both the individual projects' returns and their combination's return average
10 percent. In this case the extreme good and bad observations cancel each other out. The degree to which the total risk is reduced is a function of how the two sets of cash flows or returns
from the projects move together.

As we will see for most projects and assets, some risk can be eliminated through diversification, whereas some risk can not. This becomes an important distinction later in our studies.
*For now, we should realize that the process of diversification can reduce risk, and as a result, measuring
a project's or an asset's risk is very difficult.* A project's risk changes depending on whether you
measure it standing alone or together with other projects the company may take on.

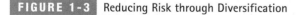

Principle 10

Ethical Behavior Means Doing the Right Thing, but Ethical Dilemmas Are Everywhere in Finance

Ethical behavior means "doing the right thing." The difficulty arises, however, in attempting to define "doing the right thing." The problem is that each of us has his or her own set
of values, which forms the basis for our personal judgments about what is the right thing
to do. However, every society adopts a set of rules or laws that prescribe what it believes to
be "doing the right thing." In a sense, we can think of laws as a set of rules that reflect the
values of the society as a whole, as they have evolved. For purposes of this text, we recognize that people have a right to disagree about what constitutes "doing the right thing," and
we seldom venture beyond the basic notion that ethical conduct involves abiding by society's rules. However, we point out some of the ethical dilemmas that have arisen in recent
years with regard to the practice of financial management. So as we embark on our study

FIGURE 1-3   Reducing Risk through Diversification

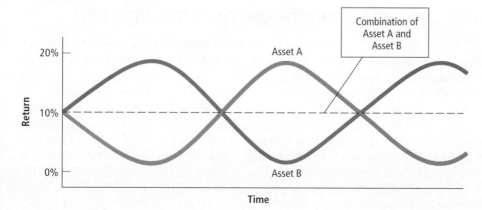

of finance and encounter ethical dilemmas, we encourage you to consider the issues and form your own opinions.

Many students ask, "Is ethics really relevant?" This is a good question and deserves an answer. First, although business errors can be forgiven, ethical errors tend to end careers and terminate future opportunities. Why? Because *unethical behavior eliminates trust, and without trust businesses cannot interact*. Second, *the most damaging event a business can experience is a loss of the public's confidence in its ethical standards*. In finance we have seen several recent examples of such events. Ethics, or rather a lack of ethics, in finance is a recurring theme in the news. Scandals like those at Salomon Brothers, Enron, WorldCom, and Tyco seem to make continuous headlines. But as the lessons of these companies illustrate, ethical errors are not forgiven in the business world. Not only is acting in an ethical manner morally correct, but also it is congruent with our goal of maximization of shareholder wealth.

Beyond the question of ethics is the question of social responsibility. In general, corporate social responsibility means that a corporation has responsibilities to society beyond the maximization of shareholder wealth. It asserts that a corporation answers to a broader constituency than its shareholders alone. As with most debates that center on ethical and moral questions, there is no definitive answer. One opinion is that because financial managers are employees of the corporation and the corporation is owned by the shareholders, the financial managers should run the corporation in such a way that shareholder wealth is maximized and then allow the shareholders to decide if they would like to fulfill a sense of social responsibility by passing on any of the profits to deserving causes. Very few corporations consistently act in this way. For example, Bristol-Myers Squibb Co. has an ambitious program to give away heart medication to those who cannot pay for it. This program came in the wake of an American Heart Association report showing that many of the nation's working poor face severe health risks because they cannot afford such medications. Clearly, Bristol-Myers Squibb felt it had a social responsibility to provide this medicine to the poor at no cost.

How do you feel about this decision?

A Final Note on the 10 Principles

Hopefully, these principles are as much statements of common sense as they are theoretical statements. They provide the logic behind what is to follow. We build on them and attempt to draw out their implications for decision making. As we continue, try to keep in mind that although the topics being treated may change from chapter to chapter, the logic driving our treatment of them is constant and rooted in these 10 principles.

Did You Get It?

1. According to Principle 1, how do investors decide where to invest their money?
2. Why is it so hard to find extremely profitable projects?
3. Why is ethics relevant?

Objective **5**

Explain what has led to the era of the multinational corporation.

FINANCE AND THE MULTINATIONAL FIRM: THE NEW ROLE

In the search for profits, U.S. corporations have been forced to look beyond our country's borders. This movement has been spurred on by the collapse of communism and the acceptance of the free market system in third world countries. All this has taken place at a time when information technology has experienced a revolution brought on by the personal computer and the Internet. Concurrently, the United States went through an unprecedented period of deregulation of industries. These changes resulted in the opening of new international markets, and U.S. firms experienced a period of price competition here at home that made it imperative that businesses look across borders for investment opportunities. The end result is that many U.S. companies, including General Electric, IBM, Walt Disney, American Express, and General Motors, have restructured their operations to expand internationally.

Ethics in Financial Management

THE ENRON LESSONS: TRUST

The bankruptcy and failure of the Enron Corporation in late 2001 and the trial of Enron's CEO, Kenneth Lay, in 2006, shook the investment community to its very core and resulted in congressional hearings that led to new regulations with far-reaching implications. Enron's failure provides a sober warning to employees and investors and a valuable set of lessons for students of business. The lesson we offer here reaches far beyond corporate finance and touches on fundamental principles that have always been true but are sometimes forgotten.

Lesson: Trust and Credibility Are Essential to Business Success

The viability of any firm hinges critically on the firm's credibility with its customers, employees, regulators, investors, and even to some degree, competitors. This is particularly critical for a trading company such as Enron, whose primary business rests on the willingness of the firm's counterpart with whom it trades to "trust" in Enron's ability to "be there" when the time to settle up arrives. When the faith of the investment community was tested with the revelation of losses from some of Enron's largest investments and the subsequent disclosure of Enron's off-balance-sheet liabilities, Enron's trading business evaporated.

We also were reminded of the fact that investors must believe that a firm's published financial reports are a fair representation of the firm's financial condition. Without this trust, outside investors would refuse to invest in the shares of publicly traded firms, and financial markets would collapse.[a]

Trust between two entities is hard to sustain when one of the parties has dual and conflicting motives. We refer to the presence of multiple motives as a conflict of interest, and the potential for conflict-of-interest problems was in abundance as Enron fell to earth. Some of the following sources of conflict apply only to Enron, whereas others apply to many firms:

- Andy Fastow, Enron's chief financial officer (CFO), attempted to serve two masters when he was both the CFO and the general partner for a series of limited partnerships used by Enron to finance its investments and hedge certain investment returns. There were times when he represented the interests of Enron in circumstances that were in direct conflict with the interests of the partners to the partnerships. It is still not clear how he handled these circumstances, but the source of concern to Enron's shareholders is obvious.

- Allegations abound that top corporate executives at Enron were selling their shares long before other employees and outside investors knew how serious the firm's problems were. Regardless of the outcome in the Enron case, this raises a serious dilemma for investors, who cannot know as much about the financial condition of the firms in which they invest as the managers know.

- The Enron failure has called into question the wisdom of relying on external auditing firms that are beholden to the firms they audit, both for their continued employment as an auditor and for consulting fees that can sometimes dwarf their audit fees.

- Finally, investors often rely on the opinions of equity analysts. Investors make the assumption that the analysts are offering unfettered, independent opinions of a company's financial prospects. However, in many cases the analysts work for investment banks that, in turn, rely on investment-banking fees from the very companies the analysts cover. The potential conflict of interest is obvious.

[a] This is simply a recasting of the famous result from microeconomics stating that where informational asymmetry problems between buyers and sellers are extreme, markets will collapse [George Akerlof, "The Market for Lemons: Qualitative Uncertainty and the Market Mechanism," *Quarterly Journal of Economics*, 84 (1970), pp. 488–500].

The bottom line is what you think of as a U.S. firm may be much more of a multinational firm than you would expect. For example, Coca-Cola earns over 80 percent of its profits from overseas sales and more money from its sales in Japan than it does from all its domestic sales. This is not uncommon. In fact, Dow Chemical, Colgate-Palmolive, 3M, Compaq, Hewlett-Packard, and Gillette make over half their sales overseas and earn over half of their profits from international sales.

In addition to U.S. firms venturing abroad, foreign firms have also made their mark in the United States. You need only look to the auto industry to see what changes the entrance of Toyota, Honda, Nissan, BMW, and other foreign car manufacturers have had on the auto industry. In addition, foreigners have bought and now own such companies as Brooks Brothers, RCA, Pillsbury, A&P, 20th Century Fox, Columbia Pictures, and Firestone Tire & Rubber. Consequently, even if we wanted to, we couldn't keep all our attention focused on the United States, and even more important, we wouldn't want to ignore the opportunities that are available across international borders.

Did You Get It? ....

1.   What has brought on the era of the multinational corporation?
2.   Has looking beyond U.S. borders been a profitable experience for U.S. corporations?

Summary

Objective **1**

Identify the goal of the firm.

This chapter outlines the framework for the maintenance and creation of shareholder wealth, which should be the goal of the firm and its managers. The commonly accepted goal of profit maximization is contrasted with the more complete goal of the maximization of shareholder wealth. Because it deals well with uncertainty and time in a real-world environment, the maximization of shareholder wealth is found to be the proper goal for the firm.

Objective **2**

Compare the various legal forms of business organization and explain why the corporate form of business is the most logical choice for a firm that is large or growing.

The legal forms of business are examined. The sole proprietorship is a business operation owned and managed by an individual. Initiating this form of business is simple and generally does not involve any substantial organizational costs. The proprietor has complete control of the firm but must be willing to assume full responsibility for its outcomes.

The general partnership, which is simply a coming together of two or more individuals, is similar to the sole proprietorship. The limited partnership is another form of partnership sanctioned by states to permit all but one of the partners to have limited liability if this is agreeable to all partners.

The corporation increases the flow of capital from public investors to the business community. Although larger organizational costs and regulations are imposed on this legal entity, the corporation is more conducive to raising large amounts of capital. Limited liability, continuity of life, and ease of transfer in ownership, which increase the marketability of the investment, have contributed greatly in attracting large numbers of investors to the corporate environment. The formal control of the corporation is vested in the parties who own the greatest number of shares. However, day-to-day operations are managed by the corporate officers, who theoretically serve on behalf of the firm's stockholders.

Objective **3**

Describe the corporate tax features that affect business decisions.

The tax environment is presented insomuch as taxes affect our business decisions. Three taxable entities exist: the individual, including partnerships; the corporation; and the fiduciary. Only information on the corporate tax environment is given here.

For the most part, taxable income for the corporation is equal to the firm's operating income plus capital gains less any interest expense. The corporation is allowed an income exclusion of 70 percent of the dividends received from another corporation.

Tax consequences, particularly marginal tax rates, have a direct bearing on the decisions of the financial manager.

Objective **4**

Explain the 10 principles that form the foundations of financial management.

An examination of the 10 principles on which finance is built is presented. The techniques and tools introduced in this text are all motivated by these 10 principles. They are

Principle 1

The Risk–Return Trade-Off—We Won't Take On Additional Risk Unless We Expect to Be Compensated with Additional Return

Principle 2

The Time Value of Money—A Dollar Received Today Is Worth More Than a Dollar Received in the Future

Principle 3

Cash—Not Profits—Is King

Principle 4

Incremental Cash Flows—It's Only What Changes That Counts

Principle 5

The Curse of Competitive Markets—Why It's Hard to Find Exceptionally Profitable Projects

Principle 6

Efficient Capital Markets—The Markets Are Quick and the Prices Are Right

Principle 7

The Agency Problem—Managers Won't Work for the Firm's Owners Unless It's in Their Best Interest

Principle 8

Taxes Bias Business Decisions

Principle 9

All Risk Is Not Equal—Some Risk Can Be Diversified Away, and Some Can Not

Principle 10

Ethical Behavior Means Doing the Right Thing, but Ethical Dilemmas Are Everywhere in Finance

With the collapse of communism and the acceptance of the free market system in third world countries, U.S. firms have been spurred on to look beyond their own boundaries for new business. The end result has been that it is not uncommon for major U.S. companies to earn over half their income from sales abroad. Foreign firms are also increasingly investing in the United States.

Objective **5**

Explain what has led to the era of the multinational corporation.

Key Terms

Agency problem   19

Capital gain (or loss)   13

Corporation   8

Depreciation   13

Efficient market   18

General partnership   8

Gross income   11

Incremental cash flow   17

Limited liability company (LLC)   9

Limited partnership   8

Marginal tax rate   12

Net operating loss carryback and carryforward   14

Partnership   7

Sole proprietorship   7

S-type corporation   9

Taxable income   11

Review Questions

1-1. What are some of the problems involved in the use of profit maximization as the goal of the firm? How does the goal of maximization of shareholder wealth deal with those problems?

1-2. Compare and contrast the goals of profit maximization and maximization of shareholder wealth.

1-3. Firms often involve themselves in projects that do not result directly in profits. For example, IBM and ExxonMobil frequently support public television broadcasts. Do these projects contradict the goal of maximization of shareholder wealth? Why or why not?

1-4. What is the relationship between financial decision making and risk and return? Would all financial managers view risk–return trade-offs similarly?

1-5. Define (a) sole proprietorship, (b) partnership, and (c) corporation.

1-6. Identify the primary characteristics of each form of legal organization.

1-7. Using the following criteria, specify the legal form of business that is favored: (a) organizational requirements and costs, (b) liability of the owners, (c) the continuity of the business, (d) the transferability of ownership, (e) management control and regulations, (f) the ability to raise capital, and (g) income taxes.

1-8. Does a partnership pay taxes on its income? Explain.

1-9. When a corporation receives a dividend from another corporation, how is it taxed?

1-10. What is the purpose of the net operating loss carryback and carryforward?

Self-Test Problem

The solution to this problem is provided at the end of the chapter.

ST-1. (*Corporate income tax*) The Dana Flatt Corporation had sales of $2 million this past year. Its cost of goods sold was $1.2 million, and its operating expenses were $400,000. Interest expenses on outstanding debts were $100,000, and the company paid $40,000 in preferred stock dividends. The corporation received $10,000 in preferred stock dividends and interest income of $12,000. The firm sold stock that had been owned for 2 years for $40,000; the original cost of the stock was $30,000. Determine the corporation's taxable income and its tax liability.

Study Problems

1-1. (*Corporate income tax*) The William B. Waugh Corporation is a regional Toyota dealer. The firm sells new and used trucks and is actively involved in the parts business. During the most recent year the company generated sales of $3 million. The combined cost of goods sold and the operating expenses were $2.1 million. Also, $400,000 in interest expense was paid during the year. The firm received $6,000 during the year in dividend income from 1,000 shares of common stock that had been purchased 3 years previously. However, the stock was sold toward the end of the year for $100 per share; its initial cost was $80 per share. The company also sold land that had been recently purchased and had been held for only 4 months. The selling price was $50,000; the cost was $45,000. Calculate the corporation's tax liability.

1-2. (*Corporate income tax*) Sales for L. B. Menielle Inc. during the past year amounted to $5 million. The firm provides parts and supplies for oil field service companies. Gross profits for the year were $3 million. Operating expenses totaled $1 million. The interest and dividend income from the securities it owned were $20,000 and $25,000, respectively. The firm's interest expense was $100,000. The firm sold securities on two occasions during the year, receiving a gain of $40,000 on the first sale but losing $50,000 on the second. The stock sold first had been owned for 4 years; the stock sold second had been purchased 3 months before the sale. Compute the corporation's tax liability.

1-3. (*Corporate income tax*) Sandersen Inc. sells minicomputers. During the past year the company's sales were $3 million. The cost of its merchandise sold came to $2 million, and cash operating expenses were $400,000; depreciation expense was $100,000, and the firm paid $150,000 in interest on its bank loans. Also, the corporation received $50,000 in dividend income but paid $25,000 in the form of dividends to its own common stockholders. Calculate the corporation's tax liability.

1-4. (*Corporate income tax*) A. Don Drennan Inc. had sales of $6 million during the past year. The company's cost of goods sold was 70 percent of sales; operating expenses, including depreciation, amounted to $800,000. The firm sold a capital asset (stock) for $75,000, which had been purchased 5 months earlier at a cost of $80,000. Determine the company's tax liability.

1-5. (*Corporate income tax*) The Robbins Corporation is an oil wholesaler. The company's sales last year were $1 million, with the cost of goods sold equal to $600,000. The firm paid interest of $200,000, and its cash operating expenses were $100,000. Also, the firm received $40,000 in dividend income while paying only $10,000 in dividends to its preferred stockholders. Depreciation expense was $150,000. Compute the firm's tax liability. Based on your answer, does management need to take any additional action?

1-6. (*Corporate income tax*) The Fair Corporation had sales of $5 million this past year. The cost of goods sold was $4.3 million, and operating expenses were $100,000. Dividend income totaled $5,000. The firm sold land for $150,000 that had cost $100,000 5 months ago. The firm received $150 per share from the sale of 1,000 shares of stock. The stock was purchased for $100 per share 3 years ago. Determine the firm's tax liability.

1-7. (*Corporate income tax*) Sales for J. P. Hulett Inc. during the past year amounted to $4 million. The firm supplies statistical information to engineering companies. Gross profits totaled $1 million, and operating and depreciation expenses were $500,000 and $350,000, respectively. Dividend income for the year was $12,000. Compute the corporation's tax liability.

1-8. (*Corporate income tax*) Anderson & Dennis Inc. sells computer software. The company's past year's sales were $5 million. The cost of its merchandise sold came to $3 million. Operating expenses were $175,000, plus depreciation expenses totaling $125,000. The firm paid $200,000 interest on loans. The firm sold stock during the year, receiving a $40,000 gain on a stock owned 6 years but losing $60,000 on stock held 4 months. Calculate the company's tax liability.

1-9. (*Corporate income tax*) G. R. Edwin Inc. had sales of $6 million during the past year. The cost of goods sold amounted to $3 million. Operating expenses totaled $2.6 million, and interest expense was $30,000. Determine the firm's tax liability.

1-10. (*Corporate income tax*) The Analtoly Corporation is an electronics dealer and distributor. Sales for the last year were $4.5 million, and cost of goods sold and operating expenses totaled $3.2 million. Analtoly also paid $150,000 in interest expense, and depreciation expense totaled $50,000. In addition, the company sold securities for $120,000 that it had purchased 4 years earlier at a price of $40,000. Compute the tax liability for Analtoly.

1-11. (*Corporate income tax*) Utsumi Inc. supplies wholesale industrial chemicals. Last year the company had sales of $6.5 million. Cost of goods sold and operating expenses amounted to 70 percent of sales, and depreciation and interest expenses were $75,000 and $160,000, respectively. Furthermore, the corporation sold 40,000 shares of Sumitomo Industries for $10 a share. These shares were purchased 1 year ago for $8 each. In addition, Utsumi received $60,000 in dividend income. Compute the corporation's tax liability.

1-12. (*Corporate income tax*) Mdyer Inc. had taxable income of $300,000. Calculate Mdyer's federal income taxes.

1-13. (*Corporate income tax*) Fighting Dyer Inc. had taxable income of $20 million. Calculate Fighting Dyer's federal income taxes.

1-14. (*Corporate income tax*) Boisjoly Productions had taxable income of $19 million.
   a. Calculate Boisjoly's federal income taxes.
   b. Now calculate Boisjoly's average and marginal tax rates.
   c. What would Boisjoly's federal income taxes be if its taxable income was $29 million?
   d. Now calculate Boisjoly's average and marginal tax rates with taxable income of $29 million.

Web Works

1-WW1. There are a lot of great business majors. Checks out the Careers in Business Web site at **www.careers-in-business.com**. It covers not only finance but also marketing, accounting, and management. Find out and provide a short write-up describing the opportunities investment banking and financial planning offer.

1-WW2. Like it or not, ethical problems seem to crop up all the time in finance. Some of the worst financial scandals are examined on the Financial Scandals Web site **www.ex.ac.uk/~RDavies/arian/scandals/classic.html**. Take a look at the write-ups dealing with "The Dot-Com Bubble and Investment Banks" and "Enron Corp. and Arthur Andersen." Provide a short write-up on the major characters in these scandals.

1-WW3. As you'll soon find out, finance has a language all its own. If you ever come across terms you aren't familiar with, try looking them up in the Investopedia financial dictionary at **www.investopedia.com/dictionary**. Look up "Ben Bernanke" and "Management Buyout-MBO" and write up the definitions you found.

1-WW4. We know that if a corporation is to maximize shareholder wealth, the interests of the managers and the shareholders must be aligned. The simplest way to align these interests is to structure executive compensation packages appropriately to encourage managers to act in the best interests of shareholders. However, has executive compensation gotten out of control? Take a look at the Executive Pay Watch Web site at **www.aflcio.org/corporatewatch/paywatch** to see to whom top salaries have gone. What are the most recent total compensation packages for the head of Home Depot (HD), Disney (DIS), and Exxon Mobil (XOM)?

Mini Case

The final stage in the interview process for an assistant financial analyst at Caledonia Products involves a test of your understanding of basic financial concepts and of the corporate tax code. You are given the following memorandum and asked to respond to the questions. Whether you are offered a position at Caledonia will depend on the accuracy of your response.

> To: Applicants for the position of Financial Analyst
> From: Mr. V. Morrison, CEO, Caledonia Products
> Re: A test of your understanding of basic financial concepts and of the corporate tax code

Please respond to the following questions:

   a. What are the differences between the goals of profit maximization and the maximization of shareholder wealth? Which goal do you think is more appropriate?
   b. What does the risk–return trade-off mean?
   c. Why are we interested in cash flows rather than accounting profits in determining the value of an asset?
   d. What is an efficient market and what are the implications of efficient markets for us?
   e. What is the cause of the agency problem and how do we try to solve it?
   f. What do ethics and ethical behavior have to do with finance?
   g. Define (1) sole proprietorship, (2) partnership, and (3) corporation.
   h. The Carrickfergus Corporation had sales of $4 million this past year. Its cost of goods sold was $2.4 million, and its operating expenses were $600,000. Interest expenses on outstanding debts were $300,000, and the company paid $60,000 in preferred stock dividends. The corporation received $30,000 in preferred stock dividends and interest income of $22,000. The firm sold stock that it had owned for 2 years for $100,000; the original cost of the stock was $60,000. Determine the corporation's taxable income and its tax liability.

Self-Test Solution

ST-1.

Sales		$2,000,000
Cost of goods sold		1,200,000
Gross profit		800,000
Tax-deductible expenses:		
Operating expenses	$400,000	
Interest expenses	100,000	500,000
		$ 300,000
Other income:		
Interest income		12,000
Preferred dividend income	$ 10,000	
Less 70% exclusion	7,000	3,000
Taxable ordinary income		$ 315,000
Gain on sale:		
Selling price	$ 40,000	
Cost	30,000	10,000
Taxable income		$ 325,000
Tax liability		

$.15 \times \$50,000 =$	$	7,500
$.25 \times \$25,000 =$		6,250
$.34 \times \$250,000 =$		85,000
5% surtax		11,250
		$ 110,000

✎ LEARNING OBJECTIVES ✎

After reading this chapter, you should be able to:

1. Describe key components of the U.S. financial market system.

2. Understand the role of the investment-banking business in the context of raising corporate capital.

3. Distinguish between privately placed securities and publicly offered securities.

4. Be acquainted with securities flotation costs and securities markets regulations.

5. Understand the rate-of-return relationships among various classes of financing vehicles that persist in the financial markets.

6. Be acquainted with recent interest rate levels and the fundamentals of interest rate determination.

7. Explain the popular theories of the term structure of interest rates.

8. Understand the relationships among the multinational firm, efficient financial markets, and intercountry risk.

CHAPTER 2

The Financial Markets and Interest Rates

Back in 1995, when they first met, Larry Page and Sergey Brin were not particularly fond of one another. Larry was on a weekend visit to Stanford University, and Sergey was in a group of students assigned to show him around. Nonetheless, in short time the two began to collaborate and even built their own computer housings in Larry's dorm room. That computer housing later became Google's first data center. From there things didn't move as smoothly as one might expect, there just wasn't the interest from the search-engine players of the day, so Larry and Sergey decided to go it alone. Stuck in a dorm room with maxed-out credit cards, the problem they faced was money—they didn't have any. So they put together a business plan and went looking for money. Fortunately for all of us that use Google today, they met up with one of the founders of Sun Microsystems, and after a short demo he had to run off somewhere and upon leaving said, "Instead of us discussing all the details, why don't I just write you a check?" It was made out to Google Inc. and was for $100,000.

With that, Google Inc. was founded, and over the next 10 years it became anything but a conventional company, with an official motto of "don't be evil"; a goal to make the world a better place; on-site meals prepared by a former caterer for the Grateful Dead; lava lamps; and a fleet of Segways to move employees about the Google campus to roller-hockey games in the parking lot and to other on-site diversions. It was not unexpected that when Google needed more money in 2004 it would raise that money in an unusual way—through a "Dutch auction." With a Dutch auction investors submit bids, saying how many shares they'd like and at what price. Next, Google used these bids to calculate an issue price that was just low enough to ensure that all the shares were sold, and everyone who bid at least that price got to buy shares at the issue price.

Eventually, Google settled on an issue price of $85 per share, and on August 19, 2004, it raised $1.76 billion dollars. How did those initial investors do? On the first day of trading Google's shares rose by 18 percent, and by mid-March 2005 the price of Google stock had risen to about $340 per share! In September 2005, Google went back to the financial markets and sold another 14.18 million shares at $295 per share, and by March 2007 it was selling at around $460 per share.

As you read this chapter you will learn about how funds are raised in the financial markets. This will help you, as an emerging business executive specializing in accounting, finance, marketing, or strategy, understand the basics of acquiring financial capital in the funds marketplace.

This chapter focuses on the market environment in which long-term financial capital is raised. Long-term funds are raised in the capital market. By the term *capital market*, we mean all institutions and procedures that facilitate transactions for long-term financial instruments, such as common stocks and bonds.

We will introduce the logic behind the determination of interest rates and required rates of return in the capital markets. We will also explore interest rate levels and risk differentials (premia) over recent time periods. This knowledge of financial market history will permit you as both a financial manager and an investor to realize that earning, say, a 40 percent annual return on a common stock investment does not occur very often.

As you work through this chapter, be on the lookout for direct applications of several of our principles that form the basics of business financial management. Specifically, your attention will be directed to: **Principle 1: The Risk–Return Trade-Off—We Won't Take On Additional Risk Unless We Expect to Be Compensated with Additional Return; Principle 6: Efficient Capital Markets—The Markets Are Quick and the Prices Are Right**; and **Principle 10: Ethical Behavior Means Doing the Right Thing, and Ethical Dilemmas Are Everywhere in Finance**.

COMPONENTS OF THE U.S. FINANCIAL MARKET SYSTEM

Objective 1

Describe key components of the U.S. financial market system.

In Chapter 1 we examined the different business forms, and we found that the ease of raising capital is the major reason for the popularity of the corporate form. After all, at times, internally generated funds will not be sufficient to finance all of the firm's proposed expenditures. In these situations, it becomes necessary to raise large amounts of financial capital externally or otherwise forgo projects that are forecast to be profitable. It is the financial markets that make all this possible.

Figure 2-1 examines the relationship between the financial markets and the corporation. (1) Initially, the corporation raises funds in the financial markets by selling securities. The corporation receives cash in return for securities—stocks and debt. (2) The corporation then invests this cash in return-generating assets—new projects for example. (3) The cash flow from those assets is then reinvested in the corporation, given back to the investors in the form of dividends or interest payments, used to repurchase stock, which should cause the stock price to rise, or given to the government in the form of tax payments.

A securities market is simply a place where you can buy or sell securities. These markets can take the form of anything from an actual building on Wall Street in New York City to an electronic hookup among security dealers all over the world. Let's take a look at five sets of dichotomous terms that are used to describe the financial markets.

Public Offerings Versus Private Placements

public offering a security offering where all investors have the opportunity to acquire a portion of the financial claims being sold.

When a corporation decides to raise external capital, those funds can be obtained by making a public offering or a private placement. In a **public offering**, both individual and institutional investors have the opportunity to purchase the securities. The securities are usually made available to the public at large by a managing investment-banking firm, which is a firm that specializes in helping other firms raise money. This process of acting as an intermediary between an issuer of a security and the investing public is called underwriting, and the investment firm that does this is referred to as an underwriter. This is a very impersonal market, and the issuing firm never actually meets the ultimate purchasers of the securities.

private placement a security offering limited to a small number of potential investors.

In a **private placement**, also called a direct placement, the securities are offered and sold directly to a limited number of investors. The firm will usually hammer out, on a face-to-face basis with the prospective buyers, the details of the offering. In this setting, the investment-banking firm may act as a finder by bringing together potential lenders and borrowers. The private placement market is a more personal market than its public counterpart. Now let's look at the role of venture capital in the private placement market.

Private placements can involve issuing both debt and equity, and venture "capitalists" can play an active role in both. For start-up companies or companies in the early stages of business, as well as firms in "turnaround" situations, venture capital is a prime source of

FIGURE 2-1 The Corporation and the Financial Markets: The Interaction

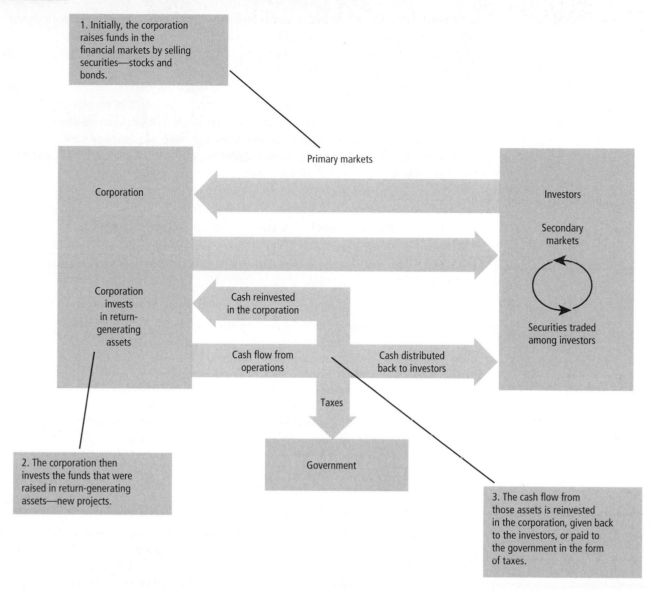

funds. **Venture capital** investments involve risky investments in generally innovative enter-prises, many times in high-technology areas. These investments are often very risky but also carry the potential for high returns. They are made when the start-up firm finds that its need for financial capital is not appealing to the broader public markets owing to the firm's (1) small absolute size, (2) very limited or no historical track record of operating results, and (3) obscure growth prospects. Thus, the venture capitalist who is willing to accept such risks jumps into these more cloudy markets in hopes of a greater return (reward). This economic logic should remind you of **Principle 2: The Risk–Return Trade-Off—We Won't Take On Additional Risk Unless We Expect to Be Compensated with Additional Return**.

The venture capitalist firm will frequently acquire a meaningful dollar stake in the start-up firm. In exchange for this risk taking, the venture capital firm will occupy a seat or seats on the young firm's board of directors and will take an active part in monitoring the com-pany's management activities, strategies, and capital-budgeting decisions.

venture capital funds made available to start-up companies or companies in the early stages of business, as well as firms in "turn-around" situations. These are risky investments, generally in innovative enterprises and many times in high-technology areas.

Primary Markets Versus Secondary Markets

A **primary market** is a market in which new, as opposed to previously issued, securities are traded. For example, if Google issues a new batch of stock, this issue would be considered a

primary market a market in which securities are offered for the first time for sale to potential investors.

In this chapter, we cover material that introduces the financial manager to the process involved in raising funds in the nation's capital markets and how interest rates in those markets are determined.

Without question the United States has a highly developed, complex, and competitive system of financial markets that allows for the quick transfer of savings from people and organizations with a surplus of savings to those with a savings deficit. Such a system of highly developed financial markets allows great ideas (such as the personal computer) to be financed and increases the overall wealth of the economy. Consider your wealth, for example, compared to that of the average family in Russia. Russia lacks the complex system of financial markets to facilitate securities transactions. As a result, real capital formation there has suffered.

Thus, we return now to **Principle 6: Efficient Capital Markets—The Markets Are Quick and the Prices Are Right**. Financial managers like the U.S. system of capital markets because they trust it. This trust stems from the fact that the markets are efficient, and so prices quickly and accurately reflect all available information about the value of the underlying securities. This means that the expected risks and expected cash flows matter more to market participants than do simpler things such as accounting changes and the sequence of past price changes in a specific security. With security prices and returns (such as interest rates) competitively determined, more financial managers (rather than fewer) participate in the markets and help ensure the basic concept of efficiency.

initial public offering, IPO
the first time a company issues its stock to the public.

seasoned equity offering, SEO
the sale of additional stock by a company whose shares are already publicly traded.

secondary market a market in which currently outstanding securities are traded.

primary market transaction. In this case, Google would issue new shares of stock and receive money from investors. The primary market is akin to the new car market. For example, the only time that Ford ever gets money for selling a car is the first time the car is sold to the public. The same is true with securities in the primary market. That's the only time the issuing firm ever gets any money for the securities, and it is the type of transaction that introduces new financial assets—for example, stocks and bonds—into the economy. The first time a company issues stock to the public is referred to as an **initial public offering** or **IPO**. This is what happened with Google on August 19, 2004, when it first sold its common stock to the public at $85 per share and raised $1.76 billion dollars. When Google went back to the primary market in September 2005 and sold more Google stock worth an addition $4.18 million, it was considered a **seasoned equity offering**, or **SEO**. A seasoned equity offering is the sale of additional shares by a company whose shares are already publicly traded and is also called a secondary share offering.

The **secondary market** is where currently outstanding securities are traded. You can think of it as akin to the used car market. If a person who bought some shares the Google stock subsequently sells them, he or she does so in the secondary market. Those shares can go from investor to investor, and Google never receives any money when they are traded. In effect, all transactions after the initial purchase in the primary market take place in the secondary market. These sales do not affect the total amount of financial assets that exists in the economy.

The job of regulation of the primary and secondary markets falls on the Security and Exchange Commission, or SEC. For example, before a firm can offer its securities for sale in the primary markets, it must register them with the SEC, and it is the job of the SEC to make sure that the information provided to investors is adequate and accurate. The SEC also regulates the secondary markets, making sure that investors are provided with enough accurate information to make intelligent decisions when buying and selling in the secondary markets.

The Money Market Versus the Capital Market

money market all institutions and procedures that facilitate transactions for short-term instruments issued by borrowers with very high credit ratings.

The key distinguishing feature between the money and capital markets is the maturity period of the securities traded in them. The **money market** refers to transactions in short-term debt instruments, with short-term meaning maturity periods of 1 year or less. Short-term securities are generally issued by borrowers with very high credit ratings. The major instruments issued and traded in the money market are U.S. Treasury bills, various federal agency securities, bankers' acceptances, negotiable certificates of deposit, and commercial paper. Stocks, either common or preferred, are not traded in the money market.

Keep in mind that the money market isn't a physical place. You do not walk into a building on Wall Street that has the words "Money Market" etched in stone over its arches. Rather, the money market is primarily a telephone and computer market.

As we explained, the **capital market** refers to the market for long-term financial instruments. Long-term here means having maturity periods that extend beyond 1 year. In the broad sense, this encompasses term loans, financial leases, and corporate stocks and bonds.

capital market all institutions and procedures that facilitate transactions in long-term financial instruments.

Spot Markets Versus Futures Markets

Cash markets are where something sells today, right now, on the spot—in fact, cash markets are often called spot markets. Futures markets are where you can buy or sell something at some future date—in effect, you sign a contract that states what you're buying, how much of it you're buying, at what price you're buying it, and when you will actually make the purchase. The difference between purchasing something in the spot market and purchasing it in the futures market is when it is delivered and when you pay for it. For example, say it is May right now and you need 250,000 euros in December. You purchase 125,000 euros today in the spot market and another 125,000 euros in the futures market for delivery in December. You get the euros you purchased in the spot market today, and you get the euros you purchased in the futures market seven months later.

Organized Security Exchanges Versus Over-the-Counter Markets

Important elements of the capital market are the organized security exchanges and the over-the-counter markets. **Organized security exchanges** are tangible entities; that is, they physically occupy space (such as a building or part of a building), and financial instruments are traded on their premises. The **over-the-counter markets** include all security markets except the organized exchanges. The money market, then, is an over-the-counter market because it doesn't occupy a physical location. Because both markets are important to financial officers concerned with raising long-term capital, some additional discussion is warranted.

organized security exchanges formal organizations that facilitate the trading of securities.

over-the-counter markets all security markets except organized exchanges. The money market is an over-the-counter market. Most corporate bonds also are traded in this market.

Organized Security Exchanges

There are seven organized exchanges in the United States, starting with the New York Stock Exchange (NYSE) and the American Stock Exchange (AMEX), and smaller exchanges in Philadelphia, Boston, Chicago, Cincinnati, and the Pacific Stock Exchange, which is headquartered in San Francisco, but doesn't actually have a trading floor—it's a totally electronic exchange. The New York Stock Exchange and the American Stock Exchange are considered national stock exchanges, and the others are generally termed *regional stock exchanges*. If a firm's stock trades on a particular exchange, it is said to be *listed* on that exchange. Securities can be listed on more than one exchange. All of these seven active exchanges are registered with the Securities and Exchange Commission (SEC). Firms whose securities are traded on the registered exchanges must comply with reporting requirements of both the specific exchange and the SEC.

The NYSE, also called the "Big Board," is the oldest of all the organized exchanges. Without question, the NYSE is the big player, with well over half of the typical trading volume taking place there. An example of the prominent stature of the NYSE is provided by the sheer number of companies that have stocks listed on this exchange. In 2005, the NYSE listed approximately 2,672 issuers, which included operating companies, along with some mutual funds and exchange-traded funds. This represents over a 40 percent increase in the number of issuers over the previous 14 years. Even though the NASDAQ, soon to be discussed, surpassed the NYSE in trading volume during the "dot-com" bubble, the NYSE remains the preeminent exchange in the United States. The collapse in market value of numerous high-tech and dot-com firms during the years of 2000 to 2001 gave the lead in trading value back to the NYSE and reinforced the importance of the NYSE to the general credibility of the U.S. financial market system. The total market value of shares listed on the NYSE in 2005 amounted to $20.8 trillion, over double what it was in 1996.

Stock Exchange Benefits

Both corporations and investors enjoy several benefits provided by the existence of organized security exchanges. These include

1. **Providing a continuous market.** This may be the most important function of an organized security exchange. A continuous market provides a series of continuous security prices. Price changes from trade to trade tend to be smaller than they would be in the absence of organized markets. The reasons are that there is a relatively large sales volume of each security traded, trading orders are executed quickly, and the range between the price asked for a security and the offered price tends to be narrow. The result is that price volatility is reduced.
2. **Establishing and publicizing fair security prices.** An organized exchange permits security prices to be set by competitive forces. They are not set by negotiations off the floor of the exchange, where one party might have a bargaining advantage. The bidding process flows from the supply and demand underlying each security. This means the specific price of a security is determined in the manner of an auction. In addition, the security prices determined at each exchange are widely publicized.
3. **Helping business raise new capital.** Because a continuous secondary market exists, it is easier for firms to float, or issue, new security offerings at competitively determined prices. This means that the comparative values of securities offered in these markets are easily observed.

Listing Requirements

To receive the benefits provided by an organized exchange, the firm must seek to have its securities listed on the exchange. An application for listing must be filed and a fee paid. The requirements for listing vary from exchange to exchange; those of the NYSE are the most stringent. The general criteria for listing fall into these categories: (1) profitability, (2) size, (3) market value, and (4) public ownership. To give you the flavor of an actual set of listing requirements, a selected sample of those set forth by the NYSE are displayed in Table 2-1.

Over-the-Counter Markets

Many publicly held firms do not meet the listing requirements of major stock exchanges. Others may want to avoid the reporting requirements and fees required to maintain a listing. As an alternative, their securities may trade in the over the counter markets. On the basis of sheer numbers (not dollar volume), more stocks are traded over the counter than on organized exchanges. As far as secondary trading in corporate bonds is concerned, the over-the-counter markets are where the action is. In a typical year, more than 90 percent of corporate bond business takes place over the counter.

Most over-the-counter transactions are done through a loose network of security traders who are known as broker-dealers and brokers. Brokers do not purchase securities for

---

TABLE 2-1   A Sample of NYSE Listing Requirements for Domestic (U.S.) Companies

PROFITABILITY (EARNINGS)

Earnings before taxes (EBT) for the most recent year must be at least $2.5 million. For the 2 years preceding that, EBT must be at least $2.0 million.

MARKET VALUE

The market value of publicly held stock must be at least $100.0 million. For initial public offerings (IPOs), the value must be at least $60.0 million.

PUBLIC OWNERSHIP (DISTRIBUTION CRITERIA)

There must be at least 1.1 million publicly held common shares.
There must be at least 2,000 holders of 100 shares or more.

Source: New York Stock Exchange, www.nysedata.com.

their own account, whereas dealers do. Broker-dealers stand ready to buy and sell specific securities at selected prices. They are said to "make a market" in those securities. Their profit is the "spread," or difference, between the price they will pay for a security (bid price) and the price at which they will sell the security (asked price).

Price Quotes and the NASDAQ

The availability of prices is not as continuous in the over-the-counter market as it is on an organized exchange. Since February 8, 1971, however, when a computerized network called NASDAQ came into existence, the availability of prices in this market has improved substantially. NASDAQ stands for National Association of Security Dealers Automated Quotation System. It is a telecommunications system that provides a national information link among the brokers and dealers operating in the over-the-counter markets. Subscribing traders have a terminal that allows them to obtain representative bids and ask prices for thousands of securities traded over the counter. NASDAQ is a quotation system, not a transactions system. The final trade is still consummated by direct negotiation between traders.

The NASDAQ system has become an increasingly important element of the U.S. financial market system in recent years. It provides a nationwide communications element that was lacking in the over-the-counter side of the securities markets. The Nasdaq Stock Market Inc. describes itself as a "screen-based, floorless market." It now is actually home to the securities of more companies than the NYSE. In 2005 some 3,300 companies were listed on NASDAQ, after reaching a peak of 5,556 in 1996. It has become highly popular as the trading mechanism of choice of several fast-growth sectors in the United States, including the high-technology sector. The common stock of computer chip maker Intel Corporation, for example, is traded via the NASDAQ, as is that of Dell, Starbucks, Whole Foods Market, and Google.

NASDAQ price quotes for many stocks are published daily in the *Wall Street Journal*, and those that aren't published in the paper are available on the online version of the *Wall Street Journal* (**www.wsj.com**).

Finance at Work

THE NEW YORK STOCK EXCHANGE—THE EXCHANGE IN CHANGE

In 2006, when the stocks on the New York Stock Exchange (NYSE) approached all-time high levels, many of the traders working on the floor of the NYSE wondered if they would be around to see stocks go much higher. That was not because they didn't expect stocks to continue to rise, but because they expected to be let go as the NYSE became computer automated. In fact, some of the large investment companies, including Credit Suisse Group, LaBranche & Co., and others, have begun to let staff go as the NYSE implements an electronic trading system that allows trades to be automatically transacted. As a result in the future when you see action from the NYSE on your nightly news report, you may not see many humans on the floor of the exchange.

This move to automate the New York Stock Exchange is aimed at making it more competitive with NASDAQ, which is completely computerized. While the NYSE is making a move toward an automated market, it isn't planning on totally doing away with the human component for some time. Actually, the NYSE is moving toward a hybrid system, which allows for greater dependence on computers.

The NYSE hopes that these improvements in technology will allow them to fend off competition from NASDAQ and the other electronic markets that have already eaten away at some of the NYSE's market share. How does this happen? Just because a stock is listed on the NYSE doesn't mean that it can only trade there. In fact, exchanges are allowed to trade each other's stocks electronically, ending the exclusive listings that once limited where stocks could be bought and sold. For example, in 2006, 69.9 percent of stocks listed on the NYSE actually traded on the NYSE; that's down from 78.6 percent just 1 year prior.

What other changes can you expect to see? You can expect to see an international expansion of the NYSE and NASDAQ. NASDAQ already purchased 25 percent of the London Stock Exchange, and the NYSE is also trying to buy Euronext, a European exchange. The bottom line here is that in the investment world the only thing that doesn't change is change.

Source: Authers, John, Norma Cohen, and Anuj Gangahar, "Clearing the floor; How a regulatory overhaul is helping rivals to close in on the Big Board," *Financial Times*, London edition, September 14, 2006, page 15; Bel Bruno, Joe, "On NYSE Floor, Concerns About the Future," Associated Press Newswires, October 20, 2006; Ceron, Gaston F., "NYSE Floor Traders Face End To Limits On Electronic Trade," Dow Jones News Service, August 25, 2006; Dow Jones News Service, "NYSE Electronic Trading System Debut Seems Smoot," October 6, 2006; Lucchetti, Aaron, "NYSE Is Set for Electronic- Trading Expansion," *Wall Street Journal*, October 5, 2006, page C1.

Did You Get It? . . . .

1. Explain the difference between (a) public offerings and private placements, (b) primary markets and secondary markets, (c) the money market and the capital market, and (d) organized security exchanges and over-the-counter markets.

2. Name the benefits derived from the existence of stock exchanges.

3. Briefly describe what is meant by the "NASDAQ system."

Objective **2**

Understand the role of the investment-banking business in the context of raising corporate capital.

investment banker a financial specialist who underwrites and distributes new securities and advises corporate clients about raising new funds.

underwriting the purchase and subsequent resale of a new security issue. The risk of selling the new issue at a satisfactory (profitable) price is assumed (underwritten) by the investment banker.

underwriter's spread the difference between the price the corporation raising money gets and the public offering price of a security.

THE INVESTMENT BANKER

Most corporations do not frequently raise long-term capital. The activities of working-capital management go on daily, but attracting long-term capital is, by comparison, episodic. The sums involved can be huge, so these situations are considered of great importance to financial managers. Because most managers are unfamiliar with the subtleties of raising long-term funds, they enlist the help of an expert. That expert is an investment banker. It is with the help of an **investment banker** serving as the underwriter that stocks and bonds are generally sold in the primary markets. An **underwriter** is a middleperson who buys the entire stock or bond issue from the issuing company and resells it to the general public in individual shares. The difference between the price the corporation gets and the public offering price is called the **underwriter's spread**. For example, Citigroup/Salomon Smith Barney, Merrill Lynch, Goldman Sachs, and Lehman Brothers all specialize in investment banking and the underwriting that goes with it.

Table 2-2 gives us some idea who the major players are within the investment-banking industry. It lists the top 10 houses in 2005 based on the dollar volume of security issues that were managed. Notice in the table that the U.S. investment-banking industry is a highly concentrated one. The top five bankers with regard to underwriting volume during 2005 accounted for over half of the total IPO offerings. This degree of concentration seems to be continuing over time.

Actually, we use the term "investment banker" to describe both the firm itself and the individuals who work for it in that capacity. Just what does this intermediary role involve? The easiest way to understand it is to look at the basic investment-banking functions.

Functions

The investment banker performs three basic functions: (1) underwriting, (2) distributing, and (3) advising.

TABLE 2-2 Initial Public Offerings of Stock, Global Offerings by U.S. Issuers, Ranked by 2005 Proceeds

MANAGER	AMOUNT (BILLIONS)	MARKET SHARE	NO. OF ISSUES
Goldman Sachs & Co.	$4.1	11.5%	24
Citigroup	4.0	11.2	30
Morgan Stanley	3.8	10.5	21
Lehman Brothers	3.6	10.1	31
Credit Suisse First Boston	3.1	8.6	23
JP Morgan	2.7	7.6	22
Merrill Lynch & Co. Inc.	2.5	7.0	19
UBS	1.8	5.0	17
Deutsche Bank AG	1.4	4.0	12
Banc of America Securities LLC	1.3	3.5	12
Top 10 Totals	$28.4	79.0%	211
Industry Totals	35.9	100.0	211

Source: *Wall Street Journal*, 2005 Underwriting Rankings, January 3, 2006, R10. Copyright 2006 by Dow Jones & Company, Inc. Reproduced with permission of Dow Jones & Company, Inc.

Underwriting

The term underwriting is borrowed from the field of insurance. It means *assuming a risk*. The investment banker assumes the risk of selling a security issued at a satisfactory price. A satisfactory price is one that generates a profit for the investment-banking house.

The procedure goes like this. The managing investment banker and its syndicate will buy the security issue from the corporation in need of funds. The **syndicate** is *a group of other investment bankers that is invited to help buy and resell the issue*. The managing house is the investment-banking firm that originated the business because its corporate client decided to raise external funds. On a specific day, the client that is raising capital is presented with a check from the managing house in exchange for the securities being issued. At this point the investment-banking syndicate owns the securities. The client has its cash, so it is immune from the possibility that the security markets might turn sour. That is, if the price of the newly issued security falls below that paid to the firm by the syndicate, the syndicate will suffer a loss. The syndicate, of course, hopes that the opposite situation will result. Its objective is to sell the new issue to the investing public at a price per security greater than its cost.

> **syndicate** a group of investment bankers who contractually assist in the buying and selling of a new security issue.

Distributing

Once the syndicate owns the new securities, it must get them into the hands of the ultimate investors. This is the distribution or selling function of investment banking. The investment banker may have branch offices across the United States, or it may have an informal arrangement with several security dealers who regularly buy a portion of each new offering for final sale. It is not unusual to have 300 to 400 dealers involved in the selling effort. The syndicate can properly be viewed as the security wholesaler, and the dealer organization can be viewed as the security retailer.

Advising

The investment banker is an expert in the issuance and marketing of securities. A sound investment-banking house will be aware of prevailing market conditions and can relate those conditions to the particular type of security and the price at which it should be sold at a given time. For example, business conditions may be pointing to a future increase in interest rates,

---

Across the Hall

MANAGEMENT AND SELECTION CRITERIA FOR AN INVESTMENT BANKER

Comments and Procedure by David R. Klock, Ph.D.
Dr. David R. Klock is past CEO and current chairman of the board of directors of CompBenefits Corporation, headquartered in Atlanta, Georgia. Dr. Klock holds a Ph.D. in finance from the University of Illinois and is a nationally known insurance economist. CompBenefits is a privately held national leader in providing a wide range of dental and vision insurance products. The firm's annual revenues are approximately $310 million. The firm continually works with venture capitalists who provide equity capital and access to debt capital in the nation's financial market system. Dr. Klock authored the following checklist that deals with selecting an investment banker within the context of seeking what are called "strategic buyers" by venture capital firms. Dr. Klock is highly familiar with the field, having spent time at the investment-banking firm of Goldman Sachs earlier in his career.

1. Competency
   - Technical skills/resources of total team
   - People skills/resources of total team
   - Knowledge of the firm
   - Knowledge of key potential buyers and their needs/ability to pay
2. Connections
   - Recent firm history of working with potential buyers
   - Individual banker's recent history of working with key potential buyers
   - Reputation of investment-banking firm with potential buyers
   - Intangibles
3. Conviction on Enterprise Value of the Firm
   - Valuation range and strength of valuation methods/matrix
   - Ability to strongly tell the firm's story and to be heard/understood by key individuals and potential buyers
   - Level of commitment to this transaction within the banking firm

so the investment banker might advise the firm to issue its bonds in a timely fashion to avoid the higher yields that are forthcoming. The banker can analyze the firm's capital structure and make recommendations about what general source of capital should be issued. In many instances the firm will invite its investment banker to sit on the board of directors. This permits the banker to observe corporate activity and make recommendations on a regular basis.

In the preceding "Across the Hall" section, a board chairman presents his checklist for selecting an investment-banking firm to work with an actual corporation. Please keep in mind that many board chairpersons and chief executive officers of business firms come from academic disciplines other than finance, for example, marketing, management, and information systems. Thus, a basic knowledge of the investment-banking industry is vital to both the employee and the employer.

Distribution Methods

Several methods are available to the corporation for placing new security offerings in the hands of investment bankers followed by final investors. The investment banker's role is different in each of these. Sometimes, in fact, it is possible to bypass the investment banker. These methods are described in this section. Private placements, because of their importance, are treated separately later in the chapter.

A Negotiated Purchase

In a negotiated underwriting, the firm that needs funds makes contact with an investment banker, and deliberations concerning the new issue begin. If all goes well, a *method* is negotiated for determining the price the investment banker and the syndicate will pay for the securities. For example, the agreement might state that the syndicate will pay $2 less than the closing price of the firm's common stock on the day before the offering date of a new stock issue. The negotiated purchase is the most prevalent method of securities distribution in the private sector. It is generally thought to be the most profitable technique as far as investment bankers are concerned.

A Competitive Bid Purchase

The method by which the underwriting group is determined distinguishes the competitive bid purchase from the negotiated purchase. In a competitive underwriting, several underwriting groups bid for the right to purchase the new issue from the corporation that is raising funds. The firm does not directly select the investment banker. Instead, the investment banker that underwrites and distributes the issue is chosen by an auction process. The one willing to pay the greatest dollar amount per new security will win the competitive bid.

Most competitive bid purchases are confined to three situations, compelled by legal regulations: (1) railroad issues, (2) public utility issues, and (3) state and municipal bond issues. The argument in favor of competitive bids is that any undue influence of an investment banker over the firm is mitigated and the price received by the firm for each security should be higher. Thus, we would intuitively suspect that the cost of capital in a competitive bidding situation would be less than in a negotiated purchase situation. Evidence on this question, however, is mixed. One problem with the competitive bidding purchase as far as the fund-raising firm is concerned is that the benefits gained from the advisory function of the investment banker are lost. It may be necessary to use an investment banker for advisory purposes and then by law exclude the banker from the competitive bid process.

A Commission or Best-Efforts Basis

Here, the investment banker acts as an agent rather than as a principal in the distribution process. The securities are *not* underwritten. The investment banker attempts to sell the issue in return for a fixed commission on each security actually sold. Unsold securities are then returned to the corporation. This arrangement is typically used for more speculative issues. The issuing firm may be smaller or less established than the banker would like. Because the underwriting risk is not passed on to the investment banker, this distribution method is less costly to the issuer than a negotiated or competitive bid purchase. On the other hand, the investment banker only has to give it his or her "best effort." A successful sale is not guaranteed.

A Privileged Subscription

Occasionally, the firm may feel that a distinct market already exists for its new securities. When a *new issue is marketed to a definite and select group of investors*, it is called a **privileged subscription**. Three target markets are typically involved: (1) current stockholders, (2) employees, or (3) customers of the firm. Of these, distributions directed at current stockholders are the most prevalent. Such offerings are called *rights offerings*. In a privileged subscription the investment banker may act only as a selling agent. It is also possible that the issuing firm and the investment banker might sign a *standby agreement*, which obligates the investment banker to underwrite the securities that are not purchased by the privileged investors.

privileged subscription the process of marketing a new security issue to a select group of investors.

Dutch Auction

As we explained at the beginning of the chapter, with a **Dutch auction**, investors first bids on the number of shares they would like to buy and the price they are willing to pay for them. Once all the bids are in, the prices that were bid along with the number of shares are ranked from the highest price to the lowest price. The selling price for the stock is then calculated, and it is calculated as the highest price that allows for all the stock to be sold. Although Google really brought this method to the public's eye, it has been used by a number of other companies including Overstock.com and Salon (**www.salon.com**). Figure 2-2 explains in more detail how a Dutch auction works.

Dutch auction a method of issuing securities (common stock) where investors place bids indicating how many shares they are willing to buy and at what price. The price the stock is then sold for becomes the lowest price at which the issuing company can sell all the available shares.

A Direct Sale

In a **direct sale** *the issuing firm sells the securities directly to the investing public without involving an investment banker*. Even among established corporate giants, this procedure is relatively rare. A variation of the direct sale involves the private placement of a new issue by the fund-raising corporation *without* the use of an investment banker as an intermediary. Texaco, Mobil Oil, and International Harvester (now Navistar) are examples of large firms that have followed this procedure.

direct sale the sale of securities by a corporation to the investing public without the services of an investment-banking firm.

FIGURE 2-2 A Dutch Auction Primer

A company is planning to use a Dutch auction to set the price of the shares in its initial public offering. Here is how the auction process will find the highest price at which all shares can be sold.

Adding it up

1 The auctioneer starts by gathering all the bids and sorting them according to price.

THE BIDS

Setting the price

2 The auctioneer works back from the highest bid until all the shares are sold.

3 The final price that fills the quota of shares to sell becomes the offering price to all successful bidders.

Number of shares

$ FINAL PRICE   HIGHEST PRICE $

SUCCESSFUL BIDDERS

Bid price per share, sorted from lowest to highest

Did You Get It? ....

1. What is the main difference between an investment banker and a commercial banker?
2. What are the three major functions that an investment banker performs?
3. What are the five key methods by which securities are distributed to final investors?

Objective **3**

Distinguish between privately placed securities and publicly offered securities.

PRIVATE PLACEMENTS

Earlier in this chapter we discussed the private placement market. Here we take a closer look at the debt side of the private placement market and how it is used by seasoned corporations as distinct from start-ups. Thus, when we talk of private placements in this section, we are focusing on debt contracts rather than stock offerings. This debt side of the private placement market is always a significant portion of the total private market.

Private placements are an alternative to the sale of securities to the public or to a restricted group of investors through a privileged subscription. Any type of security can be privately placed (directly placed). The major investors in private placements are large financial institutions. Based on the volume of securities purchased, the three most important investor groups are (1) life insurance companies, (2) state and local retirement funds, and (3) private pension funds.

In arranging a private placement, the firm may (1) avoid the use of an investment banker and work directly with the investing institutions or (2) engage the services of an investment banker. If the firm does not use an investment banker, of course, it does not have to pay a fee. However, investment bankers can provide valuable advice in the private placement process. They are usually in contact with several major institutional investors; thus, they will know who the major buyers able to invest in the proposed offering are, and they can help the firm evaluate the terms of the new issue.

Private placements have advantages and disadvantages compared with public offerings. The financial manager must carefully evaluate both sides of the question. The advantages associated with private placements are:

1. **Speed.** The firm usually obtains funds more quickly through a private placement than a public offering. The major reason is that registration of the issue with the SEC is not required.
2. **Reduced costs.** These savings result because the lengthy registration statement for the SEC does not have to be prepared, and the investment-banking underwriting and distribution costs do not have to be absorbed.
3. **Financing flexibility.** In a private placement the firm deals on a face-to-face basis with a small number of investors. This means that the terms of the issue can be tailored to meet the specific needs of the company. For example, all of the funds need not be taken by the firm at once. In exchange for a "commitment" fee, the firm can "draw down" against the established amount of credit with the investors. This provides some insurance against capital market uncertainties, and the firm does not have to borrow the funds if the need does not arise. There is also the possibility of renegotiation. The terms of the debt issue can be altered. The term to maturity, the interest rate, or any restrictive covenants can be discussed among the affected parties.

The following disadvantages of private placements must be evaluated.

1. **Interest costs.** It is generally conceded that interest costs on private placements exceed those of public issues. Whether this disadvantage is enough to offset the reduced costs associated with a private placement is a determination the financial manager must make. There is some evidence that on smaller issues, say $500,000 as opposed to $30 million, the private placement alternative would be preferable.
2. **Restrictive covenants.** A firm's dividend policy, working-capital levels, and the raising of additional debt capital may all be affected by provisions in the private-placement debt contract. This is not to say that such restrictions are always absent in public debt con-

tracts. Rather, the firm's financial officer must be alert to the tendency for these covenants to be especially burdensome in private contracts.

3. **The possibility of future SEC registration.** If the lender (investor) should decide to sell the issue to a public buyer before maturity, the issue must be registered with the SEC. Some lenders, then, require that the issuing firm agree to a future registration at their option.

Did You Get It?

1. Within the financial markets, explain what we mean by "private placements."
2. What are the possible advantages and disadvantages of private placements?

FLOTATION COSTS

The firm raising long-term capital incurs two types of **flotation costs**: (1) the underwriter's spread and (2) issuing costs. Of these two costs, the underwriter's spread is the larger. The *underwriter's spread* is simply the difference between the gross and net proceeds from a given security issue expressed as a percent of the gross proceeds. The *issue costs* include (1) the printing and engraving of the security certificates, (2) legal fees, (3) accounting fees, (4) trustee fees, and (5) several other miscellaneous components. The two most significant issue costs are printing and engraving and legal fees.

Data published by the SEC have consistently revealed two relationships about flotation costs. First, the costs associated with issuing common stock are notably greater than the costs associated with preferred stock offerings. In turn, preferred stock costs exceed those of bonds. Second, flotation costs (expressed as a percentage of gross proceeds) decrease as the size of the security issue increases.

In the first instance, the stated relationship reflects the fact that issue costs are sensitive to the risks involved in successfully distributing a security issue. Common stock is riskier to own than corporate bonds. Underwriting risk is, therefore, greater with common stock than with bonds. Thus, flotation costs just mirror these risk relationships. In the second case, a portion of the issue costs is fixed. Legal fees and accounting costs are good examples. So, as the size of the security issue rises, the fixed component is spread over a larger gross proceeds base. As a consequence, average flotation costs vary inversely with the size of the issue.

Objective **4**

Be acquainted with securities flotation costs and securities markets regulations.

flotation costs the transaction cost incurred when a firm raises funds by issuing a particular type of security.

Did You Get It?

1. What are the two major categories of flotation costs?
2. Are flotation costs greater for a new bond issue or a new common stock issue?

REGULATION AIMED AT MAKING THE GOAL OF THE FIRM WORK: THE SARBANES-OXLEY ACT

As we previously noted, in recent years the world of finance has been awash with scandals. As a result of these scandals, Congress passed the Sarbanes-Oxley Act of 2002. One of the primary inspirations for this new law was Enron, which failed financially in December 2001. Prior to that formal failure (bankruptcy) Enron's board of directors actually voted on two occasions to temporarily suspend its own "code of ethics" to permit its CFO to engage in risky personal financial ventures that involved the financial structure and cash flow streams of Enron. This should remind you of our **Principle 10: Ethical Behavior Means Doing the Right Thing, and Ethical Dilemmas Are Everywhere in Finance**.

The Sarbanes-Oxley Act holds corporate advisors (such as a firm's accountants, lawyers, company officers, and boards of directors), who have access to or influence on company decisions, strictly accountable in a legal sense for any instances of misconduct. The act very simply and directly identifies its purpose as being "to protect investors by improving the accuracy and reliability of corporate disclosures made pursuant to the securities laws, and for other purposes." In a speech given in March 2003, SEC Commissioner Paul S. Atkins directly recognized the relationship of the act to corporate valuations. He said:[1]

> Fundamentally, Sarbanes-Oxley acknowledges the importance of stockholder value. Without equity investors and their confidence, our economic growth and continued technological innovations would be slowed. Sarbanes-Oxley strengthens the role of directors as representatives of stockholders and reinforces the role of management as stewards of the stockholders' interest.

What does the Sarbanes-Oxley Act accomplish? It ensures that top managers work for the best interests of the shareholders by providing greater protection against accounting fraud and financial misconduct.

RATES OF RETURN IN THE FINANCIAL MARKETS

Objective **5**

Understand the rate-of-return relationships among various classes of financing vehicles that persist in the financial markets.

opportunity cost of funds
the next-best rate of return available to the investor for a given level of risk.

In this chapter we've discussed the process of raising funds to finance new projects. As you might expect, to raise those funds a firm must offer a rate of return *competitive* with the next-best investment alternative available to that saver (investor).

This *rate of return on the next-best investment alternative to the saver* is known as the investor's **opportunity cost of funds**. The opportunity cost concept is crucial in financial management and is referred to often.

Next we review the levels and variability in rates of return that have occurred over the lengthy period of 1926 through 2005. This review focuses on returns from a wide array of financial instruments. In Chapter 11 we discuss at length the concept of an *overall* cost of capital. Part of that overall cost of capital is attributed to interest rate levels at given points in time. So we follow this initial broad look at interest rate levels with a discussion of the more recent period of 1981 through 2005.

Rates of Return over Long Periods

History can tell us a great deal about the returns that investors earn in the financial markets. Let's look at what has taken place since 1926. First, what should we expect in terms of return and risk? From **Principle 1: The Risk–Return Trade-Off, We Won't Take On Additional Risk Unless We Expect to Be Compensated with Additional Return** we know that with higher returns we should expect to see higher risk, and that's exactly the case. Common stocks of small firms have more risk and produce higher average annual returns than large stock, with the annual return on small-company stocks averaging 17.40 percent and the annual return on large-company stocks averaging 11.60 percent.

The data is summarized visually in Figure 2-3, which presents the relationship between the average annual observed rates of return for different types of securities along with the average annual rate of inflation. Over this period, the average inflation rate was 3.2 percent. We refer to this rate as the "inflation-risk premium." The investor who earns only the rate of inflation has earned no "real return." That is, the *real* return is the return earned above the rate of increase in the general price level for goods and services in the economy, which is the inflation rate. In addition to the danger of not earning above the inflation rate, investors are concerned about the risk of the borrower defaulting, or failing to repay the loan when due. Thus, we would expect investors to earn a default-risk premium for investing in long-term corporate bonds versus long-term government bonds because corporate bonds are considered more risky. The premium for 1926 to 2005, as shown in Figure 2-3, was 1.0 percent, or what is called 100 basis points (6.2 percent on long-term corporate bonds minus 5.2 percent on long-term government bonds). We would also expect an even greater risk premium for common stocks vis-à-vis long-term corporate bonds, because the variability in average returns is greater for common stocks. The results show such a risk premium: Com-

---

[1] Paul S. Atkins, "The Sarbanes-Oxley Act of 2002: Goals, Content, and Status of Implementation," Speech by the SEC Commissioner, March 25, 2003, p. 2 of 6. See www.sec.gov/news/speech/spch032503psa.htm.

FIGURE 2-3 Rates of Return and Standard Deviations, 1926 to 2005

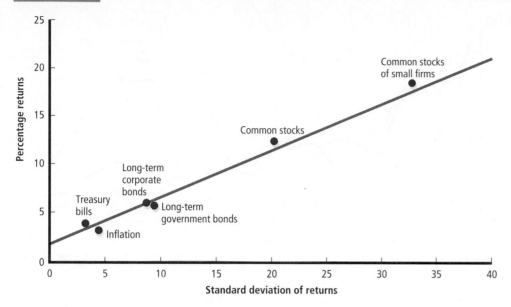

mon stocks earned 5.4 percent more than long-term corporate bonds (11.6 percent for common stocks minus 6.2 percent for long-term corporate bonds).

Remember that these returns are "averages" across many securities and over an extended period of time. However, these averages reflect the conventional wisdom regarding risk premiums: The greater the risk, the greater will be the expected returns. Such a relationship is shown in Figure 2-4, where the average returns are plotted against their standard deviations; note that higher average returns have historically been associated with higher dispersion in these returns.

INTEREST RATE LEVELS IN RECENT PERIODS

Objective   **6**

Be acquainted with recent interest rate levels and the fundamentals of interest rate determination.

The *nominal* interest rates on some key fixed-income securities are displayed within both Table 2-3 and Figure 2-4 for the most recent 1981–2005 time frame. The rate of inflation at the consumer level is also presented in those two exhibits. This allows us to observe quite easily several concepts that were mentioned in the previous section. Specifically, we can observe (1) the inflation-risk premium, (2) the default-risk premium across the several instruments, and (3) the approximate real return for each instrument. Looking at the mean (average) values for each security and the inflation rate at the bottom of Table 2-3 will facilitate the discussion.

Notice that the average inflation between 1981 and 2005 was slightly higher than it was over the 1926 through 2005 period. This was largely because of the high inflation rates over the 10-year period beginning in 1981. In recent years, this has changed and inflation rates have dropped dramatically from their levels in the 1980s, and as inflation has dropped, interest rates have come down. This only makes sense according to the logic of the financial markets. Investors *require* a nominal rate of interest that exceeds the inflation rate or else their realized *real* return will be negative. This additional return that investors require to compensate for the loss of purchasing of their investment to inflation is referred to as the inflation-risk premium. Earning a negative return over long periods of time (e.g., 25 years) is not very smart.

Table 2-3 indicates that investor rationality prevailed. For example, the average return premium demanded on U.S. Treasury bills with a 3-month maturity was 2.31 percent (or 231 basis points, where a basis point is one one-hundredth of 1 percent) in excess of the inferred inflation-risk premium of 3.37 percent. That is, an average 5.68 percent yield on Treasury bills over the period *minus* the average inflation rate of 3.37 percent over the same period produces a premium of 2.31 percent. This 2.31 percent can be thought of as the real risk-free short-term interest rate that prevailed over the 1981–2005 period.

FIGURE 2-4 Interest Rate Levels and Inflation Rates, 1981 through 2005

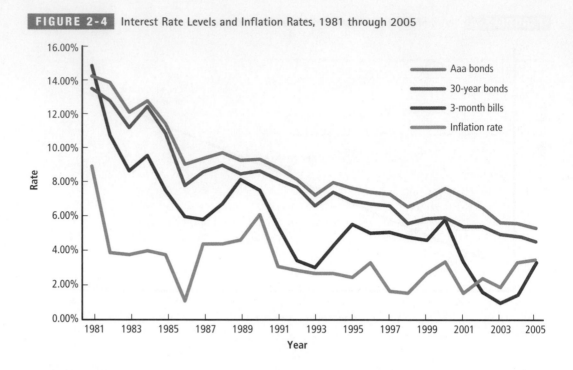

TABLE 2-3 Interest Rate Levels and Inflation Rates, 1981 through 2005

YEAR	3-MONTH TREASURY BILLS %	30-YEAR TREASURY BONDS %	Aaa-RATED CORPORATE BONDS %	INFLATION RATE %
1981	14.08	13.44	14.17	8.9
1982	10.69	12.76	13.79	3.9
1983	8.63	11.18	12.04	3.8
1984	9.52	12.39	12.71	4.0
1985	7.49	10.79	11.37	3.8
1986	5.98	7.80	9.02	1.1
1987	5.82	8.58	9.38	4.4
1988	6.68	8.96	9.71	4.4
1989	8.12	8.45	9.26	4.6
1990	7.51	8.61	9.32	6.1
1991	5.42	8.14	8.77	3.1
1992	3.45	7.67	8.14	2.9
1993	3.02	6.59	7.22	2.7
1994	4.29	7.37	7.97	2.7
1995	5.51	6.88	7.59	2.5
1996	5.02	6.71	7.37	3.3
1997	5.07	6.61	7.26	1.7
1998	4.81	5.58	6.53	1.6
1999	4.64	5.87	7.05	2.7
2000	5.82	5.94	7.62	3.4
2001	3.40	5.43	7.08	1.6
2002	1.61	5.41	6.49	2.4
2003	1.01	4.93	5.66	1.9
2004	1.37	4.86	5.63	3.3
2005	3.15	4.51	5.23	3.4
Mean	5.68	7.82	8.66	3.37

Source: U.S. Treasury, Federal Reserve Bulletin, various issues Federal Reserve Statistical Releases H. 15 (519), G. 13 (415), various issues, and www.federalreserve.gov/releases. Analysis and presentation by the Dr. Phillips Institute for the Study of American Business Activity, College of Business Administration, University of Central Florida, Orlando, June 9, 2004. The 30-year Treasury constant maturity series was discontinued on February 18, 2002, and reintroduced on February 9, 2006. From February 18, 2002, to February 9, 2006, the U.S. Treasury published a factor for adjusting the daily nominal 20-year constant maturity in order to estimate a 30-year nominal rate. The historical adjustment factor can be found at www.treas.gov/offices/domestic-finance/debt-management/interest-rate/ltcompositeindex_historical.shtml.

The default-risk premium is also evident in Table 2-3 and Figure 2-4. If we arrange the securities in these two exhibits from low risk to high risk, the following tabulation results:

SECURITY	AVERAGE YIELD
3-month Treasury bills	5.68
30-year Treasury bonds	7.82
Aaa corporate bonds	8.66

Again, the basic rationale of the financial markets prevailed. The default-risk premium on high-rated (Aaa) corporate bonds relative to long-term Treasury bonds of 30-year maturity was 0.84 percent (8.66 percent minus 7.82 percent), or 84 basis points.

The preceding array of numbers can also be used to identify another factor that affects interest rate levels. It is referred to as the *maturity premium*. The **maturity premium** can be defined as *the additional return required by investors in longer-term securities (bonds in this case) to compensate them for the greater risk of price fluctuations on those securities caused by interest rate changes.* This maturity premium arises even if securities possess equal (or approximately equal) odds of default. Notice that Treasury bonds with a 30-year maturity commanded a 2.14 percent yield differential over the shorter, 3-month-to-maturity Treasury bonds. (Both types of bonds are considered risk-free because they are issued and backed by the U.S. government.) This provides an estimate of the maturity premium demanded by all investors over this specific 1981–2005 period.

maturity premium the additional return required by investors in longer-term securities to compensate them for the greater risk of price fluctuations on those securities caused by interest rate changes.

When you study the basic mathematics of financial decisions and the characteristics of fixed-income securities in later chapters, you will learn how to quantify this maturity premium that is imbedded in nominal interest rates.

One other type of risk premium that helps determine interest rate levels needs to be identified and defined. It is known as the "liquidity premium." The **liquidity premium** is defined as *the additional return required by investors in securities that cannot be quickly converted into cash at a reasonably predictable price.* The secondary markets for small-bank stocks, especially community banks, provide a good example of the liquidity premium. A bank holding company that trades on the New York Stock Exchange, such as SunTrust Bank, will be more liquid to investors than, say, the common stock of Century National Bank of Orlando, Florida. Such a liquidity premium is reflected across the spectrum of financial assets, from bonds to stocks.

liquidity premium the additional return required by investors for securities that cannot be quickly converted into cash at a reasonably predictable price.

Remember Your Principles

Our first principle, **Principle 1: The Risk–Return Trade-Off—We Won't Take On Additional Risk Unless We Expect to Be Compensated with Additional Return**, *established the fundamental risk–return trade-offs that govern the financial markets. We are now trying to provide you with an understanding of the kinds of risks that are rewarded in the risk–return trade-off presented in* **Principle 1**.

Did You Get It?

1. What is the "opportunity cost of funds"?
2. Over long periods of time is the "real rate of return" higher on common stocks or long-term government bonds?
3. Distinguish between the concepts of the "inflation-risk premium" and the "default-risk premium."
4. Distinguish between the concepts of the "maturity premium" and the "liquidity premium."

Objective 7

Explain the popular theories of the
term structure of interest rates.

nominal rate of interest
the interest rate paid on debt
securities without an adjustment
for any loss in purchasing power.

INTEREST RATE DETERMINANTS IN A NUTSHELL

Using the logic from **Principle 1: The Risk–Return Trade-Off,** we can decompose the interest rate paid on a security into a simple equation with the **nominal** (i.e., observed) **rate of interest** being the output variable from the equation. The nominal interest rate, also called the "quoted" rate, *is the interest rate paid on debt securities without an adjustment for any loss in purchasing power.* It is the rate that you would read about in the *Wall Street Journal* for a specific fixed-income security. That equation is:

$$k = k_{rf}^* + IRP + DRP + MP + LP \qquad (2\text{-}1)$$

where k = the nominal or observed rate of interest on a specific fixed-income security.

k_{rf}^* = the real risk-free rate of interest; it is the required rate of interest on a fixed-income security that has no risk in an economic environment of zero inflation. This can be reasonably thought of as the rate of interest demanded by investors in U.S. Treasury securities during periods of no inflation.

IRP = the inflation-risk premium.

DRP = the default-risk premium.

MP = the maturity premium.

LP = the liquidity premium.

Estimating Specific Interest Rates Using Risk Premiums: An Example

By using our knowledge of various risk premia as contained in equation (2-1), the financial manager can generate useful information for the firm's financial planning process. For instance, if the firm is about to offer a new issue of corporate bonds to the investing marketplace, it is possible for the financial manager or analyst to estimate what interest rate (yield) would satisfy the market to help ensure that the bonds are actually bought by investors. It would be unwise for the firm to offer too high of a yield because it will incur unnecessary interest expenses that will negatively impact earnings. On the other hand, offering too low of a yield will hinder the bonds from being attractive to investors (savers) in a competitive marketplace. The following example should help clarify and illustrate this situation.

Problem Situation

You have been asked to provide a reasonable estimate of the nominal interest rate for a new issue of Aaa-rated bonds (that is, very high quality corporate bonds) to be offered by Big Truck Producers Inc. The final format that the CFO of Big Truck has requested is that of equation (2-1) in the text.

Some agreed-upon procedures related to generating estimates for key variables in equation (2-1) follow:

1. The current (mid-2006) financial market environment is considered representative of the prospective tone of the market near the time of offering the new bonds to the investing public. This means that current interest rates will be used as benchmarks for some of the variable estimates. All estimates will be rounded off to hundredths of a percent; thus, 6.288 becomes 6.29 percent.
2. The real risk-free rate of interest, k_{rf}^*, is the difference between the calculated average yield on 3-month Treasury bills and the inflation rate.
3. The inflation-risk premium, *IRP*, is the rate of inflation expected to occur over the life of the bond under consideration.
4. The default-risk premium, *DRP*, is estimated by the difference between the average yield on Aaa-rated bonds and 30-year Treasury bonds.
5. The maturity premium, *MP*, is estimated by the difference between the calculated average yield on 30-year Treasury bonds and 3-month Treasury bills.
6. Big Truck's bonds will be traded on the New York Exchange for Bonds, so the liquidity premium, *LP*, will be slight. It will be greater than zero; however, because the secondary market for the firm's bonds is more uncertain than that of some other truck producers. It is estimated at 3 basis points. A basis point is one one-hundredth of 1 percent.

Now place your output into the format of equation (2-1) so that the nominal interest rate can be estimated and the size of each variable can also be inspected for reasonableness and discussion with the chief financial officer.

Solution

Let's now look at the building blocks that will comprise our forecast of the nominal interest rate on Big Truck's new issue of bonds. The nominal rate (k) that is forecast to satisfy the market turns out be 6.27 percent. The following tables illustrate how we obtained this estimate. The first table provides estimates of representative interest rates. The second table is a worksheet that "builds up" the nominal interest rate. It's just equation (2-1) in worksheet form.

DATE	(1) 3-MONTH TREASURY BILLS %	(2) 20-YEAR TREASURY BONDS %	(3) Aaa-RATED CORPORATE BONDS %	(4) INFLATION RATE %
Mid-2006	4.89	5.38	6.24	3.60

TABLE COLUMNS AS SHOWN	EQUATION (2-1)	
(1)–(4)	k^*	1.29
	+	+
(4)	IRP	3.60
	+	+
(3)–(2)	DRP	0.86
	+	+
(2)–(1)	MP	0.49
	+	+
Given	LP	0.03
	=	=
	k =	6.27

Thus the real risk-free rate of interest (k_{rf}^*) is estimated to be 1.29 percent. It is the difference between the average yield on 3-month Treasury bills and the inflation rate (column 1 minus column 4). In similar fashion, the inflation-risk premium of 3.60 percent (IRP) is the change in the inflation rate (column 4). The default-risk premium (DRP) is the difference in the average rate available to investors in Aaa-rated bonds and Treasury bonds with a 20-year maturity (column 3 minus column 2). The maturity premium (MP) of 0.49 percent is the difference in the rate earned by investors in 20-year Treasury bonds and 3-month Treasury bills (column 2 minus column 1). The liquidity premium (LP) was estimated for us by a sharp analyst—such as yourself.

When we put this all together as an estimate of the nominal interest rate needed to satisfy the financial markets on Big Truck's new bond issue, we have

$$k = k_{rf}^* + IRP + DRP + MP + LP = \text{nominal rate on Big Truck's bonds}$$
$$k = 1.29 + 3.60 + 0.86 + 0.49 + 0.03 = 6.27\%$$

Understanding this analysis will help you deal with the Mini Case at the end of this chapter. We move now to an examination of the relationship between real and nominal interest rates.

Real and Nominal Rates of Interest

As we just learned, when a rate of interest is quoted, it is generally the nominal, or observed, rate. The nominal rate of interest tells you how much more money you will have. The **real rate of interest, k^*,** in contrast, represents the rate of increase in your actual purchasing power, after adjusting for inflation. In effect, the real rate of interest tells you how much more purchasing power you will have. The real rate of interest is not necessarily a risk-free rate of interest, although it can be. In effect, there are real rates of interest for all different

real rate of interest the nominal (quoted) rate of interest less any loss in purchasing power of the dollar during the time of the investment.

levels of risk. Because the real rate of interest is not necessarily a risk-free rate, it can include both the real risk-free rate of interest and any appropriate risk premiums (DRP, MP, and LP). The nominal risk-free rate can be calculated to be approximately

$$k \approx \text{(approximately equals) } k^* + IRP \tag{2-2}$$

where k = the nominal or observed rate of interest on a specific fixed-income security.
       k^* = the real rate of interest; it is the required rate of interest on a fixed-income security with risk in an economic environment of zero inflation.
    IRP = the inflation-risk premium, a premium to compensate for anticipated inflation that is equal to be the price change expected to occur over the life of the bond or investment instrument.

This equation just says that the nominal rate of interest is approximately equal to the real interest rate plus the inflation premium and provides a quick and *approximate* way of estimating the real rate of interest, k^*, by solving directly for this rate. You'll notice it is very similar to equation (2-1), except it lumps all the different risk premiums in with the real risk-free rate of interest to come up with the real rate of interest. This basic relationship in equation (2-2) contains important information for the financial decision maker. It has also been for years the subject of fascinating and lengthy discussions among financial economists. We will look more at the substance of the real rate of interest in the second section that follows here. In that discussion, we will improve on equation (2-2) by making it more precise.

As we saw in equation (2-2), a quick approximation for the nominal rate of interest is the real interest rate plus the inflation premium. Let's take a closer look at this relationship. Let's begin by assuming that you have $100 today and lend it to someone for one year at a nominal rate of interest of 11.3 percent. This means you will get back $111.30 in 1 year. But if during the year, the prices of goods and services rise by 5 percent, it will take $105 at year-end to purchase the same goods and services that $100 purchased at the beginning of the year. What was your increase in purchasing power over the year? The quick and dirty answer is found by subtracting the inflation rate from the nominal rate, $11.3\% - 5\% = 6.3\%$, but this is not exactly correct. To be more precise, let the nominal rate of interest be represented by k, the anticipated rate of inflation by IRP, and the real rate of interest by k^*. Using these notations, we can express the relationship among the nominal interest rate, the rate of inflation, and the real rate of interest as follows:

1 + the nominal or quoted rate of interest = (1 + the real rate of interest)
(1 + the rate of inflation)
$$1 + k = (1 + k^*)(1 + IRP) \tag{2-3}$$

or

$$k = k^* + IRP + (k^* \cdot IRP) \tag{2-3a}$$

Consequently, the nominal rate of interest (k) is equal to the sum of the real rate of interest (k^*), the inflation rate (IRP), and the product of the real rate and the inflation rate. This relationship among nominal rates, real rates, and the rate of inflation has come to be called the *Fisher effect*.[2] What does the product ($k^* \cdot IRP$) represent? It represents the fact that the money you earn on your investment is worth less because of inflation. All this demonstrates that the observed nominal rate of interest includes both the real rate and an *inflation premium*.

Substituting into equation (2-3a) using a nominal rate of 11.3 percent and an inflation rate of 5 percent, we can calculate the real rate of interest, k^*, as follows:

Nominal or quoted rate of interest		real rate of interest	+	inflation rate	+	product of the real rate of interest and the inflation rate
k	=	k^*	+	IRP	+	$(k^* \times IRP)$
.113	=	k^*	+	.05	+	$.05k^*$
.063	=	$1.05k^*$				
k^*	=	.06	=	6%		

---

[2] In Chapter 5 , we will study more about the time value of money.

Can You Do It?

SOLVING FOR THE REAL RATE OF INTEREST

Your banker just called and offered you the chance to invest your savings for 1 year at a quoted rate of 10 percent. You also saw on the news that the inflation rate is 6 percent. What is the real rate of interest you would be earning if you made the investment? (The solution can be found on page 52.)

Thus, at the new higher prices, your purchasing power will have increased by only 6 percent, although you have $11.30 more than you had at the start of the year. To see why, let's assume that at the outset of the year, one unit of the market basket of goods and services costs $1, so you could purchase 100 units with your $100. At the end of the year, you have $11.30 more, but each unit now costs $1.05 (remember the 5 percent rate of inflation). How many units can you buy at the end of the year? The answer is $111.30 ÷ $1.05 = 106, which represents a 6 percent increase in real purchasing power.[3]

Inflation and Real Rates of Return: The Financial Analyst's Approach

Although the algebraic methodology presented in the previous section is strictly correct, few practicing analysts or executives use it. Rather, they employ some version of the following relationship, an approximation method, to estimate the real rate of interest over a selected past time frame.

(nominal interest rate) – (inflation rate) = real interest rate

The concept is straightforward, but its implementation requires that several judgments be made. For example, which interest rate series and maturity period should be used? Suppose we settle for using some U.S. Treasury security as a surrogate for a nominal risk-free interest rate. Then, should we use the yield on 3-month U.S. Treasury bills or, perhaps, the yield on 20-year Treasury bonds? There is no absolute answer to the question.

So, we can have a real risk-free short-term interest rate, as well as a real risk-free long-term interest rate, and several variations in between. In essence, it just depends on what the analyst wants to accomplish. We could also calculate the real rate of interest on some rating class of corporate bonds (such as Aaa-rated bonds) and have a risky real rate of interest as opposed to a real risk-free interest rate.

Furthermore, the choice of a proper inflation index is equally challenging. Again, we have several choices. We could use the consumer price index, the producer price index for finished goods, or some price index out of the national income accounts, such as the gross domestic product chain price index. Again, there is no precise scientific answer as to which specific price index to use. Logic and consistency do narrow the boundaries of the ultimate choice.

Let's tackle a very basic (simple) example. Suppose that an analyst wants to estimate the approximate real interest rate on (1) 3-month Treasury bills, (2) 30-year Treasury bonds, and (3) Aaa-rated corporate bonds over the 1981–2005 time frame. Furthermore, the annual rate of change in the consumer price index (measured from December to December) is considered

---

[3] This relationship was analyzed many years ago be Irving Fisher. For those who want to explore Fisher's theory of interest in more detail, a fine overview is contained in Peter N. Ireland, "Long-Term Interest Rate and Inflation: A Fisherian Approach," Federal Reserve Bank of Richmond, *Economic Quarterly*, 82 (Winter 1996), pp. 22–26.

How Did You Do?

SOLVING FOR THE REAL RATE OF INTEREST

Nominal or quoted =	real rate of	+	inflation	+	product of the real rate of interest
rate of interest	interest		rate		and the inflation rate
k	$=$ k^*	$+$	IRP	$+$	$(k^* \times IRP)$
.10	$=$ k^*	$+$	.06	$+$	$.06k^*$
.04	$=$ $1.06k^*$				
k^*	$=$ $.0377$	$=$	3.77%		

a logical measure of past inflation experience. Most of our work is already done for us in Table 2-3. Some of the data from Table 2-3 are displayed here.

SECURITY	MEAN NOMINAL YIELD (%)	MEAN INFLATION RATE (%)	INFERRED REAL RATE (%)
3-month Treasury bills	5.68	3.37	2.31
30-year Treasury bonds	7.82	3.37	4.45
Aaa-rated corporate bonds	8.66	3.37	5.29

Notice that the mean yield over the 25 years from 1981 to 2005 on all three classes of securities has been used. Likewise, the mean inflation rate over the same time period has been used as an estimate of the inflation-risk premium (*IRP* from our earlier notation). The last column provides the approximation for the real interest rate on each class of securities.

Thus, over the 25-year examination period the real rate of interest on 3-month Treasury bills was 2.31 percent versus 4.45 percent on 30-year Treasury bonds, versus 5.29 percent on Aaa-rated corporate bonds. These three estimates (approximations) of the real interest rate provide a rough guide to the increase in real purchasing power associated with an investment position in each security. Remember that the real rate on the corporate bonds is expected to be greater than that on long-term government bonds because of the default-risk premium (*DRP*) placed on the corporate securities. We move in the next section to a more detailed discussion of the maturity-risk premium (*MRP*).

Did You Get It?

1. What is the "nominal rate of interest"? Explain how it differs from the "real rate of interest."
2. Write an equation that includes the building blocks of the nominal rate of interest.

THE TERM STRUCTURE OF INTEREST RATES

term structure of interest rates the relationship between interest rates and the term to maturity, where the risk of default is held constant.

yield to maturity the rate of return a bondholder will receive if the bond is held to maturity.

The relationship between a debt security's rate of return and the length of time until the debt matures is known as the **term structure of interest rates** or the **yield to maturity**. For the relationship to be meaningful to us, all the factors other than maturity, meaning factors such as the chance of the bond defaulting, must be held constant. Thus, *the term structure reflects observed rates or yields on similar securities, except for the length of time until maturity, at a particular moment in time.*

Figure 2-5 shows an example of the term structure of interest rates. The curve is upward sloping, indicating that longer terms to maturity command higher returns, or yields. In this hypothetical term structure, the rate of interest on a 5-year note or bond is 11.5 percent, whereas the comparable rate on a 20-year bond is 13 percent.

Can You Do It?

SOLVING FOR THE NOMINAL RATE OF INTEREST

If you would like to earn a real rate of interest of 6 percent while the inflation rate is 4 percent, what nominal rate of interest would you have to invest in? (The solution can be found on page 54.)

FIGURE 2-5 The Term Structure of Interest Rates

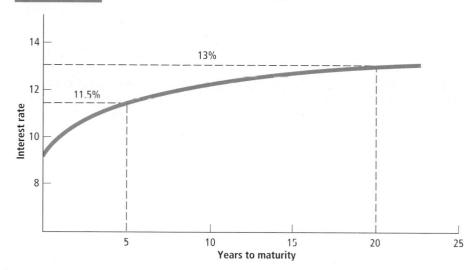

Observing the Historical Term Structures of Interest Rates

As we might expect, the term structure of interest rates changes over time, depending on the environment. The particular term structure observed today may be quite different from the term structure 1 month ago and different still from the term structure 1 month from now. A perfect example of the changing term structure, or yield curve, was witnessed during the early days of the first Persian Gulf Crisis, which occurred in August 1990. Figure 2-6 shows the yield curves 1 day before the Iraqi invasion of Kuwait and then again just 3 weeks later. The

FIGURE 2-6 Changes in the Term Structure of Interest Rates for Government Securities at the Outbreak of the First Persian Gulf Crisis

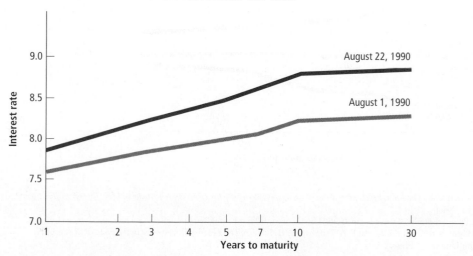

How Did You Do?

SOLVING FOR THE NOMINAL RATE OF INTEREST

Nominal or quoted rate of interest	=	real rate of interest	+	inflation rate	+	product of the real rate of interest and the inflation rate
k	=	k^*	+	IRP	+	$(k^* \times IRP)$
k	=	.06	+	.04	+	$(.06 \times .04)$
k	=	0.1024	=	10.24%		

change is noticeable, particularly for long-term interest rates. Investors quickly developed new fears about the prospect of increased inflation to be caused by the crisis and, consequently, increased their required rates of return. Although the upward-sloping term-structure curves in Figures 2-5 and 2-6 are the ones most commonly observed, yield curves can assume several shapes. Sometimes the term structure is downward sloping; at other times it rises and then falls (humpbacked); and at still other times it may be relatively flat. Figure 2-7 shows some yield curves at different points in time.

What Explains the Shape of the Term Structure?

A number of theories may explain the shape of the term structure of interest rates at any point in time. Three possible explanations are prominent: (1) the unbiased expectations theory, (2) the liquidity preference theory, and (3) the market segmentation theory.[4] Let's look at each in turn.

The Unbiased Expectations Theory

unbiased expectations theory
the theory that the shape of the term structure of interest rates is determined by an investor's expectations about future interest rates.

The **unbiased expectations theory** says that *the term structure is determined by an investor's expectations about future interest rates.*[5] To see how this works, consider the following investment problem faced by Mary Maxell. Mary has $10,000 that she wants to invest for 2 years, at which time she plans to use her savings to make a down payment on a new home. Want-

FIGURE 2-7   Historical Term Structures of Interest Rates for Government Securities

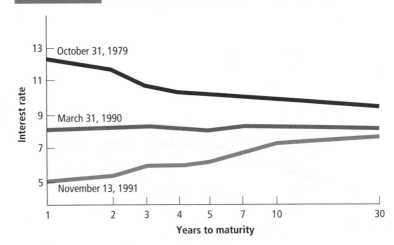

[4] See Richard Roll, *The Behavior of Interest Rates: An Application of the Efficient Market Model to U.S. Treasury Bills* (New York: Basic Books, 1970).
[5] Irving Fisher thought of this idea in 1896. The theory was later refined by J. R. Hicks in *Value and Capital* (London: Oxford University Press, 1946) and F. A. Lutz and V. C. Lutz in *The Theory of Investment in the Firm* (Princeton, NJ: Princeton University Press, 1951).

ing not to take any risk of losing her savings, she decides to invest in U.S. government securities. She has two choices. First, she can purchase a government security that matures in 2 years, which offers her an interest rate of 9 percent per year. If she does this, she will have $11,881 in 2 years, calculated as follows:[6]

Principal amount	$10,000
Plus year 1 interest (.09 × $10,000)	900
Principal plus interest at the end of year 1	$10,900
Plus year 2 interest (.09 × $10,900)	981
Principal plus interest at the end of year 2	$11,881

Alternatively, Mary could buy a government security maturing in 1 year that pays an 8 percent rate of interest. She would then need to purchase another 1-year security at the end of the first year. Which alternative Mary chooses obviously depends in part on the rate of interest she expects to receive on the government security she will purchase a year from now. We cannot tell Mary what the interest rate will be in a year; however, we can at least calculate the rate that will give her the same 2-year total savings she would get from her first choice, or $11,881. The interest rate can be calculated as follows:

Savings needed in 2 years	$11,881
Savings at the end of year 1 [$10,000(1 + .08)]	$10,800
Interest needed in year 2	$ 1,081

For Mary to receive $1,081 in the second year, she would have to earn about 10 percent on her second-year investment, computed as follows:

$$\frac{\text{interest received in year 2}}{\text{investment made at beginning of year 2}} = \frac{\$1,081}{\$10,800} = 10\%$$

So the term structure of interest rates for our example consists of the 1-year interest rate of 8 percent and the 2-year rate of 9 percent. This exercise also gives us information about the *expected* 1-year rate for investments made 1 year hence. In a sense, the term structure contains implications about investors' expectations of future interest rates; thus, this explains the unbiased expectations theory of the term structure of interest rates.

Although we can see a relationship between current interest rates with different maturities and investors' expectations about future interest rates, is this the whole story? Are there other influences? Probably, so let's continue to think about Mary's dilemma.

The Liquidity Preference Theory

In presenting Mary's choices, we have suggested that she would be indifferent to a choice between the 2-year government security offering a 9 percent return and two consecutive 1-year investments offering 8 and 10 percent, respectively. However, that would be so only if she is unconcerned about the risk associated with not knowing the rate of interest on the second 1-year security as of today. If Mary is risk averse (that is, she dislikes risk), she might not be satisfied with expectations of a 10 percent return on the second 1-year government security. She might require some additional expected return to be truly indifferent. Mary might in fact decide that she will expose herself to the uncertainty of future interest rates only if she can reasonably *expect* to earn an additional .5 percent in interest, or 10.5 percent, on the second 1-year investment. This *risk premium* (additional required interest rate) to compensate for the risk of changing future interest rates is nothing more than the maturity premium introduced earlier, and this concept underlies the liquidity preference theory of the term structure.[7] According to the **liquidity**

liquidity preference theory
the theory that the shape of the term structure of interest rates is determined by an investor's additional required interest rate in compensation of additional risks.

---

[6] We could also calculate the principal plus interest for Mary's investment using the following compound interest equation: $\$10,000(1 + .09)^2 = \$11,881$. We study the mathematics of compound interest in Chapter 5.

[7] This theory was first presented by John R. Hicks in *Value and Capital* (London: Oxford University Press, 1946), pp. 141–145, with the risk premium referred to as the liquidity premium. For our purposes we use the term *maturity premium (MP)* to describe this risk premium, thereby keeping our terminology consistent within this chapter.

preference theory, *investors require maturity premiums to compensate them for buying securities that expose them to the risks of fluctuating interest rates.*

The Market Segmentation Theory

market segmentation theory
the theory that the shape of the term structure of interest rates implies that the rate of interest for a particular maturity is determined solely by demand and supply for a given maturity. This rate is independent of the demand and supply for securities having different maturities.

The **market segmentation theory** of the term structure of interest rates is built on the notion that legal restrictions and personal preferences limit choices for investors to certain ranges of maturities. For example, commercial banks prefer short- to medium-term maturities as a result of the short-term nature of their deposit liabilities. They prefer not to invest in long-term securities. Life insurance companies, on the other hand, have long- term liabilities, so they prefer longer maturities in investments. At the extreme, the market segmentation theory implies that *the rate of interest for a particular maturity is determined solely by demand and supply for a given maturity and that it is independent of the demand and supply for securities having different maturities.* A more moderate version of the theory allows investors to have strong maturity preferences, but it also allows them to modify their feelings and preferences if significant yield changes occur.

Did You Get It?

1. Identify three prominent theories that attempt to explain the term structure of interest rates.
2. Which shape of the yield curve is considered to be the most typical?

Objective **8**

Understand the relationships among the multinational firm, efficient financial markets, and intercountry risk.

FINANCE AND THE MULTINATIONAL FIRM: EFFICIENT FINANCIAL MARKETS AND INTERCOUNTRY RISK

In this chapter we have discussed and demonstrated that the United States has a highly developed, complex, and competitive system of financial markets that allows for the quick transfer of savings from people and organizations with a surplus of savings to people and organizations with a savings deficit. Such a system of robust and credible financial markets allows great ideas (such as the personal computer) to be financed and increases the overall wealth of the given economy.

One major reason underdeveloped countries are indeed underdeveloped is that they lack a financial market system that has the confidence of those who must use it—such as the multinational firm. The multinational firm with cash to invest in foreign markets will weigh heavily the integrity of both the financial system and the political system of the prospective foreign country.

A lack of integrity on either the financial side or the political stability side retards direct investment in the lesser-developed nation. Consider the Walt Disney Company, headquartered in Burbank, California. Disney common stock trades on the NYSE (ticker symbol DIS), although the firm has significant overseas real investments such as Disneyland Paris Resort and Tokyo Disneyland. Disney has confidence in China's financial markets and those of western Europe and Japan. Disney would be less inclined to invest in a country like North Korea because it is less politically and financially stable.

Did You Get It?

1. Identify one major reason why underdeveloped countries remain underdeveloped.

Objective **1**

Describe key components of the U.S. financial market system.

Summary

This chapter centers on the market environment in which corporations raise long-term funds, including the structure of the U.S. financial markets, the institution of investment banking, and the various methods for distributing securities. It also discusses the role interest rates play in allocating savings to ultimate investment.

Corporations can raise funds through public offerings or private placements. The public market is impersonal in that the security issuer does not meet the ultimate investors in the financial instruments. In a private placement, the securities are sold directly to a limited number of institutional investors.

The primary market is the market for new issues. The secondary market represents transactions in currently outstanding securities. Both the money and capital markets have primary and secondary sides. The money market refers to transactions in short-term debt instruments. The capital market, on the other hand, refers to transactions in long-term financial instruments. Trading in the capital markets can occur in either the organized security exchanges or the over-the-counter market. The money market is exclusively an over-the-counter market.

The investment banker is a financial specialist involved as an intermediary in the merchandising of securities. He or she performs the functions of (1) underwriting, (2) distributing, and (3) advising. Major methods for the public distribution of securities include (1) the negotiated purchase, (2) the competitive bid purchase, (3) the commission or best-efforts basis, (4) privileged subscriptions, and (5) direct sales. The direct sale bypasses the use of an investment banker. The negotiated purchase is the most profitable distribution method to the investment banker. It also provides the greatest amount of investment-banking services to the corporate client.

Privately placed debt provides an important market outlet for corporate bonds. Major investors in this market are (1) life insurance firms, (2) state and local retirement funds, and (3) private pension funds. Several advantages and disadvantages are associated with private placements. The financial officer must weight these attributes and decide if a private placement is preferable to a public offering.

Flotation costs consist of the underwriter's spread and issuing costs. The flotation costs of common stock exceed those of preferred stock, which, in turn, exceed those of debt. Moreover, flotation costs as a percent of gross proceeds are inversely related to the size of the security issue.

On July 30, 2002, President Bush signed into law the Public Company Accounting Reform and Investor Protection Act. This act is commonly known as the Sarbanes-Oxley Act of 2002. Its intended purpose as stated in the act is "to protect investors by improving the accuracy and reliability of corporate disclosures made pursuant to the securities laws, and for other purposes."

The financial markets give managers an informed indication of investors' opportunity costs. The more efficient the market, the more informed the indication. This information is a useful input about the rates of return that investors require on financial claims. In turn, this becomes useful to financial managers as they estimate the overall cost of capital the firm will have to pay for its financing needs.

From **Principle 1: The Risk–Return Trade-Off,** you know that the rates of return on various securities are based on the risks that investors face when they invest in those securities. In addition to a risk-free return, investors will want to be compensated for the potential loss of purchasing power resulting from inflation. Moreover, investors require a greater return the greater the default risk, maturity premium, and liquidity premium are on the securities being analyzed.

A system of robust and credible financial markets allows great ideas to be financed and increases the overall wealth of a given economy. The multinational firm with cash to invest in foreign markets will weigh heavily the integrity of both the financial system and the political system of the prospective foreign country where the proposed investment project will be domiciled. A lack of integrity on either the financial side or the political stability side retards direct investment in a less-developed nation.

Objective **2**

Understand the role of the investment-banking business in the context of raising corporate capital.

Objective **3**

Distinguish between privately placed securities and publicly offered securities.

Objective **4**

Be acquainted with securities flotation costs and securities markets regulations.

Objective **5**

Understand the rate-of-return relationships among various classes of financing vehicles that persist in the financial markets.

Objective **6**

Be acquainted with recent interest rate levels and the fundamentals of interest rate determination.

Objective **7**

Explain the popular theories of the term structure of interest rates.

Objective **8**

Understand the relationships among the multinational firm, efficient financial markets, and intercountry risk.

Key Terms

Capital market   35

Direct sale   41

Dutch auction   41

Flotation costs   43

Initial public offering, IPO   34

Investment banker   38

Liquidity preference theory   55

Liquidity premium   47

Market segmentation theory   56

Maturity premium   47

Money market   34

Nominal rate of interest   48

Opportunity cost of funds   44

Organized security exchanges   35

Over-the-counter markets   35

Primary market   33

Private placement   32

Privileged subscription   41

Public offering   32

Real rate of interest   49

Review Questions

2-1. Distinguish between the money and capital markets.

2-2. What major benefits do corporations and investors enjoy because of the existence of organized security exchanges?

2-3. What general criteria does an organized exchange examine to determine whether a firm's securities can be listed on the exchange? (Specific numbers are not needed here but rather areas of investigation.)

2-4. Why do you think most secondary-market trading in bonds takes place over the counter?

2-5. What is an investment banker, and what major functions does he or she perform?

2-6. What is the major difference between a negotiated purchase and a competitive bid purchase?

2-7. Why is an investment-banking syndicate formed?

2-8. Why might a large corporation want to raise long-term capital through a private placement rather than a public offering?

2-9. As a recent business school graduate, you work directly for the corporate treasurer. Your corporation is going to issue a new security and is concerned with the probable flotation costs. What tendencies about flotation costs can you relate to the treasurer?

2-10. Identify three distinct ways that savings are ultimately transferred to business firms in need of cash.

2-11. Explain the term *opportunity cost* with respect to the cost of funds to the firm.

2-12. Compare and explain the historical rates of return for different types of securities.

2-13. Explain the impact of inflation on rates of return.

2-14. Define the *term structure of interest rates*.

2-15. Explain the popular theories for the rationale of the term structure of interest rates.

Study Problems

2-1. (*Real interest rates: financial analyst's method*) The CFO of your firm has asked you for an approximate answer to this question: What was the increase in real purchasing power associated with both 3-month Treasury bills and 30-year Treasury bonds over the 2000–2005 period? *Hints:* (1) Consult Table 2-3 in the text; (2) simple averages on the key variables will provide a defensible response to your boss. Also, the chief financial officer wants a short explanation should the 3-month real rate of return turn out to be *less* than the 30-year real rate of return.

2-2. (*Real interest rates: financial analyst's method*) The CFO of your firm has asked you for an approximate answer to this question: What was the increase in real purchasing power associated with both 3-month Treasury bills and 30-year Treasury bonds over the 1991–1995 period? *Hints:* (1) Consult Table 2-3 in the text; (2) simple averages on the key variables will provide a defensible response to your boss. Also, the chief financial officer wants a short explanation should the 3-month real rate turn out to be *less* than the 30-year real rate.

2-3. (*Inflation and interest rates*) What would you expect the nominal rate of interest to be if the real rate is 4 percent and the expected inflation rate is 7 percent?

2-4. (*Inflation and interest rates*) Assume the expected inflation rate to be 4 percent. If the current real rate of interest is 6 percent, what ought the nominal rate of interest be?

2-5. (*Inflation and interest rates*) Assume the expected inflation rate to be 5 percent. If the current real rate of interest is 7 percent, what would you expect the nominal rate of interest to be?

2-6. (*Term structure of interest rates*) You want to invest your savings of $20,000 in government securities for the next 2 years. Currently, you can invest either in a security that pays interest of 8 percent per year for the next 2 years or in a security that matures in 1 year but pays only 6 percent interest. If you make the latter choice, you would then reinvest your savings at the end of the first year for another year.

   a. Why might you choose to make the investment in the 1-year security that pays an interest rate of only 6 percent, as opposed to investing in the 2-year security paying 8 percent? Provide numerical support for your answer. Which theory of term structure have you supported in your answer?

   b. Assume your required rate of return on the second-year investment is 11 percent; otherwise, you will choose to go with the 2-year security. What rationale could you offer for your preference?

Web Works

2-WW1. Check out the Living Yield Curve on the SmartMoney.com Web site. It's located at **www.smartmoney.com/onebond/index.cfm?story=yieldcurve** and shows how the yield curve has changed since 1976. Once you get there, hit the play button and watch the changes in the yield curve since 1976. After looking at the latest yield curve compared with what it has been in the past, would you consider current long-term interest rates to be above or below their historical average? Would you consider the current yield curve to be normal, steep, inverted, or flat (or humped)?

2-WW2. Negative real interest rates occur when the rate of inflation exceeds the rate of interest on fixed-income financing instruments such as corporate bonds, government bonds, and U.S. Treasury bills. Negative real rates of interest generally are associated with slow periods of economic growth. During such periods, corporations usually prefer to raise external cash via new debt issues rather than equity issues. Two Web sites can give you insights into whether current real rates of interest are negative or positive. Visit **www.federalreserve.gov** to check on the H.15 Selected Interest Rates report to assess nominal interest rates. Then check on **stats.bls.gov** to assess several different inflation indices. Estimate the level of the real rate of interest on the 10-year Treasury note (and any other maturity period that excites you), using more than one inflation index. *Hint:* The consumer price index and producer price index for finished goods are two indicators commonly used by security and financial analysts.

Mini Case

On the first day of your summer internship, you've been assigned to work with the Chief Financial Officer (CFO) of SanBlas Jewels Inc. Not knowing how well trained you are, the CFO has decided to test your understanding of interest rates. Specifically, she asked you to provide a reasonable estimate of the nominal interest rate for a new issue of Aaa-rated bonds to be offered by SanBlas Jewels Inc. The final format that the chief financial officer of SanBlas Jewels has requested is that of equation (2-1) in the text. Your assignment also requires that you consult the data in Table 2-3.

Some agreed-upon procedures related to generating estimates for key variables in equation (2-1) follow.

   a. The financial market environment over the 2000–2003 period is considered representative of the prospective tone of the market near the time of the offering of the new bonds to the investing public. This means that 4-year averages will be used as benchmarks for some of the variable estimates. All estimates are rounded off to hundredths of a percent; thus, 3.688 becomes 3.69 percent.

   b. The real risk-free rate of interest is the difference between the calculated average yield on 3-month Treasury bills and the inflation rate.

   c. The default-risk premium is estimated by the difference between the average yield on Aaa-rated bonds and 30-year Treasury bonds.

   d. The maturity premium is estimated by the difference between the average yield on 30-year Treasury bonds and 3-month Treasury bills.

   e. SanBlas Jewels' bonds will be traded on the New York Bond Exchange, so the liquidity premium will be slight. It will be greater than zero, however, because the secondary market for the firm's bonds is more uncertain than that of some other jewel sellers. It is estimated at 4 basis points. A basis point is one one-hundredth of 1 percent.

Now place your output into the format of equation (2-1) so that the nominal interest rate can be estimated and the size of each variable can also be inspected for reasonableness and discussion with the CFO.

After reading this chapter, you should be able to:

1. Compute a company's profits, as reflected by its income statement.

2. Determine a firm's financial position at a point in time based on its balance sheet.

3. Measure a company's cash flows.

CHAPTER 3

Understanding Financial Statements and Cash Flows

Assume that after graduating from college, you accepted a position in the consumer electronics division of a large international corporation with a strong focus on marketing and branding. You considered the opportunity to be a great fit given your degree in marketing. You progressed well within the firm, being promoted on numerous occasions. Within time you were offered the position of president of consumer electronics for all the United States—no small achievement, to say the least.

You were thrilled to accept the challenge. There was just one problem. Although U.S. consumer electronics sales amounted to $4 billion, the division had not shown a profit in the last 15 years. When you accepted the position, the company's CEO made it clear that you must turn the situation around, saying, "If you can't get the division profitable within 3 years, it will be closed."

The situation just described is exactly where Reneir Jens found himself when he became the president of the North American consumer electronics division of Royal Philips Electronics in 2000. Philips, based in the Netherlands, is one the largest consumer electronics firms in the world, selling brands such as the Magnavox flat-screen television. However, the U.S. division had been a loser for 15 years. The CEO at Philips, Gerard Kleisterlee, made it clear to Jens that the division must be profitable within a few years or it would be history.

To make the division profitable, Jens knew his job was to focus on the few things Philips did well. He met regularly with the marketing and sales departments in a modest office, avoiding the executive suite hidden behind frosted glass. Within months of his arrival he had cut the number of products Philips sold in the United States from 600 to 100. He directed his sales reps to concentrate on only the 100 largest retailers (75% of Philips' business is conducted with the 10 largest) and abandon hundreds of smaller chains that weren't profitable for Philips. The result: In 2005, his division was profitable.

Jens now says that Philips' future growth in the United States lies in premium products, tech toys such as high-definition TVs, wireless music systems, and Blu-ray disc players. Among the new products being developed: a beautiful glass orb that wirelessly receives digital photos and videos; consumers simply shake the orb, and the photos and videos on it change. Philips' researchers are also toying with an MP3 player that senses everyone else with the same player within 90 feet, allowing you to tune in to what they are listening to and get the track information. The next two chapters will give you a framework for understanding the connection between business decisions and the resulting profits or losses.

In Chapter 2, we explained the workings of the financial markets. We found that these markets provide the means for bringing together investors (savers) with the users of capital (businesses that provide products and services to the consumer). There we looked at the world as the economist sees it, with an eye for understanding the marketplace where managers go to acquire capital. It is the investors in these financial markets who determine the value of a firm, and given our goal of maximizing shareholder value, no issue is more fundamental to our study. However, we want to alter our perspective for the time being.

In this chapter, we view the world of finance more as an accountant sees it. To begin, we examine the two basic financial statements that are used to understand how a firm is doing financially: the income statement, or what is sometimes called the profit and loss statement, and the balance sheet. We will also examine carefully how to compute a firm's cash flows. Our goal is not to make you an accountant, but instead to provide you with the tools to understand a firm's financial situation. With this knowledge, you will be able to understand the financial consequences of a company's decisions and actions—as well as your own.

The financial performance of a firm matters to a lot of groups—the company's management, its employees, and its investors, just to name a few. If you are an employee, the firm's performance is important to you because it may determine your annual bonus, your job security, and your opportunity to advance your professional career. This is true whether you are in the firm's marketing, finance, or human resources department. Moreover, an employee who can see how decisions affect a firm's finances has a competitive advantage. So regardless of your position in the firm, it is in your own best interest to know the basics of financial statements—even if accounting is not your greatest love.

Let's begin our review of financial statements by looking at the format and content of the income statement.

Objective 1

Compute a company's profits, as reflected by its income statement.

income statement (profit and loss statement) a basic accounting statement that measures the results of a firm's operations over a specified period, commonly 1 year. Also known as the profit and loss statement. The bottom line of the income statement shows the firm's profit or loss for the period.

cost of goods sold the cost of producing or acquiring a product or service to be sold in the ordinary course of business.

gross profit sales or revenue minus the cost of goods sold.

operating expense marketing and selling expenses, general and administrative expenses, and depreciation expense.

operating income (earnings before interest and taxes) sales less the cost of goods sold less operating expenses.

THE INCOME STATEMENT

An **income statement**, or **profit and loss statement**, indicates the amount of profits generated by a firm over a given time period, often 1 year. In its most basic form, the income statement may be represented as follows:

$$\text{Sales} - \text{expenses} = \text{profits} \tag{3-1}$$

The format for an income statement is shown in Figure 3-1. The income statement begins with sales or revenue, from which we subtract the **cost of goods sold** (the cost of producing or acquiring the product or service to be sold) to yield **gross profits**. Next, **operating expenses** are deducted to determine **operating income** (also called **operating profits** or **earnings before interest and taxes** or **EBIT**). Notice that the operating expenses in the income statement consist of:

1. Marketing and selling expenses—the cost of promoting the firm's products or services to customers.

FIGURE 3-1 The Income Statement: An Overview

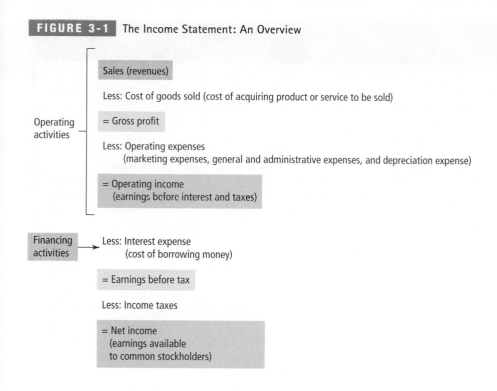

2. General and administrative expenses—the firm's overhead expenses, such as executive salaries and rent expense.
3. Depreciation expense—a noncash expense to allocate the cost of depreciable assets, such as plant and equipment, over the life of the asset.

In Figure 3-1, we see that operating income is the result of management's decisions relating only to the *operations* of the business, not its financing. In other words, the firm's *financing* expenses (its interest expense resulting from the use of debt financing) have not been subtracted to this point. Thus, the operating income of a firm reports the results of the following activities:

1. The selling price of the products or services to be sold and the number of units sold (selling price × units sold = total sales)
2. The cost of producing or acquiring the goods or services that were sold (cost of goods sold)
3. Selling and marketing expenses (the expenses related to marketing, selling, and distributing the products or services)
4. The firm's overhead expenses (general and administrative expenses, and depreciation expenses)

We then determine the **earnings before taxes**, or **taxable income**, by deducting the **financing cost** (the interest expense on the firm's debt financing) from the operating income.[1] Next, the firm's income taxes are calculated, based on its earnings before taxes and the applicable tax rate for the amount of income reported. For instance, if a firm had earnings before taxes of $100,000, and its tax rate is 28 percent, then it would owe $28,000 in taxes (0.28 × $100,000 = $28,000).

The resulting number is the **net income**, or **earnings available to common stockholders**, which represents income that may be reinvested in the firm or distributed to its owners—provided, of course, the cash is available to do so. As you will come to understand, a positive net income on an income statement does not necessarily mean that a firm has generated positive cash flows.

earnings before taxes (taxable income) operating income minus interest expense.

financing cost cost incurred by a company that often includes interest expenses and preferred dividends.

net income (earnings available to common stockholders) a figure representing a firm's profit or loss for the period. It also represents the earnings available to the firm's common and preferred stockholders.

[1] If a firm has issued preferred stock, it would pay preferred stock dividends, which would be shown in the income statement as an expense along with any interest paid on debt. For our purposes, we will assume that there is no preferred stock being used to finance the firm's assets.

Finance at Work

EVERYONE'S A CFO

At a monthly staff meeting, Maria Mantz nibbled her pen top and shuffled the spreadsheets in her lap, anxiously awaiting her turn at the podium. Mantz had good reason to be nervous. She had worked at Development Counsellors International (DCI)—a New York City public relations firm that represents dozens of cities, states, and countries—for only 5 months. And she was just 23. Nonetheless, she was about to present the monthly financial report for the company.

Mantz's anxiety seemed to abate as she stood before about 30 of her colleagues and began: "Several accounts had quite an increase in May," she said, asking her audience to refer to a DCI revenue table in their handouts. Next, she gestured to a large flip board. "Does anyone know what the five clients listed on this page have in common?" she asked.

"They're all performance-based accounts," yelled out DCI account executive Malcolm Griffiths, referring to the company's clients whose fees are based on results.

"Right," Mantz replied, handing him a gift card for Cosi, a nearby sandwich shop. "In fact, 20% of our billings for May came from performance-based accounts. Is this a good thing or a bad thing?"

Andrew Levine's, DCI's president, wants each of DCI's employees—from its receptionists to its tech support staffers—to become financially savvy. So each month, a different staffer is appointed CFO for a day and is responsible for leading DCI's monthly finance meeting. The CFO of the day goes through a breakdown of the company's sales and expenses for the previous month, pointing out irregularities and trends, taking questions from staffers, and sparking conversations about everything from cost cutting to contract negotiations. At the end of the report, the acting CFO unveils the bottom line and reveals if the company met its profit goal for the month. Each time DCI's accumulated profit hits another $100,000 in-

crement during the course of the year, 30% of it is distributed among employees along with their next paychecks.

The CFO-for-a-day idea occurred to Levine while he was trying to implement a more open management style at DCI. Initially, he simply added a financial segment to the company's monthly staff meetings. But employees seemed bored. During one staff meeting, he asked his employees how to calculate a profit. Only one employee, receptionist Sergio Barrios, knew the answer. "It was mind-boggling," Levine says.

Then Barrios's knack for figures gave Levine an idea: What if he required employees to present the financial reports themselves? They'd have to learn at least the basics, he reasoned. So for the next staff meeting, Levine appointed his receptionist CFO for the day—and was pleased to see the reactions in the room during the presentation. Unlike Levine, Barrios was new to accounting and explained things in a way that any layperson could understand. "They figured, 'Gosh, if our receptionist can get this, so can I,'" Levine says.

Since then, the approach has helped transform the most unlikely staffers into finance whizzes. At first Mantz, who recently graduated from Penn State with a degree in advertising and public relations, dreaded the idea of being CFO. "The first time I saw the numbers, it was a little nerve-wracking," Mantz says. But after several months of seeing her colleagues make sense of complex financial details, she began to see that it wasn't as hard as it looked. By the time she was selected to be CFO in June, she was ready.

As far as Mantz is concerned, it was worth the extra effort and nerves. "I'm a new, young employee," she says. "And I'm being trained not only as a PR executive, but also as a business executive."

Source: Nadine Heintz, "Everyone's a CFO," *Inc. Magazine*, September 2005, pp. 42–43. Copyright 2005 by Mansueto Ventures, LLC. Reproduced with permission of Mansueto Ventures LLC.

Table 3-1 contains the 2007 income statement for Davies Inc., a manufacturer of accessories for small technology products. We see that the firm had *sales* of $600 million for the 12-month period ended December 31, 2007. The *cost of goods sold* was $460 million, resulting in *gross profits* of $140 million. The firm then had $65 million of operating expenses. After deducting the operating expenses, the firm's *operating income (earnings before interest and taxes)* was $75 million. To this point, we have calculated the profits resulting only from operating the business, without regard for any financing costs, such as the interest paid on money borrowed.

We next deduct the $15 million in interest expense (the amount paid for borrowing money) to arrive at the company's *earnings before taxes (taxable income)* of $60 million. We then subtract the income taxes of $18 million to determine the company's *net income*, or *earnings available to common stockholders*, of $42 million.

At this point, we have completed the income statement. However, the firm's owners (common stockholders) like to know how much income the firm made on a *per share* basis, or what is called **earnings per share**. We calculate earnings per share as net income divided by the number of common stock shares outstanding. Because Davies Inc. had 20 million shares outstanding in 2007 (see Table 3-1), its earnings per share was $2.10 ($2.10 = $42 million net income ÷ 20 million shares).

Investors also want to know the amount of dividends a firm pays for each share outstanding, or the **dividends per share**. In Table 3-1 we see that Davies Inc. paid $10 million in

earnings per share net income on a per share basis.

dividends per share the amount of dividends a firm pays for each share outstanding.

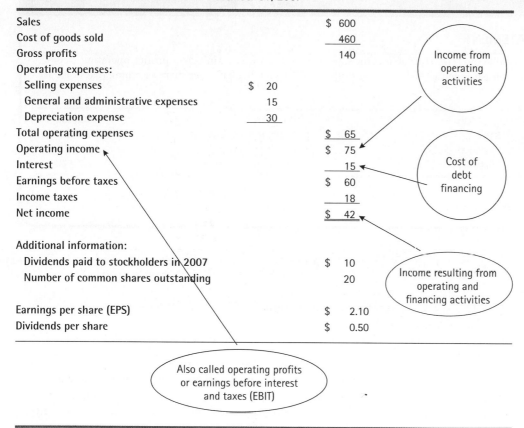

TABLE 3-1	Davies Inc.: Income Statement (expressed in millions, except per share data) for the Year Ended December 31, 2007		
Sales		$ 600	
Cost of goods sold		460	
Gross profits		140	
Operating expenses:			
Selling expenses	$ 20		
General and administrative expenses	15		
Depreciation expense	30		
Total operating expenses		$ 65	
Operating income		$ 75	
Interest		15	
Earnings before taxes		$ 60	
Income taxes		18	
Net income		$ 42	
Additional information:			
Dividends paid to stockholders in 2007		$ 10	
Number of common shares outstanding		20	
Earnings per share (EPS)		$ 2.10	
Dividends per share		$ 0.50	

TABLE 3-2	Davies Inc.: Common-Sized Income Statement for the Year Ended December 31, 2007		
		Dollars	Percentage of Sales
Sales		$ 600	100.0%
Cost of goods sold		460	76.7%
Gross profits		$ 140	23.3% ← gross profit margin
Operating expenses		$ 65	10.8%
Operating income		$ 75	12.5% ← operating profit margin
Interest		15	2.5%
Earnings before taxes		$ 60	10.0%
Income taxes		18	3.0%
Net income		$ 42	7.0% ← net profit margin

dividends during 2007. We can then determine that the firm paid $0.50 in dividends per share ($0.50 = $10 million total dividends ÷ 20 million shares outstanding).

What conclusions can we draw from Davies Inc.'s income statement? To answer this question, it is helpful to restate the numbers in the income statement as a percentage of sales. Such a revision is called a **common-sized income statement** and is presented in Table 3-2 for Davies Inc. The common-sized income statement allows us to express expenses and profits on a relative basis, so that we can more easily compare a firm's income performance across time and with competitors. The profits-to-sales relationships are defined as **profit margins**. For Davies Inc. we see that the firm earned

1. A 23.3 percent **gross profit margin** (23.3% = $140 million of gross profits ÷ $600 million of sales)

common-sized income statement an income statement in which a firm's expenses and profits are expressed as a percentage of its sales.

profit margins financial ratios (sometimes simply referred to as margins) that reflect the level of the firm's profits relative to its sales. Examples include the gross profit margin (gross profit divided by sales), operating profit margin (operating earnings divided by sales), and the net profit margin (net profit divided by sales).

gross profit margin gross profit divided by net sales. It is a ratio denoting the gross profit earned by the firm as a percentage of its net sales.

Can You Do It?

PREPARING AN INCOME STATEMENT

Given the information below for Menielle Inc., construct an income statement. What are the firm's gross profits, operating income, and net income? What is the firm's noncash expense? Calculate earnings per share and dividends per share assuming that there are 20,000 shares outstanding.

Interest expense	$35,000	Sales	$400,000
Cost of goods sold	$150,000	Common stock dividends	$15,000
Selling expenses	$40,000	Income taxes	$40,000
Administrative expenses	$30,000	Depreciation expense	$20,000

(The solution can be found on page 67.)

---

operating profit margin operating income divided by sales. This ratio serves as an overall measure of the company's operating effectiveness.

net profit margin net income divided by sales. A ratio that measures the net income of the firm as a percent of sales.

2. A 12.5 percent **operating profit margin** (12.5% = $75 million of operating profits ÷ $600 million of sales)

3. A 7 percent **net profit margin** (7% = $42 million of net profits ÷ $600 million of sales)

In practice, managers pay close attention to the firm's profit margins. Profit margins are considered to be an important measurement of how well the firm is doing financially. Managers carefully watch for any changes in margins, up or down. They also compare the firm's margins with those of competitors—something we will discuss in Chapter 4. For the time being, simply remember that profit-to-sales relationships, or *profit margins*, are important in assessing a firm's performance.

Did You Get It?

1. What can we learn by reviewing a firm's income statement?
2. What basic relationship can we see in an income statement?
3. How are gross profits, operating income, and net income different as they relate to the areas of business activity reported in the income statement?
4. What are earnings per share and dividends per share?
5. What is a profit margin? What are the different types of profit margins?

Objective **2**

Determine a firm's financial position at a point in time based on its balance sheet.

balance sheet a statement that shows a firm's assets, liabilities, and shareholder equity at a given point in time. It is a snapshot of the firm's financial position on a particular date.

THE BALANCE SHEET

A firm's income statement reports the results from operating the business *for a period of time*, such as 1 year. The firm's **balance sheet**, on the other hand, provides a snapshot of the firm's financial position *at a specific point in time*, presenting its asset holdings, liabilities, and owner-supplied capital (stockholders' equity). Figure 3-2 shows the difference in time perspectives between an income statement and a balance sheet. By examining two balance sheets, one at the beginning of a year and one at the end of the year, along with the income statement for the year, we have a more complete picture of firm's operations. For instance, we could see what a company looked like at the beginning of 2007 (by looking at its balance sheet on December 31, 2006), what happened during the year (by looking at its income statement for 2007), and the final outcome at the end of 2007 (by looking at its balance sheet on December 31, 2007).

In its simplest form, a balance sheet is represented by the following balance sheet "equation":

$$\text{Total assets} = \text{total liabilities (debt)} + \text{total shareholders' equity} \qquad (3\text{-}2)$$

How Did You Do?

PREPARING AN INCOME STATEMENT

On page 66, we provided data for Menielle Inc. and asked you to prepare an income statement based on the information. Your results should be as follows:

Sales		$400,000
Cost of goods sold		150,000
Gross profit		$250,000
Operating expenses:		
Selling and marketing expenses	$40,000	
Administrative expenses	30,000	
Depreciation expense	20,000	
Total operating expenses		$ 90,000
Operating income		$160,000
Interest expense		35,000
Earnings before tax		$125,000
Income taxes		40,000
Net income		$ 85,000
Earnings per share ($85,000 net income ÷ 20,000 shares)		$ 4.25
Dividends per share ($15,000 dividends ÷ 20,000 shares)		$ 0.75

FIGURE 3-2   The Income Statement and Balance Sheet as One Picture

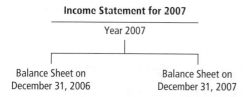

where *total assets* represent the resources owned by the firm, and *total liabilities* and *total shareholders' equity* indicate how those resources were financed.

The conventional practice is to report the value of the firm's various assets in the balance sheet by using the actual cost of acquiring them. Thus, the balance sheet does not represent the current market value of the company's assets, and consequently does not reflect the value of the company itself. Rather, *it reports historical transactions at their cost*. Therefore, the balance sheet reports a company's **accounting book value**, which is simply equal to a firm's total assets as listed in its balance sheet. It's important for you to understand that a company's accounting book value is not the same as the market value of the assets. Determining a fair or market value of a business or its assets is a different matter—an issue that we will give great attention to throughout future chapters.

Figure 3-3 shows us the basic components of a balance sheet. On the left side of Figure 3-3, the firm's assets are listed according to their type; on the right side, we see a listing of the different sources of financing a company could use to finance its assets.

accounting book value the value of an asset as shown on a firm's balance sheet. It represents the historical cost of the asset rather than its current market value or replacement cost.

Types of Assets

As shown in Figure 3-3, a company's assets fall into three categories: (1) current assets, (2) fixed assets, and (3) other assets.

FIGURE 3-3   What Goes on the Balance Sheet: An Overview

ASSETS	LIABILITIES (DEBT) AND EQUITY
Current assets: • Cash • Accounts receivable • Inventories • Other current assets **Total current assets**	**Current liabilities (debt):** • Accounts payable • Accrued expenses • Short-term notes **Total current debt**
+	+
Fixed assets: • Machinery and equipment • Buildings • Land **Total fixed assets**	**Long-term liabilities (debt)**
+	+
Other assets: • Goodwill • Patents **Total other assets**	**Equity:** • Preferred stock • Common stock • Retained earnings **Total stockholders' equity**
=	=
TOTAL ASSETS	**TOTAL DEBT AND EQUITY**

Finance at Work

WANT TO TALK TO THE CFO OF THE LARGEST COMPUTER SYSTEMS MANUFACTURER IN THE WORLD?

Want to have a little fun by listening to Dell's executives talk about an earnings announcement or some other major event? In addition to filing reports with the Securities Exchange Commission and on the news wires, Dell, along with most other publicly traded firms, allow interested people to participate in a conference call with the firm's executives when information is being released to the public. The conference calls are then archived and remain on the firm's Web site for a period of time. To access the archives for Dell, go to **www.dell.com**, click the link "About Dell" (at the bottom of the page), then choose "Investors," and finally, select "Meetings and Conference Calls." You will then see a list of dates and topics. You can even get on an e-mail list alerting you as to when you can participate in live conference calls. Give it a try!

Current Assets

Current assets, or **gross working capital**, as it is sometimes called, are those assets that are relatively *liquid*, that is, those that are expected to be converted into cash within 12 months. Current assets include a firm's cash, accounts receivable, inventories, and other current assets.

- **Cash.** Every firm must have **cash** to conduct its business operations. A reservoir of cash is needed because of the unequal flow of funds into (cash receipts) and out of (cash expenditures) the business.
- **Accounts receivable.** A firm's **accounts receivable** are the amounts owed to the firm by its customers who buy on credit.
- **Inventories.** A company's **inventories** consist of raw materials, work in process, and finished goods held by the firm for eventual sale.
- **Other current assets.** **Other current assets** include such items as prepaid expenses. For example, a company's insurance premium might be due before the actual insurance coverage begins; or the firm's rent might have to be paid in advance. These expenditures are considered assets because they represent an investment that's been made by the company. Only when, for example, the insurance premium is used up following the coverage period is the premium considered an expense.

current assets (gross working capital) current assets consist primarily of cash, marketable securities, accounts receivable, inventories, and prepaid expenses.

cash cash on hand, demand deposits, and short-term marketable securities that can quickly be converted into cash.

accounts receivable money owed by customers who purchased goods or services from the firm on credit.

inventories raw materials, work in progress, and finished goods held by the firm for eventual sale.

Fixed Assets

Fixed assets are long term in nature, such as machinery and equipment, buildings, and land. These assets will be used over a number of years.

When a firm purchases a fixed asset, it does not immediately report the cost of the asset as an expense in its income statement. Instead, it is considered to be an asset and included in the balance sheet. Some of these assets, such as machinery and equipment, will depreciate in value over time due to obsolescence or daily wear and tear; others may not, such as land.

With depreciable assets, the original cost of an asset is allocated in the income statement over the asset's expected useful life. The amount allocated as the cost each year is shown as a **depreciation expense** in the income statement. (Recall that you first encountered the term *depreciation* in Chapter 1.) The sum of all depreciation taken over the entire life of the asset is shown as **accumulated depreciation** in the balance sheet.

To illustrate, assume that a truck purchased for $20,000 is to be evenly depreciated over a 4-year life.[2] The depreciation expense to be reported in the income statement for each year would be $5,000 ($20,000 asset cost ÷ 4 years = $5,000). When a firm buys the truck, the $20,000 original cost of the asset is added to the balance sheet as a **gross fixed asset**. The cumulative depreciation taken over the asset's life is reported as *accumulated depreciation*. We subtract the accumulated depreciation each year from the gross fixed assets to determine **net fixed assets**. In this example, the income statements for each year and balance sheets over time would appear as follows:

fixed assets assets such as equipment, buildings, and land.

depreciation expense a noncash expense to allocate the cost of depreciable assets, such as plant and equipment, over the life of the asset.

accumulated depreciation the sum of all depreciation taken over the entire life of a depreciable asset.

gross fixed assets the original cost of a firm's fixed assets.

net fixed assets gross fixed assets minus the accumulated depreciation taken over the life of the assets.

Income Statement

| | FOR THE YEAR ENDING | | | |
	1	2	3	4
Depreciation expense	$5,000	$5,000	$5,000	$5,000

Balance Sheet

| | END OF YEARS | | | |
	1	2	3	4
Gross fixed assets	$20,000	$20,000	$20,000	$20,000
Accumulated depreciation	5,000	10,000	15,000	20,000
Net fixed assets	$15,000	$10,000	$ 5,000	$0

[2] In this instance, we are using a straight-line depreciation method. (As we explained in Chapter 1, other methods allow a firm to accelerate the depreciation expenses in the early years of the asset's life and report less in the later years.)

Finance at Work

LEHMAN BROTHERS ANNOUNCES SECOND QUARTER 2006 EARNINGS

Lehman Brothers is a leading investment-banking firm. Below are excerpts from the press release Lehman Brothers issued to report its second-quarter earnings for 2006. The excerpts are followed by parts of a *Wall Street Journal* article reporting on the release.

PRESS RELEASE

For Immediate Release
Media Contact: Hannah Burns
212-526-4064
Investor Contact: Shaun Butler
212-526-8381

LEHMAN BROTHERS REPORTS SECOND-QUARTER EARNINGS

- Reports 47% Increase in Net Income and 35% Increase in Net Revenues from Second Quarter of 2006 -

NEW YORK, June 12, 2006 – Lehman Brothers Holdings Inc. today reported net income of $1.0 billion, or $1.69 per common share, for the second quarter ended May 31, 2006, representing an increase of 47% and 50%, respectively, from net income of $683 million, or $1.13 per common share, reported for the second quarter of 2005. The second-quarter results represented a decrease of 8% from record net income in the first quarter of fiscal 2006 of $1.1 billion and $1.83, respectively.

Richard S. Fuld Jr., chairman and chief executive officer, said, "Our strong results for the second quarter continue to demonstrate that Lehman Brothers has the breadth, balance, and scale necessary to help our clients around the world take advantage of opportunities in a changing and challenging market environment."

A conference call, to discuss the firm's financial results and outlook, will be held at 10:00 A.M. EDT today. The call will be open to the public. Members of the public who would like to access the conference call should dial, from the United States, 888-323-4182, or from outside the United States, 517-623-4500. The pass code for all callers is LEHMAN.

And What Did the *Wall Street Journal* Have to Say?[a]

Lehman Brothers Holdings Inc. reported its second-best quarter ever, but investors focused on a weakening financial-markets environment that could crimp brokerage firm earnings going forward and sent the company's shares tumbling to their worst trading day in more than 4 years.

On a conference call, analysts peppered Lehman executives with questions about the potential for further weakness if the markets don't rebound. Lehman chief administrative officer, David Goldfarb, known on Wall Street for a rose-colored view of Lehman's operations, responded by saying that despite the stock-market drop in early May, the firm's business remained relatively steady throughout the quarter and there hasn't been a "substantial difference" in the environment since the end of May.

"Wow, that's an interesting insight," remarked Merrill Lynch & Co. analyst Guy Moszkowski. John Mayo at Prudential added on the call that he was "surprised" by Mr. Goldfarb's comment.

The firm's stock fell $3.60, or 5.5%, to $62.01. The skid was the largest percentage drop in Lehman's stock since early 2002, according to Thomson.

[a]Source: Susanne Craig, "Lehman Reports 47% Surge in Profit," the *Wall Street Journal*, June 13, 2006, p. C3.

It is important to understand the distinction between *gross* fixed assets and *net* fixed assets and how depreciation expense in the income statement relates to accumulated depreciation in the balance sheet.

Other Assets

Other assets are all of the firm's assets that are not current assets or fixed assets. They include, for example, intangible assets such as the company's patents, copyrights, and goodwill.

Types of Financing

debt liabilities consisting of such sources as credit extended by suppliers or a loan from a bank.

We now turn to the right side of the balance sheet in Figure 3-3 labeled "Liabilities (Debt) and Equity," which indicates how the firm finances its assets. **Debt** is money that has been borrowed and must be repaid at some predetermined date. **Equity**, on the other hand, represents the shareholders' (owners') investment in the company.

equity stockholders' investment in the firm and the cumulative profits retained in the business up to the date of the balance sheet.

Debt (Liabilities)

Debt capital is financing provided by a creditor. As shown in Figure 3-3, it is divided into (1) current or short-term debt and (2) long-term debt.

Current Debt

The firm's **current debt**, or **short-term liabilities**, includes borrowed money that must be repaid within the next 12 months. The sources of a firm's current debt include the following:

- **Accounts payable.** The firm's **accounts payable** represents the credit suppliers have extended the firm when it purchased inventories. The purchasing firm may have 30, 60, or even 90 days to pay for the inventory. This form of credit extension is also called **trade credit**.
- **Accrued expenses.** **Accrued expenses** are short-term liabilities that have been incurred in the firm's operations but not yet paid. For example, the company's employees might have done work for which they will not be paid until the following week or month, and these are recorded as accrued wages.
- **Short-term notes.** **Short-term notes** represent amounts borrowed from a bank or other lending source that are due and payable within 12 months.

Long-Term Debt

The firm's **long-term debt** includes loans from banks or other sources that lend money for longer than 12 months. A firm might borrow money for 5 years to buy equipment, or it might borrow money for as long as 25 or 30 years to purchase real estate, such as land and buildings. Usually a loan to finance real estate is called a **mortgage**, which means that the lender has first claim on the property in the event the borrower is unable to repay the loan.

Equity

Equity includes the shareholders' investment—both preferred stockholders and common stockholders—in the firm.

- **Preferred stockholders** generally receive a dividend that is fixed in amount. In the event of the firm being liquidated, these stockholders are paid after the firm's creditors but before the common stockholders. This is similar to bonds in that dividends are limited in amount. (p. 64)
- **Common stockholders** are the *residual owners* of a business. They receive whatever income is left over after paying all expenses. In the event the firm is liquidated, the common stockholders receive only what is left over—good or bad—after the creditors and preferred stockholders are paid. The amount of a firm's common equity as reported in the balance sheet is equal to the sum of two items:

  1. **The amount a company receives from selling stock to investors.** This amount may simply be shown as **common stock** in the balance sheet or it may be divided into **par value** (the arbitrary value a firm puts on each share of stock prior to it being offered for sale) and **additional paid-in capital** above par (or just **paid-in capital** for short). Paid-in capital is the additional amount of capital the firm raises when buyers pay more than par value for the firm's stock. The amount of common stock issued will be offset by any stock that has been repurchased by the company, which is shown as **treasury stock**.
  2. **The amount of the firm's retained earnings. Retained earnings** are the earnings (net income, to be exact) that have been retained in the business rather than being distributed to the shareholders. In other words, we take the *cumulative total of all the net income over the firm's life less the common stock dividends that have been paid over the years*. More simply, we can compute retained earnings at the end of a given year by taking the retained earnings at the end of the previous year, adding net income and subtracting dividends paid for the current year.[3] But remember, profits and cash are not the same; *so do not think of retained earnings as a big bucket of cash*. It is not!

---

[3] Sometimes retained earnings will be affected by some unusual or extraordinary accounting transactions in addition to the reported net income and the dividends paid to stockholders. However, we are ignoring this possibility when explaining the primary components of retained earnings.

TABLE 3-3   Davies Inc.
Balance Sheets ($ millions)
December 31, 2006 and 2007

		2006		2007		CHANGE
Cash		$ 21		$ 20		$ (1)
Accounts receivable		31		36		5
Inventory		51		84		33
Other current assets		3		3		0
Total current assets		$ 106		$ 143		$ 37
Gross plant and equipment	$ 371		$ 410		$ 39	
Less accumulated depreciation	(85)		(115)		(30)	
Net plant and equipment		$ 286		$ 295		$ 9
Total assets		$ 392		$ 438		$ 46
Accounts payable		$ 41		$ 42		$ 1
Accrued expenses		10		10		0
Short-term notes		14		12		(2)
Total current liabilities		$ 65		$ 64		$ (1)
Long-term debt		160		171		11
Total debt		$ 225		$ 235		$ 10
Common stockholders' equity						
Common stock—par value		$ 10		$ 11		$ 1
Paid-in capital		72		75		3
Retained earnings		85		117		32
Total common stockholders' equity		$ 167		$ 203		$ 36
Total liabilities and equity		$ 392		$ 438		$ 46

Balance sheets for Davies Inc. are presented in Table 3-3 as of December 31, 2006, and December 31, 2007, along with the changes in each account between the two years. The balance sheet data shows that the firm ended 2007 with $438 million in assets, compared to $392 million at the end of 2006, for an increase of $46 million. As shown in the far right-hand column in Table 3-3, the increase resulted from (1) the additional investment in current assets (gross working capital) of $37 million (mostly from the increase in inventories), and (2) $39 million of new investments in fixed assets (based on the change in *gross* fixed assets, not *net* fixed assets). However, $30 million of the firm's fixed assets were depreciated during the year, as reflected by the increase in accumulated depreciation. Thus, the $46 million increase in total assets can be reconciled as follows: A $37 million increase in current assets, *plus* $39 million invested in new fixed assets, *less* $30 million in the depreciation of the firm's fixed assets.

In the debt and equity section of Table 3-3, notice that the $46 million increase in total debt and equity is exactly the same amount as the increase in total assets—as it must be. (Remember total assets = total debt + total equity.) The additional financing came primarily from a $36 million increase in common equity and secondarily from borrowing $11 million in long-term debt. The increase in common equity can be explained as follows:

December 31, 2006, common equity		$167,000,000
Sale of common stock		
Increase in par value	$ 1,000,000	
Increase in additional paid-in capital	3,000,000	
Total amount received from selling stock		$ 4,000,000
Increase in retained earnings		
Net income for 2007	$ 42,000,000	
Less 2007 common stock dividends	(10,000,000)	
Total increase in retained earnings		$ 32,000,000
Increase in common equity		$ 36,000,000
December 31, 2007, common equity		$203,000,000

There are two other issues revealed in the balance sheet that deserve special note: (1) the amount of a firm's working capital and (2) the mix of debt to equity used in financing the company. Let's consider each for Davies Inc.

Working Capital

Earlier we noted that the term *current assets* is also referred to as *gross working capital*. These two terms are used interchangeably. As we explained, gross working capital is equal to a company's current assets. By contrast, **net working capital** is equal to a company's current assets *less* its current liabilities. That is,

Net working capital = current assets − current liabilities   (3-4)

> **net working capital** the difference between a firm's current assets and its current liabilities. When the term *working capital* is used, it is frequently intended to mean net working capital.

Thus, net working capital compares the amount of current assets (assets that should convert into cash within the next 12 months) to the current liabilities (debt that must be paid within 12 months). The larger the net working capital a firm has, the more able the firm will be to pay its debt as it comes due. Thus, the amount of net working capital is important to a company's lenders who are always concerned about a company's ability to repay its loans. For Davies Inc. net working capital is computed as follows:

	2006	2007
Gross working capital (current assets)	$106,000,000	$143,000,000
Current liabilities	65,000,000	64,000,000
Net working capital	$41,000,000	$79,000,000

We see that the firm's net working capital increased $38 million, from $41 million to $79 million, mostly the result of increased amounts of inventories. The increase would prompt a lender or investor to know exactly why there was such a large increase in inventories, which could be good or bad. On one hand, it might mean that the firm is anticipating higher future sales and is stocking up on inventory. On the other hand, it might mean that firm's sales have declined and unsold inventory is piling up.

Most firms have a positive amount of net working capital because their current assets are greater than their current debts. There are a few exceptions. Take Disney and Starbucks for example. These two firms actually have more current liabilities than current assets, which results in a negative net working capital position for each. How do you think this could happen? Very simply, these businesses involve mostly cash sales: The firms collect cash immediately from their customers and then quickly use it up again to keep their businesses operating. However, Disney's and Starbucks' suppliers have probably granted them 30 days or more to pay their bills. In other words, the two firms collect early and pay late.

Although bankers and accountants measure net working capital exactly as described here, there is a slightly modified measure of a firm's working capital sometimes used in finance, which is called *operating* working capital. **Operating working capital** is equal to the firm's current assets *less* non-interest-bearing current liabilities, rather than *all* current liabilities, or:

Operating working capital = current assets − non-interest-bearing current liabilities   (3-5)

> **operating working capital** the firm's current assets less its *non-interest-bearing* current liabilities (rather than *all* of its current liabilities).

A **non-interest-bearing current liability** is any current debt upon which the borrower does not have to pay interest. These liabilities primarily include accounts payable and accrued expenses, which arise from the firm's normal day-to-day operating activities of buying and selling goods. We will use this revised definition of working capital later in the chapter when we compute a firm's cash flows.

> **non-interest-bearing current liabilities (NIBCL)** current liabilities that incur no interest expense, such as accounts payable and accrued expenses.

Debt Ratio

A firm's **debt ratio** is *the percentage of a company's assets financed by debt*. Looking at Davies Inc., the debt ratios for 2006 and 2007 were 57.4 percent and 53.7 percent, respectively.

> **debt ratio** a firm's total liabilities divided by its total assets. It is a ratio that measures the extent to which a firm has been financed with debt.

	2006	2007
Debt ratio = $\dfrac{\text{total debt}}{\text{total assets}}$	$\dfrac{\$225M}{\$392M} = 57.4\%$	$\dfrac{\$235M}{\$438M} = 53.7\%$

Can You Do It?

PREPARING A BALANCE SHEET

Given the information below for Menielle Inc., construct a balance sheet. What are the firm's current assets, net fixed assets, total assets, current or short-term debt, long-term debt, total equity, and total debt and equity?

Gross fixed assets	$75,000	Accounts receivable	$50,000
Cash	10,000	Long-term bank note	5,000
Other assets	15,000	Mortgage	20,000
Accounts payable	40,000	Common stock	100,000
Retained earnings	15,000	Inventories	70,000
Accumulated depreciation	20,000	Short-term notes	20,000

(The solution can be found on page 75.)

The debt ratio is an important measure to lenders and investors because it indicates the amount of financial risk the company is bearing—the more debt a company uses to finance its assets, the greater is its financial risk. We will discuss this topic in detail in Chapter 12.

Finally, we can gain additional perspective of a company's financial position by converting the balance sheet into a **common-sized balance sheet**. On a common-sized balance sheet, each item is shown as a percentage of total assets (and total debt and equity). Table 3-4 shows common-sized balance sheets for Davies Inc.

common-sized balance sheet
a balance sheet in which a firm's assets and sources of debt and equity are expressed as a percentage of its total assets.

Now we can observe that inventories increased from 13 percent of total assets to over 19 percent. Gross fixed assets declined 1 percent, whereas net fixed assets decreased 5.6 percent as a result of the additional depreciation taken on the assets. As already noted, the firm is using a bit less debt financing on a percentage basis due to the increase in equity, specifically, its retained earnings.

TABLE 3-4   Davies Inc.
Common-Sized Balance Sheets ($ millions)
December 31, 2006 and 2007

		2006		2007		CHANGE
Cash		5.4%		4.6%		−0.8%
Accounts receivable		7.9%		8.2%		0.3%
Inventory		13.0%		19.2%		6.2%
Other current assets		0.8%		0.7%		−0.1%
Total current assets		27.0%		32.6%		5.6%
Gross plant and equipment	94.6%		93.6%		−1.0%	
Less accumulated depreciation	−21.7%		−26.3%		−4.6%	
Net plant and equipment		73.0%		67.4%		−5.6%
Total assets		100.0%		100.0%		0.0%
Debt and equity						
Accounts payable and accrued expenses		13.0%		11.9%		−1.1%
Short-term notes		3.6%		2.7%		−0.8%
Total current liabilities		16.6%		14.6%		−2.0%
Long-term debt		40.8%		39.0%		−1.8%
Total debt		57.4%		53.7%		−3.7%
Common stockholders' equity						
Common stock—par value		2.6%		2.5%		0.0%
Paid-in capital		18.4%		17.1%		−1.2%
Retained earnings		21.7%		26.7%		5.0%
Total common stockholders' equity		42.6%		46.3%		3.7%
Total liabilities and equity		100.0%		100.0%		0.0%

How Did You Do?

PREPARING A BALANCE SHEET

On page 74, we provided balance sheet data for Menielle Inc. and asked you to develop the balance sheet based on the information. Your results should be as follows:

Cash		$ 10,000	Accounts payable		$ 40,000
Accounts receivable		50,000	Short-term notes		20,000
Inventories		70,000	Total short-term debt		$ 60,000
Total current assets		$130,000	Long-term bank note	$5,000	
Gross fixed assets	$ 75,000		Mortgage	20,000	
Accumulated depreciation	20,000		Total long-term debt		$ 25,000
Net fixed assets		$ 55,000	Total debt		$ 85,000
Other assets		15,000	Common stock	100,000	
Total assets		$200,000	Retained earnings	15,000	
			Total equity		$ 115,000
			Total debt and equity		$200,000

Did You Get It? ....

1. Regarding the time frame reported, how is the balance sheet different from the income statement?
2. What does the basic balance sheet equation state, and what does it mean?
3. What is a firm's "accounting book value"?
4. What are a firm's two principal sources of financing? Of what do these sources consist?
5. What is gross working capital? Net working capital? Operating working capital?
6. What is a debt ratio?

MEASURING CASH FLOWS

Objective **3**

Measure a company's cash flows.

Although an income statement measures a company's profits, profits are not the same as cash flows; profits are calculated on an accrual basis rather than a cash basis. **Accrual basis accounting** records revenue when it is earned, whether or not the revenue has been received in cash, and records expenses when they are incurred, even if the money has not actually been paid out. For example, sales reported in the income statement include both cash sales and credit sales. Therefore, sales for a given year do not correspond exactly to the actual cash collected from sales. Similarly, a firm must purchase inventory, but some of the purchases are financed by trade credit rather than by an immediate cash payment, so the firm's expenses are not equal to its actual "out of pocket" cash flows. Also, under the accrual system, the purchase of equipment that will last for more than 1 year is not shown as an expense in the income statement. Instead, the amount is recorded as an asset and then expensed as depreciation over the useful life of the equipment. An annual depreciation expense (this is not a cash flow) is recorded as a way to match the use of the asset with sales generated from its service.

accrual basis accounting a method of accounting whereby revenue is recorded when it is earned, whether or not the revenue has been received in cash. Likewise, expenses are recorded when they are incurred, even if the money has not actually been paid out.

We could give you more examples to show why a firm's profits differ from its cash flows, but the point should be clear: *Profits and cash flows are not the same thing.* In fact, a business could be profitable but have negative cash flows, even to the point of going bankrupt. So, understanding a firm's cash flows is very important to its managers.

There are a number of different ways to measure a firm's cash flows. For one, we could use the conventional accountant's presentation called a *statement of cash flows*, which is always included in the financial section of a firm's annual report. But for our purposes, we will instead

Can You Do It?

Your brother-in-law has asked you to help him finance what he considers to be a "great investment opportunity." He plans to sell a new brand of European clothing that is becoming popular in the United States. He thinks that the university located nearby, from which you both graduated, would be an ideal location. He estimates that the financing can come mostly from a bank loan and credit from suppliers. However, the two of you will need to chip in a total of $5,000 to get the business going. He will invest $3,000, he says, and he wants you to invest the remaining $2,000.

It's not that you don't trust your brother-in-law, but you have decided to undertake your own investigation of the opportunity. After a few hours of work, you develop what you think are realistic estimates of the profits that can be earned from the venture. You also estimate how much money it will take to start the business.

There is a slight problem, however: Your new puppy chewed up your papers. After putting the dog in the backyard without any supper, you pick up the pieces and begin reconstructing your work. The remnants of your hard work—at least most of it—look as follows (numbers are in thousands):

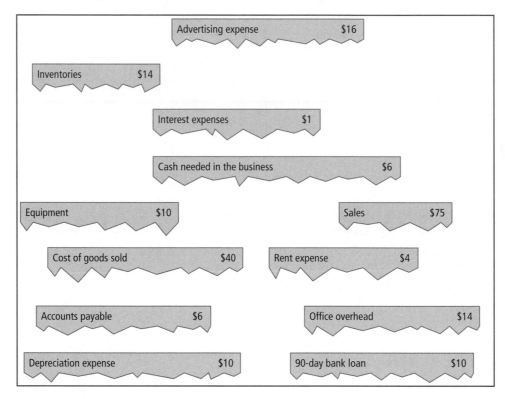

Advertising expense	$16
Inventories	$14
Interest expenses	$1
Cash needed in the business	$6
Equipment	$10
Sales	$75
Cost of goods sold	$40
Rent expense	$4
Accounts payable	$6
Office overhead	$14
Depreciation expense	$10
90-day bank loan	$10

Can you reconstruct the income statement and balance sheet using the bits of information provided above? What do you conclude about your brother-in-law's great opportunity?

See page 78 for the solution to your brother-in-law problem—hopefully after you have made a good-faith effort to solve it yourself. (The solution can be found on page 78.)

take a finance perspective when it comes to measuring cash flows and compute what we will call *free cash flows*. We will use this measurement later to put a value on the firm's capital investments and the firm itself. So, what follows is similar to a conventional cash flow statement presented as part of a company's financial statements, but it does not follow exactly the accountant's format. (We do, however, present the accountant's statement of cash flows for Davies Inc. in Appendix A.)

Free Cash Flows

We can think of a firm as a bundle of assets that produces cash flow. Once the firm has paid all of its operating expenses and taxes and made all of its investments, the remaining cash flows are *free* to be distributed to the firm's creditors and shareholders—thus, the term **free cash flows**.

During recent years, free cash flow has come to be viewed by many executives as an important measure of a firm's performance. Take for example, Jack Welch, the former CEO of General Electric, who commented that

> . . . there's cash flow, which is valuable because it just does not lie. All your other profit-and-loss numbers, like net income, have some art to them. They've been massaged through the accounting process, which is filled with assumptions. But free cash flow tells you the true condition of the business. It gives you a sense of your maneuverability—whether you can return cash to shareholders, pay down debt, borrow more to grow faster, or any combination of these options. Cash flow helps you understand and control your destiny.[4]

To measure a firm's free cash flows, we should understand that two key business areas affect cash flows:

1. The cash flow earned from the firm's operations, or normal operating activities. If the cash flow from the firm's operations is positive, it adds to the business's cash flows, but if it is negative, it reduces the business's cash flows.
2. The firm's additional investments in (1) operating working capital and (2) fixed assets and other long-term assets

Specifically, free cash flows are equal to

$$\begin{matrix} \textbf{Free cash} \\ \textbf{flows} \end{matrix} = \begin{matrix} \textbf{after-tax cash flows} \\ \textbf{from operations} \end{matrix} - \begin{matrix} \textbf{additional investment in} \\ \textbf{operating working capital} \end{matrix}$$

$$- \begin{matrix} \textbf{additional investment in fixed} \\ \textbf{assets and other long-term assets} \end{matrix} \qquad (3\text{-}6)$$

Thus, to compute a firm's free cash flows, we must take the following three steps:

1. Compute the after-tax cash flows from operations.
2. Calculate the increase or decrease in the firm's operating working capital: An increase is a negative cash flow, and a decrease is a positive cash flow.
3. Compute the increase or decrease in the firm's fixed assets and other long-term assets: An increase in these assets is a negative cash flow, and a decrease is a positive cash flow.

Let's look at each of the foregoing steps.

Step 1. *Compute the after-tax cash flows from operations.* For the first step, we compute the after-tax cash flows from operations as follows:

After-tax cash flows from operations
= operating income (earnings before interest and taxes)   (3-7)
+ depreciation expense − income taxes

Thus, we compute the after-tax cash flows from operations by adding back the firm's depreciation expense to its operating income (because depreciation expense is not a cash expense), and then subtracting the income taxes the firm owes. This gives us the cash flows from operations on an after-tax basis.[5]

To illustrate how to compute a firm's after-tax cash flows from operations, return to Davies Inc.'s income statement in Table 3-1 on page 65, where you will find the following information:

Operating income (EBIT)	$75,000,000
Depreciation expense	30,000,000
Income tax expense	18,000,000

---

[4] Jack and Suzy Welch, "How Healthy Is Your Company?," *Business Week*, May 8, 2006, p. 126.

[5] Remember that the income statement is prepared on an accrual basis, not a cash basis. We should be computing the actual taxes paid, as opposed to the income taxes reported in the income statement. However, we are taking some liberty here for the sake of simplicity.

How Did You Do?

Now that you understand how a firm's income statement and balance sheet are used, let's return to your brother-in-law's clothing-business proposition described on page 76. You have constructed the business's projected income statement and balance sheet from the fragments of paper your dog chewed up and found the following results (in $ thousands):

PROJECTED INCOME STATEMENT			PROJECTED BALANCE SHEET	
Sales		$ 75	Cash needed in the business	$ 6
Cost of goods sold		40	Inventories	14
Gross profit		$ 35	Equipment	10
			Total assets	$30
Operating expenses:				
Office overhead	$ 14		Accounts payable	$ 6
Advertising expense	16		90-day bank loan	10
Rent expense	4		Total debt	$16
Depreciation expense	10		Equity:	
Total operating expenses		$ 44	Brother-in-law	$ 3
Operating income		$ (9)	Your investment	2
Interest expense		1	Total equity	$ 5
Loss before taxes		$(10)	Total projected debt and equity	$21
Taxes		0	Additional financing needed	9
Net income		$(10)	Total debt and equity needed	$30

So, based on your estimates, the venture would expect to incur a loss of $10,000. Furthermore, the balance sheet suggests you will need $30,000 to purchase the business's assets. This would have to come from $16,000 in debt financing that you hope you can obtain, $3,000 from your brother-in-law (if he has it), and $2,000 from you, which totals $21,000. However, this is still less than the $30,000 you actually need. Thus, the business will need an additional $9,000. Maybe, just maybe, this is not quite the opportunity your brother-in-law perceives it to be.

Given this information, we compute Davies Inc.'s after-tax cash flows from operations as follows:

Operating income (EBIT)	$75,000,000
Plus depreciation	30,000,000
Less income tax expense	(18,000,000)
After-tax cash flows from operations	$87,000,000

Step 2. *Calculate the change in the firm's operating working capital.* For this step, the change in operating working capital for the year would be as follows:

$$\text{Change in operating working capital} = \text{change in current assets} - \text{change in non-interest-bearing current liabilities} \quad (3\text{-}8)$$

The change in the operating working capital can be calculated based on the firm's balance sheet data in Table 3-3. We calculate Davies Inc.'s operating working capital for 2006 and 2007 as follows:

	DECEMBER 31			
		2006		2007
Current assets		$106		$143
Accounts payable	$41		$42	
Accrued expenses	10		10	
Non-interest-bearing current liabilities		$ 51		$ 52
Operating working capital		$ 55		$ 91

Thus, in 2007 Davies Inc. increased its investment in operating working capital by $36 million (from $55 million to $91 million).

Step 3. *Compute the change in fixed assets.* The final step involves computing the change in gross fixed assets (not *net* fixed assets).[6] Again returning to Davies Inc.'s balance sheets, we see that gross fixed assets increased by $39 million (from $371 million to $410 million).

We can now compute Davies Inc.'s free cash flows as follows:

After-tax cash flows from operations		$ 87
Less:		
Investment in operating working capital	$ (36)	
Investment in long-term assets	(39)	
Total investments		(75)
Free cash flows		$ 12

We can now see that the firm's free cash flows are positive in the amount of $12 million. The firm's operations generated $87 million in cash flows, but the firm spent $75 million in additional investments to grow the business ($36 million on operating working capital and $39 million on long-term assets). Still, Davies Inc. generated $12 million more than it needed to finance its operations in 2007. Where, then, did the $12 million cash surplus go? To the investors, as we will see.

Financing Cash Flows

A firm can either receive money from or distribute money to its investors, or some of both. In general, cash flows between investors and the firm, or what we will call **financing cash flows**, occur in one of four ways. The firm can

financing cash flows cash flows paid to or received from investors and lenders.

1. Pay interest to its lenders
2. Pay dividends to its shareholders
3. Increase or decrease its interest-bearing debt, both short term and long term
4. Issue stock to new shareholders or repurchase stock from current investors

Let's again return to Davies Inc. to illustrate the process for calculating the firm's financing cash flows, which will also let us determine how the $12 million positive free cash flows that the firm generated were used.

When we speak of investors in this context, we include both lenders and shareholders. However, we do not include financing provided by non-interest-bearing current liabilities, which were recognized earlier as part of the firm's operating working capital.

Let's compute the financing cash flows for Davies Inc. We first determine the interest expense paid to lenders and the dividends paid to shareholders, which are provided in the firm's income statement (Table 3-1 on page 65). We then refer to the balance sheet (Table 3-3 on page 72) to see the changes in interest-bearing debt and common stock. The results are as follows:

Interest paid to lenders	$ (15)	Negative cash flow
Common stock dividends	(10)	Negative cash flow
Paid off (decreased) short-term interest-bearing debt	(2)	Negative cash flow
Borrowed (increased) interest-bearing debt	11	Positive cash flow
Issued common stock (increased par value + additional paid-in capital)	4	Positive cash flow
Financing cash flows	($ 12)	

---

[6] Sometimes only net fixed assets are shown in a balance sheet. If so, then we can compute the change in gross fixed assets as the change in net fixed assets plus the depreciation expense reported in the income statement. By adding back the depreciation expense, we have removed the effects of taking depreciation on the assets, leaving only the change resulting from increases or decreased in gross fixed assets.

Thus, the firm paid $15 million in interest, $10 million in dividends, and paid off $2 million of short-term interest-bearing debt.[7] The firm received $11 million by taking on additional long-term debt, and $4 million by issuing common stock. Add it all up and we find that the company paid out a net amount of $12 million to its creditors and shareholders.

It is not a coincidence that the dollar amount of Davies' free cash flows exactly equals its financing cash flows. They will always be the same except the signs will be opposite—if one is positive, the other will be negative, and vice versa. The firm's free cash flows, if positive, will be the amount distributed to investors; if the free cash flows are negative, it will be the amount investors provided to the firm to cover the shortage in free cash flows.

Interpreting Free Cash Flows

So what does it mean to have a positive or negative free cash flow? Is having a negative free cash flow bad and a positive cash flow good? Does a positive cash flow indicate that shareholder value is being increased and a negative cash flow indicate that shareholder value is being destroyed? There is no single right answer to this question. It depends on what is causing the positive or negative free cash flow. One firm may have positive free cash flows because it has no good investment opportunities. Another company may have negative cash flows because it is reinvesting heavily in great investment opportunities, which will potentially offer large positive cash flows in the future. The final answer can only be found by looking at the cash flows over time. Even so, it is good to understand why a firm's cash flows are positive or negative during a given year.

To interpret the meaning of a firm's cash flows for a single period of time, we need to think about the three different components of the free cash measurement:

- Cash flows from operations
- Cash flows related to increases or decreases in operating working capital
- Cash flows related to increases or decreases in fixed assets and other long-term assets

We then have to consider the cash flow patterns along with the financing cash flows. To help us understand the basic nature of a firm's cash flows, consider the following cash flow patterns with respect to the listed categories.

Free Cash Flows

CASH FLOW PATTERN	CASH FLOW FROM OPERATIONS	INVESTMENT IN WORKING CAPITAL	INVESTMENT IN LONG-TERM ASSETS	FREE CASH FLOWS	FINANCING CASH FLOWS
1	+	−	−	+	−
2	+	+	+	+	−
3	−	−	−	−	+
4	−	+	+	−	+

Cash flow pattern 1. Cash flow pattern 1 represents Davies Inc.'s cash flow pattern, which has (1) positive cash flows from operations, (2) negative investment cash flows, both for working capital and long-term assets, resulting in a positive free cash flow overall. Given the positive free cash flows, the firm will have negative financing cash flows. How would we describe this company? It is a firm that is using a large part of its cash flows from operations to grow the firm's operations and a smaller amount to return cash flow to the investors.

Cash flow pattern 2. In cash flow pattern 2, the firm is generating positive cash flows from operations and selling assets to pay down debt and/or pay owners. How would we describe this company? It is a firm that is downsizing the business by selling its assets and using the proceeds (along with its cash flows from operations) to pay down debt and/or equity. Perhaps the firm is anticipating that the demand for its products will be

---

[7] As mentioned with income taxes, the income statement is prepared on an accrual basis, not a cash basis. So interest expenses and dividends reported in the income statement may or may not have been paid. We should only be using the actual interest and dividends that have been paid. But again, we are going for simplicity.

Can You Do It?

MEASURING CASH FLOWS

Given the following information for Menielle Inc., compute the firm's free cash flows and financing cash flows.

Increase in current assets	$ 25	Dividends	5
Operating income	55	Change in common stock	0
Interest expense	10	Increase in gross fixed assets	55
Increase in accounts payable	20	Depreciation expense	7
Decrease in accrued expenses	5	Income Taxes	12
Increase in long-term notes payable	30		

(The solution can be found on page 82.)

lower in the future, so it is eliminating some of its debt in an effort to prepare for harder times.

Cash flow pattern 3. Cash flow pattern 3 depicts a firm that is experiencing negative cash flows from operations and negative cash flows from growing the business, all of which is being financed by the firm's investors. This firm could be an early-stage company that has not reached a break-even point in its operations and at the same time is growing the company in anticipation of future returns. Alternatively it could simply be a company in financial trouble.

Cash flow pattern 4. Cash flow pattern 4 describes a company that is encountering cash flow problems from operations, which are being covered both by selling assets and by borrowing more and/or acquiring more equity financing.

There are obviously additional possible cash flow patterns that exist (another four to be exact), but the cash flow patterns we just explained should be sufficient to help you see the process used to interpret a firm's cash flow statement.

Did You Get It?

1. Why doesn't an income statement provide a measure of a firm's cash flows?
2. What are free cash flows?
3. How do we measure free cash flows?
4. How do we compute a firm's financing cash flows?
5. What is the relationship between free cash flows and financing cash flows?

Based on our review of Davies Inc.'s financial statements, we can now draw some conclusions. To this point, we have learned that:

- For every dollar of sales, Davies earned 12.5 cents in operating income and 7 cents in net income.
- The firm finances its assets more with debt than with equity.
- The company's primary investments in 2007 were in additional inventories and fixed assets.
- Davies had positive free cash flows, which means that on net, the firm is returning cash to its investors.
- The firm paid (investors received) cash flows in the form of interest, dividends, and the repayment of debt.

We will use the information included in this chapter in Chapter 4 to dig deeper and conduct a financial analysis of Davies Inc. Read on.

How Did You Do?

MEASURING CASH FLOWS

On page 81 we asked you to calculate Menielle Inc.'s free cash flows and its financing cash flows. Your results should be as follows:

FREE CASH FLOWS

Operating income		$ 55
Depreciation expense		7
Income taxes		(12)
After-tax cash flows from operations		$ 50
Investments in operating working capital:		
Change in current assets	$(25)	
Change in non-interest-bearing current liabilities	15	
Investments in operating working capital:		$(10)
Investment in fixed assets		(55)
Total investments		$(65)
Free cash flows		$(15)

FINANCING CASH FLOWS

Interest expense	($10)
Dividends	(5)
Increase in long-term notes payable	30
Change in common stock	0
Investors' cash flows	$ 15

Objective **1**

Compute a company's profits, as reflected by its income statement.

Summary

A firm's profits may be viewed as follows:

Gross profit = sales − cost of goods sold

Earnings before interest and tax (operating profit) = sales − cost of goods sold − operating expenses

Net profit (net income) = sales − cost of goods sold − operating expenses − interest expense − taxes

The following five activities determine a company's net income:

1. The revenue derived from selling the company's product or service
2. The cost of producing or acquiring the goods or services to be sold
3. The operating expenses related to (1) marketing and distributing the product or service to the customer and (2) administering the business
4. The financing costs of doing business—namely, the interest paid to the firm's creditors
5. The payment of taxes

Objective **2**

Determine a firm's financial position at a point in time based on its balance sheet.

The balance sheet presents a company's assets, liabilities, and equity on a specific date. Its total assets represent all the investments that the firm has made in the business. The total assets must equal the firm's total debt and equity because every dollar of assets has been financed by the firm's lenders or stockholders. The firm's assets include its current assets, fixed assets, and other assets. Its debt includes both its short-term and long-term debt. The firm's equity includes (1) common stock, which may be shown as par value plus additional paid-in capital, and (2) retained earnings. All the numbers in a balance sheet are based on historical costs, rather than current market values.

In measuring a firm's cash flows we can take one of two perspectives: the cash flows produced by the firm's assets (free cash flows) or the cash flows received from or distributed to lenders and investors (financing cash flows). That is,

Objective **3**

Measure a company's cash flows.

Cash Flows

FREE CASH FLOWS	FINANCING CASH FLOWS
Operating income plus depreciation expense less additional investments in working capital and long-term assets	Interest and dividends paid to lenders and stockholders plus an increase or less a decrease in interest-bearing debt plus an increase or less a decrease in common stock

Key Terms

Accounting book value 67

Accounts payable (trade credit) 71

Accounts receivable 69

Accrual basis accounting 75

Accrued expenses 71

Accumulated depreciation 69

Additional paid-in capital 71

Balance sheet 66

Cash 69

Common-sized balance sheet 74

Common-sized income statement 65

Common stock 71

Common stockholders 71

Cost of goods sold 62

Current assets (gross working capital) 69

Current debt 71

Debt 70

Debt ratio 73

Depreciation expense 69

Dividends per share 64

Earnings before interest and taxes or EBIT 62

Earnings before taxes (taxable income) 63

Earnings per share 64

Equity 70

Financing cash flows 79

Financing cost 63

Fixed assets 69

Free cash flows 77

Gross fixed assets 69

Gross profit 62

Gross profit margin 65

Income statement (profit and loss statement) 62

Inventories 69

Long-term debt 71

Mortgage 71

Net fixed assets 69

Net income (earnings available to common stockholders) 63

Net profit margin 66

Net working capital 73

Non-interest-bearing current liabilities (NIBCL) 73

Operating expenses 62

Operating income (earnings before interest and taxes) 62

Operating profit margin 66

Operating working capital 73

Par value 71

Preferred stockholders 71

Profit margins 65

Retained earnings 71

Short-term liabilities 71

Short-term notes (debt) 71

Trade credit 71

Treasury stock 71

Review Questions

3-1. A company's financial statements consist of the balance sheet, income statement, and statement of cash flows.

   a. Describe the nature of the balance sheet and the income statement.

   b. Why have we not used the conventional statement of cash flows in our presentation, computing instead what we call free cash flows?

3-2. How do gross profits, operating profits, and net income differ?

3-3. How do dividends and interest expense differ?

3-4. Why is it that the preferred stockholders' equity section of the balance sheet changes only when new shares are sold or repurchased, whereas the common stockholders' equity section changes from year to year regardless of whether new shares are bought or sold?

3-5. What is net working capital? What is operating working capital? When is each used?

3-6. Why might one firm have positive cash flows and be headed for financial trouble, whereas another firm with negative cash flows could actually be in a good financial position?

3-7. Why is the examination of only the balance sheet and income statement not adequate in evaluating a firm?

3-8. Why do a firm's free cash flows have to equal its financing cash flows?

Self-Test Problem

The solution to this problem is provided at the end of the chapter.

ST-1. *(Interpreting financial statements and measuring cash flows)* Given the following information for the M & G Corporation:

    a. How much is the firm's net working capital, operating working capital, and what is the debt ratio for 2008?

    b. Complete (1) a common-sized income statement and (2) a common-sized balance sheet. Interpret your results for 2008.

    c. Compute free cash flows and financing cash flows for 2008. Interpret your results.

M & G Corporation Balance Sheet for December 31, 2007 and 2008

	2007	2008
Cash	$ 9,000	$ 500
Accounts receivable	12,500	16,000
Inventories	29,000	45,500
Total current assets	$ 50,500	$ 62,000
Land	20,000	26,000
Buildings and equipment	70,000	100,000
Less accumulated depreciation	(28,000)	(38,000)
Total fixed assets	$ 62,000	$ 88,000
Total assets	$112,500	$150,000
Accounts payable	$ 6,500	$ 17,000
Accrued expenses	4,000	5,000
Short-term bank notes	17,000	47,000
Total current liabilities	$ 27,500	$ 69,000
Long-term debt	28,750	22,950
Common stock	31,500	31,500
Retained earnings	24,750	26,550
Total debt and equity	$112,500	$150,000

M & G Corporation Income Statement for the Year Ending December 31, 2008

	2008
Sales (all credit)	$160,000
Cost of goods sold	96,000
Gross profit	$ 64,000
Operating expenses	
Fixed cash operating expenses	$ 21,000
Variable operating expenses	16,000
Depreciation	10,000
Total operating expenses	$ 47,000
Earnings before interest and taxes	$ 17,000
Interest expense	6,100
Earnings before taxes	$ 10,900
Income taxes	3,900
Net income	$ 7,000

Study Problems

3-1. *(Review of financial statements)* Prepare a balance sheet and income statement for Belmond Inc. from the following information.

a. How much is the firm's net working capital and operating working capital, and what is its debt ratio?

b. Complete a common-sized income statement and a common-sized balance sheet. Interpret your results.

Inventory	$ 6,500
Common stock	45,000
Cash	16,550
Operating expenses	1,350
Short-term notes payable	600
Interest expense	900
Depreciation expense	500
Net sales	12,800
Accounts receivable	9,600
Accounts payable	4,800
Long-term debt	55,000
Cost of goods sold	5,750
Buildings and equipment	$122,000
Accumulated depreciation	34,000
Taxes	1,440
General and administrative expense	850
Retained earnings	?

3-2. *(Computing cash flows)* Given the following information, compute the firm's free cash flows and financing cash flows.

Increase in current assets	$50
Operating income	75
Interest expense	25
Increase in accounts payable	35
Dividends	15
Increase in common stock	20
Increase in net fixed assets	23
Depreciation expense	12
Income taxes	17

3-3. *(Review of financial statements)* Prepare a balance sheet and income statement for the Warner Company from the following scrambled list of items.

a. What are the firm's net working capital, operating working capital, and debt ratio?

b. Complete a common-sized income statement and a common-sized balance sheet. Interpret your findings.

Depreciation expense	$ 66,000
Cash	225,000
Long-term debt	334,000
Sales	573,000
Accounts payable	102,000
General and administrative expense	79,000
Buildings and equipment	895,000
Notes payable	75,000
Accounts receivable	153,000
Interest expense	4,750
Accrued expenses	7,900
Common stock	289,000
Cost of goods sold	297,000
Inventory	99,300
Taxes	50,500
Accumulated depreciation	263,000
Prepaid expenses	14,500
Taxes payable	53,000
Retained earnings	262,900

3-4. *(Free cash flow analysis)* Interpret the following information regarding Westlake Corporation's free cash flows and financing cash flows.

Westlake Corporation Free Cash Flows and Financing Cash Flows

FREE CASH FLOWS		
Operating income (EBIT)		$ 1,020
Depreciation		125
Income taxes		(290)
After-tax cash flows from operations		$ 855
Increase in operating working capital		
Increase in current assets	(640)	
Increase in non-interest-bearing debt	201	
Increase in operating working capital		$ (439)
(current assets − non-interest-bearing debt)		
Increase in long-term assets:		
Purchase of fixed assets		(1,064)
Free cash flows		$ (648)

FINANCING CASH FLOWS	
Interest paid to lenders	$ (276)
Issued long-term debt	640
Issued common stock	348
Common stock dividends	(64)
Financing cash flow	$ 648

3-5. *(Computing cash flows)* Given the following information, compute the firm's free cash flows and financing cash flows.

Dividends	$ 25
Increase in common stock	27
Increase in current assets	135
Operating income	215
Interest expense	50
Depreciation expense	20
Increase in interest-bearing debt	48
Increase in gross fixed assets	55
Income taxes	45

3-6. *(Free cash flow analysis)* Interpret the following information regarding Maness Corporation's free cash flows and financing cash flows.

Maness Corporation Free Cash Flows and Financing Cash Flows

FREE CASH FLOWS		
Operating income (EBIT)		$ 954
Depreciation expense		60
Income taxes		(320)
After-tax cash flows from operations		$ 694
Increase in operating working capital		
Increase in current assets	$ (899)	
Increase in non-interest-bearing debt	175	
Increase in operating working capital		$ (724)
Decrease in long-term assets:		
Sale of fixed assets		2,161
Free cash flows		$ 2,131

FINANCING CASH FLOWS	
Interest paid to lenders	$ (364)
Increase in short-term interest-bearing debt	100
Repayment of long-term debt	(950)
Repurchase of common stock	(524)
Common stock dividends	(393)
Financing cash flow	($ 2,131)

3-7. *(Interpreting financial statements and measuring cash flows)* Given the information for Pamplin Inc. for 2008:

    a. How much is the firm's net working capital and operating working capital, and what is the debt ratio?

    b. Complete a common-sized income statement and a common-sized balance sheet. Interpret your results.

    c. Compute free cash flows and financing cash flows for the period. Interpret your results.

Pamplin Inc. Balance Sheet at 12/31/2007 and 12/31/2008

ASSETS

	2007	2008
Cash	$ 200	$ 150
Accounts receivable	450	425
Inventory	550	625
Current assets	$ 1,200	$ 1,200
Plant and equipment	$ 2,200	$ 2,600
Less accumulated depreciation	(1,000)	(1,200)
Net plant and equipment	$ 1,200	$ 1,400
Total assets	$ 2,400	$ 2,600

LIABILITIES AND OWNERS' EQUITY

	2007	2008
Accounts payable	$ 200	$ 150
Notes payable—current (9%)	0	150
Current liabilities	$ 200	$ 300
Bonds	$ 600	$ 600
Owners' equity		
Common stock	$ 900	$ 900
Retained earnings	700	800
Total owners' equity	$ 1,600	$ 1,700
Total liabilities and owners' equity	$ 2,400	$ 2,600

Pamplin Inc. Income Statement for Years Ending 12/31/2007 and 12/31/2008

		2007		2008
Sales		$ 1,200		$ 1,450
Cost of goods sold		700		850
Gross profit		$ 500		$ 600
Selling, general and administrative expenses	$ 30		$ 40	
Depreciation	220	250	200	240
Operating income		$ 250		$ 360
Interest expense		$ 50		64
Net income before taxes		$ 200		$ 296
Taxes (40%)		80		118
Net income		$ 120		$ 178

3-8. *(Interpreting financials statements and measuring cash flows)* Based on the information for T. P. Jarmon Company for the year ended December 31, 2008:

    a. How much is the firm's net working capital and operating working capital, and what is the debt ratio?

    b. Complete a common-sized income statement and a common-sized balance sheet. Interpret your results.

    c. Compute free cash flows and financing cash flows for the period. Interpret your results.

T. P. Jarmon Company Balance Sheet for 12/31/2007 and 12/31/2008

ASSETS

	2007	2008
Cash	$ 15,000	$ 14,000
Marketable securities	6,000	6,200
Accounts receivable	42,000	33,000
Inventory	51,000	84,000
Prepaid rent	$ 1,200	$ 1,100
Total current assets	$ 115,200	$ 138,300
Net plant and equipment	286,000	270,000
Total assets	$ 401,200	$ 408,300

LIABILITIES AND EQUITY

	2007	2008
Accounts payable	$ 48,000	$ 57,000
Accruals	6,000	5,000
Notes payable	15,000	13,000
Total current liabilities	$ 69,000	$ 75,000
Long-term debt	$ 160,000	$ 150,000
Common stockholders' equity	$ 172,200	$ 183,300
Total liabilities and equity	$ 401,200	$ 408,300

T. P. Jarmon Company Income Statement for the Year Ended 12/31/2008

Sales		$ 600,000
Less cost of goods sold		460,000
Gross profit		$ 140,000
Operating and interest expenses		
General and administrative	$ 30,000	
Interest	10,000	
Depreciation	30,000	
Total operating and interest expenses		70,000
Earnings before taxes		$ 70,000
Taxes		27,100
Net income available to common stockholders		$ 42,900
Cash dividends		31,800
Change in retained earnings		$ 11,100

3-9. (*Measuring cash flows*) Calculate the free cash flows and financing cash flows for Abrahams Manufacturing Company for the year ended December 31, 2008. Interpret your results.

Abrahams Manufacturing Company Balance Sheet for 12/31/2007 and 12/31/2008

	2007	2008
Cash	$ 89,000	$ 100,000
Accounts receivable	64,000	70,000
Inventory	112,000	100,000
Prepaid expenses	10,000	10,000
Total current assets	275,000	280,000
Gross plant and equipment	238,000	311,000
Accumulated depreciation	(40,000)	(66,000)
Total assets	$ 473,000	$ 525,000
Accounts payable	$ 85,000	$ 90,000
Accrued liabilities	68,000	63,000
Total current debt	153,000	153,000
Mortgage payable	70,000	0
Preferred stock	0	120,000
Common stock	205,000	205,000
Retained earnings	45,000	47,000
Total debt and equity	$ 473,000	$ 525,000

Abrahams Manufacturing Company Income Statement for the Year Ended 12/31/2008

	2008
Sales	$ 184,000
Cost of goods sold	60,000
Gross profit	$ 124,000
Selling, general, and administrative expenses	44,000
Depreciation expense	26,000
Operating income	$ 54,000
Interest expense	4,000
Earnings before taxes	$ 50,000
Taxes	16,000
Preferred stock dividends	10,000
Earnings available to common shareholders	$ 24,000

Additional Information

1. The only entry in the accumulated depreciation account is for 2008 depreciation.
2. The firm paid $22,000 in common stock dividends during 2008.

3-10. Interpret the cash flow patterns shown for the Erin Corporation.

CASH FLOW PATTERN	CASH FLOW FROM OPERATIONS	INVESTMENT IN WORKING CAPITAL	INVESTMENT IN LONG-TERM ASSETS	FREE CASH FLOWS	FINANCING CASH FLOWS
1	+	−	−	−	+
2	+	+	−	+	−
3	−	+	−	−	+
4	−	−	+	−	+

Web Works

3-WW1. See the annual report for the Dell Corporation by going to **www.dell.com**. Scroll to the bottom of the page, then click "About Dell," then "Investors," and finally the link "Annual Reports." Scan the list to determine which year you would like to review. Alternatively, select one of the other links (such as "Financial History") to learn additional financial information about Dell Inc.

3-WW2. Go to **www.homedepot.com** for the home page of the Home Depot Corporation. Scroll to the bottom of the page and select the "Corporate Info" option, then "Investor Relations" and finally, "Financial Reports." Look for keywords in the income statement that appear in this chapter, such as sales, gross profits, and net income. What do you learn about the firm from its financial statements that you find interesting?

3-WW3. Go to the *Wall Street Journal* home page at **www.wsj.com.** Search for Barnes & Noble (ticker symbol BKS). Find the firm's earnings announcements. What did you learn about the company from the announcements? Also, search **www.barnesandnoble.com** to find the same information.

3-WW4. In 2004, Disney was having a big stir about its CEO, Michael Eisner. Some of the Disney board members wanted to fire him. After considerable turmoil, Eisner announced that he would retire in 2007. Conduct a Web search to find out Eisner's status with Disney. Also go to the firm's Web site and look at its financial statements and see how the business is doing in terms of profits. Can you discover what parts of the business are doing well and those that are not?

Mini Case

In the 2005 and 2006 time frame, General Motors and Toyota experienced significantly different financial situations:The period was terrible for GM but wonderful for Toyota. Given here are their income statements and balance sheets for 2004 and 2005. (The financial statements, as shown, are available in Excel at **www.prenhall.com/keown/**. Using them will save you a lot of time as you solve the problem.)

   a. Prepare a common-sized income statement and common-sized balance sheet for each firm, both for 2004 and 2005.

   b. How much profit was each company making per dollar of sales? To what would you attribute any differences?

c. What differences do you notice in the common-sized balance sheets that could account for the problems of GM relative to Toyota?

d. Calculate the 2005 free cash flows for the two firms. (You need not compute the financing cash flows.) Compare your findings.

e. Conduct an Internet search on the two firms to gain additional insights as to causes of the financial differences between the firms in 2005 and continuing into 2006.

f. How are the two companies doing financially today?

Toyota Corp. Income Statement
for Year Ended December 31, 2004 and 2005 ($ millions except per share data)

	2004	2005
Sales	$ 163,637	$ 172,749
Cost of goods sold	120,262	129,100
Gross profit	$ 43,375	$ 43,649
Selling, general, and administrative expenses	19,438	18,095
Depreciation expense	9,177	9,291
Operating profit	$ 14,760	$ 16,263
Interest expense	−196	−177
Nonoperating income/expense	2,269	2,244
Extraordinary items	608	−1,297
Taxable income	$ 17,441	$ 17,033
Income taxes	6,446	6,126
Net income	$ 10,995	$ 10,907
Number of common stock shares	1,665	1,634
Earnings per share	$ 6.60	$ 6.67
Dividends per share	$ 0.83	$ 1.22

Toyota Corp. Balance Sheets
for Year Ended December 31, 2004 and 2005 ($ millions)

	DECEMBER 31	
	2004	2005
ASSETS		
Cash and equivalents	$ 21,258	$ 19,466
Net receivables	43,063	47,166
Inventories	10,250	12,168
Other current assets	9,150	9,105
Total current assets	$ 83,721	$ 87,905
Gross plant, property, and equipment	$ 126,429	$ 130,916
Accumulated depreciation	75,765	76,948
Net plant, property, and equipment	$ 50,664	$ 53,968
Investments	64,728	77,296
Intangibles	—	—
Other assets	9,424	7,435
TOTAL ASSETS	$ 208,537	$ 226,604
LIABILITIES AND EQUITY		
Accounts payable	$ 16,173	$ 17,290
Notes payable	20,712	22,179
Accrued expenses	10,723	12,006
Short-term notes	13,036	13,444
Other current liabilities	11,245	11,692
Total current liabilities	$ 71,889	$ 76,611
Long-term notes	$ 40,186	$ 46,698
Other long-term liabilities	19,079	19,070
Total liabilities	$ 131,154	$ 142,379
Common stock	$ 3,757	$ 3,697
Paid-in capital	4,685	4,616
Retained earnings	68,941	75,912
Common equity	$ 77,383	$ 84,225
TOTAL LIABILITIES AND EQUITY	$ 208,537	$ 226,604

General Motors Income Statement
for Year Ended December 31, 2004 and 2005 ($ millions except per share data)

	2004	2005
Sales	$ 190,812	$ 190,215
Cost of goods sold	144,179	155,264
Gross profit	$ 46,633	$ 34,951
Selling, general, and administrative expenses	20,394	22,734
Depreciation expense	14,152	15,769
Operating profit	$ 12,087	($3,552)
Interest expense	−11,980	−15,768
Nonoperating income/expense	3,407	2,984
Extraordinary items	−1,620	−109
Taxable income	$ 1,894	($ 16,445)
Income tax refund	911	5,878
Net income	$ 2,805	($ 10,567)
Number of common stock shares	565	565
Earnings per share	$ 4.96	$ (18.70)
Dividends per share	$ 2.00	$ 2.00

General Motors Balance Sheets
for Year Ended December 31, 2004 and 2005 ($ millions)

	DECEMBER 31	
	2004	2005
ASSETS		
Cash and equivalents	$ 35,993	$ 32,142
Net receivables	180,195	199,407
Inventories	32,181	36,219
Other current assets	10,794	8,877
Total current assets	$ 259,163	$ 276,645
Gross plant, property, and equipment	$ 124,988	$ 130,226
Accumulated depreciation	49,904	51,825
Net plant, property, and equipment	$ 75,084	$ 78,401
Investments	30,614	23,891
Intangibles	12,089	9,097
Other assets	102,653	88,044
TOTAL ASSETS	$ 479,603	$ 476,078
LIABILITIES AND EQUITY		
Accounts payable	$ 28,830	$ 29,913
Accrued expenses	21,103	65,614
Short-term notes	93,105	83,747
Other current liabilities	−	3,759
Total current liabilities	$ 143,038	$ 183,033
Long-term notes	$ 207,174	$ 203,598
Other long-term liabilities	101,665	74,850
Total liabilities	$ 451,877	$ 461,481
Common stock	$ 942	$ 943
Paid-in capital	15,241	15,285
Retained earnings	11,543	(1,631)
Total common equity	$ 27,726	$ 14,597
TOTAL LIABILITIES AND EQUITY	$ 479,603	$ 476,078

Self-Test Solution

ST-1.

a. 2008 net working capital = current assets − current liabilities
$$= \$62,000 − \$69,000$$
$$= \$(7,000)$$

2008 operating working capital = current assets − non-interest-bearing current liabilities
$$= \$62,000 − \$22,000$$
$$= \$40,000$$

$$2008 \text{ debt ratio} = \text{total liabilities} \div \text{total assets}$$
$$= \$91,950 \div 150,000$$
$$= .613 \text{ or } 61.3\%$$

(1)b. Common-sized income statement

	2008	**% OF SALES**
Sales (all credit)	$160,000	100.0%
Cost of goods sold	96,000	60.0%
Gross profit	$ 64,000	40.0%
Operating expenses		
Fixed cash operating expenses	$ 21,000	13.1%
Variable operating expenses	16,000	10.0%
Depreciation	10,000	6.3%
Total operating expenses	$ 47,000	29.4%
Earnings before interest and taxes	$ 17,000	**10.6%**
Interest expense	6,100	3.8%
Earnings before taxes	$ 10,900	6.8%
Income taxes	3,900	2.4%
Net income	$ 7,000	**4.4%**

From the common-sized income statement, we see that M&G Corporation's gross profit margin was 40 percent of sales. Furthermore, the firm earned an operating profit margin of 10.6 percent and a net profit margin of 4.4 percent.

(2) Common-sized balance sheet

Cash	$ 500	0.3%
Accounts receivable	16,000	10.7%
Inventories	45,500	30.3%
Total current assets	$62,000	41.3%
Land	$26,000	17.3%
Plant and equipment	100,000	66.7%
Accumulated depreciation	(38,000)	−25.3%
Total fixed assets	$ 88,000	58.7%
Total assets	$150,000	100.0%
Accounts payable	$ 17,000	11.3%
Accrued expenses	$ 5,000	3.3%
Short-term bank notes	47,000	31.3%
Total current liabilities	$ 69,000	46.0%
Long-term debt	22,950	15.3%
Total debt	$ 91,950	61.3%
Common stock	$ 31,500	21.0%
Retained earnings	26,550	17.7%
Total common equity	$ 58,050	38.7%
Total liabilities and equity	$150,000	100.0%

M&G Corporation has about 41 percent in current assets and 59 percent in long-term assets. A large part of its debt is short term, mostly in the form of short-term bank notes.

c. Compute the free cash flows and financing cash flows for the period. Interpret your results.

FREE CASH FLOWS		
Operating income		$ 17,000
Plus depreciation expense		10,000
Less tax expense		(3,900)
After-tax cash flows from operations		$ 23,100
Change in operating working capital		
Increase in current assets	$(11,500)	
Increase in non-interest-bearing current liabilities	11,500	
Total change in operating working capital		$0
Change in fixed assets and land		
Purchase of plant and equipment	$(30,000)	
Purchase of land	(6,000)	
Total change in fixed assets and land		$ (36,000)
Free cash flows		$ (12,900)

FINANCING CASH FLOWS

Borrowed (increased) short-term bank notes	$30,000
Paid down (decreased) long-term notes	$ (5,800)
Dividends	(5,200)
Interest expense	(6,100)
Financing cash flows	$12,900

M& G Corporation has negative free cash flows of $12,900, which is the result of:

1. Positive after-tax cash flow from operations of $23,100
2. No additional investment in operating working capital
3. A $36,000 increase in long-term assets

Thus, M&G Corporation's managers invested more in fixed assets and land than was generated in after-tax cash flows from operations. The company then borrowed enough in short-term financing to cover its shortfall in free cash flows and to pay down its long-term debt, pay interest expense, and pay dividends.

APPENDIX A

DAVIES INC. STATEMENT OF CASH FLOWS

In the chapter, we presented cash flows purely from a finance perspective, choosing free cash flows as our measure, rather than using the conventional statement of cash flows as we would observe in a firm's financial statements. Here we provide the statement of cash flows for Davies Inc.

The statement begins with net income, adds back depreciation expense, and then adds or subtracts any changes in operating working capital, with the exception of the change in cash. Investments in long-term assets—fixed assets in this case—are then subtracted. Financing activities are then added or subtracted, with the exception of interest expense, which would have been included in computing net income—no need to double count. Adding the cash flows from operations, investment activities, and financing activities gives us the change in cash for the year. We then take the beginning cash for the year and add the change in cash to give the ending cash balance at year end. That is how the accountants compute cash flows.

Davies Inc.
Statement of Cash Flows
for the Year Ending December 31, 2008 ($ millions)

Net income	$ 42
Depreciation expense	30
Increase in accounts receivable	(5)
Increase in inventories	(33)
Increase in accounts payable	1
Increase in accrued expenses	0
Cash flow from operations	$ 35
Investment activity	
Increase in fixed assets	$(39)
Financing activity	
Decrease in short-term notes	$ (2)
Increase in long-term debt	11
Increase in common stock	4
Common stock dividends	(10)
Total financing activities	$ 3
Change in cash	$ (1)
Beginning cash	21
Ending cash	$ 20

≪ LEARNING OBJECTIVES ≫

After reading this chapter, you should be able to:

1. Explain the purpose and importance of financial analysis.

2. Calculate and use a comprehensive set of measurements to evaluate a company's performance.

3. Describe the limitations of financial ratio analysis.

CHAPTER 4

Evaluating a Firm's Financial Performance

Nike, the world's largest athletic footwear and apparel manufacturer, is a winner when it comes to competition within its industry. In a special 2006 issue on winning companies, *Business Week* described Nike in glowing terms:[1]

> Many try, but few can run with Nike, a company that can handle defeats in the market and absorb global economic bumps without too much pain. It's clear that Adidas outpaced the Swoosh at this summer's FIFA World Cup in Germany and that higher oil prices are squeezing margins. But even a setback in the key soccer category hardly trips up this marathon runner. Nike veteran and new CEO Mark Parker is steeped in Nike's hypercompetitive cauldron (a sign in the plush exercise and workout center reads: "No brand X. Wear the Swoosh, please"). He's expanding in Brazil, China, India, and Russia while speeding innovation with ozone-friendly Max Air cushioning and Nike Plus with Apple, a sensor that beams data to an iPod nano while you run.

No doubt, Nike is the leader in its industry; but Nike's management makes it clear as to the company's ultimate goal: In its 2006 annual report, Nike's managers stated the firm's goal is to "deliver value to our shareholders by building a profitable portfolio of global footwear, apparel, equipment, and accessories brands."

How does Nike intend to meet that goal? According to the report, by doing the following:

> Our strategy for building this portfolio is focused in four key areas:
>
> - Deepening our relationship with consumers;
> - Delivering superior, innovative products to the marketplace;
> - Making our supply chain a competitive advantage, through operational discipline and excellence; and
> - Accelerating growth through focused execution.
>
> By executing this strategy, we aim to deliver the following long-term financial goals:
>
> - High-single-digit revenue growth;
> - Midteens earnings per share growth;
> - Increased return on invested capital and accelerated cash flows; and
> - Consistent results through effective management of our diversified portfolio of businesses.

In evaluating their 2006 performance, Nike's managers noted that the company's earnings grew 9 percent, net income grew 15 percent, and earning per share increased 18 percent. The firm's gross profit margin was 44 percent, which meant that a shoe that sold for $60 cost Nike $33.57 to produce. The end result: Nike's return on invested capital was almost 21 percent. Let there be no question, whatever Nike does eventually will be evaluated in terms of its financial performance.

[1] Harry Maurer (ed.), "The List: Here's Where the Most Driven Go-Getters Thrive," *Business Week*, August 21–28, 2006, p. 105.

This chapter is a natural extension of Chapter 3. In this chapter, we restate financial statements in relative terms to understand how a firm is performing. Specifically, we look at key financial relationships in the form of ratios to understand three basic attributes of the firm's performance:

- The ability of the firm to meet its current liabilities as they come due, or what financial analysts refer to as *liquidity*
- Whether the firm's managers deliver acceptable, and hopefully, even superior profits on the capital entrusted to the firm
- Whether the firm's managers create or destroy shareholder value

In this chapter, we look at financial measurements, or metrics, used to manage a business. Is using metrics to help us manage a business important? John Thompson, CEO, Symantec Corporation, a high-growth Internet security firm, thinks so:

> I don't believe you can manage what you don't measure. A firm needs metrics that serve as an indication for the team about what you're paying attention to. If employees know you're measuring market growth and customer satisfaction, they'll pay attention to those considerations and will behave based on indicators that you, as the leader, provide to the organization. Metrics help the team focus on what's important for an organization.
>
> The best metrics are simple to understand, are simple to communicate, and make it relatively easy for everyone to get access to the data that represents the results. That makes your metrics an effective management tool. If you make your metrics difficult to gather, manage, or communicate, they won't be effective. Simplicity is key.
>
> My experience has proven to me the importance of picking a few metrics that are the most critical for running the business. Stick with them—and communicate them to both internal and external audiences.[2]

With this advice from an experienced CEO, we begin our study of the key financial metrics that can and must be used by companies, both large and small.

Remember Your Principles

As in Chapter 3 when we talked about financial statements, a primary rationale for evaluating a company's financial performance relates to **Principle 7: The Agency Problem—Managers Won't Work for the Firm's Owners Unless It's in Their Best Interest** to do so. Thus, the firm's common stockholders need information that can be used to monitor managers' actions. Interpreting the firm's financial statements through the use of financial ratios is a key tool used in this monitoring. Of course, the firm's managers also need metrics to monitor the company's performance so corrective actions can be taken when necessary.

Principle 5: The Curse of Competitive Markets—Why It's Hard to Find Exceptionally Profitable Projects is also relevant when it comes to evaluating a firm's financial performance. By exceptionally profitable markets, we mean markets in which investments earn rates of return that exceed the opportunity cost of the money invested. Thus, rates of return are critical measures of whether or not managers are creating shareholder value. In addition, certain financial ratios can help us better know if managers are pursuing exceptionally good investments or bad ones.

Finally, **Principle 1: The Risk–Return Trade-Off—We Won't Take On Additional Risk Unless We Expect to Be Compensated with Additional Return** is also at work in this chapter. As we will see, how managers choose to finance the business affects the company's risk and, as a result, the rate of return stockholders receive on their investments.

[2] David Liss, "Ask the CEO: Management by the Numbers," *Business Week Online*, New York: McGraw-Hill, at **www.businessweek.com/technology/content/jul2003/tc20030721_6130.htm**, July 23, 2003.

THE PURPOSE OF FINANCIAL ANALYSIS

Objective 1

Explain the purpose and importance of financial analysis.

As explained in Chapter 1, the fundamental and core objective of financial management is to create shareholder value, as opposed to focusing on accounting numbers, such as earnings. In a perfect world, we would rely on market values relating to a firm's assets rather than its accounting data. However, we rarely have market values to guide decision making. Thus, accounting information can be very useful for this purpose.

However, financial analysts use accounting information differently than accountants do. Accountants focus on using the information to prepare financial statements according to generally accepted accounting principles (GAAP). By contrast, financial analysts use the information to measure a company's performance and make projections about and improve its future financial performance. The analysis is primarily based on the use of ratios that help us see critical relationships that might not otherwise be readily identifiable. Ratios are used to standardize financial information so that we can make comparisons. Otherwise, it is really difficult to compare the financial statements of two firms of different sizes or even the same firm at different times.

Financial ratios give us two ways of making meaningful comparisons of a firm's financial data: (1) We can examine the ratios across time (say, for the past 5 years) to compare a firm's current and past performance; and (2) we can compare the firm's ratios with those of other firms. In comparing a firm with other companies, we could select a peer group of companies, or we could use industry norms published by firms such as Dun & Bradstreet, Risk Management Association, Standard & Poor's, Value Line, and Prentice Hall. Dun & Bradstreet, for instance, annually publishes a set of 14 key ratios for each of 125 lines of business. The Risk Management Association (the association of bank loan and credit officers) publishes a set of 16 key ratios for more than 350 lines of business. The firms are grouped according to the North American Industrial Classification System (NAICS) codes. They are also segmented by firm size to provide the basis for more meaningful comparisons.

financial ratios accounting data restated in relative terms in order to help people identify some of the financial strengths and weaknesses of a company.

Figure 4-1 shows the financial statement information as reported by Risk Management Association (RMA) for new car dealers. The report shows the information by two asset-size and sales-size categories. In the complete report (not provided here), other size categories are presented. The balance sheet data in the report are provided as a percentage of total assets, or what we called in Chapter 3 a *common-sized balance sheet*. Likewise, the income statement data are reported as a percentage of sales, referred to as a *common-sized income statement*.[3] In presenting the financial ratios in the bottom portion of the report, RMA gives three results for each ratio—the firms at the 75th, 50th, and 25th percentiles, respectively.

Financial analysis is not just a tool for financial managers but also can be used effectively by investors, lenders, suppliers, employees, and customers. Within the firm, managers use financial ratios to:

- Identify deficiencies in the firm's performance and take corrective action.
- Evaluate employee performance and determine incentive compensation.
- Compare the financial performance of the firm's different divisions.
- Prepare, at both the firm and division levels, financial projections, such as those associated with the launch of a new product.
- Understand the financial performance of the firm's competitors.
- Evaluate the financial condition of a major supplier.

Outside the company, financial ratios can be used by:

- Lenders to decide whether or not to make a loan to the company
- Credit-rating agencies to determine the firm's creditworthiness
- Investors to decide whether or not to invest in a company
- Major suppliers to decide whether or not to grant credit terms to a company

---

[3] In Chapter 3, we presented a common-sized income statement and common-sized balance sheet for Davies Inc. (See pages 72 and 74.)

FIGURE 4-1 Financial Statement Data by Industry: Norms for New Car Dealers

RETAIL—NEW CAR DEALERS NAICS 4411 (SIC 5511)

CURRENT DATA SORTED BY ASSETS			CURRENT DATA SORTED BY SALES	
50-100MM	100-250MM		10-25MM	25MM and OVER
%	%	ASSETS	%	%
7.3	8.7	Cash and Equivalents	8.1	10.3
10.0	10.9	Trade Receivables (net)	7.3	8.7
48.3	45.5	Inventory	67.9	60.0
4.4	2.5	All Other Current	2.7	2.9
70.0	67.6	Total Current	85.9	81.9
16.3	20.9	Fixed Assets (net)	8.3	10.9
2.6	1.5	Intangibles (net)	1.4	1.6
11.1	10.0	All Other Non-current	4.3	5.6
100.0	100.0	Total	100.0	100.0
		LIABILITIES		
42.2	42.5	Notes Payable Short Term	56.5	51.8
3.5	2.4	Cur. Mat.-L/T/D	2.0	2.4
3.5	4.2	Trade Payables	4.3	4.4
.1	.2	Income Taxes Payable	.1	.2
9.7	12.8	All Other Current	9.5	11.2
59.0	62.2	Total Current	72.3	70.0
14.6	16.0	Long Term Debt	6.5	7.5
.6	.3	Deferred Taxes	.1	.2
3.4	2.3	All Other Non-current	2.7	2.2
22.5	19.2	Net Worth	18.5	20.1
100.0	100.0	Total Liabilities and Net Worth	100.0	100.0
		INCOME DATA		
100.0	100.0	Net Sales	100.0	100.0
15.6	15.6	Gross Profit	12.3	12.1
13.2	14.0	Operating Expenses	11.9	11.2
2.4	1.6	Operating Profit	.3	.9
		All Other		
−.3	.3	Expenses (net)	−.6	−.5
2.6	1.3	Profit Before Taxes	.9	1.4
		RATIOS		
1.3	1.2	Current	1.3	1.3
1.2	1.1		1.2	1.1
1.1	.9		1.1	1.0
.4	.4	Quick	.3	.4
.3	.3	(768)	.2 (1302)	.2
.2	.2		.1	.2
5 67.2	6 61.0	Sales/Receivables	3 127.5	4 102.8
10 36.1	11 33.1		5 70.6	6 60.7
17 21.6	17 21.9		9 38.6	10 37.5

CURRENT DATA SORTED BY ASSETS			CURRENT DATA SORTED BY SALES	
50-100MM	100-250MM	RATIOS	10-25MM	25MM and OVER
%	%		%	%
52 7.1	53 6.9	Cost of Sales/Inventory	60 6.1	46 8.0
67 5.4	62 5.9		76 4.8	59 6.2
80 4.5	74 5.0		93 3.9	73 5.0
3 142.6	3 111.0	Cost of Sales/Payables	1 257.4	2 209.2
4 84.3	4 81.3		3 140.6	3 123.4
8 43.8	8 43.5		5 71.2	5 77.8
16.7	30.5	Sales/Working Capital	17.5	21.9
29.7	95.3		30.6	39.4
53.0	−98.0		88.5	134.2
8.4	12.7	EBIT/Interest	6.8	11.3
(32) 4.0	(20) 4.1		(597) 2.4	(938) 4.5
1.5	2.5		1.0	1.9
8.4		Net Profit+Depr., Dep., Amort./Cur. Mat. L/T/D	4.6	6.7
(10) 1.5			(64) 1.8	(174) 2.2
1.0			.6	.9
.2	.4	Fixed Assets/Net Worth	.2	.2
.8	1.3		.4	.5
1.3	4.9		1.2	1.2
2.4	3.2	Debt/Net Worth	3.0	2.6
3.7	5.3		5.8	4.8
6.6	17.0		14.0	9.8
39.3	77.4	% Profit Before Taxes/Tangible Net Worth	36.4	50.4
(36) 23.2	(25) 22.2		(692) 17.4	(1223) 28.0
10.5	13.3		3.0	12.2
8.6	7.7	% Profit Before Taxes/Total Assets	6.1	9.2
4.4	5.0		2.3	4.8
1.5	2.9		.1	1.6
84.2	74.0	Sales/Net Fixed Assets	163.6	126.3
22.9	17.7		77.4	67.2
9.6	8.2		37.0	27.0
4.0	3.9	Sales/Total Assets	4.5	5.2
3.3	3.1		3.8	4.2
1.9	2.5		3.0	3.4
.3	.2	% Depr., Dep., Amort./Sales	.1	.1
(37) .4	(21) .5		(679) .3	(1214) .3
1.0	.8		.4	.4
.1		% Officers', Directors', Owners' Comp/Sales	.4	.2
(17) .3			(501) .6	(760) .4
1.1			1.1	1.0
7968935M	13431196M	Net Sales ($)	13318098M	95427461M
2604956M	3948948M	Total Assets ($)	3876849M	24306019M

M = $ thousand   MM = $ million

The conclusion: Financial analysis tools can help a wide group of individuals for a variety of purposes. However, in this chapter we will focus on how the firm itself uses financial ratios to evaluate its performance. But remember that personnel in marketing, human resources, information systems, and other groups within a firm can use financial ratios for a variety of other reasons.

Did You Get It?

1. What is the basic purpose of doing a financial analysis?
2. How does a firm use financial ratios? Who else might use financial ratios and why?
3. Where can we find financial ratios for different companies or for peer groups?

MEASURING KEY FINANCIAL RELATIONSHIPS

Objective **2**

Calculate and use a comprehensive set of measurements to evaluate a company's performance.

Instructors usually take one of two approaches to teach students about financial ratios. The first approach reviews the different types or categories of ratios, whereas the second approach uses ratios to answer important questions about a firm's operations. We prefer the latter approach and have chosen the following five questions to help you map out the process of using financial ratios:

1. How liquid is the firm?
2. Are the firm's managers generating adequate operating profits on the company's assets?
3. How is the firm financing its assets?
4. Are the firm's managers providing a good return on the capital provided by the shareholders?
5. Are the firm's managers creating shareholder value?

Let's look at each of these five questions in turn. In doing so, we will use Davies Inc. to illustrate the use of financial ratios. The company's financial statements, which were originally presented in Chapter 3, are shown again in Table 4-1 and Table 4-2.

To give us a basis for comparison, we also provide the average financial ratios for a peer group of businesses similar to Davies Inc. In the ratio computations, we have color coded the numbers so that you can readily determine whether a particular number is coming from the income statement (red numbers) or the balance sheet (blue numbers). (Note: An Excel spreadsheet model is available with this chapter at **www.prenhall.com/keown**. We suggest you use the model as you work through the different examples in the chapter.)

TABLE 4-1   Davies Inc. Income Statement for Year
Ending December 31, 2007 ($ millions)

Sales		$ 600
Cost of goods sold		460
Gross profits		$ 140
Operating expenses:		
Selling expenses	$ 20	
General and administrative expenses	15	
Depreciation expense	30	
Total operating expenses		$ 65
Operating income (EBIT)		$ 75
Interest		15
Earnings before taxes		$ 60
Income taxes		18
Net income		$ 42
Number of common shares outstanding (millions)		20
Earnings per share (EPS)		$ 2.10
Dividends per share (DPS)		$ 0.50

| **TABLE 4-2** | Davies Inc. Balance Sheets ($ millions) December 31, 2007 |

ASSETS

Cash	$ 20
Accounts receivable	36
Inventories	84
Other current assets	3
Total current assets	$143
Gross fixed assets	$410
Accumulated depreciation	(115)
Net fixed assets	$295
Total assets	$438

DEBT AND EQUITY

Accounts payable	$ 42
Accrued expenses	10
Short-term notes	12
Total current liabilities	$ 64
Long-term debt	$171
Total liabilities	$235
Equity	
Common stockholders' equity	
Common stock—par value	$ 11
Paid-in capital	75
Retained earnings	117
Total common equity	$203
Total liabilities and equity	$438

Question 1: How Liquid Is the Firm—Can It Pay Its Bills?

A liquid asset is one that can be converted quickly and routinely into cash at the current market price. So the **liquidity** of a business is a function of its ability to have cash available when needed to meet its financial obligations. Very simply, can we expect the company to be able to pay creditors on a timely basis?

This question can be answered by taking a look at two complementary perspectives: (1) by comparing the firm's assets that are relatively liquid (those that can be converted quickly and easily into cash) with the firm's debt owed in the near term, and (2) by examining the timeliness with which the firm's primary liquid assets—accounts receivable and inventories—are being converted into cash. Let's consider these two approaches.

liquidity a firm's ability to pay its bills on time. Liquidity is related to the ease and quickness with which a firm can convert its noncash assets into cash, as well as the size of the firm's investment in noncash assets relative to its short-term liabilities.

Measuring Liquidity: Perspective 1

The first angle for measuring liquidity is to look at the company's balance sheet and compare the firm's "liquid" assets (current assets) to its current (short-term) liabilities. Thus, the most commonly used measure of a firm's short-term solvency is the **current ratio:**

current ratio a firm's current assets divided by its current liabilities. This ratio indicates the firm's degree of liquidity by comparing its current assets to its current liabilities.

$$\text{Current ratio} = \frac{\text{current assets}}{\text{current liabilities}} \tag{4-1}$$

For Davies Inc.:

$$\text{Current ratio} = \frac{\$143M}{\$64M} = 2.23$$

| Peer group current ratio | 1.80 |

Based on the current ratio, Davies Inc. is more liquid than the average firm in the peer group. The company has $2.23 in current assets for every $1 in short-term debt, compared to a peer-group average current ratio of $1.80.

When we use the current ratio, we assume that the firm's accounts receivable will be collected and turned into cash on a timely basis and that its inventories can be sold without any extended delay. However, a company's inventory is generally less liquid than its accounts receivable because inventory must first be sold before any cash can be collected. So, if we want to have a more stringent test of a firm's liquidity, we include only the firm's cash and accounts receivable in the numerator of our liquidity measure (and not its inventory). This revised ratio is called the **acid-test** (or **quick**) **ratio**. It is calculated as follows:

$$\text{Acid-test ratio} = \frac{\text{cash} + \text{accounts receivable}}{\text{current liabilities}} \tag{4-2}$$

For Davies Inc.:

$$\text{Acid-test ratio} = \frac{\$20M + \$36M}{\$64M} = 0.88$$

Peer group acid-test ratio	0.94

acid-test (quick) ratio a firm's current assets and accounts receivable divided by its current liabilities. This ratio is a more stringent measure of liquidity than the current ratio in that it excludes inventories and other current assets (those that are least liquid) from current assets.

Based on the acid-test ratio, Davies Inc. appears to be slightly *less* liquid. It has $0.88 in cash and accounts receivable per $1 in current debt, compared to $0.94 for the average company in the peer group.

Measuring Liquidity: Perspective 2

The second angle for measuring liquidity examines the quality of a firm's accounts receivable and inventories in terms of the firm' abilty to convert these assets into cash on a timely basis. A firm might have a higher current ratio or acid-test ratio than its competitors. However, it might also have more uncollectible receivables and/or be carrying a lot of obsolete inventory. So knowing the quality of these assets is necessary if we are to have a more complete understanding of a firm's liquidity.

Converting Accounts Receivable to Cash   The conversion of accounts receivable into cash can be measured by computing *how long it takes to collect the firm's receivables*. We can answer this question by computing a firm's days of sales outstanding, or its **average collection period**, as follows:[4]

$$\text{Average collection period} = \frac{\text{accounts receivable}}{\text{annual credit sales}/365} = \frac{\text{accounts receivable}}{\text{daily credit sales}} \tag{4-3}$$

average collection period a firm's accounts receivable divided by the company's average daily credit sales (annual credit sales ÷ 365). This ratio expresses how rapidly the firm is collecting its credit accounts.

Assuming that Davies Inc. sells entirely on credit, the firm's average collection period would be found as follows:

$$\text{Average collection period} = \frac{\text{accounts receivable}}{\text{daily credit sales}}$$

For Davies Inc.:

$$\text{Average collection period} = \frac{\$36M}{\$600M/365} = \frac{\$36M}{\$1.64M/\text{day}} = 21.95 \text{ days}$$

Peer group average collection period	25.00 days

On average Davies Inc. collects its accounts receivable in 22 days compared to 25 days for the peer group, which suggests that the firm's receivables are more liquid than those of competing firms.

---

[4] When computing a given ratio that uses information from both the income statement and the balance sheet, we should remember that the income statement is for a given time period (e.g., 2007), whereas balance sheet data are at a point in time (e.g., December 31, 2007). If there has been a significant change in an asset from the beginning of the period to the end of the period, it would be better to use the average balance for the year. For example, if the accounts receivable for a company have increased from $1,000 at the beginning of the year to $2,000 at the end of the year, it would be more appropriate to use the average accounts receivable of $1,500 in our computations. Nevertheless, in an effort to simplify, we will use year-end amounts from the balance sheet in our computations.

accounts receivable turnover ratio a firm's credit sales divided by its accounts receivable. This ratio expresses how often accounts receivable are "rolled over" during a year.

We could have reached the same conclusion by measuring how many times accounts receivable are "rolled over" during a year, using the **accounts receivable turnover ratio**. If Davies Inc. collects its accounts receivable every 21.90 days, then it is collecting 16.67 times per year (16.67 times = 365 days ÷ 21.95 days). The accounts receivable turnover can also be calculated as follows:

$$\text{Accounts receivable turnover} = \frac{\text{annual credit sales}}{\text{accounts receivable}} \qquad (4\text{-}4)$$

For Davies Inc.:

$$\text{Acounts receivable turnover} = \frac{\$600M}{\$36M} = 16.67X$$

Peer group accounts receivable turnover	14.60X

Whether we use the average collection period or the accounts receivable turnover ratio, the conclusion is the same. Davies Inc. collects its accounts receivable more quickly than competing firms. In other words, Davies Inc.'s accounts receivable are of better quality than the peer group average.

Converting Inventories to Cash We now want to know the quality of Davies Inc.'s inventory, as indicated by how long the inventory is held before being sold; stated differently, we want to know *how many times the company is turning over its inventory during the year.* **Inventory turnover** is calculated as follows:[5]

inventory turnover a firm's cost of goods sold divided by its inventory. This ratio measures the number of times a firm's inventories are sold and replaced during the year, that is, the relative liquidity of the inventories.

$$\text{Inventory turnover} = \frac{\text{cost of goods sold}}{\text{inventory}} \qquad (4\text{-}5)$$

For Davies Inc.:

$$\text{Inventory turnover} = \frac{\$460M}{\$84M} = 5.48X$$

Peer group inventory turnover	7.00X

We see that Davies Inc. is moving (turning over) its inventory more slowly than the average peer group firm—5.48 times per year at Davies Inc., compared with 7.0 times for the peer group, which suggests that the firm's inventory is less liquid than that of the peer group on average.

We could also express the inventory turnover in terms of the number of days of sales in inventory. Davies Inc. turns its inventory over 5.48 times per year, so on average, it is carrying its inventory for 67 days (365 days ÷ 5.48 times per year), whereas the average peer firm carries its inventory only 52 days (365 days ÷ 7.0 times per year) on average.

To conclude, the current ratio indicates that Davies Inc. is more liquid than the competing firms on average, but this result assumes that the firm's inventory are of similar quality as the competitors, which is not the case given Davies' slower inventory turnover. The acid-test ratio, on the other hand, suggests that the firm is less liquid than its competitors, but we know that Davies' accounts receivable are more liquid than the average peer group firm. So we have a mixed outcome and cannot say definitely whether Davies Inc. is more or less liquid. Judgment suggests that Davies Inc. is probably similar in its liquidity to other firms on average.

---

[5] Note that sales has been replaced by cost of goods sold in the numerator. Because inventory (the denominator) is measured at cost, we want to use the cost-based measure of sales in the numerator. Otherwise our answer will vary from one firm to the next solely because of differences in how each firm marks up its sales over cost. However, some of the industry norms provided by financial services are computed using sales in the numerator. In those cases, we will want to use sales in our computation of inventory turnover.

Can You Do It?

EVALUATING DISNEY'S LIQUIDITY

The following information (expressed in $ millions) is taken from the Walt Disney Company's 2005 financial statements:

Current assets	$ 8,845
Accounts receivable	4,585
Cash	1,723
Inventories	1,136
Sales	31,944
Cost of goods sold	26,498
Total current liabilities	9,168

Evaluate Disney's liquidity based on the following norms in the broadcasting and entertainment industry:

Current ratio	1.17
Acid-test ratio	0.92
Accounts receivable turnover	10.08
Inventory turnover	18.32

(The solution can be found on page 104.)

Did You Get It?

1. What information about the firm is provided by liquidity measures?
2. Describe the two perspectives available for measuring liquidity.
3. Why might a very high current ratio actually indicate there's a problem with a firm's inventory or accounts receivable management? What might be another reason for a high current ratio?
4. Why might a successful (liquid) firm have an acid-test ratio that is less than 1?

Question 2: Are the Firm's Managers Generating Adequate Operating Profits on the Company's Assets?

We now switch to a different dimension of performance—the firm's profitability. The question is, "Do the firm's managers produce adequate profits from the company's assets?" From the perspective of the firm's shareholders, there is no more important question to be asked. One of the most important ways managers create shareholder value is to earn strong profits on the assets in which they have invested.

To answer this all-important question, think about the process of financing a company. In its simplest form, a firm's shareholders invest in a business. The company might also borrow additional money from other sources (banks and so forth). The cumulative effects of this process are reflected in a firm's balance sheet. For example, Figure 4-2 indicates that Davies Inc.'s shareholders have invested $203 million in the company, and the company has borrowed another $235 million to finance $438 million of assets. These assets were then used to produce $75 million in operating profits.

Notice that we are using *operating profits* (the same as *operating income* or *earnings before interest and taxes*) rather than *net income*. Operating profits is the income generated from the

FIGURE 4-2 Davies Inc. Operating Profits from Assets December 31, 2007

How Did You Do?

EVALUATING DISNEY'S LIQUIDITY

	DISNEY	INDUSTRY
Current ratio	0.96	1.17
Acid-test ratio	0.69	0.92
Accounts receivable turnover	6.97X	10.1X
Inventory turnover	23.33X	18.3X

Based on these results, Disney is not as liquid as the average firm in the industry! The company has less liquid assets relative to its current liabilities than do its competitors on average. Nor does the firm convert its receivables to cash as quickly as its competitors. However, Disney's inventories turn over more quickly then those of its competitors.

firm's assets without regard to how the assets are financed. The effect of financing will be explicitly considered in the two questions that follow, but for now we want to isolate only the operating aspects of the company's profits.

To examine the level of operating profits relative to the firm's total assets, we use the **operating return on assets (OROA)**:

operating return on assets (OROA) the ratio of a firm's operating income divided by its total assets. This ratio indicates the rate of return being earned on the firm's assets.

$$\text{Operating return on assets} = \frac{\text{operating profits}}{\text{total assets}} \tag{4-6}$$

For Davies Inc.:

$$\text{Operating return on assets} = \frac{\$75M}{\$438M} = 0.171 = 17.1\%$$

Peer group operating return on assets	17.8%

Davies Inc. is earning a slightly lower return on its assets relative to the average firm in the peer group. Managers are generating 17.1 cents of operating profits for every $1 of assets, compared to 17.8 cents on average for the peer group.

Because Davies Inc. is generating a return on the firm's assets that is less than the competition, the company's managers will want to know why the firm is not earning a competitive return on the assets. The answer lies in two areas: (1) *operations management*, which includes the day-to-day buying and selling of a firm's goods or services as reflected in the income statement, and (2) *asset management*, which relates to the balance sheet. We can relate operations management and asset management through a firm's *operating return on assets* using the product of two ratios; that is,

$$\underset{\text{on assets}}{\text{Operating return}} = \underset{\substack{\text{OPERATIONS} \\ \text{operating profit} \\ \text{margin}}}{} \times \underset{\substack{\text{ASSET MANAGEMENT} \\ \text{total asset} \\ \text{turnover}}}{} \tag{4-7a}$$

which is calculated as follows:

$$\underset{\text{on assets}}{\text{Operating return}} = \frac{\text{operating profits}}{\text{sales}} \times \frac{\text{sales}}{\text{total assets}} \tag{4-7b}$$

Managing Operations

operating profit margin a firm's operating income (earnings before interest and taxes) divided by sales. This ratio serves as an overall measure of operating effectiveness.

The first component of the operating return on assets (OROA), the **operating profit margin**, is an indicator of how well the company manages its operations—that is, how well revenues are being generated and costs controlled. The operating profit margin measures how well a firm is managing its cost of operations, in terms of both the cost of goods sold and operating expenses (marketing expenses, general and administrative expenses, and depreciation expenses) relative to the firm's revenues. All else being equal, the objective for managing operations is to keep costs and expenses low relative to sales. Thus, we often say that the operating profit margin measures *how well the firm is managing its income statement.*

$$\text{Operating profit margin} = \frac{\text{operating profits}}{\text{sales}} \qquad (4\text{-}8)$$

For Davies Inc.:

$$\text{Operating profit margin} = \frac{\$75M}{\$600M} = 0.125 = 12.5\%$$

Peer group operating profit margin	15.5%

The foregoing result clearly suggests that Davies Inc.'s managers are not as good at managing its cost of goods sold and operating expenses as comparable firms. The company has higher costs per sales dollar, which result in a lower operating profit margin. Put another way, Davies Inc. is not as good as competitors at managing its income statement.

Managing Assets

The second component in equation (4-7) is the **total asset turnover**. This ratio indicates how well the firm is managing its assets, or **asset efficiency**. It measures how efficiently a firm is using its assets to generate sales. To clarify, assume that Company A generates $3 in sales for every $1 invested in assets, whereas Company B generates the same $3 in sales but has invested $2 in assets. We can therefore conclude that Company A is using its assets more efficiently to generate sales, which leads to a higher return on the firm's investment in assets.

total asset turnover a firm's sales divided by its total assets. This ratio is an overall measure of asset efficiency based on the relation between a firm's sales and the total assets.

$$\text{Total asset turnover} = \frac{\text{sales}}{\text{total assets}} \qquad (4\text{-}8)$$

For Davies Inc.:

$$\text{Total asset turnover} = \frac{\$600M}{\$438M} = 1.37X$$

asset efficiency how well a firm is managing its assets.

Peer group total asset turnover	1.15X

Davies Inc. is using its assets more efficiently than its competitors because it generates about $1.37 in sales per dollar of assets, whereas the competition produces only $1.15 in sales from every dollar in assets.

However, we should not stop here with our analysis of Davies Inc.'s asset utilization. We have learned that in general, Davies Inc.'s managers are making effective use of the firm's assets, but this may not be the case for each and every type of asset. How well are the managers delivering on the investment the firm has made in its accounts receivable, inventories, and fixed assets, respectively?

To answer the preceding question, we examine the turnover ratios for each asset category. Of course, we already calculated the turnover ratios for the company's accounts receivable and inventories, and concluded that Davies Inc.'s managers are managing the firm's accounts receivable more efficiently than its competitors, but not its inventories. Thus, we need to compute the **fixed asset turnover** as follows:

$$\text{Fixed asset turnover} = \frac{\text{sales}}{\text{net fixed assets}} \qquad (4\text{-}9)$$

fixed asset turnover a firm's sales divided by its net fixed assets. This ratio indicates how efficiently the firm is using its fixed assets.

For Davies Inc.:

$$\text{Fixed asset turnover} = \frac{\$600M}{\$295M} = 2.03X$$

Peer group fixed asset turnover	1.75X

Finance at Work

MANAGING BY THE NUMBERS

Dorian S. Boyland is taking care of business as he bustles about his 29,000-square-foot Honda dealership, located in Greenfield, Wisconsin. He is preparing for a grand opening, even though the store has been open since 2001.

Boyland, 48, is excited about the festivities, but he intends to get a return on this investment. Make no mistake about it; he is meticulous about how he spends money, keeping the company's advertising and sales salaries less than 10 percent of gross profits, respectively. No more than 10 percent of gross profits are paid in commissions to managers, and no more than 15 percent of gross profits are paid in commissions to sales managers.

The auto dealer operates with one goal in mind: net a 3 percent to 3.5 percent profit on sales from all seven of his auto dealerships. "I never ask how many cars we sold," says Boyland. "I ask my sales managers how much profit did we make. I operate on the premise that if I sell a car for $20,000, I know that 3 percent (or $600) of that amount is going to go to my bottom line. Now, how I get that 3 percent is how we operate the store—from the bottom up."

Boyland's cost controls are a never-ending process. A financial analysis is generated monthly and reviewed by all store managers. This information sharing allows every general manager and sales manager to critique one another, exchange ideas, and establish goals and guidelines.

Volume is very important to dealers because manufacturers expect them to achieve a certain level of market penetration. But as Boyland sees it, "You can be No.1 in terms of volume, but if you are constantly losing money, you'll be taken out of business."

Boyland grows excited when discussing business strategies. "You have to have a passion for this business," he says. "There's a lot of money to be made and a lot of money to be lost. But whether you are selling cars or shoes, you go into business to make money. That's the bottom line."

Source: Carolyn M. Brown, "Maximum Overdrive," *Black Enterprise*, Vol. 33, No. 11 (June 2003), pp. 156–162. Copyright 2003 by Graves Ventures LLC.

Thus, Davies Inc. has a smaller investment in fixed assets relative to the firm's sales than the average peer group firm.

We can now look at all the asset efficiency ratios together to summarize Davies Inc.'s asset management:

	DAVIES INC.	PEER GROUP
Total asset turnover	1.37X	1.15X
Accounts receivable turnover	16.67X	14.60X
Inventory turnover	5.48X	7.00X
Fixed asset turnover	2.03X	1.75X

FIGURE 4-3   Analysis of Davies Inc. Operating Return on Assets

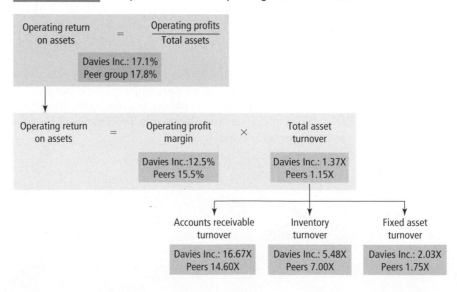

Can You Do It?

EVALUATING DISNEY'S OPERATING RETURN ON ASSETS

Given the following financial information for the Walt Disney Company (expressed in $ millions), evaluate the firm's operating return on its assets (OROA).

Accounts receivable	$ 4,585
Inventories	1,136
Sales	31,944
Operating profits	4,107
Cost of goods sold	26,498
Net fixed assets	22,395
Total assets	53,158

The industry norms are as follows:

Operating return on assets	5.09%
Operating profit margin	11.30%
Total asset turnover	0.45X
Accounts receivable turnover	10.08X
Inventory turnover	18.32X
Fixed assets turnover	1.05X

(The solution can be found on the next page.)

Davies Inc.'s situation with respect to asset management is now clear. Overall, Davies Inc.'s managers are utilizing the firm's assets efficiently, as based on the firm's total asset turnover. This overall asset efficiency results from better management of the firm's accounts receivable and fixed assets (which have higher turnovers than the peer group), but the firm is not managing its inventories as well (which has a lower turnover than the peer group).

Figure 4-3 provides a summary of our evaluation of Davies Inc.'s operating and asset management performance. We began by computing the operating return on assets to determine if managers are producing good returns on the assets. We then broke the operating return on assets into its two pieces, operations management (operating profit margin) and asset management (asset turnover ratios), to explain why Davies Inc.'s operating return on assets is lower than the peer group.

Did You Get It?

1. Which number in a company's income statement should be used to measure its profitability relative to its total assets? Why?
2. What two broad areas of the firm's management does the operating return on assets assess?
3. What factors influence the operating profit margin?
4. A low total asset turnover indicates that a firm's total assets are not being managed efficiently. What additional information would you want to know when this is the case?

Question 3: How Is the Firm Financing Its Assets?

We now turn to the matter of how a firm is financed. (We will return to the issue of profitability shortly.) Is it financed through debt or equity? To answer this question, we use two ratios. First, we ask *what percentage of the firm's assets is financed by debt*, including both short-term and long-term debt, realizing that the remaining percentage must be financed by equity. We compute the **debt ratio** as follows:[6]

$$\text{Debt ratio} = \frac{\text{total debt}}{\text{total assets}} \qquad (4\text{-}10)$$

debt ratio a firm's total liabilities divided by its total assets. This ratio measures the extent to which a firm has been financed with debt.

---

[6] Instead of using the debt ratio, we could use the debt-equity ratio. The debt-equity ratio is simply a transformation of the debt ratio:

$$\text{Debt-equity ratio} = \frac{\text{total debt}}{\text{total equity}} = \frac{\text{debt ratio}}{1 - \text{debt ratio}} \text{ and the debt ratio} = \frac{\text{debt/equity}}{1 + \text{debt/equity}}$$

How Did You Do?

EVALUATING DISNEY'S OPERATING RETURN ON ASSETS

Disney generates a higher return on its assets than the average firm in the industry, 7.73 percent compared to 5.09 percent on average for the industry. Disney provided a higher operating return on its assets, both by managing its operations better (achieving a higher operating profit margin) and by making better use of its assets. The company's higher total asset turnover is due to a higher fixed asset and inventory turnover, which makes up for the less efficient management of the firm's accounts receivable, which have a lower turnover.

	DISNEY	INDUSTRY
Operating return on assets	7.73%	5.09%
Operating profit margin	12.86%	11.30%
Total asset turnover	.60X	0.45X
Accounts receivable turnover	6.97X	10.08X
Inventory turnover	23.33X	18.32X
Fixed assets turnover	1.43X	1.05X

For Davies Inc.:

$$\text{Debt ratio} = \frac{\$235M}{\$438M} = 0.54 = 54\%$$

Peer group debt ratio	35%

Davies Inc. finances 54 percent of its assets with debt (taken from Davies Inc.'s balance sheet in Table 4-2), compared with the peer group average of 35 percent. Stated differently, Davies Inc. finances with 46 percent equity, whereas the average for the peer group is 65 percent equity. Thus, Davies Inc. uses significantly more debt than the peer group average. As we will see at several points in our study, more debt financing results in more financial risk.

Our second perspective regarding the firm's financing decisions comes by looking at the income statement. When the firm borrows money, it must at least pay the interest on what it has borrowed. Thus, it is informative to compare (1) the amount of operating income that is available to pay the interest with (2) the amount of interest that has to be paid. Stated as a ratio, we compute the number of times we are earning our interest. The **times interest earned** ratio is commonly used when examining a firm's debt position and is computed in the following manner:

times interest earned a firm's earnings before interest and taxes (EBIT) divided by interest expense. This ratio measures a firm's ability to meet its interest payments from its annual operating earnings.

$$\text{Times interest earned} = \frac{\text{operating profits}}{\text{interest expense}} \qquad (4\text{-}11)$$

For Davies Inc.:

$$\text{Times interest earned} = \frac{\$75M}{\$15M} = 5.0X$$

Peer group times interest earned	7.0X

Davies Inc.'s interest expense is $15 million, which when compared to its operating income of $75 million, indicates that its interest expense is consuming 1/5 (20.0%) of its operating profits compared to 1/7 (14.29%) for the average peer group firm.

Why would Davies Inc. have a lower times interest earned ratio than the peer group? For one thing, Davies Inc. uses significantly more debt than the average company in the peer group, which leads to more interest expense. Second, its operating return on assets is slightly less than competitors, which means the firm has less operating income to cover the interest.

Before concluding our discussion regarding times interest earned, we should understand that interest is not paid with income but with cash. Moreover, in addition to the interest that must be paid, the firm might be required to repay some of the debt principal. Thus, the times interest earned ratio is only a crude measure of the firm's capacity to service its debt.

Can You Do It?

EVALUATING DISNEY'S FINANCING DECISIONS

Given the following information (expressed in $ millions) for the Disney Corporation, calculate the firm's debt ratio and the times interest earned. How do Disney's ratios compare to those of the industry in which it operates? What are the implications of your findings?

Total debt	$26,948
Total common equity	
Common stock	9,007
Retained earnings	17,203
Total liabilities and equity	53,158
Operating profits	4,107
Interest expense	597
Industry norms:	
Debt ratio	34.21%
Times interest earned	4.50X

(The solution can be found on the next page.)

Nevertheless, it does give us a general indication of a company's financial risk and its capacity to borrow.

Did You Get It?

1. What information is provided by the debt ratio?
2. Why is it important to calculate the times interest earned ratio, even for firms that have low debt ratios?
3. Why does operating income not give a complete picture of a firm's ability to service its debt?

Question 4: Are the Firm's Managers Providing a Good Return on the Capital Provided by the Company's Shareholders?

We now want to look at the *accounting return on the common stockholders' investment*, or the **return on equity** (frequently shortened to ROE). We want to know if the earnings available to the firm's owners (shareholders) are attractive when compared with the returns earned for the owners of companies in the peer group. We measure the return on equity (ROE) as follows:

return on equity a firm's net income divided by its common book equity. This ratio is the accounting rate of return earned on the common stockholders' investment.

$$\text{Return on equity} = \frac{\text{net income}}{\text{common equity}} \qquad (4\text{-}12)$$

For Davies Inc.:

$$\text{Return on equity} = \frac{\$42\text{M}}{\$203\text{M}} = 0.207 = 20.7\%$$

Peer group return on equity	18.0%

In the preceding computation, the common equity includes all common equity in the balance sheet, including both common stock and retained earnings. (Understand that profits retained within the business are as much of an investment for the common stockholders as when the shareholders bought the company's stock.)

The return on equity for Davies Inc. and the peer group are 20.7 percent and 18.0 percent, respectively. Hence, the owners of Davies Inc. are receiving a higher return on their

How Did You Do?

EVALUATING DISNEY'S FINANCING PRACTICES

A comparison of Disney's debt ratio and times interest earned with the industry is as follows:

	DISNEY	INDUSTRY
Debt ratio	50.69%	34.21%
Times interest earned	6.88X	4.50X

Disney uses significantly more debt financing than the average firm in the industry. The higher debt ratio implies that the firm has greater financial risk. Even so, Disney appears to have no difficulty servicing its debt, covering its interest 6.88 times compared only to 4.50 times for the average firm in the industry. Disney's higher times interest earned is attributable to a significantly higher operating return on assets, which more than offsets the higher debt ratio.

equity investment than the shareholders in the peer group firms on average. How are they doing it? To answer, we need to draw on what we have already learned, namely, that:

1. Davies Inc. is receiving a lower operating return on its assets. We learned earlier that the operating return on assets was 17.1 percent for Davies Inc., compared to 17.8 percent for the competition. A lower (higher) return on the firm's assets will always result in a lower (higher) return on equity. Conversely, a higher return on the firm's assets will always result in a higher return on equity.

2. Davies Inc. uses significantly more debt (less equity) financing than the average firm in the industry—54 percent debt for Davies Inc. and 35 percent debt for the peer group. As we will see shortly, the more debt a firm uses, the higher its return on equity will be, provided that the firm is earning a return on assets greater than the interest rate on its debt. Conversely, the less debt a firm uses, the lower its return on equity will be (again, provided that the firm is earning a return on assets greater than the interest rate on its debt). Thus, Davies Inc. has increased its return for its shareholders by using more debt. That's the good news. The bad news for Davies Inc.'s shareholders is that the more debt a firm uses, the greater is the company's financial risk, which translates into more risk for the shareholders.

To help us understand the foregoing reason for Davies Inc.'s higher return on equity and its implications, consider the following example.

➤ EXAMPLE

Firms A and B are identical in size. Both have $1,000 in total assets, and both have an operating return on assets of 14 percent. However, they are different in one respect: Firm A uses all equity and no debt financing; Firm B finances 60 percent of its investments with debt and 40 percent with equity. (For the sake of simplicity, we will assume that both firms pay interest at an interest cost of 6 percent, and there are no income taxes.) The financial statements for the two companies would be as follows:

	FIRM A	FIRM B
BALANCE SHEET		
Total assets	$1,000	$1,000
Debt (6% interest rate)	$ 0	$ 600
Equity	1,000	400
Total debt and equity	$1,000	$1,000
INCOME STATEMENT		
Operating income (OROA = 14%)	$ 140	$ 140
Interest expense (6%)	0	36
Net income	$ 140	$ 104

Computing the return on equity for both companies, we see that Firm B has a more attractive return of 26 percent compared with Firm A's 14 percent. The calculations are as follows:

		FIRM A	FIRM B
Return on common equity	$= \dfrac{\text{net income}}{\text{common equity}} =$	$\dfrac{\$140}{\$1,000} = 14\%$	$\dfrac{\$104}{\$400} = 26\%$

Why the difference? The answer is straightforward. Firm B is earning 14 percent on all of its $1,000 in assets, but only having to pay 6 percent to the lenders on the $600 debt principal. The difference between the 14 percent return on the firm's assets (operating return on assets) and the 6 percent interest rate goes to the owners, thus boosting Firm B's return on equity above that of Firm A.

This is an illustration of favorable financial leverage. What's favorable, you might ask? Well, you earn 14 percent on your investments while paying only 6 percent to the bankers, thus capturing an 8 percent spread on each dollar of debt financing. The result is an increase in the return on equity to Firm B when compared to Firm A. What a great deal for Firm B's shareholders! So if debt enhances owners' returns, why doesn't Firm A borrow money or Firm B borrow even more money?

The good outcome for Firm B shareholders is based on the assumption that the firm does in fact earn 14 percent operating return on the assets. But what if the economy falls into a deep recession, business declines sharply, and Firms A and B only earn a 2 percent operating return on their assets? Let's recompute the return on equity given the new conditions:

	FIRM A	FIRM B
Operating income (OROA = 2%)	$ 20	$ 20
Less interest expense	(0)	(36)
Net income	$ 20	($ 16)
Return on equity:		
$\dfrac{\text{net income}}{\text{common equity}}$	$\dfrac{\$\ 20}{\$1,000}$	$\dfrac{(\$\ 16)}{\$400}$
Equals:	2%	−4%

Now the use of financial leverage has a negative influence on the return on equity, with Firm B earning less than Firm A for its owners. This results from Firm B earning less than the interest rate of 6 percent; consequently, the equity investors have to make up the difference. Thus, financial leverage is a two-edged sword; when times are good, financial leverage can make them very, very good, but when times are bad, financial leverage makes them very, very bad. Financial leverage can enhance the returns of the equity investors, but it also increases the possibility of losses, thereby increasing the uncertainty, or risk, for the owners. Chapter 12 will address financial leverage in greater detail.

Figure 4-4 provides a summary of our discussion of the return on equity relative to Davies Inc. and helps us visualize the two fundamental factors affecting a firm's return on equity:

1. There is a direct relationship between a firm's operating return on assets (OROA) and the resulting return on equity (ROE). As we have explained, the higher the operating return on assets (OROA), the higher will be the return on equity (ROE). Even more precisely, the greater the difference between the firm's operating return on assets (OROA) and the interest rate (i) being paid on the firm's debt, the higher the return on equity will be. So increasing the operating return on assets relative to the interest rate (OROA-i) increases the return on equity (ROE). But if OROA-i decreases, then ROE will decrease as well.

Can You Do It?

EVALUATING DISNEY'S RETURN ON EQUITY

The net income and also the common equity invested by Disney's shareholders (expressed in $ millions) are provided here, along with the average return on equity for the industry. Evaluate the rate of return being earned on the common stockholders' equity investment. In addition to comparing the Disney Corporation's return on equity to the industry, consider the implications Disney's operating return on assets and its debt financing practices have on the firm's return on equity.

Net income	$2,569
Common equity	
Common stock	9,007
Retained earnings	17,203
Industry average return on equity	4.31%

(The solution can be found on page 113.)

---

2. Increasing the amount of debt financing relative to the amount of equity (increasing the debt ratio) increases the return on equity if the operating return on assets is higher than the interest rate being paid. If the operating return on assets falls below the interest rate, more debt financing will decrease the return on equity.

In short, the return on equity is driven by (1) the spread between the operating return on assets and the interest rate (OROA-i) and (2) changes in the debt ratio.

Did You Get It?

1. How is a company's return on equity related to the firm's operating return on assets?
2. How is a company's return on equity related to the firm's debt ratio?
3. What is the upside of debt financing? What is the downside?

FIGURE 4-4   Return on Equity Relationships for Davies Inc.[7]

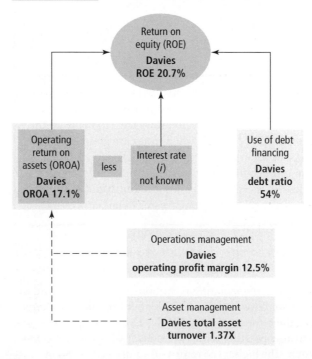

[7] This figure is a modified format of the "DuPont Analysis", which is provided for those interested at **www.prenhall.com/keown.**

How Did You Do?

EVALUATING DISNEY'S RETURN ON EQUITY

Disney's return on equity is 9.8 percent (9.8% = $2,569 million / $26,210 million common equity), compared to 4.31 percent for the industry average. Disney's return on equity is due to the firm having a higher operating return on assets and using a lot more debt financing than the average firm in the industry. Although Disney certainly provides it stockholders a higher return on equity than other firms in the industry on average, it is still low compared to the Standard & Poor's 500 firms, which have historically had an average return on equity of about 18 percent. Thus, the entire industry is struggling to give attractive returns to stockholders.

Question 5: Are the Firm's Managers Creating Shareholder Value?

To this point, we have relied exclusively on accounting data to assess the performance of a firm's managers. We now want to look at management's performance in terms of creating or destroying shareholder value. To answer this question, we use two approaches: (1) We examine market-value ratios, and (2) we estimate the value being created for shareholders, as measured by a popular technique called Economic Value Added (EVA™).

Market-Value Ratios

There are two commonly used ratios that compare the firm's stock price to the firm's earnings and the accounting book value of the equity. These two ratios indicate what investors think of management's past performance and future prospects.

Price/Earnings Ratio   The **price/earnings** (P/E) ratio indicates how much investors are willing to pay for $1 of reported earnings. Returning to Davies Inc., the firm had net income in 2007 of $42 million and 20 million shares of common stock outstanding. (See Table 4-1.) Accordingly, its earnings per share were $2.10 ($2.10 = $42 million net income ÷ 20 million shares). At the time, the firm's stock was selling for $32 per share. Thus, the price/earnings ratio was 15.24 times, calculated as follows:

> **price/earnings ratio** the price the market places on $1 of a firm's earnings. For example, if a firm has an earnings per share of $2, and a stock price of $30 per share, its price/earnings ratio is 15 ($30 ÷ $2).

$$\text{Price/earnings ratio} = \frac{\text{price per share}}{\text{earnings per share}} \qquad (4\text{-}13)$$

For Davies Inc.:

$$\text{Price/earning ratio} = \frac{\$32.00}{\$2.10} = 15.24\text{X}$$

Peer group average price/earnings ratio	19.0X

Davies Inc.'s price/earnings ratio tells us that the investors were willing to pay $15.24 for every dollar of earnings per share that Davies Inc. produced, compared to an average price/earnings ratio of 19 times for the firms making up the peer group. Thus, investors were not willing to pay as much for Davies Inc.'s earnings as were shareholders of the average peer group firm. Why might that be? The price/earnings ratio will be higher for companies that investors think have strong earnings growth prospects with less risk. Thus, investors must perceive Davies Inc. to have less growth potential and/or greater risk compared to the average company in the peer group.

Price/Book Ratio   A second frequently used indicator of investors' assessment of the firm is its **price/book ratio**. This ratio compares the market value of a share of stock to the book value per share of the firm's reported equity in its balance sheet. We already know that the market price of Davies Inc.'s common stock was $32. To determine the equity book value per share, we divide the firm's equity book value by the number of shares of stock outstanding. From Davies Inc.'s balance sheet (Table 4-2), we see that the equity book value was

> **price/book ratio** the market value of a share of the firm's stock divided by the book value per share of the firm's reported equity in the balance sheet.

Can You Do It?

COMPUTING DISNEY'S PRICE/EARNINGS RATIO AND PRICE/BOOK RATIO

Disney's stock was selling for $25.47, while its net income was $2.569 billion ($2,569 million) and its common equity in the balance sheet (book equity) was $26.21 billion ($26,210 million). There were 2.007 billion shares outstanding. What was the firm's earnings per share and its book value per share? Calculate the price/earnings ratio and the price/book ratio. What do the shareholders think about the firm's performance and future growth prospects?

   (The solution can be found on page 117.)

$203 million (including both common stock and retained earnings). Given that Davies Inc. had 20 million shares outstanding, the equity book value per share is $10.15 ($10.15 = $203 million book equity value ÷ 20 million shares). With this information, we determine the price/book ratio to be:

$$\text{Price/book ratio} = \frac{\text{price per share}}{\text{equity book value per share}} \tag{4-14}$$

For Davies Inc.:

$$\text{Price/book ratio} = \frac{\$32.00}{\$10.15} = 3.15X$$

Peer group 500 price/book ratio	3.7X

Given that the book value per share is an accounting number that reflects historical costs, we can roughly think of it as the amount shareholders have invested in the business over its lifetime. So, a ratio greater than 1 indicates that investors believe the firm is more valuable than the amount shareholders have invested in it. Conversely, a ratio less than 1 suggests that investors do not believe the stock is worth the amount shareholders have invested in it. Clearly, investors believe the stock of Davies Inc. is now worth more than shareholders paid, because they are now paying $3.15 for each dollar of book value. In comparison, the average firm in the peer group was selling for $3.70 for every $1 in book equity. Again, the investors are signaling that they believe that Davies Inc. has less growth prospects relative to its riskiness.

Economic Value Added (EVA™)

The price/book ratio, as just described, indicates whether the shareholders value the firm's equity above or below the amount of capital they originally invested. If the firm's market value is above the accounting book value (price/book > 1), then management has created value for shareholders, but if the firm's market value is below book value (price/book < 1), then management has destroyed shareholder value.

How is shareholder value created or destroyed? Quite simply, shareholder value is created when a firm earns a rate of return on the capital invested that is greater than the investors' required rate of return. If we invest in a firm and have a 12 percent required rate of return, and the firm earns 15 percent on our capital, then the firm's managers have created value for investors. If instead, the firm earns only 10 percent, then value has been destroyed. This concept is regularly applied by firms when they decide whether or not to make large capital investments in plant and equipment; however, it has not been generally applied to the analysis of a firm's day-to-day operating results. Instead, managers have traditionally focused on accounting results, such as earnings growth, profit margins, and the return on equity.

More recently, however, people have begun assessing whether or not a firm's managers are creating shareholder value and then linking this assessment to managers' compensation, mostly through bonuses. Although several techniques have been developed for making this assessment, the one that has received the most attention is Economic Value Added (EVA™).

Economic Value Added is a financial performance measure developed by the investment consulting firm, Stern Stewart & Co. EVA attempts to measure a firm's economic profit, rather than accounting profit, in a given year. Economic profits assign a cost to the equity capital (the opportunity cost of the funds provided by the shareholders) in addition to the interest cost on the firm's debt—even though accountants recognize only the interest expense as a financing cost when calculating a firm's net income.

For example, assume a firm has total assets of $1,000; 40 percent ($400) is financed with debt, and 60 percent ($600) is financed with equity. If the interest rate on the debt is 5 percent, the firm's interest expense is $20 ($20 = $400 × 0.05) and would be reported in the firm's income statement. However, there would be no cost shown for the equity financing. To compute economic profits, we compute not only the $20 in interest expense but also the opportunity cost of the $600 equity capital invested in the firm. That is, if the shareholders could earn 15 percent on another investment of similar risk (their opportunity cost is, therefore, 15 percent), then we should count this cost just as surely as we do the interest expense. This would involve subtracting not only the $20 in interest but also $90 ($90 = $600 equity × 0.15) as the cost of equity. Thus, the firm has earned an economic profit only if its operating profit exceeds $110 ($20 + $90). Stated as a percentage, the firm must earn at least an 11 percent operating return on its assets (11% = $110 ÷ $1,000) in order to meet the investors' required rate of return.

We can calculate Economic Value Added (EVA)—the value created for the shareholders—as follows:

$$\text{EVA} = \left(\begin{array}{c} \text{operating return} \\ \text{on assets} \end{array} - \begin{array}{c} \text{cost of} \\ \text{all capital} \end{array} \right) \times \text{total assets} \qquad (4\text{-}15)$$

where the cost of capital is the cost of all the firm's capital, both debt and equity. That is, the value created by management is determined by the amount the firm earns on its invested capital relative to the cost of these funds—both debt and equity—and the amount of capital invested in the firm, which are the total assets.[8]

Continuing with our previous example, assume that our company is earning a 16 percent operating return on its assets (invested capital). Then the firm's economic value added is $50, calculated as follows:

$$\text{EVA} = \left(\begin{array}{c} \text{operating return} \\ \text{on assets} \end{array} - \begin{array}{c} \text{cost of} \\ \text{all capital} \end{array} \right) \times \text{total asset}$$

$$\text{EVA} = (0.16 - 0.11) \times \$1000 = \$50$$

The foregoing explains the EVA concept in its simplest form. However, computing EVA requires converting a firm's financial statements from an accountant's perspective (GAAP) to an economic book value. This process is much more involved than we will go into here, but the basic premise involved in its computation is the same.

To conclude, with the exception of Economic Value Added, a summary of all the ratios we used to analyze the financial performance of Davies Inc. is provided in Table 4-3.

Did You Get It? ....

1. What determines if a firm is creating or destroying shareholder value?
2. What is the rationale of Economic Value Added?

---

[8] In Chapter 11, we will explain how the firm's cost of capital is calculated.

TABLE 4-3　Davies Inc. Financial Ratio Analysis

FINANCIAL RATIOS		DAVIES INC.	PEER GROUP
1. FIRM LIQUIDITY			
Current ratio	$\dfrac{\text{Current assets}}{\text{Current liabilities}}$	$\dfrac{\$143M}{\$64M} = 2.23$	1.80
Acid-test ratio	$\dfrac{\text{Cash + Accounts Receivable}}{\text{Current liabilities}}$	$\dfrac{\$20M + \$36M}{\$64M} = .88$	.94
Average collection period	$\dfrac{\text{Accounts receivable}}{\text{Daily credit sales}}$	$\dfrac{\$36M}{\$600M \div 365} = 21.95$	25
Accounts receivable turnover	$\dfrac{\text{Credit sales}}{\text{Accounts receivable}}$	$\dfrac{\$600M}{\$36M} = 16.67$	14.6
Inventory turnover	$\dfrac{\text{Cost of goods sold}}{\text{Inventory}}$	$\dfrac{\$460M}{\$84M} = 5.48$	7.00
2. OPERATING PROFITABILITY			
Operating return on assets	$\dfrac{\text{Operating profit}}{\text{Total assets}}$	$\dfrac{\$75M}{\$438M} = 17.1\%$	17.8
Operating profit margin	$\dfrac{\text{Operating profit}}{\text{Sales}}$	$\dfrac{\$75M}{\$600M} = 12.5\%$	15.5
Total asset turnover	$\dfrac{\text{Sales}}{\text{Total assets}}$	$\dfrac{\$600M}{\$438M} = 1.37$	1.15
Accounts receivable turnover	$\dfrac{\text{Sales}}{\text{Accounts receivable}}$	$\dfrac{\$600M}{\$36M} = 16.67$	14.6
Inventory turnover	$\dfrac{\text{Cost of goods sold}}{\text{Inventory}}$	$\dfrac{\$460M}{\$84M} = 5.48$	7.00
Fixed assets turnover	$\dfrac{\text{Sales}}{\text{Fixed assets}}$	$\dfrac{\$600M}{\$295M} = 2.03$	1.75
3. FINANCING DECISIONS			
Debt ratio	$\dfrac{\text{Total debt}}{\text{Total assets}}$	$\dfrac{\$235M}{\$438M} = 53.7\%$	35%
Times interest earned	$\dfrac{\text{Operating income}}{\text{Interest expense}}$	$\dfrac{\$75M}{\$15M} = 5.0X$	7.0X
4. RETURN ON EQUITY			
Return on equity	$\dfrac{\text{Net income}}{\text{Common equity}}$	$\dfrac{\$42M}{\$203M} = 20.7\%$	18%
5. MARKET-VALUE RATIOS			
Price/earnings ratio	$\dfrac{\text{Price per share}}{\text{Earnings per share}}$	$\dfrac{\$32.00}{\$2.10} = 15.24X$	19.0X
Price/book ratio	$\dfrac{\text{Price per share}}{\text{Equity book value per share}}$	$\dfrac{\$32.00}{\$10.15} = 3.15X$	3.7X

How Did You Do?

COMPUTING DISNEY'S PRICE/EARNINGS RATIO AND PRICE/BOOK RATIO

We compute Disney's price/earnings ratio and price/book ratio as follows:

$$\text{Earnings per share} = \frac{\text{net income}}{\text{number of shares}}$$

$$= \frac{\$2.569 \text{ billion}}{2.007 \text{ billion shares}} = \$1.28$$

$$\text{Equity book value per share} = \frac{\text{common equity}}{\text{number of shares}}$$

$$= \frac{\$26.21 \text{ billion}}{2.007 \text{ billion shares}} = \$13.06$$

$$\text{Price/earnings ratio} = \frac{\text{price per share}}{\text{earning per share}}$$

$$= \frac{\$25.47}{\$1.28} = 19.9$$

$$\text{Price/book ratio} = \frac{\text{price per share}}{\text{equity book value per share}}$$

$$= \frac{\$25.47}{\$13.06} = 1.95$$

Disney's stock is selling for 19.9 times its earnings and 1.95 times its book value. At the same time, the average firm in the industry was selling for 25 times its earnings and 2.19 times its book value. Thus, investors see Disney as being dissimilar in terms of its growth prospects and/or the firm's level of risk.

Finance at Work

USING ECONOMIC VALUE ADDED TO MEASURE A FIRM'S FINANCIAL PERFORMANCE

The California Public Employees' Retirement System (CalPERS) invests pension monies that fund the retirement and health benefits for more than 2,500 employers and 1.4 million California public employees, retirees, and their families. CalPERS evaluates the companies in which it invests based in part on economic value added (EVA™). Using EVA™, CalPERS' analysts can determine if a company's poor market performance is due to financial performance problems or other extraneous factors.

Each year CalPERS compiles a list of companies it feels are not performing up to their potential. For example, in 2004, the Walt Disney Company was included as one of four companies on what CalPERS calls its "Focus List." CalPERS, which had millions of dollars invested in Disney at the time, was trying to change the way in which Disney determined the long-term compensation for its managers. The fund wanted their pay based on performance measures, such as economic value added. Other earnings-based methods, such as earnings per share, provide the wrong type of motivation for managers, which eventu-

ally leads to the destruction of shareholder wealth—or so CalPERS contends.

Is CalPERS insistence that EVA be used to measure wealth creation sound? Perhaps so. A Wilshire Associates study concluded that after being put on CalPERS' Focus List, the stock values of companies subsequently outperformed the Standard & Poor's 500 Index by 8.1 percentage points over the course of 5 years. Apparently these companies took CalPERS' suggestions seriously. Wilshire Associates even went so far as to give this phenomenon a name, describing it as the "CalPERS Effect."

As for Disney, after it first appeared on the Focus List, the firm has replaced its CEO. Thereafter, the company's OROA improved from 4.36 percent to 7.73 percent, and the destruction of the wealth, as measured by economic value added, shrunk from ($2.19) billion in 2003 to ($67.3) million in 2005.

Source: "CalPERS Releases 2004 Corporate Governance Focus List." *Business Wire*. Lexis-Nexis, June 9, 2004. Copyright 2004 Business Wire, Inc. at **www.calpers.ca.gov/index.jsp?bc=/about/home.xml**. Posted June 1, 2004. Accessed February 20, 2006.

Did You Get It?

1. What measures can we use to determine whether a firm is creating shareholder value?
2. What is indicated by a price/book ratio that is greater than 1? Less than 1?
3. How does the information provided by a firm's price/book ratio differ from that provided by its price/earnings ratio?
4. How do the profits shown in an income statement differ from economic profits?
5. What is Economic Value Added? What does it tell you?

Can You Do It?

CALCULATING DISNEY'S ECONOMIC VALUE ADDED

Earlier in the chapter, we determined that Disney's operating return on assets (OROA) was 7.73 percent. If Disney's cost of capital (the cost of both its debt and equity capital) was 10 percent at that time, what was the Economic Value Added for the firm when its total assets were approximately $53 billion?

(The solution can be found on the next page.)

Objective **3**

Describe the limitations of financial ratio analysis.

THE LIMITATIONS OF FINANCIAL RATIO ANALYSIS

We conclude this chapter by offering several caveats about using financial ratios. We have described how financial ratios can be used to understand a company's financial position. That said, anyone who works with these ratios needs to be aware of the limitations related to their use. The following list includes some of the more important pitfalls you will encounter as you compute and interpret financial ratios:

1. It is sometimes difficult to determine the industry to which a firm belongs when the firm engages in multiple lines of business. In this case, you must select your own set of peer firms and construct your own norms.
2. Published peer group or industry averages are only approximations. They provide the user with general guidelines, rather than scientifically determined averages of the ratios for all, or even a representative sample, of the firms within an industry.
3. An industry average is not necessarily a desirable target ratio or norm. There is nothing magical about an industry norm. At best, an industry average provides an indication as to the financial position of the average firm within the industry. It does not mean it is the ideal or best value for the ratio. For various reasons, a well-managed company might be above the average, whereas another equally good firm might choose to be below the average.
4. Accounting practices differ widely among firms. For example, different firms choose different methods to depreciate their fixed assets. Differences such as these can make the computed ratios of different firms difficult to compare.
5. Financial ratios can be too high or too low. For example, a current ratio that exceeds the industry norm might signal the presence of excess liquidity, resulting in lower profits relative to the firm's investment in assets. On the other hand, a current ratio that falls below the norm might indicate (1) the possibility that the firm has inadequate liquidity and may at some future date be unable to pay its bills on time, or (2) the firm is managing its accounts receivable and inventories more efficiently than other similar firms.
6. Many firms experience seasonal changes in their operations. As a result, their balance sheet entries and their corresponding ratios will vary with the time of year the statements are prepared. To avoid this problem, an average account balance should be used (one calculated on the basis of several months or quarters during the year) rather than the year-end account balance. For example, an average of the firm's month-end inventory balance might be used to compute its inventory turnover ratio versus a year-end inventory balance.

In spite of their limitations, financial ratios provide us with a very useful tool for assessing a firm's financial condition. We should, however, be aware of their potential weaknesses. In many cases, the "real" value derived from the ratios is that they tell us what additional questions we need to ask about the firm.

How Did You Do?

CALCULATING DISNEY'S ECONOMIC VALUE ADDED

Disney's Economic Value Added (EVA) is calculated as follows:

$$\text{EVA} = \left(\begin{array}{c} \text{operating return} \\ \text{on assets} \end{array} - \begin{array}{c} \text{cost of} \\ \text{all capital} \end{array} \right) \times \text{total assets}$$

$$= (7.73\% - 10\%) \times \$53 \text{ billion} = (\$1.203 \text{ billion})$$

Wow! In the year we are calculating Disney's EVA, 2005, the firm destroyed $1.203 billion in shareholder value by earning a rate of return on the firm's assets that was less than the investors' required rate of return.

Did You Get It?

1. When comparing a firm to its peers, why is it difficult to determine the industry to which the firm belongs?
2. Why do differences in the accounting practices of firms limit the usefulness of financial ratios?
3. Why should you be careful when comparing a firm with industry norms?

Summary

A variety of groups find financial ratios useful. For instance, both managers and shareholders use them to measure and track a company's performance over time. Financial analysts outside of the firm who have an interest in its economic well-being also use financial ratios. An example of this group would be a loan officer of a commercial bank who wishes to determine the creditworthiness of a loan applicant and its ability to pay the interest and principal associated with the loan request.

Financial ratios are the principal tool of financial analysis. Sometimes referred to simply as benchmarks, ratios standardize the financial information of firms so comparisons can be made between firms of varying sizes.

Financial ratios can be used to answer at least five questions: (1) How liquid is the company? (2) Are the company's managers effectively generating profits on the firm's assets? (3) How is the firm financed? (4) Are the firm's managers providing a good return on the capital provided by the shareholders? (5) Are the firm's managers creating or destroying shareholder value?

Two methods can be used to analyze a firm's financial ratios. (1) We can examine the firm's ratios across time (say, for the past 5 years) to compare its current and past performance; and (2) we can compare the firm's ratios with those of other firms. In our example, a peer group was chosen for analyzing the financial position of Davies Inc.

Financial ratios provide a popular way to evaluate a firm's financial performance. However, when evaluating a company's use of its assets (capital) to create firm value, a financial ratio analysis based entirely on the firm's financial statements may not be enough. If we want to understand how the shareholders assess the performance of a company's managers, we can use the market price of the firm's stock relative to its accounting earnings and equity book value.

Economic Value Added (EVA™) provides another approach to evaluate a firm's performance in terms of shareholder value creation. EVA is equal to the return on a company's invested capital less the investors' opportunity cost of the funds times the total amount of the capital invested.

The following are some of the limitations that you will encounter as you compute and interpret financial ratios:

1. It is sometimes difficult to determine an appropriate industry within which to place the firm.
2. Published industry averages are only approximations rather than scientifically determined averages.
3. Accounting practices differ widely among firms and can lead to differences in computed ratios.
4. Some financial ratios can be too high or too low, which makes the results more difficult to interpret.

Objective **1**

Explain the purpose and importance of financial analysis.

Objective **2**

Calculate and use a comprehensive set of measurements to evaluate a company's performance.

Objective **3**

Describe the limitations of financial ratio analysis.

5. An industry average may not be a desirable target ratio or norm.
6. Many firms experience seasonal business conditions. As a result, the ratios calculated for them will vary with the time of year the statements are prepared.

In spite of their limitations, financial ratios provide us with a very useful tool for assessing a firm's financial condition.

Key Terms

Accounts receivable turnover ratio   102

Acid-test (quick) ratio   101

Asset efficiency   105

Average collection period   101

Current ratio   100

Debt ratio   107

Financial ratios   97

Fixed asset turnover   105

Inventory turnover   102

Liquidity   100

Operating profit margin   104

Operating return on assets (OROA)   104

Price/book ratio   113

Price/earnings ratio   113

Return on equity   109

Times interest earned   108

Total asset turnover   105

Review Questions

4-1. Describe the "five-question approach" to using financial ratios.

4-2. Discuss briefly the two perspectives that can be taken when performing a ratio analysis.

4-3. Where can we obtain industry norms?

4-4. What are the limitations of industry average ratios? Discuss briefly.

4-5. What is liquidity, and what is the rationale for its measurement?

4-6. Distinguish between a firm's operating return on assets and operating profit margin.

4-7. Why is a firm's operating return on assets a function of its operating profit margin and total asset turnover?

4-8. What is the difference between a firm's gross profit margin, operating profit margin, and net profit margin?

4-9. What information do the price/earnings ratio and the price/book ratio give us about the firm and its investors?

4-10. Explain what determines a company's return on equity.

4-11. What is Economic Value Added? Why is it used?

Self-Test Problems

ST-1. (*Ratio analysis and short-term liquidity*) Ray's Tool and Supply Company in Austin, Texas, has been expanding its level of operation for the past 2 years. The firm's sales have grown rapidly as a result of the expansion in the Austin economy. However, Ray's is a privately held company, and the only source of available funds it has is a line of credit with the firm's bank. The company needs to expand its inventories to meet the needs of its growing customer base but also wishes to maintain a current ratio of at least 3. If Ray's current assets are $6 million, and its current ratio is now 4, how much can it expand its inventories (finance the expansion with its line of credit) before its target current ratio is violated?

ST-2. (*Ratio analysis*) The statements for M & G Industries are presented below:

M & G Industries Balance Sheet for December 31, 2007 and 2008

	2007		2008	
Cash		$ 9,000		$ 500
Accounts receivable		12,500		16,000
Inventories		29,000		45,500
Total current assets		$ 50,500		$ 62,000
Land	20,000		26,000	
Buildings and equipment	70,000		100,000	
Less accumulated depreciation	(28,000)		(38,000)	
Total fixed assets		$ 62,000		$ 88,000
Total assets		$112,500		$150,000
Accounts payable		$ 10,500		$ 22,000
Short-term bank notes		17,000		47,000
Total current liabilities		$ 27,500		$ 69,000
Long-term debt		28,750		22,950
Common stock		31,500		31,500
Retained earnings		24,750		26,550
Total debt and equity		$112,500		$150,000

M & G Industries Income Statement for the Years Ended
December 31, 2007 and 2008

	2007		2008	
Sales (all credit)		$125,000		$160,000
Cost of goods sold		75,000		96,000
Gross profit		$ 50,000		$ 64,000
Operating expenses				
Fixed cash operating expenses	$ 21,000		$ 21,000	
Variable operating expenses	$ 12,500		16,000	
Depreciation	4,500		10,000	
Total operating expenses		$ 38,000		$ 47,000
Earnings before interest and taxes		$ 12,000		$ 17,000
Interest expense		$ 3,000		$ 6,100
Earnings before taxes		$ 9,000		10,900
Taxes		$ 4,500		$ 5,450
Net income		$ 4,500		$ 5,450

a. Based on the preceding statements, complete the following table:

M & G Industries Ratio Analysis

	INDUSTRY AVERAGES	ACTUAL 2007	ACTUAL 2008
Current ratio	1.80		
Acid-test ratio	0.70		
Average collection period	37.00		
Inventory turnover	2.50		
Debt ratio	58.0%		
Times interest earned	3.80		
Operating profit margin	10.0%		
Total asset turnover	1.14		
Fixed asset turnover	1.40		
Operating return on assets	11.4%		
Return on common equity	9.5%		

b. Evaluate the firm's financial position at the end of 2008 in terms of liquidity, operating return on assets, financing, and return on equity.

c. If in 2008 the firm has 5,000 shares of common stock outstanding selling for $15, what is the (1) firm's earnings per share, (2) price/earnings ratio, and (3) price/book ratio?

Study Problems

4-1. (*Ratio analysis*) Brashear Inc. currently has $2,145,000 in current assets and $858,000 in current liabilities. The company's managers want to increase the firm's inventory, which will be financed by a short-term note with the bank. What level of inventories can the firm carry without its current ratio falling below 2.0?

4-2. (*Ratio analysis*) The Allen Corporation had sales in 2008 of $65 million, total assets of $42 million, and total liabilities of $20 million. The interest rate on the company's debt is 6 percent and its tax rate is 30 percent. The operating profit margin was 12 percent. What was the 2008 operating income and net income? What was operating return on assets and return on equity? Assume that interest must be paid on all of the debt.

4-3. (*Ratio analysis*) Last year, Davies Inc. had sales of $400,000, with a cost of goods sold of $112,000. The firm's operating expenses were $130,000, and its increase in retained earnings was $58,000. There are currently 22,000 common stock shares outstanding and the firm pays a $1.60 dividend per share.

    a. Assuming the firm's earnings are taxed at 34 percent, construct the firm's income statement.
    b. Compute the firm's operating profit margin.
    c. What was the times interest earned?

4-4. (*Ratio analysis*) Greene Inc.'s balance sheet shows a stockholders' equity value of $750,500. The firm's earnings per share was $3, resulting in a price/earnings ratio of 12.25. There are 50,000 shares of common stock outstanding. What is the price/book ratio? What does this indicate about how shareholders view Greene Inc.?

4-5. (*Ratio analysis*) The Mitchem Marble Company has a target current ratio of 2.0 but has experienced some difficulties financing its expanding sales in the past few months. At present the firm has a current ratio of 2.5 and current assets of $2.5 million. If Mitchem expands its receivables and inventories using its short-term line of credit, how much additional short-term funding can it borrow before its current ratio standard is reached?

4-6. (*Ratio analysis*) The balance sheet and income statement for the J. P. Robard Mfg. Company arc as follows:

Balance Sheet ($000)

Cash	$ 500
Accounts receivable	2,000
Inventories	1,000
Current assets	3,500
Net fixed assets	4,500
Total assets	$8,000
Accounts payable	$ 1,100
Accrued expenses	600
Short-term notes payable	300
Current liabilities	$ 2,000
Long-term debt	2,000
Owners' equity	4,000
Total liabilities and owners' equity	$8,000

Income Statement ($000)

Net sales (all credit)	$8,000
Cost of goods sold	(3,300)
Gross profit	4,700
Operating expenses (includes $500 depreciation)	(3,000)
Operating income	$ 1,700
Interest expense	(367)
Earnings before taxes	$ 1,333
Income taxes (40%)	(533)
Net income	$ 800

Calculate the following ratios:

Current ratio	Operating return on assets
Times interest earned	Debt ratio
Inventory turnover	Average collection period
Total asset turnover	Fixed asset turnover
Operating profit margin	Return on equity

4-7. (*Analyzing operating return on assets*) The R. M. Smithers Corporation earned an operating profit margin of 10 percent based on sales of $10 million and total assets of $5 million last year.

    a. What was Smithers' total asset turnover ratio?

    b. During the coming year the company president has set a goal of attaining a total asset turnover of 3.5. How much must firm sales rise, other things being the same, for the goal to be achieved? (State your answer in both dollars and percentage increase in sales.)

    c. What was Smithers' operating return on assets last year? Assuming the firm's operating profit margin remains the same, what will the operating return on assets be next year if the total asset turnover goal is achieved?

4-8. (*Using financial ratios*) The Brenmar Sales Company had a gross profit margin (gross profits ÷ sales) of 30 percent and sales of $9 million last year. Seventy-five percent of the firm's sales are on credit and the remainder are cash sales. Brenmar's current assets equal $1.5 million, its current liabilities equal $300,000, and it has $100,000 in cash plus marketable securities.

    a. If Brenmar's accounts receivable are $562,500, what is its average collection period?

    b. If Brenmar reduces its average collection period to 20 days, what will be its new level of accounts receivable?

    c. Brenmar's inventory turnover ratio is 9 times. What is the level of Brenmar's inventories?

4-9. (*Ratio analysis*) Using Pamplin Inc.'s financial statements shown here:

    a. Compute the following ratios for both 2007 and 2008.

	INDUSTRY NORM	2007	2008
Current ratio	5.00		
Acid-test (quick) ratio	3.00		
Inventory turnover	2.20		
Average collection period	90.00		
Debt ratio	0.33		
Times interest earned	7.00		
Total asset turnover	0.75		
Fixed asset turnover	1.00		
Operating profit margin	20%		
Return on common equity	9%		

    b. How liquid is the firm?

    c. Are its managers generating an adequate operating profit on the firm's assets?

    d. How is the firm financing its assets?

    e. Are its managers generating a good return on equity?

Pamplin Inc. Balance Sheet at 12/31/2007 and 12/31/2008

ASSETS

	2007		2008	
Cash		$ 200		$ 150
Accounts receivable		450		425
Inventory		550		625
Current assets		$ 1,200		$ 1,200
Plant and equipment	$ 2,200		$ 2,600	
Less accumulated depreciation	(1,000)		(1,200)	
Net plant and equipment		$ 1,200		$ 1,400
Total assets		$ 2,400		$ 2,600

LIABILITIES AND OWNERS' EQUITY

Accounts payable		$ 200	$ 150
Notes payable–current (9%)		0	150
Current liabilities		$ 200	$ 300
Bonds (8.33% interest)		600	600
Total debt		$ 800	$ 900
Owners' equity			
Common stock	$ 300		$ 300
Paid-in capital	600		600
Retained earnings	700		800
Total owners' equity		$ 1,600	$ 1,700
Total liabilities and owner's equity		$ 2,400	$ 2,600

Pamplin Inc. Income Statement for Years Ending 12/31/2007 and 12/31/2008

		2007		2008
Sales (all credit)		$1,200		$1,450
Cost of goods sold		700		850
Gross profit		$ 500		$ 600
Operating expenses	30		40	
Depreciation	220	250	200	240
Operating income		$ 250		$ 360
Interest expense		50		64
Net income before taxes		$ 200		$ 296
Taxes (40%)		80		118
Net income		$ 120		$ 178

4-10. (*Financial ratios—investment analysis*) The annual sales for Salco Inc. were $4.5 million last year. The firm's end-of-year balance sheet was as follows:

Current assets	$ 500,000	Liabilities	$1,000,000
Net fixed assets	1,500,000	Owners' equity	1,000,000
	$2,000,000		$2,000,000

The firm's income statement for the year was as follows:

Sales	$ 4,500,000
Less cost of goods sold	(3,500,000)
Gross profit	$ 1,000,000
Less operating expenses	(500,000)
Operating income	$ 500,000
Less interest expense	(100,000)
Earnings before taxes	$ 400,000
Less taxes (50%)	(200,000)
Net income	$ 200,000

a. Calculate Salco's total asset turnover, operating profit margin, and operating return on assets.

b. Salco plans to renovate one of its plants, which will require an added investment in plant and equipment of $1 million. The firm will maintain its present debt ratio of .5 when financing the new investment and expects sales to remain constant. The operating profit margin will rise to 13 percent. What will be the new operating return on assets for Salco after the plant's renovation?

c. Given that the plant renovation in part b occurs and Salco's interest expense rises by $50,000 per year, what will be the return earned on the common stockholders' investment? Compare this rate of return with that earned before the renovation.

4-11. (*Financial analysis*) The T. P. Jarmon Company manufactures and sells a line of exclusive sportswear. The firm's sales were $600,000 for the year just ended, and its total assets exceeded $400,000. The company was started by Mr. Jarmon just 10 years ago and has been profitable every year since its inception. The chief financial officer for the firm, Brent Vehlim, has decided to seek a line of credit from the firm's bank totaling $80,000. In the past, the company has relied on its suppliers to finance a large part of its needs for inventory. However, in recent months tight money conditions have led the firm's suppliers to offer sizable cash discounts to speed up payments for purchases. Mr. Vehlim wants to use the line of credit to replace a large portion of the firm's payables during the summer, which is the firm's peak seasonal sales period.

The firm's two most recent balance sheets were presented to the bank in support of its loan request. In addition, the firm's income statement for the year just ended was provided. These statements are found in the following tables:

T. P. Jarmon Company, Balance Sheet for 12/31/2007 and 12/31/2008

	2007	2008
Cash	$ 15,000	$ 14,000
Marketable securities	6,000	6,200
Accounts receivable	42,000	33,000
Inventory	51,000	84,000
Prepaid rent	1,200	1,100
Total current assets	$ 115,200	$138,300
Net plant and equipment	286,000	270,000
Total assets	$401,200	$408,300
Accounts payable	$ 48,000	$ 57,000
Notes payable	15,000	13,000
Accruals	6,000	5,000
Total current liabilities	$ 69,000	$ 75,000
Long-term debt	160,000	150,000
Common stockholders' equity	172,200	183,300
Total liabilities and equity	$401,200	$408,300

T. P. Jarmon Company, Income Statement for the Year Ended 12/31/2008

Sales (all credit)		$600,000
Less cost of goods sold		460,000
Gross profit		$140,000
Less operating and interest expenses		
General and administrative	$ 30,000	
Interest	10,000	
Depreciation	30,000	
Total		70,000
Earnings before taxes		$ 70,000
Less taxes		27,100
Net income available to common stockholders		$ 42,900
Less cash dividends		31,800
Change in retained earnings		$ 11,100

Jan Fama, associate credit analyst for the Merchants National Bank of Midland, Michigan, was assigned the task of analyzing Jarmon's loan request.

a. Calculate the financial ratios for 2008 corresponding to the industry norms provided as follows:

RATIO	NORM
Current ratio	1.8
Acid-test ratio	0.9
Debt ratio	0.5
Times interest earned	10.0
Average collection period	20.0
Inventory turnover (based on cost of goods sold)	7.0
Return on common equity	12.0%
Operating return on assets	16.8%
Operating profit margin	14.0%
Total asset turnover	1.20
Fixed asset turnover	1.80

b. Which of the ratios reported in the industry norms do you feel should be most crucial in determining whether the bank should extend the line of credit?

c. Compute Jarmon's free cash flows for the year ended December 31, 2008. Interpret your findings.

d. Use the information provided by the financial ratios and the cash flow statement to decide if you would support making the loan.

4-12. (*Economic Value Added*) Stegemoller Inc.'s managers want to evaluate the firm's prior-year performance in terms of its contribution to shareholder value. This past year, the firm earned an operating income return on investment of 12 percent, compared to an industry norm of 11 percent. It has been estimated that the firm's investors have an opportunity cost on their funds of 14 percent. The firm's total assets for the year were $100 million. Compute the amount of economic value created or destroyed by the firm. How does your finding support or fail to support what you would conclude using ratio analysis to evaluate the firm's performance?

Web Works

4-WW1. Go to the Web site for IBM at **www.ibm.com/investor**. Click "Investor tools" and then "Investment guides" for a guide to reading financial statements. How does the guide differ from the presentation in Chapter 3 and this chapter?

4-WW2.

a. Go to **www.investor.reuters.com**. (You will need to sign up for a free membership before being able to access all the information on the site.) Type in the symbol for Starbucks (SBUX) in the "Quote" box and then click "Go." Click the "Financial Statements" link on the left side of the Web page and examine Starbucks' financial statements.

b. After becoming familiar with the financial statements for Starbucks, click on the "Ratios" link in the left margin to see a large number of ratios that have been calculated for the company. There are many more ratios than what we presented, and some have been calculated differently than we did—a problem that occurs frequently when using different sources of ratios. Which ratios are familiar to you? How have the ratios changed for Starbucks Corporation over the past 5 years (look at the 5-year averages)?

4-WW3. Being able to identify an industry to use for benchmarking your firm's results with similar companies is frequently not easy. Choose a type of business and go to **www.naics.com**. This Web site allows you to do a free search for the NAICS (North American Industry Classification System, pronounced *Nakes*) number for different types of businesses. Choose keywords such as "athletic shoes" or "auto dealers" and others to see what industry to which they have been assigned.

Mini Case

Go to **http://finance.yahoo.com/** and locate current financial information for GM and Toyota, both in terms of the company's current financial statements and stock market prices. With this information:

a. Compute the financial ratios for both firms for the most recent year, and evaluate the relative performance of the two firms in the following areas:

1. Liquidity
2. Operating profitability
3. Financing practices
4. Return on the shareholders' investment

b. What is each firm's price/earnings ratio and market/book ratio? What do these ratios tell you?

c. Assume that the cost of capital (investors' required rate of return) is 8 percent for both companies. Calculate the EVA for each company. Interpret your findings.

Self-Test Solutions

SS-1. Note that the current ratio for Ray's Tool and Supply Company before its inventory expansion is as follows:

current ratio = $6,000,000/current liabilities = 4

Thus, the firm's level of current liabilities is $1.5 million. If the expansion in inventories is financed entirely with borrowed funds, then the change in inventories is equal to the change in the firm's current liabilities. Thus, the firm's current ratio after the expansion can be defined as follows:

$$\text{current ratio} = \frac{\$6,000,000 + \text{change in inventory}}{\$1,500,000 + \text{change in inventory}} = 3$$

Note that we set the new current ratio equal to the firm's target of 3. Solving for the change in inventory in the equation, we determine that the firm can expand its inventories by $750,000, finance the expansion with current liabilities, and still maintain its target current ratio.

SS-2.

a. M & G Industries Ratio Analysis

	INDUSTRY AVERAGES	ACTUAL 2007	ACTUAL 2008
Current ratio	1.80	1.84	0.90
Acid-test ratio	0.70	0.78	0.24
Average collection period (based on a 365-day year and end-of-year figures)	37.00	36.50	36.50
Inventory turnover	2.50	2.59	2.11
Debt ratio	58%	50%	61.3%
Times interest earned	3.80	4.00	2.79
Operating profit margin	10%	9.6%	10.6%
Total asset turnover	1.14	1.11	1.07
Fixed asset turnover	1.40	2.02	1.82
Operating return on assets	11.4%	10.67%	11.3%
Return on common equity	9.5%	8.0%	9.4%

b. M & G's liquidity is poor, as suggested by its low current ratio and acid-test ratio in 2008; also, the firm's inventories are turning over slowly compared to the industry norm. In 2008, M & G's managers are doing a satisfactory job of generating profits on the firm's operating assets, as indicated by the operating return on assets. Note that the operating return on assets in 2008 is about the same as the industry average, owing to a slightly above-average operating profit margin combined with a slightly below-average total asset turnover ratio. The problem with the total asset turnover ratio comes from slow inventory turnover. M & G has increased its use of debt to the point of using slightly more debt than the average company in the industry. As a result, the firm's coverage of interest has decreased to a point well below the industry norm.

c.

1. $\text{Earnings per share} = \dfrac{\text{net income}}{\text{number of shares outstanding}} = \dfrac{\$5,450}{5,000} = \$1.09$

2. $\text{Price/earnings ratio} = \dfrac{\text{market price share}}{\text{earnings per share}} = \dfrac{\$15.00}{\$1.09} = 13.76$

3. $\text{Price/book ratio} = \dfrac{\text{market price share}}{\text{book value per share}} = \dfrac{\$15.00}{\$11.61} = 1.29$

where

$$\text{book value per share} = \frac{\text{total book equity value}}{\text{number of shares outstanding}}$$

$$= \frac{\$31,500 + \$26,550}{5,000 \text{ shares}}$$

$$= \frac{\$58,050}{5,000 \text{ shares}} = \$11.61$$

PART 2

The Valuation of Financial Assets

➤ As a partner at Ernst & Young, a national accounting and consulting firm, Don Erickson is in charge of the business valuation practice for the firm's Southwest region. Erickson's sole job for the firm is valuing companies, or what he calls a dedicated valuation practice. He has national responsibilities for valuing certain industries. In this role, he works with managers of major companies from across the nation. Although he has valued businesses of all kinds and sizes, he primarily focuses on certain industries, such as oil and gas firms and major league sports franchises. For instance, he has valued a number of major league sports clubs, including NFL, NBA, NHL, and major league baseball teams.

Erickson explains, "Valuing a company is an interesting, even intriguing, process. It requires having an understanding of the outlook of the specific business and the nature of the industry, which allows us to predict multiple scenarios of the future. More specifically, it is crucial to understand the two key value drivers: the company's risk and expected growth. If I were to name one variable that matters the most in estimating a firm's value and is the most difficult thing to determine, it would be our estimate of the firm's *growth rate*."

Erickson continues, "In valuing a business, we use several methods, the most important being a discounted cash flow approach. I am a true believer that the value of a company is the present value of the firm's expected future free cash flows."

When asked about the discount rate used in finding the present value of a firm's cash flows, he says, "In almost all cases, we use the *effective market discount rate*. In this approach, we estimate the discount rate for companies that have recently been sold. Alternatively, we may compute an *imputed discount rate* for the industry. In both cases, we will then adjust the discount rate for company-specific risk. The greater the inherent risk, the higher the discount rate.

"Let me also say that it is essential that an operating manager be familiar with what determines firm value. Due to recent changes in accounting rules for any firm that is audited, accounting and finance are becoming increasingly interconnected. The changes will make it all the more important for a manager to understand how much value is being created, not just at the firm level, but also at the division level."

The chapters in this part of the text will provide you a basic understanding of valuation concepts and procedures—the same ones that Erickson uses in valuing a company, or almost any business asset for that matter. We will explain the role of risk, which Erickson identifies as a matter of importance, and then see how to value a company's bonds and its stock.

CHAPTER 5

The Time Value of Money

In business, there is probably no other single concept with more power or applications than that of the time value of money. In his landmark book, *A History of Interest Rates*, Sidney Homer noted that if $1,000 was invested for 400 years at 8 percent interest, it would grow to $23 quadrillion—that would work out to approximately $5 million per person on earth. He was not giving a plan to make the world rich but effectively pointing out the power of the time value of money.

The time value of money is certainly not a new concept. Benjamin Franklin had a good understanding of how it worked when he left £1,000 each to Boston and Philadelphia. With the gift, he left instructions that the cities were to lend the money, charging the going interest rate, to worthy apprentices. Then, after the money had been invested in this way for 100 years, they were to use a portion of the investment to build something of benefit to the city and hold some back for the future. Two hundred years later, Franklin's Boston gift resulted in the construction of the Franklin Union, has helped countless medical students with loans, and still has over $3 million left in the account. Philadelphia, likewise, has reaped a significant reward from his gift with its portion of the gift growing to over $2 million. Bear in mind that all this has come from a gift of £2,000 with some serious help from the time value of money.

The power of the time value of money can also be illustrated through a story Andrew Tobias tells in his book *Money Angles*. There he tells of a peasant who wins a chess tournament put on by the king. The king then asks the peasant what he would like as the prize. The peasant answers that he would like for his village one piece of grain to be placed on the first square of his chessboard, two pieces of grain on the second square, four pieces on the third, eight on the fourth, and so forth. The king, thinking he was getting off easy, pledged on his word of honor that it would be done. Unfortunately for the king, by the time all 64 squares on the chessboard were filled, there were 18.5 million trillion grains of wheat on the board—the kernels were compounding at a rate of 100 percent over the 64 squares of the chessboard. Needless to say, no one in the village ever went hungry; in fact, that is so much wheat that if each kernel were one-quarter inch long (quite frankly, I have no idea how long a kernel of wheat is, but Andrew Tobias's guess is one-quarter inch), if laid end to end, they could stretch to the sun and back 391,320 times.

Understanding the techniques of compounding and moving money through time is critical to almost every business decision. It will help you to understand such varied things as how stocks and bonds are valued, how to determine the value of a new project, how much you should save for children's education, and how much your mortgage payments will be.

In the next five chapters, we focus on determining the value of the firm and the desirability of the investments it considers making. A key concept that underlies this material is the time value of money; that is, a dollar today is worth more than a dollar received a year from now. Intuitively this idea is easy to understand. We are all familiar with the concept of interest. This concept illustrates what economists call an opportunity cost of passing up the earning potential of a dollar today. This opportunity cost is the time value of money.

To evaluate and compare investment proposals, we need to examine how dollar values might accrue from accepting these proposals. To do this, all the dollar values must first be comparable. In other words, we must move all dollar flows back to the present or out to a common future date. An understanding of the time value of money is essential, therefore, to an understanding of financial management, whether basic or advanced.

<table>
<tr><td>Objective   1</td><td></td></tr>
</table>

Explain the mechanics of compounding, that is how money grows over time when it is invested.

compound interest the situation in which interest paid on an investment during the first period is added to the principal. During the second period, interest is earned on the original principal plus the interest earned during the first period.

COMPOUND INTEREST AND FUTURE VALUE

Most of us encounter the concept of compound interest at an early age. Anyone who has ever had a savings account or purchased a government savings bond has received compound interest. **Compound interest** occurs when *interest paid on the investment during the first period is added to the principal; then, during the second period, interest is earned on this new sum.*

For example, suppose we place $100 in a savings account that pays 6 percent interest, compounded annually. How will our savings grow? At the end of the first year we have earned 6 percent, or $6 on our initial deposit of $100, giving us a total of $106 in our savings account. The mathematical formula illustrating this phenomenon is

$$FV_1 = PV(1 + i) \tag{5-1}$$

where FV_1 = the future value of the investment at the end of one year
$\quad\quad i$ = the annual interest (or discount) rate
$\quad\quad PV$ = the present value, or original amount invested at the beginning of the first year

In our example

$$\begin{aligned} FV_1 &= PV(1 + i) \\ &= \$100(1 + .06) \\ &= \$100(1.06) \\ &= \$106 \end{aligned}$$

Carrying these calculations one period further, we find that we now earn the 6 percent interest on a principal of $106, which means we earn $6.36 in interest during the second year. Why do we earn more interest during the second year than we did during the first? Simply because we now earn interest on the sum of the original principal and the interest we earned in the first year. In effect we are now earning interest on interest; this is the concept of compound interest. Examining the mathematical formula illustrating the earning of interest in the second year, we find

$$FV_2 = FV_1(1 + i) \tag{5-2}$$

which, for our example, gives

$$\begin{aligned} FV_2 &= \$106(1.06) \\ &= \$112.36 \end{aligned}$$

▰▰▰ *Remember Your Principles*

In this chapter we develop the tools to incorporate **Principle 2: The Time Value of Money—A Dollar Received Today Is Worth More Than a Dollar Received in the Future** into our calculations. In coming chapters we use this concept to measure value by bringing the benefits and costs from a project back to the present.

Looking back at equation (5-1), we can see that FV_1, or $106, is actually equal to $PV(1 + i)$, or $100(1 + .06)$. If we substitute these values into equation (5-2), we get

$$FV_2 = PV(1 + i)(1 + i)$$
$$= PV(1 + i)^2$$

(5-3)

Carrying this forward into the third year, we find that we enter the year with $112.36 and we earn 6 percent, or $6.74 in interest, giving us a total of $119.10 in our savings account. Expressing this mathematically:

$$FV_3 = FV_2(1 + i)$$

(5-4)

which, for our example, gives

$$FV_3 = \$112.36(1.06)$$
$$= \$119.10$$

If we substitute the value in equation (5-3) for FV_2 into equation (5-4), we find

$$FV_3 = PV(1 + i)(1 + i)(1 + i)$$
$$= PV(1 + i)^3$$

(5-5)

By now a pattern is becoming apparent. We can generalize this formula to illustrate the value of our investment if it is compounded annually at a rate of i for n years to be

$$FV_n = PV(1 + i)^n$$

(5–6)

where FV_n = the future value of the investment at the end of n years
  n = the number of years during which the compounding occurs
  i = the annual interest (or discount) rate
  PV = the present value or original amount invested at the beginning of the first year

Table 5-1 illustrates how this investment of $100 would continue to grow for the first 10 years at a compound interest rate of 6 percent. Notice how the amount of interest earned annually increases each year. Again, the reason is that each year interest is received on the sum of the original investment plus any interest earned in the past.

Keep in mind that future cash flows are assumed to occur at the end of the time period (t) during which they accrue. For example, if a cash flow of $100 occurs in time period 5 (or year 5, as in Table 5-1), it is assumed to occur at the end of time period 5, which is also the beginning of time period 6 (year 6). In addition, cash flows that occur in time $t = 0$ occur right now; that is, they are already in present dollars.

When we examine the relationship between the number of years an initial investment is compounded for and its future value as shown graphically in Figure 5-1, we see that we can increase the future value of an investment by either increasing the number of years for which we let it compound or by compounding it at a higher interest rate. We can also see this from equation (5-6) because an increase in either i or n while PV is held constant results in an increase in FV_n.

TABLE 5-1   An Illustration of Compound Interest Calculations

YEAR	BEGINNING VALUE	INTEREST EARNED	ENDING VALUE
1	$100.00	$ 6.00	$106.00
2	106.00	6.36	112.36
3	112.36	6.74	119.10
4	119.10	7.15	126.25
5	126.25	7.57	133.82
6	133.82	8.03	141.85
7	141.85	8.51	150.36
8	150.36	9.02	159.38
9	159.38	9.57	168.95
10	168.95	10.13	179.08

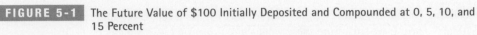

FIGURE 5-1 The Future Value of $100 Initially Deposited and Compounded at 0, 5, 10, and 15 Percent

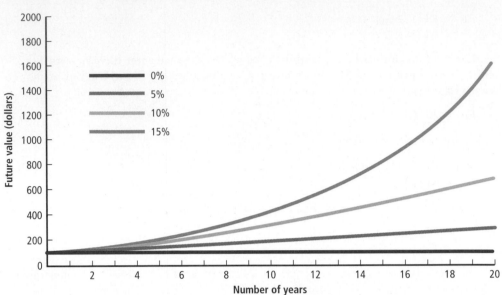

➤ EXAMPLE

If we place $1,000 in a savings account paying 5 percent interest compounded annually, how much will our account accrue to in 10 years? Substituting $PV = \$1,000$, $i = 5$ percent, and $n = 10$ years into equation (5-6), we get

$$FV_n = PV(1 + i)^n$$
$$= \$1,000(1 + .05)^{10}$$
$$= \$1,000(1.62889)$$
$$= \$1,628.89$$

Thus, at the end of 10 years we will have $1,628.89 in our savings account.

Objective **2**

Be able to move money through time using time value of money tables, financial calculators, and spreadsheets.

TABLES, CALCULATORS, AND SPREADSHEETS— THREE ALTERNATIVES TO SOLVING TIME VALUE OF MONEY PROBLEMS

There are three different approaches that you can use to solve a time value of money problem. The first is to use the time value of money tables that appear in Appendix B in the back of the book. These tables do much of the math for you and solve for the present or future value of $1 for a range of i and n values. Financial calculators are a second alternative, and there are a number of them that do a good job of solving time value of money problems. Based on many years of experience, the Texas Instruments BA II Plus calculator would be an excellent choice. Finally, spreadsheets can move money through time, and in the real world, they are without question the tool of choice. Now let's take a look at all three alternatives.

The Time Value of Money (TVM) Tables Solution

future-value interest factor
$(FVIF_{i, n})$ the value $(1 + i)^n$ used as a multiplier to calculate an amount's future value.

Because determining an investment's future value can be quite time consuming when it is held for a number of years, the **future-value interest factor** for i and n ($FVIF_{i, n}$), defined as $(1 + i)^n$, has been compiled in the back of the book for various values of i and n. An abbreviated compound interest, or future-value interest, factor table appears in Table 5-2, a more comprehensive version of this table appearing in Appendix B at the back of this book. Alternatively, the $FVIF_{i, n}$ values can easily be determined using a calculator. Note that the

TABLE 5-2 $FVIF_{i,n}$, or the Compound Sum of $1

n	1%	2%	3%	4%	5%	6%	7%	8%	9%	10%
1	1.010	1.020	1.030	1.040	1.050	1.060	1.070	1.080	1.090	1.100
2	1.020	1.040	1.061	1.082	1.102	1.124	1.145	1.166	1.188	1.210
3	1.030	1.061	1.093	1.125	1.158	1.191	1.225	1.260	1.295	1.331
4	1.041	1.082	1.126	1.170	1.216	1.262	1.311	1.360	1.412	1.464
5	1.051	1.104	1.159	1.217	1.276	1.338	1.403	1.469	1.539	1.611
6	1.062	1.126	1.194	1.265	1.340	1.419	1.501	1.587	1.677	1.772
7	1.072	1.149	1.230	1.316	1.407	1.504	1.606	1.714	1.828	1.949
8	1.083	1.172	1.267	1.369	1.477	1.594	1.718	1.851	1.993	2.144
9	1.094	1.195	1.305	1.423	1.551	1.689	1.838	1.999	2.172	2.358
10	1.105	1.219	1.344	1.480	1.629	1.791	1.967	2.159	2.367	2.594
11	1.116	1.243	1.384	1.539	1.710	1.898	2.105	2.332	2.580	2.853
12	1.127	1.268	1.426	1.601	1.796	2.012	2.252	2.518	2.813	3.138
13	1.138	1.294	1.469	1.665	1.886	2.133	2.410	2.720	3.066	3.452
14	1.149	1.319	1.513	1.732	1.980	2.261	2.579	2.937	3.342	3.797
15	1.161	1.346	1.558	1.801	2.079	2.397	2.759	3.172	3.642	4.177

compounding factors given in these tables represent the value of $1 compounded at rate i at the *end* of the nth year. Thus, to calculate the future value of an initial investment, we need only to determine the $FVIF_{i,n}$ using a calculator or the tables at the end of the text and multiply this times the initial investment. In effect, we can rewrite equation (5-6) as follows:

$$FV_n = PV(1 + i)^n = PV(FVIF_{i,n}) \tag{5-6a}$$

➤ EXAMPLE

If we invest $500 in a bank where it will earn 8 percent compounded annually, how much will it be worth at the end of 7 years? Looking at Table 5-2 in the row $n = 7$ and column $i = 8\%$, we find that $FVIF_{8\%,\,7\,yr}$ has a value of 1.714. Substituting this into equation (5-6a), we find

$$FV_n - PV(1 + .08)^7 = PV(FVIF_{8\%,\,7\,yr})$$
$$= \$500(1.714)$$
$$= \$857$$

Thus, we will have $857 at the end of 7 years.

In the future we will find several uses for equation (5-6a); not only can we find the future value of an investment, but we can also solve for PV, i, or n. In any case, you will be given three of the four variables and will have to solve for the fourth.

➤ EXAMPLE

Solving for n: Let's assume that the DaimlerChrysler Corporation has guaranteed that the price of a new Jeep will always be $20,000, and you'd like to buy one but currently have only $7,752. How many years will it take for your initial investment of $7,752 to grow to $20,000 if it is invested at 9 percent compounded annually? We can use equation (5-6a) to solve for this problem as well. Substituting the known values in equation (5-6a), you find

$$FV_n = PV(1 + i)^n = PV(FVIF_{i,n})$$
$$\$20,000 = \$7,752(FVIF_{9\%,\,n\,yr})$$
$$\frac{\$20,000}{\$7,752} = \frac{\$7,752(FVIF_{9\%,\,n\,yr})}{\$7,752}$$
$$2.58 = FVIF_{9\%,\,n\,yr}$$

Thus, you are looking for a value of 2.58 in the $FVIF_{i,n}$ tables, and you know it must be in the 9% column. To finish solving the problem, look down the 9% column for the value closest to 2.58. You find that it occurs in the $n = 11$ row. Thus it will take 11 years for an initial investment of $7,752 to grow to $20,000 if it is invested at 9 percent compounded annually.

➤ **EXAMPLE**

Solving for i: Now let's solve for the compound annual growth rate, and let's go back to that Jeep that always costs $20,000. In 10 years, you'd really like to have $20,000 to buy a new Jeep, but you only have $11,167. At what rate must your $11,167 be compounded annually for it to grow to $20,000 in 10 years? Substituting the known variables into equation (5-6a), you get

$$FV_n = PV(1 + i)^n = PV(FVIF_{i,n})$$
$$\$20,000 = \$11,167(FVIF_{i,10\,yr})$$
$$\frac{\$20,000}{\$11,167} = \frac{\$11,167(FVIF_{i,10\,yr})}{\$11,167}$$
$$1.791 = FVIF_{i,10\,yr}$$

You know to look in the $n = 10$ row of the $FVIF_{i,n}$ tables for a value of 1.791, and you find this in the $i = 6\%$ column. Thus, if you want your initial investment of $11,167 to grow to $20,000 in 10 years, you must invest it at 6 percent.

➤ **EXAMPLE**

Solving for i: At what rate must $100 be compounded annually for it to grow to $179.10 in 10 years? In this case we know the initial investment, $PV = \$100$; the future value of this investment at the end of n years, $FV_n = \$179.10$; and the number of years that the initial investment will compound for, $n = 10$ years. Substituting into equation (5-6), we get

$$FV_n = PV(1 + i)^n$$
$$\$179.10 = \$100(1 + i)^{10}$$
$$1.791 = (1 + i)^{10}$$

We know to look in the $n = 10$ row of the $FVIF_{i,n}$ table for a value of 1.791, and we find this in the $i = 6\%$ column. Thus, if we want our initial investment of $100 to accrue to $179.10 in 10 years, we must invest it at 6 percent.

Just how powerful is the time value of money? Manhattan Island was purchased by Peter Minuit from the Native Americans in 1626 for $24 in "knickknacks" and jewelry. If at the end of 1626 the Native Americans had invested their $24 at 8 percent compounded annually, it would be worth over $120 trillion today (by the end of 2006, 380 years later). That's certainly enough to buy back all of Manhattan—in fact, with $120 trillion in the bank, the $80 billion to $90 billion you'd have to pay to buy back all of Manhattan would seem like pocket change. This story illustrates the incredible power of time in compounding. There simply is no substitute for it.

One of the problems with using the time value of money tables is that they express interest rates only in whole numbers. Unfortunately, in the real world interest rates are quoted to the second, third, or fourth decimal place. As a result, the time value of money tables have fallen out of favor and been replaced by financial calculators and spreadsheets, which we discuss next.

The Financial Calculator Solution

Time value of money calculations can be made simple with the aid of a *financial calculator*. To solve time value of money problems with a financial calculator, you will be given three of four variables and will have to solve for the fourth. Before presenting any solutions using a financial calculator, we introduce the calculator's five most common keys. (In most time value of money problems, only four of these keys are relevant.) These keys are

N I/Y PV PMT FV

where:

N stores (or calculates) the total number of payments or compounding periods.

I/Y stores (or calculates) the interest or discount rate.

PV stores (or calculates) the present value of a cash flow or series of cash flows.

FV stores (or calculates) the future value, that is, the dollar amount of a final cash flow or the compound value of a single flow or series of cash flows.

PMT stores (or calculates) the dollar amount of each annuity payment deposited or received at the end of each year.

As previously stated, in any problem you will be given three of four variables. These four variables will always include *N* and *I/Y*; in addition, two out of the final three variables—*PV*, *FV*, and *PMT*—will also be included. To solve a time value of money problem using a financial calculator, all you need to do is enter the appropriate numbers for three of the four variables and then press the key of the final variable to calculate its value. It is also a good idea to enter zero for any of the five variables not included in the problem in order to clear that variable.

Now let's solve the previous example using a financial calculator. We were trying to find at what rate $100 must be compounded annually for it to grow to $179.10 in 10 years. The solution using a financial calculator would be as follows:

CALCULATOR SOLUTION

Data Input	Function Key
10	N
−100	PV
179.10	FV
0	PMT

Function Key	Answer
CPT	
I/Y	6.00

Any of the problems in this chapter can easily be solved using a financial calculator, and the solutions to many examples using a Texas Instruments BA II Plus financial calculator are provided in the margins.

Calculators are pretty easy to use. When people have problems with calculators, it is usually the result of a few common mistakes. Before you take a crack at solving a problem using a financial calculator:

1. Set your calculator to one payment per year. Some financial calculators use monthly payments as the default; change it to annual payments.
2. Set your calculator to display at least four decimal places. Most calculators are preset to display only two decimal places. Because interest rates are so small, change your decimal setting to at least four.
3. Set your calculator to the "end" mode. Your calculator will assume cash flows occur at the end of each time period.

When you're ready to work a problem, remember:

1. Every problem will have at least one positive and one negative number.
2. You must enter a zero for any variable that isn't used in a problem, or you have to clear the calculator before beginning a new problem. If you don't clear your calculator or enter a value for one of the variables, your calculator won't assume that that variable is zero. Instead, your calculator will assume it carries the same number as it did during the previous problem.

3. Enter the interest rate as a percent, not a decimal. That means 10% must be entered as 10 rather than .10.

Without question, the two most popular financial calculators are the Texas Instruments BA II Plus (TI BA II Plus) and the Hewlett-Packard 10BII (HP 10BII). If you're using one of these calculators and encounter any problems, just take a look at Appendix A at the end of the book—it provides a tutorial for both of these calculators.

Also, you will notice that solutions using the present-value tables versus solutions using a calculator may vary slightly—this is a result of rounding errors in the tables.

Obviously, the choice of the interest rate plays a critical role in how much an investment grows, but do small changes in the interest rate have much of an impact on future values? To answer this question, let's look back at Peter Minuit's purchase of Manhattan. If the Native Americans had invested their $24 at 10 percent rather than 8 percent compounded annually at the end of 1626, they would have over $128 quadrillion by the end of 2006 (380 years later). That is 128 followed by 15 zeros, or $128,000,000,000,000,000. Actually, that is enough to buy back not only Manhattan Island but also the entire world and still have plenty left over! Now let's assume a lower interest rate—say 6 percent. In that case the $24 would have only grown to a mere $99.2 billion—less than one one-thousandth of what it grew to at 8 percent, and less than one-millionth of what it would have grown to at 10 percent. With today's real estate prices, you'd have a tough time buying Manhattan with $99.2 billion, and if you did, you probably couldn't pay your taxes! To say the least, the interest rate is extremely important in investing.

The Spreadsheet Solution

Without question, in the real world most calculations involving moving money through time will be carried out with the help of a spreadsheet. Although there are several competing spreadsheets, the most popular one is Microsoft Excel. Just as with the keystroke calculations on a financial calculator, a spreadsheet can make easy work of most common financial calculations. Listed here are some of the most common functions used with Excel when moving money through time:

Calculation	Formula
Present value	= PV(rate,number of periods,payment,future value,type)
Future value	= FV(rate,number of periods,payment,present value,type)
Payment	= PMT(rate,number of periods,present value,future value,type)
Number of periods	= $NPER$(rate,payment,present value,future value,type)
Interest rate	= $RATE$(number of periods,payment,present value,future value,type, guess)

where | rate | = i, the interest rate or discount rate
| | number of periods | = n, the number of years or periods
| | payment | = PMT, the annuity payment deposited or received at the end of each period
| | future value | = FV, the future value of the investment at the end of n periods or years
| | present value | = PV, the present value of the future sum of money
| | type | = when the payment is made (0 if omitted)
| | | 0 = at end of period
| | | 1 = at beginning of period
| | guess | = a starting point when calculating the interest rate; if omitted, the calculations begin with a value of 0.1 or 10%

Just like with a financial calculator, the outflows have to be entered as negative numbers. In general, each problem will have two cash flows: one positive and one negative. The idea is that you deposit money at some point in time (an outflow or negative value), and at some point later in time, you withdraw your money (an inflow or positive value). For example, let's look back on the example on page 135.

	A	B	C	D	E	F	G
1							
2		Spreadsheets and the Time Value of Money					
3							
4	If we invest $500 in a bank where it will earn 8 percent compounded						
5	annually, how much will it be worth at the end of 7 years?						
6							
7			rate (i) =	8%			
8		number of periods (n) =		7			
9		payment (PMT) =		$0			
10		present value (PV) =		$500			
11		type (0 = at end of period) =		0			
12							
13			Future value =	$856.91			
14							
15	Excel formula: =FV(rate,number of periods,payment,present value,type)						
16							
17	Entered value in cell d13: =FV(d7,d8,d9,–d10,d11)						
18	Notice that present value ($500) took on a negative value.						
19							

Entered values in cell d13:
=FV(d7,d8,d9,–d10,d11)

	A	B	C	D	E	F	G	H
1								
2			Spreadsheets: Solving for i					
3								
4	In 10 years you'd like to have $20,000 to buy a new Jeep, but you only							
5	have $11,167. At what rate must your $11,167 be compounded							
6	annually for it to grow to $20,000 in 10 years?							
7								
8		number of periods (n) =		10				
9		payment (PMT) =		$0				
10		present value (PV) =		$11,167				
11		future value (FV) =		$20,000				
12		type (0 = at end of period) =		0				
13			guess =					
14								
15			i =	6.00%				
16								
17	Excel formula: =RATE(number of periods,payment,present value,future value,type,guess)							
18								
19	Entered value in cell d15: =RATE(d8,d9, d10,d11,d12,d13)							
20								
21	Notice that present value ($11,167) took on a negative value.							
22	Also note that if you didn't assign a value to guess, it would begin calculations							
23	with a value of 0.1 or 10%. If it could not come up with a value for i after							
24	20 iterations, you would receive the #NUM! error message. Generally a							
25	guess between 10 and 100 percent will work.							
26								

Entered values in cell d15:
=RATE(d8,d9,–d10,d11,d12,d13)

Did You Get It?

1. Principle 2 states that "a dollar received today is worth more than a dollar received in the future." Explain this statement.
2. How does compound interest differ from simple interest?
3. Explain the formula $FV_n = PV(1 + i)^n$.

PRESENT VALUE

Up to this point we have been moving money forward in time; that is, we know how much we have to begin with and are trying to determine how much that sum will grow in a certain number of years when compounded at a specific rate. We are now going to look at the reverse question: What is the value in today's dollars of a sum of money to be received in the future? The answer to this question will help us determine the desirability of investment projects in Chapters 9 and 10. In this case we are moving future money back to the present. We will determine the **present value** of a lump sum, which in simple terms is the *current value of a future payment*. In fact, we will be doing nothing other than inverse compounding.

Objective **3**

Discuss the relationship between compounding and bringing the value of money back to the present.

present value the value in today's dollars of a future payment discounted back to present at the required rate of return.

The differences in these techniques come about merely from the investor's point of view. In compounding, we talked about the compound interest rate and the initial investment; in determining the present value, we will talk about the discount rate and present value of future cash flows. Determining the discount rate is the subject of Chapter 11 and can be defined as the rate of return available on an investment of equal risk to what is being discounted. Other than that, the technique and the terminology remain the same, and the mathematics are simply reversed. In equation (5-6) we were attempting to determine the future value of an initial investment. We now want to determine the initial investment or present value. By dividing both sides of equation (5-6) by $(1 + i)^n$, we get

$$PV = FV_n \left[\frac{1}{(1 + i)^n} \right] \tag{5-7}$$

where FV_n = the future value of the investment at the end of n years
n = the number of years until the payment will be received
i = the annual discount (or interest) rate
PV = the present value of the future sum of money

Because the mathematical procedure for determining the present value is exactly the inverse of determining the future value, we also find that the relationships among n, i, and PV are just the opposite of those we observed in future value. The present value of a future sum of money is inversely related to both the number of years until the payment will be received and the discount rate. This relationship is shown in Figure 5–2. Although the present value equation [equation (5-7)] is used extensively to evaluate new investment proposals, it should be stressed that the equation is actually the same as the future value, or compounding equation [equation (5-6)], only it is solved for PV instead of FV.

➤ EXAMPLE

What is the present value of $500 to be received 10 years from today if our discount rate is 6 percent? Substituting $FV_{10} = \$500$, $n = 10$, and $i = 6$ percent into equation (5-7), we find

$$PV = \$500 \left[\frac{1}{(1 + .06)^{10}} \right]$$

$$= \$500 \left(\frac{1}{1.791} \right)$$

$$= \$500(.558)$$

$$= \$279$$

Thus, the present value of the $500 to be received in 10 years is $279.

CALCULATOR SOLUTION

Data Input	Function Key
10	N
6	I/Y
500	FV
0	PMT

Function Key	Answer
CPT	
PV	−279.20

present-value interest factor ($PVIF_{i, n}$) the value $[1/(1 + i)^n]$ used as a multiplier to calculate an amount's present value.

To help you compute present values, the **present-value interest factor** for i and n (**$PVIF_{i, n}$**), defined as $[1/(1 + i)^n]$, has been compiled for various combinations of i and n and appears in Appendix C at the back of this book. An abbreviated version of Appendix C appears in Table 5-3. A close examination shows that the values in Table 5-3 are merely the inverse of those found in Table 5-2 and Appendix B. This, of course, is as it should be because the values in Appendix B are $(1 + i)^n$, and those in Appendix C are $[1/(1 + i)^n]$. Now, to determine the present value of a sum of money to be received at some future date, we need only determine the value of the appropriate $PVIF_{i, n}$, by either using a calculator or consulting the tables, and multiply it by the future value. In effect we can use our new notation and rewrite equation (5-7) as follows:

$$PV = FV_n \left[\frac{1}{(1 + i)^n} \right] = FV_n(PVIF_{i, n}) \tag{5-7a}$$

FIGURE 5-2 The Present Value of $100 to Be Received at a Future Date and Discounted Back to the Present at 0, 5, 10, and 15 Percent

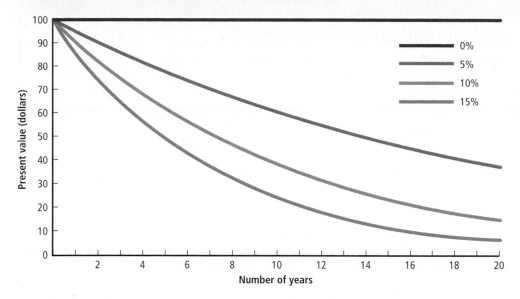

➤ EXAMPLE

You're on vacation in a rather remote part of Florida and see an advertisement stating that if you take a sales tour of some condominiums "you will be given $100 just for taking the tour." However, the $100 that you get is in the form of a savings bond that will not pay you the $100 for 10 years. What is the present value of $100 to be received 10 years from today if your discount rate is 6 percent? By looking at the $n = 10$ row and $i = 6\%$ column of Table 5-3, you find the $PVIF_{6\%, 10\,yr}$ is .558. Substituting $FV_{10} = \$100$ and $PVIF_{6\%, 10\,yr} = .558$ into equation (5-7a), you find

$$PV = \$100\left[\frac{1}{(1 + .06)^{10}}\right] = \$100(PVIF_{6\%, 10\,yr})$$

$$= \$100(.558)$$

$$= \$55.80$$

Thus, the value in today's dollars of that $100 savings bond is only $55.80.

CALCULATOR SOLUTION

Data Input	Function Key
10	N
6	I/Y
100	FV
0	PMT

Function Key	Answer
CPT	
PV	−55.84

TABLE 5-3 $PVIF_{i, n}$, or the Present Value of $1

n	1%	2%	3%	4%	5%	6%	7%	8%	9%	10%
1	.990	.980	.971	.962	.952	.943	.935	.926	.917	.909
2	.980	.961	.943	.925	.907	.890	.873	.857	.842	.826
3	.971	.942	.915	.889	.864	.840	.816	.794	.772	.751
4	.961	.924	.888	.855	.823	.792	.763	.735	.708	.683
5	.951	.906	.863	.822	.784	.747	.713	.681	.650	.621
6	.942	.888	.837	.790	.746	.705	.666	.630	.596	.564
7	.933	.871	.813	.760	.711	.655	.623	.583	.547	.513
8	.923	.853	.789	.731	.677	.627	.582	.540	.502	.467
9	.914	.837	.766	.703	.645	.592	.544	.500	.460	.424
10	.905	.820	.744	.676	.614	.558	.508	.463	.422	.386
11	.896	.804	.722	.650	.585	.527	.475	.429	.388	.350
12	.887	.789	.701	.625	.557	.497	.444	.397	.356	.319
13	.879	.773	.681	.601	.530	.469	.415	.368	.326	.290
14	.870	.758	.661	.577	.505	.442	.388	.340	.299	.263
15	.861	.743	.642	.555	.481	.417	.362	.315	.275	.239

Can You Do It?

SOLVING FOR THE PRESENT VALUE WITH TWO FLOWS IN DIFFERENT YEARS

What is the present value of an investment that yields $500 to be received in 5 years and $1,000 to be received in 10 years if the discount rate is 4 percent?

(The solution can be found on page 143.)

Again, we have only one present-value–future-value equation; that is, equations (5-6) and (5-7) are identical. We have introduced them as separate equations to simplify our calculations; in one case we are determining the value in future dollars, and in the other case the value in today's dollars. In either case the reason is the same: to compare values on alternative investments and to recognize that the value of a dollar received today is not the same as that of a dollar received at some future date. In other words, we must measure the dollar values in dollars of the same time period. For example, if we looked at these projects—one that promised $1,000 in 1 year, one that promised $1,500 in 5 years, and one that promised $2,500 in 10 years—the concept of present value allows us to bring their flows back to the present and make those projects comparable. Moreover, because all present values are comparable (they are all measured in dollars of the same time period), we can add and subtract the present value of inflows and outflows to determine the present value of an investment. Let's now look at an example of an investment that has two cash flows in different time periods and determine the present value of this investment.

STEP 1:

CALCULATOR SOLUTION

Data Input	Function Key
7	N
6	I/Y
1,000	FV
0	PMT

Function Key	Answer
CPT	
PV	−665.06

STEP 2:

CALCULATOR SOLUTION

Data Input	Function Key
10	N
6	I/Y
1,000	FV
0	PMT

Function Key	Answer
CPT	
PV	−558.39

STEP 3:

Add the two present values that you just calculated together:

$ 665.06
 558.39
$1,223.45

➤ EXAMPLE

What is the present value of an investment that yields $1,000 to be received in 7 years and $1,000 to be received in 10 years if the discount rate is 6 percent? Substituting the values of $n = 7$, $i = 6$ percent, and $FV_7 = \$1,000$; and $n = 10$, $i = 6$ percent, and $FV_{10} = \$1,000$ into equation (5-7) and adding these values together, we find

$$PV = \$1,000\left[\frac{1}{(1 + .06)^7}\right] + \$1,000\left[\frac{1}{(1 + .06)^{10}}\right]$$
$$= \$1,000(.66506) + \$1,000(.55839)$$
$$= \$665.06 + \$558.39 = \$1,223.45$$

Again, present values are comparable because they are measured in the same time period's dollars.

With a financial calculator, this becomes a three-step solution. First, you'll solve for the present value of the $1,000 received at the end of 7 years, then you'll solve for the present value of the $1,000 received at the end of 10 years, and finally, you'll add the two present values together. Remember, once you've found the present value of those future cash flows you can add them together because they're measured in the same period's dollars.

Did You Get It?

1. What is the relationship between the present-value equation (5-7) and the future-value, or compounding, equation (5-6)?
2. Why is the present value of a future sum always less than that sum's future value?

How Did You Do?

SOLVING FOR THE PRESENT VALUE WITH TWO FLOWS IN DIFFERENT YEARS

There are several different ways you can solve this problem—using the mathematical formulas, the time value of money tables, a financial calculator, or a spreadsheet—each one giving you the same answer.

1. **Using the Mathematical Formulas.** Substituting the values of $n = 5$, $i = 4$ percent, and $FV_5 = \$500$; and $n = 10$, $i = 4$ percent, and $FV_{10} = \$1,000$ into equation 5-7 and adding these values together, we find

$$PV = \$500 \left[\frac{1}{(1 + .04)^5} \right] + \$1,000 \left[\frac{1}{(1 + .04)^{10}} \right]$$
$$= \$500(.822) + \$1,000(.676)$$
$$= \$411 + \$676 = \$1,087$$

Again, present values are comparable and can be added together because they are measured in the same time period's dollars.

2. **Using the Time Value of Money Tables.** Simply calculate the present value of each cash flow individually, and then add the present values together.

Step 1: Determine the present value of $500 at the end of year 5 at 4%:

By looking at the $n = 5$ row and $i = 4\%$ column of Table 5-3, you find the $PVIF_{4\%,5\ yr}$ is .822. Substituting $FV_5 = \$500$ and $PVIF_{4\%,5\ yr} = .822$ into equation (5-7a), you find

$$PV = FV_n(PVIF_{i,n})$$
$$PV = \$500(0.822) = \$411$$

Step 2: Determine the present value of $1,000 at the end of year 10 at 4%:

By looking at the $n = 10$ row and $i = 4\%$ column of Table 5-3, you find the $PVIF_{4\%,10\ yr}$ is .676. Substituting $FV_{10} = \$100$ and $PVIF_{4\%,10\ yr} = .676$ into equation (5-7a), you find

$$PV = FV_n(PVIF_{i,n})$$
$$PV = \$1,000(0.676) = \$676$$

Step 3: Add the two present values together:

$$PV = \$411 + \$676 = \$1,087$$

3. **Using a Financial Calculator.** Again, it is a three-step process. First calculate the present value of each cash flow individually, and then add the present values together.

STEP 1: CALCULATOR SOLUTION		STEP 2: CALCULATOR SOLUTION		STEP 3:
Data Input	**Function Key**	**Data Input**	**Function Key**	Add the two present values that you just calculated together:
5	N	10	N	$ 410.96
4	I/Y	4	I/Y	675.56
500	FV	1,000	FV	$1,086.52
0	PMT	0	PMT	
Function Key	**Answer**	**Function Key**	**Answer**	
CPT		CPT		
PV	−410.96	PV	−675.56	

4. **Using an Excel Spreadsheet.** Using Excel, the cash flows are brought back to the present using the =PV function and then added together using the = SUM function with a negative sign inserted in the = SUM function, making it =–SUM. This allows the sum of the present values to take on a positive sign.

Objective **4**

Define an ordinary annuity and calculate its compound or future value.

annuity a series of equal dollar payments made for a specified number of years.

ordinary annuity an annuity where the cash flows occur at the end of each period.

compound annuity depositing an equal sum of money at the end of each year for a certain number of years and allowing it to grow.

ANNUITIES

An **annuity** is a *series of equal dollar payments for a specified number of years*. When we talk about annuities, we are referring to **ordinary annuities** unless otherwise noted. With an ordinary annuity *the payments occur at the end of each period*. Because annuities occur frequently in finance—for example, as bond interest payments—we treat them specially. Although compounding and determining the present value of an annuity can be dealt with using the methods we have just described, these processes can be time consuming, especially for larger annuities. Thus, we have modified the formulas to deal directly with annuities.

Compound Annuities

A **compound annuity** involves *depositing or investing an equal sum of money at the end of each year for a certain number of years and allowing it to grow*. Perhaps we are saving money for education, a new car, or a vacation home. In any case, we want to know how much our savings will have grown at some point in the future.

Actually, we can find the answer by using equation (5-6), our compounding equation, and compounding each of the individual deposits to its future value. For example, if to provide for a college education we are going to deposit $500 at the end of each year for the next 5 years in a bank where it will earn 6 percent interest, how much will we have at the end of 5 years? Compounding each of these values using equation (5-6), we find that we will have $2,818.50 at the end of 5 years.

$$
\begin{aligned}
FV_5 &= \$500(1 + 0.6)^4 + \$500(1 + 0.6)^3 + \$500(1 + 0.6)^2 + \$500(1 + 0.6) + \$500 \\
&= \$500(1.262) + \$500(1.191) + \$500(1.124) + \$500(1.060) + \$500 \\
&= \$631.00 + \$595.50 + \$562.00 + \$530.00 + \$500.00 \\
&= \$2,818.50
\end{aligned}
$$

By examining the mathematics involved and the graph of the movement of money through time in Table 5-4, we can see that all we are really doing is adding up the future values of different cash flows that initially occurred in different time periods. Fortunately, there is also an equation that helps us calculate the future value of an annuity:

$$
FV_n \text{ of an annuity} = PMT \left[\frac{FVIF_{i,n} - 1}{i} \right] \tag{5-8}
$$

$$
= PMT \left[\frac{(1 + i)^n - 1}{i} \right] \tag{5-8a}
$$

where FV_n = the future value of the annuity at the end of the nth year
PMT = the annuity payment deposited or received at the end of each year
i = the annual interest (or discount) rate
n = the number of years for which the annuity will last

TABLE 5-4   Growth of a 5-Year, $500 Annuity Compounded at 6 Percent

YEAR	0	1	2	3	4	5
Dollar deposits at end of year		500	500	500	500	500
						$ 500.00
						530.00
						562.00
						595.50
						631.00
Future value of the annuity						$2,818.50

TABLE 5-5	*FVIFA$_{i,n}$*, or the Sum of an Annuity of $1 for *n* Years

n	1%	2%	3%	4%	5%	6%	7%	8%	9%	10%
1	1.000	1.000	1.000	1.000	1.000	1.000	1.000	1.000	1.000	1.000
2	2.010	2.020	2.030	2.040	2.050	2.060	2.070	2.080	2.090	2.100
3	3.030	3.060	3.091	3.122	3.152	3.184	3.215	3.246	3.278	3.310
4	4.060	4.122	4.184	4.246	4.310	4.375	4.440	4.506	4.573	4.641
5	5.101	5.204	5.309	5.416	5.526	5.637	5.751	5.867	5.985	6.105
6	6.152	6.308	6.468	6.633	6.802	6.975	7.153	7.336	7.523	7.716
7	7.214	7.434	7.662	7.898	8.142	8.394	8.654	8.923	9.200	9.487
8	8.286	8.583	8.892	9.214	9.549	9.897	10.260	10.637	11.028	11.436
9	9.368	9.755	10.159	10.583	11.027	11.491	11.978	12.488	13.021	13.579
10	10.462	10.950	11.464	12.006	12.578	13.181	13.816	14.487	15.193	15.937
11	11.567	12.169	12.808	13.486	14.207	14.972	15.784	16.645	17.560	18.531
12	12.682	13.412	14.192	15.026	15.917	16.870	17.888	18.977	20.141	21.384
13	13.809	14.680	15.618	16.627	17.713	18.882	20.141	21.495	22.953	24.523
14	14.947	15.974	17.086	18.292	19.598	21.015	22.550	24.215	26.019	27.975
15	16.097	17.293	18.599	20.023	21.578	23.276	25.129	27.152	29.361	31.772

To simplify our discussion, we will refer to the value in brackets in equation (5-8a) as the **future-value interest factor for an annuity (FVIFA$_{i,n}$)**. It is defined as $\left[\dfrac{(1+i)^n - 1}{i}\right]$, which is provided in Appendix D for various combinations of *n* and *i*. An abbreviated version of the appendix is shown in Table 5-5.

Using this new notation, we can rewrite equation (5-8) as follows:

$$FV_n = PMT\left[\frac{(1+i)^n - 1}{i}\right] = PMT(FVIFA_{i,n}) \tag{5-8b}$$

future-value interest factor for an annuity (FVIFA$_{i,n}$) the value used as a multiplier to calculate the future value of an annuity.

Let's now reexamine the previous example: To determine the value after 5 years of $500 deposited in the bank at 6 percent at the end of each of the next 5 years, we would look in the *i* = 6% column and *n* = 5 row and find the value of the *FVIFA$_{6\%,\,5\,yr}$* to be 5.637. Substituting this value into equation (5-8b), we get

$$FV_5 = \$500(5.637)$$
$$= \$2,818.50$$

This is the same answer we obtained earlier using equation (5-6).

Rather than asking how much we will accumulate if we deposit an equal sum in a savings account each year, a more common question to ask is how much we must deposit each year to accumulate a certain amount of savings. This problem frequently occurs with respect to saving for large expenditures and pension funding obligations.

For example, if we know that we need $10,000 for college in 8 years, how much must we deposit in the bank at the end of each year at 6 percent interest to have the college money ready? In this case we know the values of *n*, *i*, and *FV$_n$* in equation (5-8b); what we do not know is the value of *PMT*. Substituting these example values in equation (5-8b), we find

$$\$10,000 = PMT\left[\frac{(1+.06)^8 - 1}{.06}\right] = PMT(FVIFA_{6\%,\,8\,yr})$$
$$\$10,000 = PMT(9.8975)$$
$$\frac{\$10,000}{9.8975} = PMT$$
$$\$1,010.36 = PMT$$

Thus, we must deposit $1,010.36 in the bank at the end of each year for 8 years at 6 percent interest to accumulate $10,000 at the end of 8 years.

CALCULATOR SOLUTION

Data Input	Function Key
5	N
6	I/Y
0	PV
500	PMT

Function Key	Answer
CPT	
FV	−2,818.55

CALCULATOR SOLUTION

Data Input	Function Key
8	N
6	I/Y
10,000	FV
0	PV

Function Key	Answer
CPT	
PMT	−1,010.36

> # EXAMPLE

How much must we deposit in an 8 percent savings account at the end of each year to accumulate $5,000 at the end of 10 years? Substituting the values $FV_{10} = \$5,000$, $n = 10$, and $i = 8$ percent into equation (5-8b), we find

$$\$5,000 = PMT\left[\frac{(1 + .08)^{10} - 1}{.08}\right] = PMT(FVIFA_{8\%,\ 10\ \text{yr}})$$

$$\$5,000 = PMT(14.487)$$

$$\frac{5,000}{14.487} = PMT$$

$$\$345.14 = PMT$$

Thus, we must deposit $345.14 per year for 10 years at 8 percent to accumulate $5,000.

The Present Value of an Annuity

Pension payments, insurance obligations, and the interest owed on bonds all involve annuities. To compare these three types of investments we need to know the present value of each. Although we can find this by using the present-value table in Appendix C, this can be time consuming, particularly when the annuity lasts for several years. For example, if we wish to know what $500 received at the end of each of the next 5 years is worth given a discount rate of 6 percent, we can simply substitute the appropriate values into equation (5-7), such that

$$PV = \$500\left[\frac{1}{(1 + .06)^1}\right] + \$500\left[\frac{1}{(1 + .06)^2}\right] + \$500\left[\frac{1}{(1 + .06)^3}\right]$$

$$+ \$500\left[\frac{1}{(1 + .06)^4}\right] + \$500\left[\frac{1}{(1 + .06)^5}\right]$$

$$= \$500(.943) + \$500(.890) + \$500(.840) + \$500(.792) + \$500(.747)$$

$$= \$2,106$$

Thus, the present value of this annuity is $2,106.00. By examining the mathematics involved and the graph of the movement of money through time in Table 5-6, we can see that all we are really doing is adding up the present values of different cash flows that initially occurred in different time periods. Fortunately, there is also an equation that helps us calculate the present value of an annuity:

$$PV \text{ of an annuity} = PMT\left[\frac{1 - PVIF_{i,\ n}}{i}\right] \tag{5-9}$$

$$= PMT\left[\frac{1 - (1 + i)^{-n}}{i}\right] \tag{5-9a}$$

where PMT = the annuity payment deposited or received at the end of each year
$\quad\quad\ i$ = the annual discount (or interest) rate
$\quad\quad PV$ = the present value of the future annuity
$\quad\quad\ n$ = the number of years for which the annuity will last

present-value interest factor for an annuity ($PVIFA_{i,\ n}$) the value used as a multiplier to calculate the present value of an annuity.

To simplify our discussion, we will refer to the value in the brackets in equation (5-9a) as the **present-value interest factor for an annuity ($PVIFA_{i,n}$)**. It is defined as $\left[\dfrac{1 - (1 + i)^{-n}}{i}\right]$, which has been compiled for various combinations of i and n in Appendix E. An abbreviated version of the appendix is provided in Table 5-7.

TABLE 5-6 Illustration of a 5–Year, $500 Annuity Discounted to the Present at 6 Percent

YEAR	0	1	2	3	4	5
Dollars received at end of year		500	500	500	500	500
	$ 471.50 ←					
	445.00 ←					
	420.00 ←					
	396.00 ←					
	373.50 ←					
Present value of the annuity	$2,106.00					

TABLE 5-7 *PVIFA*$_{i,n}$, or the Present Value of an Annuity of $1

n	1%	2%	3%	4%	5%	6%	7%	8%	9%	10%
1	0.990	0.980	0.971	0.962	0.952	0.943	0.935	0.926	0.917	0.909
2	1.970	1.942	1.913	1.886	1.859	1.833	1.808	1.783	1.759	1.736
3	2.941	2.884	2.829	2.775	2.723	2.673	2.624	2.577	2.531	2.487
4	3.902	3.808	3.717	3.630	3.546	3.465	3.387	3.312	3.240	3.170
5	4.853	4.713	4.580	4.452	4.329	4.212	4.100	3.993	3.890	3.791
6	5.795	5.601	5.417	5.242	5.076	4.917	4.767	4.623	4.486	4.355
7	6.728	6.472	6.230	6.002	5.786	5.582	5.389	5.206	5.033	4.868
8	7.652	7.326	7.020	6.733	6.463	6.210	5.971	5.747	5.535	5.335
9	8.566	8.162	7.786	7.435	7.108	6.802	6.515	6.247	5.995	5.759
10	9.471	8.983	8.530	8.111	7.722	7.360	7.024	6.710	6.418	6.145
11	10.368	9.787	9.253	8.760	8.306	7.887	7.499	7.139	6.805	6.495
12	11.255	10.575	9.954	9.385	8.863	8.384	7.943	7.536	7.161	6.814
13	12.134	11.348	10.635	9.986	9.394	8.853	8.358	7.904	7.487	7.103
14	13.004	12.106	11.296	10.563	9.899	9.295	8.746	8.244	7.786	7.367
15	13.865	12.849	11.938	11.118	10.380	9.712	9.108	8.560	8.061	7.606

Using this new notation we can rewrite equation (5-9) as follows:

$$PV = PMT\left[\frac{1 - (1 + i)^{-n}}{i}\right] = PMT(PVIFA_{i,n}) \tag{5-9b}$$

Solving the previous example to find the present value of $500 received at the end of each of the next 5 years discounted back to the present at 6 percent, we look in the $i = 6\%$ column and $n = 5$ row and find the $PVIFA_{6\%, \, 5 \, yr}$ to be 4.212. Substituting the appropriate values into equation (5-9b), we find

$$PV = \$500(4.212)$$
$$= \$2,106$$

This, of course, is the same answer we calculated when we individually discounted each cash flow to the present. The reason is that we really have only *one* table; the Table 5-7 value for an *n*-year annuity for any discount rate *i* is merely the sum of the first *n* values in Table 5-3. We can see this by comparing the value in the present-value-of-an-annuity table (Table 5-7) for $i = 8$ percent and $n = 6$ years, which is 4.623, with the sum of the values in the $i = 8\%$ column and $n = 1$, $n = 2$, $n = 3$, $n = 4$, $n = 5$, and $n = 6$ rows of the present-value table (Table 5-3). Notice that the sum of these values is also equal to 4.623, as shown in Table 5-8.

CALCULATOR SOLUTION

Data Input	Function Key
5	N
6	I/Y
500	PMT
0	FV

Function Key	Answer
CPT	
PV	−2,106.18

TABLE 5-8   Present Value of a 6–Year Annuity Discounted at 8 Percent

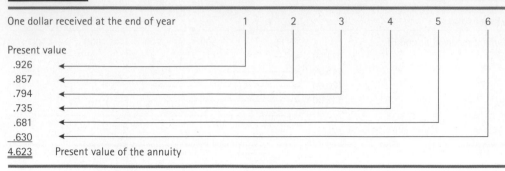

One dollar received at the end of year	1	2	3	4	5	6

Present value
.926
.857
.794
.735
.681
.630
4.623   Present value of the annuity

CALCULATOR SOLUTION

Data Input	Function Key
10	N
5	I/Y
1,000	PMT
0	FV

Function Key	Answer
CPT	
PV	−7,721.73

▶ EXAMPLE

What is the present value of a 10-year $1,000 annuity discounted back to the present at 5 percent? Substituting $n = 10$ years, $i = 5$ percent, and $PMT = \$1,000$ into equation (5-9b), we find

$$PV = \$1,000\left[\frac{1 - (1 + .05)^{-10}}{.05}\right] = \$1,000(PVIFA_{5\%,\,10\,yr})$$

Determining the value for the $PVIFA_{5\%,\,10\,yr}$ from Table 5-7, row $n = 10$, column $i = 5\%$, and substituting it in, we get

$$PV = \$1,000(7.722)$$
$$= \$7,722$$

Thus, the present value of this annuity is $7,722.

As with our other compounding and present-value tables, given any three of the four unknowns in equation (5-9b), we can solve for the fourth. In the case of the present-value-of-an-annuity table, we might be interested in solving for PMT, if we know i, n, and PV. The financial interpretation of this action would be: How much can be withdrawn, perhaps as a pension or to make loan payments, from an account that earns i percent compounded annually for each of the next n years if we wish to have nothing left at the end of n years? For example, if we have $5,000 in an account earning 8 percent interest, how large of an annuity can we draw out each year if we want nothing left at the end of 5 years? In this case the present value, PV, of the annuity is $5,000, $n = 5$ years, $i = 8$ percent, and PMT is unknown. Substituting this into equation (5-9b), we find

CALCULATOR SOLUTION

Data Input	Function Key
5	N
8	I/Y
5,000	PV
0	FV

Function Key	Answer
CPT	
PMT	−1,252.28

$$\$5,000 = PMT\left[\frac{1 - (1 + .08)^{-5}}{.08}\right] = PMT(3.993)$$

$$\$1,252.19 = PMT$$

Thus, this account will fall to zero at the end of 5 years if we withdraw $1,252.19 at the end of each year.

Did You Get It?

1. Could you determine the future value of a 3-year annuity using the formula for the future value of a single cash flow? How?

2. What is the $PVIFA_{10\%,\,3\,yr}$? Now add up the values for the $PVIF_{10\%,\,n\,yr}$ for $n = 1, 2$, and 3. What is this value? Why do these values have the relationship they do?

ANNUITIES DUE

Annuities due are really just *ordinary annuities in which all the annuity payments have been shifted forward by 1 year.* Compounding them and determining their present value is actually quite simple. With an annuity due, each annuity payment occurs at the beginning of each period rather than at the end of the period. Let's first look at how this affects our compounding calculations.

Because an annuity due merely shifts the payments from the end of the year to the beginning of the year, we now compound the cash flows for one additional year. Therefore, the compound sum of an annuity due is simply

$$FV_n(\text{annuity due}) = PMT\left[\frac{(1+i)^n - 1}{i}\right](1+i) = PMT(FVIFA_{i,n})(1+i) \qquad (5\text{-}10)$$

For example, earlier we calculated the value of a 5-year ordinary annuity of $500 invested in the bank at 6 percent to be $2,818.50. If we now assume this to be a 5-year annuity due, its future value increases from $2,818.50 to $2,987.61.

$$FV_5 = \$500\left[\frac{(1+.06)^5 - 1}{.06}\right](1+.06) = \$500(FVIFA_{6\%,\,5\,yr})(1+.06)$$
$$= \$500(5.637)(1.06)$$
$$= \$2,987.61$$

Likewise, with the present value of an annuity due, we simply receive each cash flow 1 year earlier—that is, we receive it at the beginning of each year rather than at the end of each year. Thus, because each cash flow is received 1 year earlier, it is discounted back for one less period. To determine the present value of an annuity due, we merely need to find the present value of an ordinary annuity and multiply that by $(1+i)$, which in effect cancels out 1 year's discounting.

$$PV(\text{annuity due}) = PMT\left[\frac{1-(1+i)^{-n}}{i}\right](1+i) = PMT(PVIFA_{i,n})(1+i) \qquad (5\text{-}11)$$

Reexamining the earlier example in which we calculated the present value of a 5-year ordinary annuity of $500 given a discount rate of 6 percent, we now find that if it is an annuity due rather than an ordinary annuity, the present value increases from $2,106 to $2,232.36.

$$PV = \$500\left[\frac{1-(1+.06)^{-5}}{.06}\right](1+.06) = \$500(PVIFA_{6\%,\,5\,yr})(1+.06)$$
$$= \$500(4.212)(1.06)$$
$$= \$2,232.36$$

With a financial calculator, you have two choices. First, you can reset your financial calculator to "Beginning Mode." Just as easy is to approach this as a two-step problem. First, treat it as if it were an ordinary annuity and find the present value. Then multiply the present value times $(1+i)$, in this case times 1.06; this is shown in the margin.

The result of all this is that both the future and present values of an annuity due are larger than those of an ordinary annuity because in each case all payments are received earlier. Thus, when *compounding*, an annuity due compounds for one additional year, whereas when *discounting*, an annuity due discounts for one less year. Although annuities due are used with some frequency in accounting, their usage is quite limited in finance. Therefore, in the remainder of this text, whenever the term *annuity* is used, you should assume that we are referring to an ordinary annuity.

► EXAMPLE

The Virginia State Lottery runs like most other state lotteries: You must select 6 out of 44 numbers correctly in order to win the jackpot. If you come close, there are some significantly lesser prizes, which we ignore for now. For each million dollars in the lottery

Objective **5**

Differentiate between an ordinary annuity and an annuity due and determine the future and present value of an annuity due.

annuity due an annuity in which the payments occur at the beginning of each period.

Future value of an annuity due:

STEP 1:
CALCULATOR SOLUTION

Data Input	Function Key
5	N
6	I/Y
0	PV
500	PMT

Function Key	Answer
CPT	
FV	−2,818.55

STEP 2:
$2,818.55
× 1.06
$2,987.66

Present value of an annuity due:

STEP 1:
CALCULATOR SOLUTION

Data Input	Function Key
5	N
6	I/Y
500	PMT
0	FV

Function Key	Answer
CPT	
PV	−2,106.18

STEP 2:
$2,106.18
× 1.06
$2,232.55

Present value of an annuity due:

STEP 1:

CALCULATOR SOLUTION

Data Input	Function Key
20	N
10	I/Y
100,000	PMT
0	FV

Function Key	Answer
CPT	
PV	–851,356

STEP 2:

$851,356
×1.10
$936,492

jackpot, you receive $50,000 per year for 20 years, and your chance of winning is 1 in 7.1 million. A recent advertisement for the Virginia State Lottery went as follows: "Okay, you got two kinds of people. You've got the kind who play Lotto all the time, and the kind who play Lotto some of the time. You know, like only on a Saturday when they stop in at the store on the corner for some peanut butter cups and diet soda and the jackpot happens to be really big. I mean, my friend Ned? He's like 'Hey, it's only $2 million this week.' Well, hellloooo, anybody home? I mean, I don't know about you, but I wouldn't mind having a measly 2 mill coming *my* way. . . ."

What is the present value of these payments? The answer to this question depends on what assumption you make about the time value of money. In this case, let's assume that your required rate of return on an investment with this level of risk is 10 percent. Keeping in mind that the Lotto is an annuity due—that is, on a $2 million lottery you would get $100,000 immediately and $100,000 at the end of each of the next 19 years. Thus, the present value of this 20-year annuity due discounted back to present at 10 percent becomes

$$PV(\text{annuity due}) = PMT\left[\frac{1 - (1 + i)^{-n}}{i}\right](1 + i) = PMT(PVIFA_{i,n})(1 + i)$$

$$= \$100,000\left[\frac{1 - (1 + .10)^{-20}}{.10}\right](1 + .10)$$

$$= \$100,000\ (8.514)(1.10)$$

$$= \$851,400(1.10)$$

$$= \$936,540$$

Just as before, you can either reset your financial calculator to "Beginning Mode" or use the two-step process. With the two-step process, in step 1, you treat the jackpot as if it were an ordinary annuity and find the present value. Then multiply the present value times $(1 + i)$, in this case times 1.10; this is shown in the margin. You'll notice this answer is a bit different from the answer you got using the tables. That's because of rounding error in the tables.

Thus, the present value of the $2 million Lotto jackpot is less than $1 million if 10 percent is the discount rate. Moreover, because the chance of winning is only 1 in 7.1 million, the expected value of each dollar "invested" in the lottery is only $(1/7.1 \text{ million}) \times (\$936,540) = 13.19¢$. That is, for every dollar you spend on the lottery you should expect to get, *on average*, about 13 cents back—not a particularly good deal. Although this ignores the minor payments for coming close, it also ignores taxes. In this case, it looks like "my friend Ned" is doing the right thing by staying clear of the lottery. Obviously, the main value of the lottery is entertainment. Unfortunately, without an understanding of the time value of money, it can sound like a good investment.

Did You Get It?

1. How does an annuity due differ from an ordinary annuity?
2. Why are both the future and present values greater for an annuity?

Objective

Explain loan amortization.

AMORTIZED LOANS

amortized loan a loan that is paid off in equal periodic payments.

The procedure of solving for *PMT*, the annuity payment value when *i*, *n*, and *PV* are known, is also used to determine what payments are associated with paying off a loan in equal installments over time. *Loans that are paid off this way, in equal periodic payments,* are called **amortized loans**. Actually, the word *amortization* comes from the Latin word meaning "about to die." When you pay off a loan using regular, fixed payments, that loan is amortized. Although the payments are fixed, different amounts of each payment are applied toward the principal and the interest. With each payment you owe a bit less toward the principal. As a result, the amount that has to go toward the interest payment declines with

FIGURE 5-3   The Amortization Process

Number of payments

each payment, whereas the portion of each payment that goes toward the principal increases. Figure 5-3 illustrates the process of amortization.

For example, suppose a firm wants to purchase a piece of machinery. To do this, it borrows $6,000 to be repaid in four equal payments at the end of each of the next 4 years, and the interest rate that is paid to the lender is 15 percent on the outstanding portion of the loan. To determine what the annual payments associated with the repayment of this debt will be, we simply use equation (5-9b) and solve for the value of *PMT*, the annual annuity. Again we know three of the four values in that equation: *PV*, *i*, and *n*. *PV*, the present value of the future annuity, is $6,000; *i*, the annual interest rate, is 15 percent; and *n*, the number of years for which the annuity will last, is 4 years. *PMT*, the annuity payment received (by the lender and paid by the firm) at the end of each year, is unknown. Substituting these values into equation (5-9b), we find

$$\$6,000 = PMT \left[\frac{1 - (1 + .15)^{-4}}{.15} \right] = PMT\,(PVIFA_{15\%,\,4\,\mathrm{yr}})$$

$$\$6,000 = PMT\,(2.855)$$

$$\$2,101.58 = PMT$$

To repay the principal and interest on the outstanding loan in 4 years, the annual payments would be $2,101.58. The breakdown of interest and principal payments is given in the *loan amortization schedule* in Table 5-9, with very minor rounding error. As you can see, the interest portion of the payment declines each year as the loan outstanding balance declines.

CALCULATOR SOLUTION

Data Input	Function Key
4	N
15	I/Y
6,000	PV
0	FV

Function Key	Answer
CPT	
PMT	−2,101.59

TABLE 5-9   Loan Amortization Schedule Involving a $6,000 Loan at 15 Percent to Be Repaid in 4 Years

YEAR	ANNUITY	INTEREST PORTION OF THE ANNUITY[a]	REPAYMENT OF THE PRINCIPAL PORTION OF THE ANNUITY[b]	OUTSTANDING LOAN BALANCE AFTER THE ANNUITY PAYMENT
0	0	0	0	$6,000
1	$2,101.58	$900.00	$1,201.58	4,798.42
2	2,101.58	719.76	1,381.82	3,416.60
3	2,101.58	512.49	1,589.09	1,827.51
4	2,101.58	274.13	1,827.45	

[a]The interest portion of the annuity is calculated by multiplying the outstanding loan balance at the beginning of the year by the interest rate of 15 percent. Thus, for year 1 it was $6,000 × .15 = $900.00, for year 2 it was $4,798.42 × .15 = $719.76, and so on.

[b]Repayment of the principal portion of the annuity was calculated by subtracting the interest portion of the annuity (column 2) from the annuity (column 1).

Did You Get It? ....

1. What is an amortized loan?

Now let's use a spreadsheet and look at a loan amortization problem in which the payment occurs monthly.

To buy a new house, you take out a 25-year mortgage for $100,000. What will your monthly payments be if the interest rate on your mortgage is 8 percent?

	A	B	C	D	E	F	G
1	Two things to keep in mind when you're working this problem: first, you'll						
2	have to convert the annual rate of 8 percent into a monthly rate by dividing it						
3	by 12, and second, you'll have to convert the number of periods into months						
4	by multiplying 25 times 12 for a total of 300 months.						
5							
6	Excel formula: =PMT(rate,number of periods,present value,future value,type)						
7							
8			rate (I) =	8%/12			
9			number of periods (n) =	300			
10			present value (PV) =	$100,000			
11			future value (FV) =	$0			
12			type (0 = at end of period) =	0			
13						Entered values	
14	Entered values in cell d16: =PMT((8/12)%,d9,d10,d11,d12)					in cell d16: =PMT((8/12)%,	
15						d9,d10,d11,d12)	
16		monthly mortgage payment =		($771.82)			
17							
18	Notice that monthly payments take on a negative value because you						
19	pay them.						
20							

You can also use Excel to calculate the interest and principal portion of any loan amortization payment. You can do this using the following Excel functions:

Calculation	Formula
Interest portion of payment	= *IPMT*(rate,period,number of periods,present value,future value,type)
Principal portion of payment	= *PPMT*(rate,period,number of periods,present value,future value,type)

where period refers to the number of an individual periodic payment.

	A	B	C	D	E	F
1	If you would like to determine how much of the 48th monthly					
2	payment went toward interest and principle, you would solve as follows:					
3						
4			rate (I) =	8%/12		
5		number of periods (n) =		300		
6		present value (PV) =		$100,000		
7		future value (FV) =		$0		
8	type (0 = at end of period) =			0		
9						
10	Interest portion of payment 48:			Entered values in cell c12:		
11				=IPMT((8/12)%,48,d5,d6,		
12			($628.12)	d7,d8)		
13						
14	Entered values in cell c12: =IPMT((8/12)%,48,d5,d6,d7,d8)					
15						
16	The principle portion of payment 48:			Entered values in cell c18:		
17				=PPMT((8/12)%,48,d5,d6,		
18			($143.69)	d7,d8)		
19						
20	Entered values in cell c18: =PPMT((8/12)%,48,d5,d6,d7,d8)					

MAKING INTEREST RATES COMPARABLE

Objective **7**

Determine the future or present value of a sum when there are nonannual compounding periods.

In order to make intelligent decisions about where to invest or borrow money, it is important that we make the stated interest rates comparable. Unfortunately, some rates are quoted as compounded annually, whereas others are quoted as compounded quarterly or compounded daily. But we already know that it is not fair to compare interest rates with different compounding periods to each other. Thus, the only way interest rates can logically be compared is to convert them to a common compounding period.

In order to understand the process of making different interest rates comparable, it is first necessary to define the nominal, or quoted, interest rate. The nominal, or quoted, rate is the rate of interest stated on the contract. For example, if you shop around for loans and are quoted 8 percent compounded annually and 7.85 percent compounded quarterly, then 8 percent and 7.85 percent would both be nominal rates. Unfortunately, because on one rate the interest is compounded annually, but on the other interest is compounded quarterly, the two rates are not comparable. In fact, it is never appropriate to compare nominal rates *unless* they include the same number of compounding periods per year. To make them comparable, we must calculate their equivalent rate at some common compounding period. We do this by calculating the **annual percentage yield (APY), or effective annual rate (EAR)**. This is the annual compound rate that produces the same return as the nominal or quoted rate.

annual percentage yield (APY) or **effective annual rate (EAR)** the annual compound rate that produces the same return as the nominal, or quoted, rate when something is compounded on a nonannual basis. In effect, the APY, or EAR, provides the true rate of return.

Let's assume that you are considering borrowing money from a bank at 12 percent compounded monthly. If you invested $1 at 1 percent per month for 12 months you'd have,

$$\$1.00(1.01)^{12} = \$1.126825$$

In effect, your dollar investment grew by 12.6825 percent rather than just by 12 percent. Thus, the APY for 12 percent compounded monthly is 12.6825. It tells us the annual rate that would produce the same return as the nominal rate. In other words, you'll end up with the same amount of money if it's invested at 12.6825 percent compounded annually, or 12 percent compounded monthly. Thus, 12.6825 is the annual percentage yield (APY), or effective annual rate (EAR), for 12 percent compounded monthly.

Generalizing on this process, we can calculate the *APY* using the following equation:

$$APY = \left(1 + \frac{\text{quoted rate}}{m}\right)^m - 1 \tag{5-12}$$

where *APY*, or *EAR*, is the annual percentage yield and *m* is the number of compounding periods within a year. Given the wide variety of compounding periods used by businesses and banks, it is important to know how to make these rates comparable so that logical decisions can be made.

➤ EXAMPLE

You've just received your first credit card and the problem is the rate. It looks pretty high to you. The APR, or annual percentage rate, is listed at 21.7 percent, and when you look closer, you notice that the interest is compounded daily. What's the APY, or effective annual rate, on your credit card?

To calculate the APY we can use equation (5-12)

$$APY \text{ or } EAR = \left[1 + \frac{\text{quoted rate}}{m}\right]^m - 1$$

where the quoted rate is 21.7 percent, or 0.217, and *m* is 365. Substituting, we get

$$APY \text{ or } EAR = \left[1 + \frac{0.217}{365}\right]^{365} - 1$$

$$APY \text{ or } EAR = 1.242264 - 1 = 0.242264 \text{ or } 24.2264 \text{ percent}$$

Thus, in reality, the APY, or effective annual rate, is actually 24.2264 percent.

TABLE 5-10 The Value of $100 Compounded at Various Intervals

	FOR 1 YEAR AT *i* PERCENT			
i =	2%	5%	10%	15%
Compounded annually	$102.00	$105.00	$110.00	$115.00
Compounded semiannually	102.01	105.06	110.25	115.56
Compounded quarterly	102.02	105.09	110.38	115.87
Compounded monthly	102.02	105.12	110.47	116.08
Compounded weekly (52)	102.02	105.12	110.51	116.16
Compounded daily (365)	102.02	105.13	110.52	116.18
	FOR 10 YEARS AT *i* PERCENT			
i =	2%	5%	10%	15%
Compounded annually	$121.90	$162.89	$259.37	$404.56
Compounded semiannually	122.02	163.86	265.33	424.79
Compounded quarterly	122.08	164.36	268.51	436.04
Compounded monthly	122.1	164.70	270.70	444.02
Compounded weekly (52)	122.14	164.83	271.57	447.20
Compounded daily (365)	122.14	164.87	271.79	448.03

Finding Present and Future Values with Nonannual Periods

The same logic that applies to calculating APY or EAR also applies to calculating present and future values when the periods are semiannual, quarterly, or any other nonannual period. Previously when we moved money through time we assumed that the cash flows occurred annually and the compounding or discounting period was always annual. However, it need not be, as evidenced by the fact that bonds generally pay interest semiannually and most mortgages require monthly payments.

For example, if we invest our money for 5 years at 8 percent interest compounded semiannually, we are really investing our money for 10 6-month periods during which we receive 4 percent interest each period. If it is 8 percent compounded quarterly for 5 years, we receive 2 percent interest per period for 20 3-month periods. This process can easily be generalized, giving us the following formula for finding the future value of an investment for which interest is compounded in nonannual periods:

$$FV_n = PV\left[1 + \frac{i}{m}\right]^m \tag{5-13}$$

where FV_n = the future value of the investment at the end of n years
n = the number of years during which the compounding occurs
i = annual interest (or discount) rate
PV = the present value or original amount invested at the beginning of the first year
m = the number of times compounding occurs during the year

We can see the value of intrayear compounding by examining Table 5-10. Because "interest is earned on interest" more frequently as the length of the compounding period declines, there is an inverse relationship between the length of the compounding period and the effective annual interest rate: The shorter the compounding period is, the higher the effective interest rate will be. Conversely, the longer the compounding period is, the lower the effective interest rate will be.

The Financial Calculator Solution to Nonannual Periods

With a financial calculator, the easiest way to solve a problem involving nonannual periods is to reset the "payments per year" or P/Y feature on your calculator to match the problem. Although you'll want to make sure you understand how your financial calculator works, you

Can You Do It?

HOW MUCH CAN YOU AFFORD TO SPEND ON A HOUSE?
AN AMORTIZED LOAN WITH MONTHLY PAYMENTS

You've been house shopping and aren't sure how big a house you can afford. You figure you can handle monthly mortgage payments of $1,250, and you can get a 30-year loan at 6.5 percent. How big of a mortgage can you afford? In this problem, you are solving for *PV*, which is the amount of money you can borrow today.

(The solution can be found on page 156.)

should keep in mind that on most financial calculators N is the number of compounding periods. Thus, for problems with annual compounding, P/Y should be set to 1, and for problems with monthly compounding, P/Y should be set to 12. If you have a TI BA II Plus calculator, to reset the P/Y feature you must first hit the 2ⁿᵈ button, then the I/Y button (you'll notice just above the I/Y button, P/Y is listed). From there, you enter 12, then hit the ENTER button on the top row, and finally hit CE/C , and then CE/C again. (Hitting the CE/C button twice serves to clear the display.) Once again, once you've got the "payments per year" button set, N then becomes the number of compounding periods, so if your problem involves 10 years of monthly compounding, then N equals 120, the number of months in 10 years.

➤ EXAMPLE

First let's solve this problem without resetting the "payments per year" or P/Y feature on your calculator. If we place $100 in a savings account that yields 12 percent compounded quarterly, what will our investment grow to at the end of 5 years? Substituting $n = 5$, $m = 4$, $i = 12$ percent, and $PV = \$100$ into equation (5-13), we find

$$FV_5 = \$100\left(1 + \frac{.12}{4}\right)^{4\cdot5}$$
$$= \$100(1 + .03)^{20}$$
$$= \$100(1\ .806)$$
$$= \$180.60$$

Thus, we will have $180.60 at the end of 5 years. Notice that the calculator solution is slightly different because of rounding errors in the tables, and it also takes on a negative value. Also notice that while N becomes the number of quarters in 5 years, but I/Y remains the annual interest rate.

CALCULATOR SOLUTION

First, set P/Y = 4

Data Input	Function Key
20	N
12	I/Y
100	PV
0	PMT

Function Key	Answer
CPT	
FV	−180.61

➤ EXAMPLE

In 2006 the average U.S. household owed nearly $10,000 in credit card debt, and the average interest rate on credit card debt was 13.0 percent. On many credit cards the minimum monthly payment is 4 percent of the debt balance. If the average household paid off 4 percent of the initial amount it owed each month, that is, made payments of $400 each month, how many months would it take to repay this credit card debt? Use a financial calculator to solve this problem. Don't forget to set your payments per year button (P/Y) to 12.

You'll notice in the solution that appears in the margin that the value for *PMT* goes in as a negative. The answer is over 29 months.

CALCULATOR SOLUTION

First, set P/Y = 12

Data Input	Function Key
13.0	I/Y
10,000	PV
−400	PMT
0	FV

Function Key	Answer
CPT	
N	29.3

How Did You Do?

HOW MUCH CAN YOU AFFORD TO SPEND ON A HOUSE? AN AMORTIZED LOAN WITH MONTHLY PAYMENTS

There are several different ways you can solve this problem—using the mathematical formulas, the time value of money tables, a financial calculator, or a spreadsheet—each one giving you the same answer.

1. **Using the Mathematical Formulas.** Again, you need to multiply n time m, and divide i by m, where m is the number of compounding periods per year. Thus,

$$PV = \$1,250\left[\frac{1 - \dfrac{1}{\left(1 + \dfrac{.065}{12}\right)^{30\cdot12}}}{\dfrac{.065}{12}}\right]$$

$$PV = \$1,250\left[\frac{1 - \dfrac{1}{(1 + .00541667)^{360}}}{.00541667}\right]$$

$$PV = \$1,250\left[\frac{1 - \dfrac{1}{6.99179797}}{.00541667}\right]$$

$$PV = \$1,250\,(158.2107222)$$

$$PV = \$197,763.40$$

2. **Using the Time Value of Money Tables.** Because there aren't time value of money table values for 0.541667 percent, this problem can't be solved using the tables.

3. **Using a Financial Calculator.** There are two ways you can solve this problem using a financial calculator, you could either convert everything to monthly measures or use the P/Y button.

   Converting to Monthly Measures: First, you must convert everything to months. To do this you would first convert n into months by multiplying n times m (30 times 12) and enter this enter into N. Next you would enter the interest rate as a monthly rate by dividing i by m and enter this number into I/Y. Finally, make sure that the value entered as PMT is a monthly figure, that is, it is the monthly payment value.

CALCULATOR SOLUTION

Data Input	Function Key
360	N
6.5/12	I/Y
1,250	PMT
0	FV

Function Key	Answer
CPT	
PV	−197,763.52

Using the P/Y *Button:* If you use the P/Y button and the payments are made on a monthly basis, P/Y must be set to 12. To do this, if you have a TI BA II Plus calculator, you must first hit the 2nd button, then the I/Y button; at that point you have activated the P/Y. You would then enter 12 and hit the ENTER button, which is located on the top row. Finally, hit the CE/C button twice, which will clear the display. The value entered for n becomes the number of compounding periods, which in this case is months. Because there are 360 months in 30 years, 360 is entered for n, and 6.5 is entered for i, 1250 is entered for PMT, 0 for the FV, and you then solve for PV.

CALCULATOR SOLUTION

First, set P/Y = 12

Data Input	Function Key
360	N
6.5	I/Y
1,250	PMT
0	FV

Function Key	Answer
CPT	
PV	−197,763.52

4. **Using an Excel Spreadsheet.** Notice the interest rate is entered as a decimal, rather than a percentage.

◇	A	B	C
1	rate (i) =	0.54167%	
2	number of periods (n) =	360	
3	payment (PMT) =	1,250	
4	future value (FV) =	0	
5	type (0 = at end of period) =		
6			
7	present value (PV) =	($197,762.70)	
8			
9	Equation:		
10	=PV(i,n,PMT,FV,type) = PV(b1,b2,b3,b4,b5)		
11			
12			

Did You Get It?

1. Why does the future value of a given amount increase when interest is compounded nonannually as opposed to annually?
2. How do you adjust the present- and future-value formulas when interest is compounded monthly?

THE PRESENT VALUE OF AN UNEVEN STREAM

Although some projects will involve a single cash flow, and some will involve annuities, many projects will involve uneven cash flows over several years. Chapter 9, which examines investments in fixed assets, presents this situation repeatedly. There we will be comparing not only the present value of cash flows generated by different projects but also the cash inflows and outflows generated by a particular project to determine that project's present value. However, this will not be difficult because the present value of any cash flow is measured in today's dollars and thus can be compared, through addition for inflows and subtraction for outflows, to the present value of any other cash flow also measured in today's dollars. For example, if we wished to find the present value of the following cash flows

YEAR	CASH FLOW	YEAR	CASH FLOW
1	$ 0	6	500
2	200	7	500
3	−400	8	500
4	500	9	500
5	500	10	500

given a 6 percent discount rate, we would merely discount the flows back to the present and total them by adding in the positive flows and subtracting the negative ones. However, this problem is complicated by the annuity of $500 that runs from years 4 through 10. To accommodate this, we can first discount the annuity back to the beginning of period 4 (or end of period 3) by multiplying it by the value of $PVIFA_{6\%, 7\,yr}$ and get its present value at that point in time. We then multiply this value times the $PVIF_{6\%, 3\,yr}$ in order to bring this single cash flow (which is the present value of the 7-year annuity) back to the present. In effect we discount twice, first back to the end of period 3, then back to the present. This is shown graphically in Table 5-11 and numerically in Table 5-12. Thus, the present value of this uneven stream of cash flows is $2,186.44.

TABLE 5-11 The Present Value of an Uneven Stream Involving One Annuity Discounted to the Present at 6 Percent: An Example

YEAR		0	1	2	3	4	5	6	7	8	9	10
Dollars received at end of year		0	200	−400	500	500	500	500	500	500	500	
	$ 178.00 ←											
	−336.00 ←											
				$2,791 ←								
	2,344.44 ←											
Total present value	$2,186.44											

TABLE 5-12 Determining the Present Value of an Uneven Stream Involving One Annuity Discounted to the Present at 6 Percent: An Example

1. Present value of $200 received at the end of 2 years = $200(.890) = **$178.00**
2. Present value of a $400 outflow at the end of 3 years = −400(.840) = **−336.00**
3. (a) Value at end of year 3 of a $500 annuity, years 4–10 = $500(5.582) = $2,791.00
   (b) Present value of $2,791.00 received at the end of year 3 = $2,791(.840) = **2,344.44**
4. Total present value = **$2,186.44**

STEP 4:
Bring the value we just calculated, which is the value of the 7-year annuity of $500 at the end of year 3, back to present.

CALCULATOR SOLUTION

Data Input	Function Key
3	N
6	I/Y
2,791.19	FV
0	PMT

Function Key	Answer
CPT	
PV	−2,343.54

STEP 5:
And the present value of the cash inflows and subtract the present value of the cash outlfow (the $400 from the end of year 3) calculated in steps 1, 2, and 4.

$ 178.00
−335.85
+2,343.54
$ 2,185.69

Objective **9**

Determine the present value of a perpetuity.

perpetuity an annuity with an infinite life.

Remember, once the cash flows from an investment have been brought back to the present, they can be combined by adding and subtracting to determine the project's total present value.

Did You Get It?

1. How would you calculate the present value of an investment that produced cash flows of $100 received at the end of year 1 and $700 at the end of year 2?

PERPETUITIES

A **perpetuity** is *an annuity that continues forever*; that is, every year following its establishment this investment pays the same dollar amount. An example of a perpetuity is preferred stock that pays a constant dollar dividend infinitely. Determining the present value of a perpetuity is delightfully simple; we merely need to divide the constant flow by the discount rate. For example, the present value of a $100 perpetuity discounted back to the present at 5 percent is $100/.05 = $2,000. Thus, the equation representing the present value of a perpetuity is

$$PV = \frac{PP}{i} \qquad (5\text{-}14)$$

where: PV = the present value of the perpetuity
PP = the constant dollar amount provided by the perpetuity
i = the annual interest (or discount) rate

➤ **EXAMPLE**

What is the present value of a $500 perpetuity discounted back to the present at 8 percent? Substituting PP = $500 and i = .08 into equation (5-14), we find

$$PV = \frac{\$500}{.08} = \$6,250$$

Thus, the present value of this perpetuity is $6,250.

Did You Get It?

1. What is a perpetuity?
2. When *i*, the annual interest (or discount) rate, increases, what happens to the present value of a perpetuity? Why?

Objective **10**

Explain how the international setting complicates the time value of money.

THE MULTINATIONAL FIRM: THE TIME VALUE OF MONEY

From **Principle 1: The Risk–Return Trade-Off—We Won't Take On Additional Risk Unless We Expect to Be Compensated with Additional Return**, we found that investors demand a return for delaying consumption, as well as an additional return for taking on added risk. The discount rate that we use to move money through time should reflect this return for delaying consumption; and as the Fisher effect showed in Chapter 2, this discount rate should reflect anticipated inflation. In the United States, anticipated inflation is quite low, although it does tend to fluctuate over time. Elsewhere in the world, however, the inflation rate is difficult to predict because it can be dramatically high and fluctuate tremendously.

Let's look at Argentina, keeping in mind that similar examples abound in Central and South America and Eastern Europe. At the beginning of 1992, Argentina introduced its fifth currency in 22 years, the new peso. The austral, the currency that was replaced, was intro-

TABLE 5-13	Summary of Time Value of Money Equations[a]
CALCULATION	**EQUATION**
Future value of a single payment	$FV_n = PV(1 + i)^n\ PV(FVIF_{i,n})$
Present value of a single payment	$PV = FV_n\left[\dfrac{1}{(1 + i)^n}\right] = FV_n(PVIF_{i,n})$
Future value of an annuity	$FV\text{ of an annuity} = PMT\left[\dfrac{FVIF_{i,n} - 1}{i}\right] = PMT\left[\dfrac{(1 + i)^n - 1}{i}\right] = PMT(FVIFA_{i,n})$
Present value of an annuity	$PV\text{ of an annuity} = PMT\left[\dfrac{1 - PVIF_{i,n}}{i}\right] = PMT\left[\dfrac{1 - (1 + i)^{-n}}{i}\right] = PMT(PVIFA_{i,n})$
Future value of an annuity due	$FV_n(\text{annuity due}) = PMT(FVIFA_{i,n})(1 + i)$
Present value of an annuity due	$PV(\text{annuity due}) = PMT(PVIFA_{i,n})(1 + i)$
Annual percentage yield (APY) or Equivalent annual return (EAR) =	$\left[1 + \dfrac{\text{quoted rate}}{m}\right]^m - 1$
Future value of a single payment with nonannual compounding	$FV_n = PV\left(1 + \dfrac{i}{m}\right)^{mn}$
Present value of a perpetuity	$PV = \dfrac{PP}{i}$

Notations: FV_n = the future value of the investment at the end of n years
       n = the number of years until payment will be received or during which compounding occurs
       i = the annual interest or discount rate
      PV = the present value of the future sum of money
      m = the number of times compounding occurs during the year
    PMT = the annuity payment deposited or received at the end of each year
     PP = the constant dollar amount provided by the perpetuity

[a]Related tables appear in Appendixes B through E at the end of the book.

duced in June 1985 and was initially equal in value to $1.25 U.S. currency. Five and a half years later, it took 100,000 australs to equal $1. Inflation had reached the point at which the stack of money needed to buy a candy bar was bigger and weighed more than the candy bar itself, and many workers received their week's wages in grocery bags. Needless to say, if we were to move australs through time, we would have to use an extremely high interest or discount rate.

Unfortunately, in countries suffering from hyperinflation, inflation rates tend to fluctuate dramatically, and this makes estimating the expected inflation rate even more difficult. For example, in 1989 the inflation rate in Argentina was 4,924 percent; in 1990 it dropped to 1,344 percent; in 1991 it was only 84 percent; in 1992, only 18 percent; in 2000 it was close to zero, and by 2005 it climbed up again, to 12.3 percent. However, as inflation in Argentina dropped, inflation in Brazil heated up, going from 426 percent in 1991 to 1,094 percent in 1995. By 2000, the inflation rate in Brazil had dropped to 7 percent, and it slowly fell to 5.7% in 2005. However, in 2000 the inflation rate in Uzbekistan, our ally in the war against terrorists based in Afghanistan, reached 1,568 percent and has since dropped to 26 percent. Finally, at the extreme, in 1993 in Serbia the inflation rate reached 360,000,000,000,000,000 percent.

The bottom line on all this is that for companies doing business internationally, dramatic fluctuations in inflation rates can make choosing the appropriate discount rate to move money through time an extremely difficult process.

Did You Get It?

1. How does the international setting complicate the choice of the appropriate interest rate to use when discounting cash flows back to the present?

Objective 1

Explain the mechanics of compounding, that is, how money grows over time when it is invested.

Objective 2

Be able to move money through time using time value of money tables, financial calculators, and spreadsheets.

Objective 3

Discuss the relationship between compounding and bringing the value of money back to the present.

Objective 4

Define an ordinary annuity and calculate its compound or future value.

Objective 5

Differentiate between an ordinary annuity and an annuity due and determine the future and present value of an annuity due.

Objective 6

Explain loan amortization.

Objective 7

Determine the future or present value of a sum when there are nonannual compounding periods.

Objective 8

Determine the present value of an uneven stream of payments.

Objective 9

Determine the present value of a perpetuity.

Objective 10

Explain how the international setting complicates the time value of money.

Summary

Compound interest occurs when interest paid on an investment during the first period is added to the principal; then, during the second period, interest is earned on this new sum. The formula for this appears in Table 5-13.

Although there are several ways to move money through time, they all give you the same result. In the business world, the primary method is through the use of a financial spreadsheet, with Excel being the most popular. If you can use a financial calculator, you can easily apply your skills to a spreadsheet.

Actually, we have only one formula with which to calculate both present value and future value—we simply solve for different variables—FV and PV. This single compounding formula is $FV_n = PV(1 + i)^n$ and is presented in Table 5-13.

An annuity is a series of equal payments made for a specified number of years. In effect, it is calculated as the sum of the present or future value of the individual cash flows over the life of the annuity. The formula for an annuity due is given in Table 5-13.

If the cash flows from an annuity occur at the end of each period, the annuity is referred to as an ordinary annuity. If the cash flows occur at the beginning of each period, the annuity is referred to as an annuity due. We will assume that cash flows occur at the end of each period unless otherwise stated.

The procedure for solving for PMT, the annuity payment value when i, n, and PV are known, is also used to determine what payments are associated with paying off a loan in equal installments over time. Loans that are paid off this way, in equal periodic payments, are called amortized loans. Although the payments are fixed, different amounts of each payment are applied toward the principal and the interest. With each payment you make, you owe a bit less on the principal. As a result, the amount that goes toward the interest payment declines with each payment made, whereas the portion of each payment that goes toward the principal increases.

With nonannual compounding, interest is earned on interest more frequently because the length of the compounding period is shorter. As a result, there is an inverse relationship between the length of the compounding period and the effective annual interest rate. The formula for solving for the future value of a single payment with nonannual compounding is given in Table 5-13.

Although some projects will involve a single cash flow, and some will involve annuities, many projects will involve uneven cash flows over several years. However, finding the present or future value of these flows is not difficult because the present value of any cash flow measured in today's dollars can be compared, by adding the inflows and subtracting the outflows, to the present value of any other cash flow also measured in today's dollars.

A perpetuity is an annuity that continues forever; that is, every year following its establishment the investment pays the same dollar amount. An example of a perpetuity is preferred stock, which pays a constant dollar dividend infinitely. Determining the present value of a perpetuity is delightfully simple. We merely need to divide the constant flow by the discount rate.

For companies doing business internationally, dramatic fluctuations in inflation rates from country to country can make choosing the appropriate discount rate to move money through time an extremely difficult process.

Key Terms

Amortized loan   150

Annual percentage yield (APY) or effective annual rate (EAR)   153

Annuity   144

Annuity due   149

Compound annuity   144

Compound interest   132

Future-value interest factor ($FVIF_{i, n}$)   134

Future-value interest factor for an annuity ($FVIFA_{i, n}$)   145

Ordinary annuity   144

Perpetuity   158

Present value   139

Present-value interest factor ($PVIF_{i, n}$)   140

Present-value interest factor for an annuity ($PVIFA_{i, n}$)   146

Review Questions

5-1. What is the time value of money? Why is it so important?

5-2. The process of discounting and compounding are related. Explain this relationship.

5-3. How would an increase in the interest rate (i) or a decrease in the holding period (n) affect the future value (FV_n) of a sum of money? Explain why.

5-4. Suppose you were considering depositing your savings in one of three banks, all of which pay 5 percent interest; bank A compounds annually, bank B compounds semiannually, and bank C compounds daily. Which bank would you choose? Why?

5-5. What is the relationship between the $PVIF_{i,n}$ (Table 5-3) and the $PVIFA_{i,n}$ (Table 5-7)? What is the $PVIFA_{10\%,\,10\,yr}$? Add up the values of the $PVIF_{10\%,n}$ for $n = 1, \ldots, 10$. What is this value? Why do these values have the relationship they do?

5-6. What is an annuity? Give some examples of annuities. Distinguish between an annuity and a perpetuity.

Self-Test Problems

Solutions to these problems are provided at the end of the chapter.

ST-1. You place $25,000 in a savings account paying an annual compound interest of 8 percent for 3 years and then move it into a savings account that pays 10 percent interest compounded annually. By how much will your money have grown at the end of 6 years?

ST-2. You purchase a boat for $35,000 and pay $5,000 down. You also agree to pay the rest over the next 10 years in 10 equal end-of-the-year payments plus 13 percent compound interest on the unpaid balance. What will be the amount of each payment?

Study Problems

5-1. (*Compound interest*) To what amount will the following investments accumulate?

  a. $5,000 invested for 10 years at 10 percent compounded annually
  b. $8,000 invested for 7 years at 8 percent compounded annually
  c. $775 invested for 12 years at 12 percent compounded annually
  d. $21,000 invested for 5 years at 5 percent compounded annually

5-2. (*Compound value solving for n*) How many years will the following take?

  a. $500 to grow to $1,039.50 if invested at 5 percent compounded annually
  b. $35 to grow to $53.87 if invested at 9 percent compounded annually
  c. $100 to grow to $298.60 if invested at 20 percent compounded annually
  d. $53 to grow to $78.76 if invested at 2 percent compounded annually

5-3. (*Compound value solving for i*) At what annual rate would the following have to be invested?

  a. $500 to grow to $1,948.00 in 12 years
  b. $300 to grow to $422.10 in 7 years
  c. $50 to grow to $280.20 in 20 years
  d. $200 to grow to $497.60 in 5 years

5-4. (*Present value*) What is the present value of the following future amounts?

  a. $800 to be received 10 years from now discounted back to the present at 10 percent
  b. $300 to be received 5 years from now discounted back to the present at 5 percent
  c. $1,000 to be received 8 years from now discounted back to the present at 3 percent
  d. $1,000 to be received 8 years from now discounted back to the present at 20 percent

5-5. (*Compound annuity*) What is the accumulated sum of each of the following streams of payments?

  a. $500 a year for 10 years compounded annually at 5 percent
  b. $100 a year for 5 years compounded annually at 10 percent
  c. $35 a year for 7 years compounded annually at 7 percent
  d. $25 a year for 3 years compounded annually at 2 percent

5-6. (*Present value of an annuity*) What is the present value of the following annuities?

    a. $2,500 a year for 10 years discounted back to the present at 7 percent

    b. $70 a year for 3 years discounted back to the present at 3 percent

    c. $280 a year for 7 years discounted back to the present at 6 percent

    d. $500 a year for 10 years discounted back to the present at 10 percent

5-7. (*Compound value*) Stanford Simmons, who recently sold his Porsche, placed $10,000 in a savings account paying annual compound interest of 6 percent.

    a. Calculate the amount of money that will have accrued if he leaves the money in the bank for 1, 5, and 15 years.

    b. If he moves his money into an account that pays 8 percent or one that pays 10 percent, rework part (a) using these new interest rates.

    c. What conclusions can you draw about the relationship between interest rates, time, and future sums from the calculations you have completed in this problem?

5-8. (*Compound interest with nonannual periods*) Calculate the amount of money that will be in each of the following accounts at the end of the given deposit period.

ACCOUNT	AMOUNT DEPOSITED	ANNUAL INTEREST RATE	COMPOUNDING PERIOD (MONTHS)	DEPOSIT PERIOD (YEARS)
Theodore Logan III	$ 1,000	10%	12 *(1)*	10
Vernell Coles	95,000	12	1 *(12)*	1
Thomas Elliott	8,000	12	2 *(6)*	2
Wayne Robinson	120,000	8	3 *(4)*	2
Eugene Chung	30,000	10	6 *(2)*	4
Kelly Cravens	15,000	12	4 *(3)*	3

5-9. (*Compound interest with nonannual periods*)

    a. Calculate the future sum of $5,000, given that it will be held in the bank 5 years at an annual interest rate of 6 percent.

    b. Recalculate part (a) using compounding periods that are (1) semiannual and (2) bimonthly.

    c. Recalculate parts (a) and (b) for a 12 percent annual interest rate.

    d. Recalculate part (a) using a time horizon of 12 years (annual interest rate is still 6 percent).

    e. With respect to the effect of changes in the stated interest rate and holding periods on future sums in parts (c) and (d), what conclusions do you draw when you compare these figures with the answers found in parts (a) and (b)?

5-10. (*Solving for i with annuities*) Nicki Johnson, a sophomore mechanical engineering student, receives a call from an insurance agent, who believes that Nicki is an older woman ready to retire from teaching. He talks to her about several annuities that she could buy that would guarantee her an annual fixed income. The annuities are as follows:

ANNUITY	INITIAL PAYMENT INTO ANNUITY (AT *t* = 0)	AMOUNT OF MONEY RECEIVED PER YEAR	DURATION OF ANNUITY (YEARS)
A	$50,000	$8,500	12
B	$60,000	$7,000	25
C	$70,000	$8,000	20

If Nicki could earn 11 percent on her money by placing it in a savings account, should she place it instead in any of the annuities? Which ones, if any? Why?

5-11. (*Future value*) Sales of a new finance book were 15,000 copies this year and were expected to increase by 20 percent per year. What are expected sales during each of the next 3 years? Graph this sales trend and explain.

5-12. (*Future value*) Barry Bonds hit 73 home runs in 2001. If his home-run output grew at a rate of 10 percent per year, what would it have been over the following 5 years?

5-13. (*Loan amortization*) Mr. Bill S. Preston, Esq., purchased a new house for $80,000. He paid $20,000 down and agreed to pay the rest over the next 25 years in 25 equal end-of-year payments plus 9 percent compound interest on the unpaid balance. What will these equal payments be?

5-14. (*Solving for PMT of an annuity*) To pay for your child's education, you wish to have accumulated $15,000 at the end of 15 years. To do this you plan on depositing an equal amount into the bank at the end of each year. If the bank is willing to pay 6 percent compounded annually, how much must you deposit each year to reach your goal?

5-15. (*Solving for i in compound interest*) If you were offered $1,079.50 10 years from now in return for an investment of $500 currently, what annual rate of interest would you earn if you took the offer?

5-16. (*Future value of an annuity*) In 10 years you are planning on retiring and buying a house in Oviedo, Florida. The house you are looking at currently costs $100,000 and is expected to increase in value each year at a rate of 5 percent. Assuming you can earn 10 percent annually on your investments, how much must you invest at the end of each of the next 10 years to be able to buy your dream home when you retire?

5-17. (*Compound value*) The Aggarwal Corporation needs to save $10 million to retire a $10 million mortgage that matures in 10 years. To retire this mortgage, the company plans to put a fixed amount into an account at the end of each year for 10 years, with the first payment occurring at the end of 1 year. The Aggarwal Corporation expects to earn 9 percent annually on the money in this account. What equal annual contribution must it make to this account to accumulate the $10 million in 10 years?

5-18. (*Compound interest with nonannual periods*) After examining the various personal loan rates available to you, you find that you can borrow funds from a finance company at 12 percent compounded monthly or from a bank at 13 percent compounded annually. Which alternative is more attractive?

5-19. (*Present value of an uneven stream of payments*) You are given three investment alternatives to analyze. The cash flows from these three investments are as follows:

END OF YEAR	INVESTMENT		
	A	B	C
1	$10,000		$10,000
2	10,000		
3	10,000		
4	10,000		
5	10,000	$10,000	
6		10,000	50,000
7		10,000	
8		10,000	
9		10,000	
10		10,000	10,000

Assuming a 20 percent discount rate, find the present value of each investment.

5-20. (*Present value*) The Kumar Corporation is planning on issuing bonds that pay no interest but can be converted into $1,000 at maturity, 7 years from their purchase. To price these bonds competitively with other bonds of equal risk, it is determined that they should yield 10 percent, compounded annually. At what price should the Kumar Corporation sell these bonds?

5-21. (*Perpetuities*) What is the present value of the following?

   a. A $300 perpetuity discounted back to the present at 8 percent
   b. A $1,000 perpetuity discounted back to the present at 12 percent
   c. A $100 perpetuity discounted back to the present at 9 percent
   d. A $95 perpetuity discounted back to the present at 5 percent

5-22. (*Solving for n with nonannual periods*) About how many years would it take for your investment to grow fourfold if it were invested at 16 percent compounded semiannually?

5-23. (*Complex present value*) How much do you have to deposit today so that beginning 11 years from now you can withdraw $10,000 a year for the next 5 years (periods 11 through 15) plus an *additional* amount of $20,000 in that last year (period 15)? Assume an interest rate of 6 percent.

5-24. (*Loan amortization*) On December 31, Beth Klemkosky bought a yacht for $50,000, paying $10,000 down and agreeing to pay the balance in 10 equal end-of-year installments and 10 percent interest on the declining balance. How big would the annual payments be?

5-25. (*Solving for i of an annuity*) You lend a friend $30,000, which your friend will repay in five equal annual end-of-year payments of $10,000, with the first payment to be received 1 year from now. What rate of return does your loan receive?

5-26. (*Solving for i in compound interest*) You lend a friend $10,000, for which your friend will repay you $27,027 at the end of 5 years. What interest rate are you charging your "friend"?

5-27. (*Loan amortization*) A firm borrows $25,000 from the bank at 12 percent compounded annually to purchase some new machinery. This loan is to be repaid in equal installments at the end of each year over the next 5 years. How much will each annual payment be?

5-28. (*Present-value comparison*) You are offered $1,000 today, $10,000 in 12 years, or $25,000 in 25 years. Assuming that you can earn 11 percent on your money, which should you choose?

5-29. (*Compound annuity*) You plan on buying some property in Florida 5 years from today. To do this you estimate that you will need $20,000 at that time for the purchase. You would like to accumulate these funds by making equal annual deposits in your savings account, which pays 12 percent annually. If you make your first deposit at the end of this year, and you would like your account to reach $20,000 when the final deposit is made, what will be the amount of your deposits?

5-30. (*Complex present value*) You would like to have $50,000 in 15 years. To accumulate this amount you plan to deposit each year an equal sum in the bank, which will earn 7 percent interest compounded annually. Your first payment will be made at the end of the year.

    a. How much must you deposit annually to accumulate this amount?
    b. If you decide to make a large lump-sum deposit today instead of the annual deposits, how large should this lump-sum deposit be? (Assume you can earn 7 percent on this deposit.)
    c. At the end of 5 years you will receive $10,000 and deposit this in the bank toward your goal of $50,000 at the end of 15 years. In addition to this deposit, how much must you deposit in equal annual deposits to reach your goal? (Again assume you can earn 7 percent on this deposit.)

5-31. (*Comprehensive present value*) You are trying to plan for retirement in 10 years, and currently you have $100,000 in a savings account and $300,000 in stocks. In addition you plan on adding to your savings by depositing $10,000 per year in your savings account at the end of each of the next 5 years and then $20,000 per year at the end of each year for the final 5 years until retirement.

    a. Assuming your savings account returns 7 percent compounded annually, and your investment in stocks will return 12 percent compounded annually, how much will you have at the end of 10 years? (Ignore taxes.)
    b. If you expect to live for 20 years after you retire, and at retirement you deposit all of your savings in a bank account paying 10 percent, how much can you withdraw each year after retirement (20 equal withdrawals beginning 1 year after you retire) to end up with a zero balance upon your death?

5-32. (*Loan amortization*) On December 31, Son-Nan Chen borrowed $100,000, agreeing to repay this sum in 20 equal end-of-year installments and 15 percent interest on the declining balance. How large must the annual payments be?

5-33. (*Loan amortization*) To buy a new house you must borrow $150,000. To do this you take out a $150,000, 30-year, 10 percent mortgage. Your mortgage payments, which are made at the end of each year (one payment each year), include both principal and 10 percent interest on the declining balance. How large will your annual payments be?

5-34. (*Present value*) The state lottery's million-dollar payout provides for $1 million to be paid over 19 years in 20 payments of $50,000. The first $50,000 payment is made immediately, and the 19 remaining $50,000 payments occur at the end of each of the next 19 years. If 10 percent is the appropriate discount rate, what is the present value of this stream of cash flows? If 20 percent is the appropriate discount rate, what is the present value of the cash flows?

5-35. (*Solving for i in compound interest—financial calculator needed*) In September 1963, the first issue of the comic book *X-MEN* was issued. The original price for that issue was $0.12. By September 2002, 39 years later, the value of this comic book had risen to $7,500. What annual rate of interest would you have earned if you had bought the comic in 1963 and sold it in 2002?

5-36. (*Comprehensive present value*) You have just inherited a large sum of money, and you are trying to determine how much you should save for retirement and how much you can spend now. For retirement, you will deposit today (January 1, 2008) a lump sum in a bank account paying 10 percent compounded annually. You don't plan on touching this deposit until you retire in 5 years (on January 1, 2013), and you plan on living for 20 additional years and then dropping dead on December 31, 2032. During your retirement you would like to receive income of $50,000 per year to be received the first day of each year, with the first payment on January 1, 2013, and the last payment on January 1, 2032. Complicating this objective is your desire to have one final 3-year fling during which time you'd like to track down all the living original cast members of *Leave It to Beaver* and *The Brady Bunch* and get their autographs. To finance this effort you want to receive $250,000 on

January 1, 2028, and *nothing* on January 1, 2029, and January 1, 2030, as you will be on the road. In addition, after you pass on (January 1, 2033), you would like to have a total of $100,000 to leave to your children.

   a. How much must you deposit in the bank at 10 percent on January 1, 2008, to achieve your goal? (Use a timeline to answer this question.)
   b. What kinds of problems are associated with this analysis and its assumptions?

5-37. (*Spreadsheet problem*) If you invest $900 in a bank in which it will earn 8 percent compounded annually, how much will it be worth at the end of 7 years? Use a spreadsheet to do your calculations.

5-38. (*Spreadsheet problem*) In 20 years you'd like to have $250,000 to buy a vacation home, but you have only $30,000. At what rate must your $30,000 be compounded annually for it to grow to $250,000 in 20 years? Use a spreadsheet to calculate your answer.

5-39. (*Spreadsheet problem*) To buy a new house you take out a 25-year mortgage for $300,000. What will your monthly payments be if the interest rate on your mortgage is 8 percent? Use a spreadsheet to calculate your answer. Now, calculate the portion of the 48th monthly payment that goes toward interest and principal.

5-40. (*Future and present value using a calculator*) Over the past few years Microsoft founder Bill Gates's net worth has fluctuated between $20 billion and $130 billion. In 2006 Gates was worth about $28 billion after he reduced his stake in Microsoft from 21 percent to around 14 percent by moving billions into his charitable foundation. Let's see what Bill Gates can do with his money in the following problems.

   a. I'll take Manhattan? Manhattan's native tribe sold Manhattan Island to Peter Minuit for $24 in 1626. Now, 781 years later in 2007, Bill Gates wants to buy the island from the "current natives." How much would Bill have to pay for Manhattan if the "current natives" want a 6 percent annual return on the original $24 purchase price? Could he afford it?
   b. (*Nonannual compounding using a calculator*) How much would Bill have to pay for Manhattan if the "current natives" want a 6% return compounded monthly on the original $24 purchase price?
   c. Microsoft Seattle? Bill Gates decides to pass on Manhattan and instead plans to buy the city of Seattle, Washington, for $60 billion in 10 years. How much would Mr. Gates have to invest today at 10 percent compounded annually in order to purchase Seattle in 10 years?
   d. Now assume Bill Gates wants to invest only about half his net worth today, $14 billion, in order to buy Seattle for $60 billion in 10 years. What annual rate of return would he have to earn in order to complete his purchase in 10 years?
   e. Margaritaville? Instead of buying and running large cities, Bill Gates is considering quitting the rigors of the business world and retiring to work on his golf game. To fund his retirement, Bill Gates would invest his $28 billion fortune in safe investments with an expected annual rate of return of 7 percent. Also, Mr. Gates wants to make 40 equal annual withdrawals from this retirement fund beginning a year from today. How much can Mr. Gates's annual withdrawal be in this case?

5-41. (*Compounding using a calculator*) Bart Simpson, age 10, wants to be able to buy a really cool new car when he turns 16. His really cool car costs $15,000 today, and its cost is expected to increase 3 percent annually. Bart wants to make one deposit today (he can sell his mint-condition original *Nuclear Boy* comic book) into an account paying 7.5 percent annually in order to buy his car in 6 years. How much will Bart's car cost, and how much does Bart have to save today in order to buy this car at age 16?

5-42. (*Compounding using a calculator*) Lisa Simpson wants to have $1 million in 45 years by making equal annual end-of-the-year deposits into a tax-deferred account paying 8.75 percent annually. What must Lisa's annual deposit be?

5-43. (*Compounding using a calculator*) Springfield mogul Montgomery Burns, age 80, wants to retire at age 100 in order to steal candy from babies full time. Once Mr. Burns retires, he wants to withdraw $1 billion at the beginning of each year for 10 years from a special offshore account that will pay 20 percent annually. In order to fund his retirement, Mr. Burns will make 20 equal end-of-the-year deposits in this same special account that will pay 20 percent annually. How much money will Mr. Burns need at age 100, and how large of an annual deposit must he make to fund this retirement account?

5-44. (*Compounding using a calculator and annuities due*) Imagine Homer Simpson actually invested $100,000 5 years ago at a 7.5 percent annual interest rate. If he invests an additional $1,500 a year at the beginning of each year for 20 years at the same 7.5 percent annual rate, how much money will Homer have 20 years from now?

5-45. (*Nonannual compounding using a calculator*) Prof. Finance is thinking about trading cars. He estimates he will still have to borrow $25,000 to pay for his new car. How large will Prof. Finance's monthly car loan payment be if he can get a 5-year (60 equal monthly payments) car loan from the university's credit union at 6.2 percent?

5-46. (*Nonannual compounding using a calculator*) Bowflex's television ads say you can get a fitness machine that sells for $999 for $33 a month for 36 months. What rate of interest are you paying on this Bowflex loan?

5-47. (*Nonannual compounding using a calculator*) Ford's current incentives include 4.9 percent financing for 60 months or $1,000 cash back for a Mustang. Let's assume Suzie Student wants to buy the premium Mustang convertible, which costs $25,000, and she has no down payment other than the cash back from Ford. If she chooses the $1,000 cash back, Suzie can borrow from the VTech Credit Union at 6.9 percent for 60 months (Suzie's credit isn't as good as Prof. Finance's). What will Suzie Student's monthly payment be under each option? Which option should she choose?

5-48. (*Nonannual compounding using a calculator*) Ronnie Rental plans to invest $1,000 at the end of each quarter for 4 years into an account that pays 6.4 percent compounded quarterly. He will use this money as a down payment on a new home at the end of the 4 years. How large will his down payment be 4 years from today?

5-49. (*Nonannual compounding using a calculator*) Dennis Rodman has a $5,000 debt balance on his Visa card that charges 12.9 percent compounded monthly. Dennis's current minimum monthly payment is 3 percent of his debt balance, which is $150. How many months (round up) will it take Dennis to pay off his credit card if he pays the current minimum payment of $150 at the end of each month?

5-50. (*Nonannual compounding using a calculator*) Should we have bet the kids' college fund at the dog track? In the early 2000s investors suffered substantial declines on tax-sheltered college savings plans (called 529 plans) around the country. Let's look at one specific case of a college professor (let's call him Prof. ME) with two young children. Two years ago Prof. ME invested $160,000 hoping to have $420,000 available 12 years later when the first child started college. However, the account's balance is now only $140,000. Let's figure out what is needed to get Prof. ME's college savings plan back on track.

    a. What was the original annual rate of return needed to reach Prof. ME's goal when he started the fund 2 years ago?

    b. Now with only $140,000 in the fund and 10 years remaining until his first child starts college, what annual rate of return would the fund have to earn to reach Prof. ME's $420,000 goal if he adds nothing to the account?

    c. Shocked by his experience of the past 2 years, Prof. ME feels the college mutual fund has invested too much in stocks. He wants a low-risk fund in order to ensure he has the necessary $420,000 in 10 years, and he is willing to make end-of-the-month deposits to the fund as well. He later finds a fund that promises to pay a guaranteed return of 6 percent compounded monthly. Prof. ME decides to transfer the $140,000 to this new fund and make the necessary monthly deposits. How large of a monthly deposit must Prof. ME make into this new fund to meet his $420,000 goal?

    d. Now Prof. ME gets sticker shock from the necessary monthly deposit he has to make into the guaranteed fund in the preceding question. He decides to invest the $140,000 today and $500 at the end of each month for the next 10 years into a fund consisting of 50 percent stock and 50 percent bonds and hope for the best. What annual rate of return would the fund have to earn in order to reach Prof. ME's $420,000 goal?

5-51. (*Complex annuity*) Upon graduating from college 35 years ago, Dr. Nick Riviera was already thinking of retirement. Since then he has made deposits into his retirement fund on a quarterly basis in the amount of $300. Nick has just completed his final payment and is at last ready to retire. His retirement fund has earned 9% interest compounded quarterly.

    a. How much has Nick accumulated in his retirement account?

    b. In addition to all this, 15 years ago, Nick received an inheritance check for $20,000 from his beloved uncle. He decided to deposit the entire amount into his retirement fund. What is his current balance in the fund?

5-52. (*Solving for i in an annuity*) Your folks just called and would like some advice from you. An insurance agent just called them and offered them the opportunity to purchase an annuity for $21,074.25 that will pay them $3,000 per year for 20 years, but they don't have the slightest idea what return they would be making on their investment of $21,074.25. What rate of return will they be earning?

5-53. *(Complex annuity and future value)* Milhouse, 22, is about to begin his career as a rocket scientist for a NASA contractor. Being a rocket scientist, Milhouse knows that he should begin saving for retirement immediately. Part of his inspiration came from reading an article on Social Security in *Newsweek*, where he saw that the ratio of workers paying taxes to retirees collecting checks will drop dramatically in the future. In fact the ratio was 8.6 workers for every retiree in 1955; today the ratio is 3.3, and it will drop to 2 workers for every retiree in 2040. Milhouse's retirement plan pays 9 percent interest annually and allows him to make equal yearly contributions. Upon retirement Milhouse plans to buy a new boat, which he estimates will cost him $300,000 in 43 years (he plans to retire at age 65). He also estimates that in order to live comfortably he will require a yearly income of $80,000 for each year after he retires. Based on family history, Milhouse expects to live until age 80 (that is, he would like to receive 15 payments of $80,000 at the end of each year). When he retires, Milhouse will purchase his boat in one lump sum and place the remaining balance into an account, which pays 6% interest, from which he will withdraw his $80,000 per year. If Milhouse's first contribution is made 1 year from today, and his last is made the day he retires, how much money must he contribute each year to his retirement fund?

Web Works

5-WW1. How fast will my money grow? Use the financial calculator provided by Financenter (**http://partners.financenter.com/financenter/calculate/us-eng/savings14.fcs**) to determine how long it will take $50,000 to grow to $90,000 if it earns 10 percent. If you start with $50,000 and invest an additional $250 per month every month, how long will it take to grow to $90,000 if it earns 10 percent?

5-WW2. How much money will you need to start with if you make no additional investments? You want to have $90,000 in 6 years, and your investment will grow at 10 percent. Again, use the financial calculator provided by Financenter (**http://partners.fmancenter.com/financenter/ calculate/us-eng/ savings14.fcs**) to determine how much money you will need to start with.

5-WW3. Financial calculators. Compare some of the different financial calculators that are available on the Internet. Look at both the Dinky Town Calculators (**www.dinkytown.net**) and *USA Today's* consumer loan, tuition, new car, mortgage, retirement, and 401(k) calculators (**www.usatoday.com/money/perfi/calculators/calculator.htm**). Also check out the ABC News Online calculators (**abcnews.go.com/Business/Calculators/story?id=133188**), which include investing, banking, and financial planning online calculators. Finally look at Interest.com calculators (**calculators interest.com/index.asp**). Which financial calculators do you find to be the most useful? Why?

5-WW4. Understanding annuities. Home mortgage payments are an annuity, and so are any loans in which the payments remain constant. In effect, if you can understand annuities, you'll understand how mortgages and other loans are calculated. What would your monthly loan payments be if you bought a new 60-inch television for $3,400? Assume you put $300 down and plan to finance the loan over 36 months at 12 percent interest. In addition, when you bought the new television, you received $100 for the trade-in of your old set. Use an online financial calculator (**www.moneychimp.com/calculator/annuity_calculator.htm**) to determine your answer.

5-WW5. College savings planning. Try out the MSN Money Tuition Savings Calculator (**http://moneycentral.msn.com/investor/calcs/n_college/main.asp**). Assume you live in Virginia, begin with an initial balance of $1,000, and there are 11 years until your child goes to college. The rate of return on your college investments is 9 percent, and this is a taxable investment with a marginal tax rate of 22.35 percent. You do not pay capital gains tax when you cash out your college investments, the rate of tuition cost increase is 6 percent annually, and the current annual cost of college is $10,000 each year for 4 years. How much do you need to save annually to cover the cost of college, and how much in total will be available for college?

Mini Case

For your job as the business reporter for a local newspaper, you are given the task of putting together a series of articles that explain the power of the time value of money to your readers. Your editor would like you to address several specific questions in addition to demonstrating for the readership the use of time value of money techniques by applying them to several problems. What would be your response to the following memorandum from your editor?

To: Business Reporter
From: Perry White, Editor, *Daily Planet*
Re: Upcoming Series on the Importance and Power of the Time Value of Money

In your upcoming series on the time value of money, I would like to make sure you cover several specific points. In addition, before you begin this assignment, I want to make sure we are all reading from the same script, as accuracy has always been the cornerstone of the *Daily Planet*. In this regard, I'd like a response to the following questions before we proceed:

a. What is the relationship between discounting and compounding?

b. What is the relationship between the $PVIF_{i,n}$ and $PVIFA_{i,n}$?

c. 1. What will $5,000 invested for 10 years at 8 percent compounded annually grow to?

   2. How many years will it take $400 to grow to $1,671 if it is invested at 10 percent compounded annually?

   3. At what rate would $1,000 have to be invested to grow to $4,046 in 10 years?

d. Calculate the future sum of $1,000, given that it will be held in the bank for 5 years and earn 10 percent compounded semiannually.

e. What is an annuity due? How does this differ from an ordinary annuity?

f. What is the present value of an ordinary annuity of $1,000 per year for 7 years discounted back to the present at 10 percent? What would be the present value if it were an annuity due?

g. What is the future value of an ordinary annuity of $1,000 per year for 7 years compounded at 10 percent? What would be the future value if it were an annuity due?

h. You have just borrowed $100,000, and you agree to pay it back over the next 25 years in 25 equal end-of-year payments plus 10 percent compound interest on the unpaid balance. What will be the size of these payments?

i. What is the present value of a $1,000 perpetuity discounted back to the present at 8 percent?

j. What is the present value of a $1,000 annuity for 10 years, with the first payment occurring at the end of year 10 (that is, ten $1,000 payments occurring at the end of year 10 through year 19), given a discount rate of 10 percent?

k. Given a 10 percent discount rate, what is the present value of a perpetuity of $1,000 per year if the first payment does not begin until the end of year 10?

Self–Test Solutions

SS-1. This is a compound interest problem in which you must first find the future value of $25,000 growing at 8 percent compounded annually for 3 years and then allow that future value to grow for an additional 3 years at 10 percent. First, the value of the $25,000 after 3 years growing at 8 percent is

$$FV_3 = PV(1 + i)^n$$
$$FV_3 = \$25,000(1 + 0.8)^3$$
$$FV_3 = \$25,000(1.260)$$
$$FV_3 = \$31,500$$

Thus, after 3 years you have $31,500. Now this amount is allowed to grow for 3 years at 10 percent. Plugging this into equation (5-6), with $PV = \$31,500$, $i = 10$ percent, and $n = 3$ years, we solve for FV_3.

$$FV_3 = \$31,500(1 + .10)^3$$
$$FV_3 = \$31,500(1.331)$$
$$FV_3 = \$41,926.50$$

Thus, after 6 years the $25,000 will have grown to $41,926.50.

SS-2. This loan amortization problem is actually just a present-value-of-an-annuity problem in which we know the values of i, n, and PV and are solving for PMT. In this case the value of i is 13 percent, n is 10 years, and PV is $30,000. Substituting these values into equation (5-9b) we find

$$\$30,000 = PMT(PVIFA_{13\%,\ 10\ yr})$$
$$\$30,000 = PMT(5.426)$$
$$\$5,528.93 = PMT$$

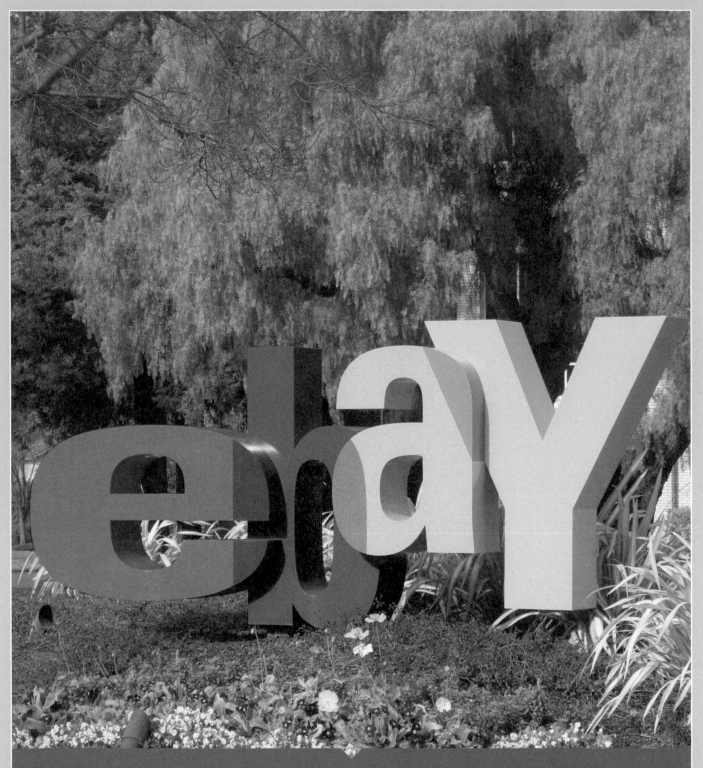

CHAPTER 6

The Meaning and Measurement of Risk and Return

One of the most important concepts in all of finance deals with risk and return, and our first principle addresses this topic. As an illustration of risk and return, consider what has happened with Internet stocks in recent years.

Company names such as Amazon, eBay, Google, and Yahoo! are familiar to us all. Hardly a week goes by, if not a day, that we do not access the Web sites of these firms—and many other Internet companies. But far fewer of us have ever directly invested in Internet companies.

Following a 17.5 percent decline in Internet stock prices during the first half of 2006, Jonathan Post, an analyst for Merrill Lynch, recommended that investors should consider purchasing Internet stocks. In an investor report in early summer 2006, Post wrote:

> [T]he recent sell-off in Internet stocks has created a buying opportunity given the stocks' valuations and long-term growth opportunities. . . . While the Internet sector could drift sideways into the summer. . . , we expect improved sentiment on operating margins and believe the group is well positioned for a positive move in the second half [of the year].[1]

[1] Mary Crane, "Buy-Time For Undervalued Large-Cap Internet Stocks," **www.forbes.com/markets/2006/06/01/google-yahoo-ebay-0601markets03.html**, accessed July 30, 2006.

Would you have followed Post's recommendation to invest? After all, how could you go wrong with Google, Amazon, Yahoo!, and eBay? Before deciding, you should have taken the time to learn a little history about investing in Internet stocks.

If you had invested as early as February 1, 2001, 2 months later your investment would have been worth only half of what it was originally. But April 2001 would have been good to you; your investment would have gained 32 percent in value. However, 5 months later, at the end of September, you would have seen the value of your stocks decline by 58 percent. Then in 2003, your investment would have increased 82 percent in value, followed by 24 percent in 2004. Finally, in 2005 your portfolio of Internet stocks would have increased a meager 9 percent, followed by an 18 percent decrease in the first 6 months of 2006.

Clearly, owning Internet stocks has not been for the faint of heart. These stocks have produced high rates of return for a few investors depending on when they invested, but punished many others. To say the least, these investments have offered investors the potential of high returns, but only for those who were willing to assume great amounts of risk. As the owner of Internet stocks, you may eat well if they continue to increase in the future, but you certainly won't sleep very well some nights. Welcome to the world of high risk.

Remember Your Principles

This chapter has one primary objective, that of helping you understand **Principle 1: The Risk–Return Trade-Off—We Won't Take On Additional Risk Unless We Expect to Be Compensated with Additional Return**.

The need to recognize risk in financial decisions has already been apparent in earlier chapters. In Chapter 2, we referred to the discount rate, or the interest rate, as the opportunity cost of funds, but we did not look at the reasons why that rate might be high or low. For example, we did not explain why in July 2006 you could buy bonds issued by SBC Communications that promised to pay a 6.1 percent rate of return, or why you could buy Ford Motor Company Corporation bonds that would give you a 10.1 percent rate of return, provided that both firms make the payments to the investors as promised.

In this chapter, we learn that risk is an integral force underlying rates of return. To begin our study, we define expected return and risk and offer suggestions about how these important concepts of return and risk can be measured quantitatively. We also compare the historical relationship between risk and rates of return. We then explain how diversifying investments can affect the expected return and riskiness of those investments. We also consider how the riskiness of an investment should affect the required rate of return on an investment.

Let's begin our study by looking at what we mean by the expected rate of return and how it can be measured.

Objective **1**

Define and measure the expected rate of return of an individual investment.

EXPECTED RETURN DEFINED AND MEASURED

The expected benefits, or returns, an investment generates come in the form of cash flows. Cash flow, not accounting profit, is the relevant variable the financial manager uses to measure returns. This principle holds true regardless of the type of security, whether it is a debt instrument, preferred stock, common stock, or any mixture of these (such as convertible bonds).

Accurately measuring expected future cash flows is not easy in a world of uncertainty. To illustrate, assume you are considering an investment costing $10,000, for which the future cash flows from owning the security depend on the state of the economy, as estimated in Table 6-1.

In any given year, the investment could produce any one of three possible cash flows, depending on the particular state of the economy. With this information, how should we select the cash flow estimate that means the most for measuring the investment's expected rate of return? One approach is to calculate an *expected* cash flow. The expected cash flow is simply the weighted average of the *possible* cash flow outcomes such that the weights are the probabilities of the various states of the economy occurring. Let X_i designate the ith possible cash flow, n reflect the number of possible states of the economy, and P_i indicate the probability

Remember Your Principles

Remember that future cash flows, not reported earnings, determine the investor's rate of return. That is, **Principle 3: Cash—Not Profits—Is King**.

TABLE 6-1   Measuring the Expected Return of an Investment

STATE OF THE ECONOMY	PROBABILITY OF THE STATES[a]	CASH FLOWS FROM THE INVESTMENT	PERCENTAGE RETURNS (CASH FLOW ÷ INVESTMENT COST)
Economic recession	20%	$1,000	10% ($1,000 ÷ $10,000)
Moderate economic growth	30%	1,200	12% ($1,200 ÷ $10,000)
Strong economic growth	50%	1,400	14% ($1,400 ÷ $10,000)

[a] The probabilities assigned to the three possible economic conditions have to be determined subjectively, which requires managers to have a thorough understanding of both the investment cash flows and the general economy.

Can You Do It?

COMPUTING EXPECTED RETURN

You are contemplating making a $5,000 investment that would have the following possible outcomes in cash flow each year. What is the expected value of the future cash flows and the expected rate of return?

PROBABILITY	CASH FLOW
0.30	$350
0.50	625
0.20	900

(The solution can be found on page 174.)

that the *i*th cash flow, or state of economy, will occur. The expected cash flow, $\overline{X}$, may then be calculated as follows:

$$\overline{X} = P_1 X_1 + P_2 X_2 + \cdots + P_n X_n \tag{6-1}$$

For the present illustration:

$$\overline{X} = (.2)(\$1,000) + (.3)(\$1,200) + (.5)(\$1,400) = \$1,260$$

In addition to computing an expected dollar return from an investment, we can also calculate an **expected rate of return** earned on the $10,000 investment. Similar to the expected cash flow, the expected rate of return is *a weighted average of all the possible returns, weighted by the probability that each return will occur.* As the last column in Table 6-1 shows, the $1,400 cash inflow, assuming strong economic growth, represents a 14 percent return ($1,400 ÷ $10,000). Similarly, the $1,200 and $1,000 cash flows result in 12 percent and 10 percent returns, respectively. Using these percentage returns in place of the dollar amounts, the expected rate of return, $\overline{k}$ can be expressed as follows:

$$\overline{k} = P_1 k_1 + P_2 k_2 + \cdots + P_n k_n \tag{6-2}$$

In our example:

$$\overline{k} = (.2)(10\%) + (.3)(12\%) + (.5)(14\%) = 12.6\%$$

With our concept and measurement of expected returns, let's consider the other side of the investment coin: risk.

expected rate of return (1) the discount rate that equates the present value of the future cash flows of a bond (interest and maturity value) with the current market price of the bond. It is the rate of return an investor will earn if the bond is held to maturity. (2) The rate of return the investor expects to receive on an investment by paying the market price of the security. (3) The arithmetic mean or average of all possible outcomes where those outcomes are weighted by the probability that each will occur.

Did You Get It?

1. When we speak of "benefits" from investing in an asset, what do we mean?
2. Why is it difficult to measure future cash flows?
3. Define *expected rate of return*.

RISK DEFINED AND MEASURED

Objective **2**

Define and measure the riskiness of an individual investment.

Because we live in a world where events are uncertain, the way we see risk is vitally important in almost all dimensions of our life. The Greek poet and statesman Solon, writing in the sixth century B.C., put it this way:

There is risk in everything that one does, and no one knows where he will make his landfall when his enterprise is at its beginning. One man, trying to act effectively, fails to foresee something and falls into great and grim ruination, but to another man, one who is acting ineffectively, a god gives good fortune in everything and escape from his folly.[2]

[2] Translated by Arthur W. H. Adkins from the Greek text of Solon's poem "Prosperity, Justice, and the Hazards of Life," in M. L. West, ed., *Iambi et Elegi Gracci ante Alexandrum Canttati*, vol. 2 (Oxford: Clarendon Press, 1972).

How Did You Do?

COMPUTING EXPECTED RETURN

	POSSIBLE		EXPECTED	
PROBABILITY	CASH FLOW	RETURN	CASH FLOW	RETURN
0.30	$350	7.0%	$105.00	2.1%
0.50	625	12.5%	312.50	6.3%
0.20	900	18.0%	180.00	3.6%
Expected cash flow and rate of return			$597.50	12.0%

The possible returns are equal to the possible cash flows divided by the $5,000 investment. The expected cash flow and return are equal to the possible cash flows and possible returns multiplied by the probabilities.

Solon would have given more of the credit to Zeus than we would for the outcomes of our ventures. However, his insight reminds us that little is new in this world, including the need to acknowledge and compensate as best we can for the risks we encounter. In fact, the significance of risk and the need for understanding what it means in our lives is noted by Peter Bernstein in the following excerpt:

> What is it that distinguishes the thousands of years of history from what we think of as modern times? The answer goes way beyond the progress of science, technology, capitalism, and democracy.
>
> The distant past was studded with brilliant scientists, mathematicians, inventors, technologists, and political philosophers. Hundreds of years before the birth of Christ, the skies had been mapped, the great library of Alexandria built, and Euclid's geometry taught. Demand for technological innovation in warfare was as insatiable then as it is today. Coal, oil, iron, and copper have been at the service of human beings for millennia, and travel and communication mark the very beginnings of recorded civilization.
>
> The revolutionary idea that defines the boundary between modern times and the past is the mastery of risk: the notion that the future is more than a whim of the gods and that men and women are not passive before nature. Until human beings discovered a way across that boundary, the future was a mirror of the past or the murky domain of oracles and soothsayers who held a monopoly over knowledge of anticipated events.[3]

In our study of risk, we want to consider these questions:

1. What is risk?
2. How do we know the amount of risk associated with a given investment; that is, how do we measure risk?
3. If we choose to diversify our investments by owning more than one asset, as most of us do, will such diversification reduce the riskiness of our combined portfolio of investments?

Without intending to be trite, risk means different things to different people, depending on the context and on how they feel about taking chances. For the student, risk is the possibility of failing an exam or the chance of not making his or her best grades. For the coal miner or the oil field worker, risk is the chance of an explosion in the mine or at the well site. For the retired person, risk means perhaps not being able to live comfortably on a fixed income. For the entrepreneur, risk is the chance that a new venture will fail.

While certainly acknowledging these different kinds of risk, we limit our attention to the risk inherent in an investment. In this context, **risk** is the *potential variability in future cash flows*. The wider the range of possible events that can occur, the greater the risk. If we think about it, this is a relatively intuitive concept.

risk potential variability in future cash flows. The likely variability associated with revenue or income streams. Risk can be measured as the standard deviation or beta.

[3] Peter Bernstein, *Against the Gods: The Remarkable Story of Risk*. John Wiley & Sons, Inc., New York, 1996, p. 1.

To help us grasp the fundamental meaning of risk within this context, consider two possible investments:

1. The first investment is a U.S. Treasury bill, a government security that matures in 90 days and promises to pay an annual return of 6 percent. If we purchase and hold this security for 90 days, we are virtually assured of receiving no more and no less than 6 percent on an annualized basis. For all practical purposes, the risk of loss is nonexistent.
2. The second investment involves the purchase of the stock of a local publishing company. Looking at the past returns of the firm's stock, we have made the following estimate of the annual returns from the investment:

CHANCE OF OCCURRENCE	RATE OF RETURN ON INVESTMENT
1 chance in 10 (10% chance)	0%
2 chances in 10 (20% chance)	5%
4 chances in 10 (40% chance)	15%
2 chances in 10 (20% chance)	25%
1 chance in 10 (10% chance)	30%

Investing in the publishing company could conceivably provide a return as high as 30 percent if all goes well, or no return (0 percent) if everything goes against the firm. However, in future years, both good and bad, we could expect a 15 percent return on average.[4]

$$\overline{k} = (.10)(0\%) + (.20)(5\%) + (.40)(15\%) + (.20)(25\%) + (.10)(30\%) = 15\%$$

Comparing the Treasury bill investment with the publishing company investment, we see that the Treasury bill offers an expected 6 percent annualized rate of return, whereas the publishing company has an expected rate of return of 15 percent. However, our investment in the publishing firm is clearly more "risky"—that is, there is greater uncertainty about the final outcome. Stated somewhat differently, there is a greater variation or dispersion of possible returns, which in turn implies greater risk.[5] Figure 6–1 shows these differences graphically in the form of discrete probability distributions.

Although the return from investing in the publishing firm is clearly less certain than for Treasury bills, quantitative measures of risk are useful when the difference between two investments is not so evident. The standard deviation is such a measure. The **standard deviation** is

standard deviation a statistical measure of the spread of a probability distribution calculated by squaring the difference between each outcome and its expected value, weighting each value by its probability, summing over all possible outcomes, and taking the square root of this sum.

FIGURE 6-1 The Probability Distribution of the Returns on Two Investments

Treasury bill

Publishing company

---

[4] We assume that the particular outcome or return earned in 1 year does *not* affect the return earned in the subsequent year. Technically speaking, the distribution of returns in any year is assumed to be independent of the outcome in any prior year.

[5] How can we possibly view variations above the expected return as risk? Should we even be concerned with the positive deviations above the expected return? Some would say "no," viewing risk as only the negative variability in returns from a predetermined minimum acceptable rate of return. However, as long as the distribution of returns is symmetrical, the same conclusions will be reached.

Ethics in Financial Management

THE TYCO SCANDAL: WHEN IT COMES TO ETHICS, LEADERSHIP MATTERS

Tyco International is a multinational conglomerate with business units selling products in the electronic-component, health care, fire safety, security, and fluid-control industries. In 1992, Dennis Kozlowski became CEO of Tyco, and for the next 10 years, the company went on an aggressive acquisitions spree. By some accounts, the firm acquired over 1,000 companies under Kozlowski's leadership, including businesses such as ADT Security, Curad, and divisions of Siemens, Raytheon, and AT&T.

Throughout the 1990s, Tyco's earnings improved steadily each year, and Kozlowski was touted as one of the best managers in the country. Most investors considered Tyco's stock to be a blue chip, in fact. However, after it came to light in 2002 that Tyco's success was an illusion generated by the way in which the firm reported its financial earnings, the company's shares plummeted. At one point the shares had been trading for $60 apiece. After the scandal broke, the trading price dropped to just $8.

Kozlowski and Tyco's chief financial officer at the time, Mark Swartz, were later charged with stealing $170 million from the company and pocketing $430 million from fraudulent sales of Tyco's stock. Although both men were ultimately convicted, neither admitted wrongdoing.

Fortunately for its investors and employees, Tyco recovered from the scandal. In late 2006, its shares sold for $30—still only half of what they had once sold for, but definitely up from their all-time low. Tyco's current managers have vowed, via a new company mission statement, to base their leadership on integrity and ensure accountability at all levels within the organization. Unfortunately, almost all managers embroiled in scandals have crafted mission statements such as this for their companies. Obviously, what counts is what you do, not what you say.

So what can we learn from the Tyco debacle? Much can be said for having good managerial controls and processes in place to reduce the chances of fraud and unethical behavior. But if a company's leaders are determined to act unethically, no controls will prevent this from happening. Thus, it's paramount for the firm's current managers to genuinely commit to ethical standards that will ultimately permeate down through the entire organization.

simply *the square root of the weighted average squared deviation of each possible return from the expected return*; that is,

$$\sigma = \sqrt{\sum_{i=1}^{n} (k_i - \bar{k})^2 P_i} \tag{6-3}$$

where n = the number of possible outcomes or different rates of return on the investment

k_i = the value of the ith possible rate of return

P_i = the chance or probability that the ith return will occur

$\bar{k}$ = the expected value of the rates of return

For the publishing company, the standard deviation would be 9.22 percent, determined as follows:

$$\sigma = \left[\begin{array}{l} (\ 0\% - 15\%)^2(.10) + (\ 5\% - 15\%)^2(.20) \\ + (15\% - 15\%)^2(.40) + (25\% - 15\%)^2(.20) \\ + (30\% - 15\%)^2(.10) \end{array} \right]^{\frac{1}{2}}$$

$$= \sqrt{85\%} = 9.22\%$$

Although the standard deviation of returns provides us with a quantitative measure of an asset's riskiness, how should we interpret the result? What does it mean? Is the 9.22 percent standard deviation for the publishing company investment good or bad? First, we should remember that statisticians tell us that two-thirds of the time, an event will fall within one standard deviation of the expected value (assuming the distribution is normally distributed; that is, it is shaped like a bell). Thus, given a 15 percent expected return and a standard deviation of 9.22 percent for the publishing company investment, we can reasonably anticipate that the actual returns will fall between 5.78 percent and 24.22 percent (15% ± 9.22%) two-thirds of the time. In other words, there is not much certainty with this investment.

A second way of answering the question about the meaning of the standard deviation comes by comparing the investment in the publishing firm against other investments. Obviously the attractiveness of a security with respect to its return and risk cannot be deter-

Can You Do It?

COMPUTING THE STANDARD DEVIATION

In the preceding problem check, we computed the expected cash flow of $597.50 and the expected return of 12 percent on a $5,000 investment. Now let's calculate the standard deviation of the returns. The probabilities of possible returns are given as follows:

PROBABILITY	RETURNS
0.30	7.0%
0.50	12.5%
0.20	18.0%

(The solution can be found on page 178.)

mined in isolation. Only by examining other available alternatives can we reach a conclusion about a particular investment's risk. For example, if another investment, say, an investment in a firm that owns a local radio station, has the same expected return as the publishing company, 15 percent, but with a standard deviation of 7 percent, we would consider the risk associated with the publishing firm, 9.22 percent, to be excessive. In the technical jargon of modern portfolio theory, the radio station investment is said to "dominate" the publishing firm investment. In common sense terms, this means that the radio station investment has the same expected return as the publishing company investment, but is less risky.

What if we compare the investment in the publishing company with one in a quick oil-change franchise, an investment in which the expected rate of return is an attractive 24 percent but the standard deviation is estimated at 13 percent? Now what should we do? Clearly, the oil-change franchise has a higher expected rate of return, but it also has a larger standard deviation. In this example, we see that the real challenge in selecting the better investment comes when one investment has a higher expected rate of return but also exhibits greater risk. *Here the final choice is determined by our attitude toward risk, and there is no single right answer.* You might select the publishing company, whereas I might choose the oil-change investment, and neither of us would be wrong. We would simply be expressing our tastes and preferences about risk and return.

Did You Get It?

1. How is risk defined?
2. How does the standard deviation help us measure the riskiness of an investment?
3. Does greater risk imply a bad investment?

Finance at Work

A DIFFERENT PERSPECTIVE OF RISK

The first Chinese symbol shown here represents danger; the second stands for opportunity. The Chinese define risk as the combination of danger and opportunity. Greater risk, according to the Chinese, means we have greater opportunity to do well, but also greater danger of doing badly.

How Did You Do?

STANDARD DEVIATION

DEVIATION (POSSIBLE RETURN − 12% EXPECTED RETURN)	DEVIATION SQUARED	PROBABILITY	PROBABILITY × DEVIATION SQUARED
−5.0%	.25%	0.30	.075%
0.5%	.0025%	0.50	.00125%
6.0%	.36%	0.20	.072%
Sum of squared deviations × probability			.14825%
Standard deviation			3.85%

Objective **3**

Compare the historical relationship between risk and rates of return in the capital markets.

RATES OF RETURN: THE INVESTOR'S EXPERIENCE

So far, we have mostly used hypothetical examples of expected rates of return and risk; however, it is also interesting to look at returns that investors have actually received on different types of securities. For example, we could compare the long-term historical annual rates of return for the following types of investments:

1. Common stocks of large companies
2. Common stocks of small firms
3. Long-term corporate bonds
4. Long-term U.S. government bonds
5. Intermediate-term U.S. government bonds
6. U.S. Treasury bills (short-term government securities)

Before comparing these returns, we should think about what to expect. First, we would intuitively expect a Treasury bill (short-term government securities) to be the least risky of the six portfolios. Because a Treasury bill has a short-term maturity date, the price is less volatile (less risky) than the price of an intermediate- or long-term government security. In turn, because there is a chance of default on a corporate bond, which is essentially nonexistent for government securities, a long-term government bond is less risky than a long-term corporate bond. Finally, the common stocks of large companies are more risky than corporate bonds, with small-company stocks being more risky than large-firm stocks.

With this in mind, we could reasonably expect different rates of return to the holders of these varied securities. If the market rewards an investor for assuming risk, the average annual rates of return should increase as risk increases.

A comparison of the annual rates of return for the six respective portfolios for the years 1926 to 2005 is provided in Figure 6-2. Four aspects of these returns are included: (1) the nominal average annual rate of return; (2) the standard deviation of the returns, which measures the volatility, or riskiness, of the returns; (3) the real average annual rate of return, which is the nominal return less the inflation rate; and (4) the risk premium, which represents the additional return received beyond the risk-free rate (Treasury bill rate) for assuming risk. Looking at the first two columns of nominal average annual returns and standard deviations, we get a good overview of the risk–return relationships that have existed over the 80 years ending in 2005. In every case, there has been a positive relationship between risk and return, with Treasury bills being least risky and small-company stocks being most risky.

The return information in Figure 6-2 clearly demonstrates that only common stock has in the long run served as an inflation hedge and provided any substantial risk premium. However, it is equally apparent that the common stockholder is exposed to a sizable amount of risk, as is demonstrated by the 20 percent standard deviation for large-company stocks and the 33 percent standard deviation for small-company stocks. In fact, in the 1926 to 2005 time frame, common shareholders of large firms received negative returns in 22 of the 80 years, compared with only 1 (1938) in 80 years for Treasury bills.

Finance At Work

WANT TO GET BETTER RETURNS WITH LESS RISK? TRY MIDCAPS

Investment advisors are frequently looking for ways to "beat the market," which usually means doing better on average than the companies listed in the Standard & Poor's 500 Index or the New York Stock Exchange. As noted in Figure 6-2, small-company stocks have had higher average annual rates of return than large-company stocks over the past 80 years. But small-company stocks are also seen to be much more risky than large-company stocks, as measured by the variability in their prices (standard deviation). Also, there have been shorter periods in which large-company stocks have provided higher returns than small-company stocks.

One investment advisor, Jim Lowell, editor of *Forbes ETF Advisor*, believes too much attention has been given to small- and large-company stocks. Lowell contends that investors should not be focusing on large companies or small companies, but middle-sized companies, or what are called *midcaps*. Midcaps include all of the companies found in the Standard & Poor's 400 Index, with total equity values between $1 billion and $4 billion. The most widely known midcaps include Legg Mason, Chico's, Sandisk, and Whole Foods.

By mid-2006, Lowell observed that although the Dow Jones Industrial Average had provided better returns than other major U.S. stock indices, it had, over longer periods of time, underperformed indices comprised of midcap stocks, such as the Russell 2000 and the S&P MidCap 400. He explains, "If you go back to the beginning of 1999, you will find that midcaps have climbed over 80 percent, compared to 62 percent for the Russell 2000, 24 percent for the Dow Jones Industrial Average, and 4 percent for the S&P 500 Index." Lowell argues that midcaps are a better haven for long-term investors because they have better risk–return profiles than large caps and small caps.

Says Lowell: "Midcaps represent companies with real history, real products, real management, and real profitability. For those investors with a time horizon of 18 months rather than 18 seconds, midcaps offer superior returns for the risk."

So what do you think? Could you get higher rates of return with less risk by investing in midcaps?

Source: Matthew Schifrin, "Midcaps Win the Marathon," *Forbes.com*, June 14, 2006, **www.forbes.com/etf/2006/06/14/mdy-etf-sandisk-in_ms_0614gurusow_inl.html**, accessed August 16, 2006. Reprinted by permission of Forbes Magazine © 2007 Forbes Media LLC.

Did You Get It?

1. What is the additional compensation for assuming greater risk called?
2. In Figure 6-2, which rate of return is the risk-free rate? Why?

FIGURE 6-2 Historical Rates of Return

Securities	Nominal Average Annual Returns	Standard Deviation of Returns	Real Average Annual Returns[a]	Risk Premium[b]
Large-company stocks	11.7%	20.0%	8.5%	8.0%
Small-company stocks	17.4%	33.0%	14.2%	13.7%
Corporate bonds	6.2%	8.5%	3.0%	2.5%
Government bonds	5.2%	5.7%	2.0%	1.5%
U.S. Treasury bills	3.7%	3.1%	0.5%	0.0%
Inflation	3.2%	4.3%		

[a]The real return equals the nominal returns less the inflation rate of 3.2 percent.
[b]The risk premium equals the nominal security return than the average risk-free rate (Treasury bills) of 3.7 percent.

Objective 4

Explain how diversifying investments affects the riskiness and expected rate of return of a portfolio or combination of assets.

RISK AND DIVERSIFICATION

More can be said about risk, especially about its nature, when we own more than one asset in our investment portfolio. Let's consider for the moment how risk is affected if we diversify our investment by holding a variety of securities.

Let's assume that you graduated from college in May 2006. Not only did you get the good job you had hoped for, but you also finished the year with a little nest egg—not enough to take that summer fling to Europe like some of your college friends but a nice surplus. Besides, you suspected that they used credit cards to go anyway. So, you made two stock investments with your nest egg—one in Harley Davidson and one in Starbucks. (As the owner of a Harley Softail motorcycle, you've had a passion for riding since your college days. And you give Starbucks credit for helping you get through many long study sessions.) You then focused on your career and seldom thought about your investments. Your first extended break from work came on Labor Day weekend. After a lazy Saturday morning, you decided to get on the Internet to see how your investments did over the previous several months. You bought Harley for $48, and the stock was now trading at almost $60. "Not bad," you thought. But then the bad news—Starbucks was selling for $32, compared to the $40 that you paid for the stock. After a little checking, you found out that Starbucks had announced that sales for the month of July had not met expectations.

Clearly, what we have described about Harley Davidson and Starbucks were events unique to these two companies, and as we would expect, investors reacted accordingly; that is, the value of the stock changed in light of the new information. Although we might have wished we had owned only Harley Davidson stock at the time, most of us would prefer to avoid such uncertainties; that is, we are risk averse. Instead, we would like to reduce the risk associated with our investment portfolio, without having to accept a lower expected return. Good news: It is possible by diversifying your portfolio!

Diversifying Away the Risk

If we diversify our investments across different securities rather than invest in only one stock, the variability in the returns of our portfolio should decline. The reduction in risk will occur if the stock returns within our portfolio do not move precisely together over time—that is, if they are not perfectly correlated. Figure 6-3 shows graphically what we could expect to happen to the variability of returns as we add additional stocks to the portfolio. The reduction occurs because some of the volatility in returns of a stock are unique to that security. The unique variability of a single stock tends to be countered by the uniqueness of another security. However, we should not expect to eliminate all risk from our portfolio. In practice, it would be rather difficult to cancel all the variations in returns of a portfolio, because stock prices have some tendency to move together. Thus, we can divide the total risk (total vari-

FIGURE 6-3 Variability of Returns Compared with Size of Portfolio ability) of our portfolio into two types of risk: (1) **company-unique risk**, or **unsystematic risk**, and (2) **market risk**, or **systematic risk**. Company-unique risk might also be called **diversifiable risk**, in that it *can be diversified away*. Market risk is **nondiversifiable risk**; it *cannot be eliminated through random diversification*. These two types of risk are shown graphically in Figure 6–3. Total risk declines until we have approximately 20 securities, and then the decline becomes very slight.

The remaining risk, which would typically be about 40 percent of the total risk, is the portfolio's systematic, or market, risk. At this point, our portfolio is highly correlated with all securities in the marketplace. Events that affect our portfolio now are not so much unique events as changes in the general economy, major political events, and sociological changes. Examples include changes in interest rates in the economy, changes in tax legislation that affect all companies, or increasing public concern about the effect of business practices on the environment. Our measure of risk should, therefore, measure how responsive a stock or portfolio is to changes in a market portfolio, such as the New York Stock Exchange or the S&P 500 Index.[6]

Measuring Market Risk

To help clarify the idea of systematic risk, let's examine the relationship between the common stock returns of Barnes & Noble Inc. and the returns of the S&P 500 Index.

The monthly returns for Barnes & Noble Inc. and the S&P 500 Index for the 24 months ending March 2006 are presented in Table 6-2 and Figure 6-4. These *monthly returns*, or **holding-period returns**, as they are often called, are calculated as follows.[7]

$$k_t = \frac{P_t}{P_{t-1}} - 1 \tag{6-4}$$

where: k_t = the holding period return in month t for a particular firm, such as Barnes & Noble, or for a portfolio such as the S&P 500 Index

P_t = a firm's stock price, such as Barnes & Noble (or the S&P 500 Index), at the end of month t

For instance, the holding-period return for Barnes & Noble and the S&P 500 Index for March 2006 is computed as follows:

$$\text{The Barnes \& Noble return} = \frac{\text{stock price at end of March 2006}}{\text{stock price at end of February 2006}} - 1$$

$$= \frac{\$43.10}{\$43.07} - 1 = .0007 = .07\%$$

$$\text{The S\&P 500 Index return} = \frac{\text{index value at end of March 2006}}{\text{index value at end of February 2006}} - 1$$

$$= \frac{\$1,291.24}{\$1,280.66} - 1 = .0083 = .83\%$$

At the bottom of Table 6-2, we have also computed the averages of the returns for the 24 months, for both Barnes & Noble and the S&P 500 Index, and the standard deviation for these returns. Because we are using historical return data, we assume each observation has

company-unique risk see Unsystematic risk.

unsystematic risk the risk related to an investment return that can be eliminated through diversification. Unsystematic risk is the result of factors that are unique to the particular firm. Also called company-unique risk or diversifiable risk.

market risk see Systematic risk.

systematic risk (1) the risk related to an investment return that cannot be eliminated through diversification. Systematic risk results from factors that affect all stocks. Also called market risk or nondiversifiable risk. (2) The risk of a project from the viewpoint of a well-diversified shareholder. This measure takes into account that some of the project's risk will be diversified away as the project is combined with the firm's other projects, and, in addition, some of the remaining risk will be diversified away by shareholders as they combine this stock with other stocks in their portfolios.

diversifiable risk see Unsystematic risk.

nondiversifiable risk see Systematic risk.

holding-period return the return an investor would receive from holding a security for a designated period of time. For example, a monthly holding-period return would be the return for holding a security for a month.

---

[6] The New York Stock Exchange Index is an index that reflects the performance of all stocks listed on the New York Stock Exchange. The Standard & Poor's (S&P) 500 Index is similarly an index that measures the combined stock-price performance of the companies that constitute the 500 largest companies in the United States, as designated by Standard & Poor's.

[7] For simplicity's sake, we are ignoring the dividend that the investor receives from the stock as part of the total return. In other words, letting D_t equal the dividend received by the investor in month t, the holding-period return would more accurately be measured as

$$k_1 = \frac{P_t + D_t}{P_{t-1}} - 1 \tag{6-5}$$

TABLE 6-2　Monthly Holding–Period Returns, Barnes & Noble Inc. versus the S&P 500 Index, April 2004 through March 2006

MONTH AND YEAR	BARNES & NOBLE PRICE	BARNES & NOBLE RETURNS (%)	S&P 500 INDEX PRICE	S&P 500 INDEX RETURNS (%)
2004				
March	$32.60		$1,126.21	
April	29.87	−8.37%	1,107.30	−1.68%
May	29.94	0.23%	1,120.68	1.21%
June	33.98	13.49%	1,140.84	1.80%
July	34.38	1.18%	1,101.72	−3.43%
August	34.56	0.52%	1,104.24	0.23%
September	37.00	7.06%	1,114.58	0.94%
October	33.27	−10.08%	1,130.20	1.40%
November	27.08	−18.61%	1,173.82	3.86%
December	32.27	19.17%	1,211.92	3.25%
2005				
January	32.70	1.33%	1,181.27	−2.53%
February	34.16	4.46%	1,203.60	1.89%
March	34.49	0.97%	1,180.59	−1.91%
April	35.60	3.22%	1,156.85	−2.01%
May	37.85	6.32%	1,191.50	3.00%
June	38.80	2.51%	1,191.33	−0.01%
July	41.02	5.72%	1,234.18	3.60%
August	37.77	−7.92%	1,220.33	−1.12%
September	37.70	−0.19%	1,228.81	0.69%
October	36.16	−4.08%	1,207.01	−1.77%
November	40.34	11.56%	1,249.48	3.52%
December	42.67	5.78%	1,248.29	−0.10%
2006				
January	42.42	−0.59%	1,280.08	2.55%
February	43.07	1.53%	1,280.66	0.05%
March	43.10	0.07%	1,291.24	0.83%
Average monthly return		1.47%		0.59%
Standard deviation		7.88%		2.12%

an equal probability of occurrence. Thus, the average return, $\bar{k}$, is found by summing the returns and dividing by the number of months; that is,

$$\text{Average return} = \bar{k} = \frac{\sum\limits_{t=1}^{n} \text{return in month } t}{\text{number of months}} = \frac{\sum\limits_{t=1}^{n} (k_t)}{n} \tag{6-6}$$

and the standard deviation σ is computed as

$$\text{Standard deviation} = \sqrt{\frac{\sum\limits_{t=1}^{n} (\text{return in month } t - \text{average return})^2}{\text{number of months} - 1}}$$

$$\sigma = \sqrt{\frac{\sum\limits_{t=1}^{n} (k_t - \bar{k})^2}{n - 1}} \tag{6-7}$$

In looking at Table 6-2 and Figure 6-4, we notice the following things about Barnes & Noble's holding-period returns over the 2 years ending in March 2006.

1. Barnes & Noble's stockholders have had significantly higher average monthly returns than the average stock in the S&P 500 Index, 1.47 percent compared to .59 percent.

FIGURE 6-4 Monthly Holding–Period Returns: Barnes & Noble versus the S&P 500 Index, April 2004 through March 2006

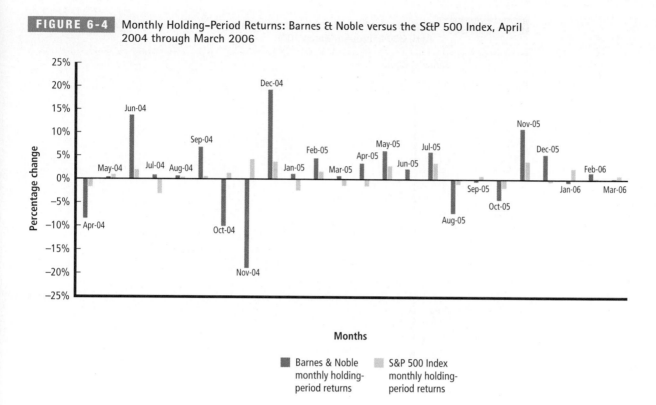

2. The bad news is Barnes & Noble's greater volatility of returns—in other words, greater risk—as evidenced by Barnes & Noble's higher standard deviation. As shown at the bottom of Table 6-2, the standard deviation of the returns is 7.88 percent for Barnes & Noble versus 2.12 percent for the S&P 500 Index. Barnes & Noble's more volatile returns are also evident in Figure 6-4, where we see Barnes & Noble's returns frequently being higher and lower than the corresponding S&P 500 returns.

3. We should also notice the tendency, although far from perfect, of Barnes & Noble's stock price to increase when the value of the S&P 500 Index increases and vice versa. This was the case in 14 of the 24 months. That is, there is a moderate positive relationship between Barnes & Noble's stock returns and the S&P 500 Index returns.

With respect to our third observation, that there is a relationship between the stock returns of Barnes & Noble and the S&P 500 Index, it is helpful to see this relationship by graphing Barnes & Noble's returns against the S&P 500 Index returns. We provide such a graph in Figure 6-5. In the figure, we have plotted Barnes & Noble's returns on the vertical axis and the returns for the S&P 500 Index on the horizontal axis. Each of the 24 dots in the figure represents the returns of Barnes & Noble and the S&P 500 Index for a particular month. For instance, the returns for February 2005 for Barnes & Noble and the S&P 500 Index were 4.46 percent and 1.89 percent, respectively, which are noted in the figure.

In addition to the dots in the graph, we have drawn a line of "best fit," which we call the **characteristic line**. *The slope of the characteristic line measures the average relationship between a stock's returns and those of the S&P 500 Index:* or stated differently, *the slope of the line indicates the average movement in a stock's price in response to a movement in the S&P 500 Index price.* For Barnes & Noble, the slope of the line is 1.4, which simply equals the rise of the line relative to the run of the line.[8] A slope of 1.4, as for Barnes & Noble, means that as the market return (S&P 500 Index returns) increases or decreases 1 percentage point, the return for Barnes & Noble on average increases or decreases 1.4 percentage points.

characteristic line the line of "best fit" through a series of returns for a firm's stock relative to the market's returns. The slope of the line, frequently called beta, represents the average movement of the firm's stock returns in response to a movement in the market's returns.

---

[8] Linear regression is the statistical technique used to determine the slope of the line of best fit.

FIGURE 6-5 Monthly Holding–Period Returns for Barnes & Noble versus the S&P 500 Index, April 2004 through March 2006

We can also think of the 1.4 slope of the characteristic line as indicating that Barnes & Noble's returns are 1.4 times as volatile on average as those of the overall market (S&P 500 Index). This slope has come to be called **beta** in investor jargon, and it *measures the average relationship between a stock's returns and the market's returns*. It is a term you will see almost any time you read an article written by a financial analyst about the riskiness of a stock.

beta the relationship between an investment's returns and the market's returns. This is a measure of the investment's nondiversifiable risk.

Looking once again at Figure 6-5, we see that the dots (returns) are scattered all about the characteristic line—most of the returns do not fit neatly on the characteristic line. That is, the average relationship may be 1.4, but the variation in Barnes & Noble's returns is only partly explained by the stock's average relationship with the S&P 500 Index. There are other driving forces unique to Barnes & Noble that also affect the firm's stock returns. (Earlier, we called this company-unique risk.) If we were, however, to diversify our holdings and own, say, 20 stocks with betas of 1.4, we could essentially eliminate the variation about the characteristic line. That is, we would remove almost all the volatility in returns, except for that caused by the general market, which is represented by the slope of the line in Figure 6-5. If we plotted the returns of our 20-stock portfolio against the S&P 500 Index, the points in our new graph would fit nicely along a straight line with a slope of 1.4, which means that the beta of the portfolio is also 1.4. The new graph would look something like the one shown in Figure 6-6. In other words, by diversifying our portfolio, we can essentially eliminate the variations about the characteristic line, leaving only the variation in returns for a company that comes from variations in the general market returns.

So beta—the slope of the characteristic line—is a measure of a firm's market risk or systematic risk, which is the risk that remains for a company even after we have diversified our portfolio. It is this risk—and only this risk—that matters for investors who have broadly diversified portfolios.

Although we have said that beta is a measure of a stock's systematic risk, how should we interpret a specific beta? For instance, when is a beta considered low and when is it considered high? In general, a stock with a beta of zero has no systematic risk; a stock with a beta

Finance At Work

THREE WISE MEN OF FINANCE: THEIR INSIGHTS INTO THE LINKS BETWEEN RISK AND RETURN REVOLUTIONIZED INVESTING FOREVER

In 2004, *Business Week* published a series of profiles of the greatest innovators of the past 75 years—some were in science or technology, others were in management, finance, marketing, or government.

For finance, three individuals were recognized for their innovation: Harry Markowitz, William Sharpe, and the late Merton Miller. Their work changed the way investors and managers think about financial markets and won them the Nobel Prize for economics in 1990. Key concepts in investing and corporate finance that are today accepted as obvious can be traced back to their research—everything from the existence of a systematic trade-off between risk and return, to the concept that markets are efficient.

Markowitz, Sharpe, and Miller demolished many cherished Wall Street ideas. One example: that it's possible to beat the market consistently by savvy stock picking. This is impossible, they said, because thousands of investors collectively have factored everything that is known about stocks into current prices.

Sharpe, a charming, if sometimes blunt, computer whiz, devised the capital asset pricing model (CAPM), which quantified the idea that investors demand extra returns for taking on more risk. Souped-up versions of the CAPM are still used widely today in business to guide investment decision making. Miller,

along with Franco Modigliani, showed that any company's value depends on its earning power rather than its book value. That insight was a real shocker to the professional money managers on Wall Street.

But it was Markowitz, a self-described nerd whose father was a Chicago grocer, who initially got the ball rolling. In 1952, the University of Chicago economist published a 14-page paper called "Portfolio Selection." Another renowned economist said that Markowitz's basic idea of diversifying a portfolio of stocks in order to produce the maximum potential returns given the amount of risk an investor is prepared to take on was "the most famous insight in the history of modern finance." Of course, the notion of not putting all one's eggs in the same basket had been a truism for centuries. (It's mentioned in the Talmud and in the works of Shakespeare among other places.) Money managers around the world still follow Markowitz's precepts daily.

Now, a new generation of financial economists is challenging the work of Miller, Sharpe, and Markowitz, often improving on it. But it's the Nobel trio who helped us change how we should understand risk and return.

Source: Adapted from Christopher Farrell, "Three Wise Men of Finance," *Business Week*, October 14, 2004, accessed at **www.businessweek.com/magazine/content/04_41/b3903015_mz072.htm?chan=search**.

of 1 has systematic or market risk equal to the "typical" stock in the marketplace; and a stock with a beta exceeding 1 has more market risk than the typical stock. Most stocks, however, have betas between 0.60 and 1.60.

We should also realize that calculating beta is not an exact science. The final estimate of a firm's beta is heavily dependent on one's methodology. For instance, it matters whether

FIGURE 6-6 Holding–Period Returns for a Hypothetical Portfolio and the S&P 500 Index

Can You Do It?

ESTIMATING BETA

To the right, we provide the end-of-month prices for McDonald's stock and the Standard & Poor's 500 Index for December 2005 and the first 6 months of 2006. Given the information, compute the following both for McDonald's and the S&P 500: (1) the monthly holding-period returns, (2) the average monthly returns, and (3) the standard deviation of the returns. Next, graph the holding-period returns of McDonald's on the vertical axis against the holding-period returns of the S&P 500 on the horizontal axis. Draw a line on your graph similar to what we did in Figure 6-5 to estimate the average relationship between the stock returns of McDonald's and the returns of the overall market as represented by the S&P 500. What is the approximate slope of your line? What does this tell you?

(In working this problem, it would be easier if you used a computer spreadsheet. One is available for this chapter at **www.prenhall.com/keown** to help you.)

	MCDONALD'S CORP.	S&P 500
Dec-05	$33.72	$1,248.29
Jan-06	35.01	1,280.08
Feb-06	34.91	1,280.66
Mar-06	34.36	1,291.24
Apr-06	34.57	1,310.61
May-06	33.17	1,270.09
Jun-06	33.60	1,270.20

(The solution can be found on page 188.)

you use 24 months in your measurement or 60 months, as most professional investment companies do. Take our computation of Barnes & Noble's beta. We said Barnes & Noble's beta is 1.4 but Standard & Poor's, a well-known investment service, has estimated Barnes & Noble's beta to be 1.05. Standard & Poor's beta estimates for a number of firms are as follows:

	VALUE LINE
Coca-Cola	0.35
Exxon Mobil	0.63
General Motors	1.37
General Electric	0.84
IBM	1.54
Merck	0.66
Nike	0.52
PepsiCo	0.48
Wal-Mart	0.59

Thus, although close in many instances, even the professionals may not agree in their measurement of a given firm's beta.

To this point, we have talked about measuring an individual stock's beta. We will now consider how to measure the beta for a portfolio of stocks.

Measuring a Portfolio's Beta

portfolio beta the relationship between a portfolio's returns and the market returns. It is a measure of the portfolio's nondiversifiable risk.

What if we were to diversify our portfolio, as we have just suggested, but instead of acquiring stocks with the same beta as Barnes & Noble (1.40), we buy 8 stocks with betas of 1.0 and 12 stocks with betas of 1.5. What would the beta of our portfolio become? As it works out, the **portfolio beta** is merely the average of the individual stock betas. It is a *weighted average of the individual securities' betas, with the weights being equal to the proportion of the portfolio invested in each security.* Thus, the beta (β) of a portfolio consisting of n stocks is equal to

$$\beta_{\text{portfolio}} = \sum_{j=1}^{n} [(\text{percentage invested in stock } j) \times (\beta \text{ of stock } j)] \qquad (6\text{-}8)$$

FIGURE 6-7 Holding–Period Returns: High– and Low–Beta Portfolios and the S&P 500 Index

So, assuming we bought equal amounts of each stock in our new 20-stock portfolio, the beta would simply be 1.3, calculated as follows:

$$\text{Portfolio beta} = \left(\frac{8}{20} \times 1.0\right) + \left(\frac{12}{20} \times 1.50\right) = 1.3$$

Thus, whenever the general market increases or decreases 1 percent, our new portfolio's returns would change 1.3 percent on average, which means that our new portfolio has more systematic, or market, risk than the market has as a whole.

We can conclude that the beta of a portfolio is determined by the betas of the individual stocks. If we have a portfolio consisting of stocks with low betas, then our portfolio will have a low beta. The reverse is true as well. Figure 6-7 presents these situations graphically.

Before leaving the subject of risk and diversification, we want to share a study that demonstrates the effects of diversifying our investments, not just across different stocks but also across different types of securities.

Risk and Diversification Demonstrated[9]

Having described the effect of diversification on risk and return in a general way, let's now look at some actual numbers to demonstrate how risk and return change as you diversify your portfolio. As it was stated earlier in the chapter, our source of information is Ibbotson Associates, a firm that gathers extensive return data on a large group of investments.

To show the effect of diversification on risk and rates of return, Ibbotson compared three portfolios (A, B, and C), consisting of the following investments:

	INVESTMENT MIX IN PORTFOLIO (%)		
TYPES OF SECURITIES	**A**	**B**	**C**
Short-term government securities (Treasury bills)	0%	63%	34%
Long-term government bonds	100	12	14
Large-company stocks	0	25	52
	100%	100%	100%

How Did You Do?

ESTIMATING BETA

The holding-period returns, average monthly returns, and the standard deviations for McDonald's and the S&P 500 data are as follows:

	MCDONALD'S CORP.		S&P 500	
Dec-05	$33.72		1,248.29	
Jan-06	35.01	3.83%	1,280.08	2.55%
Feb-06	34.91	−0.29%	1,280.66	0.05%
Mar-06	34.36	−1.58%	1,291.24	0.83%
Apr-06	34.57	0.61%	1,310.61	1.50%
May-06	33.17	−4.05%	1,270.09	−3.09%
Jun-06	33.60	1.30%	1,270.20	0.01%
Average return		−0.03%		0.31%
Standard deviation		2.67%		1.91%

The graph would appear as follows:

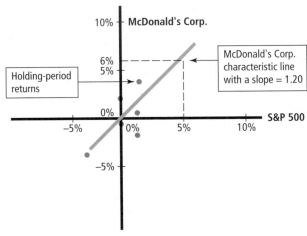

The average relationship between McDonald's stock returns and the S&P 500's returns, as estimated by the slope of the characteristic line in the graph above, appears to be about 1.20, where the rise of the line is 6.0 relative to a run (horizontal axis) of 5.0 (1.20 = 6.0/5.0). If our estimates fairly represent the relationships, then McDonald's stock returns are more volatile than the market's returns. When the market rises (or falls) 1 percent, McDonald's stock will rise (or fall) 1.2 percent. (We should, however be hesitant to draw any firm conclusions here, given the limited number of return observations.)

Figure 6-8 shows the average returns and standard deviations of the three portfolios. The results show that an investor can use diversification to improve the risk–return characteristics of a portfolio. Specifically, we can see that

1. Portfolio A, which consists entirely of long-term government bonds, had an average annual return of 5.5 percent with a standard deviation of 11.3 percent.[10]
2. In portfolio B, we diversified across all three security types, with the majority of the funds (63%) invested in Treasury bills and a lesser amount in stocks (25%) and long-term government bonds (12%). The effects are readily apparent. The average returns of the two portfolios were identical, but the risk associated with portfolio B was almost half that of portfolio A—a standard deviation of 6.1 percent for portfolio B compared with 11.3 percent for portfolio A. Notice that risk was less in portfolio B even though stocks, a far more risky security, were included in the portfolio. How could this be? Quite sim-

[10] In this example, Ibbotson Associates uses 1970 to 1993 data to compute the standard deviation for the long-term government bonds; all other computations use the total 1926 to 1993 time frame.

FIGURE 6-8 The Effect of Diversification on Average Returns and Risk

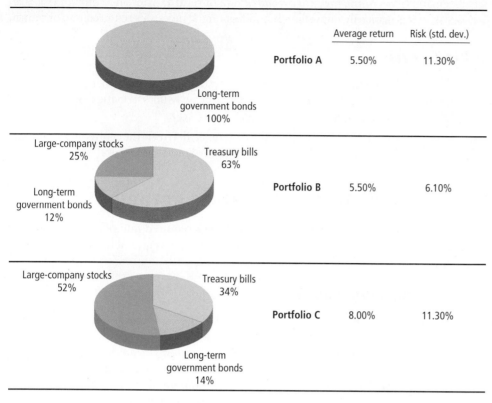

Source: Adapted from Ibbotson Associates, Inc. Copyright © 1994, Ibbotson Assoc., Inc., Chicago.

ply, stocks behave differently than both government bonds and Treasury bills, with the effect being a less risky (lower standard deviation) portfolio.

3. Whereas portfolio B demonstrates how an investor can reduce risk while keeping returns constant, portfolio C, with its increased investment in stocks (52%), shows how an investor can increase average returns while keeping risk constant. This portfolio had a risk level identical to that of long-term government bonds alone (portfolio A), but it achieved a higher average return of 8 percent, compared with 5.5 percent for the government bond portfolio.

The conclusion to be drawn from this example is clear. The market rewards diversification. We can indeed lower risk without sacrificing expected returns, and/or we can increase expected returns without having to assume more risk by diversifying our investments.

This example gives us real-world evidence about the merits of diversification; however, a clarification is in order. Note that the diversification in our example is across different asset types—Treasury bills versus long-term government bonds versus common stocks. *Diversifying among different kinds of assets* is called **asset allocation**, compared with diversification within the different asset classes. The benefit we receive from diversifying is far greater through effective asset allocation than from astutely selecting individual stocks to include within an asset category. For instance, Brinson, Singer, and Beebower studied quarterly data from 82 large U.S. pension funds over the period 1977 to 1987.[11] They found that the asset allocation decision accounted for over 91 percent of the differences among the returns of pension funds. Deciding what specific securities to hold accounted for only 4.6 percent of the variation in the different pension returns.[12] The point is investors in the capital markets should focus more attention on asset allocation than on selecting individual securities.

asset allocation identifying and selecting the asset classes appropriate for a specific investment portfolio and determining the proportions of those assets within the portfolio.

[11] Gary P. Brinson, Ronald F. Singer, and Gilbert L. Beebower, "Determinants of Portfolio Performance," *Financial Analysts Journal* (May–June 1991) 40–47.

[12] It is also interesting to know that Brinson, Singer, and Beebower found that timing investments explained a meager 1.8 percent of the variation in pension fund returns. That is, none of the investors of these pension funds were any better than their peers at timing market movements when making investments.

In the next section, we complete our study of risk and returns by connecting risk— market or systematic risk—to the investor's *required* rate of return. After all, although risk is an important issue, it is primarily important in its effect on the investor's required rate of return.

Did You Get It?

1. Give specific examples of systematic and unsystematic risk. How many different securities must be owned to essentially diversify away unsystematic risk?
2. What method is used to measure a firm's market risk?
3. After reviewing Figure 6-5, explain the difference between the plotted dots and the firm's characteristic line. What must be done to eliminate the variations?

Objective **5**

Explain the relationship between an investor's required rate of return on an investment and the riskiness of the investment.

THE INVESTOR'S REQUIRED RATE OF RETURN

In this section, we examine the concept of the investor's required rate of return, especially as it relates to the riskiness of an asset, and then we see how the required rate of return might be measured.

The Required Rate of Return Concept

required rate of return minimum rate of return necessary to attract an investor to purchase or hold a security.

An investor's **required rate of return** can be defined as the *minimum rate of return necessary to attract an investor to purchase or hold a security*. This definition considers the investor's opportunity cost of funds of making an investment in *the next-best investment*. This forgone return is an opportunity cost of undertaking the investment and, consequently, is the investor's required rate of return. In other words, we invest with the intention of achieving a rate of return sufficient to warrant making the investment. The investment will be made only if the purchase price is low enough relative to expected future cash flows to provide a rate of return greater than or equal to our required rate of return.

To help us better understand the nature of an investor's required rate of return, we can separate the return into its basic components: the risk-free rate of return plus a risk premium. Expressed as an equation:

$$k = k_{rf} + k_{rp} \tag{6-9}$$

where k = the investor's required rate of return
k_{rf} = the risk-free rate of return
k_{rp} = the risk premium

risk-free rate of return the rate of return on risk-free investments. The interest rates on short-term U.S. government securities are commonly used to measure this rate.

risk premium the additional return expected for assuming risk.

The **risk-free rate of return** is the *required rate of return, or discount rate, for riskless investments*. Typically, our measure for the risk-free rate of return is the U.S. Treasury bill rate. The **risk premium**, k_{rp}, is the *additional return we must expect to receive for assuming risk*. As the level of risk increases, we will demand additional expected returns. Even though we may or may not actually receive this incremental return, we must have reason to expect it; otherwise, why expose ourselves to the chance of losing all or part of our money?

► EXAMPLE

Assume you are considering the purchase of a stock that you believe will provide a 14 percent return over the next year. If the expected risk-free rate of return, such as the rate of return for 90-day Treasury bills, is 5 percent, then the risk premium you are demanding to assume the additional risk is 9 percent (14% − 5%).

Measuring the Required Rate of Return

We have seen that (1) systematic risk is the only relevant risk—the rest can be diversified away, and (2) the required rate of return, k, equals the risk-free rate, k_{rf}, plus a risk premium, k_{rp}. We will now examine how we can estimate investors' required rates of return.

Finance at Work

DOES BETA ALWAYS WORK?

At the start of 1998, Apple Computer was in deep trouble. As a result, its stock price fluctuated wildly—far more than other computer firms, such as IBM. However, based on the capital asset pricing model (CAPM) and its measure of beta, the required return of Apple's investors would have been only 8 percent, compared with 12 percent for IBM's stockholders. Equally interesting, when Apple's situation improved in the spring of that year, and its share price became less volatile, Apple's investors, at least according to the CAPM, would have required a rate of return of 11 percent—a 3 percentage point increase from the earlier required rate of return. That is not what intuition would suggest should have happened.

So what should we think? Just when Apple's future was most in doubt and its shares most volatile, its beta was only 0.47, suggesting that Apple's stock was only half as volatile as the overall stock market. In reality, beta is meaningless here. The truth is that Apple was in such a dire condition that its stock price simply "decoupled" itself from the stock market. So, as IBM and its peer stock prices moved up and down with the rest of the market, Apple shares reacted solely to news about the company,

without regard for the market's movements. The stock's beta thus created the false impression that Apple shares were more stable than the stock market.

The lesson here is that beta may at times be misleading when used with individual companies. Instead, its use is far more reliable when applied to a portfolio of companies. If a firm that was interested in acquiring Apple Computer in 1998, for instance, had used the beta in computing the required rate of return for the acquisition, it would without a doubt have overvalued Apple.

So does that mean that CAPM is worthless? No, not as long as company-unique risk is not the main driving force in a company's stock price movements or if investors are able to diversify away specific company risk. Then they would bid up the price of such shares until they reflected only market risk. For example, a mutual fund that specializes in "distressed stocks" might purchase a number of "Apple Computer-type companies," each with its own problems, but for different reasons. For such investors, betas work pretty well. Thus, the moral of the story is to exercise common sense and judgment when using a beta.

The finance profession has had difficulty in developing a practical approach to measure an investor's required rate of return; however, financial managers often use a method called the **capital asset pricing model (CAPM)**. The capital asset pricing model is *an equation that equates the expected rate of return on a stock to the risk-free rate plus a risk premium for the stock's systematic risk*. Although certainly not without its critics, the CAPM provides an intuitive approach for thinking about the return that an investor should require on an investment, given the asset's systematic or market risk.

Equation (6-9) provides the natural starting point for measuring the investor's required rate of return and sets us up for using the CAPM. Rearranging this equation to solve for the risk premium (k_{rp}), we have

$$k_{rp} = k - k_{rf} \tag{6-10}$$

which simply says that the risk premium for a security, k_{rp}, equals the required return, k, less the risk-free rate existing in the market, k_{rf}. For example, if the required return is 15 percent, and the risk-free rate is 5 percent, the risk premium is 10 percent. Also, if the required return for the market portfolio, k_m, is 12 percent, and the risk-free rate, k_{rf}, is 5 percent, the risk premium, k_{rp}, for the market would be 7 percent. This 7 percent risk premium would apply to any security having systematic (nondiversifiable) risk equivalent to the general market, or a beta of 1.

In this same market, a security with a beta (β) of 2 should provide a risk premium of 14 percent, or twice the 7 percent risk premium existing for the market as a whole. Hence, in general, the appropriate required rate of return for the jth security, k_j, should be determined by

$$k_j = k_{rf} + \beta_j (k_m - k_{rf}) \tag{6-11}$$

Equation (6–11) is the CAPM. This equation designates the risk–return trade-off existing in the market, where risk is measured in terms of beta. Figure 6-9 graphs the CAPM as

capital asset pricing model (CAPM) an equation stating that the expected rate of return on a project is a function of (1) the risk-free rate, (2) the investment's systematic risk, and (3) the expected risk premium for the market portfolio of all risky securities.

FIGURE 6-9 Security Market Line

security market line the return line that reflects the attitudes of investors regarding the minimum acceptable return for a given level of systematic risk associated with a security.

the **security market line**.[13] The security market line is *the graphic representation of the CAPM. It is the line that shows the appropriate required rate of return given a stock's systematic risk*. As presented in this figure, securities with betas equal to 0, 1, and 2 should have required rates of return as follows:

$$\text{If } \beta_j = 0: k_j = 5\% + 0(12\% - 5\%) = 5\%$$
$$\text{If } \beta_j = 1: k_j = 5\% + 1(12\% - 5\%) = 12\%$$
$$\text{If } \beta_j = 2: k_j = 5\% + 2(12\% - 5\%) = 19\%$$

where the risk-free rate, k_{rf}, is 5 percent, and the required return for the market portfolio, k_m, is 12 percent.

Remember Your Principles

The conclusion of the matter is that **Principle 1** is alive and well. It tells us, **We Won't Take On Additional Risk Unless We Expect to Be Compensated with Additional Return**. That is, there is a risk–return trade-off in the market.

---

[13] Two key assumptions are made in using the security market line. First, we assume that the marketplace where securities are bought and sold is highly efficient. Market efficiency indicates that the price of an asset responds quickly to new information, thereby suggesting that the price of a security reflects all available information. As a result, the current price of a security is considered to represent the best estimate of its future price. Second, the model assumes that a perfect market exists. A perfect market is one in which information is readily available to all investors at a nominal cost. Also, securities are assumed to be infinitely divisible, with any transaction costs incurred in purchasing or selling a security being negligible. Furthermore, investors are assumed to be single-period wealth maximizers who agree on the meaning and significance of the available information. Finally, within the perfect market, all investors are *price takers*, which simply means that a single investor's actions cannot affect the price of a security. These assumptions are obviously not descriptive of reality. However, from the perspective of positive economics, the mark of a good theory is the accuracy of its predictions, not the validity of the simplifying assumptions that underlie its development.

Can You Do It?

COMPUTING AN EXPECTED RATE OF RETURN

Determine a fair expected (or required) rate of return for a stock that has a beta of 1.25 when the risk-free rate is 5 percent, and the expected market return is 9 percent.

(The solution can be found on page 194.)

Did You Get It?

1. How does opportunity cost affect an investor's required rate of return?
2. What are the two components of the investor's required rate of return?
3. How does beta fit into factoring the risk premium in the CAPM equation?
4. Assuming the market is efficient, what is the relationship between a stock's price and the security market line?

Summary

In Chapter 2, we referred to the discount rate as the interest rate, or the opportunity cost of funds. At that point, we considered a number of important factors that influence interest rates, including the price of time, expected or anticipated inflation, and the risk premium related to maturity (liquidity) and the variability of future returns. In this chapter, we have returned to our study of rates of return and looked ever so carefully at the relationship between risk and rates of return.

In a world of uncertainty, we cannot make forecasts with certitude. Thus, we must speak in terms of *expected* events. The expected return on an investment may therefore be stated as a weighted average of all possible returns, weighted by the probability that each will occur.

Risk for our purposes is the variability of returns and can be measured by the standard deviation.

Ibbotson and Sinquefield have provided us with annual rates of return earned on different types of security investments as far back as 1926. Ibbotson Associates summarizes, among other things, the annual returns for six portfolios of securities made up of

1. Common stocks of large companies
2. Common stocks of small firms
3. Long-term corporate bonds
4. Long-term U.S. government bonds
5. Intermediate-term U.S. government bonds
6. U.S. Treasury bills

A comparison of the annual rates of return for these respective portfolios for the years 1926 to 2005 shows a positive relationship between risk and return, with Treasury bills being least risky and common stocks of small firms being most risky. From the data, we are able to see the benefit of diversification in terms of improving the return–risk relationship. Also, the data clearly demonstrate that only common stock has in the long run served as an inflation hedge, and that the risk associated with common stock can be reduced if investors are patient in receiving their returns.

We made an important distinction between nondiversifiable risk and diversifiable risk. We concluded that the only relevant risk, given the opportunity to diversify our portfolio, is a security's nondiversifiable risk, which we called by two other names: systematic risk and market-related risk.

The capital asset pricing model provides an intuitive framework for understanding the risk–return relationship. The CAPM suggests that investors determine an appropriate required rate of return, depending upon the amount of systematic risk inherent in a security. This minimum acceptable rate of return is equal to the risk-free rate plus a risk premium for assuming risk.

Objective **1**

Define and measure the expected rate of return of an individual investment.

Objective **2**

Define and measure the riskiness of an individual investment.

Objective **3**

Compare the historical relationship between risk and rates of return in the capital markets.

Objective **4**

Explain how diversifying investments affects the riskiness and expected rate of return of a portfolio or combination of assets.

Objective **5**

Explain the relationship between the investor's required rate of return on an investment and the riskiness of the investment.

How Did You Do?

COMPUTING AN EXPECTED RATE OF RETURN

The appropriate rate of return would be:

Expected return = risk-free rate + [beta × (market return − risk-free rate)]
$$= 5\% + 1.25 \times (9\% - 5\%)$$
$$= 10\%$$

Key Terms

Asset allocation   189

Beta   184

Capital asset pricing model (CAPM)   191

Characteristic line   183

Company-unique risk   181

Diversifiable risk   181

Expected rate of return   173

Holding-period return   181

Market risk   181

Nondiversifiable risk   181

Portfolio beta   186

Required rate of return   190

Risk   174

Risk-free rate of return   190

Risk premium   190

Security market line   192

Standard deviation   175

Systematic risk   181

Unsystematic risk   181

Review Questions

6-1. a. What is meant by the investor's required rate of return?

   b. How do we measure the riskiness of an asset?

   c. How should the proposed measurement of risk be interpreted?

6-2. What is (a) unsystematic risk (company-unique or diversifiable risk) and (b) systematic risk (market or nondiversifiable risk)?

6-3. What is a beta? How is it used to calculate k, the investor's required rate of return?

6-4. What is the security market line? What does it represent?

6-5. How do we measure the beta of a portfolio?

6-6. If we were to graph the returns of a stock against the returns of the S&P 500 Index, and the points did not follow a very ordered pattern, what could we say about that stock? If the stock's returns tracked the S&P 500 returns very closely, then what could we say?

6-7. Over the past 6 decades, we have had the opportunity to observe the rates of return and the variability of these returns for different types of securities. Summarize these observations.

6-8. What effect will diversifying your portfolio have on your returns?

Self-Test Problems

(The solutions to the following problems are found at the end of the chapter.)

ST-1. (*Expected return and risk*) Universal Corporation is planning to invest in a security that has several possible rates of return. Given the following probability distribution of returns, what is the expected rate of return on the investment? Also compute the standard deviations of the returns. What do the resulting numbers represent?

PROBABILITY	RETURN
.10	−10%
.20	5%
.30	10%
.40	25%

ST-2. (*Capital asset pricing model*) Using the CAPM, estimate the appropriate required rate of return for the three stocks listed here, given that the risk-free rate is 5 percent, and the expected return for the market is 17 percent.

STOCK	BETA
A	.75
B	.90
C	1.40

ST-3. (*Average expected return and risk*) Given the holding-period returns shown here, calculate the average returns and the standard deviations for the Kaifu Corporation and for the market.

MONTH	KAIFU CORP.	MARKET
1	4%	2%
2	6	3
3	0	1
4	2	−1

ST-4. (*Holding-period returns*) From the price data that follow, compute the holding-period returns for periods 2 through 4.

PERIOD	STOCK PRICE
1	$10
2	13
3	11
4	15

ST-5. (*Security market line*)

a. Determine the expected return and beta for the following portfolio:

STOCK	PERCENTAGE OF PORTFOLIO	BETA	EXPECTED RETURN
1	40%	1.00	12%
2	25	0.75	11
3	35	1.30	15

b. Given the foregoing information, draw the security market line and show where the securities fit on the graph. Assume that the risk-free rate is 8 percent and that the expected return on the market portfolio is 12 percent. How would you interpret these findings?

Study Problems

6-1. (*Expected rate of return and risk*) Carter Inc. is evaluating a security. One-year Treasury bills are currently paying 9.1 percent. Calculate the investment's expected return and its standard deviation. Should Carter invest in this security?

PROBABILITY	RETURN
.15	6%
.30	9%
.40	10%
.15	15%

6-2. (*Expected rate of return and risk*) Summerville Inc. is considering an investment in one of two common stocks. Given the information that follows, which investment is better, based on the risk (as measured by the standard deviation) and return of each?

COMMON STOCK A		COMMON STOCK B	
PROBABILITY	RETURN	PROBABILITY	RETURN
.30	11%	.20	−5%
.40	15%	.30	6%
.30	19%	.30	14%
		.20	22%

6-3. (*Expected rate of return and risk*) Richland Manufacturing Inc. has prepared the following information regarding two investments under consideration. Which investment should be accepted?

COMMON STOCK A		COMMON STOCK B	
PROBABILITY	RETURN	PROBABILITY	RETURN
.20	−2%	.10	4%
.50	18%	.30	6%
.30	27%	.40	10%
		.20	15%

6-4. (*Required rate of return using CAPM*)

    a. Compute a fair rate of return for Intel common stock, which has a 1.2 beta. The risk-free rate is 6 percent, and the market portfolio (New York Stock Exchange stocks) has an expected return of 16 percent.

    b. Why is the rate you computed a fair rate?

6-5. (*Estimating beta*) From this graph relating the holding-period returns for Aram Inc. to the S&P 500 Index, estimate the firm's beta.

6-6. (*Capital asset pricing model*) Levine Manufacturing Inc. is considering several investments. The rate on Treasury bills is currently 6.75 percent, and the expected return for the market is 12 percent. What should be the required rates of return for each investment (using the CAPM)?

SECURITY	BETA
A	1.50
B	.90
C	.70
D	1.15

6-7. (*Capital asset pricing model*) MFI Inc. has a beta of .86. If the expected market return is 11.5 percent and the risk-free rate is 7.5 percent, what is the appropriate required return of MFI (using the CAPM)?

6-8. (*Capital asset pricing model*) The expected return for the general market is 12.8 percent, and the risk premium in the market is 4.3 percent. Tasaco, LBM, and Exxos have betas of .864, .693, and .575, respectively. What are the corresponding required rates of return for the three securities?

6-9. (*Computing holding-period returns*)

    a. From the price data here, compute the holding-period returns for Jazman and Solomon for periods 2 through 4.

PERIOD	JAZMAN	SOLOMON
1	$9	$27
2	11	28
3	10	32
4	13	29

    b. How would you interpret the meaning of a holding-period return?

6-10. (*Measuring risk and rates of return*)

a. Given the holding-period returns shown here, compute the average returns and the standard deviations for the Zemin Corporation and for the market.

MONTH	ZEMIN CORP.	MARKET
1	6%	4%
2	3	2
3	−1	1
4	−3	−2
5	5	2
6	0	2

b. If Zemin's beta is 1.54 and the risk-free rate is 8 percent, what would be an appropriate required return for an investor owning Zemin? (*Note:* Because the returns of Zemin Corporation are based on monthly data, you will need to annualize the returns to make them compatible with the risk-free rate. For simplicity, you can convert from monthly to yearly returns by multiplying the average monthly returns by 12.)

c. How does Zemin's historical average return compare with the return you believe to be a fair return, given the firm's systematic risk?

6-11. (*Portfolio beta and security market line*) You own a portfolio consisting of the following stocks:

STOCK	PERCENTAGE OF PORTFOLIO	BETA	EXPECTED RETURN
1	20%	1.00	16%
2	30	0.85	14
3	15	1.20	20
4	25	0.60	12
5	10	1.60	24

The risk-free rate is 7 percent. Also, the expected return on the market portfolio is 15.5 percent.

a. Calculate the expected return of your portfolio. (*Hint:* The expected return of a portfolio equals the weighted average of the individual stocks' expected returns, where the weights are the percentage invested in each stock.)

b. Calculate the portfolio beta.

c. Given the foregoing information, plot the security market line on paper. Plot the stocks from your portfolio on your graph.

d. From your plot in part c, which stocks appear to be your winners and which ones appear to be losers?

e. Why should you consider your conclusion in part d to be less than certain?

6-12. (*Expected return, standard deviation, and capital asset pricing model*) The following are the end-of-month prices for both the Standard & Poor's 500 Index and Ford Motor Company's common stock.

a. Using the data here, calculate the holding-period returns for each of the months.

MONTH AND YEAR	S&P 500 INDEX	FORD
March-05	$1,180.59	$11.33
April-05	1,156.85	9.11
May-05	1,191.50	9.98
June-05	1,191.33	10.24
July-05	1,234.18	10.74
August-05	1,220.33	9.97
September-05	1,228.81	9.86
October-05	1,207.01	8.32
November-05	1,249.48	8.13
December-05	1,248.29	7.72
January-06	1,280.08	8.58
February-06	1,280.66	7.97
March-06	1,291.24	7.96

b. Calculate the average monthly return and the standard deviation for both the S&P 500 and Ford.

c. Develop a graph that shows the relationship between the Ford stock returns and the S&P 500 Index. (Show the Ford returns on the vertical axis and the S&P 500 Index returns on the horizontal axis as done in Figure 6-5.)

d. From your graph, describe the nature of the relationship between Ford stock returns and the returns for the S&P 500 Index.

Web Works

6-WW1. Go to **www.moneychimp.com**. Select the link "Volatility". Complete the retirement planning calculator, making the assumptions that you believe are appropriate for you. Then go to the Monte Carlo simulation calculator. Assume that you invest in large-company common stocks during your working years and then invest in long-term corporate bonds during retirement. Use the nominal average returns and standard deviations shown in Figure 6-2. What did you learn?

6-WW2. Go to **www.cgi.money.cnn.com/tools**. Choose "Asset Allocator." Answer the questions and click "Calculate." Try different options and see how the calculator suggests you allocate your investments.

6-WW3. Access **http://finance.yahoo.com**. On the left side of the page, scroll down to and select "Investing" and then choose "Education." Next select "Glossary" and find "Expected Return" and "Expected Value." What did you learn from the definitions of these terms?

6-WW4. Go to **www.investopedia.com/university/beginner**, where there is an article on "Investing 101: A Tutorial for Beginning Investors." Read the article and explain what it says about risk tolerance.

Mini Case

Note: Although not absolutely necessary, you are advised to use a computer spreadsheet to work the following problem. A spreadsheet (Chapter 6 Mini Case) with the following data is available at **www.prenhall.com/keown**.

    a. Use the price data from the table that follows for the Standard & Poor's 500 Index, Wal-Mart, and Target to calculate the holding-period returns for the 24 months from March 2004 through March 2006.

MONTH	S&P 500	WAL-MART	TARGET
Mar-04	$928.62	$59.69	$45.04
Apr-04	876.99	57.00	43.37
May-04	854.74	55.73	44.70
Jun-04	834.75	52.50	42.47
Jul-04	864.03	53.01	43.60
Aug-04	917.77	52.67	44.58
Sep-04	953.08	53.20	45.25
Oct-04	981.06	53.92	50.02
Nov-04	989.58	52.06	51.22
Dec-04	999.31	52.82	51.93
Jan-05	1,002.14	52.40	50.77
Feb-05	1,049.29	51.61	50.82
Mar-05	1,055.61	50.11	50.02
Apr-05	1,108.55	47.14	46.41
May-05	1,131.20	47.23	53.70
Jun-05	1,142.93	48.20	54.41
Jul-05	1,123.93	49.35	58.75
Aug-05	1,118.54	44.96	53.75
Sep-05	1,120.00	43.82	51.93
Oct-05	1,134.30	47.31	55.69
Nov-05	1,099.91	48.56	53.51
Dec-05	1,102.80	46.80	54.97
Jan-06	1,111.39	46.11	54.75
Feb-06	1,125.23	45.36	54.40
Mar-06	1,180.54	47.24	52.01

    b. Calculate the average monthly holding-period returns and the standard deviation of these returns for the S&P 500 Index, Wal-Mart, and Target.

c. Plot (1) the holding-period returns for Wal-Mart against the Standard & Poor's 500 Index, and (2) the Target holding-period returns against the Standard & Poor's 500 Index. (Use Figure 6-5 as the format for your graph.)

d. From your graphs in part c, describe the nature of the relationship between the stock returns for Wal-Mart and the returns for the S&P 500 Index. Make the same comparison for Target.

e. Assume that you have decided to invest one-half of your money in Wal-Mart and the remainder in Target. Calculate the monthly holding-period returns for your two-stock portfolio. (*Hint:* The monthly return for the portfolio is the average of the two stocks' monthly returns.)

f. Plot the returns of your two-stock portfolio against the Standard & Poor's 500 Index as you did for the individual stocks in part c. How does this graph compare to the graphs for the individual stocks? Explain the difference.

g. The following table shows the returns on an *annualized* basis that were realized from holding long-term government bonds for the same period. Calculate the average *monthly* holding-period returns and the standard deviations of these returns. (*Hint:* You will need to convert the annual returns to monthly returns by dividing each return by 12 months.)

MONTH AND YEAR	ANNUALIZED RATE OF RETURN (%)
Apr-04	4.50%
May-04	4.66%
Jun-04	4.62%
Jul-04	4.47%
Aug-04	4.13%
Sep-04	4.12%
Oct-04	4.03%
Nov-04	4.36%
Dec-04	4.22%
Jan-05	4.13%
Feb-05	4.36%
Mar-05	4.50%
Apr-05	4.20%
May-05	4.01%
Jun-05	3.94%
Jul-05	4.29%
Aug-05	4.02%
Sep-05	4.33%
Oct-05	4.56%
Nov-05	4.50%
Dec-05	4.39%
Jan-06	4.53%
Feb-06	4.55%
Mar-06	4.86%

h. Now assuming that you have decided to invest equal amounts of money in Wal-Mart, Target, and long-term government securities, calculate the monthly returns for your three-asset portfolio. What is the average return and the standard deviation?

i. Make a comparison of the average returns and the standard deviations for all the individual assets and the two portfolios that we designed. What conclusions can be reached by your comparison?

j. According to Standard & Poor's, the betas for Wal-Mart and Target are 0.59 and 1.02, respectively. Compare the meaning of these betas relative to the standard deviations calculated above.

k. The Treasury bill rate at the end of March 2006 was 4.5 percent. Given the betas for Wal-Mart and Target and using the above data for the S&P 500 Index as a measure for the market portfolio expected return, estimate an appropriate required rate of return given the level of systematic risk for each stock.

Self-Test Solutions

SS-1.

(A) PROBABILITY $P(k_i)$	(B) RETURN (k_i)	EXPECTED $\bar{k}$ $(A) \times (B)$	WEIGHTED DEVIATION $(k_i - \bar{k})^2 P(k_i)$
.10	−10%	−1%	52.9%
.20	5	1	12.8
.30	10	3	2.7
.40	25	10	57.6
		$\bar{k} = 13\%$	$\sigma^2 = 126.0\%$
			$\sigma = 11.22\%$

From our studies in statistics, we know that if the distribution of returns were normal, then Universal could expect a return of 13 percent, with a 67 percent possibility that this return would vary up or down by 11.22 percent between 1.78 percent (13% − 11.22%) and 24.22 percent (13% + 11.22%). However, it is apparent from the probabilities that the distribution is not normal.

SS-2.

Stock A: 5% + .75 (17% − 5%) = 14.0%
Stock B: 5% + .90 (17% − 5%) = 15.8%
Stock C: 5% + 1.40 (17% − 5%) = 21.8%

SS-3.

KAIFU	MARKET

Average return: $\dfrac{4\% + 6\% + 0\% + 2\%}{4} = 3\%$ Average return: $\dfrac{2\% + 3\% + 1\% - 1\%}{4} = 1.25\%$

Standard deviation: $\sqrt{\dfrac{[(4\% - 3\%)^2 + (6\% - 3\%)^2 + (0\% - 3\%)^2 + (2\% - 3\%)^2]}{4 - 1}} = 2.58\%$

Standard deviation: $\sqrt{\dfrac{[(2\% - 1.25\%)^2 + (3\% - 1.25\%)^2 + (1\% - 1.25\%)^2 + (-1\% - 1.25\%)^2]}{4 - 1}} = 1.71\%$

SS-4.

TIME	STOCK PRICE	HOLDING-PERIOD RETURN
1	$10	
2	13	($13 ÷ $10) − 1 = 30.0%
3	11	($11 ÷ $13) − 1 = −15.4%
4	15	($15 ÷ $11) − 1 = 36.4%

SS-5. a. Portfolio expected return:

$(.4 \times 12\%) + (.25 \times 11\%) + (.35 \times 15\%) = 12.8\%$

Portfolio beta:

$(.4 \times 1) + (.25 \times .75) + (.35 \times 1.3) = 1.04$

b.

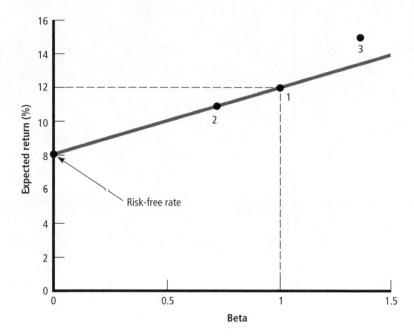

Stocks 1 and 2 seem to be right in line with the security market line, which suggest that they are earning a fair return, given their systematic risk. Stock 3, on the other hand, is earning more than a fair return (above the security market line). We might be tempted to conclude that security 3 is undervalued. However, we may be seeing an illusion; it is possible to mis-specify the security market line by using bad estimates in our data.

✍ LEARNING OBJECTIVES ❧

After reading this chapter, you should be able to:

1. Distinguish between different kinds of bonds.

2. Explain the more popular features of bonds.

3. Define the term *value* as used for several different purposes.

4. Explain the factors that determine value.

5. Describe the basic process for valuing assets.

6. Estimate the value of a bond.

7. Compute a bondholder's expected rate of return.

8. Explain three important relationships that exist in bond valuation.

CHAPTER 7

The Valuation and Characteristics of Bonds

If you have ever shopped at Neiman Marcus, you know it sells only very high-quality products, which for many of us means *expensive*.

For many years Neiman Marcus' stock had been traded on the New York Stock Exchange, but that ended in 2005, when a private investment group, including Texas Pacific Group and Warburg Pincus LLC, bought the firm for $5.1 billion. To buy the stock, the investors borrowed a lot of money to finance the purchase, and then they provided the equity financing to complete it. In this type of financing arrangement, known as a *leveraged buyout*, or LBO, the new owners work with the firm's managers to make it more efficient and then eventually sell it to other investors or take the firm public. By 2005, LBOs were taking on significantly more debt than in the past to make their purchases. Consequently, the owners of these firms were finding it more difficult to sell the companies or to take them public. So, they began paying themselves large dividends, which meant that there was less money available to service the companies' debt.

In announcing the sale, Richard A. Smith, Neiman Marcus' CEO and chairman of the board, remarked, "This transaction provides outstanding shareholder value and represents an endorsement of the excellent performance of our entire team." But although Smith considered the sale to be a good deal for the firm's stock-holders, the firm's bondholders, who had loaned the company money, were not happy.

In the Neiman Marcus case, the bondholders made an unusual demand of the shareholders: For the interest they were to be paid as part of the buyout, they agreed to accept new bonds rather than cash—a provision known as a *payment in kind*, or PIK. But they insisted that Neiman Marcus must not pay any dividends to the new shareholders with the money that was saved by the trade, or PIK.

Although the PIK provision does provide, as CFO James Skinner notes, "a security blanket in case of financial stress," the fact is, bondholders did not want to see shareholders rewarded at their expense. "You want to make sure there's enough cash available to pay debt [rather than see it] go out to the equity holders," observed Paul Scanlon, a manager at Putnam Investments, which bought more than $13 million of the bonds.

"LBO activity has firmly established its place atop the list of bondholder concerns," wrote the authors of a Morgan Stanley report. Given the increasingly aggressive terms of the deals, they added, "All we need is Michael Douglas to squeeze back into his bespoke suit, his Gucci loafers, and release *Wall Street II*, and we'll know the end of the LBO boom can't be far behind."

Source: Adapted from Ronald Fink, "Bondholder Backlash," *CFO Magazine*, February 01, 2006, pp. 51–55, and **www.neimanmarcusgroup.com**

Knowing the fair value or price of an asset is no easy matter. The *Maxims* by the French writer La Rouchefoucauld, written over 3 centuries ago, still speak to us: "The greatest of all gifts is the power to estimate things at their true worth."

Understanding how to value financial securities is essential if managers are to meet the objective of maximizing the value of the firm. If they are to maximize the investors' value, they must know what drives the value of an asset. Specifically, they need to understand how bonds and stocks are valued in the marketplace; otherwise, they cannot act in the best interest of the firm's investors.

A bond is one form of a company's long-term debt. In this chapter, we begin by identifying the different kinds of bonds. We next look at the features or characteristics of most bonds. We then examine the concepts of and procedures for valuing an asset and apply these ideas to valuing bonds.

We now begin our study by considering the different kinds of bonds.

Objective **1**

Distinguish between different kinds of bonds.

bond a long-term (10-year or more) promissory note issued by the borrower, promising to pay the owner of the security a predetermined, fixed amount of interest each year.

TYPES OF BONDS

A **bond** is a *type of debt or long-term promissory note, issued by the borrower, promising to pay its holder a predetermined and fixed amount of interest per year and the face value of the bond at maturity*. However, there is a wide variety of such creatures. Just to mention a few, we have

Debentures	Zero and very low coupon bonds
Subordinated debentures	Junk bonds
Mortgage bonds	Convertible bonds
Eurobonds	

The following sections briefly explain each of these types of bonds.

Debentures

debenture any unsecured long-term debt.

The term **debenture** applies to *any unsecured long-term debt*. Because these bonds are unsecured, the earning ability of the issuing corporation is of great concern to the bondholder. They are also viewed as being more risky than secured bonds and, as a result, must provide investors with a higher yield than secured bonds provide. Often the firm issuing debentures attempts to provide some protection to the holder of the debenture by agreeing not to issue more secured long-term debt that would further tie up the firm's assets. To the issuing firm, the major advantage of debentures is that no property has to be secured by them. This allows the firm to issue debt and still preserve some future borrowing power.

Subordinated Debentures

subordinated debenture a debenture that is subordinated to other debentures in terms of its payments in case of insolvency.

Many firms have more than one issue of debentures outstanding. In this case a hierarchy may be specified, in which some debentures are given *subordinated standing in case of insolvency*. The claims of the **subordinated debentures** are honored only after the claims of secured debt and unsubordinated debentures have been satisfied.

Mortgage Bonds

mortgage bond a bond secured by a lien on real property.

A **mortgage bond** is a *bond secured by a lien on real property*. Typically, the value of the real property is greater than that of the mortgage bonds issued. This provides the mortgage bondholders with a margin of safety in the event the market value of the secured property declines. In the case of foreclosure, *trustees*, who represent the bondholders and act on their behalf, have the power to sell the secured property and use the proceeds to pay the bondholders. The bond trustee, usually a banking institution or trust company, oversees the relationship between the bondholder and the issuing firm, protecting the bondholder and seeing that the terms of the indenture are carried out. In the event that the proceeds from this sale do not cover the bonds, the bondholders become general creditors, similar to debenture bondholders, for the unpaid portion of the debt.

Eurobonds

Eurobonds are not so much a different type of security. They are simply securities, in this case *bonds, issued in a country different from the one in which the currency of the bond is denominated*. For example, a bond that is issued in Europe or in Asia by an American company and that pays interest and principal to the lender in U.S. dollars would be considered a Eurobond. Thus, even if the bond is not issued in Europe, it merely needs to be sold in a country different from the one in which the bond's currency is denominated to be considered a Eurobond.

The primary attractions of Eurobonds to borrowers, aside from favorable rates, are the relative lack of regulation (Eurobonds are not registered with the Securities and Exchange Commission [SEC]), less-rigorous disclosure requirements than those of the SEC, and the speed with which they can be issued. Interestingly, not only are Eurobonds not registered with the SEC, but they may not be offered to U.S. citizens and residents.

eurobond a bond issued in a country different from the one in which the currency of the bond is denominated; for example, a bond issued in Europe or Asia by an American company that pays interest and principal to the lender in U.S. dollars.

Zero and Very Low Coupon Bonds

Zero and very low coupon bonds allow the issuing firm to issue *bonds at a substantial discount from their $1,000 face value with a zero or very low coupon rate*. The investor receives a large part (or all with zero coupon bonds) of the return from the appreciation of the bonds. For example, American Music issued $3 billion of debt maturing in 2036 with a zero coupon rate. In 2006, these bonds sold at an 80 percent discount from their par value; that is, investors paid only $200 for a bond with a $1,000 par value. Investors who purchased these bonds for $200 and hold them until they mature in 2036 will receive an effective interest rate of 5.5 percent, with all of this return coming from the appreciation of the bond. Furthermore, the firm will have no cash outflows until these bonds mature; however, at that time it will have to pay back $3 billion, even though it only received approximately $600 million when the bonds were issued.

As with any form of financing, there are both advantages and disadvantages of issuing zero and very low coupon bonds. As already mentioned, one disadvantage is, when the bonds mature, American Music will face an extremely large cash outflow, much greater than the cash inflow it experienced when the bonds were issued. There are several advantages of zero coupon bonds from the issuing firm's perspective. First, the annual cash outflows associated with interest payments do not occur with zero coupon bonds and are at a relatively low level with low coupon bonds. Second, because there is relatively strong investor demand for this type of debt, the investors will frequently accept a lower effective interest rate. For instance, American Music was able to issue zero coupon bonds at about half a percent less than it would have been if they had been traditional interest-paying bonds. Finally, the firm is able to deduct the annual amortization of the discount from taxable income, which will provide a positive annual cash flow to American Music.

zero and very low coupon bond a bond issued at a substantial discount from its $1,000 face value and that pays little or no interest.

Junk Bonds (High-Yield Bonds)

Junk bonds are high-risk debt with *ratings of BB or below* by Moody's and Standard & Poor's. The lower the rating, the higher the chance of default. The lowest rating is CC for Standard & Poor's and Ca for Moody's. Originally, the term "junk bonds" was used to describe bonds issued by "fallen angels," that is, firms with sound financial histories that were facing severe financial problems and suffering from poor credit ratings. Junk bonds are also called **high-yield bonds** because of the high interest rates they pay the investor. Typically, they have an interest rate of between 3 and 5 percent more than AAA-grade long-term debt.

Before the mid-1970s, smaller firms simply did not have access to the capital markets because of the reluctance of investors to accept speculative-grade bonds. However, by the late 1980s, junk bonds became the way to finance hostile takeovers—buying a firm without the approval of its managers. For example, the purchase of RJR Nabisco for about $20 billion by

junk bond any bond rated BB or below.

high-yield bond see Junk bond.

the investment group KKR was largely accomplished by junk bond financing. However, the eventual bankruptcy of Drexel Burnham Lambert, the investment bank most responsible for developing the large junk bond market, the criminal activity (and jailing) of the "king of junk bonds," Michael Milken, and increasing interest rates brought an end to the extensive use of junk bonds for financing corporate takeovers. (Michael Milken, a partner at Drexel Burnham Lambert, used to have an annual conference in Beverly Hills, California, nicknamed "The Predator's Ball" to attract takeover investors and corporate raiders who needed junk bond financing to accomplish their takeovers.)

When corporate takeovers subsided from their highs, most people thought the junk bond was forever dead. By 1990, the junk bond market was virtually nonexistent. Then, in 1992, when the economy rebounded and investors began looking for higher interest rates, the junk bond market was revitalized. The following year, new junk bond issues reached a record $62 billion. Also, by 1995, less than 20 percent of the proceeds from junk bonds was being used to finance mergers and acquisitions, compared with 60 percent in the 1980s. Between 1997 and 2000, corporations issued $382 billion in junk bonds, suggesting that this type of debt continued to be a significant source of capital to finance corporate growth. However, the increase came with increased risk as well, with such giants as W. R. Grace, Lucent, and Pacific Gas & Electric defaulting on their debt. Junk bonds continue to be a source of financing for a number of companies providing higher potential returns for investors— but with greater risk as well.

Convertible Bonds

convertible bond a debt security that can be converted into a firm's stock at a prespecified price.

Convertible bonds are debt securities that can be converted into a firm's stock at a prespecified price. For instance, you might have a convertible bond with a face, or par, value of $1,000 that pays 6 percent interest, or $60, each year. The bond matures in 5 years, at which time the company must pay the $1,000 par value to the bondholder. However, at the time the bond was issued, the firm gave the bondholder the option of either collecting the $1,000 or receiving shares of the firm's stock at a conversion price of $50. In other words, the bondholder would receive 20 shares (20 = $1,000 par value ÷ $50 conversion price). What would you do if you were the bondholder? If the stock were selling for more than $50, then you would want to give up the $1,000 par value and take the stock. Thus, it's the investor's choice either to take the $1,000 promised when the bond was issued or to convert the bond into the firm's stock.

Consider TiVo, the firm that developed the TiVo recorder for television. In 2001, TiVo issued $51.8 million of 7 percent convertible debt. The bonds can be converted at any time into TiVo common stock at a conversion price of $6.73 per share. Because the par value for each bond is $1,000, a bondholder can convert one bond into 148.59 shares (148.59 shares = $1,000 ÷ $6.73 price per share.) This option allows the investor to be repaid the $1,000 par value or to convert into stock if the value of the stock exceeds $1,000.

Did You Get It?

1. How do debentures, subordinated debentures, and mortgage bonds differ with regard to their risk? How would investors respond to the varying types of risk?
2. How does an investor receive a return from a zero or very low coupon bond? Why would a company be able to deduct the amortized interest over the life of the bond even though there are no cash outflows associated with the interest?
3. Why do junk bonds typically have a higher interest rate than other types of bonds? Why has this market been revitalized?

▇ *Remember Your Principles*

Some have thought junk bonds were fundamentally different from other securities, but they are not. They are bonds with a great amount of risk and, therefore, promise high expected returns. Thus, **Principle 1: The Risk–Return Trade-Off—We Won't Take On Additional Risk Unless We Expect to Be Compensated with Additional Return**.

Now that you have an understanding of the kinds of bonds firms might issue, let's look at some of the characteristics and terminology of bonds.

TERMINOLOGY AND CHARACTERISTICS OF BONDS

Objective **2**

Explain the more popular features of bonds.

Before valuing bonds, we first need to understand the terminology related to bonds. Then we will be better prepared to determine the value of a bond.

When a firm or nonprofit institution needs financing, one source is bonds. As already noted, this type of financing instrument is simply a long-term promissory note, issued by the borrower, promising to pay its holder a predetermined and fixed amount of interest each year. Some of the more important terms and characteristics that you might hear about bonds are as follows:

Claims on assets and income   Call provision
Par value   Indenture
Coupon interest rate   Bond ratings
Maturity

Let's consider each in turn.

Claims on Assets and Income

In the case of insolvency, claims of debt, including bonds, are generally honored before those of both common stock and preferred stock. In general, if the interest on bonds is not paid, the bond trustees can classify the firm as insolvent and force it into bankruptcy. Thus, the bondholders' claim on income is more likely to be honored than that of the common stockholders, whose dividends are paid at the discretion of the firm's management. However, different types of debt can have a hierarchy among themselves as to the order of their claims on assets.

Par Value

The **par value** of a bond is its *face value, which is returned to the bondholder at maturity*. In general, corporate bonds are issued in denominations of $1,000, although there are some exceptions to this rule. Also, when bond prices are quoted, either by financial managers or in the financial press, prices are generally expressed as a percentage of the bond's par value. For example, a Time-Warner bond was recently quoted as selling for 113.68. That does not mean you can buy the bond for $113.68. It means that this bond is selling for 113.68 percent of its par value of $1,000. Hence, the market price of this bond is actually $1,136.80. At maturity in 2028 the bondholder will receive $1,000.

par value on the face of a bond, the stated amount that the firm is to repay upon the maturity date.

Coupon Interest Rate

The **coupon interest rate** on a bond indicates the *percentage of the par value of the bond that will be paid out annually in the form of interest*. Thus, regardless of what happens to the price of a bond with an 8 percent coupon interest rate and a $1,000 par value, it will pay out $80 annually in interest until maturity (.08 × $1,000 = $80). However, as we will observe later, the interest may be paid semiannualy, perhaps in June and December. In the foregoing example, the interest would be $40 semiannually, but the coupon rate is still calculated on the annual interest of $80.

coupon interest rate the interest rate contractually owed on a bond as a percent of its par value.

Maturity

The **maturity** of a bond indicates *the length of time until the bond issuer returns the par value to the bondholder and terminates or redeems the bond.*

maturity the length of time until the bond issuer returns the par value to the bondholder and terminates the bond.

Call Provision

If a company issues bonds and then later the prevailing interest rate declines, the firm may want to pay off the bonds early and then issue new bonds with a lower interest rate. To do so, the bond must be **callable**, or **redeemable**; otherwise, the firm cannot force the bondholder

callable bond (redeemable bond) an option available to a company issuing a bond whereby the issuer can call (redeem) the bond before it matures. This is usually done if interest rates decline below what the firm is paying on the bond.

call protection period
a prespecified time period during which a company cannot recall a bond.

to accept early payment. The issuer, however, usually must pay the bondholders a premium, such as 1 year's interest. Also, there frequently is a **call protection period** where the firm cannot call the bond for a prespecified time period.

Indenture

indenture the legal agreement between the firm issuing bonds and the bond trustee who represents the bondholders, providing the specific terms of the loan agreement.

An **indenture** is the *legal agreement between the firm issuing the bonds and the trustee who represents the bondholders.* The indenture provides the specific terms of the loan agreement, including a description of the bonds, the rights of the bondholders, the rights of the issuing firm, and the responsibilities of the trustee. This legal document may run 100 pages or more in length, with the majority of it devoted to defining protective provisions for the bondholder.

Typically, the restrictive provisions included in the indenture attempt to protect the bondholders' financial position relative to that of other outstanding securities. Common provisions involve (1) prohibiting the sale of the firm's accounts receivable, (2) limiting common stock dividends, (3) restricting the purchase or sale of the firm's fixed assets, and (4) setting limits on additional borrowing by the firm. Not allowing the sale of accounts receivable is specified because such sales would benefit the firm's short-run liquidity position at the expense of its future liquidity position. Common stock dividends may not be allowed if the firm's liquidity falls below a specified level, or the maximum dividend payout might be limited to some fraction, say, 50 or 60 percent of earnings. Fixed-asset restrictions generally require permission before they can be liquidated or used as collateral on new loans. Constraints on additional borrowing usually involve limiting the amount and type of additional long-term debt that can be issued. All these restrictions have one thing in common: They attempt to prohibit actions that would improve the status of other securities at the expense of bonds, and to protect the status of bonds from being weakened by any managerial action.

Bond Ratings

John Moody first began to rate bonds in 1909. Since that time three rating agencies—Moody's, Standard & Poor's, and Fitch Investor Services—have provided ratings on corporate bonds. These ratings involve a judgment about the future risk potential of the bonds. Although they deal with expectations, several historical factors seem to play a significant role in their determination. Bond ratings are favorably affected by (1) a greater reliance on eq-

TABLE 7-1	Standard & Poor's Corporate Bond Ratings

AAA	This is the highest rating assigned by Standard & Poor's for debt obligation and indicates an extremely strong capacity to pay principal and interest.
AA	Bonds rated AA also qualify as high-quality debt obligations. Their capacity to pay principal and interest is very strong, and in the majority of instances, they differ from AAA issues only by a small degree.
A	Bonds rated A have a strong capacity to pay principal and interest, although they are somewhat more susceptible to the adverse effects of changes in circumstances and economic conditions.
BBB	Bonds rated BBB are regarded as having an adequate capacity to pay principal and interest. Whereas they normally exhibit adequate protection parameters, adverse economic conditions or changing circumstances are more likely to lead to a weakened capacity to pay principal and interest for bonds in this category than for bonds in the A category.
BB B CCC CC	Bonds rated BB, B, CCC, and CC are regarded, on balance, as predominately speculative with respect to the issuer's capacity to pay interest and repay principal in accordance with the terms of the obligation. BB indicates the lowest degree of speculation and CC the highest. Although such bonds will likely have some quality and protective characteristics, these are outweighed by large uncertainties or major risk exposures to adverse conditions.
C	The rating C is reserved for income bonds on which no interest is being paid.
D	Bonds rated D are in default, and payment of principal and/or interest is in arrears.

Plus (+) or Minus (−): To provide more detailed indications of credit quality, the ratings from AA to BB may be modified by the addition of a plus or minus sign to show relative standing within the major rating categories.

Source: Adapted from **www.standardandpoors.com**, December 2005.

Finance at Work

FORD'S DEBT RATING GETS DOWNGRADED TWO NOTCHES

In 2006, Ford Motor Co. faced sliding revenues as consumers bought fewer big, gas-guzzling trucks. On June 8, 2006, Fitch Ratings downgraded the auto maker's credit rating two notches and analyzed how creditors might fare in the event of a bankruptcy court filing. The following are excerpts from an article that appeared in the *Wall Street Journal* on June 9, 2006.

> Ford Motor Co. faces new questions about its lineup of vehicles and its ability to reverse sliding revenue as consumers shift away from big trucks, after Fitch Ratings downgraded the auto maker's credit rating two notches and analyzed how creditors might fare in the event of a bankruptcy court filing.
>
> How is Ford Motor doing now? Currently it is struggling to halt falling U.S. vehicle sales and cut costs. Fitch's decision to downgrade Ford's debt rating to a highly speculative single-B-plus from BB highlights a growing concern among investors and industry executives that Ford's North American turnaround plan, dubbed the "Way Forward," is encountering strong headwinds from external competition and internal problems that have slowed down the development of new models.
>
> Fitch based its action in part on a "relatively sparse [Ford] product lineup over the next year" and concerns that Ford would be unable to cut product costs because of a beleaguered supply base and rising costs for commodities like steel, aluminum, and copper. Fitch also predicted Ford's important F-series pickup would

be hurt by new big pickup trucks produced in late 2006 by General Motors Corp. and Toyota Motor Corp. In short, Fitch's outlook for Ford was negative.

> "There is little to point to in terms of a turnaround for Ford in North America through 2007. The cost side of the business is also unfavorable with Ford having to prop up suppliers," said Mark Oline, Fitch managing director.
>
> Ford spokeswoman Becky Sanch said the auto maker pays attention to the downgrades but feels it is making progress on its turnaround plan. "We remain committed to our North American turnaround plan. We're always watching those ratings actions, but we are making progress on our plans as expected," she said.
>
> Fitch says companies with a single-B-plus rating fall into bankruptcy about 24 percent of the time within five years. It estimated debtholders would get back 50 percent to 70 percent of their investment from Ford and 70 percent to 90 percent of their investment in Ford Credit, the lending arm of Ford Motor Co.
>
> Ford declined to comment on Fitch's bankruptcy recovery analysis for its North American operations. Ford's ratings are still higher than its crosstown rival GM, which is rated B3 by Moody's Investors Service and single-B by Standard & Poor's and Fitch.

Source: Jeffrey McCracken, "Ford's Debt Rating is Downgraded Two Notches," the *Wall Street Journal*, June 9, 2006, p. A3.

Remember Your Principles

When we say that a lower bond rating means a higher interest rate charged by the investors (bondholders), we are observing an application of **Principle 1: The Risk–Return Trade-Off—We Won't Take On Additional Risk Unless We Expect to Be Compensated with Additional Return.**

uity as opposed to debt in financing the firm, (2) profitable operations, (3) a low variability in past earnings, (4) large firm size, and (5) little use of subordinated debt. In turn, the rating a bond receives affects the interest rate demanded on the bond by the investors. The poorer the bond rating, the higher the interest rate demanded by investors. (Table 7-1 describes these ratings.) Thus, bond ratings are extremely important for the financial manager. They provide an indicator of default risk that in turn affects the interest rate that must be paid on borrowed funds.

We are now ready to think about bond valuation. To begin, we must first clarify precisely what we mean by value. Next, we need to understand the basic concepts of valuation and the process for valuing an asset. Then we may apply these concepts to valuing a bond, and in Chapter 8, to valuing stocks.

Did You Get It?

1. What are some of the important features of a bond? Which features determine the cash flows associated with a bond?

2. What restrictions are typically included in an indenture in order to protect the bondholder?

3. How does the bond rating affect an investor's required rate of return? What actions could a firm take to receive a more favorable rating?

Objective **3**

Define the term *value* as used for several different purposes.

book value (1) the value of an asset as shown on the firm's balance sheet. It represents the historical cost of the asset rather than its current market value or replacement cost. (2) The depreciated value of a company's assets (original cost less accumulated depreciation) less outstanding liabilities.

liquidation value the dollar sum that could be realized if an asset were sold.

market value the value observed in the marketplace.

intrinsic, or economic, value the present value of an asset's expected future cash flows. This value is the amount the investor considers to be fair value, given the amount, timing, and riskiness of future cash flows.

fair value the present value of an asset's expected future cash flows.

DEFINING VALUE

The term *value* is often used in different contexts, depending on its application. **Book value** is the *value of an asset as shown on a firm's balance sheet*. It represents the historical cost of the asset rather than its current worth. For instance, the book value of a company's common stock is the amount the investors originally paid for the stock and, therefore, the amount the firm received when the stock was issued.

Liquidation value is the *dollar sum that could be realized if an asset were sold individually and not as part of a going concern*. For example, if a firm's operations were discontinued and its assets were divided up and sold, the sales price would represent the asset's liquidation value.

The **market value** of an asset is the *observed value for the asset in the marketplace*. This value is determined by supply and demand forces working together in the marketplace, whereby buyers and sellers negotiate a mutually acceptable price for the asset. For instance, the market price for Ford's common stock on October 30, 2006, was $5.40 per share. This price was reached by a large number of buyers and sellers working through the New York Stock Exchange. In theory, a market price exists for all assets. However, many assets have no readily observable market price because trading seldom occurs. For instance, the market price for the common stock of Vision Research Organization, a recent start-up firm in Dallas, Texas, would be more difficult to establish than the market value of Ford's common stock.

The **intrinsic, or economic, value** of an asset—also called the **fair value**—is the *present value of the asset's expected future cash flows*. This value is the amount an investor should be willing to pay for the asset given the amount, timing, and riskiness of its future cash flows. Once the investor has estimated the intrinsic value of a security, this value could be compared with its market value when available. If the intrinsic value is greater than the market value, then the security is undervalued in the eyes of the investor. Should the market value exceed the investor's intrinsic value, then the security is overvalued.

We hasten to add that if the securities market is working efficiently, the market value and the intrinsic value of a security will be equal. Whenever a security's intrinsic value differs from its current market price, the competition among investors seeking opportunities to make a profit will quickly drive the market price back to its intrinsic value. Thus, we may define an efficient market as one in which the values of all securities at any instant fully reflect all available public information, which results in the market value and the intrinsic value being the same. If the markets are efficient, it is extremely difficult for an investor to make extra profits from an ability to predict prices.

The idea of market efficiency has been the backdrop for an intense battle between professional investors and university professors. The academic community has contended that someone throwing darts at the list of securities in the *Wall Street Journal* could do as well as a professional money manager. Market professionals retort that academicians are grossly mistaken in this view. The war has been intense but also one that the student of finance should find intriguing.

Did You Get It?

1. Explain the different types of value.
2. Why should the market value equal the intrinsic value?

Remember Your Principles

The fact that investors have difficulty identifying stocks that are undervalued relates to **Principle 6: Efficient Capital Markets—The Markets Are Quick and the Prices Are Right**. In an efficient market, the price reflects all available public information about the security and, therefore, it is priced fairly.

Objective **4**

Explain the factors that determine value.

WHAT DETERMINES VALUE?

For our purposes, *the value of an asset is its intrinsic value or the present value of its expected future cash flows*, when these cash flows are discounted back to the present using the investor's required rate of return. This statement is true for valuing all assets, and it serves as the basis of almost all that we do in finance. Thus, value is affected by three elements:

1. The amount and timing of the asset's expected cash flows
2. The riskiness of these cash flows
3. The investor's required rate of return for undertaking the investment

The first two factors are characteristics of the asset. The third one, the required rate of return, is the minimum rate of return necessary to attract an investor to purchase or hold a security. This rate of return is determined by *the rates of return available on similar investments*, or what we learned in Chapter 2 is called the opportunity cost of funds. This rate must be high enough to compensate the investor for risk perceived in the asset's future cash flows. (The required rate of return was explained in Chapter 6.)

Figure 7-1 depicts the basic factors involved in valuation. As the figure shows, finding the value of an asset involves the following steps:

1. Assessing the asset's characteristics, which include the amount and timing of the expected cash flows and the riskiness of these cash flows
2. Determining the investor's required rate of return, which embodies the investor's attitude about assuming risk and the investor's perception of the riskiness of the asset
3. Discounting the expected cash flows back to the present, using the investor's required rate of return as the discount rate

Thus, intrinsic value is a function of the cash flows yet to be received, the riskiness of these cash flows, and the investor's required rate of return.

Did You Get It?

1. What are the three important elements of asset valuation?

FIGURE 7-1 Basic Factors Determining an Asset's Value

Ethics in Financial Management

KEEPING PERSPECTIVE

Most business school graduates become competent executives, managing people and resources for the benefit of society. They understand that the rewards—the titles and money—are merely byproducts of doing a good job. However, ethical and moral lapses in the business and financial community, academia, politics, and religion fill the daily press. It is particularly disturbing that these incidents frequently involve recent graduates of top business and law schools with six-figure incomes and brilliant careers ahead of them.

Most of these individuals appear to be very bright, highly motivated overachievers, driven by peer rivalries to win a game in which the score has a dollar sign in front of it. Most have sold their futures for $20,000 to $50,000 of illicit profits. Essentially, they have missed the point—that life is a marathon, not a sprint.

To illustrate the point, consider the owner of a small company who had the opportunity to acquire a contract with a large

Fortune 500 company to produce a product for the large firm. A verbal agreement was reached on the deal, but when the owner met with the president of the large company to sign the contract, the price to be received by the small firm was $0.25 per unit higher than originally agreed upon—in the small company owner's favor. When questioned, the president of the large firm informed the small firm owner she was to open a personal bank account in the president's name in Mexico and then deposit part of the difference in the account.

Should the small firm owner have accepted the terms given that it would have increased her firm's profits significantly? How about the president of the large company? Why would he be willing to act unethically for what would have meant $40,000 or $50,000 to him?

What happened? The entrepreneur walked away from the deal. She explained, "I could not have lived with myself." As a result, the contract was given to another company.

Objective **5**

Describe the basic process for valuing assets.

VALUATION: THE BASIC PROCESS

The valuation process can be described as follows: It is assigning value to an asset by calculating the present value of its expected future cash flows using the investor's required rate of return as the discount rate. The investor's required rate of return, k, is determined by the level of the risk-free rate of interest and risk premium that the investor feels is necessary compensation. Therefore, a basic asset valuation model can be defined mathematically as follows:

$$V = \frac{C_1}{(1 + k)^1} + \frac{C_2}{(1 + k)^2} + \ldots + \frac{C_n}{(1 + k)^n} \tag{7-1}$$

where V = the intrinsic value, or present value, of an asset producing expected future cash flows, C_t, in years 1 through n
$\quad\quad C_t$ = cash flow to be received at time t
$\quad\quad k$ = the investor's required rate of return

Using equation (7-1), there are three basic steps in the valuation process:

Step 1. Estimate the C_t in equation (7-1), which is the amount and timing of the future cash flows the security is expected to provide.
Step 2. Determine k, the investor's required rate of return.
Step 3. Calculate the intrinsic value, V, as the present value of expected future cash flows discounted at the investor's required rate of return.

Equation (7-1), which measures the present value of future cash flows, is the basis of the valuation process. It is the most important equation in this chapter because all the remaining equations in this chapter and in Chapter 8 are merely reformulations of this one equation. If we understand equation (7-1), all the valuation work we do, and a host of other topics as well, will be much clearer in our minds.

With the foregoing principles of valuation as our foundation, let's now look at how bonds are valued.

Can You Do It?

COMPUTING AN ASSET'S VALUE

You purchased an asset that is expected to provide $5,000 cash flow per year for 4 years. If you have a 12 percent required rate of return, what is the value of the asset for you?

(The solution can be found on page 214.)

FIGURE 7-2 Data Requirements for Bond Valuation

(A) Cash flow information	Periodic interest payments. For example, $65 per year. Principal amount or par value. For example, $1,000.
(B) Term to maturity	For example, 12 years.
(C) Investor's required rate of return	For example, 8%.

VALUING BONDS

The value of a bond is the present value of both the future interest to be received and the par or maturity value of the bond. It's that simple.

The process for valuing a bond, as depicted in Figure 7-2, requires knowing three essential elements: (1) the amount and timing of the cash flows to be received by the investor, (2) the time to maturity of the bond, and (3) the investor's required rate of return. The amount of cash flows is dictated by the periodic interest to be received and by the par value to be paid at maturity. Given these elements, we can compute the value of the bond, or the present value.

Objective **6**

Estimate the value of a bond.

➤ EXAMPLE

Consider a bond issued by Toyota with a maturity date of 2010 and a stated annual coupon rate of 4.35 percent.[1] In December 2005, with 5 years left to maturity, investors owning the bonds were requiring a 3.6 percent rate of return. We can calculate the value of the bonds to these investors using the following three-step valuation procedure:

Step 1. Estimate the amount and timing of the expected future cash flows. Two types of cash flows are received by the bondholder:
   a. Annual interest payments equal to the coupon rate of interest times the face value of the bond. In this example, the bond's coupon interest rate is 4.35 percent; thus, the annual interest payment is $43.5 = .0435 × $1,000. Assuming that 2005 interest payments have already been made, these cash flows will be received by the bondholder in each of the 5 years before the bond matures (2006 through 2010 = 5 years).
   b. The face value of $1,000 to be received in 2010.

---

[1] Toyota pays interest to its bondholders on a semiannual basis on June 15 and December 15. However, for the moment, assume the interest is to be received annually. The effect of semiannual payments is examined shortly.

How Did You Do?

COMPUTING AN ASSET'S VALUE

The value of an asset generating $5,000 per year for 4 years, given a 12 percent required rate of return, would be $15,186.75. Using a TI BA II Plus calculator, we find the answer as follows:

CALCULATOR SOLUTION

Data Input	Function Key
12	I/Y
4	N
5,000	PMT
0	FV

Function Key	Answer
CPT PV	−15,186.75

To summarize, the cash flows received by the bondholder are as follows:

YEARS	1	2	3	4	5
	$43.50	$43.50	$43.50	$43.50	$ 43.50
					$1,000.00
					$1,043.50

Step 2. Determine the investor's required rate of return by evaluating the riskiness of the bond's future cash flows. A 3.6 percent required rate of return for the bondholders is given. However, we should recall from Chapter 6 that an investor's required rate of return is equal to a rate earned on a risk-free security plus a risk premium for assuming risk.

Step 3. Calculate the intrinsic value of the bond as the present value of the expected future interest and principal payments discounted at the investor's required rate of return.

In general, the present value of a bond is found as follows:

$$\text{Bond value} = V_b = \frac{\$ \text{ interest in year 1}}{(1 + \text{required rate of return})^1} \tag{7-2a}$$

$$+ \frac{\$ \text{ interest in year 2}}{(1 + \text{required rate of return})^2}$$

$$+ \frac{\$ \text{ interest in year 3}}{(1 + \text{required rate of return})^3}$$

$$+ \dots$$

$$+ \frac{\$ \text{ interest in year } n}{(1 + \text{required rate of return})^n}$$

$$+ \frac{\$ \text{ maturity value of bond}}{(1 + \text{required rate of return})^n}$$

Using I_t to represent the interest payment in year t, M to represent the bond's maturity (or par) value, and k_b to equal the bondholder's required rate of return, we can express the value of a bond maturing in year n as follows:

$$V_b = \frac{\$I_1}{(1 + k_b)^1} + \frac{\$I_2}{(1 + k_b)^2} + \frac{\$I_3}{(1 + k_b)^3} + \dots + \frac{\$I_n}{(1 + k_b)^n} + \frac{\$M}{(1 + k_b)^n} \tag{7-2b}$$

Notice that equation (7-2b) is a restatement of equation (7-1), where now the cash flows are represented by the interest received each period and the par value of the bond when it matures. In either equation, the value of an asset is the present value of its future cash flows. The equation for finding the value of the Toyota bonds would be as follows:

$$V_b = \frac{\$43.50}{(1 + 0.036)^1} + \frac{\$43.50}{(1 + 0.036)^2} + \frac{\$43.50}{(1 + 0.036)^3} + \frac{\$43.50}{(1 + 0.036)^4} + \frac{\$43.50}{(1 + 0.036)^5} + \frac{\$1,000}{(1 + 0.036)^5}$$

Finding the value of the Toyota bonds can be represented graphically as follows:

YEAR	0	1	2	3	4	5
Dollars received at end of year		$43.50	$43.50	$43.50	$43.50	$43.50 + $1,000.00 $1,043.50
Present value	$1033.77					

Using a TI BA II Plus financial calculator, we find the value of the bond to be $1,033.77, as calculated in the margin.[2] Thus, if investors consider 3.6 percent to be an appropriate required rate of return in view of the risk level associated with Toyota bonds, paying a price of $1,033.77 would satisfy their return requirement.

We can also solve for the value of Toyota's bonds using a spreadsheet. The solution using Excel appears as follows:

	A	B	C	D
1	**Required rate of return**	**Rate**	3.6%	
2	**Periods left to maturity**	**Nper**	5	
3	**Annual interest payment**	**Pmt**	43.50	
4	**Future value**	**FV**	1,000	
5	**Present value**	**PV**	($1,033.77)	
6				
7	Equation:			
8	=PV (Rate, Nper, Pmt, FV) = PV(C1,C2,C3,C4)			
9				
10				

CALCULATOR SOLUTION

Data Input	Function Key
5	N
3.6	I/Y
43.50	PMT
1000	FV

Function Key	Answer
CPT PV	−1,033.77

Did You Get It?

1. What two factors determine an investor's required rate of return?
2. How does the required rate of return affect a bond's value?

In the preceding Toyota illustration, the interest payments were assumed to be paid annually. However, companies typically pay interest to bondholders semiannually. For example, Toyota actually pays a total of $43.50 per year, but disburses the interest semiannually ($21.75 each June 15 and December 15).

Several steps are involved in adapting equation (7-2b) for semiannual interest payments.[3] First, thinking in terms of *periods* instead of years, a bond with a life of n years paying interest semiannually has a life of $2n$ periods. In other words, a 5-year bond ($n = 5$) that remits its interest on a semiannual basis actually makes 10 payments. Although the number of periods has doubled, the *dollar* amount of interest being sent to the investors for each period and the bondholders' required rate of return are half of the equivalent annual

[2] As noted in Chapter 5, we are using the TI BA II Plus. You may want to return to the Chapter 5 section "Moving Money Through Time with the Aid of a Financial Calculator" or Appendix A, to see a more complete explanation of using the TI BA II Plus. For an explanation of other calculators, see the study guide that accompanies this text.
[3] The logic for calculating the value of a bond that pays interest semiannually is similar to the material presented in Chapter 5, where compound interest with nonannual periods was discussed.

Can You Do It?

COMPUTING A BOND'S VALUE

La Fiesta Restaurants issued bonds that have a 6 percent coupon interest rate. Interest is paid annually. The bonds mature in 12 years. If your required rate of return is 8 percent, what is the value of a bond to you?

(The solution can be found on page 217.)

figures. I_t becomes $I_t/2$ and k_b is changed to $k_b/2$; thus, for semiannual compounding, equation (7-2b) becomes

$$V_b = \frac{\$I_1/2}{\left(1 + \dfrac{k_b}{2}\right)^1} + \frac{\$I_2/2}{\left(1 + \dfrac{k_b}{2}\right)^2} + \frac{\$I_3/2}{\left(1 + \dfrac{k_b}{2}\right)^3} + \dots + \frac{\$I_n/2}{\left(1 + \dfrac{k_b}{2}\right)^{2n}} + \frac{\$M}{\left(1 + \dfrac{k_b}{2}\right)^{2n}} \quad (7\text{-}3)$$

CALCULATOR SOLUTION

Data Input	Function Key
$2n \rightarrow 2 \times 5 \rightarrow 10$	N
$3.6 \div 2 \rightarrow 1.8$	I/Y
$\$43.50 \div 2 \rightarrow 21.75$	PMT
1000	FV

Function Key	Answer
CPT PV	$-1,034.04$

We can now compute the value of the Toyota bonds, recognizing that interest is being paid semiannually. We simply change the number of periods from 5 years to 10 semiannual periods and the required rate of return from 3.6 percent annually to 1.8 percent per semiannual period and divide interest payment by 2 to get $21.75. The value of the bond would now be $1,034.04.

This solution can be found using a calculator as shown in the margin or a spreadsheet that would look as follows:

	A	B	C	D	E
1	Required rate of return	Rate	1.8%		
2	Years left to maturity	Nper	10		
3	Annual interest payment	Pmt	21.75		
4	Future value	FV	1,000		
5	Present value	PV	($1,034.04)		
6					
7		Equation:			
8		=PV (Rate, Nper, Pmt, FV) = PV(C1,C2,C3,C4)			
9					
10					
11					

Did You Get It?

1. How do semiannual interest payments affect the asset valuation equation?

Now that we know how to value a bond, we will next examine a bondholder's rate of return from investing in a bond, or what is called bond yields.

Objective **7**

Compute a bond's expected rate of return.

BOND YIELDS

There are two calculations used to measure the rate of return a bondholder receives from owning a bond: the yield to maturity and the current yield.

Yield to Maturity

Theoretically, each bondholder could have a different required rate of return for a particular bond. However, the financial manager is interested only in the expected rate of return that is implied by the market prices of the firm's bonds, or what we call the yield to maturity.

How Did You Do?

COMPUTING A BOND'S VALUE

A bond with a 6 percent coupon rate pays $60 in interest per year ($60 = 0.06 coupon rate × $1,000 par value). Thus, you would receive $60 per year for 12 years plus the $1,000 in par value in year 12. Assuming an 8 percent required rate of return, the value of the bond would be $849.28.

CALCULATOR SOLUTION

Data Input	Function Key
8	I/Y
12	N
60	PMT
1,000	FV

Function Key	Answer
CPT PV	−849.28

Finance at Work

AT&T BOND PRICES FALL, THANKS TO WORLDCOM

When WorldCom announced to the public the accounting misfeasance that had occurred within the company, the firm's bond prices fell sharply—as would be expected. But the news also sent shock waves through the industry. AT&T's bonds, for example, suffered one of their worst 1-day losses in years. Investors were worried that the telephone giant would run into the same troubles as WorldCom.

AT&T's 10-year bonds fell to about 82 percent of their par value, down from about 90 percent the day before—a significant fall for an investment-grade-rated bond. A week earlier, the bonds had traded at around 96 percent of par value.

The spread, or difference in yield, between AT&T's bonds and U.S. Treasuries surged to about 4.3 percentage points, up from almost 3.8 percentage points earlier, suggesting investors were demanding more compensation for the risk of buying the bonds.

AT&T was being treated as if it had a "junk" bond rating, even though it belonged firmly in the investment-grade category. In the words of Philip Olesen, an analyst at UBS Warburg, "There was nothing but selling . . . ; it was brutal."

Source: Gregory Zuckerman, Richard A. Bravo, and Christine Richard, "AT&T's Bonds Tumble in Sell-Off as WorldCom Woes Spark Fears," the *Wall Street Journal*, May 2, 2002, p. A2.

To measure the bondholder's **expected rate of return**, $\bar{k}_b$, we would find the *discount rate that equates the present value of the future cash flows (interest and maturity value) with the current market price of the bond*.[4] It is also the *rate of return the investor will earn if the bond is held to maturity*, thus the name **yield to maturity**. So, when referring to bonds, the terms *expected rate of return* and *yield to maturity* are often used interchangeably.

To illustrate this concept, consider the Brister Corporation's bonds, which are selling for $1,100. The bonds carry a coupon interest rate of 9 percent and mature in 10 years. (Remember, the coupon rate determines the interest payment—coupon rate × par value.)

To determine the expected rate of return $(\bar{k}_b)$ implicit in the current market price, we need to find the rate that discounts the anticipated cash flows back to a present value of $1,100, the current market price (P_0) for the bond.

expected rate of return (1) the discount rate that equates the present value of the future cash flows (interest and maturity value) of a bond with its current market price. It is the rate of return an investor will earn if the bond is held to maturity. (2) The rate of return the investor expects to receive on an investment by paying the existing market price of the security.

yield to maturity (1) see Term structure of interest rates. (2) The rate of return a bondholder will receive if the bond is held to maturity. (It is equivalent to the expected rate of return.)

[4] When we speak of computing an expected rate of return, we are not describing the situation very accurately. Expected rates of return are ex ante (before the fact) and are based on "expected and unobservable future cash flows" and, therefore, can only be "estimated."

The expected return for the Brister Corporation bondholders is 7.54 percent, which can be found as presented in the margin by using the TI BA II Plus calculator, or by using a computer spreadsheet, as follows:

	A	B	C	D	E
1	Years left to maturity	Nper	10		
2	Annual interest payment	Pmt	90		
3	Present value	PV	−1,100		
4	Future value	FV	1,000		
5	Required rate of return	Rate	7.54%		
6					
7					
8		Equation:			
9		= RATE(Nper, Pmt, PV,FV) = RATE(C1,C2,C3,C4)			
10					

Current Yield

current yield the ratio of a bond's annual interest payment to its market price.

The **current yield** on a bond refers to the *ratio of the annual interest payment to the bond's current market price*. If, for example, we have a bond with an 8 percent coupon interest rate, a par value of $1,000, and a market price of $700, it would have a current yield of 11.4 percent:

$$\text{Current yield} = \frac{\text{annual interest payment}}{\text{current market price of the bond}} \tag{7-4}$$

In our example

$$\text{Current yield} = \frac{0.08 \times \$1,000}{\$700} = \frac{\$80}{\$700} = 0.114 = 11.4\%$$

We should understand that the current yield, although frequently quoted in the popular press, is an incomplete picture of the expected rate of return from holding a bond. The current yield indicates the cash income that results from holding a bond in a given year, but it fails to recognize the capital gain or loss that will occur if the bond is held to maturity. As such, it is not an accurate measure of the bondholder's expected rate of return.

BOND VALUATION: THREE IMPORTANT RELATIONSHIPS

Objective **8**

Explain three important relationships that exist in bond valuation.

We have now learned to find the value of a bond (V_b), given (1) the amount of interest payments (I_t), (2) the maturity value (M), (3) the length of time to maturity (n periods), and (4) the investor's required rate of return, k_b. We also know how to compute the expected rate of return ($\bar{k}_b$), which also happens to be the current interest rate on the bond, given (1) the current market value (P_0), (2) the amount of interest payments (I_t), (3) the maturity value (M), and (4) the length of time to maturity (n periods). We now have the basics. But let's go further in our understanding of bond valuation by studying several important relationships:

1. The value of a bond is inversely related to changes in the investor's present required rate of return. In other words, as interest rates increase (decrease), the value of the bond decreases (increases).

    To illustrate, assume that an investor's required rate of return for a given bond is 12 percent. The bond has a par value of $1,000 and annual interest payments of $120, indicating a 12 percent coupon interest rate ($120 ÷ $1,000 = 12%). Assuming a 5-year maturity date, the bond would be worth $1,000, computed as follows:

$$V_b = \frac{\$I_1}{(1 + k_b)^1} + \cdots + \frac{\$I_n}{(1 + k_b)^n} + \frac{\$M}{(1 + k_b)^n}$$

Can You Do It?

COMPUTING THE YIELD TO MATURITY AND CURRENT YIELD

The Argon Corporation bonds are selling for $925. They have a 5 percent coupon interest rate paid annually and mature in 8 years. What is the yield to maturity for the bonds if an investor buys them at the $925 market price? What is the current yield?

(The solution can be found on page 220.)

In our example

$$V_b = \frac{\$120}{(1 + 0.12)^1} + \frac{\$120}{(1 + 0.12)^2} + \frac{\$120}{(1 + 0.12)^3} + \frac{\$120}{(1 + 0.12)^4} + \frac{\$120}{(1 + 0.12)^5} + \frac{\$1,000}{(1 + 0.12)^5}$$

Using a calculator, we find the value of the bond to be $1,000.

CALCULATOR SOLUTION

Data Input	Function Key
12	I/Y
5	N
120	PMT
1,000	FV

Function Key	Answer
CPT PV	−1,000

If, however, the investors' required rate of return increases from 12 percent to 15 percent, the value of the bond would decrease to $899.44, computed as follows:

CALCULATOR SOLUTION

Data Input	Function Key
15	I/Y
5	N
120	PMT
1,000	FV

Function Key	Answer
CPT PV	−899.44

On the other hand, if the investor's required rate of return decreases to 9 percent, the bond would increase in value to $1,116.69.

CALCULATOR SOLUTION

Data Input	Function Key
9	I/Y
5	N
120	PMT
1,000	FV

Function Key	Answer
CPT PV	−1,116.69

How Did You Do?

COMPUTING THE YIELD TO MATURITY AND CURRENT YIELD

The Argon bonds pay $50 in interest per year ($50 = 0.05 coupon rate × $1,000 par value) for the duration of the bond, or for 8 years. The investor will then receive $1,000 at the bond's maturity. Given a market price of $925, the yield to maturity would be 6.2 percent.

CALCULATOR SOLUTION

Data Input	Function Key
8	N
925	PV
50	+/− PMT
1,000	+/− FV

Function Key	Answer
CPT I/Y	6.22

$$\text{Current yield} = \frac{\text{annual interest payment}}{\text{current market price of the bond}}$$

$$= \frac{\$50}{\$925} = 0.0541 = 5.41\%$$

---

interest rate risk (1) the variability in a bond's value (risk) caused by changing interest rates. (2) The uncertainty that envelops the expected returns from a security caused by changes in interest rates. Price changes induced by interest rate changes are greater for long-term than for short-term financial instruments.

This inverse relationship between the investor's required rate of return and the value of a bond is presented in Figure 7-3. Clearly, as investors demand a higher rate of return, the value of the bond decreases: The higher rate of return can be achieved only by paying less for the bond. Conversely, a lower required rate of return yields a higher market value for the bond.

Changes in bond prices represent an element of uncertainty for the bond investor. If the current interest rate (required rate of return) changes, the price of the bond also fluctuates. An increase in interest rates causes the bondholder to incur a loss in market value. Because future interest rates and the resulting bond value cannot be predicted with certainty, a bond investor is exposed to the *risk of changing values as interest rates vary*. This risk has come to be known as **interest rate risk**.

FIGURE 7-3 Value and Required Rates for a 5-Year Bond at a 12 Percent Coupon Rate

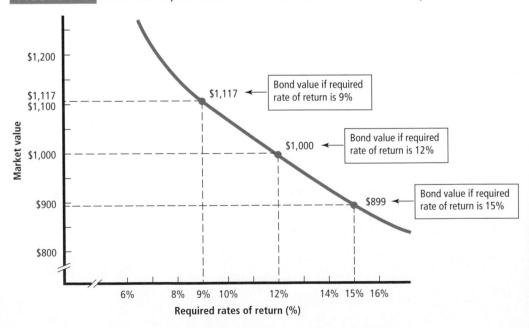

2. The market value of a bond will be less than the par value if the required rate of return of investors is above the coupon interest rate; but it will be valued above par value if the required rate of return of investors is below the coupon interest rate.

Using the previous example, we observed that

- The bond has a *market value* of $1,000, equal to the par, or maturity, value, when the required rate of return demanded by investors equals the 12 percent coupon interest rate. In other words, if

required rate = coupon rate, then *market value = par value*
    12%   =   12%,   then $1,000   = $1,000

- When the required rate is 15 percent, which exceeds the 12 percent coupon rate, the market value of the bond falls below par value to $899.44; that is, if

required rate > coupon rate, then *market value < par value*
    15%   >   12%,   then $899.44   < $1,000

In this case the *bond sells at a discount below par value*; thus, it is called a **discount bond**.

- When the required rate is 9 percent, or less than the 12 percent coupon rate, the market value, $1,116.69, exceeds the bond's par value. In this instance, if

required rate < coupon rate, then *market value > par value*
    9%   <   12%,   then $1,116.69   > $1,000

The *bond is now selling at a premium above par value*; thus, it is a **premium bond**.

> **discount bond** a bond that sells at a discount, or below par value.

> **premium bond** a bond that is selling above its par value.

3. Long-term bonds have greater interest rate risk than do short-term bonds.

As already noted, a change in current interest rates (the required rate of return) causes an inverse change in the market value of a bond. However, the impact on value is greater for long-term bonds than it is for short-term bonds.

In Figure 7-3 we observed the effect of interest rate changes on a 5-year bond paying a 12 percent coupon interest rate. What if the bond did not mature until 10 years from today instead of 5 years? Would the changes in market value be the same? Absolutely not. The changes in value would be more significant for the 10-year bond. For example, what if the current interest rates increase from 9 percent to 12 percent and then to 15 percent? In this case, a 10-year bond's value would drop more sharply than a 5-year bond's value would. The values for both the 5-year and the 10-year bonds are shown here.

	MARKET VALUE FOR A 12% COUPON-RATE BOND MATURING IN	
REQUIRED RATE	5 YEARS	10 YEARS
9%	$1,116.69	$1,192.53
12%	1,000.00	1,000.00
15%	899.44	849.44

The reason long-term bond prices fluctuate more than short-term bond prices in response to interest rate changes is simple. Assume an investor bought a 10-year bond yielding a 12 percent interest rate. If the current interest rate for bonds of similar risk increased to 15 percent, the investor would be locked into the lower rate for 10 years. If, on the other hand, a shorter term bond had been purchased—say, one maturing in 2 years—the investor would have to accept the lower return for only 2 years and not the full 10 years. At the end of year 2, the investor would receive the maturity value of $1,000 and could buy a bond offering the higher 15 percent rate for the remaining 8 years. Thus, interest rate risk is determined, at least in part, by the length of time an investor is required to commit to an investment.

Using these values and the required rates, we can graph the changes in values for the two bonds relative to different interest rates. These comparisons are provided in

FIGURE 7-4   The Market Values of a 5-Year and a 10-Year Bond at Different Required Rates of Return

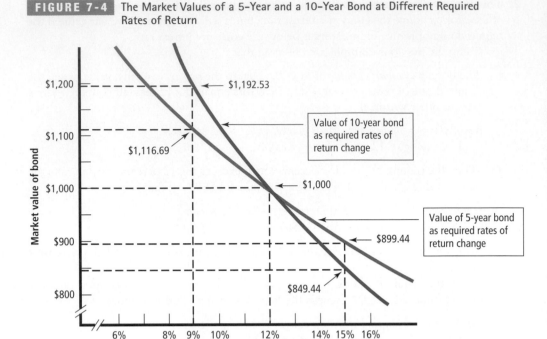

Figure 7-4. The figure clearly illustrates that the price of a long-term bond (say, 10 years) is more responsive or sensitive to interest rate changes than the price of a short-term bond (say, 5 years). However, the holder of a long-term bond can take some comfort from the fact that long-term interest rates are usually not as volatile as short-term rates. If the short-term rate changed 1 percentage point, for example, it would not be unusual for the long-term rate to change only .3 percentage points.

Did You Get It?

1. Why does a bond sell at a discount when the coupon rate is lower than the required rate of return and vice versa?
2. As interest rates increase, why does the price of a long-term bond decrease more than a short-term bond?

Summary

Objective **1**

Distinguish between different kinds of bonds.

Understanding how to compute the value of a security underlies much of what we do in finance. Only if we know what matters to our investors can we maximize the firm's value.

There is a variety of types of bonds, including:

Debentures	Zero coupon bonds
Subordinated debentures	Very low coupon bonds
Mortgage bonds	Junk bonds
Eurobonds	Convertible bonds

Objective **2**

Explain the more popular features of bonds.

Some of the more popular terms and characteristics used to describe bonds include the following:

Call provision	Maturity
Claims on assets and income	Indenture
Par value	Bond ratings
Coupon interest rate	

Value is defined differently depending on the context. But for us, value is the present value of future cash flows expected to be received from an investment, discounted at the investor's required rate of return.

Three basic factors determine an asset's value: (1) the amount and timing of future cash flows, (2) the riskiness of the cash flows, and (3) the investor's attitude about the risk.

The valuation process can be described as follows: It is assigning value to an asset by calculating the present value of its expected future cash flows using the investor's required rate of return as the discount rate. The investor's required rate of return, k, equals the risk-free rate of interest plus a risk premium to compensate the investor for assuming risk.

The value of a bond is the present value of both future interest to be received and the par or maturity value of the bond.

To measure the bondholder's expected rate of return, we find the discount rate that equates the present value of the future cash flows (interest and maturity value) with the current market price of the bond. The expected rate of return for a bond is also the rate of return the investor will earn if the bond is held to maturity, or the yield to maturity. We may also compute the current yield as the annual interest payment divided by the bond's current market price, but this is not an accurate measure of a bondholder's expected rate of return.

Certain key relationships exist in bond valuation, these being:

1. A decrease in interest rates (the required rates of return) will cause the value of a bond to increase; by contrast, an interest rate increase will cause a decrease in value. The change in value caused by changing interest rates is called interest rate risk.
2. If the required rate of return (current interest rate):
   a. Equals the coupon interest rate, the bond will sell at par, or maturity value.
   b. Exceeds the bond's coupon rate, the bond will sell below par value, or at a discount.
   c. Is less than the bond's coupon rate, the bond will sell above par value, or at a premium.
3. A bondholder owning a long-term bond is exposed to greater interest rate risk than one owning a short-term bond.

Objective **3**

Define the term *value* as used for several different purposes.

Objective **4**

Explain the factors that determine value.

Objective **5**

Describe the basic process for valuing assets.

Objective **6**

Estimate the value of a bond.

Objective **7**

Compute a bond's expected rate of return.

Objective **8**

Explain three important relationships that exist in bond valuation.

Key Terms

Bond 204	Interest rate risk 220
Book value 210	Intrinsic, or economic, value (fair value) 210
Callable bond (redeemable bond) 207	Junk bond 205
Call protection period 208	Liquidation value 210
Convertible bond 206	Market value 210
Coupon interest rate 207	Maturity 207
Current yield 218	Mortgage bond 204
Debenture 204	Par value 207
Discount bond 221	Premium bond 221
Eurobond 205	Subordinated debenture 204
Expected rate of return 217	Yield to maturity 217
Fair value 210	Zero and very low coupon bond 205
High-yield bond 205	
Indenture 208	

Review Questions

7-1. Distinguish between debentures and mortgage bonds.

7-2. Define (a) Eurobonds, (b) zero coupon bonds, and (c) junk bonds.

7-3. Describe the bondholder's claim on the firm's assets and income.

7-4. a. How does a bond's par value differ from its market value?

    b. Explain the difference between a bond's coupon interest rate, current yield, and required rate of return.

7-5. What factors determine a bond's rating? Why is the rating important to the firm's manager?

7-6. What are the basic differences between book value, liquidation value, market value, and intrinsic value?

7-7. What is a general definition of the intrinsic value of an asset?

7-8. Explain the three factors that determine the intrinsic, or economic, value of an asset.

7-9. Explain the relationship between the required rate of return and the value of a security.

7-10. Define the expected rate of return to bondholders.

Self-Test Problems

(The solution to the following problems are found at the end of the chapter.)

ST-1. (*Bond valuation*) Trico bonds have an annual coupon rate of 8 percent and a par value of $1,000 and will mature in 20 years. If you require a return of 7 percent, what price would you be willing to pay for the bond? What happens if you pay *more* for the bond? What happens if you pay *less* for the bond?

ST-2. (*Bond valuation*) Sunn Co.'s bonds, maturing in 7 years, pay 8 percent interest on a $1,000 face value. However, interest is paid semiannually. If your required rate of return is 10 percent, what is the value of the bond? How would your answer change if the interest were paid annually?

ST-3. (*Bondholders' expected rate of return*) Sharp Co. bonds are selling in the market for $1,045. These 15-year bonds pay 7 percent interest annually on a $1,000 par value. If they are purchased at the market price, what is the expected rate of return?

Study Problems

7-1. You own a 20-year, $1,000 par value bond paying 7 percent interest annually. The market price of the bond is $875, and your required rate of return is 10 percent.
    a. Compute the bond's expected rate of return.
    b. Determine the value of the bond to you, given your required rate of return.
    c. Should you sell the bond or continue to own it?

7-2. (*Bond valuation*) Calculate the value of a bond that will mature in 14 years and has a $1,000 face value. The annual coupon interest rate is 7 percent, and the investor's required rate of return is 10 percent.

7-3. At the beginning of the year, you bought a $1,000 par value corporate bond with a 6 percent annual coupon rate and a 10-year maturity date. When you bought the bond, it had an expected yield to maturity of 8 percent. Today the bond sells for $1,060.
    a. What did you pay for the bond?
    b. If you sold the bond at the end of the year, what would be your one-period return on the investment?

7-4. (*Bond valuation*) Shelly Inc. bonds have a 10 percent coupon rate. The interest is paid semiannually, and the bonds mature in 8 years. Their par value is $1,000. If your required rate of return is 8 percent, what is the value of the bond? What is the value if the interest is paid annually?

7-5. Crawford Inc. has two bond issues outstanding, both paying the same annual interest of $85, called Series A and Series B. Series A has a maturity of 12 years, whereas Series B has a maturity of 1 year.
    a. What would be the value of each of these bonds when the going interest rate is (1) 5 percent, (2) 8 percent, and (3) 12 percent? Assume that there is only one more interest payment to be made on the Series B bonds.
    b. Why does the longer-term (12-year) bond fluctuate more when interest rates change than does the shorter-term (1-year) bond?

7-6. (*Bondholders' expected rate of return*) The market price is $900 for a 10-year bond ($1,000 par value) that pays 8 percent interest (4 percent semiannually). What is the bond's expected rate of return?

7-7. You own a bond that has a par value of $1,000 and matures in 5 years. It pays a 9 percent annual coupon rate. The bond currently sells for $1,200. What is the bond's expected rate of return?

7-8. (*Bond valuation*) ExxonMobil 20-year bonds pay 9 percent interest annually on a $1,000 par value. If bonds sell at $945, what is the bonds' expected rate of return?

7-9. (*Bondholders' expected rate of return*) Zenith Co.'s bonds mature in 12 years and pay 7 percent interest annually. If you purchase the bonds for $1,150, what is your expected rate of return?

7-10. (*Bond valuation*) National Steel 15-year, $1,000 par value bonds pay 8 percent interest annually. The market price of the bonds is $1,085, and your required rate of return is 10 percent.

   a. Compute the bond's expected rate of return.

   b. Determine the value of the bond to you, given your required rate of return.

   c. Should you purchase the bond?

7-11. (*Bond valuation*) You own a bond that pays $100 in annual interest, with a $1,000 par value. It matures in 15 years. Your required rate of return is 12 percent.

   a. Calculate the value of the bond.

   b. How does the value change if your required rate of return (1) increases to 15 percent or (2) decreases to 8 percent?

   c. Explain the implications of your answers in part b as they relate to interest rate risk, premium bonds, and discount bonds.

   d. Assume that the bond matures in 5 years instead of 15 years. Recompute your answers in part b.

   e. Explain the implications of your answers in part d as they relate to interest rate risk, premium bonds, and discount bonds.

7-12. (*Bond valuation*) New Generation Public Utilities issued a bond with a $1,000 par value that pays $80 in annual interest. It matures in 20 years. Your required rate of return is 7 percent.

   a. Calculate the value of the bond.

   b. How does the value change if your required rate of return (1) increases to 10 percent or (2) decreases to 6 percent?

   c. Explain the implications of your answers in part b as they relate to interest rate risk, premium bonds, and discount bonds.

   d. Assume that the bond matures in 10 years instead of 20 years. Recompute your answers in part b.

   e. Explain the implications of your answers in part d as they relate to interest rate risk, premium bonds, and discount bonds.

7-13. (*Bond valuation—zero coupon*) The Logos Corporation is planning on issuing bonds that pay no interest but can be converted into $1,000 at maturity, 7 years from their purchase. To price these bonds competitively with other bonds of equal risk, it is determined that they should yield 9 percent, compounded annually. At what price should the Logos Corporation sell these bonds?

7-14. (*Bond valuation*) You are examining three bonds with a par value of $1,000 (you receive $1,000 at maturity) and are concerned with what would happen to their market value if interest rates (or the market discount rate) changed. The three bonds are

   Bond A—a bond with 3 years left to maturity that has a 10 percent annual coupon interest rate, but the interest is paid semiannually.

   Bond B—a bond with 7 years left to maturity that has a 10 percent annual coupon interest rate, but the interest is paid semiannually.

   Bond C—a bond with 20 years left to maturity that has a 10 percent annual coupon interest rate, but the interest is paid semiannually.

What would be the value of these bonds if the market discount rate were

   a. 10 percent per year compounded semiannually?

   b. 4 percent per year compounded semiannually?

   c. 16 percent per year compounded semiannually?

   d. What observations can you make about these results?

Web Works

7-WW1. Go to **http://bond.yahoo.com**. Under "Find Bonds by Name," type in the company name "Boeing." How many bonds has "Boeing" issued? How are they different? Click on one of the issues. What do you learn about the issue? Choose another one and see how the two issues are different.

7-WW2. At the Web site **http://bond.yahoo.com** there are links under "Tools." Choose "Bond Screener." Then identify the type of bond. Make up some examples to see what you learn from using the screen.

7-WW3. Find the Web site **www.investopedia.com/university/bonds**. Scroll down the table of contents and choose the option on how to read a bond table. Describe what you find.

7-WW4. Go to the following Web site: **http://nalu.hpu.edu/mlane/BusinessFinanceOnline/BV/BondValuation.html**. Then choose the link, "bond quiz," on the left side of the page. Take the quiz and see how you do.

Mini Case

Here are data on $1,000 par value bonds issued by Bell South, Dole, and Xerox at the end of 2006. Assume you are thinking about buying these bonds as of January 2007. Answer the following questions:

   a. Calculate the values of the bonds if your required rates of return are as follows: Bell South, 7 percent; Dole, 7.5 percent; and Xerox, 10 percent; where

	BELL SOUTH	DOLE	XEROX
Coupon interest rate	6.375%	7.875%	7.2%
Years to maturity	3	8	11

   b. At the end of 2006, the bonds were selling for the following amounts:

Bell South	$ 983.75
Dole	$1,030.00
Xerox	$1,047.50

   What were the expected rates of return for each bond?

   c. How would the value of the bonds change if (1) your required rate of return (k_b) increased 2 percentage points or (2) decreased 2 percentage points?

   d. Explain the implications of your answers in part b in terms of interest rate risk, premium bonds, and discount bonds.

   e. Should you buy the bonds? Explain.

Self-Test Solutions

SS-1.

$$\text{Value } (V_b) = \frac{\$80}{(1.07)^1} + \frac{\$80}{(1.07)^2} + \; \cdots \; + \frac{\$80}{(1.07)^{20}} + \frac{\$1000}{(1.07)^{20}}$$

Using a financial calculator, we find the value of the bond to be $1,105.94:

CALCULATOR SOLUTION

Data Input	Function Key
7	I/Y
20	N
80	PMT
1,000	FV

Function Key	Answer
CPT PV	−1,105.94

If you pay more for the bond, your required rate of return will not be satisfied. In other words, by paying an amount for the bond that exceeds $1,105.94, the expected rate of return for the bond is less than the required rate of return. If you have the opportunity to pay less for the bond, the expected rate of return exceeds the 7 percent required rate of return.

SS-2. If interest is paid semiannually:

$$\text{Value } (V_b) = \frac{\$40}{(1.05)^1} + \; \cdots \; + \frac{\$40}{(1.05)^{14}} + \frac{\$1,000}{(1.05)^{14}}$$

The value of the bond would be $901.01:

CALCULATOR SOLUTION	
Data Input	Function Key
5	I/Y
14	N
40	PMT
1,000	FV
Function Key	Answer
CPT PV	−901.01

If interest is paid annually:

$$\text{Value } (V_b) = \frac{\$80}{(1.10)^1} + \ldots + \frac{\$80}{(1.10)^7} + \frac{\$1,000}{(1.10)^7}$$

The value of the bond would be $902.63:

CALCULATOR SOLUTION	
Data Input	Function Key
10	I/Y
7	N
80	PMT
1,000	FV
Function Key	Answer
CPT PV	−902.63

SS-3. Finding the bond's yield to maturity, the expected rate of return is based on the following equation:

$$\$1,045 = \frac{\$70}{(1 + \bar{k}_b)^1} + \ldots + \frac{\$70}{(1 + \bar{k}_b)^{15}} + \frac{\$1,000}{(1 + \bar{k}_b)^{15}}$$

Using a financial calculator, we find the yield to maturity to be 6.52 percent:

CALCULATOR SOLUTION	
Data Input	Function Key
15	N
70	+/− PMT
1000	+/− FV
1045	PV
Function Key	Answer
CPT I/Y	6.52

CHAPTER 8

The Valuation and Characteristics of Stock

If success is having your firm's name become a verb in languages around the world, then the founders of Google, Sergey Brin and Larry Page, have, without any question, succeeded. Today students "google" research topics; most of us "google" before shopping for a product; and patients "google" their symptoms before visiting their doctors. Many single people "google" their prospective dates. Google has clearly been a phenomenal success.

But as early as 2002–2004, Google's board of directors was deliberating about how to translate the firm's "success" into money. The answer came in the decision to issue Google stock to the public. They planned to auction off about 20 million shares for between $108 to $135 per share. Some experts were estimating that Google's stock would have a total market value of as much as $25 billion or more.

There were some skeptics, however, who questioned if Google would be the next overhyped stock to make its founders rich, only to later lose value, as so many other Internet stocks had done.

But by late October 2006, Google's stock was selling for almost $500 per share, with a total firm stock value of almost $150 billion. No problem there. How is the stock doing today?

In Chapter 7, we developed a general concept about valuation, and economic value was defined as the present value of the expected future cash flows generated by an asset. We then applied that concept to valuing bonds.

We continue our study of valuation in this chapter, but we now give our attention to valuing stocks, both preferred stock and common stock. As already noted at the outset of our study of finance and on several occasions since, the financial manager's objective should be to maximize the value of the firm's common stock. Thus, we need to understand what determines stock value. Also, only with an understanding of valuation can we compute a firm's cost of capital, a concept essential to making effective capital investment decisions—an issue to be discussed in Chapter 12.

PREFERRED STOCK

preferred stock a hybrid security with characteristics of both common stock and bonds. Preferred stock is similar to common stock in that it has no fixed maturity date, the nonpayment of dividends does not bring on bankruptcy, and dividends are not deductible for tax purposes. Preferred stock is similar to bonds in that dividends are limited in amount.

Preferred stock is often referred to as a *hybrid security* because it has *many characteristics of both common stock and bonds*. Preferred stock is similar to common stock in that (1) it has no fixed maturity date, (2) if the firm fails to pay dividends, it does not bring on bankruptcy, and (3) dividends are not deductible for tax purposes. On the other hand, preferred stock is similar to bonds in that dividends are fixed in amount.

The amount of the preferred stock dividend is generally fixed either as a dollar amount or as a percentage of the par value. For example, Texas Utility Electric (TXU) has preferred stock outstanding that pays an annual dividend of $1.81, whereas AT&T has some 8.25 percent preferred stock outstanding. The AT&T preferred stock has a par value of $25; hence, each share pays 8.25 percent × $25, or $2.06 in dividends annually.

To begin, we first discuss several features associated with almost all preferred stock. Then we take a brief look at methods of retiring preferred stock. We close by learning how to value preferred stock.

Objective **1**

Identify the basic characteristics of preferred stock.

The Characteristics of Preferred Stock

Although each issue of preferred stock is unique, a number of characteristics are common to almost all issues. Some of these more frequent traits include

- Multiple series of preferred stock
- Preferred stock's claim on assets and income
- Cumulative dividends
- Protective provisions
- Convertibility
- Retirement provisions

All these features are presented in the discussion that follows.

Multiple Series

If a company desires, it can issue more than one series of preferred stock, and each series can have different characteristics. In fact, it is quite common for firms that issue preferred stock to issue more than one series. These issues can be differentiated in that some are convertible into common stock and others are not, and they have varying protective provisions in the event of bankruptcy. For instance, the Xerox Corporation has a Series B and Series C preferred stock.

Claim on Assets and Income

Preferred stock has priority over common stock with regard to claims on assets in the case of bankruptcy. The preferred stock claim is honored after that of bonds and before that of common stock. Multiple issues of preferred stock may be given an order of priority. Preferred stock also has a claim on income before common stock. That is, the firm must pay its preferred stock dividends before it pays common stock dividends. Thus, in terms of risk, preferred stock is safer than common stock because it has a prior claim on assets and income. However, it is riskier than long-term debt because its claims on assets and income come after those of bonds.

Cumulative Dividends

Most preferred stocks carry a **cumulative feature** that *requires all past, unpaid preferred stock dividends be paid before any common stock dividends are declared*. The purpose is to provide some degree of protection for the preferred shareholder.

Protective Provisions

In addition to the cumulative feature, protective provisions are common to preferred stock. These **protective provisions** generally *allow for voting rights in the event of nonpayment of dividends, or they restrict the payment of common stock dividends if the preferred stock payments are not met or if the firm is in financial difficulty*. For example, consider the stocks of Tenneco Corporation and Reynolds Metals. The Tenneco preferred stock has a protective provision that provides preferred stockholders with voting rights whenever six quarterly dividends are in arrears. At that point the preferred shareholders are given the power to elect a majority of the board of directors. The Reynolds Metals preferred stock includes a protective provision that precludes the payment of common stock dividends during any period in which the preferred stock payments are in default. Both provisions offer preferred stockholders protection beyond that provided by the cumulative provision and further reduce their risk. Because of these protective provisions, preferred stockholders do not require as high a rate of return. That is, they will accept a lower dividend payment.

Convertibility

Much of the preferred stock that is issued today is **convertible preferred stock;** that is, *at the discretion of the holder, the stock can be converted into a predetermined number of shares of common stock*. In fact, today about one-third of all preferred stock issued has a convertibility feature. The convertibility feature is, of course, desirable to the investor and, thus, reduces the cost of the preferred stock to the issuer.

Retirement Provisions

Although preferred stock does not have a set maturity date associated with it, issuing firms generally provide for some method of retiring the stock, usually in the form of a call provision or a sinking fund. A **call provision** *entitles a company to repurchase its preferred stock from holders at stated prices over a given time period*. In fact, the Securities and Exchange Commission discourages firms from issuing preferred stock without some call provision. For example, on January 9, 2006, Dynex Capital Inc. redeemed (called) its Series D preferred stock.

The call feature on preferred stock usually requires buyers to pay an initial premium of approximately 10 percent above the par value or issuing price of the preferred stock. Then, over time, the call premium generally falls. By setting the initial call price above the initial issue price and allowing it to decline slowly over time, the firm protects the investor from an early call that carries no premium. A call provision also allows the issuing firm to plan the retirement of its preferred stock at predetermined prices.

A **sinking-fund provision** *requires the firm to periodically set aside an amount of money for the retirement of its preferred stock*. This money is then used to purchase the preferred stock in the open market or to call the stock, whichever method is cheaper. The use of a call provision in addition to a sinking fund can effectively create a maturity date for preferred stock. For instance, Xerox Corporation has two preferred stock issues, one that has a 7-year sinking-fund provision and another with a 17-year sinking-fund provision.

Valuing Preferred Stock

As already explained, the owner of preferred stock generally receives a constant dividend from the investment in each period. In addition, most preferred stocks are perpetuities (nonmaturing). In this instance, finding the value (present value) of preferred stock, (V_{ps}), with a level cash-flow stream continuing indefinitely, may best be explained by an example.

cumulative feature a requirement that all past, unpaid preferred stock dividends be paid before any common stock dividends are declared.

protective provisions provisions for preferred stock that protect the investor's interest. The provisions generally allow for voting in the event of nonpayment of dividends, or they restrict the payment of common stock dividends if sinking-fund payments are not met or if the firm is in financial difficulty.

convertible preferred stock preferred shares that can be converted into a predetermined number of shares of common stock, if investors so choose.

call provision a provision that entitles the corporation to repurchase its preferred stock from investors at stated prices over specified periods.

sinking-fund provision a protective provision that requires the firm periodically to set aside an amount of money for the retirement of its preferred stock. This money is then used to purchase the preferred stock in the open market or through the use of the call provision, whichever method is cheaper.

Objective **2**
Value preferred stock.

Finance at Work

READING A STOCK QUOTE IN THE WALL STREET JOURNAL

Following is a section of the *Wall Street Journal* that gives the quotes on July 12, 2006, for some of the stocks traded on the New York Stock Exchange that day.

The stocks listed include familiar companies—such as General Electric (GE), General Mills, and General Motors— that are listed in the *Wall Street Journal* on a daily basis. To help us understand how we read the quotes, consider General Electric.

- The 52-week *high* column shows General Electric stock reached a high of 36.34 ($36.34) during the past year.
- The 52-week *low* column shows that General Electric sold at a low of 32.21 ($32.21) during the past year.
- The *stock* (GenElec) and *div* columns give an abbreviated version of the corporation's name and the amount of divi-

dend that General Electric paid its common stockholders in the last year; $1.00 per share.
- *Yld%* (3.0) is the stock's dividend yield—the amount of the dividend divided by the day's closing price ($1.00 ÷ 33.26).
- *PE* (21) gives the current market price (33.26) divided by the firm's earnings per share.
- The amount of General Electric stock traded on July 12, 2006, is represented in the *Vol 100s* column, or 22,295,500 shares.
- The previous day's closing price is subtracted from the closing price (*close*) of 33.26 for July 12, 2006, for a net change (*Net Chg*) of −0.19.

| 52 WEEKS | | | | | | | |
HI	LO	STOCK (DIV)	YLD%	PE	VOL 100S	CLOSE	NET CHG
36.34	32.21	GenElec 1.00	3.0	21	222,955	33.26	−0.19
52.32	39.60	GenGrthProp 1.64	3.6	cc	9,953	45.71	−0.06
45.26	30.34	GenMaritime 4.52e	12.0	7	2,440	37.66	−0.45
53.15	44.67	GenMills 1.40f	2.7	18	21,101	52.79	0.17
37.70	18.33	GenMotor 1.00	3.4	dd	73,482	29.50	0.12
43.72	31.93	Genesco		13	3,087	31.90	−0.34

➤ EXAMPLE

Consider Xerox's Series C preferred stock issue. In similar fashion to valuing bonds in Chapter 7, we use a three-step valuation procedure.

Step 1. Estimate the amount and timing of the receipt of the future cash flows the preferred stock is expected to provide. Xerox's preferred stock pays an annual dividend of $6.25. The shares do not have a maturity date; that is, they are a perpetuity.

Step 2. Evaluate the riskiness of the preferred stock's future dividends and determine the investor's required rate of return. The investor's required rate of return is assumed to equal 5 percent for the Xerox preferred stock.[1]

Step 3. Calculate the economic, or intrinsic, value of the Xerox share of preferred stock, which is the present value of the expected dividends discounted at the investor's required rate of return. The valuation model for a share of preferred stock, V_{ps}, is, therefore, defined as follows:

$$V_{ps} = \frac{\text{dividend in year 1}}{(1 + \text{required rate of return})^1}$$
$$+ \frac{\text{dividend in year 2}}{(1 + \text{required rate of return})^2}$$
$$+ \cdots + \frac{\text{dividend in infinity}}{(1 + \text{required rate of return})^\infty} \tag{8-1}$$
$$= \frac{D_1}{(1 + k_{ps})^1} + \frac{D_2}{(1 + k_{ps})^2} + \cdots + \frac{D_\infty}{(1 + k_{ps})^\infty}$$

[1] In Chapter 6, we learned about measuring an investor's required rate of return.

Can You Do It?

VALUING PREFERRED STOCK

If a preferred stock pays 4 percent on its par, or stated, value of $100, and your required rate of return is 7 percent, what is the stock worth to you?

(The solution can be found on page 234.)

Notice that equation (8-1) is a restatement in a slightly different form of equation (7-1) in Chapter 7. Recall that equation (7-1) states that the value of an asset is the present value of future cash flows to be received by the investor.

Because the dividends in each period are equal for preferred stock, equation (8-1) can be reduced to the following relationship:[2]

$$V_{ps} = \frac{\text{annual dividend}}{\text{required rate of return}} = \frac{D}{k_{ps}} \qquad (8\text{-}2)$$

Equation (8-2) represents the present value of an infinite stream of cash flows, when the cash flows are the same each year. We can determine the value of the Xerox preferred stock, using equation (8-2), as follows:

$$V_{ps} = \frac{D}{k_{ps}} = \frac{\$6.25}{0.05} = \$125.00$$

In summary, the value of a preferred stock is the present value of all future dividends. But because most preferred stocks are nonmaturing—the dividends continue to infinity—we rely on a shortcut for finding value as represented by equation (8-2).

Did You Get It?

1. What features of preferred stock are different from bonds?
2. What provisions are available to protect a preferred stockholder?
3. What cash flows associated with preferred stock are included in the valuation model equation (8-1)? Why is the valuation model simplified in equation (8-2)?

---

[2] To verify this result, we begin with equation (8-1):

$$V_{ps} = \frac{D_1}{(1 + k_{ps})^1} + \frac{D_2}{(1 + k_{ps})^2} + \cdots + \frac{D_n}{(1 + k_{ps})^n}$$

If we multiply both sides of this equation by $(1 + k_{ps})$, we have

$$V_{ps}(1 + k_{ps}) = D_1 + \frac{D_2}{(1 + k_{ps})} + \cdots + \frac{D_n}{(1 + k_{ps})^{n-1}} \qquad (8\text{-}1\text{i})$$

Subtracting (8-1) from (8-1i) yields

$$V_{ps}(1 + k_{ps} - 1) = D_1 - \frac{D_n}{(1 + k_{ps})^n} \qquad (8\text{-}1\text{ii})$$

As n approaches infinity, $D_n/(1 + k_{ps})^n$ approaches zero. Consequently,

$$V_{ps}k_{ps} = D_1 \text{ and } V_{ps} = \frac{D_1}{k_{ps}} \qquad (8\text{-}1\text{iii})$$

Because $D_1 = D_2 = \ldots = D_n$, we need not designate the year. Therefore,

$$V_{ps} = \frac{D}{k_{ps}} \qquad (8\text{-}2)$$

How Did You Do?

VALUING PREFERRED STOCK

The value of the preferred stock would be $57.14:

$$\text{Value} = \frac{\text{dividend}}{\text{required rate of return}} = \frac{0.04 \times \$100}{0.07} = \frac{\$4}{0.07} = \$57.14$$

Remember Your Principles

Valuing preferred stock relies on three of our principles presented in Chapter 1, namely:

Principle 1: The Risk–Return Trade-Off—We Won't Take On Additional Risk Unless We Expect to Be Compensated with Additional Return.

Principle 2: The Time Value of Money—A Dollar Received Today Is Worth More Than a Dollar Received in the Future.

Principle 3: Cash—Not Profits—Is King.

Determining the economic worth, or value, of an asset always relies on these three principles. Without them, we would have no basis for explaining value. With them, we can know that the amount and timing of cash, not earnings, drives value. Also, we must be rewarded for taking risk; otherwise, we will not invest.

COMMON STOCK

common stock shares that represent the ownership in a corporation.

Common stock is *a certificate that indicates ownership in a corporation.* In effect, bondholders and preferred stockholders can be viewed as creditors, whereas the common stockholders are the true owners of the firm. Common stock does not have a maturity date but exists as long as the firm does. Nor does common stock have an upper limit on its dividend payments. Dividend payments must be declared each period (usually quarterly) by the firm's board of directors. In the event of bankruptcy, the common stockholders, as owners of the corporation, will not receive any payment until the firm's creditors, including the bondholders and preferred shareholders, have been paid. Next we look at several characteristics of common stock. Then we focus on valuing common stock.

The Characteristics of Common Stock

Objective **3**

Identify the basic characteristics of common stock.

We now examine common stock's claim on income and assets, its limited liability feature, and holders' voting and preemptive rights.

Claim on Income

As the owners of a corporation, the common shareholders have the right to the residual income after bondholders and preferred stockholders have been paid. This income may be paid directly to the shareholders in the form of dividends or retained within the firm and reinvested in the business. Although it is obvious the shareholder benefits immediately from the distribution of income in the form of dividends, the reinvestment of earnings also benefits the shareholder. Plowing back earnings into the firm should result in an increase in the value of the firm, its earning power, future dividends, and, ultimately, an increase in the value of the stock. In effect, residual income is distributed directly to shareholders in the form of dividends or indirectly in the form of capital gains (value increases) on their common stock.

The right to residual income has advantages and disadvantages for the common stockholder. The advantage is that the potential return is limitless. Once the claims of the most

Finance at Work

DOES STOCK BY ANY OTHER NAME SMELL AS SWEET?

All publicly traded stocks have ticker symbols, or abbreviations used to identify them. During 2005–2006, Harley-Davidson Inc.'s investor-relations personnel thought about changing their firm's stock ticker symbol, HDI: It wasn't exactly evocative of the motorcycle maker's image. And there was something better available: HOG (biker-slang for a Harley motorcycle). Interestingly, after Harley-Davidson adopted the new symbol in mid-August 2006, its shares gained nearly 16 percent in 5 weeks, compared with about 4 percent for the Standard & Poor's 500 Index.

It wasn't the first time a stock had risen after adopting a catchy ticker symbol. Counterintuitive as it may seem, research suggests that companies with clever symbols do better than other companies. Any suggestion of a cause-and-effect relationship may be hokum, but tickers that make investors chuckle—think Sotheby's BID, Advanced Medical Optics Inc.'s EYE, or PORK for Premium Standard Farms Inc.—also may make them richer, at least for a time. In one study, researchers at Princeton University found that companies with pronounceable symbols do better soon after an IPO than companies with symbols that can't be said as a word. In another study, researchers found that a portfolio of stocks with clever ticker symbols returned 23.6 percent compounded annually during the years 1990–2004, compared with 12.3 percent for a hypothetical index of all NYSE and Nasdaq stocks. The clever stocks included such well-known stocks as Anheuser Busch Cos. (BUD) and Southwest Airlines Co. (LUV), along with compa-

nies eventually delisted or acquired, such as Grand Havana Enterprises Inc. (PUFF) and Lion Country Safari (GRRR).

Some companies are more deliberate in aligning their ticker symbol with their brand. Yum Brands Inc., which runs restaurant chains including KFC, Pizza Hut, and Long John Silver's, actually changed its name in 2002, in part, to reflect its ticker symbol, YUM. The company, formerly known as Tricon Global Restaurants Inc., is trying to attract individual investors by advertising its name and ticker symbol at events such as the Kentucky Derby.

"It's easy for people to remember and puts a smile on their face," said Virginia Ferguson, a Yum spokeswoman. With a share price of $53.01, the stock is up about 230 percent from its 1997 debut price of $16, adjusted for splits, and has risen 68 percent since the name change to Yum Brands.

Michael Cooper, an associate professor of finance at the University of Utah, who has studied investor behavior, said that both papers were "intriguing," but that he would need to see further study before accepting the results.

The researchers themselves say it probably wouldn't behoove investors to make decisions based on their studies. "We certainly don't recommend that people make trading decisions based on our findings," said one researcher. "Rather, our findings suggest that economic models should take psychological factors into account if they are designed to faithfully capture how the markets operate in practice."

Source: Adapted from Jennifer Valentino, "Does Stock by Any Other Name Smell as Sweet?" the *Wall Street Journal*, September 28, 2006, P. C1.

senior securities (bonds and preferred stock) have been satisfied, the remaining income flows to the common stockholders in the form of dividends or capital gains. The disadvantage is that if the bond and preferred stock claims on income totally absorb earnings, common shareholders receive nothing. In years when earnings fall, it is the common shareholders who suffer first.

Claim on Assets

Just as common stock has a residual claim on income, it also has a residual claim on assets in the case of liquidation. Unfortunately, when bankruptcy does occur, the claims of the common shareholders generally go unsatisfied because debt holders and preferred stockholders have first and second claims on the assets. This residual claim on assets adds to the risk of common stock. Thus, although common stocks have historically provided a large return, averaging 12 percent annually since the late 1920s, there is also a higher risk associated with them.

Limited Liability

Although the common shareholders are the actual owners of the corporation, their *liability in the case of bankruptcy is limited to the amount of their investment*. The advantage is that investors who might not otherwise invest their funds in the firm become willing to do so. This **limited liability** feature aids the firm in raising funds.

limited liability a protective provision whereby the investor is not liable for more than the amount he or she has invested in the firm.

Voting Rights

The common stock shareholders are entitled to elect the board of directors and are, in general, the only security holders given a vote. Common shareholders have the right not only

Finance at Work

WHAT DOES A STOCK LOOK LIKE?

Antone Common Stock

John B. Doe
100 Main St
Anywhere, U.S.A 12345

* * * * * * * One-thousand, two-hundred shares * * * * * * *

FULL-PAID AND NON-ASSESSABLE SHARES OF THE COMMON STOCK OF

Date issued: December 14, 1996

---

proxy a means of voting in which a designated party is provided with the temporary power of attorney to vote for the signee at the corporation's annual meeting.

proxy fight a battle between rival groups for proxy votes in order to control the decisions made in a stockholders' meeting.

majority voting voting in which each share of stock allows the shareholder one vote, and each position on the board of directors is voted on separately. As a result, a majority of shares has the power to elect the entire board of directors.

cumulative voting voting in which each share of stock allows the shareholder a number of votes equal to the number of directors being elected. The shareholder can then cast all of his or her votes for a single candidate or split them among the various candidates.

to elect the board of directors but also to approve any change in the corporate charter. A typical change might involve the authorization to issue new stock or to accept a merger proposal. Voting for directors and charter changes occurs at the corporation's annual meeting. Although shareholders can vote in person, the majority generally vote by proxy. A **proxy** *gives a designated party the temporary power of attorney to vote for the signee at the corporation's annual meeting.* The firm's management generally solicits proxy votes, and, if the shareholders are satisfied with the firm's performance, has little problem securing them. However, in times of financial distress or when managerial takeovers are threatened, **proxy fights**—*battles between rival groups for proxy votes*—occur.

Although each share of stock carries the same number of votes, the voting procedure is not always the same from company to company. The two procedures commonly used are majority and cumulative voting. Under **majority voting**, *each share of stock allows the shareholder one vote, and each position on the board of directors is voted on separately.* Because each member of the board of directors is elected by a simple majority, a majority of shares has the power to elect the entire board of directors.

With **cumulative voting**, *each share of stock allows the stockholder a number of votes equal to the number of directors being elected.* The shareholder can then cast all of his or her votes for a single candidate or split them among the various candidates. The advantage of a cumulative voting procedure is that it gives minority shareholders the power to elect a director.

In theory, the shareholders pick the corporate board of directors, generally through proxy voting, and the board of directors, in turn, picks the management. In reality, shareholders are offered a slate of nominees selected by management from which to choose. The end result is that management effectively selects the directors, who then may have more allegiance to the managers than to the shareholders. This sets up the potential for agency problems in which a divergence of interests between managers and shareholders is allowed to exist, with the board of directors not monitoring the managers on behalf of the shareholders as they should.

Finance at Work

WHAT DO YOU TELL YOUR SHAREHOLDERS?

If you want a higher share price, what would you tell your investors? Suppose that someone asks you whether your company's share price is too high, too low, or just right. What should you say? If you think the answer depends on the circumstances, then you had best think again.

Most chief executives understand that they are, above all, salespersons, trying to convince the financial markets that their company is a good buy. But whereas ordinary salespeople are told that the customer is always right, most CEOs act as if the investors are always wrong. The CEO complains about the market's short-term focus and has little appreciation for analysts who follow the firm's stock.

Pleasing investors, however, is becoming more complicated. Besides the usual backward-looking financial measures, investors also want managers to be specific about their firm's future prospects, and they want more nonfinancial information to help them fill in the picture. Some advocates also want firms to provide more details about their "corporate governance" practices, such as boardroom procedures and ethical guidelines.

In a study by Shelley Taylor & Associates, "The Care and Feeding of Institutional Investors," the researchers examined the demands of the largest institutional investors in America, Britain, and continental Europe and compared these with what firms actually disclose. The study found that investors rate one measure above all else: *free cash flow*.

Most managers, however, have refused to believe this. Instead, they continue to rely on accrual accounting measures to make decisions, frequently destroying value in the process. This has discouraged firms from being frank with shareholders. Although the disclosure of cash flow itself is easy enough (and is required by many accounting standards), Shelley Taylor's research suggests that information that helps investors gauge future cash flows is guarded closely.

There was another interesting finding. Of the 19 kinds of corporate governance information considered, only one—executive pay—ranked among the top 20 issues investors care about. Specifically, they are concerned about the way in which pay relates to performance, not with just the amount. The rationale: An executive's incentives have a large effect on future performance.

Preemptive Rights

The **preemptive right** *entitles the common shareholder to maintain a proportionate share of ownership in the firm.* When new shares are issued, common shareholders have the first right of refusal. If a shareholder owns 25 percent of the corporation's stock, then he or she is entitled to purchase 25 percent of the new shares. *Certificates issued to the shareholders giving them an option to purchase a stated number of new shares of stock at a specified price during a 2- to 10-week period* are called **rights**. These rights can be exercised (generally at a price set by management below the common stock's current market price), allowed to expire, or sold in the open market.

preemptive right the right entitling the common shareholder to maintain his or her proportionate share of ownership in the firm.

right a certificate issued to common stockholders giving them an option to purchase a stated number of new shares at a specified price during a 2- to 10-week period.

Valuing Common Stock

Like bonds and preferred stock, a common stock's value is equal to the present value of all future cash flows expected to be received by the stockholder. However, in contrast to bonds, common stock does not promise its owners interest income or a maturity payment at some specified time in the future. Given the uniqueness of common stock, compared with bonds and preferred stock, we will consider two approaches to valuing common stock:

Objective **4**

Value common stock.

1. The value of a common stock is equal to the present value of all future dividends—the same approach just used in valuing preferred stock, but with some twists and turns, as we will see.
2. The value of a common stock is equal to the total firm value less the firm's outstanding debt, where the firm's value is equal to the present value of the firm's *free cash flows*.

Each of these approaches will now be explained.

Common Stock Value: The Present Value of Future Dividends

In contrast to preferred stock dividends, common stock does not provide the investor with a predetermined, constant dividend. For common stock, the dividend is based on the profitability of the firm and its decision to pay dividends or to retain the profits for reinvestment. As a consequence, dividend streams tend to increase with the growth in corporate earnings. Thus, the growth of future dividends is a prime distinguishing feature of common stock.

The Growth Factor in Valuing Common Stock   What is meant by the term *growth* when used in the context of valuing common stock? A company can grow in a variety of ways. It can become larger by borrowing money to invest in new projects. Likewise, it can issue new stock for expansion. Managers can also acquire another company to merge with the existing firm, which would increase the firm's assets. Although it can accurately be said that the firm has grown, the original stockholders may or may not participate in this growth. Growth is realized through the infusion of new capital. The firm size clearly increases, but unless the original investors increase their investment in the firm, they will own a smaller portion of the expanded business.

Another means of growing is **internal growth**, which requires that *managers retain some or all of the firm's profits for reinvestment in the firm*, resulting in the growth of future earnings and, hopefully, the value of the common stock. This process underlies the essence of potential growth for the firm's current stockholders and is the only relevant growth for our purposes of valuing a firm's common shares.[3]

internal growth a firm's growth rate resulting from reinvesting the company's profits rather than distributing them as dividends. The growth rate is a function of the amount retained and the return earned on the retained funds.

> **EXAMPLE** _____

To illustrate the nature of internal growth, assume that the return on equity for PepsiCo is 16 percent.[4] If PepsiCo decides to pay all the profits out in dividends to its stockholders, the firm will experience no growth internally. It might become larger by borrowing more money or issuing new stock, but internal growth will come only through the retention of profits. If, on the other hand, PepsiCo retains all of the profits, the stockholders' investment in the firm would grow by the amount of profits retained, or by 16 percent. If, however, PepsiCo keeps only 50 percent of the profits for reinvestment, the common shareholders' investment would increase only by half of the 16 percent return on equity, or by 8 percent. We can express this relationship by the following equation:

$$g = ROE \times r$$

where g = the growth rate of future earnings and the growth in the common stockholders' investment in the firm

ROE = the return on equity (net income/common book value)

r = *the company's percentage of profits retained*, called the **profit-retention rate**[5]

profit-retention rate the company's percentage of profits retained.

Therefore, if only 25 percent of the profits were retained by PepsiCo, we would expect the common stockholders' investment in the firm and the value of the stock price to increase, or grow, by 4 percent; that is,

$$g = 16\% \times 0.25 = 4\%$$

In summary, common stockholders frequently rely on an increase in the stock price as a source of return. If the company is retaining a portion of its earnings for reinvestment, future profits and dividends should grow. This growth should be reflected by an increase in the market price of the common stock in future periods. Therefore, both types of return (dividends and price appreciation) must be recognized in valuing common stock.

Dividend Valuation Model   The value of a common stock when defining value as the present value of future dividends relies on the same basic equation that we used with preferred stock

---

[3] We are not arguing that the existing common stockholders never benefit from the use of external financing; however, such benefit is nominal if capital markets are efficient.

[4] The return on equity is the accounting rate of return on the common shareholders' investment in the company and is computed as follows:

$$\text{Return on equity} = \frac{\text{net income}}{(\text{common stock} + \text{retained earnings})}$$

dividend-payout ratio dividends as a percentage of earnings.

[5] The retention rate is also equal to (1 − the percentage of profits paid out in dividends). *The percentage of profits paid out in dividends* is often called the **dividend-payout ratio**.

Can You Do It?

MEASURING JOHNSON & JOHNSON'S GROWTH RATE

In 2005, Johnson & Johnson had a return on equity of 27.49 percent. The firm's earnings per share was $3.46, and the firm paid $1.275 in dividends per share. If these relationships hold in the future, what will be the firm's internal growth rate?

$$ROE = \frac{\text{net income}}{\text{common stock} + \text{retained earning}}$$

$$= \frac{10,411}{37,871}$$

$$= 27.49\%$$

(The solution can be found on page 240.)

[equation (8-1)], with the exception that we are using the required rate of return of common stockholders, k_{cs}. That is,

$$V_{cs} = \frac{D_1}{(1 + k_{cs})^1} + \frac{D_2}{(1 + k_{cs})^2} + \cdots + \frac{D_n}{(1 + k_{cs})^n} + \cdots + \frac{D_\infty}{(1 + k_{cs})^\infty} \tag{8-3}$$

If you turn back to Chapter 7 and compare equation (7-1) with equation (8-3), you will notice that equation (8-3) is merely a restatement of equation (7-1). Recall that equation (7-1), which is the basis for our work in valuing securities, states that the value of an asset is the present value of future cash flows to be received by the investor. Equation (8-3) simply applies equation (7-1) to valuing common stock.

Equation (8-3) indicates that we are discounting the dividend at the end of the first year, D_1, back 1 year; the dividend in the second year, D_2, back 2 years; the dividend in the nth year back n years; and the dividend in infinity back an infinite number of years. The required rate of return is k_{cs}. In using equation (8-3), note that the value of the stock is established at the beginning of the year, say January 1, 2007. The most recent past dividend, D_0, would have been paid the previous day, December 31, 2006. Thus, if we purchased the stock on January 1, the first dividend would be received in 12 months, on December 31, 2007, which is represented by D_1.

Fortunately, equation (8-3) can be reduced to a much more manageable form if dividends grow each year at a constant rate, g. The constant-growth, common-stock valuation equation can be presented as follows:[6]

---

[6] When common stock dividends grow at a constant rate of g every year, we can express the dividend in any year in terms of the dividend paid at the end of the previous year, D_0. For example, the expected dividend year 1 hence is simply $D_0(1 + g)$. Likewise, the dividend at the end of t years is $D_0(1 + g)^t$. Using this notation, the common-stock valuation equation in (8-3) can be rewritten as follows:

$$V_{cs} = \frac{D_0(1 + k_{cs})^1}{(1 + g)^1} + + \frac{D_0(1 + g)^2}{(1 + k_{cs})^2} + \cdots + \frac{D_0(1 + g)^n}{(1 + k_{cs})^n} + \cdots + \frac{D_0(1 + g)^\infty}{(1 + k_{cs})^\infty} \tag{8-3i}$$

If both sides of equation (8-3i) are multiplied by $(1 + k_{cs})/(1 + g)$ and then equation (8-4) is subtracted from the product, the result is

$$\frac{V_{cs}(1 + k_{cs})}{1 + g} - V_{cs} = D_0 - \frac{D_0(1 + g)^\infty}{(1 + k_{cs})^\infty} \tag{8-3ii}$$

If $k_{cs} > g$, which normally should hold, $[D_0(1 + g)(1 + k_{cs}^\infty]$ approaches zero. As a result,

$$\frac{V_{cs}(1 + k_{cs})}{1 + g} - V_{cs} = D_0$$

$$V_{cs}\left(\frac{1 + k_{cs}}{1 + g}\right) - V_{cs}\left(\frac{1 + g}{1 + g}\right) = D_0$$

$$V_{cs}\left[\frac{(1 + k_{cs}) - (1 + g)}{1 + g}\right] = D_0 \tag{8-3iii}$$

$$V_{cs}(k_{cs} - g) = D_0(1 + g)$$

$$V_{cs} = \frac{D_1}{k_{cs} - g}$$

How Did You Do?

MEASURING JOHNSON & JOHNSON'S GROWTH RATE

Johnson & Johnson's internal growth rate would be 17.36 percent. The firm is paying out 36.85 percent of its earnings in dividends (36.85% = $1.275 dividends per share ÷ $3.46 earnings per share), which means that the firm is retaining 63.15 percent of its earnings (63.15% = 100% − 36.85%). Given that the firm has a 27.49 percent return on equity, its internal growth rate would be 17.36 percent (17.36% = 27.49% return on equity × 63.15% earnings or profits retained per dollar of earnings).

$$\text{Common stock value} = \frac{\text{dividend in year 1}}{\text{required rate of return} - \text{growth rate}} \tag{8-4}$$

$$V_{cs} = \frac{D_1}{k_{cs} - g}$$

In other words, the intrinsic value (present value) of a share of common stock whose dividends grow at a constant annual rate can be calculated using equation (8-4). Although the interpretation of this equation might not be intuitively obvious, simply remember that it solves for the present value of the future dividend stream growing at a rate, g, to infinity, assuming that k_{cs} is greater than g.

> ### ➤ EXAMPLE

Consider the valuation of a share of common stock that paid a $2 dividend at the end of last year and is expected to pay a cash dividend every year from now to infinity. Each year the dividends are expected to grow at a rate of 10 percent. Based on an assessment of the riskiness of the common stock, the investor's required rate of return is 15 percent. Using this information, we would compute the value of the common stock as follows:

1. Because the $2 dividend was paid last year, we must compute the next dividend to be received, that is, D_1, where

$$\begin{aligned} D_1 &= D_0(1 + g) \\ &= \$2(1 + .10) \\ &= \$2.20 \end{aligned}$$

2. Now, using equation (8-4),

$$\begin{aligned} V_{cs} &= \frac{D_1}{k_{cs} - g} \\ &= \frac{\$2.20}{.15 - .10} \\ &= \$44 \end{aligned}$$

We have argued that the value of a common stock is equal to the present value of all future dividends, which is without question a fundamental premise of finance. In practice, however, managers, along with many security analysts, often talk about the relationship between stock value and earnings, rather than dividends. We would encourage you to be very

Can You Do It?

CALCULATING COMMON STOCK VALUE

The Abraham Corporation paid $1.32 in dividends per share *last year*. The firm's projected growth rate is 6 percent for the foreseeable future. If the investor's required rate of return for a firm with Abraham's level of risk is 10 percent, what is the value of the stock?
   (The solution can be found on page 242.)

Remember Your Principles

Valuing common stock is no different from valuing preferred stock; only the pattern of the cash flows changes. Thus, the valuation of common stock relies on the same three principles developed in Chapter 1 that were used in valuing preferred stock:

Principle 1: The Risk–Return Trade-Off—We Won't Take On Additional Risk Unless We Expect to Be Compensated with Additional Return.

Principle 2: The Time Value of Money—A Dollar Received Today Is Worth More Than a Dollar Received in the Future.

Principle 3: Cash—Not Profits—Is King.

   Determining the economic worth, or value, of an asset always relies on these three principles. Without them, we would have no basis for explaining value. With them, we can know that the amount and timing of cash, not earnings, drives value. Also, we must be rewarded for taking risk; otherwise, we will not invest.

cautious in using earnings to value a stock. Even though it may be a popular practice, significant available evidence suggests that investors look to the cash flows generated by the firm, not the earnings, for value. A firm's value truly is the present value of the cash flows it produces.

   We now turn to our second approach for estimating the value of a common stock—the present value of free cash flows.

Did You Get It?

1. What features of common stock indicate ownership in the corporation versus preferred stock or bonds?
2. In what two ways does a shareholder benefit from ownership?
3. How does internal growth versus the infusion of new capital affect the original shareholders?
4. Describe the process for common stock valuation.

Common Stock Value: The Present Value of Free Cash Flows

Free cash flow valuation defines the value of a firm as the present value of its expected future cash flows. In other words, a firm's economic, or intrinsic, value is equal to the present value of its future free cash flows discounted at the company's cost of capital—the required rate of return of the firm's investors. We then compute shareholder value as the value of the firm less the value of its outstanding interest-bearing debt, such as bonds and bank notes.

free cash flow valuation valuing a firm as the present value of its expected future cash flows.

How Did You Do?

CALCULATING COMMON STOCK VALUE

Abraham's stock value would be $35:

$$\text{Value} = \frac{\text{dividend year 1}}{\text{required rate of return} - \text{growth rate}}$$

$$= \frac{\$1.32 \times (1 + .06)}{0.10 - 0.06} = \frac{\$1.40}{0.04} = \$35$$

Finance at Work

A DARKER SIDE OF STARBUCKS

In October 2006, Howard Schultz, the CEO of Starbucks, was planning to more than triple the number of its stores (to 40,000) in an effort to challenge Yum Brands and McDonald's. Schultz, with his usual flair, also wanted Starbucks to become an arbiter of culture, announcing that the company had reached an agreement with Apple that would give consumers the ability to preview, buy, and download a variety of Starbucks' Hear Music titles from iTunes. And for the 2006 holiday season, Starbucks would begin selling a specially packaged DVD of White Christmas at its coffee shops.

News of the ramped-up expansion plans impressed Wall Street, as the company's stock jumped 8 percent, registering the biggest one-day gain in nearly a year. In fact, Starbucks' shares were selling for a staggering price/earnings multiple of 55, even slightly more expensive than Google at the time, which was trading at 51 times earnings.

Although Starbucks' lofty P/E ratio indicated that investors were highly enthusiastic about the stock, not everyone was so perky about the company's prospects. David Trainer, the founder of New Constructs, an independent equity research firm, thought that Starbucks would have to achieve extraordinary growth to justify its value. Trainer estimated that Starbucks would have to boost revenues nearly 25 percent each year for the next 10 years and improve returns on capital by 30 percent to justify its current stock price. That would only happen, Trainer argued, if more consumers were willing to pay up for Starbucks' premium-priced coffee. But Trainer, for one, wouldn't bet on it: "People who play in these popular stocks where expectations are so high are playing a fool's game," he said.

At the time, Starbucks (SBUX) was selling for $37 per share, and earnings per share were $0.72. Was Trainer right? Go to **http://finance.yahoo.com/** and check it out.

Source: Adapted from "A Darker View of Starbucks," *Fortune*, November 13, 2006, p. 197.

In Chapter 3 we learned to compute a firm's historical free cash flows. We specifically said that a firm's free cash flows are determined as follows:

Operating Income

+ depreciation and amortization
− tax expense
= after-tax cash flows from operations
− the investment (increase) in the firm's assets (both net working capital and capital expenditures in plant and equipment)
= free cash flows

We are now interested in predicting the firm's *future*, rather than its *historical*, free cash flows and then finding the present value of these cash flows as a measure of firm value. The actual process is as follows:

competitive-advantage period the number of years a firm's managers believes it can sustain a competitive advantage, given the company's present strategies.

1. We decide on a **competitive-advantage period**, which represents the number of years the firm's managers believe it can sustain a competitive advantage, given the company's present strategies.

2. We estimate the free cash flows for each year of the competitive-advantage period. For instance, if managers thinks the firm has a 5-year competitive-advantage period, they will estimate the free cash flows for each year through the fifth year.

3. We next make an assumption that the free cash flows in all subsequent years (for example, the sixth year onward) will grow at a constant growth rate each year, much like we did when we were using the dividend-valuation approach described earlier. With this assumption, we can determine the free cash flow for the first year of the residual period, for example, year 6.

4. Given the projected cash flows, we

   a. Calculate the present value of the free cash flows (FCF_t) during the competitive-advantage period expected to continue through year T, discounted at the cost of capital, k.

$$\begin{array}{c}\text{Present value} \\ \text{competitive-advantage period}\end{array} = PV_{\text{CAP}} = \frac{FCF_1}{(1+k)^1} + \frac{FCF_2}{(1+k)^2} + \frac{FCF_3}{(1+k)^3} \qquad (8\text{-}5)$$

$$+ \ \dots \ + \frac{FCF_T}{(1+k)^T}$$

   b. Compute the firm's **residual value** as of the end of the competitive-advantage period, where the residual value is the present value of the post-competitive-advantage period cash flows.

   residual value the present value of a firm's post-competitive-advantage period cash flows.

   By assuming that the firm's free cash flows will grow at a constant growth rate, we can compute the firm's residual value (RV_T) as of year T, based on free cash flows (FCF_t) beginning 1 year later at $T + 1$.

$$\begin{array}{c}\text{Residual value} \\ \text{(year } T)\end{array} = RV_T = \frac{FCF_{T+1}}{k - g} \qquad (8\text{-}6)$$

   c. Calculate the present value of the residual value (RV_0).

$$\begin{array}{c}\text{Present value} \\ \text{of the} \\ \text{residual value}\end{array} = RV_0 = \frac{\text{residual value year } T}{(1+k)^T} \qquad (8\text{-}7)$$

   d. Find the firm value as follows:

$$\begin{array}{c}\text{Firm} \\ \text{value}\end{array} = \text{present value} \left(\begin{array}{c}\text{competitive–advantage} \\ \text{period cash flows}\end{array}\right) + \text{present value} \left(\begin{array}{c}\text{residual} \\ \text{value}\end{array}\right) \qquad (8\text{-}8)$$

   e. Subtract the firm's outstanding debt from the firm value to determine the shareholder or stock value:

$$\text{Shareholder value} = \text{firm value} - \text{debt} \qquad (8\text{-}9)$$

   f. Divide the shareholder value by the number of shares outstanding to arrive at the value per share.

We just gave you a lot of things (steps) to do to find the fair value of a firm's stock. We can best clarify the free cash flow valuation method by an illustration. Let's assume the following facts and estimates about the M. K. Green Corporation:

- Sales for the most recent period (last year) were $1,000.
- Managers anticipate sales to grow at 12 percent annually for 2 years, 8 percent in years 3 through 5, and 4 percent thereafter.
- The firm's operating profit margin (operating income ÷ sales) is expected to be 12 percent.
- The corporation's tax rate is 40 percent.
- The firm's assets as a percentage of sales are expected to be 45 percent for the foreseeable future. That is, for each increase in sales of $1, we would expect assets to increase $0.45.
- The firm's cost of capital (the discount rate) is 12 percent.
- The company has $250 of debt outstanding.
- The firm has 100 shares of common stock outstanding.

TABLE 8-1   Free Cash Flow Valuation: M. K. Green Corporation

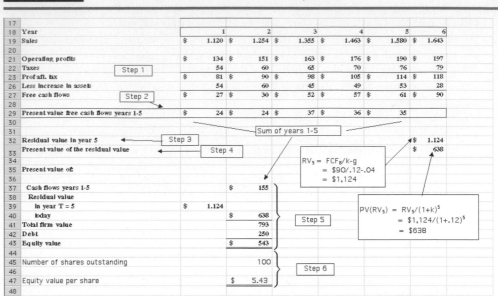

Note that the numbers have been rounded to the nearest dollars, which may create rounding differences.

The Excel spreadsheet used to compute the M. K. Green Corporation's shareholder value is shown in Table 8-1. (This spreadsheet is available at **www.prenhall.com/keown**.) The calculations involve the following steps:

1. Based on the assumptions given, we compute the annual free cash flows for the competitive-advantage period (years 1 through 5) and for the first year of the post-competitive-advantage period (year 6). For instance, the free cash flow in the first year is computed below. (The numbers have been rounded to the nearest dollar, which may create rounding differences.)

Sales	$1,120	[$1,000 last year's sales × (1 + 12% growth rate)]
Operating profits	134	[$1,120 sales × 12% operating profit margin]
Taxes	54	[$134 operating profits × 40% tax rate]
After-tax profits	$ 81	[operating profits − taxes]
Increase in assets	54	[(increase in sales $1,120 − $1,000 = $120) × 45% assets-to-sales ratio]
Free cash flows	$ 27	[after-tax profits − increase in assets]

Note that free cash flows are found by computing after-tax operating profits and subtracting the *incremental* investments, where the incremental investments are determined by computing the *change in sales for the year* multiplied by the percentage of the assets-to-sales relationship.

Also, observe that we did not add back depreciation expense, as is usually done in computing free cash flow. Instead, it is common practice in a free cash flow model to assume that the depreciation expense equals the cost of replacing fixed assets. That is, accounting depreciation is assumed to equal the economic depreciation—the actual cost of replacing depreciating assets. Therefore, we do not add back any depreciation expense, but neither do we show a cash outflow for the cost of replacing already existing fixed assets. Additions to fixed assets include only those investments resulting from firm growth, not from replacements.

2. Find the present value of the cash flows during the competitive-advantage period (years 1 to 5) by discounting each year's cash flows back to the present and summing the results:

$$\text{Present value} = \frac{\$27}{(1+0.12)^1} + \frac{\$30}{(1+0.12)^2} + \frac{\$52}{(1+0.12)^3} + \frac{\$57}{(1+0.12)^4} + \frac{\$61}{(1+0.12)^5}$$

$$= \$24 + \$24 + \$37 + \$36 + \$35 = \$155$$

Can You Do It?

COMPUTING STOCK VALUE (A FREE CASH FLOW APPROACH)

You have been asked to determine the stock value for the Davies Corporation, a small computer supplies business. Given the following information, calculate the firm's stock value based on the free cash flow valuation approach.

1. The firm had sales last year of $2 million, and the owner expects sales to grow at 10 percent for 2 years and 4 percent thereafter.
2. The operating profit margin is expected to be 15 percent with a tax rate of 30 percent.
3. The firm has maintained a 45 percent asset-to-sales relationship, which should continue into the future. That is, for every $1 of sales, the firm has $0.40 in assets.
4. The company has $500,000 in outstanding debt.
5. The firm's cost of capital (discount rate for finding the present value of future cash flows) is 12 percent.
6. There are 150,000 shares outstanding.

(The solution can be found on page 247.)

3. Determine the residual value (value of all future free cash flows beginning in year 6 and beyond) as of year 5 as follows:

$$\text{Residual value}_5 = \frac{FCF_6}{k - g} = \frac{\$90}{.12 - .04} = \$1,125$$

4. Discount the residual value in year 5 back to the present, giving us a value of

$$\frac{\text{Present value}}{\text{of the residual value}} = \frac{\text{residual value year 5}}{(1 + k)^5} = \frac{\$1,125}{(1 + 12)^5} = \$638$$

5. Combine the two present values to determine a firm value of $794, and subtract the debt of $250 to find the shareholder value of $544.
6. Divide the shareholder value, $544, by the number of shares outstanding (100) to determine a value per share of $5.44.

The foregoing approach to valuing a firm and its shareholder value has become relatively popular in practice. We will see that this same basic approach is used to assign value to individual, fixed-asset investments when we look at capital budgeting decisions—so don't forget the process of valuing an asset or a firm based on the present value of its free cash flows.

THE EXPECTED RATE OF RETURN OF STOCKHOLDERS

Objective **5**

Calculate a stock's expected rate of return.

As stated in Chapter 7, the expected rate of return, or yield to maturity, on a bond is the return the bondholder expects to receive on the investment by paying the existing market price for the security. This rate of return is of interest to the financial manager because it tells the manager about investors' expectations. The same can be said for the financial manager needing to know the expected rate of return of the firm's stockholders, which is the topic of this section.

The Expected Rate of Return of Preferred Stockholders

To compute the expected rate of return of preferred stockholders, we use the valuation equation for preferred stock. Earlier, equation (8-2) specified the value of a preferred stock, V_{ps}, as

$$V_{ps} = \frac{\text{annual dividend}}{\text{required rate of return}} = \frac{D}{k_{ps}}$$

Finance at Work

EARNINGS PER SHARE? PHOOEY!

In June 2006, Ivan P. Feinseth, director of research at the Manhattan broker-dealer firm Matrix USA, rated almost 40 percent of the stocks he followed—1,200 out of 3,100 stocks—as "sell" or "strong sell." Given that a third of the stocks were down near the end of May that year, Feinseth's recommendations seemed far more realistic than many other analysts were recommending.

What made Feinseth's analysis unique is his fixation on something other than earnings. He views traditional corporate earnings as being vastly overrated as an investment gauge. The question, he says, is whether a company is creating real, hard value for its shareholders. Earnings per share, he says, is just an accounting measure of profit. The real key to the stock price is economic profit. Companies manage analysts' expectations quite carefully—so they can beat them. But they can't fudge economic profit, which Feinseth defines as the extent of a company's return above its cost of capital.

Skeptics point out that by focusing primarily on data, Feinseth misses out on the nuances and "body language" that other analysts pick up on as they study companies and their executives. Feinseth doesn't seem to care. "We don't talk with the compa-

nies," he says, swiveling around to four computer monitors brimming with charts in Matrix' modest, disheveled midtown office. "What we're doing is a deep analysis of the numbers."

As an example of Feinseth's analysis, as of June 2006, Microsoft's shares were at a multiyear low. At that time, many analysts were down on Microsoft. But Feinseth's analysis suggested investors buy the stock. The reason: The company's enviable 39 percent return on capital dwarfed both its borrowing costs and the 4 percent it was earning on its $35 billion cash in the bank. In fact, he considered it a great opportunity for Microsoft to acquire its own shares at a "bargain."

Feinseth believes his reasoning will prove correct, as grandly stated in his company's literature. "Accounting-based models of valuation should be buried right alongside Communism," reads one packet. "If the Berlin Wall can come down, so, too, can the assertions that stock prices are based on reported accounting earnings."

So how is Microsoft doing today?

Source: Adapted from Roben Farzad, "Earnings Per Share? Phooey!" *Business Week*, June 12, 2006, p. 66.

Solving equation (8-2) for k_{ps}, we have

$$k_{ps} = \frac{\text{annual dividend}}{\text{preferred stock value}} = \frac{D}{V_{ps}} \tag{8-10}$$

Thus, the *required* rate of return of preferred stockholders simply equals the stock's annual dividend divided by the stock's intrinsic value. We can also restate equation (8-8) to solve for a preferred stock's *expected* rate of return, $\bar{k}_{ps}$, as follows:[7]

$$\bar{k}_{ps} = \frac{\text{annual dividend}}{\text{preferred stock market price}} = \frac{D}{P_{ps}} \tag{8-11}$$

expected rate of return (1) the discount rate that equates the present value of the future cash flows (interest and maturity value) of a bond with the current market price of the bond. It is the rate of return an investor will earn if the bond is held to maturity. (2) The rate of return investors expect to receive on an investment by paying the current market price of the security. (3) The arithmetic mean, or average, of all possible outcomes where those outcomes are weighted by the probability that each will occur.

Note that we have merely substituted the current market price, P_{ps}, for the intrinsic value, V_{ps}. The expected rate of return, $\bar{k}_{ps}$, therefore, equals the annual dividend relative to the price the stock is currently selling for, P_{ps}. Thus, the **expected rate of return**, $\bar{k}_{ps}$, *is the rate of return the investor can expect to earn from the investment if it is bought at the current market price.*

For example, if the present market price of the preferred stock is $50, and it pays a $3.64 annual dividend, the expected rate of return implicit in the present market price is

$$\bar{k}_{ps} = \frac{D}{P_{ps}} = \frac{\$3.64}{\$50} = 7.28\%$$

Therefore, investors (who pay $50 per share for a preferred security that is paying $3.64 in annual dividends) are expecting a 7.28 percent rate of return.

---

[7] We will use $\bar{k}$ to represent a security's *expected* rate of return versus k for investors' *required* rate of return.

How Did You Do?

COMPUTING STOCK VALUE (A FREE CASH FLOW APPROACH)

The solution to this problem involves the following steps:

Step 1. Compute the free cash flows for the 3 years of data given, where sales are growing at 10 percent for 2 years, followed by growth of 4 percent beginning in year 3 and continuing in perpetuity.

Step 2. Find the present value of the first 2 years of free cash flows.

Step 3. Using year 3 as the first year of the perpetual constant growth rate, we compute the residual value of the firm, as of year 2.

Step 4. Compute the present value of the residual value.

Step 5. Sum the present value of the cash flows, both for years 1 and 2 and for the residual value to determine the firm value, and then subtract the firm's debt to find the total equity value.

Step 6. Divide the total equity value by the number of shares outstanding to arrive at the equity value per share.

Using an Excel spreadsheet, the value per share is found to be $18.64, computed as follows (numbers rounded to the nearest dollars):

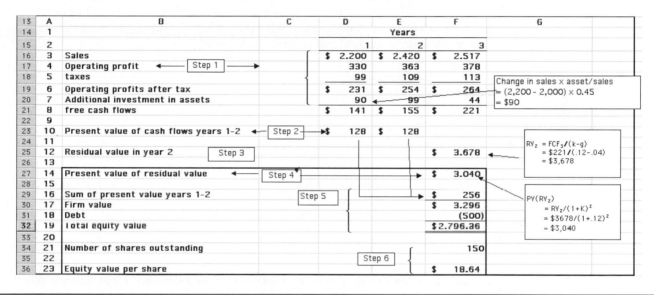

The Expected Rate of Return of Common Stockholders

The valuation equation for common stock was defined earlier in equation (8-3) as

$$\text{Common stock value} = \frac{\text{dividend in year 1}}{(1 + \text{required rate of return})^1} + \frac{\text{dividend in year 2}}{(1 + \text{required rate of return})^2}$$
$$+ \cdots + \frac{\text{dividend in year infinity}}{(1 + \text{required rate of return})^\infty}$$

$$V_{cs} = \frac{D_1}{(1 + k_{cs})^1} + \frac{D_2}{(1 + k_{cs})^2} + \cdots + \frac{D_\infty}{(1 + k_{cs})^\infty}$$

Owing to the difficulty of discounting to infinity, we made the key assumption that the dividends, D_t, increase at a constant annual compound growth rate of g. If this assumption is valid, equation (8-4) was shown to be equivalent to

$$\text{Common stock value} = \frac{\text{dividend in year 1}}{\text{required rate of return} - \text{growth rate}}$$

$$V_{cs} = \frac{D_1}{k_{cs} - g}$$

Can You Do It?

COMPUTING THE EXPECTED RATE OF RETURN

Calculate the expected rate of return for the two following stocks:

Preferred stock: The stock is selling for $80 and pays a 5 percent dividend on its $100 par or stated value.

Common stock: The stock paid a dividend of $4 last year and is expected to increase each year at a 5 percent growth rate. The stock sells for $75.

(The solution can be found on page 249.)

Thus, V_{cs} represents the maximum value that investors having a required rate of return of k_{cs} would pay for a security having an anticipated dividend in year 1 of D_1 that is expected to grow in future years at rate g. Solving equation (8-4) for k_{cs}, we can compute the common stockholders' required rate of return as follows:[8]

$$k_{cs} = \frac{D_1}{V_{cs}} + g \qquad \text{(8-12)}$$

divided yield

annual growth rate

According to this equation, the required rate of return is equal to the dividend yield plus a growth factor. Although the growth rate, g, applies to the growth in the company's dividends, given our assumptions, the stock's value can also be expected to increase at the same rate. For this reason, g represents the annual percentage growth in the stock value. In other words, the required rate of return of investors is satisfied by their receiving dividends *and* capital gains, as reflected by the expected percentage growth rate in the stock price.

As was done for preferred stock earlier, we may revise equation (8-12) to measure a common stock's *expected* rate of return, $\bar{k}_{cs}$. Replacing the intrinsic value, V_{cs}, in equation (8-12) with the stock's current market price, P_{cs}, we may express the stock's expected rate of return as follows:

$$\bar{k}_{cs} = \frac{\text{dividend in year 1}}{\text{market price}} + \text{growth rate} = \frac{D_1}{P_{cs}} + g \qquad \text{(8-13)}$$

Most of the returns on stocks come from price appreciation, or capital gains, with a smaller part of the return coming from dividends. The Standard & Poor's 500 Index, for example, returned a 10 percent annual return on average over the past 10 years. But the dividend yield (dividend ÷ stock price) accounted for only about 2 percent of the return. The remaining 10 percent resulted from price appreciation.

As a final note, we should understand that the *expected* rate of return implied by a given market price equals the *required* rate of return for investors at the margin. For these investors, the expected rate of return is just equal to their required rate of return and, therefore, they are willing to pay the current market price for the security. These investors' required rate of return is of particular significance to the financial manager because it represents the cost of new financing to the firm.

---

[8] At times the expected dividend at year-end (D_1) is not given. Instead, we might only know the most recent dividend (paid yesterday), that is, D_0. If so, equation (8-4) must be restated as follows:

$$V_{cs} = \frac{D_1}{(k_{cs} - g)} = \frac{D_0(1 + g)}{(k_{cs} - g)}$$

How Did You Do?

COMPUTING THE EXPECTED RATE OF RETURN

Preferred stock:

$$\text{Expected return} = \frac{\text{dividend}}{\text{stock price}} = \frac{\$5}{\$80} = 0.0625 \text{ or } 6.25\%$$

Common stock:

$$\text{Expected return} = \frac{\text{dividend}}{\text{stock price}} + \text{growth rate}$$

$$= \frac{\$4 \times (1 + 0.05)}{\$75} + 5\% = \frac{\$4.20}{\$75} + 5\%$$

$$= 5.6\% + 5\% = 10.6\%$$

Remember Your Principles

We have just learned that, on average, the expected return will be equal to the investor's required rate of return. This equilibrium condition is achieved by investors paying for an asset only the amount that will exactly satisfy their required rate of return. Thus, finding the expected rate of return based on the current market price for the security relies on two of the principles given in Chapter 1:

Principle 1: The Risk–Return Trade-Off—We Won't Take On Additional Risk Unless We Expect to Be Compensated with Additional Return.

Principle 2: The Time Value of Money—A Dollar Received Today Is Worth More Than a Dollar Received in the Future.

Did You Get It?

1. In computing the required rate of return, why should the growth factor be added to the dividend yield?
2. How does an efficient market affect the required and expected rates of return?

Summary

Valuation is an important process in financial management. An understanding of valuation, both the concepts and procedures, supports the financial officer's objective of maximizing the value of the firm.

Preferred stock has no fixed maturity date, and the dividends are fixed in amount. Some of the more common characteristics of preferred stock include the following:

Objective **1**

Identify the basic characteristics of preferred stock.

- There are multiple classes of preferred stock.
- Preferred stock has a priority claim on assets and income over common stock.
- Any dividends, if not paid as promised, must be paid before any common stock dividends may be paid; that is, they are cumulative.
- Protective provisions are included in the contract with the shareholder to reduce the investor's risk.
- Many preferred stocks are convertible into common stock shares.

In addition, there are provisions frequently used to retire an issue of preferred stock, such as the ability of the firm to call its preferred stock or to use a sinking-fund provision.

Objective **2**

Value preferred stock.

Value is the present value of future cash flows discounted at the investor's required rate of return. Although the valuation of any security entails the same basic principles, the procedures used in each situation vary. For example, we learned in Chapter 7 that valuing a bond involves calculating the present value of the future interest to be received plus the present value of the principal returned to the investor at the maturity of the bond.

For securities with cash flows that are constant in each year but with no specified maturity, such as preferred stock, the present value equals the dollar amount of the annual dividend divided by the investor's required rate of return of investors; that is,

$$\text{Preferred stock value} = \frac{\text{annual dividend}}{\text{required rate of return}}$$

Objective **3**

Identify the basic characteristics of common stock.

Common stock involves ownership in the corporation. In effect, bondholders and preferred stockholders can be viewed as creditors, whereas common stockholders are the owners of the firm. Common stock does not have a maturity date but exists as long as the firm does. Nor does common stock have an upper limit on its dividend payments. Dividend payments must be declared by the firm's board of directors before they are issued. In the event of bankruptcy, the common stockholders, as owners of the corporation, cannot exercise claims on assets until the firm's creditors, including its bondholders and preferred shareholders, have been satisfied. However, common stockholders' liability is limited to the amount of their investment.

The common stockholders are entitled to elect the firm's board of directors and are, in general, the only security holders given a vote. Common shareholders also have the right to approve any change in the company's corporate charter. Although each share of stock carries the same number of votes, the voting procedure is not always the same from company to company.

The preemptive right entitles the common shareholder to maintain a proportionate share of ownership in the firm.

When future dividends are expected to increase at a constant growth rate, the value of the common stock may be given by the following equation:

Objective **4**

Value common stock.

$$\text{Common stock value} = \frac{\text{dividend in year 1}}{\text{required rate of return} - \text{growth rate}}$$

Growth here relates to *internal* growth only—growth achieved by retaining part of the firm's profits and reinvesting them in the firm—as opposed to growth achieved by issuing new stock or acquiring another firm.

Growth in and of itself does not mean that a firm is creating value for its stockholders. Only if profits are reinvested at a rate of return greater than the investor's required rate of return will growth result in increased stockholder value.

A second approach for calculating common stock value is based on the present value of the firm's projected free cash flows. Here we compute the expected free cash flows and find their present value. The process involves identifying the anticipated time frame for the firm's existing competitive advantage and determining the value of the cash flows during this time period and adding the present value of the cash flows during the post-competitive-advantage period, or what we call the residual value. The basic concept suggests that the value of an asset, or even an entire firm, is equal to the present value of the asset's future free cash flows.

The expected rate of return on a security is the required rate of return of investors who are willing to pay the present market price for the security, but no more. This rate of return is important to the financial manager because it equals the required rate of return of the firm's investors.

Objective **5**

Calculate a stock's expected rate of return.

The expected rate of return for preferred stock is computed as follows:

$$\text{Expected return, preferred stock} = \frac{\text{annual dividend}}{\text{market price}}$$

The expected rate of return for common stock is calculated as follows:

$$\text{Expected return, common stock} = \frac{\text{dividend in year 1}}{\text{market price}} + \text{growth rate}$$

Key Terms

Call provision   231

Common stock   234

Competitive-advantage period   242

Convertible preferred stock   231

Cumulative feature   231

Cumulative voting   236

Dividend-payout ratio   238

Expected rate of return   246

Free cash flow valuation   241

Internal growth   238

Limited liability   235

Majority voting   236

Preemptive right   237

Preferred stock   230

Profit-retention rate   238

Protective provisions   231

Proxy   236

Proxy fight   236

Residual value   243

Right   237

Sinking-fund provision   231

Review Questions

8-1. Why is preferred stock referred to as a hybrid security? It is often said to combine the worst features of common stock and bonds. What is meant by this statement?

8-2. Because preferred stock dividends in arrears must be paid before common stock dividends, should they be considered a liability and appear on the right-hand side of the balance sheet?

8-3. Why would a preferred stockholder want the stock to have a cumulative dividend feature and protective provisions?

8-4. Why is preferred stock frequently convertible? Why is it callable?

8-5. Compare valuing preferred stock and common stock.

8-6. Define investors' expected rate of return.

8-7. State how investors' expected rate of return is computed.

8-8. The common stockholders receive two types of return from their investment. What are they?

Self-Test Problems

(The solutions to the following problems are found at the end of the chapter.)

ST-1. (*Preferred stock valuation*) What is the value of a preferred stock when the dividend rate is 16 percent on a $100 par value? The appropriate discount rate for a stock of this risk level is 12 percent.

ST-2. (*Preferred stockholder expected return*) You own 250 shares of Dalton Resources preferred stock, which currently sells for $38.50 per share and pays annual dividends of $3.25 per share.

  a. What is your expected return?
  b. If you require an 8 percent return, given the current price, should you sell or buy more stock?

ST-3. (*Preferred stock valuation*) The preferred stock of Armlo pays a $2.75 dividend. What is the value of the stock if your required return is 9 percent?

ST-4. (*Common stock valuation*) Crosby Corporation common stock paid $1.32 in dividends last year and is expected to grow indefinitely at an annual 7 percent rate. What is the value of the stock if you require an 11 percent return?

ST-5. (*Common stockholder expected return*) Blackburn & Smith common stock currently sells for $23 per share. The company's executives anticipate a constant growth rate of 10.5 percent and an end-of-year dividend of $2.50.

  a. What is your expected rate of return?
  b. If you require a 17 percent return, should you purchase the stock?

Study Problems

8-1. (*Preferred stock expected return*) You are planning to purchase 100 shares of preferred stock and must choose between Stock A and Stock B. Stock A pays an annual dividend of $4.50 and is currently selling for $35. Stock B pays an annual dividend of $4.25 and is selling for $36. If your required return is 12 percent, which stock should you choose?

8-2. (*Measuring growth*) The Fisayo Corporation wants to achieve a steady 7 percent growth rate. If it can achieve a 12 percent return on equity, what percentage of earnings must Fisayo retain for investment purposes?

8-3. (*Common stock valuation*) Dalton Inc. has an 11.5 percent return on equity and retains 55 percent of its earnings for reinvestment purposes. It recently paid a dividend of $3.25 and the stock is currently selling for $40.

    a. What is the growth rate for Dalton Inc.?
    b. What is the expected return for Dalton's stock?
    c. If you require a 13 percent return, should you invest in the firm?

8-4. (*Common stock valuation*) Bates Inc. pays a dividend of $1 and is currently selling for $32.50. If investors require a 12 percent return on their investment from buying Bates stock, what growth rate would Bates Inc. have to provide the investors?

8-5. (*Preferred stock valuation*) What is the value of a preferred stock when the dividend rate is 14 percent on a $100 par value? The appropriate discount rate for a stock of this risk level is 12 percent.

8-6. (*Preferred stockholder expected return*) Solitron preferred stock is selling for $42.16 per share and pays $1.95 in dividends. What is your expected rate of return if you purchase the security at the market price?

8-7. (*Preferred stockholder expected return*) You own 200 shares of Somner Resources preferred stock, which currently sells for $40 per share and pays annual dividends of $3.40 per share.

    a. What is your expected return?
    b. If you require an 8 percent return, given the current price, should you sell or buy more stock?

8-8. (*Common stock valuation*) You intend to purchase Marigo common stock at $50 per share, hold it 1 year, and then sell it after a dividend of $6 is paid. How much will the stock price have to appreciate for you to satisfy your required rate of return of 15 percent?

8-9. (*Common stockholder expected return*) Made-It common stock currently sells for $22.50 per share. The company's executives anticipate a constant growth rate of 10 percent and an end-of-year dividend of $2.

    a. What is your expected rate of return if you buy the stock for $22.50?
    b. If you require a 17 percent return, should you purchase the stock?

8-10. (*Common stock valuation*) Header Motor Inc. paid a $3.50 dividend last year. At a constant growth rate of 5 percent, what is the value of the common stock if the investors require a 20 percent rate of return?

8-11. (*Measuring growth*) Given that a firm's return on equity is 18 percent and management plans to retain 40 percent of earnings for investment purposes, what will be the firm's growth rate?

8-12. (*Common stockholder expected return*) The common stock of Zaldi Co. is selling for $32.84 per share. The stock recently paid dividends of $2.94 per share and has a projected constant growth rate of 9.5 percent. If you purchase the stock at the market price, what is your expected rate of return?

8-13. (*Common stock valuation*) Honeywag common stock is expected to pay $1.85 in dividends next year, and the market price is projected to be $42.50 per share by year-end. If investors require a rate of return of 11 percent, what is the current value of the stock?

8-14. (*Common stockholder expected return*) The market price for Hobart common stock is $43 per share. The price at the end of 1 year is expected to be $48, and dividends for next year should be $2.84. What is the expected rate of return?

8-15. (*Preferred stock valuation*) Pioneer preferred stock is selling for $33 per share in the market and pays a $3.60 annual dividend.

    a. What is the expected rate of return on the stock?

    b. If an investor's required rate of return is 10 percent, what is the value of the stock for that investor?

    c. Should the investor acquire the stock?

8-16. (*Common stock valuation*) The common stock of NCP paid $1.32 in dividends last year. Dividends are expected to grow at an 8 percent annual rate for an indefinite number of years.

    a. If NCP's current market price is $23.50 per share, what is the stock's expected rate of return?

    b. If your required rate of return is 10.5 percent, what is the value of the stock for you?

    c. Should you make the investment?

8-17. (*Preferred stock valuation*) Calculate the value of a preferred stock that pays a dividend of $6 per share if your required rate of return is 12 percent.

8-18. (*Measuring growth*) Pepperdine Inc.'s return on equity is 16 percent, and the management plans to retain 60 percent of earnings for investment purposes. What will be the firm's growth rate?

8-19. (*Common stock valuation: free cash flows*) Given the information here, calculate the shareholder value for Hokie Inc.

Cost of capital	10%
Most recent year's sales	$2,000
Debt	$ 250
Operating profit margin	12%
Assets/sales	40%
Tax rate	40%
Forecasted sales growth:	
1 to 2 years	14%
3 to 5 years	9%
6 to ∞	3%

Web Works

8-WW1. Preferred stock is frequently used by venture capitalists when investing in a private company. Go to **www.jbv.com/lessons/lesson26.htm** and learn about the terms and conditions frequently used by venture capitalists when investing using preferred stock.

8-WW2. Go to **http://finance.yahoo.com**. Click on the Mutual Fund icon at the top of the page. Then go to "Inside Mutual Fund Education." What do you learn about investing in mutual funds?

8-WW3. Go to **http://finance.yahoo.com**. Look up Chevron Texaco (ticker symbol CVX). Then click on "Key Statistics." What is the firm's dividend yield (dividend ÷ stock price)? Under the "Growth Estimates" link, what is the firm's projected growth rate for the next 5 years? Assuming your required rate of return is 10 percent, what is the Chevron Texaco stock worth to you? What is the expected rate of return for the stock? Should you buy Chevron given your required rate of return?

8-WW4. CNBC and MSN cosponsor the Web site MSN Money at **http://moneycentral. msn.com/home.asp**. The site provides all kinds of good information related both to personal and business finance. For now, go to the Web site and click on "Investing." Check out the "Financial News Center" for many of the latest financial news stories. Then choose a company of your interest and explore all the "Stock" options in the left-hand margin of the Web page.

8-WW5. Go to **http://finance.yahoo.com/**. Choose the "Investing" link, followed by the "Stocks" link. In the left margin choose "Stock Screener." In the space allowed to specify a ticker symbol, type in "YHOO," the symbol for Yahoo. What information is provided about the firm? Now choose the "Analysts Coverage" link in the left margin. Choose one of the links for a specific analyst and see what the person says about Yahoo. Now do the same for a firm of your interest.

Mini Case

You have finally saved $10,000 and are ready to make your first investment. You have the three following alternatives for investing that money:

- A CBS bond with a par value of $1,000, an interest rate of 7.625 percent, and a maturity of 10 years. The bond is selling for $986.
- Alabama Power Company preferred stock with a $50 par value and a dividend of $2.8125 per year. The stock is currently trading at $39 per share.
- Emerson Electric common stock that is selling for $80 with a par value of $5. This stock recently paid a $2.10 dividend, and the firm's earnings per share have increased from $2.40 to $4.48 in the past 5 years. An equivalent amount of growth in the dividend is expected.

Your required rates of return for these investments are 6 percent for the bond, 7 percent for the preferred stock, and 15 percent for the common stock. Using this information, answer the following questions.

    a. Calculate the value of each investment based on your required rate of return.
    b. Which investment would you select? Why?
    c. Assume Emerson Electric's managers expect an earnings downturn and a resulting decrease in growth of 3 percent. How does this affect your answers to parts 1 and 2?
    d. What required rates of return would make you indifferent to all three options?

Self-Test Solutions

SS-1. Value $(V_{ps}) = \dfrac{0.16 \times \$100}{0.12}$

$= \dfrac{\$16}{0.12}$

$= \$133.33$

SS-2. a. Expected return $= \dfrac{\text{dividend}}{\text{market price}} = \dfrac{\$3.25}{\$38.50} = 0.0844 = 8.44\%$

b. Given your 8 percent required rate of return, the stock is worth $40.62 to you:

Value $= \dfrac{\text{dividend}}{\text{required rate of return}} = \dfrac{\$3.25}{0.08} = \$40.63$

Because the expected rate of return (8.44%) is greater than your required rate of return (8%) or because the current market price ($38.50) is less than $40.63, the stock is undervalued and you should buy.

SS-3. Value $(V_{ps}) = \dfrac{\text{dividend}}{\text{required rate of return}} = \dfrac{\$2.75}{0.09} = \$30.56$

SS-4. Value $(V_{cs}) = \dfrac{\text{last year dividend } (1 + \text{growth rate})}{\text{required rate of return} - \text{growth rate}}$

$= \dfrac{\$1.32(1.07)}{0.11 - 0.07}$

$= \$35.31$

SS-5. a. Expected rate of return $(\bar{k}_{cs}) = \dfrac{\text{dividend in year 1}}{\text{market price}} + \text{growth rate}$

$$\bar{k}_{cs} = \dfrac{\$2.50}{\$23.00} + 0.105 = 0.2137$$

$$\bar{k}_{cs} = 21.37\%$$

b. $V_{cs} = \dfrac{\$2.50}{0.17 - 0.105} = \$38.46$

The expected rate of return exceeds your required rate of return, which means that the value of the security to you is greater than the current market price. Thus, you should buy the stock.

PART 3

Investment in Long-Term Assets

➤ Harken Energy is an energy company located in Houston, Texas. The firm explores for oil and gas in the southwestern part of the United States and in Central and South America.

Jim Denny supervises the technical analysis for evaluating exploration prospects, acquisitions, and divestitures. In a conversation with Denny, he talked about the capital-budgeting process at Harken.

In the oil and gas industry, the heart of capital budgeting requires a strong program for ranking drilling opportunities based on their potential risk and reward. The decisions made based on our capital-budgeting analysis greatly affect the long-term welfare of the firm—not to mention the value for the firm's shareholders.

When we evaluate drilling prospects in oil fields where we already have experience, we use a "deterministic approach." We essentially use a decision tree to assess the likelihood of high, medium, and low oil production—and resulting cash flows. For instance, we consider such factors as drilling risk, pricing, and infrastructure. The decision tree also incorporates the chance of a dry hole or results that

are economically unattractive. The probabilities assigned to the different possible events are a function of a number of technical factors, such as the structural formation, the organic matter from which the oil and gas will originate, and the ability of rock to store and flow hydrocarbons.

When we are considering drilling in geographical areas that are unfamiliar to us, we use a "probabilistic" approach. Here we build a probability distribution of outcomes. We then calculate what must happen for the drilling investment to be economically rewarding and compare these numbers against the probability distribution. Then if, for example, there is only a 20% chance of making the targeted numbers, we would reject the investment.

Once we have evaluated individual prospects, we then have to decide on a portfolio of investments, given the size of the total drilling budget. A primary concern is not running out of money before the drilling plan has been executed. To make this decision requires the assessment of a lot of intangible factors that are qualitative in nature. A decision is made and then we begin the drilling program.

CHAPTER 9
CAPITAL-BUDGETING
TECHNIQUES AND
PRACTICE

CHAPTER 10
CASH FLOWS AND
OTHER TOPICS IN
CAPITAL BUDGETING

CHAPTER 11
THE COST OF CAPITAL

❧ LEARNING OBJECTIVES ❧

After reading this chapter, you should be able to:

1. Discuss the difficulty encountered in finding profitable projects in competitive markets and the importance of the search.

2. Determine whether a new project should be accepted or rejected using the payback period, the net present value, the profitability index, and the internal rate of return.

3. Explain how the capital-budgeting decision process changes when a dollar limit is placed on the capital budget.

4. Discuss the problems encountered in project ranking.

5. Explain the importance of ethical considerations in capital-budgeting decisions.

6. Discuss the trends in the use of different capital-budgeting criteria.

7. Explain how foreign markets provide opportunities for finding new capital-budgeting projects.

CHAPTER 9

Capital-Budgeting Techniques and Practice

Back in 1955, the Walt Disney Company changed the face of entertainment when it opened Disneyland, its first theme park in Anaheim, California, at a cost of $17.5 million. Since then Disney has opened theme parks in Orlando, Florida, Tokyo, Japan, Paris, France, and in September 2005, 香港迪士尼樂園, or Hong Kong Disneyland was opened. This $3.5 billion project, with much of that money provided by the Hong Kong government, was opened in hopes of reaching what has largely been an untapped Chinese market. For Disney, a market this size was simply too large to pass up.

Disney decided not to skimp on anything. In fact, when Hong Kong Disneyland opened, it was wildly spectacular, with more than 250,000 annual flowering plants, 15,000 canopy trees, plenty of rides and attractions, and, as its centerpiece, Sleeping Beauty's castle, complete with its trademark blue-pointed turret. And that's just the start. Through 2008, more attractions, including the Pirates of the Caribbean, It's a Small World, Peter Pan's Flight, Big Thunder Mountain Railroad, and the Haunted Mansion, will be added.

For Disney, this is an important move. Keeping its theme parks and resorts division healthy is extremely important because this division accounts for over one-quarter of the company's revenues. Certainly, there are opportunities for Disney in China; with a population of 1.26 billion people, it accounts for 20 percent of the entire world's total population. In fact, in 2006, local officials in Shanghai sought approval from the central government to allow Disney to build a theme park there.

To say the least, the stakes involved with an investment of this size are so large that the outcome of this decision will have a major effect on Disney's future. Whether this was a good or a bad decision, only time will tell. The question we will ask in this chapter is: How did Disney go about making this decision to enter the Chinese market and build Hong Kong Disneyland? The answer is that the company did it using the decision criteria we will examine in this chapter.

This chapter is actually the first of two chapters dealing with the process of decision making with respect to making investments in fixed assets—that is, should a proposed project be accepted or rejected? We will refer to this process as capital budgeting. In this chapter we will look at the methods used to evaluate new projects. In deciding whether to accept a new project, we will focus on free cash flows. Free cash flows represent the benefits generated from accepting a capital-budgeting proposal. We will assume we know what level of free cash flows is generated by a project and will work on determining whether that project should be accepted. In the following chapter, we will examine what a free cash flow is and how we measure it. We will also look at how risk enters into this process.

FINDING PROFITABLE PROJECTS

Objective **1**

Discuss the difficulty encountered in finding profitable projects in competitive markets and the importance of the search.

capital budgeting the process of decision making with respect to investments made in fixed assets—that is, should a proposed project be accepted or rejected.

Without question it is easier to evaluate profitable projects or investments in fixed assets, a process referred to as **capital budgeting**, than it is to find them. In competitive markets, generating ideas for profitable projects is extremely difficult. The competition is brisk for new profitable projects, and once they have been uncovered, competitors generally rush in, pushing down prices and profits. For this reason a firm must have a systematic strategy for generating capital-budgeting projects based on these ideas. Without this flow of new projects and ideas, the firm cannot grow or even survive for long. Instead, it will be forced to live off the profits from existing projects with limited lives. So where do these ideas come from for new products, or for ways to improve existing products or make them more profitable? The answer is from inside the firm—from everywhere inside the firm, in fact.

Typically, a firm has a research and development (R&D) department that searches for ways of improving existing products or finding new products. These ideas may come from within the R&D department or may be based on referral ideas from executives, sales personnel, anyone in the firm, or even customers. For example, at Ford Motor Company before the 1990s, ideas for product improvements had typically been generated in Ford's R&D department. Unfortunately, this strategy was not enough to keep Ford from losing much of its market share to Japanese competitors. In an attempt to cut costs and improve product quality, Ford moved from strict reliance on an R&D department to seeking the input of employees at all levels for new ideas. Bonuses are now provided to workers for their cost-cutting suggestions, and assembly-line personnel who can see the production process from a hands-on point of view are now brought into the hunt for new projects. The effect on Ford has been positive and significant. Although not all suggested projects prove to be profitable, many new ideas generated from within the firm turn out to be good ones.

Another way an existing product can be applied to a new market is illustrated by Kimberly-Clark, the manufacturer of Huggies disposable diapers. The company took its existing diaper product line, made the diapers more waterproof, and began marketing them as disposable swim pants called Little Swimmers. Sara Lee Hosiery boosted its market by expanding its offerings to appeal to more customers and more customer needs. For example, Sara Lee Hosiery introduced Sheer Energy pantyhose for support, Just My Size pantyhose aimed at larger-women sizes, and Silken Mist pantyhose in shades better suited for African American women.

Big investments such as these go a long way toward determining the future of the company, but they don't always work as planned. Just look at Burger King's development of its new french fries. It looked like a slam dunk great idea. Burger King took an uncooked french fry and coated it with a layer of starch that made it crunchier and kept it hot longer. The

Remember Your Principles

The fact that profitable projects are difficult to find relates directly to **Principle 5: The Curse of Competitive Markets—Why It's Hard to Find Exceptionally Profitable Projects**. When we introduced that principle, we stated that successful investments depend on reducing competition by creating barriers to entry through either product differentiation or cost advantages. The key to locating profitable projects is to understand how and where they exist.

company spent over $70 million on the new fries, and even gave away 15 million orders on a "Free Fryday." Unfortunately, the product didn't go down with consumers, and Burger King was left to eat the loss. Given the size of the investment we're talking about, you can see why such a decision is so important.

Did You Get It?

1. Why is it so difficult to find an exceptionally profitable project?
2. Why is the search for new profitable projects so important?

CAPITAL-BUDGETING DECISION CRITERIA

As we explained, when deciding whether to accept a new project, we focus on cash flows because cash flows represent the benefits generated from accepting a capital-budgeting proposal. In this chapter we assume a given cash flow is generated by a project and work on determining whether that project should be accepted.

We consider four commonly used criteria for determining the acceptability of investment proposals. The first one is the least sophisticated in that it does not incorporate the time value of money into its calculations; the other three do take it into account. For the time being, the problem of incorporating risk into the capital-budgeting decision is ignored. This issue is examined in Chapter 10. In addition, we assume that the appropriate discount rate, required rate of return, or cost of capital is given. (The determination of the cost of capital is the topic of Chapter 11.)

Objective **2**

Determine whether a new project should be accepted or rejected using the payback period, the net present value, the profitability index, and the internal rate of return.

The Payback Period

The **payback period** is the *number of years needed to recover the initial cash outlay related to an investment*. Because this criterion measures how quickly the project will return its original investment, it deals with free cash flows, which measure the true timing of the benefits, rather than accounting profits. Unfortunately, it also ignores the time value of money and does not discount these free cash flows back to the present. Rather, the accept/reject criterion centers on whether the project's payback period is less than or equal to the firm's maximum desired payback period. For example, if a firm's maximum desired payback period is 3 years, and an investment proposal requires an initial cash outlay of $10,000 and yields the following set of annual cash flows, what is its payback period? Should the project be accepted?

payback period The number of years it takes to recapture a project's initial outlay.

YEAR	FREE CASH FLOW
1	$2,000
2	4,000
3	3,000
4	3,000
5	1,000

In this case, after 3 years the firm will have recaptured $9,000 on an initial investment of $10,000, leaving $1,000 of the initial investment to be recouped. During the fourth year $3,000 will be returned from this investment, and, assuming it will flow into the firm at a constant rate over the year, it will take one-third of the year ($1,000/$3,000) to recapture the remaining $1,000. Thus, the payback period on this project is 3⅓ years, which is more than the desired payback period. Using the payback period criterion, the firm would reject this project without even considering the $1,000 cash flow in year 5.

Although the payback period is used frequently, it does have some rather obvious drawbacks that are best demonstrated through the use of an example. Consider two investment projects, A and B, which involve an initial cash outlay of $10,000 each and produce the annual cash flows shown in Table 9-1. Both projects have a payback period of 2 years; therefore, in terms of the payback criterion both are equally acceptable. However, if we had our choice, it is clear we

TABLE 9-1 Payback Period Example		
	PROJECTS	
	A	B
Initial cash outlay	−$10,000	−$10,000
Annual free cash inflows		
Year 1	$6,000	$ 5,000
2	4,000	5,000
3	3,000	0
4	2,000	0
5	1,000	0

would select A over B, for at least two reasons. First, regardless of what happens after the payback period, project A returns more of our initial investment to us faster within the payback period ($6,000 in year 1 versus $5,000). Thus, because there is a time value of money, the cash flows occurring within the payback period should not be weighted equally, as they are. In addition, all cash flows that occur after the payback period are ignored. This violates the principle that investors desire more in the way of benefits rather than less—a principle that is difficult to deny, especially when we are talking about money.

Although these deficiencies limit the value of the payback period as a tool for investment evaluation, the payback period has several positive features. First, it deals with cash flows, as opposed to accounting profits, and therefore focuses on the true timing of the project's benefits and costs, even though it does not adjust the cash flows for the time value of money. Second, it is easy to visualize, quickly understood, and easy to calculate. Third, the payback period may make sense for the capital-constrained firm, that is, the firm that needs funds and is having problems raising additional money. These firms need cash flows early on to allow them to continue in business and to take advantage of future investments. Finally, although the payback period has serious deficiencies, it is often used as a rough screening device to eliminate projects whose returns do not materialize until later years. This method emphasizes the earliest returns, which in all likelihood are less uncertain, and provides for the liquidity needs of the firm. Although its advantages are certainly significant, its disadvantages severely limit its value as a discriminating capital-budgeting criterion.

The Net Present Value

net present value (*NPV*)
the present value of an investment's annual free cash flows less the investment's initial outlay.

The **net present value (*NPV*)** of an investment proposal is equal to the *present value of its annual free cash flows less the investment's initial outlay.* The net present value can be expressed as follows:

$$NPV = (\text{present value of all the future annual free cash flows}) - (\text{the initial cash outlay})$$

$$= \frac{FCF_1}{(1 + k)^1} + \frac{FCF_2}{(1 + k)^2} + \ldots + \frac{FCF_n}{(1 + k)^n} - IO \qquad (9\text{-}1)$$

where FCF_t = the annual free cash flow in time period t (this can take on either positive or negative values)

k = the appropriate discount rate; that is, the required rate of return or cost of capital[1]

IO = the initial cash outlay

n = the project's expected life

A project's *NPV* measures of the net value of the investment proposal in terms of today's dollars. Because all cash flows are discounted back to the present, comparing the difference between the present value of the annual cash flows and the investment outlay does not violate the time value of money assumption. The difference between the present value of the

---

[1] The required rate of return or cost of capital is the rate of return necessary to justify raising funds to finance the project or, alternatively, the rate of return necessary to maintain the firm's current market price per share. These terms are defined in greater detail in Chapter 11.

Finance at Work

FINDING PROFITABLE PROJECTS IN COMPETITIVE MARKETS—CREATING THEM BY DEVELOPING A COST ADVANTAGE

As we learned in **Principle 5: The Curse of Competitive Markets**, it is extremely difficult to find exceptionally profitable projects. We also noted that if you have the ability to produce at a cost below the competition, there is the opportunity for exceptionally large profits. Federal Express is one example of a company that has done exactly this.

Federal Express redefined the production-cost chain for rapid delivery of small parcels. Traditional firms such as Emery and Airborne Express operated by collecting freight packages of varying sizes, shipping them to their destination points via air freight and commercial airlines, and then delivering them to the addressee. Federal Express opted to focus only on the market for overnight delivery of small packages and documents. These were collected at local drop points during the late afternoon hours; flown on company-owned planes during early evening hours to a central hub in Memphis, Tennessee, where from 11 P.M. to 3 A.M. each night all parcels were sorted; and then reloaded on company planes and flown during the early morning hours to their destination points, from which they were delivered that morning by company personnel using company trucks. The cost structure achieved by Federal Express was low enough to permit guaranteed overnight delivery of a small parcel anywhere in the United States for a price as low as $11.

Remember Your Principles

The final three capital-budgeting criteria all incorporate **Principle 2: The Time Value of Money—A Dollar Received Today Is Worth More Than a Dollar Received in the Future** in their calculations. If we are to make rational business decisions, we must recognize that money has a time value. In examining the following three capital-budgeting techniques, you will notice that this principle is the driving force behind each of them.

annual cash flows and the initial outlay determines the net value of accepting the investment proposal in terms of today's dollars. Whenever the project's NPV is greater than or equal to zero, we will accept the project; whenever the NPV is negative, we will reject the project. If the project's NPV is zero, then it returns the required rate of return and should be accepted. This accept/reject criterion is illustrated here:

$NPV \geq 0.0$: accept
$NPV < 0.0$: reject

The following example illustrates the use of NPV as a capital-budgeting criterion.

➤ EXAMPLE

Ski-Doo is considering new machinery that would reduce manufacturing costs associated with its Mach Z snowmobile for which the free cash flows are shown in Table 9-2. If the firm has a 12 percent required rate of return, the present value of the free cash flow is $47,675, as calculated in Table 9-3. Subtracting the $40,000 initial outlay leaves an NPV of $7,675. Because this value is greater than zero, the NPV criterion indicates that the project should be accepted.

Note in the Ski-Doo example that the worth of the NPV calculation is a function of the accuracy of the cash flow predictions.

The NPV criterion is the capital-budgeting decision tool we find most favorable for several reasons. First of all, it deals with free cash flows rather than accounting profits. In this regard it is sensitive to the true timing of the benefits resulting from the project. Moreover, recognizing the time value of money allows the benefits and costs to be compared in a logical manner. Finally, because projects are accepted only if a positive NPV is associated with them,

TABLE 9-2 Ski-Doo's Investment in New Machinery and Its Associated Free Cash Flows

	FREE CASH FLOW
Initial outlay	−$40,000
Inflow year 1	15,000
Inflow year 2	14,000
Inflow year 3	13,000
Inflow year 4	12,000
Inflow year 5	11,000

TABLE 9-3 Calculating the *NPV* of Ski-Doo's Investment in New Machinery

	PRESENT VALUE			
	FREE CASH FLOW	×FACTOR AT 12 PERCENT	=	PRESENT VALUE
Inflow year 1	$15,000	$\times$ $\dfrac{1}{(1+.12)^1}$	=	$ 13,393
Inflow year 2	14,000	$\times$ $\dfrac{1}{(1+.12)^2}$	=	11,161
Inflow year 3	13,000	$\times$ $\dfrac{1}{(1+.12)^3}$	=	9,253
Inflow year 4	12,000	$\times$ $\dfrac{1}{(1+.12)^4}$	=	7,626
Inflow year 5	11,000	$\times$ $\dfrac{1}{(1+.12)^5}$	=	6,242
Present value of free cash flows				$ 47,675
Initial outlay				−40,000
Net present value				$ 7,675

the acceptance of a project using this criterion will increase the value of the firm, which is consistent with the goal of maximizing the shareholders' wealth.

The disadvantage of the *NPV* method stems from the need for detailed, long-term forecasts of the free cash flows accruing from the project's acceptance. Despite this drawback, the *NPV* is the most theoretically correct criterion that we will examine. The following example provides an additional illustration of its application.

➤ EXAMPLE

A firm is considering the purchase of a new computer system, which will cost $30,000 initially, to aid in credit billing and inventory management. The free cash flows resulting from this project are provided in Table 9-4. The required rate of return demanded by the firm is 10 percent. To determine the system's *NPV*, the 3-year $15,000 cash flow annuity is first discounted back to the present at 10 percent. The present value of the $15,000 annuity can be found using a calculator (as is done in the margin), using the relationship,

$$PV = PMT \left[\frac{1 - \dfrac{1}{(1+i)^n}}{i} \right]$$, or from Appendix E in the back of this book. Using the

mathematical relationship we get:

$$PV = \$15,000 \left[\frac{1 - \dfrac{1}{(1+.10)^3}}{.10} \right] = \$15,000 \,(2.4869 = \$37,303\,)$$

Alternatively, from Appendix E in the back of this book, we find that $PVIFA_{10\%,\,3\,\text{yr}}$ is 2.487. Thus, the present value of this $15,000 annuity is $37,305 (notice the slight rounding error).

TABLE 9-4 The Initial Outlay and Free Cash Flows Associated with a New Computer System

	FREE CASH FLOW
Initial outlay	−$30,000
Inflow year 1	15,000
Inflow year 2	15,000
Inflow year 3	15,000

Seeing that the cash inflows have been discounted back to the present, they can now be compared with the initial outlay because both of the flows are now stated in terms of today's dollars. Subtracting the initial outlay ($30,000) from the present value of the cash inflows ($37,305), we find that the system's *NPV* is $7,305. Because the *NPV* on this project is positive, the project should be accepted.

Using Spreadsheets to Calculate the Net Present Value

Although we can calculate the *NPV* by hand, it is more commonly done with the help of a spreadsheet. Just as with the keystroke calculations on a financial calculator, a spreadsheet can make easy work of *NPV* calculations. The only real glitch here is that Excel, along with most other spreadsheets, calculates the present value of only the future cash flows and ignores the initial outlay in its *NPV* calculations. Sounds strange? Well, it is. It is essentially just a carryforward of an error in one of the first spreadsheets. That means that the actual *NPV* is the Excel-calculated *NPV*, minus the initial outlay:

Actual *NPV* = Excel-calculated *NPV* − initial outlay

This can be input into a spreadsheet cell as:

= NPV (rate, inflow 1, inflow 2, . . . inflow 29)-initial outlay

Looking back at the Ski-Doo example in Table 9-2, we can use a spreadsheet to calculate the net present value of the investment in machinery as long as we remember to subtract the initial outlay in order to get the correct number.

	A	B	C	D	E
2	**Spreadsheets and NPV − the Ski−Doo Example**				
3					
4	Looking at the example in Table 9.2, given a 12 percent				
5	discount rate and the following after−tax cash flows, the				
6	Net Present Value could be calculated as follows:				
7					
8			rate (i) =	12%	
9					
10			Year	Cash Flow	
11			Initial Outlay	($40,000)	
12			1	$15,000	
13			2	$14,000	
14			3	$13,000	
15			4	$12,000	
16			5	$11,000	
17					
18		NPV =	$7,674.63		
19					
20	Excel formula: =NPV(rate,inflow 1, inflow2, ...,inflow 29)				
21					
22	Again, from the Excel NPV calculation we must then				
23	subtract out the initial outlay in order to calculate the				
24	actual NPV.				
25					
26					
27					

Entered value in cell c15:
=NPV(D8,D12:D16)−40000

Can You Do It?

DETERMINING THE NPV OF A PROJECT

Determine the *NPV* for a new project that costs $7,000, is expected to produce 10 years' worth of annual free cash flows of $1,000 per year, and the required rate of return on this project is 5 percent.

(The solution can be found on page 267.)

Across the Hall

MARKETING'S CAPITAL-BUDGETING ROLE

When it comes to capital-budgeting decisions, marketing and finance have to work together to make good decisions. To do this, you, as a marketing major, have to know how your input is going to be used, how the capital-budgeting decision process works, and how the firm creates wealth. Capital budgeting doesn't just involve coming up with great ideas. It also involves taking those ideas and developing them into a product that consumers are going to embrace—a product that creates wealth for the firm. Whether that good idea makes it through the capital-budgeting process and becomes a new product depends on whether the present value of the expected benefits, measured by the free cash inflows, outweighs the present value of the costs. In a marketing position, you'll be working on pricing, promotional, and sales strategies that help sell lots of the product. But great sales numbers aren't the goal—the goal is to create wealth for the company. In effect, your pricing, promotional, design, and sales strategies will be evaluated in light of the net present value capital-budgeting technique we described earlier. Unfortunately, a mistake in any one of these areas can bring down an otherwise great product.

Marketing a new product is complicated enough without understanding how that new product will create wealth for the company. But with a better understanding of how capital-budgeting decisions are made, you as a marketer will be better able to understand that great sales or excellent quality alone will not guarantee success. There is an almost unlimited list of examples of excellent new products that turned out to be flops and actually destroyed wealth for companies. For example, Gillette's "For Oily Hair Only" shampoo failed not because it wasn't a good product but because its name reminded consumers of something they would rather not be reminded of—that they had oily hair. Ben-Gay Aspirin, Exxon Fruit Punch, Smucker's Ketchup, and Singles (Gerber's food for adults with flavors such as blueberry delight, pureed sweet and sour pork, and chicken Madeira) failed because although they all might have been excellent products, consumers simply couldn't get past the brand names they were associated with and wouldn't buy them. Perhaps with a better understanding of how the firm creates wealth and how the capital-budgeting process actually works, marketers could have avoided these types of mistakes.

The Profitability Index (Benefit–Cost Ratio)

profitability index (*PI*) or benefit–cost ratio the ratio of the present value of an investment's future free cash flows to the investment's initial outlay.

The **profitability index (*PI*), or benefit–cost ratio**, is the *ratio of the present value of the future free cash flows to the initial outlay*. Although the *NPV* investment criterion gives a measure of the absolute dollar desirability of a project, the profitability index provides a relative measure of an investment proposal's desirability—that is, the ratio of the present value of its future net benefits to its initial cost. The profitability index can be expressed as follows:

$$PI = \frac{\text{present value of all the future annual free cash flows}}{\text{initial cash outlay}}$$

$$= \frac{\dfrac{FCF_1}{(1+k)^1} + \dfrac{FCF_2}{(1+k)^2} + \cdots + \dfrac{FCF_n}{(1+k)^n}}{IO} \tag{9-2}$$

where FCF_t = the annual free cash flow in time period t (this can take on either positive or negative values)

k = the appropriate discount rate; that is, the required rate of return or cost of capital

IO = the initial cash outlay

n = the project's expected life

How Did You Do?

DETERMINING THE NPV OF A PROJECT

You were asked to determine the *NPV* for a project with an initial outlay of $7,000 and free cash flows in years 1 through 10 of $1,000, given a 5 percent required rate of return.

NPV = (present value of all future free cash flows) − (initial outlay)

1. **Using the Mathematical Formulas.**

   Step 1. Determine the present value of the future cash flows.
   Substituting these example values in equation (5-9a), we find

$$PV = \$1,000 \left[\frac{1 - \dfrac{1}{(1 + .05)^{10}}}{.05} \right]$$

$$= \$1,000 \left[(1 - 1/1.62889463)/.05 \right]$$
$$= \$1,000 \left[(1 - .61391325)/.05 \right]$$
$$= \$1,000 \,(7.72173493) = \$7,721.73$$

   Step 2. Subtract the initial outlay from the future value of the free cash flows.

   $$\begin{array}{r} \$7,721.73 \\ -\ \underline{\$7,000.00} \\ \$\ \ \ 721.73 \end{array}$$

2. **Using the Time Value of Money Tables.** First, solving for the present value of all future cash flows:

   Step 1. Determine the present value of the future cash flows.
   Determining the value for the *PVIFA*$_{5\%, 10yrs}$ from Appendix E, row n = 10, column i = 5%, and substituting it in equation (5-9b), we get:

   $$PV = PMT\,(PVIFA_{5\%,\ 10yrs}) = \$1,000(7.722) = \$7,722$$

   Step 2. Subtract the initial outlay from the future value of the free cash flows.

   $$\begin{array}{r} -\$7,722 \\ \underline{\$7,000} \\ \$\ \ \ 722 \end{array}$$

3. **Using a Financial Calculator.**

   Step 1. Determine the present value of the future cash flows.

Data Input	Function Key
10	N
5	I/Y
1,000	PMT
0	FV

Function Key	Answer
CPT	
PV	−7,721.73

   Step 2. Subtract the initial outlay from future value of the free cash flows.

   $$\begin{array}{r} \$7,721.73 \\ -\underline{\$7,000.00} \\ \$\ \ \ 721.73 \end{array}$$

   Alternatively, you could use the CF button on your calculator (using a TI BA II Plus).

Data and Key Input	Display
CF ; 2nd ; CF/C	CF0 = 0. (this clears out any past cash flows)
−7,000; ENTER	CF0 = −7,000.
↓ ; 1,000; ENTER	C01 = 1,000.
↓ ; 10; ENTER	F01 = 10.00
NPV	I = 0.
5; ENTER	I = 5.00
↓	NPV = 0.
CPT	NPV = 721.73

The decision criterion is to accept the project if the *PI* is greater than or equal to 1.00 and to reject the project if the *PI* is less than 1.00.

   PI ≥ 1.0: accept
   PI < 1.0: reject

Looking closely at this criterion, we see that it yields the same accept/reject decision as the *NPV* criterion. Whenever the present value of the project's free cash flows is greater than the initial cash outlay, the project's *NPV* will be positive, signaling a decision to accept. When this is true, then the project's *PI* will also be greater than 1 because the present value of the free cash flows (the *PI*'s numerator) is greater than the initial outlay (the *PI*'s denominator). Thus, these two decision criteria will always yield the same decision, although they will not necessarily rank acceptable projects in the same order. This problem of conflicting ranking is dealt with at a later point.

Because the *NPV* and *PI* criteria are essentially the same, they have the same advantages over the other criteria examined. Both employ free cash flows, recognize the timing of the cash flows, and are consistent with the goal of maximizing shareholders' wealth. The major disadvantage of the *PI* criterion, similar to the *NPV* criterion, is that it requires long, detailed free cash flow forecasts.

➤ EXAMPLE

A firm with a 10 percent required rate of return is considering investing in a new machine with an expected life of 6 years. The free cash flows resulting from this investment are given in Table 9-5. Discounting the project's future net free cash flows back to the present yields a present value of $53,682; dividing this value by the initial outlay of $50,000 yields a profitability index of 1.0736, as shown in Table 9-6. This tells us that the present value of the future benefits accruing from this project is 1.0736 times the level of the initial outlay. Because the profitability index is greater than 1.0, the project should be accepted.

TABLE 9-5   The Free Cash Flows Associated with an Investment in New Machinery

	FREE CASH FLOW
Initial outlay	−$50,000
Inflow year 1	15,000
Inflow year 2	8,000
Inflow year 3	10,000
Inflow year 4	12,000
Inflow year 5	14,000
Inflow year 6	16,000

TABLE 9-6   Calculating the *PI* of an Investment in New Machinery

	FREE CASH FLOW ×	PRESENT VALUE FACTOR AT 10 PERCENT =	PRESENT VALUE
Inflow year 1	15,000 ×	$\dfrac{1}{(1 + .10)^1}$ =	13,636
Inflow year 2	8,000 ×	$\dfrac{1}{(1 + .10)^2}$ =	6,612
Inflow year 3	10,000 ×	$\dfrac{1}{(1 + .10)^3}$ =	7,513
Inflow year 4	12,000 ×	$\dfrac{1}{(1 + .10)^4}$ =	8,196
Inflow year 5	14,000 ×	$\dfrac{1}{(1 + .10)^5}$ =	8,693
Inflow year 6	16,000 ×	$\dfrac{1}{(1 + .10)^6}$ =	9,032

$$PI = \frac{\dfrac{FCF_1}{(1 + k)^1} + \dfrac{FCF_2}{(1 + k)^2} + \cdots + \dfrac{FCF_n}{(1 + k)^n}}{IO}$$

$$= \frac{\$13,636 + \$6,612 + \$7,513 + \$8,196 + \$8,693 + \$9,032}{\$50,000}$$

$$= \frac{\$53,682}{\$50,000}$$

$$= 1.0736$$

The Internal Rate of Return

The **internal rate of return (IRR)** attempts to answer the question, what rate of return does this project earn? For computational purposes, the internal rate of return is defined as *the discount rate that equates the present value of the project's free cash flows with the project's initial cash outlay*. Mathematically, the internal rate of return is defined as the value *IRR* in the following equation:

IRR = the rate of return that equates the present value of the project's free cash flows with the initial outlay

$$IO = \frac{FCF_1}{(1 + IRR\%)^1} + \frac{FCF_2}{(1 + IRR\%)^2} + \cdots + \frac{FCF_n}{(1 + IRR\%)^n} \qquad (9\text{-}3)$$

where FCF_t = the annual free cash flow in time period t (this can take on either positive or negative values)

IO = the initial cash outlay

n = the project's expected life

IRR = the project's internal rate of return

In effect, the *IRR* is analogous to the concept of the yield to maturity for bonds, which was examined in Chapter 6. In other words, a project's *IRR* is simply the rate of return that the project earns.

The decision criterion is to accept the project if the *IRR* is greater than or equal to the required rate of return. We reject the project if its *IRR* is less than the required rate of return. This accept/reject criterion can be stated as

$IRR \geq$ required rate of return: accept

$IRR <$ required rate of return: reject

If the *IRR* on a project is equal to the shareholders' required rate of return, then the project should be accepted because the firm is earning the rate that its shareholders are demanding. By contrast, accepting a project with an *IRR* below the investors' required rate of return will decrease the firm's stock price.

If the *NPV* is positive, then the *IRR* must be greater than the required rate of return, k. Thus, all the discounted cash flow criteria are consistent and will result in similar accept/reject decisions. One other disadvantage of the *IRR* relative to the *NPV* deals with the implied reinvestment rate assumptions made by these two methods. The *NPV* assumes that cash flows over the life of the project are reinvested back in projects that earn the required rate of return. That is, if we have a mining project with a 10-year expected life that produces a $100,000 cash flow at the end of the second year, the *NPV* technique assumes that this $100,000 is reinvested over years 3 though 10 at the required rate of return. The use of the *IRR*, however, implies that cash flows over the life of the project can be reinvested at the *IRR*. Thus, if the mining project we just looked at has a 40 percent *IRR*, the use of the *IRR* implies that the $100,000 cash flow that is received at the end of year 2 could be reinvested at 40 percent over the remaining life of the project. In effect, *the NPV method implicitly assumes that cash flows over the life of the project can be reinvested at the project's required rate of return, whereas the use of the IRR method implies that these cash flows could be reinvested at the IRR.* The better assumption is the one made by the *NPV*—that the cash flows can be reinvested at the required rate of return because they can either be (1) returned in the form of dividends to shareholders, who demand the required rate of return on their investments, or (2) reinvested in a new investment project. If these cash flows are invested in a new project, then they are simply substituting for external funding on which the required rate of return is again demanded. Thus, the opportunity cost of these funds is the required rate of return.

The bottom line of all this is that the *NPV* method makes the best reinvestment rate assumption, and, as such, is superior to the *IRR* method. Why should we care which method is used if both methods result in similar accept/reject decisions? The answer, as we will see, is that although they may result in the same accept/reject decision, they may rank projects differently in terms of desirability.

internal rate of return (IRR) the rate of return that the project earns. For computational purposes, the internal rate of return is defined as the discount rate that equates the present value of the project's free cash flows with the project's initial cash outlay.

Computing the *IRR* with a Financial Calculator

With today's calculators, determining an *IRR* is merely a matter of a few keystrokes. In Chapter 5, whenever we were solving time value of money problems for *i*, we were really solving for the *IRR*. For instance, in the example on page XXX, when we solved for the rate at which $100 must be compounded annually for it to grow to $179.10 in 10 years, we were actually solving for that problem's *IRR*. Thus, with financial calculators we need only input the initial outlay, the cash flows, and their timing and then input the function key "I/Y" or the "IRR" button to calculate the *IRR*. On some calculators it is necessary to press the compute key, CPT, before pressing the function key to be calculated.

Computing the *IRR* with a Spreadsheet

Calculating the *IRR* using a spreadsheet is extremely simple. Once the cash flows have been entered on the spreadsheet, all you need to do is input the Excel *IRR* formula into a spreadsheet cell and let the spreadsheet do the calculations for you. Of course, at least one of the cash flows must be positive and at least one must be negative. The *IRR* formula to be input into a spreadsheet cell is: **=IRR(values)**, where "values" is simply the range of cells in which the cash flows are stored.

	A	B	C	D	E
1					
2		**Spreadsheets and the IRR**			
3					
4	The three investment proposals just examined have the following				
5	cash flows:				
6					
7	Year	Project A	Project B	Project C	
8	Initial Outlay	($10,000)	($10,000)	($10,000)	
9	1	3,362	0	1,000	
10	2	3,362	0	3,000	
11	3	3,362	0	6,000	
12	4	3,362	13,605	7,000	
13					
14	IRR=	13.001%	8.000%	19.040%	
15					
16	Excel Formula: =IRR(values)				
17					
18	where:				
19	values =	the range of cells where the cash flows are stored.			
20		Note: There must be at least one positive and one			
21		negative cash flow.			
22					
23	Entered value in cell B14:=IRR(B8:B12)				
24	Entered value in cell C14:=IRR(C8:C12)				
25	Entered value in cell D14:=IRR(D8:D12)				
26					

Entered value in cell B14:=IRR(B8:B12)
Entered value in cell C14:=IRR(C8:C12)
Entered value in cell D14:=IRR(D8:D12)

Computing the *IRR* for Even Cash Flows Using the TVM Tables

In this section we are going to put our calculators aside and obtain a better understanding of the *IRR* by examining the mathematical process of calculating internal rates of return.

The calculation of a project's *IRR* can be either very simple or relatively complicated. As an example of a straightforward solution, assume that a firm with a required rate of return of 10 percent is considering a project that involves an initial outlay of $45,555. If the investment is undertaken, the free cash flows are expected to be $15,000 per annum over the project's 4-year life. In this case, the internal rate of return is equal to *IRR* in the following equation:

$$\$45,555 = \frac{\$15,000}{(1 + IRR)^1} + \frac{\$15,000}{(1 + IRR)^2} + \frac{\$15,000}{(1 + IRR)^3} + \frac{\$15,000}{(1 + IRR)^4}$$

From our discussion of the present value of an annuity in Chapter 5, we know that this equation can be reduced to

$$\$45,555 = \$15,000 \ (PVIFA_{i, \ 4 \ yr})$$

which can be solved using Appendix E. Dividing both sides by $15,000, this becomes

$$3.037 = PVIFA_{i, \ 4 \ yr}$$

Hence, we are looking for $PVIFA_{i, \ 4 \ yr}$ of 3.037 in the 4-year row of Appendix E. This value occurs when i equals 12 percent, which means that 12 percent is the IRR for the investment. Therefore, because 12 percent is greater than the 10 percent required return, the project should be accepted.

Computing the *IRR* for Uneven Cash Flows

Unfortunately, although solving for the IRR is quite easy when using a financial calculator or spreadsheet, it can be solved directly in the tables only when the future free cash flows are in the form of an annuity or a single payment. With a calculator the process is simple: One need only key in the initial cash outlay, the cash flows, and their timing and press the "IRR" button. Let's take a look at how you might solve a problem with uneven cash flows using a financial calculator. Every calculator works a bit differently, so you'll want to be familiar with how to input data into yours, but that being said, they all work essentially the same way. As you'd expect, you will enter all the cash flows, then solve for the project's IRR. With a Texas Instruments BA II Plus calculator, CFo indicates the initial outlay, which you'll want to give a negative value; C01 is the first free cash flow; and F01 is the number of years in which the first free cash flow appears. Thus, if the free cash flows in years 1, 2, and 3 are all $1,000, then F01 = 3. C02 then becomes the second free cash flow, and F02 is the number of years in which the second free cash flow appears. You'll notice that you move between the different cash flows using the down arrow ($\downarrow$) located on the top row of your calculator. Once you have inputted the initial outlay and all the free cash flows, you then calculate the project's IRR by hitting the "IRR" button followed by "CPT," the compute button. Let's look at a quick example. Consider the following investment proposal:

Initial outlay	−$5,000
FCF in year 1	2,000
FCF in year 2	2,000
FCF in year 3	3,000

CALCULATOR SOLUTION

Data Input	Function Key
4	N
−45,555	PV
15,000	PMT
0	FV

Function Key	Answer
CPT	
I/Y	12.01

CALCULATOR SOLUTION
(USING A TI BA II PLUS):

Data and Key Input	Display
CF; −5,000; ENTER	CFo = −5,000.00
↓ 2,000; ENTER	C01 = 2,000.00
↓ 2; ENTER	F01 = 2.00
↓ 3,000; ENTER	C02 = 3,000.00
↓ 1; ENTER	F02 = 1.00
IRR ; CPT	IRR = 17.50%

Thus, the IRR on this project is 17.50 percent. When a financial calculator is not available and these flows are in the form of an uneven series of flows, a trial-and-error approach is necessary. To do this, we first determine the present value of the future free cash flows using an arbitrary discount rate. If the present value of the future cash flows at this discount rate is larger than the initial outlay, the rate is increased; if it is smaller than the initial outlay, the discount rate is lowered and the process begins again. This search routine is continued until the present value of the future free cash flows is equal to the initial outlay. In effect, because the present value of the free cash inflows is equal to the initial outlay, the NPV must equal zero at this point. The interest rate that creates this situation is the IRR. This is the same basic process that a financial calculator uses to calculate an IRR.

Can You Do It?

DETERMINING THE IRR OF A PROJECT

Determine the *IRR* for a new project that costs $5,019 and is expected to produce 10 years' worth of annual free cash flows of $1,000 per year.

(The solution can be found on page 273.)

➤ **EXAMPLE**

Consider the following investment proposal:

Initial outlay	−$10,010
FCF in year 1	1,000
FCF in year 2	3,000
FCF in year 3	6,000
FCF in year 4	7,000

CALCULATOR SOLUTION

(USING A TI BA II PLUS)

Data and Key Input	Display
CF; −10,010; ENTER	CF0 = −10,010.00
↓ 1,000; ENTER	C01 = 1,000.00
↓ 1; ENTER	F01 = 1.00
↓ 3,000; ENTER	C02 = 3,000.00
↓ 1; ENTER	F02 = 1.00
↓ 6,000; ENTER	C03 = 6,000.00
↓ 1; ENTER	F03 = 1.00
↓ 7,000; ENTER	C04 = 7,000.00
↓ 1; ENTER	F04 = 1.00
IRR ; CPT	IRR = 19.00%

TRIAL-AND-ERROR SOLUTION

Try different discount rates. The one that makes the present value of the free cash inflows equal to the initial outlay (i.e., makes the *NPV* equal to zero) is the *IRR*.

Discount Rate Guesses	NPV
15%	$ 1,075
20%	−$ 245
19%	$ 0

Thus, 19 percent is the project's *IRR*.

Viewing the *NPV–IRR* Relationship: The Net Present Value Profile

net present value profile a graph showing how a project's *NPV* changes as the discount rate changes.

Perhaps the easiest way to understand the relationship between the *IRR* and the *NPV* value is to view it graphically through the use of a **net present value profile**. A net present value profile is simply *a graph showing how a project's NPV changes as the discount rate changes*. To graph a project's net present value profile, you simply need to determine the project's *NPV*, first using a 0 percent discount rate, then slowly increasing the discount rate until a representative curve has been plotted. How does the *IRR* enter into the net present value profile? The *IRR* is the discount rate at which the *NPV* is zero.

How Did You Do?

DETERMINING THE IRR OF A PROJECT

You were asked to determine the *IRR* for a project with an initial outlay of $5,019 and free cash flows in years 1 through 10 of $1,000.

1. **Using the Time Value of Money Tables.** The problem with the time value of money tables is that the numbers in them correspond only to whole interest rates. Thus, if the answer does not come out to a percent that is listed in the tables, you would have to interpolate between two percentages. In this case, that's not a problem. Using equation (9-3),

$$IO = \frac{FCF_1}{(1 + IRR)^1} + \frac{FCF_2}{(1 + IRR)^2} + \cdots + \frac{FCF_n}{(1 + IRR)^n}$$

Because this is an annuity,

$$IO = FCF(PVIFA_{IRR\%, n})$$

$$\$5,019 = \$1,000(PVIFA_{IRR\%, 15\ yr})$$

$$5.019 = PVIFA_{IRR\%, 10\ yr}$$

Thus, we know we are looking for a $PVIFA_{IRR\%, 15\ yr}$ value of 5.019 in the $n=10$ row of Appendix E, and we find it in the 15 percent column. Thus, 15 percent is the project's *IRR*.

2. **Using a Financial Calculator.** Substituting in a financial calculator, we are solving for *i*.

Data Input	Function Key
10	N
−5,019	PV
1,000	PMT
0	FV

Function Key	Answer
CPT	
I/Y	15

Alternatively, you could use the CF button on your calculator (using a TI BA II Plus):

Data and Key Input	Display
CF ; −5,019; ENTER	CF0 = −5,019.
↓ ; 1,000; ENTER	C01 = 1,000.
↓ ; 10; ENTER	F01 = 10.00
IRR ; CPT	IRR = 15

3. **Using Excel.** Using Excel, the *IRR* could be calculated using the **=IRR** function.

Let's look at an example of a project that involves an after-tax initial outlay of $105,517 with free cash flows expected to be $30,000 per year over the project's 5-year life. Calculating the *NPV* of this project at several different discount rates results in the following:

Discount Rate	Project's *NPV*
0%	$44,483
5%	$24,367
10%	$ 8,207
13%	$ 0
15%	−$ 4,952
20%	−$15,798
25%	−$24,839

Plotting these values yields the net present value profile in Figure 9-1.

Where is the *IRR* in this figure? Recall that the *IRR* is the discount rate that equates the present value of the inflows with the present value of the outflows; thus, the *IRR* is the point at which the *NPV* is equal to zero—in this case, 13 percent. This is exactly the process that we use in computing the *IRR* for a series of uneven cash flows—we simply calculate the project's *NPV* using different discount rates and the discount rate that makes the *NPV* equal to zero is the project's *IRR*.

From the net present value profile you can easily see how a project's *NPV* varies inversely with the discount rate—as the discount rate is raised, the *NPV* drops. By analyzing a project's net present value profile, you can also see how sensitive the project is to your selection of the discount rate. The more sensitive the *NPV* is to the discount rate, the more important it is that you use the correct one in your calculations.

Complications with the *IRR*: Multiple Rates of Return

Although any project can have only one *NPV* and one *PI*, a single project under certain circumstances can have more than one *IRR*. The reason for this can be traced to the calculations

FIGURE 9-1 An Example of the Net Present Value Profile of a Project

involved in determining the *IRR*. Equation (9-3) states that the *IRR* is the discount rate that equates the present value of the project's future net cash flows with the project's initial outlay:

$$IO = \frac{FCF^1}{(1 + IRR)^1} + \frac{FCF^2}{(1 + IRR)^2} + \ldots + \frac{FCF^n}{(1 + IRR)^n} \tag{9-3}$$

However, because equation (9-3) is a polynomial of a degree *n*, it has *n* solutions. Now if the initial outlay (*IO*) is the only negative cash flow and all the annual free cash flows (*FCF*) are positive, then all but one of these *n* solutions is either a negative or imaginary number and there is no problem. But problems occur when there are sign reversals in the cash flow stream; in fact, there can be as many solutions as there are sign reversals. A normal, or "conventional," pattern with a negative initial outlay and positive annual free cash flows after that (−, +, +, +, . . . , +) has only one sign reversal, hence, only one positive *IRR*. However, an "unconventional" pattern with more than one sign reversal can have more than one *IRR*.[2]

	FREE CASH FLOW
Initial outlay	−$ 1,600
Year 1 free cash flow	+$10,000
Year 2 free cash flow	−$10,000

In this pattern of cash flows, there are two sign reversals: one from −$1,600 to +$10,000 and one from +$10,000 to −$10,000, so there can be as many as two positive *IRR*s that will make the present value of the free cash flows equal to the initial outlay. In fact, two internal rates of return solve this problem: 25 percent and 400 percent. Graphically, what we are solving for is the discount rate that makes the project's *NPV* equal to zero. As Figure 9-2 illustrates, this occurs twice.

Which solution is correct? The answer is that neither solution is valid. Although each fits the definition of *IRR*, neither provides any insight into the true project returns. In summary, when there is more than one sign reversal in the cash flow stream, the possibility of multiple *IRR*s exists, and the normal interpretation of the *IRR* loses its meaning. In this case, try the *NPV* criterion instead.

---

[2] This example is taken from James H. Lorie and Leonard J. Savage, "Three Problems in Rationing Capital," *Journal of Business* 28 (October 1955): 229–39.

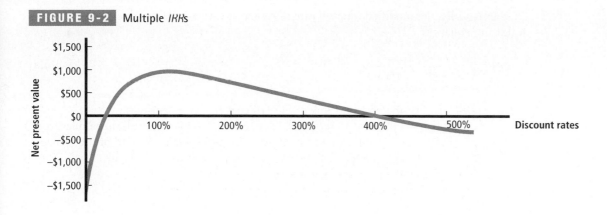

FIGURE 9-2 Multiple *IRR*s

The Modified Internal Rate of Return (*MIRR*)[3]

Problems with multiple rates of return and the reinvestment rate assumption make the *NPV* superior to the *IRR* as a capital-budgeting technique. However, because of the ease of interpretation, the *IRR* is preferred by many practitioners. Recently, a new technique, the modified internal rate of return (*MIRR*), has gained popularity as an alternative to the *IRR* method because it allows the decision maker to directly specify the appropriate reinvestment rate. As a result, the *MIRR* provides the decision maker with the intuitive appeal of the *IRR* coupled with an improved reinvestment rate assumption.

Is this really a problem? The answer is yes. One of the problems of the *IRR* is that it creates unrealistic expectations both for the corporation and for its shareholders. For example, the consulting firm McKinsey & Company examined one firm that approved 23 major projects over 5 years based on average *IRR*s of 77 percent.[4] However, when McKinsey adjusted the reinvestment rate on these projects to the firm's required rate of return, this return rate fell to 16 percent. The ranking of the projects also changed with the top-ranked project falling to the 10th most attractive project. Moreover, the returns on the highest-ranked projects with *IRR*s of 800, 150, and 130 percent dropped to 15, 23, and 22 percent, respectively, once the reinvestment rate was adjusted downward.

The driving force behind the *MIRR* is the assumption that all free cash flows over the life of the project are reinvested at the required rate of return until the termination of the project. Thus, to calculate the *MIRR*, we:

Step 1. Determine the present value of the project's free cash *out*flows. We do this by discounting all the free cash *out*flows back to the present at the required rate of return. If the initial outlay is the only free cash *out*flow, then the initial outlay is the present value of the free cash *out*flows.

Step 2. Determine the future value of the project's free cash *in*flows. Take all the annual free cash *in*flows and find their future value at the end of the project's life, compounded forward at the required rate of return. We will call this the project's *terminal value*, or *TV*.

Step 3. Calculate the *MIRR*. The *MIRR* is the discount rate that equates the present value of the free cash outflows with the project's terminal value.[5]

---

[3] This section is relatively complex and can be omitted without loss of continuity.

[4] John C. Kellecher and Justin J. MacCormack, "Internal Rate of Return: A Cautionary Tale," *McKinsey Quarterly*, September 24, 2004, pp. 1–4.

[5] You will notice that we differentiate between annual cash inflows and annual cash outflows, compounding all the inflows to the end of the project and bringing all the outflows back to the present as part of the present value of the cost. Although there are alternative definitions of the *MIRR*, this is the most widely accepted definition. For an excellent discussion of the *MIRR*, see William R. McDaniel, Daniel E. McCarty, and Kenneth A. Jessell, "Discounted Cash Flow with Explicit Reinvestment Rates: Tutorial and Extension," *The Financial Review* (August 1988): 369–85.

Mathematically, the modified internal rate of return is defined as the value of *MIRR* in the following equation:

$$PV_{\text{outflows}} = \frac{TV_{\text{inflows}}}{(1 + MIRR)^n} \qquad (9\text{-}4)$$

where PV_{outflows} = the present value of the project's free cash *out*flows
TV_{inflows} = the project's terminal value, calculated by taking all the annual free cash *in*flows and finding their future value at the end of the project's life, compounded forward at the required rate of return
n = the project's expected life
$MIRR$ = the project's modified internal rate of return

➤ EXAMPLE : CALCULATING THE *MIRR*

Let's look at an example of a project with a 3-year life and a required rate of return of 10 percent assuming the following cash flows are associated with it:

	FREE CASH FLOWS		FREE CASH FLOWS
Initial outlay	−$6,000	Year 2	$3,000
Year 1	2,000	Year 3	4,000

The calculation of the *MIRR* can be viewed as a three-step process, which is also shown graphically in Figure 9-3.

Step 1. Determine the present value of the project's free cash *out*flows. In this case, the only *out*flow is the initial outlay of $6,000, which is already at the present; thus, it becomes the present value of the cash *out*flows.

Step 2. Determine the terminal value of the project's free cash *in*flows. To do this, we merely use the project's required rate of return to calculate the future value of the project's three cash *in*flows at the termination of the project. In this case, the *terminal value* becomes $9,720.

Step 3. Determine the discount rate that equates the present value of the *terminal value* and the present value of the project's cash *out*flows. Thus, the *MIRR* is calculated to be 17.446 percent.

For our example, the calculations are as follows:

$$\$6,000 = \frac{TV_{\text{infows}}}{(1 + MIRR)^n}$$

$$\$6,000 = \frac{\$2,000(1 + .10)^2 + \$3,000(1 + .10)^1 + \$4,000(1 + .10)^0}{(1 + MIRR)^3}$$

$$\$6,000 = \frac{\$2,420 + \$3,300 + \$4,000}{(1 + MIRR)^3}$$

$$\$6,000 = \frac{\$9,720}{(1 + MIRR)^3}$$

$$MIRR = 17.446\%$$

Thus, the *MIRR* for this project (17.446 percent) is less than its *IRR*, which comes out to 20.614 percent. In this case, it only makes sense that the *IRR* should be greater than the *MIRR*, because the *IRR* allows intermediate cash *in*flows to grow at the *IRR* rather than the required rate of return.

In terms of decision rules, if the project's *MIRR* is greater than or equal to the project's required rate of return, then the project should be accepted; if not, it should be rejected:

$MIRR \geq$ required rate of return: accept
$MIRR <$ required rate of return: reject

FIGURE 9-3   Calculating the *MIRR*

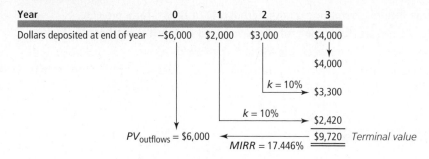

Because of the frequent use of the *IRR* in the real world as a decision-making tool and its limiting reinvestment rate assumption, the *MIRR* has become increasingly popular as an alternative decision-making tool.

Using Spreadsheets to Calculate the *MIRR*

As with other financial calculations using a spreadsheet, calculating the *MIRR* is extremely simple. The only difference between this calculation and that of the traditional *IRR* is that with a spreadsheet you also have the option of specifying both a *financing rate* and a *reinvestment rate*. The financing rate refers to the rate at which you borrow the money needed for the investment, whereas the reinvestment rate is the rate at which you reinvest the cash flows. Generally, it is assumed that these two values are one and the same. Thus, we enter the value of k, the appropriate discount rate, for both of these values. Once the cash flows have been entered on the spreadsheet, all you need to do is input the Excel *MIRR* formula into a spreadsheet cell and let the spreadsheet do the calculations for you. Of course, as with the *IRR* calculation, at least one of the cash flows must be positive and at least one must be negative. The *MIRR* formula to be input into a spreadsheet cell is: **=MIRR(values,finance rate,reinvestment rate)**, where values is simply the range of cells where the cash flows are stored, and k is entered for both the finance rate and the reinvestment rate.

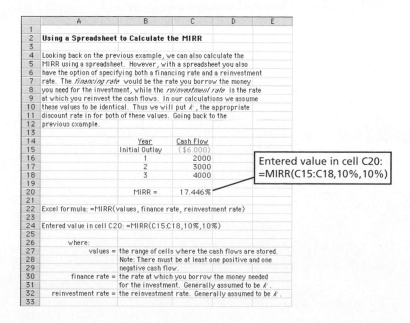

Did You Get It? ....

1. Provide an intuitive definition of an internal rate of return for a project.
2. What does a net present value profile tell you, and how is it constructed?
3. What is the difference between the *IRR* and the *MIRR*?
4. Why do the net present value and profitability index always yield the same accept or reject decision for any project?

Objective **3**

Explain how the capital-budgeting decision process changes when a dollar limit is placed on the capital budget.

capital rationing placing a limit on the dollar size of the capital budget.

CAPITAL RATIONING

The use of our capital-budgeting decision rules developed in this chapter implies that the size of the capital budget is determined by the availability of acceptable investment proposals. However, a firm may *place a limit on the dollar size of the capital budget*. This situation is called **capital rationing**. As we will see, examining capital rationing not only better enables us to deal with complexities of the real world but also serves to demonstrate the superiority of the *NPV* method over the *IRR* method for capital budgeting. It is always somewhat uncomfortable to deal with problems associated with capital rationing because, under rationing, projects with positive net present values are rejected. This is a situation that violates the firm's goal of shareholder wealth maximization. However, in the real world, capital rationing does exist, and managers must deal with it. Often when firms impose capital constraints, they are recognizing that they do not have the ability to profitably handle more than a certain number of new and/or large projects.

Using the *IRR* as the firm's decision rule, a firm accepts all projects with an *IRR* greater than the firm's required rate of return. This rule is illustrated in Figure 9-4, where projects A through E would be chosen. However, when capital rationing is imposed, the dollar size of the total investment is limited by the budget constraint. In Figure 9-4, the budget constraint of $X precludes the acceptance of an attractive investment, project E. This situation obviously contradicts prior decision rules. Moreover, choosing the projects with the highest *IRR* is complicated by the fact that some projects are indivisible. For example, it may be illogical to recommend that half of project D be undertaken.

The Rationale for Capital Rationing

In general, three principal reasons are given for imposing a capital-rationing constraint. First, managers may think market conditions are temporarily adverse. In the period surrounding the downturn in the economy in the early 2000s, this reason was frequently given. At that time stock prices were depressed, which made the cost of funding projects high. Second, there may be a shortage of qualified managers to direct new projects; this can happen when projects are of a highly technical nature. Third, there may be intangible considerations. For example, managers may simply fear debt, wishing to avoid interest payments at any cost. Or perhaps the firm wants to limit the issuance of common stock to maintain a stable dividend policy.

FIGURE 9-4 Projects Ranked by the *IRR*

TABLE 9-7   Capital Rationing: Choosing among Five Indivisible Projects

PROJECT	INITIAL OUTLAY	PROFITABILITY INDEX	NET PRESENT VALUE
A	$200,000	2.4	$280,000
B	200,000	2.3	260,000
C	800,000	1.7	560,000
D	300,000	1.3	90,000
E	300,000	1.2	60,000

So what is capital rationing's effect on the firm? In brief, the effect is negative. To what degree it is negative depends on the severity of the rationing. If the rationing is minor and short-lived, the firm's share price will not suffer to any great extent. In this case, capital rationing can probably be excused, although it should be noted that any capital-rationing action that rejects projects with positive *NPV*s is contrary to the firm's goal of maximization of shareholders' wealth. If the capital rationing is a result of the firm's decision to limit dramatically the number of new projects or to use only internally generated funds for projects, then this policy will eventually have a significantly negative effect on the firm's share price. For example, a lower share price will eventually result from lost competitive advantage if, because of a decision to arbitrarily limit its capital budget, a firm fails to upgrade its products and manufacturing processes.

Capital Rationing and Project Selection

If a firm decides to impose a capital constraint on its investment projects, the appropriate decision criterion is to select the set of projects with the highest *NPV* subject to the capital constraint. In effect, it should select the projects that increase shareholders' wealth the most. This guideline may preclude merely taking the highest-ranked projects in terms of the *PI* or the *IRR*. If the projects shown in Figure 9-4 are divisible, the last project accepted will be only partially accepted. Although partial acceptance may be possible, as we have said, in some cases, the indivisibility of most capital investments prevents it. For example, purchasing half a sales outlet or half a truck is impossible.

Consider a firm with a budget constraint of $1 million and five indivisible projects available to it, as given in Table 9-7. If the highest-ranked projects were taken, projects A and B would be taken first. At that point there would not be enough funds available to take on project C; hence, projects D and E would be taken on. However, a higher total *NPV* is provided by the combination of projects A and C. Thus, projects A and C should be selected from the set of projects available. This illustrates our guideline: to select the set of projects that maximizes the firm's *NPV*.

Did You Get It?

1. What is capital rationing?
2. How might capital rationing conflict with the goal of maximizing shareholders' wealth?
3. What are mutually exclusive projects? How might they complicate the capital-budgeting process?

RANKING MUTUALLY EXCLUSIVE PROJECTS

Objective **4**

Discuss the problems encountered in project ranking.

In the past, we have proposed that all projects with a positive *NPV*, a *PI* greater than 1.0, or an *IRR* greater than the required rate of return be accepted, assuming there is no capital rationing. However, this acceptance is not always possible. In some cases, when two projects

mutually exclusive projects
projects that, if undertaken, would serve the same purpose. Thus, accepting one will necessarily mean rejecting the others.

are judged acceptable by the discounted cash flow criteria, it may be necessary to select only one of them because they are mutually exclusive. **Mutually exclusive projects** *are projects that, if undertaken, would serve the same purpose.* For example, a company considering the installation of a computer system might evaluate three or four systems, all of which have positive *NPV*s. However, the acceptance of one system automatically means rejection of the others. In general, to deal with mutually exclusive projects, we simply rank them by means of the discounted cash flow criteria and select the project with the highest ranking. On occasion, however, problems of conflicting ranking may arise. As we will see, in general, the *NPV* method is the preferred decision-making tool because it leads to the selection of the project that increases shareholder wealth the most.

When dealing with mutually exclusive projects, there are three general types of ranking problems: the size-disparity problem, the time-disparity problem, and the unequal-lives problem. Each involves the possibility of conflict in the ranks yielded by the various discounted cash flow, capital-budgeting criteria. As noted previously, when one discounted cash flow criterion gives an accept signal, they will all give an accept signal, but they will not necessarily rank all projects in the same order. In most cases this disparity is not critical; however, for mutually exclusive projects the ranking order is important.

The Size-Disparity Problem

The size-disparity problem occurs when mutually exclusive projects of unequal size are examined. This problem is most easily clarified with an example.

➤ EXAMPLE

Suppose a firm is considering two mutually exclusive projects, A and B; both have required rates of return of 10 percent. Project A involves a $200 initial outlay and a cash inflow of $300 at the end of 1 year, whereas project B involves an initial outlay of $1,500 and a cash inflow of $1,900 at the end of 1 year. The net present values, profitability indexes, and internal rates of return for these projects are given in Table 9-8.

In this case, if the *NPV* criterion is used, project B should be accepted; whereas if the *PI* or *IRR* criterion is used, project A should be chosen. The question now becomes, which project is better? The answer depends on whether capital rationing exists. Without capital rationing, project B is better because it provides the largest increase in shareholders' wealth; that is, it has a larger *NPV*. If there is a capital constraint, the problem then focuses on what can be done with the additional $1,300 that is freed up if project A is chosen (costing $200, as opposed to $1,500). If the firm can earn more on project A plus the project financed with the additional $1,300 than it can on project B, then project A and the marginal project should be accepted. In effect, we are attempting to select the set of projects that maximizes the firm's *NPV*. Thus, if the marginal project has an *NPV* greater than $154.55 ($227.28 − $72.73), selecting it plus project A with an *NPV* of $72.73 will provide an *NPV* greater than $227.28, the *NPV* for project B.

TABLE 9-8   The Size–Disparity Ranking Problem

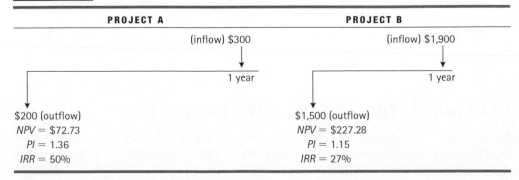

PROJECT A	PROJECT B
(inflow) $300	(inflow) $1,900
1 year	1 year
$200 (outflow)	$1,500 (outflow)
NPV = $72.73	*NPV* = $227.28
PI = 1.36	*PI* = 1.15
IRR = 50%	*IRR* = 27%

In summary, whenever the size-disparity problem results in conflicting rankings between mutually exclusive projects, the project with the largest *NPV* will be selected, provided there is no capital rationing. When capital rationing exists, the firm should select the set of projects with the largest *NPV*.

The Time-Disparity Problem

The time-disparity problem and the conflicting rankings that accompany it result from the differing reinvestment assumptions made by the net present value and internal rate of return decision criteria. The *NPV* criterion assumes that cash flows over the life of the project can be reinvested at the required rate of return or cost of capital, whereas the *IRR* criterion implicitly assumes that the cash flows over the life of the project can be reinvested at the *IRR*. One possible solution to this problem is to use the *MIRR* method introduced earlier. As you recall, this method allows you to explicitly state the rate at which cash flows over the life of the project will be reinvested. Again, this problem may be illustrated through the use of an example.

➤ EXAMPLE

Suppose a firm with a required rate of return or cost of capital of 10 percent and with no capital constraint is considering the two mutually exclusive projects illustrated in Table 9-9. The *NPV* and *PI* indicate that project A is the better of the two, whereas the *IRR* indicates that project B is the better. Project B receives its cash flows earlier than project A, and the different assumptions made about how these flows can be reinvested result in the difference in rankings. Which criterion would be followed depends on which reinvestment assumption is used. The *NPV* criterion is preferred in this case because it makes the most acceptable assumption for the wealth-maximizing firm. It is certainly the most conservative assumption that can be made, because the required rate of return is the lowest possible reinvestment rate. Moreover, as we have already noted, the *NPV* method maximizes the value of the firm and the shareholders' wealth.

The Unequal-Lives Problem

The final ranking problem to be examined asks whether it is appropriate to compare mutually exclusive projects with different life spans. The incomparability of projects with different lives arises because future, profitable investment proposals will be precluded without ever having been considered. For example, let's say you own an older hotel on some prime beachfront property on Hilton Head Island, and you're considering either remodeling the hotel, which will extend its life by 5 years, or tearing it down and building a new hotel that has an expected life of 10 years. Either way you're going to make money because beachfront property is exactly where everyone would like to stay. But clearly, you can't do both.

TABLE 9-9   The Time-Disparity Ranking Problem

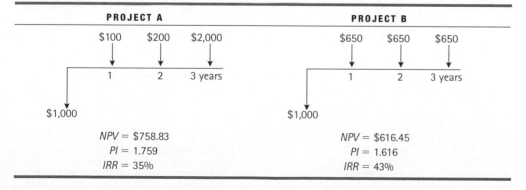

Is it fair to compare the *NPVs* on these two projects? No. Why not? Because if you accept the 10-year project, you will not only be rejecting the 5-year project but also the chance to do something else profitable with the property in years 5 through 10. In effect, if the project with the shorter life were taken, at its termination you could either remodel again or rebuild and receive additional benefits, whereas accepting the project with the longer life would exclude this possibility, which is not included in the analysis. The key question thus becomes: Does today's investment decision include all future profitable investment proposals in its analysis? If not, the projects are not comparable.

➤ EXAMPLE

Suppose a firm with a 10 percent required rate of return must replace an aging machine and is considering two replacement machines, one with a three-year life and one with a six-year life. The relevant cash flow information for these projects is given in Figure 9-5.

Examining the discounted cash flow criteria, we find that the net present value and profitability index criteria indicate that project B is the better project, whereas the internal rate of return favors project A. This ranking inconsistency is caused by the different life spans of the projects being compared. In this case, the decision is a difficult one because the projects are not comparable.

There are several methods to deal with this situation. The first option is to assume that the cash inflows from the shorter-lived investment will be reinvested at the required rate of return until the termination of the longer-lived asset. Although this approach is the simplest because it merely involves calculating the net present value, it actually ignores the problem at hand—the possibility of undertaking another replacement opportunity with a positive net present value. Thus, the proper solution involves projecting reinvestment opportunities into the future—that is, making assumptions about possible future investment opportunities. Unfortunately, whereas the first method is too simplistic to be of any value, the second is extremely difficult, requiring extensive cash flow forecasts. The final technique for confronting the problem is to assume that the firm's reinvestment opportunities in the future will be similar to its current ones. The two most common ways of doing this are by creating a replacement chain to equalize the life spans of projects or by calculating the equivalent annual annuity (*EAA* of the projects). Using a replacement chain, the present example would call for the creation of a two-chain cycle for project A; that is, we assume that project A can be replaced with a similar investment at the end of 3 years. Thus, project A would be viewed as two A projects occurring back to back, as illustrated in Figure 9-6. The net present value on this replacement chain is $426.32, which can be compared with project B's net present value. Therefore, project A should be accepted because the net present value of its replacement chain is greater than the net present value of project B.

One problem with replacement chains is that, depending on the life of each project, it can be quite difficult to come up with equivalent lives. For example, if the two projects had 7- and 13-year lives, because the lowest common denominator is $7 \times 13 = 91$, a 91-year re-

FIGURE 9-5 Unequal Lives Ranking Problem

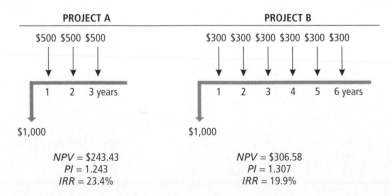

FIGURE 9-6   Replacement Chain Illustration: Two Project A's Back to Back

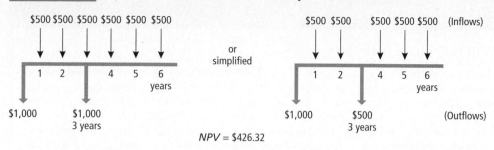

$NPV = \$426.32$

placement chain would be needed to establish equivalent lives. In this case, it is easier to determine the project's **equivalent annual annuity (EAA)**. A project's *EAA* is simply an annuity cash flow that yields the same present value as the project's *NPV*. To calculate an *EAA*, we need only calculate a project's *NPV* and then determine what annual annuity (PMT on your financial calculator) it is equal to. This can be done in two steps as follows:

Step 1. Calculate the project's *NPV*. In Figure 9-5 we determined that project A had an *NPV* of $243.43, whereas project B had an *NPV* of $306.58.

Step 2. Calculate the *EAA*. The *EAA* is determined by using the *NPV* as the project's present value (PV), the number of years in the project as *n* (N), the required rate of return as *i* (I/Y), entering a 0 for the future value (FV), and solving for the annual annuity (PMT). This determines the level of an annuity cash flow that would produce the same *NPV* as the project. For project A the calculations are:

CALCULATOR SOLUTION

Date Input	Function Key
3	N
10	I/Y
−243.43	PV
0	FV

Function Key	Answer
CPT	
PMT	97.89

For project B, the calculations are:

CALCULATOR SOLUTION

Data Input	Function Key
6	N
10	I/Y
−306.58	PV
0	FV

Function Key	Answer
CPT	
PMT	70.39

How do we interpret the *EAA*? For a project with an *n*-year life, it tells us what the dollar value is of an *n*-year annual annuity that would provide the same *NPV* as the project. Thus, for project A, it means that a 3-year annuity of $97.89 with a discount rate of 10 percent would produce a net present value the same as project A's net present value, which is $243.43. We can now compare the equivalent annual annuities directly to determine which project is better. We can do this because we now have found the level of annual annuity that produces an *NPV* equivalent to the project's *NPV*. Thus, because they are both annual annuities, they are comparable.

equivalent annual annuity (EAA) an annuity cash flow that yields the same present value as the project's *NPV*.

Ethics in Financial Management

THE FINANCIAL DOWNSIDE OF POOR ETHICAL BEHAVIOR

As we learned in **Principle 10: Ethical Behavior Means Doing the Right Thing, but Ethical Dilemmas Are Everywhere in Finance**. Knowing the inevitable outcome—for truth does percolate—why do bright and experienced people ignore it? For even if the truth is known only within the confines of the company, it will get out. Circumstances beyond even the best manager's control take over once the chance has passed to act on the moment of truth. Consider the following cases:

Dow Corning didn't deserve its bankruptcy or the multibillion-dollar settlements for its silicone implants because the science didn't support the alleged damages. However, there was a moment of truth when those implants, placed on a blotter, left a stain. The company could have disclosed the possible leakage, researched the risk, and warned doctors and patients. Given the congressional testimony on the implants, many women would have chosen them despite the risk. Instead, they sued because they were not warned.

Beech-Nut's crisis was a chemical concoction instead of apple juice in its baby food products. Executives there ignored an in-house chemist who tried to tell them they were selling adulterated products.

Kidder-Peabody fell despite warnings from employees about a glitch in its accounting system that was reporting bond swaps as sales and income.

In 2004, Merck removed one of the world's best-selling painkillers from the market after a study showed Vioxx caused an increased risk of serious cardiovascular events, such as stroke and heart attack. Producing Vioxx wasn't Merck's problem, its problem was that, according to an editorial in the *New England Journal of Medicine*, Merck was alleged to have withheld data and information that would affect conclusions drawn in an earlier study that appeared in the *New England Journal of Medicine*

in 2000. Now, Merck faces thousands of lawsuits, and studies continue to deliver bad news about the drug. In fact, in one case, a jury awarded $51 million to a retired FBI agent who suffered a heart attack after taking the drug.

These cases all have several things in common. First, their moments of truth came and went while the companies took no action. Second, employees who raised the issue were ignored or, in some cases, fired. Third, there were lawyers along for the ride, as they were with Ford and Firestone.

Never rely on a lawyer in these moments of truth. Lawyers are legal experts but are not particularly good at controlling damage. They shouldn't make business decisions; managers should. More importantly, moments of truth require managers with strong ethics who will do more than the law requires and less than the law allows.

As a now-infamous memo reveals, Ford and Firestone did not feel obligated to reveal to the U.S. Transportation Department that certain tires were being recalled in overseas markets. The companies should have realized that it was not a question of whether the recall would be reported, but by whom.

Do businesses ever face a moment of truth wisely? One example is Foxy brand lettuce, which in 2006, shortly after E. coli-contaminated spinach was linked to three deaths, recalled all its lettuce after they discovered irrigation water on their farms tested positive for the bacterium. Although their lettuce was not found to be carrying any bacterium, they did everything possible to protect the public and, as a result, have very loyal customers.

Did You Get It?

1. What are the three general types of ranking problems?

Objective **5**

Explain the importance of ethical considerations in capital-budgeting decisions.

ETHICS IN CAPITAL BUDGETING

Although it may not seem obvious, ethics play a role in capital budgeting. Firestone and Ford, Merck, Dow Corning, and Beech-Nut provide examples of how ethical rules have been violated in the past and what the consequences can be. The "Ethics in Financial

Remember Your Principles

Ethics and ethical considerations continually crop up when capital-budgeting decisions are being made. This brings us back to **Principle 10: Ethical Behavior Means Doing the Right Thing, but Ethical Dilemmas Are Everywhere in Finance**. As the "Ethics in Financial Management" article points out, the most damaging event a business can experience is a loss of the public's confidence in the business's ethical standards. In making capital-budgeting decisions, we must be aware of this and that ethical behavior is doing the right thing and is the right thing to do.

Management" article, The Financial Downside to Poor Ethical Behavior, explains how important it is for firms to not only tell the truth but also make sure that consumers have all the facts they need.

A GLANCE AT ACTUAL CAPITAL-BUDGETING PRACTICES

Objective 6

Discuss the trends in the use of different capital-budgeting criteria.

During the past 40 years, the popularity of each of the capital-budgeting methods has shifted rather dramatically. In the 1950s and 1960s, the payback period method dominated capital budgeting. Through the 1970s and 1980s, the *IRR* and the *NPV* techniques slowly gained popularity and are used by the majority of major corporations today.

Interestingly, a recent survey of 392 CFOs by John Graham and Campbell Harvey of Duke University found that 74.9 percent of CFOs always or almost always use net present value and 75.7 percent always or almost always use the internal rate of return.[6] The payback period was also found to be very popular; 56.7 percent indicated that they always or almost always use the payback period. The profitability index was found to be considerably less popular; only 11.9 percent of the CFOs surveyed indicated that they always or almost always use it. Moreover, the survey found that in firms headed by older CEOs and those without an MBA, the use of the payback period was more common.

The survey also found that large firms are significantly more likely to use *NPV* to evaluate capital-budgeting projects than are small firms. On the other hand, when it comes to capital budgeting, small firms use the payback period almost as frequently as they use *NPV* and *IRR*. Apart from the survey, one of the reasons commonly given for the use of the payback period approach is that it makes sense for the capital-constrained firm. However, the survey didn't find any evidence of this being the case.

Without taking on new projects, a company simply wouldn't continue to exist. For example, Polaroid's inability to come up with a product to replace its instant camera resulted in that company going under in 2001. Finding new profitable projects and correctly evaluating them are central to a firm's continued existence—and that's what capital budgeting is all about. In fact, much of what is done within a business involves the capital-budgeting process. Many times it's referred to as strategic planning, but it generally involves capital-budgeting decisions. For example, you may be involved in market research dealing with a proposed new product or its marketing plan, or be analyzing its costs—these are all part of the capital-budgeting process. Once all this information has been gathered, it is analyzed using the techniques and tools that we have presented in this chapter. Actually, almost any business decision can be analyzed using the framework we presented here. That's because the *NPV* method "values" the project under consideration. That is, it looks at the present value of its benefits relative to the present value of its costs, and if the present value of the benefits outweighs the costs, the project is accepted. That's a pretty good decision rule, and it can be applied to any decision a business faces.

Did You Get It?

1. What capital-budgeting criteria seem to be used most frequently in the real world? Why do you think this is so?

FINANCE AND THE MULTINATIONAL FIRM: CAPITAL BUDGETING

Objective 7

Explain how foreign markets provide opportunities for finding new capital-budgeting projects.

Without question, the key to success in capital budgeting is to identify good projects, and for many companies these good projects are overseas. Just look at the success that Coca-Cola has had in the international markets. More than 80 percent of its beverage profits come from

[6] John R. Graham and Campbell R. Harvey, "The Theory and Practice of Corporate Finance: Evidence from the Field," *Journal of Financial Economics* 60, 1–2 (May/June 2001), 187–243.

foreign markets, and the company earns more in Japan than in the United States. Likewise, ExxonMobil earns over half its profits from abroad and is involved in gas and oil exploration projects in West Africa, the Caspian Sea, Russia, the Gulf of Mexico, and South America.

But how do you enter these markets initially? One approach that has been used successfully is through international joint ventures or strategic alliances. Under these arrangements two or more corporations merge their skills and resources on a specific project, trading things such as technology and access to marketing channels. For example, GM and Suzuki Motors have a strategic alliance that provides Suzuki with access to Europe, North America, South America, and Africa, where GM has a strong presence, and provides GM with access to the Asia Pacific region, where Suzuki is well established.

Similarly, U.S. oil giant Armco formed a joint venture with Mitsubishi to sell Armco's lightweight plastics in Japan. Georgia-Pacific and Canfor Japan Corporation have a joint venture in which Georgia-Pacific gained access to Canfor's marketing expertise in Japan to sell pulp and paper products there. Likewise, H. J. Heinz Co. announced a joint venture with an Indonesian firm to gain access to its Indonesian marketing channels. Joint ventures also provide a way to get around trade barriers. For example, India and Mexico require joint ventures for entry into their markets. As a result, U.S. firms such as Apple Computer and Hewlett-Packard have been forced to enter into Mexican joint ventures in order to be allowed to ship their products into Mexico.

What is the alternative to not looking abroad for projects? It is losing out on potential revenues. Keep in mind that firms such as Xerox, Hewlett-Packard, Dow Chemical, IBM, and Gillette all earn more than 50 percent of their profits from sales abroad. International boundaries no longer apply in finance.

Did You Get It? ....

1. What methods do corporations use to enter international markets?

Summary

The process of capital budgeting involves decision making with respect to investments in fixed assets. Before a profitable project can be adopted, it must be identified or found. Unfortunately, coming up with ideas for new products, for ways to improve existing products, or for ways to make existing products more profitable is extremely difficult. In general, the best source of ideas for new, potentially profitable products is within the firm.

We examine four commonly used criteria for determining the acceptance or rejection of capital-budgeting proposals. The first method, the payback period, does not incorporate the time value of money into its calculations. However, the net present value, profitability index, and internal rate of return methods do account for the time value of money. These methods are summarized in Table 9-10 on pages 287–288.

There are several complications related to the capital-budgeting process. First, we examined capital rationing and the problems it can create by imposing a limit on the dollar size of the capital budget. Although capital rationing does not, in general, maximize shareholders' wealth, it does exist. The goal of maximizing shareholders' wealth remains, but it is now subject to a budget constraint.

There are a number of problems associated with evaluating mutually exclusive projects. Mutually exclusive projects occur when different investments, if undertaken, would serve the same purpose. In general, to deal with mutually exclusive projects, we rank them by means of the discounted cash flow criteria and select the project with the highest ranking. Conflicting rankings can arise because of the projects' size disparities, time disparities, and unequal lives. The incomparability of projects with different life spans is not simply a result of the different life spans; rather, it arises because future profitable investment proposals will be rejected without being included in the initial analysis. Replacement chains and equivalent annual annuities can solve this problem.

Ethics and ethical decisions continuously crop up in capital budgeting. Just as with all other areas of finance, violating ethical considerations results in a loss of public confidence, which can have a significant negative effect on shareholder wealth.

Over the past 40 years, the discounted capital-budgeting techniques have continued to gain in popularity and today dominate in the decision-making process.

Objective **1**

Discuss the difficulty encountered in finding profitable projects in competitive markets and the importance of the search.

Objective **2**

Determine whether a new project should be accepted or rejected using the payback period, the net present value, the profitability index, and the internal rate of return.

Objective **3**

Explain how the capital-budgeting decision process changes when a dollar limit is placed on the capital budget.

Objective **4**

Discuss the problems encountered in project ranking.

Objective **5**

Explain the importance of ethical considerations in capital-budgeting decisions.

Objective **6**

Discuss the trends in the use of different capital-budgeting criteria.

TABLE 9-10   Capital-Budgeting Methods: A Summary

1. Payback period = number of years required to recapture the initial investment
   Accept if payback period $\leq$ maximum acceptable payback period
   Reject if payback period > maximum acceptable payback period

   Advantages:
   - Uses free cash flows.
   - Is easy to calculate and understand.
   - Benefits the capital-constrained firm.
   - May be used as rough screening device.

   Disadvantages:
   - Ignores the time value of money.
   - Ignores cash flows occurring after the payback period.
   - Selection of the maximum acceptable payback period is arbitrary.

2. Net present value = present value of the annual free cash flows less the investment's initial outlay
   NPV = present value of all the future annual free cash flows − the initial cash outlay

   $$= \frac{FCF_1}{(1 + k)^1} + \frac{FCF_2}{(1 + k)^2} + \cdots + \frac{FCF_n}{(1 + k)^n} - IO$$

   where FCF_t = the annual free cash flow in time period t (this can take on either positive or negative values)
   k = the appropriate discount rate; that is, the required rate of return or the cost of capital
   IO = the initial cash outlay
   n = the project's expected life

   Accept if $NPV \geq 0.0$
   Reject if $NPV < 0.0$

   Advantages:
   - Uses free cash flows.
   - Recognizes the time value of money.
   - Is consistent with the firm's goal of shareholder wealth maximization.

   Disadvantages:
   - Requires detailed long-term forecasts of a project's cash flows.

3. Profitability index = the ratio of the present value of the future free cash flows to the initial outlay.

   $$PI = \frac{\text{present value of all the future annual free cash flows}}{\text{initial cash outlay}}$$

   $$= \frac{\dfrac{FCF_1}{(1 + k)^1} + \dfrac{FCF_2}{(1 + k)^2} + \cdots + \dfrac{FCF_n}{(1 + k)^n}}{IO}$$

   Accept if $PI \geq 1.0$
   Reject if $PI < 1.0$

   Advantages:
   - Uses free cash flows.
   - Recognizes the time value of money.
   - Is consistent with the firm's goal of shareholder wealth maximization.

   Disadvantages:
   - Requires detailed long-term forecasts of a project's cash flows.

4. Internal rate of return = the discount rate that equates the present value of the project's future free cash flows with the project's initial outlay

   IRR = the rate of return that equates the present value of the project's free cash flows with the initial outlay

   $$IO = \frac{FCF_1}{(1 + IRR\%)^1} + \frac{FCF_2}{(1 + IRR\%)^2} + \cdots + \frac{FCF_n}{(1 + IRR\%)^n}$$

   where IRR = the project's internal rate of return

   Accept if $IRR \geq$ required rate of return
   Reject if $IRR <$ required rate of return

   Advantages:
   - Uses free cash flows.
   - Recognizes the time value of money.
   - Is, in general, consistent with the firm's goal of shareholder wealth maximization.

   Disadvantages:
   - Requires detailed long-term forecasts of a project's cash flows.
   - Possibility of multiple IRRs.
   - Assumes cash flows over the life of the project can be reinvested at the IRR.

5. Modified internal rate of return = the rate of return that equates the present value of the cash outflows with the terminal value of the cash inflows

$$PV_{outflows} = \frac{TV_{inflows}}{(1 + MIRR)^n}$$

where $PV_{outflows}$ = the present value of the project's free cash outflows

$TV_{inflows}$ = the project's terminal value, calculated by taking all the annual free cash *in*flows and finding their future value at the end of the project's life, compounded forward at the required rate of return

$MIRR$ = the project's modified internal rate of return

Accept if $MIRR \geq$ required rate of return
Reject if $MIRR <$ required rate of return

Advantages:
• Uses free cash flows.
• Recognizes the time value of money.
• Is consistent with the firm's goal of shareholder wealth maximization.
• Allows reinvestment rate to be directly specified.

Disadvantages:
• Requires detailed long-term cash flow forecasts.

Objective **7**

Explain how foreign markets provide opportunities for finding new capital-budgeting projects.

The international markets provide another source for finding good capital-budgeting projects. In fact, many times a new project simply involves taking an existing product and selling it in a foreign market. Joint ventures and strategic alliances have been successfully used to enter foreign markets.

Key Terms

Capital budgeting   260
Capital rationing   278
Equivalent annual annuity (*EAA*)   283
Internal rate of return (*IRR*)   269
Mutually exclusive projects   280

Net present value (*NPV*)   262
Net present value profile   272
Payback period   261
Profitability index *(PI)* or benefit–cost ratio   266

Review Questions

9-1. Why is capital budgeting such an important process? Why are capital-budgeting errors so costly?

9-2. What are the disadvantages of using the payback period as a capital-budgeting technique? What are its advantages? Why is it so frequently used?

9-3. In some countries, the expropriation (seizure) of foreign investments is a common practice. If you were considering an investment in one of those countries, would the use of the payback period criterion seem more reasonable than it otherwise might? Why or why not?

9-4. Briefly compare and contrast the *NPV, PI,* and *IRR* criteria. What are the advantages and disadvantages of using each of these methods?

9-5. What are mutually exclusive projects? Why might the existence of mutually exclusive projects cause problems in the implementation of the discounted cash flow capital-budgeting criteria?

9-6. What are common reasons for capital rationing? Is capital rationing rational?

9-7. How should managers compare two mutually exclusive projects of unequal size? Should the approach change if capital rationing is a factor?

9-8. What causes the time-disparity ranking problem? What reinvestment rate assumptions are associated with the *NPV* and *IRR* capital-budgeting criteria?

9-9. When might two mutually exclusive projects having unequal lives be incomparable? How should managers deal with this problem?

Self-Test Problem

(The solution to this problem is provided at the end of this chapter.)

ST-1. You are considering buying a machine that will require an initial outlay of $54,200. The machine has an expected life of 5 years and will generate free cash flows to the company as a whole of $20,608 at the end of each year over its 5-year life. In addition to the $20,608 cash flow from operations during the fifth and final year, there will be an additional free cash inflow of $13,200 at the end of the fifth year associated with the salvage value of the machine, making the cash flow in year 5 equal to $33,808. Thus, the cash flows associated with this project look like this:

	CASH FLOW
Initial outlay	−$54,200
Inflow year 1	20,608
Inflow year 2	20,608
Inflow year 3	20,608
Inflow year 4	20,608
Inflow year 5	33,808

Given a required rate of return of 15 percent, calculate the following:

    a. Payback period **b.** *NPV* **c.** *PI* **d.** *IRR*

Should this project be accepted?

Study Problems

9-1. (*IRR calculation*) Determine the *IRR* on the following projects:

    a. An initial outlay of $10,000 resulting in a single free cash flow of $17,182 after 8 years

    b. An initial outlay of $10,000 resulting in a single free cash flow of $48,077 after 10 years

    c. An initial outlay of $10,000 resulting in a single free cash flow of $114,943 after 20 years

    d. An initial outlay of $10,000 resulting in a single free cash flow of $13,680 after 3 years

9-2. (*IRR calculation*) Determine the *IRR* on the following projects:

    a. An initial outlay of $10,000 resulting in a free cash flow of $1,993 at the end of each year for the next 10 years

    b. An initial outlay of $10,000 resulting in a free cash flow of $2,054 at the end of each year for the next 20 years

    c. An initial outlay of $10,000 resulting in a free cash flow of $1,193 at the end of each year for the next 12 years

    d. An initial outlay of $10,000 resulting in a free cash flow of $2,843 at the end of each year for the next 5 years

9-3. (*IRR calculation*) Determine to the nearest percent the *IRR* on the following projects:

    a. An initial outlay of $10,000 resulting in a free cash flow of $2,000 at the end of year 1, $5,000 at the end of year 2, and $8,000 at the end of year 3

    b. An initial outlay of $10,000 resulting in a free cash flow of $8,000 at the end of year 1, $5,000 at the end of year 2, and $2,000 at the end of year 3

    c. An initial outlay of $10,000 resulting in a free cash flow of $2,000 at the end of years 1 through 5 and $5,000 at the end of year 6

9-4. (*NPV, PI, and IRR calculations*) Fijisawa Inc. is considering a major expansion of its product line and has estimated the following cash flows associated with such an expansion. The initial outlay would be $1,950,000, and the project would generate incremental free cash flows of $450,000 per year for 6 years. The appropriate required rate of return is 9 percent.

    a. Calculate the *NPV*.

    b. Calculate the *PI*.

    c. Calculate the *IRR*.

    d. Should this project be accepted?

9-5. (*Payback period, NPV, PI, and IRR calculations*) You are considering a project with an initial cash outlay of $80,000 and expected free cash flows of $20,000 at the end of each year for 6 years. The required rate of return for this project is 10 percent.

    a. What is the project's payback period?

    b. What is the project's *NPV*?

     c. What is the project's *PI*?

     d. What is the project's *IRR*?

9-6. (*NPV, PI, and IRR calculations*) You are considering two independent projects, project A and project B. The initial cash outlay associated with project A is $50,000, and the initial cash outlay associated with project B is $70,000. The required rate of return on both projects is 12 percent. The expected annual free cash inflows from each project are as follows:

	PROJECT A	PROJECT B
Initial outlay	−$50,000	−$70,000
Inflow year 1	12,000	13,000
Inflow year 2	12,000	13,000
Inflow year 3	12,000	13,000
Inflow year 4	12,000	13,000
Inflow year 5	12,000	13,000
Inflow year 6	12,000	13,000

Calculate the *NPV*, *PI*, and *IRR* for each project and indicate if the project should be accepted.

9-7. (*Payback period calculations*) You are considering three independent projects, project A, project B, and project C. Given the following cash flow information, calculate the payback period for each.

	PROJECT A	PROJECT B	PROJECT C
Initial outlay	−$1,000	−$10,000	−$5,000
Inflow year 1	600	5,000	1,000
Inflow year 2	300	3,000	1,000
Inflow year 3	200	3,000	2,000
Inflow year 4	100	3,000	2,000
Inflow year 5	500	3,000	2,000

If you require a 3-year payback before an investment can be accepted, which project(s) would be accepted?

9-8. (*NPV with varying required rates of return*) Dowling Sportswear is considering building a new factory to produce aluminum baseball bats. This project would require an initial cash outlay of $5,000,000 and will generate annual free cash inflows of $1,000,000 per year for 8 years. Calculate the project's *NPV* given:

     a. A required rate of return of 9 percent

     b. A required rate of return of 11 percent

     c. A required rate of return of 13 percent

     d. A required rate of return of 15 percent

9-9. (*IRR calculations*) Given the following free cash flows, determine the *IRR* for the three independent projects A, B, and C.

	PROJECT A	PROJECT B	PROJECT C
Initial outlay	−$50,000	−$100,000	−$450,000
Cash inflows:			
Year 1	$10,000	$125,000	$200,000
Year 2	15,000	25,000	200,000
Year 3	20,000	25,000	200,000
Year 4	25,000	25,000	—
Year 5	30,000	25,000	—

9-10. (*NPV with varying required rates of return*) Big Steve's, a maker of swizzle sticks, is considering the purchase of a new plastic stamping machine. This investment requires an initial outlay of $100,000 and will generate free cash inflows of $18,000 per year for 10 years.

     a. If the required rate of return is 10 percent, what is the project's *NPV*?

     b. If the required rate of return is 15 percent, what is the project's *NPV*?

     c. Would the project be accepted under part a or b?

     d. What is the project's *IRR*?

9-11. (*IRR with uneven cash flows*) The Boisjoly Corporation is considering introducing a new low-carb pasta product line. The required rate of return on this project is 12 percent. What is the *IRR* on this project if it is expected to produce the following cash flows?

Initial outlay	−$653,803
FCF in year 1	300,000
FCF in year 2	300,000
FCF in year 3	200,000
FCF in year 4	100,000

9-12. (*IRR with uneven cash flows*) The Tiffin Barker Corporation is considering introducing a new currency verifier that has the ability to identify counterfeit dollar bills. The required rate of return on this project is 12 percent. What is the *IRR* on this project if it is expected to produce the following cash flows?

Initial outlay	−$927,917
FCF in year 1	200,000
FCF in year 2	300,000
FCF in year 3	300,000
FCF in year 4	200,000
FCF in year 5	200,000
FCF in year 6	160,000

9-13. (*MIRR calculation*) Artie's Wrestling Stuff is considering building a new plant. This plant would require an initial cash outlay of $8 million and will generate annual free cash inflows of $2 million per year for 8 years. Calculate the project's *MIRR* given:

   a. A required rate of return of 10 percent
   b. A required rate of return of 12 percent
   c. A required rate of return of 14 percent

9-14. (*Size-disparity problem*) The D. Dorner Farms Corporation is considering purchasing one of two fertilizer-herbicides for the upcoming year. The more expensive of the two is better and will produce a higher yield. Assume these projects are mutually exclusive and that the required rate of return is 10 percent. Given the following free cash flows:

	PROJECT A	PROJECT B
Initial outlay	−$500	−$5,000
Inflow year 1	700	6,000

   a. Calculate the *NPV* of each project.
   b. Calculate the *PI* of each project.
   c. Calculate the *IRR* of each project.
   d. If there is no capital-rationing constraint, which project should be selected? If there is a capital-rationing constraint, how should the decision be made?

9-15. (*Time-disparity problem*) The State Spartan Corporation is considering two mutually exclusive projects. The free cash flows associated with those projects are as follows:

	PROJECT A	PROJECT B
Initial outlay	−$50,000	−$50,000
Inflow year 1	15,625	0
Inflow year 2	15,625	0
Inflow year 3	15,625	0
Inflow year 4	15,625	0
Inflow year 5	15,625	100,000

The required rate of return on these projects is 10 percent.

   a. What is each project's payback period?
   b. What is each project's *NPV*?
   c. What is each project's *IRR*?
   d. What has caused the ranking conflict?
   e. Which project should be accepted? Why?

9-16. (*Capital rationing*) The Cowboy Hat Company of Stillwater, Oklahoma, is considering seven capital investment proposals for which the total funds available are limited to a maximum of $12 million. The projects are independent and have the following costs and profitability indexes associated with them:

PROJECT	COST	PROFITABILITY INDEX
A	$4,000,000	1.18
B	3,000,000	1.08
C	5,000,000	1.33
D	6,000,000	1.31
E	4,000,000	1.19
F	6,000,000	1.20
G	4,000,000	1.18

    a. Under strict capital rationing, which projects should be selected?

    b. What problems are there with capital rationing?

Web Works

9-WW1. Since 2000, Harley Davidson has introduced several new products aimed directly at 18- to 34-year-old Generation X-ers in hopes of bringing a new generation of customers into motorcycling. One is the Buell Blast, a fun-to-ride, sporty motorcycle that is low cost and lightweight, and the other is a lower version of its 833 Sportster aimed at shorter riders. Harley was facing the problem that its customer base was rapidly aging. In fact, over the past 10 years the average age of a Harley rider has risen from 38 to 46. In addition, Harley wanted to add more women to its customer base. How did it go about doing this? Through its Buell motorcycle division that produces smaller, sportier, and less-expensive motorcycles, which are more appropriate for less-experienced motorcyclists, Harley hopes that once these new customers find the fun in motorcycling, they will eventually graduate to Harleys.

Take a look at the Harley Davidson Web site (**www.harley-davidson.com**). What type of customer do you think the Harley Davidson motorcycles appeal to? Now find the Buell Motorcycle Company Web site (**www.buell.com/en_us**). What type of customer do these motorcycles appeal to? What do you think of Harley's strategic plan?

9-WW2. Capital budgeting involves coming up not only with new products but also with new ways of selling old products. A good example of this is the battle between Amazon.com (**www.amazon.com**) and Barnes and Noble, which introduced BarnesandNoble.com (**www.barnesandnoble.com**) in 1997 after giving Amazon.com a 2-year lead. Take a look at these two sites. Which one do you think will dominate in the future and why?

9-WW3. The same principles that guide our capital-budgeting decisions should also guide our personal finance decisions. Take a look at the excellent selection of personal finance calculators; check out the Dinkytown Web site (**www.dinkytown.net**). Which personal finance calculator do you feel will be most helpful to you in the future? Now, plug some numbers into that calculator, print out the results, and comment on those results.

Mini Case

Your first assignment in your new position as assistant financial analyst at Caledonia Products is to evaluate two new capital-budgeting proposals. Because this is your first assignment, you have been asked not only to provide a recommendation but also to respond to a number of questions aimed at assessing your understanding of the capital-budgeting process. This is a standard procedure for all new financial analysts at Caledonia, and it will serve to determine whether you are moved directly into the capital-budgeting analysis department or are provided with remedial training. The memorandum you received outlining your assignment follows.

    To: The New Financial Analysts

    From: Mr. V. Morrison, CEO, Caledonia Products

    Re: Capital-Budgeting Analysis

Provide an evaluation of two proposed projects, both with 5-year expected lives and identical initial outlays of $110,000. Both of these projects involve additions to Caledonia's highly successful

Avalon product line, and as a result, the required rate of return on both projects has been established at 12 percent. The expected free cash flows from each project are as follows:

	PROJECT A	PROJECT B
Initial outlay	−$110,000	−$110,000
Inflow year 1	20,000	40,000
Inflow year 2	30,000	40,000
Inflow year 3	40,000	40,000
Inflow year 4	50,000	40,000
Inflow year 5	70,000	40,000

In evaluating these projects, please respond to the following questions:

   a. Why is the capital-budgeting process so important?
   b. Why is it difficult to find exceptionally profitable projects?
   c. What is the payback period on each project? If Caledonia imposes a 3-year maximum acceptable payback period, which of these projects should be accepted?
   d. What are the criticisms of the payback period?
   e. Determine the *NPV* for each of these projects. Should they be accepted?
   f. Describe the logic behind the *NPV*.
   g. Determine the *PI* for each of these projects. Should they be accepted?
   h. Would you expect the *NPV* and *PI* methods to give consistent accept/reject decisions? Why or why not?
   i. What would happen to the *NPV* and *PI* for each project if the required rate of return increased? If the required rate of return decreased?
   j. Determine the *IRR* for each project. Should they be accepted?
   k. How does a change in the required rate of return affect the project's internal rate of return?
   l. What reinvestment rate assumptions are implicitly made by the *NPV* and *IRR* methods? Which one is better?
   You have also been asked for your views on three unrelated sets of projects. Each set of projects involves two mutually exclusive projects. These projects follow.
   m. Caledonia is considering two investments with 1-year lives. The more expensive of the two is the better and will produce more savings. Assume these projects are mutually exclusive and that the required rate of return is 10 percent. Given the following free cash flows:

	PROJECT A	PROJECT B
Initial outlay	−$195,000	−$1,200,000
Inflow year 1	240,000	1,650,000

   1. Calculate the *NPV* for each project.
   2. Calculate the *PI* for each project.
   3. Calculate the *IRR* for each project.
   4. If there is no capital-rationing constraint, which project should be selected? If there is a capital-rationing constraint, how should the decision be made?

   n. Caledonia is considering two additional mutually exclusive projects. The free cash flows associated with these projects are as follows:

	PROJECT A	PROJECT B
Initial outlay	−$10,000	−$100,000
Inflow year 1	32,000	0
Inflow year 2	32,000	0
Inflow year 3	32,000	0
Inflow year 4	32,000	0
Inflow year 5	32,000	200,000

The required rate of return on these projects is 11 percent.

   1. What is each project's payback period?
   2. What is each project's *NPV*?
   3. What is each project's *IRR*?
   4. What has caused the ranking conflict?
   5. Which project should be accepted? Why?

Self-Test Solution

SS-1.

a. Payback period $= \dfrac{\$54{,}200}{\$20{,}608} = 2.630$ years

b. NPV = present value of all the future annual free cash flows − the initial cash outlay

$$= \frac{FCF_1}{(1+k)^1} + \frac{FCF_2}{(1+k)^2} + \cdots + \frac{FCF_n}{(1+k)^n} - IO$$

$= \$20{,}608(2.855) + \$33{,}808(.497) - \$54{,}200$
$= \$58{,}836 + \$16{,}803 - \$54{,}200$
$= \$21{,}439$

c. $PI = \dfrac{\text{present value of all the future annual free cash flows}}{\text{initial cash outlay}}$

$$= \frac{\dfrac{FCF_1}{(1+k)^1} + \dfrac{FCF_2}{(1+k)^2} + \cdots + \dfrac{FCF_n}{(1+k)^n}}{IO}$$

$= \dfrac{\$75{,}639}{\$54{,}200}$

$= 1.396$

d. IRR = the rate of return that equates the present value of the project's free cash flows with the initial outlay

$$= \frac{FCF_1}{(1+IRR\%)^1} + \frac{FCF_2}{(1+IRR\%)^2} + \cdots + \frac{FCF_n}{(1+IRR\%)^n}$$

$\$54{,}200 = \$20{,}608\,(PVIFA_{IRR\%,\,4\,yr}) + \$33{,}808\,(PVIF_{IRR\%,\,5\,yr})$

Try 29 percent:

$\$54{,}200 = \$20{,}608(2.203) + \$33{,}808(.280)$
$\phantom{\$54{,}200} = \$45{,}399 + \$9{,}466$
$\phantom{\$54{,}200} = \$54{,}865$

Try 30 percent:

$\$45{,}200 = \$20{,}608(2.166) + \$33{,}808(.269)$
$\phantom{\$45{,}200} = \$44{,}637 + \$9{,}094$
$\phantom{\$45{,}200} = \$53{,}731$

Thus, the *IRR* is just below 30 percent and the project should be accepted because the *NPV* is positive, the *PI* is greater than 1.0, and the *IRR* is greater than the required rate of return of 15 percent. On alternatively, use your financial calculator:

CALCULATOR SOLUTION
(USING A TI BA II PLUS):

Data and Key Input	Display
CF ; −54,200; ENTER	CF0 = −54,200.
↓ ; 20,608; ENTER	C01 = 20,608.
↓ ; 4; ENTER	F01 = 4.00
↓ ; 33,808; ENTER	C02 = 33,808.
↓ ; 1; ENTER	F02 = 1.00
NPV	I = 0.00
15;	I = 15.00
↓ ; CPT	NPV = 21,444.
IRR ; CPT	IRR = 29.5907

Notice the slight rounding error difference between these answers and the previous answers.

CHAPTER 10

Cash Flows and Other Topics in Capital Budgeting

In 2001, when Toyota introduced the first-generation model of its gas-electric hybrid car, the Prius, it seemed more like a little science experiment than real competition for the auto industry. In fact, in 2004, General Motors vice chairman Bob Lutz dismissed hybrids as "an interesting curiosity." But that's all changed. As gas prices climbed to around $3 a gallon in 2006, suddenly the gas-electric hybrid car seemed to be the way to go. About that time, Toyota announced it would double the number of Prius cars that it sends to the U.S. market to 100,000 units annually, making it the Japanese automaker's third-best-selling sedan.

How did Toyota gain leadership in the gas-electric hybrid car market? Its capital-budgeting decision to enter the gas-electric hybrid car market with the Prius vaulted Toyota into the lead, and that decision involved a very large investment—in excess of $1 billion. This decision could leave Toyota in great shape to take on the future if strategic management consulting firm Booz Allen Hamilton is right in its forecast that cars equipped with hybrid engines could make up 20 percent of the overall car market by 2010 and 80 percent by 2015.

Still, according to many analysts, Toyota has yet to make a dime on the Prius. In fact, when the Prius first came out, Toyota had it priced so that it was losing about $3,000 on each car it sold. Although now Toyota claims to be finally making money on the Prius, many analysts feel that the automaker is really just breaking even.

Toyota's decision to introduce the Prius and enter the hybrid car market was a difficult one. Would it simply move Toyota customers from one Toyota car to another, or would it bring new customers to Toyota? Was this a chance to gain a foothold on the new technology of the future, or were hybrid cars simply a fad? It was indeed a difficult decision, especially when you consider the size of the investment.

Where is Toyota going next? In 2006 Toyota announced that it would start selling a flexible-fuel vehicle, which can run on up to 85 percent ethanol or ordinary gasoline by 2008. How did Toyota make the decision to go ahead with the Prius and the flexible-fuel car? It used the basic techniques described in the previous chapter; but before it could apply those techniques, Toyota had to come up with the cash flow forecasts and adjust for the risk associated with the project. That's what we'll be looking at in this chapter.

This chapter continues our discussion of decision-making rules for deciding when to invest in new projects. First, we examine what a relevant cash flow is and how to calculate it. We then turn our attention to the problem of capital budgeting under uncertainty. When we discussed capital-budgeting techniques in the preceding chapter, we implicitly assumed the level of risk associated with each investment proposal was the same. In this chapter we lift that assumption and examine various ways in which risk can be incorporated into the capital-budgeting decision.

Objective   **1**

Identify guidelines by which we measure cash flows.

GUIDELINES FOR CAPITAL BUDGETING

To evaluate investment proposals, we must first set guidelines by which we measure the value of each proposal. In effect, we are deciding what is and what isn't a relevant cash flow.

Use Free Cash Flows Rather than Accounting Profits

We use free cash flows, not accounting profits, as our measurement tool. The firm receives and is able to reinvest free cash flows, whereas accounting profits are shown when they are earned rather than when the money is actually in hand. Unfortunately, a firm's accounting profits and free cash flows may not be timed to occur together. For example, capital expenses, such as vehicles and plant and equipment, are depreciated over several years, with their annual depreciation subtracted from profits. Free cash flows correctly reflect the timing of benefits and costs—that is, when the money is received, when it can be reinvested, and when it must be paid out.

Think Incrementally

Unfortunately, calculating free cash flows from a project may not be enough. Decision makers must ask, *What new free cash flows will the company as a whole receive if the company takes on a given project?* What if the company does not take on the project? Interestingly, we may find that not all cash flows a firm expects from an investment proposal are incremental in nature. When measuring free cash flows, however, the trick is to think incrementally. In doing so, we will see that only **incremental after-tax free cash flows** matter. As such, our guiding rule in deciding if a free cash flow is incremental is to look at the company with, versus without, the new project. As you will see in the upcoming sections, this may be easier said than done.

incremental after-tax free cash flows the funds that the firm receives and is able to reinvest, as opposed to accounting profits, which are shown when they are earned rather than when the money is actually in hand.

Beware of Cash Flows Diverted from Existing Products

Assume for a moment that we are managers of a firm considering a new product line that might compete with one of our existing products and possibly reduce its sales. In determining the free cash flows associated with the proposed project, we should consider only the incremental sales brought to the company as a whole. New-product sales achieved at the cost

---

Remember Your Principles

If we are to make intelligent capital-budgeting decisions, we must accurately measure the timing of a project's benefits and costs, that is, when we receive money and when it leaves our hands. **Principle 3: Cash—Not Profits—Is King** speaks directly to this. Remember, it is cash inflows that can be reinvested and cash outflows that involve paying out money.

Remember Your Principles

In order to measure the true effects of our decisions, we analyze the benefits and costs of projects on an incremental basis, which relates directly to **Principle 4: Incremental Cash Flows—It's Only What Changes That Counts**. In effect, we ask ourselves what the cash flows will be if the project is taken on versus what they will be if the project is not taken on.

of losing sales of other products in our line are not considered a benefit. For example, when Quaker Oats introduced Cap'n Crunch's Cozmic Crunch, the product competed directly with the company's Cap'n Crunch and Crunch Berries cereals. (In fact Cozmic Crunch was almost identical to Crunch Berries, with the shapes changed to stars and moons, along with a packet of orange space dust that turns milk green.) Quaker meant to target the market niche held by Post Fruity Pebbles, but there was no question that sales recorded by Cozmic Crunch bit into—literally cannibalized—Quaker's existing product line.

Remember that we are interested only in the sales dollars to the firm if the project is accepted, as opposed to what the sales dollars would be if the project were rejected. Just moving sales from one product line to a new product line does not bring anything new into the company. But if sales are captured from competitors or if sales that would have been lost to new competing products are retained, then these are relevant incremental free cash flows.

Look for Incidental or Synergistic Effects

Although in some cases a new project may take sales away from a firm's current projects, in other cases a new effort might actually bring new sales to the existing line.

For example, in 2006, GM's Saturn division introduced the Sky, a two-seat sports car that looks more like a Honda S2000 than a car from the Saturn division. For years, the Saturn division of GM had been criticized for not keeping pace with the rest of the automotive industry. Its cars remained unchanged, and Saturn division sales steadily declined. Saturn hoped that introducing the Sky would send a message to car buyers that the division was back on track and had something new to offer—that the Sky would bring curious customers to showrooms, and those customers would, in turn, either buy a Sky or lock on to another of Saturn's products. This is called a *synergistic* effect. The cash flow comes from any Saturn sale that would not have occurred if a customer had not visited a Saturn showroom to see a Sky. Synergistic effects are quite common in the business world.

If you owned a convenience store and were considering adding gas pumps, would you evaluate the project looking only at cash flows from the sale of gas? No. You would look at any new sales to any part of your business that the new gas pumps brought in. No doubt the additional traffic that the gas pumps bring in would increase your convenience-store sales. As such, these cash flows would be considered in evaluating whether or not to install the gas pumps. In effect, you should look at any change in cash flow to the company as a whole that results from the project being evaluated.

Work in Working-Capital Requirements

Many times a new project involves an additional investment in working capital. This may take the form of new inventory to stock a sales outlet, an additional investment in accounts receivable resulting from additional credit sales, or an increased investment in free cash to operate cash registers, and more. Working-capital requirements are considered a free cash flow even though they do not leave the company. Generally, working-capital requirements are tied up over the life of the project. When the project terminates, there is usually an offsetting cash inflow as the working capital is recovered, although this offset is not perfect because of the time value of money.

Consider Incremental Expenses

Just as cash inflows from a new project are measured on an incremental basis, expenses, or cash outflows, should also be measured on an incremental basis. For example, if introducing a new product line necessitates training the sales staff, the after-tax cash flow associated with the training program must be considered a cash outflow and charged against the project. Likewise, if accepting a new project dictates that a production facility be reengineered, the cash flows associated with that capital investment should be charged against the project, and they will then be depreciated over the life of the project. Again, any incremental after-tax cash flow affecting the company as a whole is a relevant cash flow, whether it is flowing in or flowing out.

Remember That Sunk Costs Are Not Incremental Cash Flows

Only cash flows that are affected by the decision making at the moment are relevant in capital budgeting. The manager asks two questions: (1) Will this cash flow occur if the project is accepted? (2) Will this cash flow occur if the project is rejected? Yes to the first question and no to the second equals an incremental cash flow. For example, let's assume you are considering introducing a new taste treat called Puddin' in a Shoe. You would like to do some test-marketing before production. If you are considering the decision to test-market and have not yet done so, the costs associated with the test-marketing are relevant cash flows. Conversely, if you have already test-marketed, the cash flows involved in testing-marketing are no longer relevant to the project's evaluation. It's a matter of timing. Regardless of what you might decide about future production, the cash flows allocated to the marketing test have already occurred. Cash flows that have already taken place are often referred to as "sunk costs" because they have been sunk into the project and cannot be undone. As a rule, any cash flows that are not affected by the accept/reject criterion should not be included in capital-budgeting analysis.

Account for Opportunity Costs

Now we will focus on the cash flows that are lost because a given project consumes scarce resources that would have produced cash flows if that project had been rejected. This is the opportunity cost of doing business. For example, a product consumes valuable floor space in a production facility. Although the cash flow is not obvious, the real question remains: What else could be done with this space? The space could have been rented out, or another product could have been stored there. The key point is that opportunity-cost cash flows should reflect the net cash flows that would have been received if the project under consideration were rejected. Again, we are analyzing the cash flows to the company as a whole, with or without the project.

Decide If Overhead Costs Are Truly Incremental Cash Flows

Although we certainly want to include any incremental cash flows resulting in changes from overhead expenses such as utilities and salaries, we also want to make sure that these are truly incremental cash flows. Many times, overhead expenses—heat, light, rent—would occur whether a given project were accepted or rejected. There is often not a single, specific project to which these expenses can be allocated. Thus, the question is not whether the project benefits from the overhead costs a firm spends but whether they are incremental cash flows associated with the project and relevant to capital budgeting.

Ignore Interest Payments and Financing Flows

To evaluate new projects and determine cash flows, we must separate the investment decision from the financing decision. Interest payments and other financing cash flows that might result from raising funds to finance a project should not be considered incremental cash flows. If accepting a project means we have to raise new funds by issuing bonds, the interest charges associated with raising funds are not a relevant cash outflow. Why? Because when we discount the incremental cash flows back to the present at the required rate of return, we are implicitly accounting for the cost of raising funds to finance the new project. In essence, the required rate of return reflects the cost of the funds needed to support the project. Managers first determine the desirability of the project and then determine how best to finance it.

Did You Get It?

1. What is an incremental cash flow? What is a sunk cost? Why must you account for opportunity costs?

2. If Ford introduces a new auto line, might some of the cash flows from that new car line be diverted from existing product lines? How should you deal with this?

Finance at Work

UNIVERSAL STUDIOS

A major capital-budgeting decision led Universal Studios to build its Islands of Adventure theme park. The purpose of this $2.6 billion investment by Universal was to get first crack at the tourist's dollar in Orlando, Florida. Although this capital-budgeting decision may, on the surface, seem like a relatively simple decision, forecasting the expected cash flows associated with the theme park was, in fact, quite complicated.

To begin with, Universal was introducing a product that competes directly with itself. The original Universal Studios park features rides such as "Back to the Future" and "Jaws." Were there enough tourist dollars to support both theme parks, or would the new Islands of Adventure park simply cannibalize ticket sales from the older Universal Studios park? In addition, what would happen when Disney countered with a new park of its own?

In the case of Universal's Islands of Adventure, we could ask what would happen to attendance at the original Universal Studios park if the new park were not opened versus what the attendance would be with the new park. Would tourist traffic

through the Islands of Adventure lead to additional sales of the other brands and businesses visibly promoted and available in the new park that fall under Universal's and Seagrams's corporate umbrella?

From Universal's point of view, the objective may have been threefold: to increase its share of the tourist market; to keep from losing market share as tourists look for the latest in technological rides and entertainment; and to promote Universal's, and its parent company Seagrams's, other brands and products. However, for companies in very competitive markets, the evolution and introduction of new products may serve more to preserve market share than to expand it. Certainly, that's the case in the computer market, where Dell, Compaq, and IBM introduce upgraded models that continually render current models obsolete. The bottom line here is that, with respect to estimating cash flows, things are many times more complicated than they first appear. As such, we have to dig deep to understand how a firm's free cash flows are affected by the decision at hand.

AN OVERVIEW OF THE CALCULATIONS OF A PROJECT'S FREE CASH FLOWS

Objective **2**

Explain how a project's benefits and costs—that is, its free cash flows—are calculated.

As we have explained, in measuring cash flows, we will focus our attention on the difference in the firm's after-tax cash flows *with* versus *without* the project—the project's *free cash flows*. The worth of our decision depends on the accuracy of our cash flow estimates. For this reason, we first examined the question of which cash flows are relevant. Now we will see that, in general, a project's free cash flows will fall into one of three categories: (1) the initial outlay, (2) the differential flows over the project's life, and (3) the terminal cash flow. Once we have taken a look at these categories, we will take on the task of measuring these free cash flows.

What Goes Into the Initial Outlay

The **initial outlay** is the immediate cash outflow necessary to purchase the asset and put it in operating order. This amount includes the cost of installing the asset (the asset's purchase price plus any expenses associated with shipping or installation) and any nonexpense cash outlays, such as increased working-capital requirements. If we are considering a new sales outlet, there might be additional cash flows associated with making a net investment in working capital in the form of increased inventory and cash necessary to operate the outlet. Although these cash flows are not included in the cost of the asset or even expensed on the books, they must be included in our analysis. The after-tax cost of expense items incurred as a result of the new investment must also be included as cash outflows—for example, any training expenses that would not have been incurred otherwise.

initial outlay the immediate cash outflow necessary to purchase the asset and put it in operating order.

Finally, if the investment decision is a replacement decision, the cash inflow associated with the selling price of the old asset, in addition to any tax effects resulting from its sale, must be included. It should be stressed that the incremental nature of the cash flow is of great importance. In many cases, if the project is not accepted, then status quo for the firm will simply not continue. Thus, we must be realistic in estimating what the cash flows to the company would be if the new project were not accepted.

Potentially, one of the most confusing initial outlay calculations is for a replacement project involving the incremental tax payment associated with the sale of an old asset. There are three possible tax situations dealing with the sale of an old asset:

1. The old asset is sold for a price above the depreciated value. Here the difference between the old machine's selling price and its depreciated value is considered a taxable gain and is taxed at the marginal corporate tax rate. If, for example, the old machine was originally purchased for $15,000, had a book value of $10,000, and was sold for $17,000, assuming the firm's marginal corporate tax rate is 34 percent, the taxes due from the gain would be ($17,000 − $10,000) × (.34), or $2,380.

2. The old asset is sold for its depreciated value. In this case, no taxes result, because there is neither a gain nor a loss in the asset's sale.

3. The old asset is sold for less than its depreciated value. In this case, the difference between the depreciated book value and the salvage value of the asset is a taxable loss and can be used to offset capital gains and thus results in a tax savings. For example, if the depreciated book value of the asset is $10,000 and it is sold for $7,000, we have a $3,000 loss. Assuming the firm's marginal corporate tax rate is 34 percent, the cash inflow from the tax savings is ($10,000 − $7,000) × (.34), or $1,020.

What Goes Into the Annual Free Cash Flows over the Project's Life

Annual free cash flows come from operating cash flows (that is, what you've made as a result of taking on the project), changes in working capital, and any capital spending that might take place. In our calculations we'll begin with our pro forma statements and work from there. We will have to make adjustments for interest, depreciation, and working capital, along with any capital expenditures that might occur.

Before we look at the calculations, let's look at the types of adjustments that we're going to have to make to go from operating cash flows to free cash flows. To do this we'll have to make adjustments for:

- **Depreciation and taxes**   When accountants calculate a firm's net income, one of the expenses they subtract out is depreciation. However, depreciation is a non–cash flow expense. If you think about it, depreciation occurs because you bought a fixed asset (for example, you built a plant) in an earlier period, and now, through depreciation, you're expensing it over time—but depreciation does not involve a cash flow. That means the firm's net income understates cash flows by this amount. Therefore, we'll want to compensate for this by adding depreciation back into our measure of accounting income when calculating cash flows.

  In addition, although depreciation is not a cash flow item, it lowers profits, which, in turn, lowers taxes. For students developing a foundation in corporate finance, it is the concept of depreciation, not the calculation of it, that is important. The reason the calculation of depreciation is deemphasized is that it is extremely complicated, and its calculation changes every few years as Congress enacts new tax laws. That said, bear in mind that although depreciation is not a cash flow item, it does affect cash flows by lowering the level of profits on which taxes are calculated.

  A modified version of the IRS's accelerated cost recovery system (ACRS) is used for most tangible depreciable property. Under this method, the life of the asset is determined according to the asset's class life, which is assigned by the IRS; for example, most computer equipment has a 5-year asset life. ACRS also allows for only a half-year's deduction in the first year and a half-year's deduction in the year after the recovery period. The asset is then depreciated using the 200 percent declining balance method or an optional straight-line method.

  For our purposes, depreciation is calculated using a simplified straight-line method. This simplified process ignores the half-year convention that allows only a half-year's deduction in the year the project is placed in service and a half-year's deduction in the first year after the recovery period. By ignoring the half-year convention and assuming a zero salvage value, we are able to calculate annual deprecialet or simply additional investment in accounts receivable. There also may be some spontaneous short-term financing—for example, increases in accounts payable—that result from the new project. Thus, the change in net working capital is the additional investment in current assets minus any additional short-term liabilities that were generated.

Step 3. *Calculate the cash flows from the change in the firm's capital spending.* Although there is generally a large cash outflow associated with a project's initial outlay, there may also be additional capital-spending requirements over the life of the project. For example, you may know ahead of time that the plant will need some minor retooling in the second year of the project in order to keep the project abreast of new technological changes that are expected to take place. In effect, we will look at the company with and without the new project, and any changes in capital spending that occur are relevant.

Step 4. *Putting it together: calculating a project's free cash flows.* Thus, a project's free cash flows are:

Project's free cash flows = change in earnings before interest and taxes (EBIT)
− change in taxes
+ change in depreciation
− change in net working capital
− change in capital spending

To estimate the changes in EBIT, taxes, depreciation, net working capital, and capital spending we start with estimates of how many units we expect to sell, what the costs—both fixed and variable—will be, what the selling price will be, and what the required capital investment will be. From there we can put together a pro forma statement that should provide us with the data we need to estimate the project's free cash flows. However, you must keep in mind that our capital-budgeting decision will only be as good as our estimates of the costs and future demand associated with the project. In fact, most capital-budgeting decisions that turn out to be bad decisions are not so because of using a bad decision rule but because the estimates of future demand and costs were inaccurate. Let's look at an example.

➤ EXAMPLE

You are considering expanding your product line that currently consists of Lee's Press-on Nails to take advantage of the fitness craze. The new product you are considering introducing is "Press-on Abs." You feel you can sell 100,000 of these per year for 4 years (after which time this project is expected to shut down because forecasters predict looking healthy will no longer be in vogue, and looking like a couch potato will). The Press-on Abs would sell for $6.00 each, with are variable cost of $3.00 for each one produced. Annual fixed costs associated with production would be $90,000. In addition, there would be a $200,000 initial expenditure associated with the purchase of new production equipment. It is assumed that this initial expenditure will be depreciated, using the simplified, straight-line method, down to zero over 4 years. The project will also require a one-time initial investment of $30,000 in net working capital associated with the inventory. Finally, assume that the firm's marginal tax rate is 34 percent.

INITIAL OUTLAY

Let's begin by estimating the initial outlay. In this example, the initial outlay is the $200,000 initial expenditure plus the investment of $30,000 in net working capital, for a total of $230,000.

ANNUAL FREE CASH FLOWS

Table 10-1 calculates the annual change in earnings before interest and taxes. This calculation begins with the change in sales (Δ Sales) and subtracts the change in fixed and

TABLE 10-1   Calculating the Annual Change in Earnings before Interest and Taxes for the Press-on Abs Project

Δ Sales (100,000 units at $6.00/unit)	$ 600,000
Less: Δ Variable costs (variable cost $3.00/unit)	$ 300,000
Less: Δ Fixed costs	$ 90,000
Equals: EBITDA (assuming amortization is 0)	$ 210,000
Less: Δ Depreciation ($200,000/4 years)	$ 50,000
Equals: Δ EBIT	$ 160,000
Less: Δ Taxes: (taxed at 34%)	$ 54,400
Equals: Δ Net income	$ 105,600

variable costs in addition to the change in depreciation, to arrive at the change in earnings before interest and taxes (ΔEBIT). Depreciation is calculated using the simplified, straight-line method, which is simply the depreciable value of the asset ($200,000 divided by the asset's expected life of 4 years). Taxes are then calculated assuming a 34 percent marginal tax rate. Once we have calculated EBIT and taxes, we don't need to go any further, because these are the only two values from the income statement that we need. In addition, in this example there is not any annual increase in working capital associated with the project under consideration. Also notice that we have ignored any interest payments and financing flows that might have occurred. As mentioned earlier, when we discount the free cash flows back to the present at the required rate of return, we are implicitly accounting for the cost of the funds needed to support the project.

The project's annual *change in operating cash flow* is calculated in Table 10-2.

Remember: **The project's annual *free cash flow* is simply the *change in operating cash flow* less any *change in net working capital* and less any *change in capital spending*.** In this example there are no changes in net working capital and capital spending over the life of the project. This is not the case for all projects that you will consider. For example, on a project where sales increase annually, it is likely that working capital will also increase each year to support a larger inventory and a higher level of accounts receivable. Similarly, on some projects the capital expenditures may be spread out over several years. The point here is that what we are trying to do is look at the firm with this project and without this project and measure the change in cash flows other than any interest payments and financing flows that might occur.

TERMINAL CASH FLOW

For this project, the terminal cash flow is quite simple. The only unusual cash flow at the project's termination is the recapture of the net working capital associated with the project. In effect, the investment in inventory of $30,000 is liquidated when the project is shut down in 4 years. Keep in mind that in calculating free cash flow we subtract out the change in net working capital, but because the change in net working capital is negative (we are reducing our investment in inventory), we are subtracting a negative number, which has the effect of adding it back in. Thus, working capital was a negative cash flow when the project began and we invested in inventory, but at termination it becames a positive offsetting cash flow when the inventory was liquidated. The calculation of the terminal free cash flow is illustrated in Table 10-3.

TABLE 10-2   Calculating the Annual Change in Operating Cash Flow, Press-on Abs Project

Δ Earnings before interest and taxes (EBIT)	$160,000
Minus: Δ Taxes	− $ 54,400
Plus: Δ Depreciation	+ $ 50,000
Equals: Δ Operating cash flow	$155,600

Can You Do It?

CALCULATING OPERATING CASH FLOWS

Assume that a new project will generate revenues of $300,000 annually, and the annual cash expenses, including both fixed and variable costs, will be $190,000 per year. Depreciation will be $20,000 per year. In addition, the firm's marginal tax rate is 40 percent. Calculate the operating cash flows.

(The solution can be found on page 308.)

TABLE 10-3 Calculating the Terminal Free Cash Flow, Press-on Abs Project

Δ Earnings before interest and taxes (EBIT)	$160,000
Minus: Δ Taxes	−$ 54,400
Plus: Δ Depreciation	+ $ 50,000
Minus: Δ Net working capital	−($ 30,000)
Equals: Δ Free cash flow	$185,600

FIGURE 10-1 Free Cash Flow Diagram for Press-on Abs

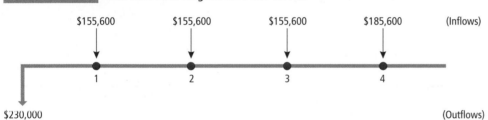

If we were to construct a free cash flow diagram from this example (Figure 10-1), it would have an initial outlay of $230,000, the free cash flows during years 1 through 3 would be $155,600, and the free cash flow in the terminal year would be $185,600. Free cash flow diagrams similar to Figure 10-1 will be used throughout the remainder of this chapter with arrows above the time line indicating cash inflows and arrows below the time line denoting outflows.

A Comprehensive Example: Calculating Free Cash Flows

Now let's put what we know about capital budgeting together and look at a capital-budgeting decision for a firm in the 34 percent marginal tax bracket with a 15 percent required rate of return or cost of capital. The project we are considering involves the introduction of a new electric scooter line by Raymobile. Our first task is that of estimating cash flows. This project is expected to last 5 years and then, because this is somewhat of a fad product, be terminated. Thus, our first task becomes that of estimating the initial outlay, the annual free cash flows, and the terminal free cash flow. Given the information in Table 10-4, we want to determine the free cash flows associated with the project. Once we have that, we can easily calculate the project's net present value, the profitability index, and the internal rate of return and apply the appropriate decision criteria.

To determine the differential annual free cash flows, we first need to determine the annual change in operating cash flow. To do this we will take the change in EBIT, subtract out the change in taxes, and then add in the change in depreciation. This is shown in Section II of Table 10-5. We first determine what the change in sales revenue will be by multiplying the units sold times the sale price. From the change in sales revenue, we subtract out variable costs,

How Did You Do?

CALCULATING OPERATING CASH FLOWS

You were asked to determine the operating cash flows for a project. Operating cash flows are calculated as:

Operating cash flows = change in earnings before interest and taxes (EBIT)
  − change in taxes
  + change in depreciation

Step 1. Calculate the change in EBIT

Revenue	$300,000
−Cash fixed and variable expenses	− 190,000
−Depreciation	− 20,000
=EBIT	= $ 90,000

Step 2. Calculate taxes by multiplying the increase in EBIT times the marginal tax rate of 40 percent

Change in EBIT	$90,000
Times: Taxes (40%)	= 36,000

Step 3. Calculate operating cash flows

Operating cash flows = change in earnings before interest and taxes (EBIT)
  − change in taxes
  + change in depreciation
  = $90,000 − $36,000 + $20,000 = $74,000

TABLE 10-4 Raymobile Scooter Line Capital–Budgeting Example

Cost of new plant and equipment	$9,700,000
Shipping and installation costs	$ 300,000
Unit sales	

YEAR	UNITS SOLD
1	50,000
2	100,000
3	100,000
4	70,000
5	50,000

Sales price per unit	$150/unit in years 1 through 4, $130/unit in year 5
Variable cost per unit	$80/unit
Annual fixed costs	$500,000
Working–capital requirements	There will be an initial working-capital requirement of $100,000 just to get production started. Then, for each year, the *total* investment in net working capital will be equal to 10 percent of the dollar value of sales for that year. Thus, the investment in working capital will increase during years 1 and 2, then decrease in year 4. Finally, all working capital will be liquidated at the termination of the project at the end of year 5.
The depreciation method	We use the simplified straight-line method over 5 years. It is assumed that the plant and equipment will have no salvage value after 5 years. Thus, annual depreciation is $2,000,000/year for 5 years.

Across the Hall

TEST-MARKETING NEW PRODUCTS

A capital-budgeting decision is only as good as its free cash flow forecasts. Coming up with those cash flow forecasts and analyzing them involves an intersection of finance and marketing—and for you, the marketing student, understanding how this information is used by the folks in finance will help you do your job better. Although finance prepares the analysis used by the firm's managers to make the go/no-go decision on new products, marketers generally supply the sales forecasts that, in turn, feed into the cash flow forecasts on which those decisions are based.

It is impossible to overstate the importance of the marketing input. One way marketers can improve the quality of cash flow forecasts is to test-market the new product. With test-marketing the firm can gain a better handle on how consumers will react to the product and thereby make more accurate cash flow forecasts. Test-marketing results also allow the firm to make adjustments that might improve the new product's chances in the marketplace. However, not only is test-marketing expensive, but it also alerts the competition to what is on the way and allows them to develop their own alternatives.

Whether to go ahead with test-marketing is generally a decision that is handled outside of finance—in the marketing area—and its impact on whether the eventual capital-budgeting decision is good or not can be considerable. Look, for example, at Nabisco, which tried to take its Teddy Grahams (crackers) to the breakfast table in the form of a breakfast cereal. Nabisco initially introduced a chocolate, cinnamon, and honey version of the cereal, but consumers weren't thrilled with it. So Nabisco reworked the formula, improved the taste, and immediately put it out without test-marketing it. Unfortunately, although it tasted better, it didn't do that well in milk, leaving a gooey paste on the bottom of the cereal bowl. Consumers rejected it, store managers refused to restock it, and Nabisco dropped the project. In effect, the decision not to test-market the reformulated Teddy Grahams Breakfast Cereal turned a potentially good capital-budgeting project into a failure.

which are $80 per unit. Then, the change in fixed costs is subtracted out, and the result is earnings before interest, taxes, depreciation, and amortization (EBITDA). Subtracting the change in depreciation and amortization, which in this case is assumed to be zero, from EBITDA then leaves us with the change in earnings before interest and taxes (EBIT). From the change in EBIT, we can then calculate the change in taxes, which are assumed to be 34 percent of EBIT.

Using the calculations provided in Section I of Table 10-5, we then calculate the operating cash flow in Section II of Table 10-5. As you recall, the operating cash flow is simply EBIT minus taxes, plus depreciation.

To calculate the free cash flow from this project, we subtract the change in net working capital and the change in capital spending from operating cash flow. Thus, the first step becomes determining the change in net working capital, which is shown in Section III of Table 10-5. The change in net working capital generally includes both increases in inventory and increases in accounts receivable that naturally occur as sales increase from the introduction of the new product line. Some of the increase in accounts receivable may be offset by increases in accounts payable, but, in general, most new projects involve some type of increase in net working capital. In this example, there is an initial working capital requirement of $100,000. In addition, for each year the total investment in net working capital will be equal to 10 percent of sales for each year. Thus, the investment in working capital for year 1 is $750,000 (because sales are estimated to be $7,500,000). Working capital will already be at $100,000, so the change in net working capital will be $650,000. Net working capital will continue to increase during years 1 and 2, then decrease in year 4. Finally, all working capital is liquidated at the termination of the project at the end of year 5.

With the operating cash flow and the change in net working capital already calculated, the calculation of the project's free cash flow becomes easy. All that is missing is the change in capital spending, which in this example will simply be the $9,700,000 for plant and equipment plus the $300,000 for shipping and installation. Thus, the change in capital spending becomes $10,000,000. We then need merely to take operating cash flow and subtract from it both the change in net working capital and the change in capital spending. This is done in Section IV of Table 10-5. A free cash flow diagram for this project is provided in Figure 10-2.

Using the information provided in Section IV of Table 10-5 and Figure 10-2, we can easily calculate the *NPV*, *PI*, and *IRR* for this project.

TABLE 10-5 Calculating the Free Cash Flow for Raymobile Scooters

YEAR	0	1	2	3	4	5
SECTION I. CALCULATE THE CHANGE IN EBIT, TAXES, AND DEPRECIATION						
(THIS BECOMES AN INPUT IN THE CALCULATION OF OPERATING CASH FLOW IN SECTION II)						
Units sold		50,000	100,000	100,000	70,000	50,000
Sales price		$150	$150	$150	$150	$130
Sales revenue		$7,500,000	$15,000,000	$15,000,000	$10,500,000	$6,500,000
Less: Variable costs		4,000,000	8,000,000	8,000,000	5,600,000	4,000,000
Less: Fixed costs		500,000	500,000	500,000	500,000	500,000
Equals: EBITDA		$3,000,000	$ 6,500,000	$ 6,500,000	$ 4,400,000	$2,000,000
Less: Depreciation (amortization is assumed to be 0)		2,000,000	2,000,000	2,000,000	2,000,000	2,000,000
Equals: EBIT		$1,000,000	$ 4,500,000	$ 4,500,000	$ 2,400,000	0
Taxes (@34%)		340,000	1,530,000	1,530,000	816,000	0
SECTION II. CALCULATE OPERATING CASH FLOW						
(THIS BECOMES AN INPUT IN THE CALCULATION OF FREE CASH FLOW IN SECTION IV)						
Operating cash flow:						
EBIT		$1,000,000	$4,500,000	$4,500,000	$2,400,000	$ 0
Minus: Taxes		340,000	1,530,000	1,530,000	816,000	0
Plus: Depreciation		2,000,000	2,000,000	2,000,000	2,000,000	2,000,000
Equals: Operating cash flows		$2,660,000	$4,970,000	$4,970,000	$3,584,000	$2,000,000
SECTION III. CALCULATE THE NET WORKING CAPITAL						
(THIS BECOMES AN INPUT IN THE CALCULATION OF FREE CASH FLOW IN SECTION IV)						
Change in net working capital:						
Revenue		$7,500,000	$15,000,000	$15,000,000	$10,500,000	$6,500,000
Initial working-capital requirement	$100,000					
Net working-capital needs		750,000	1,500,000	1,500,000	1,050,000	650,000
Liquidation of working capital						650,000
Change in working capital	100,000	650,000	750,000	0	(450,000)	(1,050,000)
SECTION IV. CALCULATE FREE CASH FLOW						
(USING INFORMATION CALCULATED IN SECTIONS II AND III, IN ADDITION TO THE CHANGE IN CAPITAL SPENDING)						
Free cash flow:						
Operating cash flow		$2,660,000	$4,970,000	$4,970,000	$3,584,000	$ 2,000,000
Minus: Change in net working capital	$ 100,000	650,000	750,000	0	(450,000)	(1,050,000)
Minus: Change in capital spending	10,000,000	0	0	0	0	0
Equals: Free cash flow	$(10,100,000)	$2,010,000	$4,220,000	$4,970,000	$4,034,000	$3,050,000

Did You Get It? ....

1. In general, a project's cash flows will fall into one of three categories. What are these categories?
2. What is a free cash flow? How do we calculate it?
3. Although depreciation is not a cash flow item, it plays an important role in the calculation of cash flows. How does depreciation affect a project's cash flows?

FIGURE 10-2 Free Cash Flow Diagram for the Raymobile Scooter Line

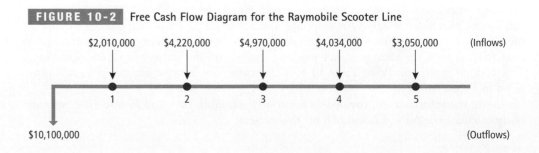

Can You Do It?

CALCULATING FREE CASH FLOWS

Hurley's Hidden Snacks is introducing a new product and has an expected change in EBIT of $800,000. Hurley's Hidden Snacks has a 40 percent marginal tax rate. This project will also produce $100,000 of depreciation per year. In addition, this project will also cause the following changes in year 1:

	WITHOUT THE PROJECT	WITH THE PROJECT
Accounts receivable	$35,000	$63,000
Inventory	65,000	70,000
Accounts payable	70,000	90,000

What is the project's free cash flow in year 1?

(The solution can be found on page 312.)

Remember Your Principles

In this chapter, it is easy to get caught up in the calculations and forget that before the calculations can be made, someone has to come up with the idea for the project. In some of the example problems, you may see projects that appear to be extremely profitable. Unfortunately, as we learned in **Principle 5: The Curse of Competitive Markets—Why It's Hard to Find Exceptionally Profitable Projects**, it is unusual to find projects with dramatically high returns because of the very competitive nature of business. Thus, keep in mind that capital budgeting not only involves the estimation and evaluation of the project's cash flows, but it also includes the process of coming up with the idea for the project in the first place.

OPTIONS IN CAPITAL BUDGETING

Objective **3**

Explain the importance of options, or flexibility, in capital budgeting.

The use of discounted cash flow decision criteria, such as the *NPV* method, provides an excellent framework within which to evaluate projects. However, what happens if the project being analyzed has the potential to be modified after some future uncertainty has been resolved? For example, if a project that had an expected life of 10 years turns out to be better than anticipated, it may be expanded or continued past 10 years, perhaps going on for 20 years. On the other hand, if its cash flows do not meet expectations, it may not last a full 10 years and be scaled back, abandoned, or sold. In addition, suppose the project were delayed for a year or two. This flexibility is something that the *NPV* and our other decision-making criteria have difficulty dealing with. In fact, the *NPV* may actually understate the value of the project if the future opportunities associated with modifying it have a positive value. It is this value of flexibility that we will be examining using options.

Three of the most common option types that can add value to a capital-budgeting project are (1) the option to delay a project until the future cash flows are more favorable—this option is common when the firm has exclusive rights, perhaps a patent, to a product or technology; (2) the option to expand a project, perhaps in size or even to develop new products that would not have otherwise been feasible; and (3) the option to abandon a project if the future cash flows fall short of expectations.

The Option to Delay a Project

There is no question that the estimated cash flows associated with a project can change over time. In fact, as a result of changing expected cash flows, a project that currently has a negative net present value may have a positive net present value in the future. Let's take another

How Did You Do?

CALCULATING FREE CASH FLOWS

You were asked to determine the free cash flows in year 1 for a new product being introduced by Hurley's Hidden Snacks.

Step 1. Calculate the change in net working capital.

The change in net working capital equals the increase in accounts receivable and inventory less the increase in accounts payable = $28,000 + $5,000 − $20,000 = $13,000.

Step 2. Calculate the change in free cash flows.

Project's free cash flows = change in earnings before interest and taxes (EBIT)

− change in taxes

+ change in depreciation

− change in net working capital

− change in capital spending

= $800,000 − ($800,000 × .40) + $100,000 − $13,000 − $0 = $567,000

look at the gas-electric hybrid car market we examined in the introduction to this chapter. This time, let's assume that you've developed a high-voltage, nickel-metal hydride battery that can be used to increase the mileage on hybrid cars to up to 150 miles per gallon. However, as you examine the costs of producing this new battery, you realize that it is still relatively expensive to manufacture and that, given the costs, the market for a car using this battery is quite small right now. Does that mean that the rights to the high-voltage, nickel-metal hydride battery have no value? No, they have value because you may be able to improve on this technology in the future and make the battery even more efficient and less expensive. They also have value because oil prices might rise even further, which would lead to a bigger market for super-fuel-efficient cars. In effect, the ability to delay this project with the hope that technological and market conditions will change, making this project profitable, lends value to the project.

Another example of the option to delay a project until the future cash flows are more favorable involves a firm that owns the oil rights to some oil-rich land and is considering an oil-drilling project. Suppose after all of the costs and the expected oil output are considered, the project has a negative net present value. Does that mean the firm should give away its oil rights or that those oil rights have no value? Certainly not. There is a chance that in the future oil prices could rise to the point that this negative *NPV* project could become a positive *NPV* project. It is this ability to delay development that provides value. Thus, the value in this seemingly negative *NPV* project is provided by the option to delay the project until the future cash flows are more favorable.

The Option to Expand a Project

Just as we saw with the option to delay a project, the estimated cash flows associated with a project can change over time, making it valuable to expand a project. Again, this flexibility to adjust production to demand has value. For example, a firm might deliberately build a production plant with excess capacity so that if the product has more-than-anticipated demand, the firm can simply increase production. Alternatively, taking on this project might provide the firm with a foothold in a new industry and lead to other products that would not have otherwise been feasible. This reasoning has led many firms to expand into e-businesses, hoping to gain know-how and expertise that will lead to other profitable projects down the line. It also provides some of the rationale for research and development expenditures to explore new markets.

Let's go back to our example of the gas-electric hybrid car and examine the option to expand that project. One of the reasons that most of the major automobile firms are introducing gas-electric hybrid cars is that they feel that if gas prices keep moving beyond the $2 per gallon price, these hybrids may become the future of the industry, and the only way to gain the know-how and expertise to produce a hybrid is to do it. As the cost of technology declines and the demand increases—perhaps pushed on by increases in gas prices—then the companies will be ready to expand into full-fledged production. This strategy becomes clear when you look at Honda, which first introduced the Insight in 2000, and Toyota, which introduced the Prius in 2001.

When hybrids were first introduced, analysts estimated that Honda was losing about $8,000 on each Insight it sold, whereas Toyota was losing about $3,000 per car, but both firms expected to break even in a few years. Still, these projects made sense because they allowed these automakers to gain the technological and production expertise to profitably produce a gas-electric hybrid car. And with production estimates reaching 1 million by 2009, it is a big market they're looking at. Moreover, the technology Honda and Toyota developed with the Insight and Prius may have profitable applications for other cars or in other areas. In effect, it is the option of expanding production in the future that brings value to this project.

The Option to Abandon a Project

The option to abandon a project as the estimated cash flows associated with it change over time also has value. Again, it is this flexibility to adjust to new information that provides the value. For example, a project's sales in the first year or two might not live up to expectations, with the project being barely profitable. The firm might then decide to liquidate the project and sell the plant and all of the equipment. That liquidated value may be more than the value of keeping the project going.

Again, let's go back to our example of the gas-electric hybrid car and, this time, examine the option to abandon that project. If after a few years the cost of gas falls dramatically while the cost of technology remains high, the gas-electric hybrid car might not become profitable. At that point the manufacturer might decide to abandon the project and sell the technology, including all the patent rights to it. In effect, the original project, the gas-electric hybrid car, may not be of value, but the technology that has been developed might be. In effect, the value of abandoning the project and selling the technology might be more than the value of keeping the project running. Again, it is the value of flexibility associated with the possibility of modifying the project in the future—in this case abandoning the project—that can produce positive value.

Options in Capital Budgeting: The Bottom Line

Because of the potential to be modified in the future after some future uncertainty has been resolved, we may find that a project with a negative net present value based upon its expected free cash flows is a "good" project and should be accepted. This demonstrates the value of options. In addition, we may find that a project with a positive net present value may be of more value if its acceptance is delayed. Options also explain the logic that drives firms to take on negative *NPV* projects that allow them to enter new markets. The option to abandon a project explains why firms hire employees on a temporary basis rather than permanently, why they lease rather than buy equipment, and why they enter into contracts with suppliers on an annual basis rather than long term.

Did You Get It?

1. Give an example of an option to delay a project. Why might this be of value?
2. Give an example of an option to expand a project. Why might this be of value?
3. Give an example of an option to abandon a project. Why might this be of value?

RISK AND THE INVESTMENT DECISION

Objective 4

Explain what the appropriate measure of risk is for capital-budgeting purposes.

Up to this point we have ignored risk in capital budgeting; that is, we have discounted expected cash flows back to the present and ignored any uncertainty that there might be surrounding that estimate. In reality the future cash flows associated with the introduction of

FIGURE 10-3   A Cash Flow Diagram Based on Possible Outcomes

a new sales outlet or a new product are estimates of what is *expected* to happen in the future, not necessarily what will happen. For example, when Coca-Cola decided to replace Classic Coke with "New Coke," you can bet that the expected cash flows it based its decision on were nothing like the cash flows it realized. As a result, it didn't take Coca-Cola long to reintroduce Classic Coke. The cash flows we have discounted back to the present so far have only been our best estimate of the expected future cash flows. A cash flow diagram based on the possible outcomes of an investment proposal rather than the expected values of these outcomes appears in Figure 10-3.

In this section, we assume that we do not know beforehand what cash flows will actually result from a new project. However, we do have expectations concerning the possible outcomes and are able to assign probabilities to these outcomes. Stated another way, although we do not know what the cash flows resulting from the acceptance of a new project will be, we can formulate the probability distributions from which the flows will be drawn. As we learned in Chapter 6, risk occurs when there is some question about the future outcome of an event.

In the remainder of this chapter, we assume that although future cash flows are not known with certainty, the probability distribution from which they are derived can be estimated. Also, because we have illustrated that the dispersion of possible outcomes reflects risk, we are prepared to use a measure of dispersion, or variability, later in the chapter when we quantify risk.

In the pages that follow, remember that there are only two basic issues that we address: (1) What is risk in terms of capital-budgeting decisions, and how should it be measured? and (2) How should risk be incorporated into a capital-budgeting analysis?

What Measure of Risk Is Relevant in Capital Budgeting?

Before we begin our discussion of how to adjust for risk, it is important to determine just what type of risk we are to adjust for. In capital budgeting, a project's risk can be looked at on three levels. First, there is the **project standing alone risk**, which is a *project's risk ignoring the fact that much of this risk will be diversified away as the project is combined with the firm's other projects and assets*. Second, we have the project's **contribution-to-firm risk**, which is the *amount of risk that the project contributes to the firm as a whole; this measure considers the fact that some of the project's risk will be diversified away as the project is combined with the firm's other projects and assets, but it ignores the effects of the diversification of the firm's shareholders*. Finally, there is **systematic risk**, which is the *risk of the project from the viewpoint of a well-diversified shareholder; this measure takes into account that some of a project's risk will be diversified away as the project is combined with the firm's other projects, and, in addition, some of the remaining risk will be diversified away by shareholders as they combine this stock with other stocks in their portfolios*. Graphically, this is shown in Figure 10-4.

Should we be interested in the project standing alone risk? The answer is no. Perhaps the easiest way to understand why not is to look at an example. Let's take the case of research and development projects at Johnson & Johnson. Each year Johnson & Johnson takes on hundreds of new R&D projects, knowing that they have only about a 10 percent probabil-

project standing alone risk
a project's risk ignoring the fact that much of this risk will be diversified away as the project is combined with the firm's other projects and assets.

contribution-to-firm risk
the amount of risk that the project contributes to the firm as a whole; this measure considers the fact that some of the project's risk will be diversified away as the project is combined with the firm's other projects and assets, but ignores the effects of diversification of the firm's shareholders.

systematic risk the risk of the project from the viewpoint of a well-diversified shareholder; this measure takes into account that some of a project's risk will be diversified away as the project is combined with the firm's other projects, and, in addition, some of the remaining risk will be diversified away by shareholders as they combine this stock with other stocks in their portfolios.

FIGURE 10-4   Looking at Three Measures of a Project's Risk

| Perspective | Measures of Risk | Risk That Is Diversified Away |

Project standing alone: Ignores diversification within the firm and within the shareholder's portfolio.

Project standing alone risk

Project from the company's perspective: Ignores diversification within the shareholder's portfolio, but allows for diversification within the firm.

Project's contribution-to-firm risk

Risk diversified away within the firm as this project is combined with the firm's other projects and assets

Project from the shareholder's perspective: Allows for diversification within the firm and within the shareholder's portfolio.

Systematic risk

Risk diversified away by shareholders as securities are combined to form diversified portfolios; also called unsystematic risk

ity of being successful. If they are successful, the profits can be enormous; if they fail, the investment is lost. If the company has only one project, and it is an R&D project, the company would have a 90 percent chance of failure. Thus, if we look at these R&D projects individually and measure their stand-alone risk, we would have to judge them to be enormously risky. However, if we consider the effect of the diversification that comes about from taking on several hundred independent R&D projects a year, all with a 10 percent chance of success, we can see that each R&D project does not add much risk to Johnson & Johnson. In short, because much of a project's risk is diversified away within the firm, the project standing alone risk is an inappropriate measure of the meaningful level of risk of a capital-budgeting project.

Should we be interested in the project's contribution-to-firm risk? Once again, at least in theory, the answer is no, provided investors are well diversified and there is no chance of bankruptcy. From our earlier discussion of risk in Chapter 6, we saw that as shareholders, if we combined an individual security with other securities to form a diversified portfolio, much of the risk of the individual security would be diversified away. In short, all that affects the shareholders is the systematic risk of the project and, as such, it is all that is theoretically relevant for capital budgeting.

Measuring Risk for Capital-Budgeting Purposes with a Dose of Reality— Is Systematic Risk All There Is?

According to the capital asset pricing model (CAPM) we discussed in Chapter 6, systematic risk is the only relevant risk for capital-budgeting purposes. However, reality complicates this somewhat. In many instances a firm will have undiversified shareholders, including owners of small corporations. Because they are not diversified, for those shareholders the relevant measure of risk is the project's contribution-to-firm risk.

The possibility of bankruptcy also affects our view of what measure of risk is relevant. As you recall in developing the CAPM, we made the assumption that bankruptcy costs were zero. Because the project's contribution-to-firm risk can affect the possibility of bankruptcy, this may be an appropriate measure of risk: Quite obviously, there is a cost associated with bankruptcy. First, if a firm fails, its assets, in general, cannot be sold for their true economic value. Moreover, the amount of money actually available for distribution to stockholders is further reduced by liquidation and legal fees that must be paid. Finally, the opportunity cost associated with the delays related to the legal process further reduces the funds available to the shareholder. Therefore, because costs are associated with bankruptcy, reducing the chance of a bankruptcy has a very real value associated with it.

The indirect costs of bankruptcy also affect other areas of the firm, including production, sales, and the quality and efficiency of management. For example, firms with a higher probability of bankruptcy may have a more difficult time recruiting and retaining quality managers because jobs with that firm are viewed as being less secure. Suppliers may be less willing to sell to the firm on credit. Finally, customers may lose confidence and fear that the firm will not be around to honor a warranty or supply spare parts for products in the future. As a result, as the probability of bankruptcy increases, an eventual bankruptcy can become self-fulfilling as potential customers and suppliers flee. The end result is that because a project's contribution-to-firm risk affects the probability of bankruptcy for the firm, it is a relevant risk measure for capital budgeting.

Finally, problems in measuring a project's systematic risk make its implementation extremely difficult. It is much easier talking about a project's systematic risk than measuring it.

Given all this, what risk measure do we use? The answer is that we will give consideration to both systematic risk and contribution-to-firm risk measures. We know in theory systematic risk is correct. We also know that bankruptcy costs and undiversified shareholders violate the assumptions of the theory, which makes the concept of a project's contribution-to-firm risk a relevant measure. Still, the concept of systematic risk holds value for capital-budgeting decisions because that is the risk that shareholders are compensated for assuming. Therefore, we will concern ourselves with both the project's contribution-to-firm risk and the project's systematic risk and not try to make any specific allocation of importance between the two for capital-budgeting purposes.

Did You Get It?

1. In terms of capital budgeting, a project's risk can be looked at on three levels. What are they and what are the measures of risk?
2. Is a project's standing alone risk the appropriate level of risk for capital budgeting? Why or why not?
3. What is systematic risk?
4. What problems are associated with using systematic risk as the measure for risk in capital budgeting?

Objective **5**

Determine the acceptability of a new project using the risk-adjusted discount method of adjusting for risk.

risk-adjusted discount rate
a method of risk adjustment when the risk associated with the investment is greater than the risk involved in a typical endeavor. Using this method, the discount rate is adjusted upward to compensate for this added risk.

INCORPORATING RISK INTO CAPITAL BUDGETING

Because different investment projects do in fact contain different levels of risk, let's now look at the risk-adjusted discount rate, which is based on the notion that investors require higher rates of return on more risky projects.

Risk-Adjusted Discount Rates

The use of **risk-adjusted discount rates** is based on the concept that investors demand higher returns for more risky projects. This is the basic principle behind **Principle 1** and the CAPM and is illustrated graphically in Figure 10-5.

As we know from **Principle 1**, the expected rate of return on any investment should include compensation for delaying consumption equal to the risk-free rate of return, plus compensation for any risk taken on. Under the risk-adjusted discount rate approach, if the

Remember Your Principles

All the methods used to compensate for risk in capital budgeting find their roots in **Principle 1: The Risk–Return Trade-Off—We Won't Take On Additional Risk Unless We Expect to Be Compensated with Additional Return**. In fact, the risk-adjusted discount method puts this concept directly into play.

FIGURE 10-5   The Risk–Return Relationship

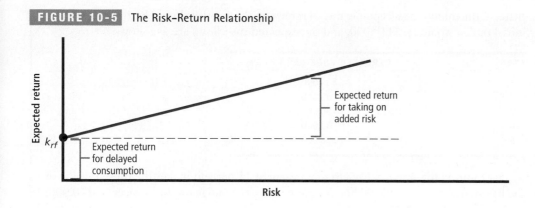

risk associated with the investment is greater than the risk involved in a typical endeavor, the discount rate is adjusted upward to compensate for this added risk. Once the firm determines the appropriate required rate of return for a project with a given level of risk, the cash flows are discounted back to the present at the risk-adjusted discount rate. Then the normal capital-budgeting criteria are applied, except in the case of the *IRR*. For the *IRR*, the hurdle rate with which the project's *IRR* is compared now becomes the risk-adjusted discount rate. Expressed mathematically, the *NPV* using the risk-adjusted discount rate becomes

$$NPV = \begin{bmatrix} \text{present value of all the} \\ \text{future annual free cash} \\ \text{flows discounted back} \\ \text{to present at the risk-adjusted} \\ \text{rate of return} \end{bmatrix} - \begin{bmatrix} \text{the initial cash outlay} \end{bmatrix} \qquad (10\text{-}1)$$

$$= \frac{FCF_1}{(1 + k^*)^1} + \frac{FCF_2}{(1 + k^*)^2} + \cdots + \frac{FCF_n}{(1 + k^*)^n} - IO$$

where FCF_t = the annual free cash flow expected in time period t
  IO = the initial cash outlay
  k^* = the risk-adjusted discount rate
  n = the project's expected life

The logic behind the risk-adjusted discount rate stems from the idea that if the level of risk associated with a project is different from that of the typical project, then managers must incorporate the shareholders' probable reaction to this new endeavor into the decision-making process. For example, if the project has more risk than a typical project, then a higher required rate of return should apply. Otherwise, marginal projects will lower the firm's share price—that is, reduce shareholders' wealth. This will occur as the market raises its required rate of return on the firm to reflect the addition of the more risky project, because the incremental cash flows resulting from it might not be large enough to offset this risk. By the same logic, if the project has less than normal risk, a reduction in the required rate of return is appropriate. Thus, the risk-adjusted discount method attempts to apply more stringent standards—that is, require a higher rate of return—to projects that will increase the firm's risk level.

➤ EXAMPLE

A toy manufacturer is considering introducing a line of fishing equipment with an expected life of 5 years. In the past, the firm has been quite conservative in its investment in new products, sticking primarily to standard toys. In this context, the introduction of a line of fishing equipment is considered an abnormally risky project. Management thinks that the normal required rate of return for the firm of 10 percent is not sufficient.

Instead, the minimum acceptable rate of return on this project should be 15 percent. The initial outlay would be $110,000, and the expected cash flows are as follows:

YEAR	EXPECTED FREE CASH FLOW
1	$30,000
2	30,000
3	30,000
4	30,000
5	30,000

Discounting this annuity back to the present at 15 percent makes the present value of the future free cash flows $100,560. Because the initial outlay on this project is $110,000, the *NPV* becomes −$9,435, and the project should be rejected. If the normal required rate of return of 10 percent had been used as the discount rate, the project would have been accepted with a *NPV* of $3,724.

In practice, when the risk-adjusted discount rate is used, projects are generally grouped according to purpose, or risk class; then the discount rate preassigned to that purpose or risk class is used. For example, a firm with a required rate of return of 12 percent might use the following rate-of-return categorization:

PROJECT	REQUIRED RATE OF RETURN (%)
Replacement decision	12
Modification or expansion of existing product line	15
Project unrelated to current operations	18
Research and development operations	25

The purpose of this categorization of projects is to make their evaluation easier, but it also introduces a sense of arbitrariness into the calculations that makes the evaluation less meaningful. The trade-offs involved in the preceding classification are obvious: Time and effort are minimized but only at the cost of precision.

Measuring a Project's Systematic Risk

When we initially talked about systematic risk or the beta, we were talking about measuring it for the entire firm. As you recall, although we could estimate a firm's beta using historical data, we did not have complete confidence in our results. As we will see, estimating the appropriate level of systematic risk for a single project is even more fraught with difficulties. To truly understand what it is we are trying to do and the difficulties we will encounter, let's step back a bit and examine systematic risk and the risk adjustment for a project.

What we are trying to do is use the CAPM to determine the level of risk and the appropriate risk–return trade-offs for a particular project. We then take the expected return on this project and compare it to the required return suggested by the CAPM to determine whether the project should be accepted. If the project appears to be a typical one for the firm, using the CAPM to determine the appropriate risk–return trade-offs and then judging the project against them may be a warranted approach. But if the project is not a typical project, what do we do? Historical data generally do not exist for a new project. In fact, for some capital investments—for example, a truck or a new building—historical data would not have much meaning. What we need to do is make the best of a bad situation. We either (1) fake it—that is, use historical accounting data, if available, to substitute for historical price data in estimating systematic risk—or (2) attempt to find a substitute firm in the same industry as the capital-budgeting project and use the substitute firm's estimated systematic risk as a proxy for the project's systematic risk.

Using Accounting Data to Estimate a Project's Beta

When we are dealing with a project that is identical to the firm's other projects, we need only estimate the level of systematic risk for the firm and use that estimate as a proxy for the project's risk. Unfortunately, when projects are not typical of the firm, this approach does not work. For example, when Altria, which owns Philip Morris, the tobacco company, and Kraft Foods, introduces a new food through one of its food products divisions, this new product most likely carries with it a different level of systematic risk than what is typical for Altria as a whole.

To get a better approximation of the systematic risk level on this project, we estimate the level of systematic risk for the food division and use that as a proxy for the project's systematic risk. Unfortunately, historical stock price data are available only for the company as a whole, and as you recall, historical stock return data are generally used to estimate a firm's beta. Thus, we are forced to use accounting return data rather than historical stock return data for the division to estimate the division's systematic risk. To estimate a project's beta using accounting data we need only run a time-series regression of the division's return on assets (net income/total assets) on the market index (the S&P 500). The regression coefficient from this equation would be the project's accounting beta and would serve as an approximation for the project's true beta, or measure of systematic risk. Alternatively, a multiple regression model based on accounting data could be developed to explain betas. The results of this model could then be applied to firms that are not publicly traded to estimate their betas.

How good is the accounting beta technique? It certainly is not as good as a direct calculation of the beta. In fact, the correlation between the accounting beta and the beta calculated on historical stock return data is only about 0.6. However, better luck has been experienced with multiple regression models used to predict betas. Unfortunately, in many cases there may not be any realistic alternative to the calculation of the accounting beta. Because adjusting for a project's risk is so important, the accounting beta method is much preferred to doing nothing.

Whereas the accounting beta method attempts to directly estimate a project's or division's beta, the **pure play method** attempts to identify publicly traded firms that are engaged solely in the same business as the project or division. Once the proxy or pure play firm is identified, its systematic risk is determined and then used as a proxy for the project's or division's level of systematic risk. What we are doing is *looking for a publicly traded firm with a project like ours and using that firm's required rate of return to judge our project.* In doing so we are presuming that the systematic risk and the capital structure of the proxy firm are identical to those of the project.

In using the pure play method it should be noted that a firm's capital structure is reflected in its beta. When the capital structure of the proxy firm is different from that of the project's firm, some adjustment must be made for this difference. Although not a perfect approach, it does provide some insights about the level of systematic risk a project might have.

pure play method a method for estimating a project's or division's beta that attempts to identify publicly traded firms engaged solely in the same business as the project or division.

Did You Get It?

1. What is the most commonly used method for incorporating risk into the capital-budgeting decision? How is this technique related to Principle 1?
2. Describe two methods for estimating a project's systematic risk.

simulation a method for dealing with risk where the performance of the project under evaluation is estimated by randomly selecting observations from each of the distributions that affect the outcome of the project and continuing with this process until a representative record of the project's probable outcome is assembled.

EXAMINING A PROJECT'S RISK THROUGH SIMULATION

Simulation: Explained and Illustrated

Another method for evaluating risk in the investment decision is through the use of **simulation**. The risk-adjusted discount rate approach provided us with a single value for the risk-adjusted *NPV*, whereas a simulation approach gives us a probability distribution for the investment's *NPV* or *IRR*. Simulation *involves the process of imitating the performance of*

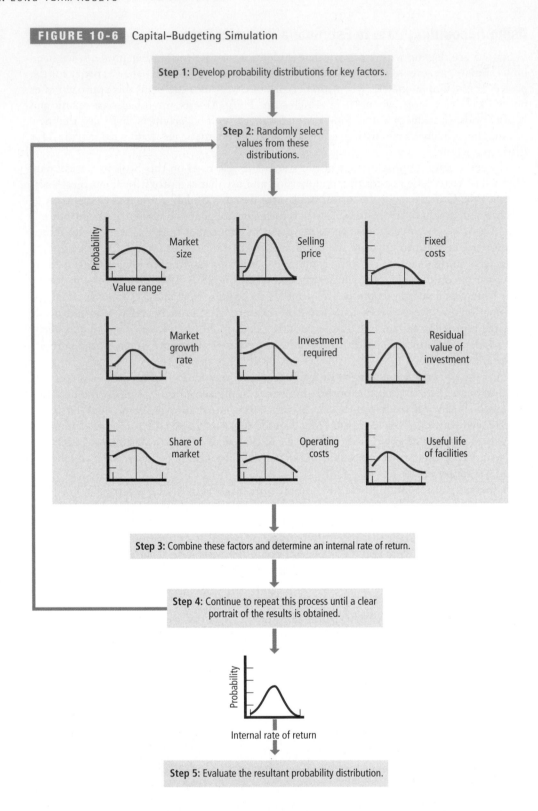

FIGURE 10-6   Capital–Budgeting Simulation

Step 1: Develop probability distributions for key factors.

Step 2: Randomly select values from these distributions.

Step 3: Combine these factors and determine an internal rate of return.

Step 4: Continue to repeat this process until a clear portrait of the results is obtained.

Step 5: Evaluate the resultant probability distribution.

the project under evaluation. This is done by randomly selecting observations from each of the distributions that affect the outcome of the project and continuing with this process until a representative record of the project's probable outcome is assembled.

The easiest way to develop an understanding of the computer simulation process is to follow through an example simulation for an investment project evaluation. Suppose a chemical producer is considering an extension to its processing plant. The simulation process is portrayed in Figure 10-6. First, the probability distributions are determined for

FIGURE 10-7   Output from Simulation

all the factors that affect the project's returns. In this case, let us assume there are nine such variables:

1. Market size
2. Selling price
3. Market growth rate
4. Share of market (which results in physical sales volume)
5. Investment required
6. Residual value of investment
7. Operating costs
8. Fixed costs
9. Useful life of facilities

Then the computer randomly selects one observation from each of the probability distributions, according to its chance of actually occurring in the future. These nine observations are combined, and an *NPV* or *IRR* figure is calculated. This process is repeated as many times as desired, until a representative distribution of possible future outcomes is assembled. Thus, the inputs to a simulation include all the principal factors affecting the project's profitability, and the simulation output is a probability distribution of net present values or internal rates of return for the project. The decision maker bases the decision on the full range of possible outcomes. The project is accepted if the decision maker feels that enough of the distribution lies above the normal cutoff criteria (*NPV* ≥ 0 or *IRR* ≥ required rate of return).

Suppose the output from the simulation of a chemical producer's project is as shown in Figure 10-7. This output provides the decision maker with the probability of different outcomes occurring in addition to the range of possible outcomes. Sometimes called **scenario analysis**, it *identifies the range of possible outcomes under the worst, best, and most likely cases*. The firm's management then examines the distribution to determine the project's level of risk and makes the appropriate decisions.

You'll notice that although the simulation approach helps us to determine the amount of total risk a project has, it does not differentiate between systematic and unsystematic risk. Because systematic risk cannot be diversified away for free, the simulation approach does not provide a complete method of risk assessment. However, it does provide important insights about the total risk level of a given investment project. Now we will look briefly at how the simulation approach can be used to perform sensitivity analysis.

Conducting a Sensitivity Analysis through Simulation

Sensitivity analysis involves *determining how the distribution of possible net present values or internal rates of return for a particular project is affected by a change in one particular input variable*. This is done by changing the value of one input variable while holding all other input variables constant. The distribution of possible net present values or internal rates of return that is generated is then compared with the distribution of possible returns generated before the

scenario analysis a simulation approach for gauging a project's risk under the worst, best, and most likely outcomes. The firm's management examines the distribution of the outcomes to determine the project's level of risk and then makes the appropriate adjustment.

sensitivity analysis a method for dealing with risk where the change in the distribution of possible net present values or internal rates of return for a particular project resulting from a change in one particular input variable is calculated. This is done by changing the value of one input variable while holding all other input variables constant.

change was made to determine the effect of the change. For this reason sensitivity analysis is commonly called *what-if analysis*.

For example, the chemical producer that is considering a possible expansion to its plant may wish to determine the effect of a more pessimistic forecast of the anticipated market growth rate. After the more pessimistic forecast replaces the original forecast in the model, the simulation is rerun. The two outputs are then compared to determine how sensitive the results are to the revised estimate of the market growth rate.

Did You Get It?

1. Explain how simulations work.
2. What is a scenario analysis? What is a sensitivity analysis? When would you perform a sensitivity analysis?

Objective **7**

Explain why a multinational firm faces a more difficult time estimating cash flows along with increased risks.

FINANCE AND THE MULTINATIONAL FIRM: CALCULATING CASH FLOWS AMID THE INTERNATIONAL DIMENSION OF RISK

The process of measuring a project's incremental, after-tax cash flows relative to the company as a whole gets a bit more complicated when we are dealing with competition from abroad. One area in which this is certainly true is in calculating the right base case—that is, what the firm's incremental after-tax cash flows would be if the project is not taken on. In determining future cash flows we must always be aware of potential competition from abroad. We need only look to the auto industry to see that competition from abroad can be serious. During the 1970s, who would have thought that firms such as Toyota, Honda, and Nissan could enter the U.S. markets and actually challenge the likes of Ford and GM? The end result of opening markets to international competition has led not only to increased opportunities but also to increased risks.

Just as competition from around the world can challenge U.S. firms, U.S. firms can also move into international markets. For example, Yum! Brands, the parent firm for KFC, Long John Silver's, Pizza Hut, and Taco Bell, has been recently registering double-digit sales growth in its China division, which covers mainland China, Thailand, and Taiwan, with its third-quarter 2006 sales jumping 25 percent from 1 year prior.

Along with all the benefits from going multinational come the risks. One of the major risks involves currency fluctuations. For example, in 2002, Toyota finalized its plans for the introduction of the second-generation Prius, which it manufactures in Japan and imports to the United States. These plans included a pricing strategy to have the Prius sell below $30,000, at $29,990, because Toyota was worried that by crossing the $30,000 price threshold it might seriously lose sales. But at that time, the Japanese yen was trading at around 134 yen per U.S. dollar. Unfortunately for Toyota, the yen-to-U.S. dollar exchange rate fell, to 111 Japanese yen per dollar in the middle of 2006. What did this mean for Toyota? It meant that Toyota received only 83 percent as many yen on each Prius it sold in the United States. Because Toyota pays its workers in yen and its material costs are in yen, this placed a real strain on its profits.

Did You Get It?

1. In what ways does the process of measuring the incremental after-tax cash flows to the company as a whole get a bit more complicated when we are dealing with competition from abroad?
2. What new risks does a firm face when it enters the international markets?

Objective **1**

Identify guidelines by which we measure cash flows.

Summary

In this chapter, we examined the measurement of the incremental cash flows associated with a firm's investment proposals and methods used to evaluate those proposals. Relying on **Principle 3: Cash—Not Profits—Is King**, and **Principle 4: Incremental Cash Flows—It's Only What**

Changes That Count, we focused only on the incremental, or differential, after-tax cash flows attributed to an investment proposal. Care is taken to beware of cash flows diverted from existing products, look for incidental or synergistic effects, consider working-capital requirements, consider incremental expenses, ignore sunk costs, account for opportunity costs, examine overhead costs carefully, and ignore interest payments and financing flows.

To measure a project's benefits, we use the project's free cash flows:

Project's free cash flows = project's change in operating cash flows
         − change in net working capital
         − change in capital spending

We can rewrite this, inserting our calculation for the project's change in operating cash flows, to get

Project's free cash flows = change in earnings before interest and taxes
         − change in taxes
         + change in depreciation
         − change in net working capital
         − change in capital spending

Options, or flexibility, can make it worthwhile to pursue projects that would otherwise be rejected or make projects undertaken more valuable. Three of the most common types of options that can add value to a capital-budgeting project are (1) the option to delay a project until the future cash flows are more favorable (this option is common when the firm has an exclusive right, perhaps a patent, to a product or technology); (2) the option to expand a project, perhaps in size or even to introduce new products that would not have otherwise been feasible; and (3) the option to abandon a project if its future cash flows fall short of expectations.

There are three types of capital-budgeting risk: the project standing alone risk, the project's contribution-to-firm risk, and the project's systematic risk. In theory, systematic risk is the appropriate risk measure, but bankruptcy costs and the issue of undiversified shareholders also give weight to considering a project's contribution-to-firm risk as the appropriate risk measure. Both measures of risk are valid, and we avoid making any specific allocation of the importance between the two.

The risk-adjusted discount rate involves an upward adjustment of the discount rate to compensate for risk. This method is based on the concept that investors demand higher returns for riskier projects. Thus, projects are evaluated using the appropriate, or risk-adjusted, discount rate.

The simulation method is used to provide information about the location and shape of the distribution of possible outcomes of the project. Decisions can be based directly on this method or used as an input to make decisions using the risk-adjusted discount rate method.

The process of measuring the free cash flows to the company as a whole becomes more complicated when we are dealing with competition from abroad. One area in which this is certainly true is in calculating the right base case—that is, what the firm's free cash flows would be if the project is not taken on. Another complication involves the risks associated with currency fluctuations.

Objective 2

Explain how a project's benefits and costs—that is, its free cash flows—are calculated.

Objective 3

Explain the importance of options, or flexibility, in capital budgeting.

Objective 4

Explain what the appropriate measure of risk is for capital-budgeting purposes.

Objective 5

Determine the acceptability of a new project using the risk-adjusted discount method of adjusting for risk.

Objective 6

Explain the use of simulating for imitating the performance of a project under evaluation.

Objective 7

Explain why a multinational firm faces a more difficult time estimating cash flows along with increased risks.

Key Terms

Contribution-to-firm risk   314

Incremental after-tax free cash flows   298

Initial outlay   301

Project standing alone risk   314

Pure play method   319

Risk-adjusted discount rate   316

Scenario analysis   321

Sensitivity analysis   321

Simulation   319

Systematic risk   314

Review Questions

10-1. Why do we focus on cash flows rather than accounting profits in making our capital-budgeting decisions? Why are we interested only in incremental cash flows rather than total cash flows?

10-2. If depreciation is not a cash flow expense, does it affect the level of cash flows from a project in any way? Why?

10-3. If a project requires an additional investment in working capital, how should this be treated when calculating the project's cash flows?

10-4. How do sunk costs affect the determination of cash flows associated with an investment proposal?

10-5. In the preceding chapter we examined the payback period capital-budgeting criterion. Often this capital-budgeting criterion is used as a risk-screening device. Explain the rationale behind its use.

10-6. The use of the risk-adjusted discount rate assumes that risk increases over time. Justify this assumption.

10-7. Explain how simulation works. What is the value in using a simulation approach?

Self–Test Problem

(The solution to this problem is provided at the end of the chapter.)

ST-1. The Easterwood Corporation, a firm in the 34 percent marginal tax bracket with a 15 percent required rate of return or cost of capital, is considering a new project. The project involves the introduction of a new product. The project is expected to last 5 years and then, because this is somewhat of a fad product, be terminated. Given the following information, determine the free cash flows associated with the project, the project's net present value, the profitability index, and the internal rate of return. Apply the appropriate decision criteria.

Cost of new plant and equipment	$20,900,000
Shipping and installation costs	$ 300,000
Unit sales	

YEAR	UNITS SOLD
1	100,000
2	130,000
3	160,000
4	100,000
5	60,000

Sales price per unit	$500/unit in years 1 through 4, $380/unit in year 5
Variable cost per unit	$260/unit
Annual fixed costs	$300,000
Working-capital requirements	There will be an initial working-capital requirement of $500,000 just to get production started. For each year, the total investment in net working capital will be equal to 10 percent of the dollar value of sales for that year. Thus, the investment in working capital will increase during years 1 through 3, then decrease in year 4. Finally, all working capital is liquidated at the termination of the project at the end of year 5.
The depreciation method	Use the simplified straight-line method over 5 years. Assume that the plant and equipment will have no salvage value after 5 years.

Study Problems

10-1. (*Capital gains tax*) The J. Harris Corporation is considering selling one of its old assembly machines. The machine, purchased for $30,000 5 years ago, had an expected life of 10 years and an expected salvage value of zero. Assume Harris uses simplified straight-line depreciation (depreciation of $3,000 per year) and could sell this old machine for $35,000. Also assume Harris has a 34 percent marginal tax rate.

    a. What would be the taxes associated with this sale?
    b. If the old machine were sold for $25,000, what would be the taxes associated with this sale?
    c. If the old machine were sold for $15,000, what would be the taxes associated with this sale?
    d. If the old machine were sold for $12,000, what would be the taxes associated with this sale?

10-2. (*Relevant cash flows*) Captins' Cereal is considering introducing a variation of its current breakfast cereal, Crunch Stuff. The new cereal will be similar to the old with the exception that it will contain sugarcoated marshmallows shaped in the form of stars and called Crunch Stuff n' Stars. It is estimated that the sales for the new cereal will be $25 million; however, 20 percent of those sales will be former Crunch Stuff customers who have switched to Crunch Stuff n' Stars but who would not have switched if the new product had not been introduced. What is the relevant sales level to consider when deciding whether to introduce Crunch Stuff n' Stars?

10-3. (*Calculating free cash flows*) Racin' Scooters is introducing a new product and has an expected change in EBIT of $475,000. Racin' Scooters has a 34 percent marginal tax rate. The project will also produce $100,000 of depreciation per year. In addition, the project will also cause the following changes in year 1:

	WITHOUT THE PROJECT	WITH THE PROJECT
Accounts receivable	$45,000	$63,000
Inventory	65,000	80,000
Accounts payable	70,000	94,000

What is the project's free cash flow in year 1?

10-4. (*Calculating free cash flows*) Visible Fences is introducing a new product and has an expected change in EBIT of $900,000. Visible Fences has a 34 percent marginal tax rate. This project will also produce $300,000 of depreciation per year. In addition, in year 1 this project will also cause the following changes:

	WITHOUT THE PROJECT	WITH THE PROJECT
Accounts receivable	$55,000	$63,000
Inventory	55,000	70,000
Accounts payable	90,000	106,000

What is the project's free cash flow in year 1?

10-5. (*Calculating operating cash flows*) Assume that a new project will annually generate revenues of $2,000,000. Cash expenses including both fixed and variable costs will be $800,000, and depreciation will increase by $200,000 per year. In addition, let's assume that the firm's marginal tax rate is 34 percent. Calculate the operating cash flows.

10-6. (*Calculating operating cash flows*) Assume that a new project will annually generate revenues of $3,000,000. Cash expenses including both fixed and variable costs will be $900,000, and depreciation will increase by $400,000 per year. In addition, let's assume that the firm's marginal tax rate is 34 percent. Calculate the operating cash flows.

10-7. (*Calculating free cash flows*) You are considering expanding your product line that currently consists of skateboards to include gas-powered skateboards, and you feel you can sell 10,000 of these per year for 10 years (after which time this project is expected to shut down because solar-powered skateboards will become more popular). The gas skateboards would sell for $100 each and have a variable cost of $40 each. The annual fixed costs associated with production would be $160,000. In addition, there would be a $1,000,000 initial expenditure associated with the purchase of new production equipment. It is assumed that this initial expenditure will be depreciated using the simplified straight-line method down to zero over 10 years. This project will also require a one-time initial investment of $50,000 in net working capital associated with inventory, and that working-capital investment will be recovered when the project is shut down. Finally, assume that the firm's marginal tax rate is 34 percent.

   a. What is the initial outlay associated with the project?
   b. What are the annual free cash flows associated with the project for years 1 through 9?
   c. What is the terminal cash flow in year 10 (that is, what is the free cash flow in year 10 plus any additional cash flows associated with the termination of the project)?
   d. What is the project's *NPV* given a 10 percent required rate of return?

10-8. (*Calculating free cash flows*) You are considering new elliptical trainers and you feel you can sell 5,000 of these per year for 5 years (after which time this project is expected to shut down when it is learned that being fit is unhealthy). The elliptical trainers would sell for $1,000 each and have a variable cost of $500 each. The annual fixed costs associated with production would be $1,000,000. In addition, there would be a $5,000,000 initial expenditure associated with the purchase of new production equipment. It is assumed that this initial expenditure will be depreciated using the simplified straight-line method down to zero over 5 years. This project will also require a one-time initial investment of $1,000,000 in net working capital associated with inventory, and that working-capital investment will be recovered when the project is shut down. Finally, assume that the firm's marginal tax rate is 34 percent.

   a. What is the initial outlay associated with this project?
   b. What are the annual free cash flows associated with this project for years 1 through 4?
   c. What is the terminal cash flow in year 5 (that is, what is the free cash flow in year 5 plus any additional cash flows associated with the termination of the project)?
   d. What is the project's *NPV* given a 10 percent required rate of return?

10-9. (*New project analysis*) The Chung Chemical Corporation is considering the purchase of a chemical analysis machine. Although the machine being considered will result in an increase in earnings before interest and taxes of $35,000 per year, it has a purchase price of $100,000, and it would cost an additional $5,000 to properly install the machine. In addition, to properly operate the machine, inventory must be increased by $5,000. This machine has an expected life of 10 years, after which it will have no salvage value. Also, assume simplified straight-line depreciation and that this machine is being depreciated down to zero, a 34 percent marginal tax rate, and a required rate of return of 15 percent.

    a. What is the initial outlay associated with this project?

    b. What are the annual after-tax cash flows associated with this project for years 1 through 9?

    c. What is the terminal cash flow in year 10 (what is the annual after-tax cash flow in year 10 plus any additional cash flows associated with the termination of the project)?

    d. Should this machine be purchased?

10-10. (*New project analysis*) Raymobile Motors is considering the purchase of a new production machine for $500,000. The purchase of this machine will result in an increase in earnings before interest and taxes of $150,000 per year. To operate this machine properly, workers would have to go through a brief training session that would cost $25,000 after taxes. It would cost $5,000 to install the machine properly. Also, because the machine is extremely efficient, its purchase would necessitate an increase in inventory of $30,000. This machine has an expected life of 10 years, after which it will have no salvage value. Assume simplified straight-line depreciation and that this machine is being depreciated down to zero, a 34 percent marginal tax rate, and a required rate of return of 15 percent.

    a. What is the initial outlay associated with this project?

    b. What are the annual after-tax cash flows associated with this project for years 1 through 9?

    c. What is the terminal cash flow in year 10 (what is the annual after-tax cash flow in year 10 plus any additional cash flows associated with the termination of the project)?

    d. Should the machine be purchased?

10-11. (*New project analysis*) Garcia's Truckin' Inc. is considering the purchase of a new production machine for $200,000. The purchase of this machine will result in an increase in earnings before interest and taxes of $50,000 per year. To operate the machine properly, workers would have to go through a brief training session that would cost $5,000 after taxes. It would cost $5,000 to install the machine properly. Also, because this machine is extremely efficient, its purchase would necessitate an increase in inventory of $20,000. This machine has an expected life of 10 years, after which it will have no salvage value. Finally, to purchase the new machine, it appears that the firm would have to borrow $100,000 at 8 percent interest from its local bank, resulting in additional interest payments of $8,000 per year. Assume simplified straight-line depreciation and that the machine is being depreciated down to zero, a 34 percent marginal tax rate, and a required rate of return of 10 percent.

    a. What is the initial outlay associated with this project?

    b. What are the annual after-tax cash flows associated with this project for years 1 through 9?

    c. What is the terminal cash flow in year 10 (what is the annual after-tax cash flow in year 10 plus any additional cash flows associated with the termination of the project)?

    d. Should the machine be purchased?

10-12. (*Comprehensive problem*) Traid Winds Corporation, a firm in the 34 percent marginal tax bracket with a 15 percent required rate of return or cost of capital, is considering a new project. This project involves the introduction of a new product. The project is expected to last 5 years and then, because this is somewhat of a fad product, be terminated. Given the following information, determine the free cash flows associated with the project, the project's net present value, the profitability index, and the internal rate of return. Apply the appropriate decision criteria.

Cost of new plant and equipment	$14,800,000
Shipping and installation costs	$ 200,000
Unit sales	

YEAR	UNITS SOLD
1	70,000
2	120,000
3	120,000
4	80,000
5	70,000

Sales price per unit	$300/unit in years 1 through 4, $250/unit in year 5
Variable cost per unit	$140/unit
Annual fixed costs	$700,000
Working-capital requirements	There will be an initial working-capital requirement of $200,000 just to get production started. For each year, the total investment in net working capital will be equal to 10 percent of the dollar value of sales for that year. Thus, the investment in working capital will increase during years 1 and 2, then decrease in year 4. Finally, all working capital is liquidated at the termination of the project at the end of year 5.
The depreciation method	Use the simplified straight-line method over 5 years. Assume that the plant and equipment will have no salvage value after 5 years.

10-13. (*Comprehensive problem*) The Shome Corporation, a firm in the 34 percent marginal tax bracket with a 15 percent required rate of return or cost of capital, is considering a new project. The project involves the introduction of a new product. This project is expected to last 5 years and then, because this is somewhat of a fad product, be terminated. Given the following information, determine the free cash flows associated with the project, the project's net present value, the profitability index, and the internal rate of return. Apply the appropriate decision criteria.

Cost of new plant and equipment	$6,900,000
Shipping and installation costs	$ 100,000
Unit sales	

YEAR	UNITS SOLD
1	80,000
2	100,000
3	120,000
4	70,000
5	70,000

Sales price per unit	$250/unit in years 1 through 4, $200/unit in year 5
Variable cost per unit	$130/unit
Annual fixed costs	$300,000
Working-capital requirements	There will be an initial working-capital requirement of $100,000 just to get production started. For each year, the total investment in net working capital will be equal to 10 percent of the dollar value of sales for that year. Thus, the investment in working capital will increase during years 1 through 3, then decrease in year 4. Finally, all working capital is liquidated at the termination of the project at the end of year 5.
The depreciation method	Use the simplified straight-line method over 5 years. Assume that the plant and equipment will have no salvage value after 5 years.

10-14. (*Risk-adjusted NPV*) The Hokie Corporation is considering two mutually exclusive projects. Both require an initial outlay of $10,000 and will operate for 5 years. Project A will produce expected cash flows of $5,000 per year for years 1 through 5, whereas project B will produce expected cash flows of $6,000 per year for years 1 through 5. Because project B is the riskier of the two projects, the management of Hokie Corporation has decided to apply a required rate of return of 15 percent to its evaluation but only a 12 percent required rate of return to project A. Determine each project's risk-adjusted net present value.

10-15. (*Risk-adjusted discount rates and risk classes*) The G. Wolfe Corporation is examining two capital-budgeting projects with 5-year lives. The first, project A, is a replacement project; the second, project B, is a project unrelated to current operations. The G. Wolfe Corporation uses the risk-adjusted discount rate method and groups projects according to purpose, and then it uses a required rate of return or discount rate that has been preassigned to that purpose or risk class. The expected cash flows for these projects are given here:

	PROJECT A	PROJECT B
Initial investment	−$250,000	−$400,000
Cash inflows:		
Year 1	$130,000	$135,000
Year 2	40,000	135,000
Year 3	50,000	135,000
Year 4	90,000	135,000
Year 5	130,000	135,000

The purpose/risk classes and preassigned required rates of return are as follows:

PURPOSE	REQUIRED RATE OF RETURN
Replacement decision	12%
Modification or expansion of existing product line	15
Project unrelated to current operations	18
Research and development operations	20

Determine each project's risk-adjusted net present value.

Web Works

10-WW1. You've decided to use the pure play method for estimating a project's beta. Let's assume that your new product is in the pharmaceutical industry. The first thing you'll have to do is to calculate the beta of a drug company—let's pick Pfizer for this—that most closely matches your new product. To do this let's use the MoneyCentral site, which is a research site for the Microsoft network. If you have the company's ticker symbol, which is a unique one- to four-place alphabetical "nickname" for a company—for Pfizer the ticker symbol is pfe—you can go to a company report (**moneycentral.msn.com/investor/research/profile.asp?**). The report provides a one-page overview of the company, including its beta. Here you'll have to enter the symbol to get to the Pfizer page. The beta is listed as "Volatility (beta)."

You can also find the beta on Yahoo! Finance:

1. From the Yahoo homepage (**www.yahoo.com**), choose "Yahoo! Finance."
2. Enter the ticker symbol in the first box and click on "Go"; choose "Key Statistics" from the left-hand column under "Company."
3. Go to the table under "Trading Information" and "Stock Price History" toward the bottom of the page on the right. The beta will be the first item in the first column.

Just as with MoneyCentral, in order to get the information for a given firm, you need to know its ticker symbol. The MoneyCentral site is a place to find the ticker symbol if you don't know it.

Let's look up four companies using both MoneyCentral and Yahoo! Finance:

- Pfizer (pfe)
- Amazon.com (amzn)
- Aetna (aet)
- Intel (intc)

What do you think the betas would be for these companies? Remember the beta of the market is 1.0. Less risky companies would be less than 1, and more risky companies would be more than 1.

Were you close? Are the betas on both sites the same? Why might there be differences in the betas?

Mini Case

It's been 2 months since you took a position as an assistant financial analyst at Caledonia Products. Although your boss has been pleased with your work, he is still a bit hesitant about unleashing you without supervision. Your next assignment involves both the calculation of the cash flows associated with a new investment under consideration and the evaluation of several mutually exclusive projects. Given your lack of tenure at Caledonia, you have been asked not only to provide a recommendation but also to respond to a number of questions aimed at judging your understanding of the capital-budgeting process. The memorandum you received outlining your assignment follows:

> To: The Assistant Financial Analyst
> From: Mr. V. Morrison, CEO, Caledonia Products
> Re: Cash Flow Analysis and Capital Rationing

We are considering the introduction of a new product. Currently we are in the 34 percent marginal tax bracket with a 15 percent required rate of return or cost of capital. This project is expected to last 5 years and then, because this is somewhat of a fad product, be terminated. The following information describes the new project:

Cost of new plant and equipment	$7,900,000
Shipping and installation costs	$ 100,000
Unit sales	

YEAR	UNITS SOLD
1	70,000
2	120,000
3	140,000
4	80,000
5	60,000

Sales price per unit	$300/unit in years 1 through 4, $260/unit in year 5
Variable cost per unit	$180/unit
Annual fixed costs	$200,000
Working-capital requirements	There will be an initial working-capital requirement of $100,000 just to get production started. For each year, the total investment in net working capital will be equal to 10 percent of the dollar value of sales for that year. Thus, the investment in working capital will increase during years 1 through 3, then decrease in year 4. Finally, all working capital is liquidated at the termination of the project at the end of year 5.
The depreciation method	Use the simplified straight-line method over 5 years. Assume that the plant and equipment will have no salvage value after 5 years.

a. Should Caledonia focus on cash flows or accounting profits in making its capital-budgeting decisions? Should the company be interested in incremental cash flows, incremental profits, total free cash flows, or total profits?

b. How does depreciation affect free cash flows?

c. How do sunk costs affect the determination of cash flows?

d. What is the project's initial outlay?

e. What are the differential cash flows over the project's life?

f. What is the terminal cash flow?

g. Draw a cash flow diagram for this project.

h. What is its net present value?

i. What is its internal rate of return?

j. Should the project be accepted? Why or why not?

k. In capital budgeting, risk can be measured from three perspectives. What are those three measures of a project's risk?

l. According to the CAPM, which measurement of a project's risk is relevant? What complications does reality introduce into the CAPM view of risk, and what does that mean for our view of the relevant measure of a project's risk?

m. Explain how simulation works. What is the value in using a simulation approach?

n. What is sensitivity analysis and what is its purpose?

Self-Test Solution

SS-1.

YEAR	0	1	2	3	4	5
		SECTION I. CALCULATE THE CHANGE IN EBIT, TAXES, AND DEPRECIATION				
		(THIS BECOMES AN INPUT IN THE CALCULATION OF OPERATING CASH FLOW IN SECTION II)				
Units sold		100,000	130,000	160,000	100,000	60,000
Sales price		$ 500	$ 500	$ 500	$ 500	$ 380
Sales revenue		$50,000,000	$ 65,000,000	$ 80,000,000	$ 50,000,000	$22,800,000
Less: Variable costs		26,000,000	33,800,000	41,600,000	26,000,000	15,600,000
Less: Fixed costs		$ 300,000	$ 300,000	$ 300,000	$ 300,000	$ 300,000
Equals: EBITDA (assuming amortization is 0)		$23,700,000	$ 30,900,000	$ 38,100,000	$ 23,700,000	$ 6,900,000
Less: Depreciation		$ 4,240,000	$ 4,240,000	$ 4,240,000	$ 4,240,000	$ 4,240,000
Equals: EBIT		$19,460,000	$ 26,660,000	$ 33,860,000	$ 19,460,000	$ 2,660,000
Taxes (@ 34%)		$6,616,400	$ 9,064,400	$ 11,512,400	$6,616,400	$ 904,400
		SECTION II. CALCULATE OPERATING CASH FLOW				
		(THIS BECOMES AN INPUT IN THE CALCULATION OF FREE CASH FLOW IN SECTION IV)				
Operating cash flow:						
EBIT		$19,460,000	$ 26,660,000	$ 33,860,000	$ 19,460,000	$ 2,660,000
Minus: Taxes		$ 6,616,400	$ 9,064,400	$ 11,512,400	$ 6,616,400	$904,400
Plus: Depreciation		$ 4,240,000	$ 4,240,000	$ 4,240,000	$ 4,240,000	$ 4,240,000
Equals: Operating cash flow		$17,083,600	$ 21,835,600	$ 26,587,600	$ 17,083,600	$ 5,995,600
		SECTION III. CALCULATE THE NET WORKING CAPITAL				
		(THIS BECOMES AN INPUT IN THE CALCULATION OF FREE CASH FLOW IN SECTION IV)				
Change in net working capital:						
Revenue		$50,000,000	$ 65,000,000	$ 80,000,000	$ 50,000,000	$22,800,000
Initial working-capital requirement	$ 500,000					
Net working-capital needs		$ 5,000,000	$ 6,500,000	$ 8,000,000	$ 5,000,000	$ 2,280,000
Liquidation of working capital						$ 2,280,000
Change in working capital	$ 500,000	$ 4,500,000	$ 1,500,000	$ 1,500,000	($ 3,000,000)	($ 5,000,000)
		SECTION IV. CALCULATE FREE CASH FLOW				
		(USING INFORMATION CALCULATED IN SECTIONS II AND III, IN ADDITION TO CHANGE IN CAPITAL SPENDING)				
Free cash flow:						
Operating cash flow		$17,083,600	$ 21,835,600	$ 26,587,600	$ 17,083,600	$ 5,995,600
Minus: Change in net working capital	$ 500,000	$4,500,000	$ 1,500,000	$ 1,500,000	($ 3,000,000)	($ 5,000,000)
Minus: Change in capital spending	$21,200,000	0	0	0	0	0
Equals: Free cash flow	($ 21,700,000)	$12,583,600	$ 20,335,600	$ 25,087,600	$ 20,083,600	$10,995,600

NPV	$38,064,020; Accept project; *NPV* is positive
PI	2.75; Accept project; *PI* is greater than 1.0
IRR	73.6%; Accept project; *IRR* is greater than the required rate of return.

LEARNING OBJECTIVES

After reading this chapter, you should be able to:

1. Describe the concepts underlying the firm's cost of capital (technically, its weighted average cost of capital) and the purpose for its calculation.

2. Calculate the after-tax cost of debt, preferred stock, and common equity.

3. Calculate a firm's weighted average cost of capital.

4. Describe the procedure used by PepsiCo to estimate the cost of capital for a multidivisional firm.

5. Use the cost of capital to evaluate new investment opportunities.

6. Compute the economic profit earned by the firm and use this quantity to calculate incentive-based compensation.

7. Calculate equivalent interest rates for different countries.

The Cost of Capital

On January 30, 2006, ExxonMobil Corp. (XOM) announced the biggest quarterly and annual earnings for any U.S. company, ever! The earnings were $10.71 billion for the fourth quarter of 2005, and $36.13 billion for 2005 as a whole. But is ExxonMobil creating value for its shareholders? The key to answering this question rests not just on the level of the firm's earnings but also on (i) how large an investment has been made in the company in order to produce these earnings and (ii) how risky the firm's investors perceive the company's investments to be. In other words, we need to know two things: What *rate* of return did the company earn on its invested capital, and what is the *market's required rate of return* on that invested capital (the company's cost of capital)?

The firm's cost of capital provides an estimate of just how much return the firm's combined investors expect from the company. Estimating a firm's cost of capital is very intuitive in theory but can be somewhat tedious in practice. In theory, what is required is the following: One, identifying all of the firm's sources of capital and their relative importance (that is, what fraction of the firm's invested capital comes from each source). Two, estimating the market's required rate of return for each source of capital the firm uses. Three, calculating an average of the required

rates of return for each source of capital where the required rate of return for each source has been weighted by its contribution to the total capital invested in the firm.

Not to hold you in suspense any longer, ExxonMobil Corp. earned a whopping 18.9 percent return on its invested capital in 2005, and its cost of capital was only 6.1 percent. Consequently, the company realized a huge premium over its capital cost, which made it the fourth-highest "value creator" for 2005, as ranked by Stern Stewart and Co.[1]

The cost of capital is not only important when evaluating the company's overall performance, but is also used when evaluating individual investment decisions made by the firm. For example, when ExxonMobil is considering the development of a new oil production property in Nigeria, the company needs to estimate just how much return is needed to justify the investment. Similarly, when it is considering a chemical plant in Southeast Asia or Louisiana, the company's analysts need a benchmark return to compare to the investment's expected return. The cost of capital provides this benchmark.

[1] This data is based on the 2006 version of the Stern Stewart Performance 1000 database.

Having studied the connection between risk and rates of return for securities (Chapter 9) and the valuation of bonds and stocks (Chapters 7 and 8), we are prepared to consider the firm's cost of capital. A firm's cost of capital serves as the link between the firm's financing decisions and its investment decisions. The cost of capital becomes the hurdle rate that must be achieved by an investment before it will increase shareholder wealth. The term *cost of capital* is commonly used interchangeably with the firm's *required rate of return*, the *hurdle rate for new investments*, the *discount rate for evaluating a new investment*, and the firm's *opportunity cost of funds*. Regardless of the term used, the basic concept is the same. The cost of capital is the rate that must be earned on an investment project if the project is to increase the value of the common stockholders' investment. The cost of capital is also the appropriate basis for evaluating the performance of a division or even an entire firm.

In this chapter, we discuss the fundamental determinants of a firm's cost of capital and the rationale for its calculation and use. This entails developing the logic for estimating the cost of debt capital, preferred stock, and common stock. Chapter 13 takes up consideration of the impact of the firm's financing mix on the cost of capital.

THE COST OF CAPITAL: KEY DEFINITIONS AND CONCEPTS

Opportunity Costs, Required Rates of Return, and the Cost of Capital

Objective 1

Describe the concepts underlying the firm's cost of capital (technically, its weighted average cost of capital) and the purpose for its calculation.

In Chapter 9, we referred to the discount rate used in calculating net present value (*NPV*) simply as the appropriate discount rate. In this chapter, we define what we mean by this term. Specifically, the appropriate discount rate primarily reflects the investor's required rate of return, or the *minimum rate of return necessary to attract an investor to purchase or hold a security*. This rate of return considers the investor's opportunity cost of making the investment. This opportunity cost equals the return on the investor's next-best investment that is forgone should the project under consideration be accepted. This forgone return is the opportunity cost of undertaking the investment and, consequently, is the investor's required rate of return.

Is the investor's required rate of return the same thing as the cost of capital? Not exactly. Two factors drive a wedge between the investor's required rate of return and the cost of capital to the firm.

1. **Taxes.**   When a firm borrows money to finance the purchase of an asset, the interest expense is deductible for federal income tax calculations. Consider a firm that borrows at 9 percent and then deducts its interest expense from its revenues before paying taxes at a rate of 34 percent. For each dollar of interest it pays, the firm reduces its taxes by $0.34. Consequently, the actual cost of borrowing to the firm is only 5.94% [.09 − (.34 × .09) = .09(1 − .34) = 0.0594, or 5.94%].

2. **Transaction costs.**   Here we are referring to the costs the firm incurs *when it raises funds by issuing a particular type of security*. As you learned in Chapter 2, these are sometimes called flotation costs. For example, if a firm sells new shares for $25 per share but incurs transaction costs of $5 per share, then the cost of capital for the new common equity is increased. Assume that the investor's required rate of return is 15 percent for each $25 share; then .15 × $25 = $3.75 must be earned each year to satisfy the investor's required return. However, the firm has only $20 to invest, so the cost of capital (*k*) is calculated as the rate of return that must be earned on the $20 net proceeds that will produce a return of $3.75; that is,

$$\$20k = \$25 \times .15 = \$3.75$$

$$k = \frac{\$3.75}{\$20.00} = .1875, \text{ or } 18.75\%$$

We will have more to say about both these considerations when we discuss the costs of the individual sources of capital to the firm shortly.

The Firm's Financial Policy and the Cost of Capital

financial policy the firm's policies regarding the sources of financing it plans to use and the particular mix (proportions) in which they will be used.

A firm's **financial policy**—that is, *the policies regarding the sources of finances it plans to use and the particular mix (proportions) in which they will be used*—governs its use of debt and equity fi-

Can You Do It?

DETERMINING HOW FLOTATION COSTS AFFECT THE COST OF CAPITAL

McDonald's Corporation sold a portion of its ownership interest in its rapidly growing fast-food Mexican restaurant Chipotle in January of 2006 for $22.00 per share. If the investor's required rate of return on these shares was 18 percent, and McDonald's incurred transaction costs totaling $2.00 per share, what was the cost of capital to McDonald's after adjusting for the effects of the transaction costs?

(The solution can be found on page 336.)

nancing. The particular mixture of debt and equity that the firm uses can impact the firm's cost of capital. However, in this chapter, we assume that the firm maintains a fixed financial policy that is reflected in a fixed debt–equity ratio. Determining the target mix of debt and equity financing is the subject of Chapter 12.

The firm's overall cost of capital reflects the combined costs of all the sources of financing used by the firm. We refer to this overall cost of capital as the firm's **weighted average cost of capital**. The weighted average cost of capital is *the weighted average of the after-tax costs of each of the sources of capital used by a firm to finance a project, where the weights reflect the proportion of total financing raised from each source.* Consequently, the weighted average cost of capital is the rate of return that the firm must earn on its investments so that it can compensate both its creditors and stockholders with their individual required rates of return. Let's now turn to a discussion of how the costs of debt and equity can be estimated.

weighted average cost of capital a composite of the individual costs of financing incurred by each capital source. A firm's weighted cost of capital is a function of (1) the individual costs of capital, (2) the capital structure mix, and (3) the level of financing necessary to make the investment.

Did You Get It?

1. How is an investor's required rate of return related to an opportunity cost?
2. How do flotation costs impact the firm's cost of capital?

DETERMINING THE COSTS OF THE INDIVIDUAL SOURCES OF CAPITAL

Objective **2**

Calculate the after-tax cost of debt, preferred stock, and common equity.

In order to attract new investors, companies have created a wide variety of financing instruments or securities. In this chapter, we stick to three basic types: debt, preferred stock, and common stock. In calculating the respective cost of financing from each of these types of financing instruments, we estimate the investor's required rate of return after properly adjusting for any transaction or flotation costs. In addition, because we will be discounting after-tax cash flows, we adjust our cost of capital for the effects of corporate taxes. In summary, the cost of a particular source of capital is equal to the investor's required rate of return after adjusting for the effects of both flotation costs and corporate taxes.

The Cost of Debt

As you have learned, the investor's required rate of return on debt is simply the return that creditors demand on new borrowing. We learned in Chapter 6 that we could calculate the value of a bond that has 3 years to maturity and pays interest annually plus the principal amount of the debt (M) at the end of 3 years as follows:

$$\text{Bond price } (P_d) = \frac{\text{interest for year 1 } (\$I_1)}{(1 + \text{bondholder's required rate of return } (R_d))}$$
$$+ \frac{\$I_2}{(1 + R_d)^2} + \frac{\$I_3 + \text{principal } (\$M)}{(1 + R_d)^3}$$

(11-1)

How Did You Do?

DETERMINING HOW FLOTATION COSTS AFFECT THE COST OF CAPITAL

If the required rate of return on the shares was 18 percent, and the shares sold for $22.00 with $2.00 in transaction costs incurred per share, then the cost of equity capital for Chipotle Mexican Grill is found by grossing up the investor's required rate of return as follows:

$$Cost\ of\ equity\ capital = \frac{investor's\ required\ rate\ of\ return}{(1\ -\ \%\ flotation\ costs)} = \frac{18\%}{1\ -\ \left(\dfrac{\$2.00}{\$22.00}\right)} = 19.80\%$$

Incidentally, although the shares were sold to the public for $22.00 per share, they doubled to $44.00 by the end of the day after being traded in the secondary market.

Because firms must pay flotation costs when they issue new debt, the net proceeds from the bond issuance (NP_d) will be less than the bond price paid by the investor who buys it. The difference (the flotation costs) consists of the fees paid to an investment banker to prepare the documents needed to issue new bonds and the sales commissions involved in selling them. Consequently, the cost of debt capital, k_d, will be higher than the investor's required rate of return, R_d. Specifically, we calculate the cost of capital for a firm's new three-year debt as follows:

$$\text{Net proceeds } (NP_d) = \frac{\$I_1}{1\ +\ \text{cost of debt capital } (k_d))^1} + \frac{\$I_2}{(1\ +\ k_d)^2} + \frac{\$I_3\ +\ \$M}{(1\ +\ k_d)^3} \quad (11\text{-}2a)$$

Note that the adjustment for flotation costs simply involves replacing the market price of the bond with the net proceeds per bond (NP_d) received by the firm after paying these costs. The result of this adjustment is that the discount rate that solves equation (11-2a) is now the firm's cost of debt financing before adjusting for the effect of corporate taxes—that is, the before-tax cost of debt (k_d). The final adjustment we make is to account for the fact that interest is tax deductible. Thus, the after-tax cost of debt capital is simply $k_d (1\ -\ T_c)$, where T_c is the corporate tax rate.

As we learned in Chapter 6, the interest payments on bonds are generally the same for each period. Under these conditions, equation (11-2a) can be restated using the interest factors in the present value tables found in the appendixes at the back of the book, as follows:

$$NP_d = \$I_1(PVIFA_{k_d,\ n}) + \$M(PVIF_{k_d,\ n}) \quad (11\text{-}2b)$$

Remember Your Principles

When we calculate the bondholder's required rate of return, we are discounting the interest and principal payments to the bondholder back to the present using a discount rate that makes this present value equal the current price of the firm's bonds. In essence, we are valuing the bond, relying on two basic principles of finance: **Principle 1: The Risk–Return Trade-Off—We Won't Take On Additional Risk Unless We Expect to Be Compensated with Additional Return** and **Principle 2: The Time Value of Money—A Dollar Received Today Is Worth More Than a Dollar Received in the Future**.

In addition, the calculation of the bondholder's required rate of return relies on the observed market price of the firm's bonds to be an accurate reflection of their worth. Buyers and sellers stop trading only when they are convinced that the price properly reflects all available information. **Principle 6: Efficient Capital Markets—The Markets Are Quick and the Prices Are Right**. What we mean here, very simply, is that investors are ever vigilant and quickly act on information that affects the riskiness and, consequently, the price of a firm's bonds and other securities.

Remember Your Principles

The tax deductibility of interest expense makes debt financing less costly to the firm. This is an example of **Principle 8: Taxes Bias Business Decisions**. The tax deductibility of interest, other things remaining constant, serves to encourage firms to use more debt in their capital structure than they might otherwise use.

➤ EXAMPLE

Synopticom Inc. plans a bond issue for the near future and wants to estimate its current cost of debt capital. After talking with the firm's investment banker, the firm's chief financial officer has determined that a 20-year maturity bond with a $1,000 face value and 8 percent coupon (paying $8\% \times \$1,000 = \$80$ per year in interest) can be sold to investors for $908.32. As we illustrated earlier in Chapter 7, equation (11-1) can be generalized to solve for the investor's required rate of return (R_d) for a 20-year bond. In this instance the bond pays 20 annual interest payments of $80 plus a $1,000 principal amount in the 20th year; that is,

$$\$908.32 = \frac{\$80}{(1+R_d)^1} + \frac{\$80}{(1+R_d)^2} + \frac{\$80}{(1+R_d)^3} + \cdots + \frac{\$80}{(1+R_d)^{19}} + \frac{\$80+\$1,000}{(1+R_d)^{20}}$$

In this case, Synopticom's creditors require a 9 percent rate of return. The cost of capital to the firm is higher than 9 percent, however, because the firm will have to pay flotation costs of $58.32 per bond when it issues the securities. The flotation costs reduce the net proceeds to Synopticom to $850. Substituting into the above equation, we find that the before-tax cost of capital for the bond issue (k_d) is 9.73 percent, that is,

$$\$850.00 = \frac{\$80}{(1+k_d)^1} + \frac{\$80}{(1+k_d)^2} + \frac{\$80}{(1+k_d)^3} + \cdots + \frac{\$80}{(1+k_d)^{19}} + \frac{\$80+\$1,000}{(1+k_d)^{20}}$$

Once again, we can solve equation (11-2a) using a financial calculator, as we illustrate in the margin.

One final adjustment is necessary to obtain the firm's after-tax cost of debt capital. Assuming that Synopticom is in the 34 percent corporate income tax (T_c) bracket, we estimate the after-tax cost of debt capital as follows:

$$\text{After-tax cost of debt} = k_d(1 - T_c)$$
$$= 9.73\%(1 - .34) = 6.422\%$$

CALCULATOR SOLUTION

Data Input	Function Key
20	N
−850	PV
80	PMT
1000	FV

Function Key	Answer
CPT I/Y	9.73

The Cost of Preferred Stock

Determining the cost of preferred stock is very straightforward because of the simple nature of the cash flows paid to the holders of preferred shares. You will recall from Chapter 7 that the value of a preferred stock is simply

$$\text{Price of preferred stock } (P_{ps}) = \frac{\text{preferred stock dividend}}{\text{required rate of return for preferred stockholder}} \qquad (11\text{-}3)$$

where P_{ps} is the current market price of the preferred shares. Solving for the preferred stockholder's required rate of return, we get the following:

$$\text{Required rate of return for preferred stockholder} = \frac{\text{preferred stock dividend}}{\text{price of preferred stock}} \qquad (11\text{-}4)$$

Once again, because flotation costs are usually incurred when new preferred shares are sold, the investor's required rate of return is less than the cost of preferred capital to the firm. To calculate the cost of preferred stock, we must adjust the required rate of return to reflect these flotation costs. We replace the price of a preferred share in equation (11-4) with the net proceeds per share from the sale of new preferred shares (NP_{ps}). The resulting formula can be used to calculate the cost of preferred stock to the firm.

$$\text{Cost of preferred stock } (k_{ps}) = \frac{\text{preferred stock dividend}}{\text{net proceeds per preferred share}} \tag{11-5}$$

Note that the net proceeds per share are equal to the price per share of preferred stock minus flotation cost per share of newly issued preferred stock.

What about corporate taxes? In the case of preferred stock, no tax adjustment must be made because, unlike interest payments, preferred dividends are not tax deductible.

➤ EXAMPLE

El Paso Edison has issued preferred stock that pays an annual dividend of $4.25 per share. On November 23, 2006, the stock closed at $58.50. Assume that if the firm were to sell an issue of preferred stock with the same characteristics as its outstanding issue, it would incur flotation costs of $1.375 per share and the shares would sell for their November 23, 2006, closing price. What is El Paso Edison's cost of preferred stock?

Substituting into equation (11-5), we get the following cost of preferred stock for El Paso Edison:

$$k_{ps} = \frac{\$4.25}{(\$58.50 - \$1.375)} = .0744, \text{ or } 7.44\%$$

Note that there is no adjustment for taxes because preferred dividends are not tax deductible—that is, preferred dividends are paid after corporate taxes, unlike bond interest, which is paid with before-tax dollars.

The Cost of Common Equity

Common equity is unique in two respects. First, the cost of common equity is more difficult to estimate than the cost of debt or cost of preferred stock because the common stockholder's required rate of return is not observable. For example, there is no stated coupon rate or set dividend payment they receive. This results from the fact that common stockholders are the residual owners of the firm, which means that their return is equal to what is left of the firm's earnings after paying the firm's bondholders their contractually set interest and principal payments and the preferred stockholders their promised dividends. Second, common equity can be obtained either from the retention of firm earnings or through the sale of new shares. The costs associated with each of these sources are different from one another because the firm does not incur any flotation costs when it retains earnings, but it does incur costs when it sells new common shares.

We discuss two methods for estimating the common stockholder's required rate of return, which is the foundation for our estimate of the firm's cost of equity capital. These methods are based on the dividend growth model and the capital asset pricing model, which were both discussed in Chapter 7 when we discussed stock valuation.

The Dividend Growth Model

Recall from Chapter 7 that the value of a firm's common stock is equal to the present value of all future dividends. When dividends are expected to grow at a rate g forever, and g is less than the investor's required rate of return, k_{cs}, then the value of a share of common stock, P_{cs}, can be written as

$$P_{cs} = \frac{D_1}{k_{cs} - g} \tag{11-6}$$

where D_1 is the dividend expected to be received by the firm's common shareholders 1 year hence. The expected dividend is simply the current dividend multiplied by 1 plus the annual rate of growth in dividends (that is, $D_1 = D_0(1 + g)$). The investor's required rate of return then is found by solving equation (11-6) for k_{cs}.

$$k_{cs} = \frac{D_1}{P_{cs}} + g \qquad (11\text{-}7)$$

Note that k_{cs} is the investor's required rate of return for investing in the firm's stock. It also serves as our estimate of the cost of equity capital, where new equity capital is obtained by retaining a part of the firm's current-period earnings. Recall that common equity financing can come from one of two sources: the retention of earnings or the sale of new common shares. When the firm retains earnings, it doesn't incur any flotation costs; thus, the investor's required rate of return is the same as the firm's cost of new equity capital in this instance.

If the firm issues new shares to raise equity capital, then it incurs flotation costs. Once again we adjust the investor's required rate of return for flotation costs by substituting the net proceeds per share, NP_{cs}, for the stock price, P_{cs}, in equation (11-7) to estimate the cost of new common stock, k_{ncs}.

$$k_{ncs} = \frac{D_1}{NP_{cs}} + g \qquad (11\text{-}8)$$

➤ EXAMPLE

The Talbot Corporation's common shareholders anticipate receiving a $2.20 per share dividend next year, based on the fact that they received $2 last year and expect dividends to grow 10 percent next year. Furthermore, analysts predict that dividends will continue to grow at a rate of 10 percent into the foreseeable future. Given that the firm's stock is

How Did You Do?

CALCULATING THE COST OF DEBT FINANCING

General Auto Parts Corporation receives $18 million from the sale of the bonds (after paying flotation costs) and is required to make principal plus interest payments at the end of the next 2 years. The total cash flows (both the inflow and the outflows) are summarized below:

	TODAY	YEAR 1	YEAR 2
Principal	$18 million	($0.00 million)	($20 million)
Interest		(0.99 million)	(0.99 million)
Total	$18 million	($0.99 million)	($20.99 million)

We can estimate the before-tax cost of capital from the bond issue by solving for k_d in the following bond valuation equation:

$$\text{Net bond proceeds}_{today} = \frac{\text{interest paid in year 1}}{(1 + k_d)^1} + \frac{\text{interest paid in year 2}}{(1 + k_d)^2} + \frac{\text{principal paid in year 2}}{(1 + k_d)^2}$$

$$\$18,000,000 = \frac{\$990,000}{(1 + k_d)^1} + \frac{\$990,000}{(1 + k_d)^2} + \frac{\$20,000,000}{(1 + k_d)^2}$$

$$k_d = 10.77\%$$

How Did You Do?

CALCULATING THE COST OF PREFERRED STOCK FINANCING

Carson Enterprises sold its shares of preferred stock for net proceeds of $2.25 a share, and each share entitles the holder to a $0.25 cash dividend every year. Because the dividend payment is constant for all future years, we can calculate the cost of capital raised by the sale of preferred stock (k_{ps}) as follows:

$$\text{Cost of preferred stock } (k_{ps}) = \frac{\text{preferred stock dividend}}{\text{net proceeds}_{per \, preferred \, share}} = \frac{\$0.25}{\$2.25} = 11.11\%$$

trading for $50 per share, we can calculate the investor's required rate of return (and the cost of retained earnings) as follows:

$$k_{cs} = \frac{D_1}{P_{cs}} + g = \frac{\$2.20}{\$50.00} + .10 = .144, \text{ or } 14.4\%$$

Should Talbot decide to issue new common stock, then it would incur a cost of $7.50 per share, or 15 percent of the current stock price. The resulting cost of new common equity capital would be

$$k_{ncs} = \frac{D_1}{NP_{cs}} + g = \frac{\$2.20}{\$50 - \$7.50} + .10 = .1518, \text{ or } 15.18\%$$

Thus, Talbot faces two costs of capital with respect to common equity. If it uses retained earnings, then the cost of capital to the firm is 14.4 percent, and if it issues new common stock, the corresponding cost is 15.18 percent. This difference will prove to be important later when we calculate the overall or weighted average cost of capital for the firm.

The dividend growth model for common stock valuation relies on three of the fundamental principles of finance. First, a stock's value is equal to the present value of its expected future dividends. This reflects **Principle 2: The Time Value of Money—A Dollar Received Today Is Worth More Than a Dollar Received in the Future**. Furthermore, dividends represent actual cash receipts to stockholders and are incorporated into the valuation model in a manner that reflects the timing of their receipt. This attribute of the dividend growth model reflects **Principle 3: Cash—Not Profits—Is King**. Finally, the rate used to discount the expected future dividends back to the present reflects the riskiness of the dividends. The higher the riskiness of the dividend payments, the higher the investor's required rate of return. This reflects **Principle 1: The Risk–Return Trade-Off—We Won't Take On Additional Risk Unless We Expect to Be Compensated with Additional Return**.

Issues in Implementing the Dividend Growth Model

The principal advantage of the dividend growth model as a basis for calculating the firm's cost of capital as it relates to common stock is the model's simplicity. To estimate an investor's required rate of return, the analyst needs only to observe the current dividend and stock price and to estimate the rate of growth in future dividends. The primary drawback relates to the applicability or appropriateness of the valuation model. That is, the dividend growth model is based on the fundamental assumption that dividends are expected to grow at a constant rate g forever. To avoid this assumption, analysts frequently utilize more complex valuation models in which dividends are expected to grow for, say, 5 years at one rate and then grow at a lower rate from year 6 forward. We do not consider these more complex models here.

Even if the constant growth rate assumption is acceptable, we must arrive at an estimate of that growth rate. We could estimate the rate of growth in historical dividends ourselves or go to published sources of growth rate expectations. Investment advisory services such as Value Line provide their own analysts' estimates of earnings growth rates (generally spanning up to 5 years), and the Institutional Brokers' Estimate System (I/B/E/S) collects and publishes earnings per share forecasts made by more than 1,000 analysts for a broad list of stocks. These estimates are helpful but still require the careful judgment of an analyst in their use because they relate to earnings (not dividends) and extend only 5 years into the future (not forever, as required by the dividend growth model). Nonetheless, these estimates provide a useful guide to making your initial dividend growth rate estimate.

The Capital Asset Pricing Model

Recall from Chapter 8 that the capital asset pricing model (CAPM) provides a basis for determining the investor's expected or required rate of return from investing in common stock. The model depends on three things:

1. The risk-free rate, k_{rf}
2. The systematic risk of the common stock's returns relative to the market as a whole, or the stock's beta coefficient, β
3. The market-risk premium, which is equal to the difference in the expected rate of return for the market as a whole, that is, the expected rate of return for the "average security" minus the risk-free rate, or in symbols, $k_m - k_{rf}$

Using the CAPM, the investor's required rate of return can be written as follows:

$$k_c = k_{rf} + \beta(k_m - k_{rf}) \tag{11-9}$$

➤ **EXAMPLE**

Talbot Corporation's common stock has a beta coefficient of 1.40. Furthermore, the risk-free rate is currently 3.75 percent, and the expected rate of return on the market portfolio of all risky assets is 12 percent. Using the CAPM from equation (11-9), we can estimate Talbot's cost of capital as follows:

$$k_c = k_{rf} + \beta(k_m - k_{rf})$$
$$= .0375 + 1.4(.12 - .0375) = .153, \text{ or } 15.3\%$$

Note that the required rate of return we have estimated is the cost of internal common equity because no transaction costs are considered.

Issues in Implementing the CAPM

The CAPM approach has two primary advantages when it comes to calculating a firm's cost of capital as it relates to common stock. First, the model is simple and easy to understand and implement. The model variables are readily available from public sources, with the possible exception of beta coefficients for small firms and/or privately held firms. Second, because the model does not rely on dividends or any assumption about the growth rate in dividends, it can be applied to companies that do not currently pay dividends or are not expected to experience a constant rate of growth in dividends.

Of course, using the CAPM requires that we obtain estimates of each of the three model variables—k_{rf}, β, and $(k_m - k_{rf})$. Let's consider each in turn. First, the analyst has a wide range of U.S. government securities on which to base an estimate of the risk-free rate (k_{rf}). Treasury securities with maturities from 30 days to 20 years are readily available. Unfortunately, the CAPM offers no guidance about the appropriate choice. In fact, the model itself assumes that there is but one risk-free rate, and it corresponds to a one-period return (the length of the period is not specified, however). Consequently, we are left to our own judgment about which maturity we should use to represent the risk-free rate. For applications of the cost of capital involving long-term capital expenditure decisions, it seems reasonable to select a risk-free rate of comparable maturity. So, if we are calculating the cost of capital to be used as the basis for evaluating investments that will provide returns over the next 20 years, it seems appropriate to use a risk-free rate corresponding to a U.S. Treasury bond of comparable maturity.

Second, estimates of security beta (β) coefficients are available from a wide variety of investment advisory services, including Merrill Lynch and Value Line, among others. Alternatively, we could collect historical stock market returns for the company of interest as well as a general market index (such as the Standard and Poor's 500 Index) and estimate the stock's beta as the slope of the relationship between the two return series—as we did in Chapter 8. However, because beta estimates are widely available for a large majority of publicly traded firms, analysts frequently rely on published sources for betas.

Finally, estimating the market-risk premium (k_m) can be accomplished by looking at the history of stock returns and the premium earned over (under) the risk-free rate of interest. In Chapter 8, we reported a summary of the historical returns earned on risk-free securities and common stocks in Figure 8-2. We saw that on average over the past 70 years, common stocks have earned a premium of roughly 7 percent over long-term government bonds. Thus, for our purposes, we will utilize this estimate of the market-risk premium ($k_m - k_{rf}$) when estimating the investor's required rate of return on equity using the CAPM.

In addition to the historical average market-risk premium, we can also utilize surveys of professional economists' opinions regarding future premiums.[2] For example, in a survey conducted in 1998 by Yale economist Ivo Welch, the median 30-year market-risk premium for all survey participants was 7 percent. When the survey was repeated in 2000, the corresponding market-risk premium had fallen to 5 percent. These results suggest two things. First, the

---

[2] The results reported here come from Ivo Welch, "Views of Financial Economists on the Equity Premium and on Professional Controversies," *Journal of Business* 73–74 (October 2000): pp. 501–537; and Ivo Welch, "The Equity Premium Consensus Forecast Revisited," Cowles Foundation Discussion Paper No. 1325 (September 2001).

Can You Do It?

CALCULATING THE COST OF NEW COMMON STOCK USING THE DIVIDEND GROWTH MODEL

In March of 2007, the Mayze Corporation sold an issue of common stock in a public offering. The shares sold for $100 per share. Mayze's dividend in 2008 was $8 per share, and analysts expect that the firm's earnings and dividends will grow at a rate of 6 percent per year for the foreseeable future. What is the common stock investor's required rate of return (and the cost of retained earnings)?

Although the shares sold for $100 per share, Mayze received net proceeds from the issue of only $95 per share. The difference represents the flotation cost paid to the investment banker.

What is your estimate of the cost of new equity for Mayze using the dividend growth model?
(The solution can be found on page 345.)

Can You Do It?

CALCULATING THE COST OF COMMON STOCK USING THE CAPM

The Mayze Corporation issued common stock in March 2007, for $100 per share. However, before the issue was made, the firm's chief financial officer (CFO) asked one of his financial analysts to estimate the cost of the common stock financing using the CAPM. The analyst looked on Yahoo! Finance and got an estimate of .90 for the firm's beta coefficient. She also consulted online sources to get the current yield on a 10-year U.S. Treasury bond, which was 5.5 percent. The final estimate she needed to complete her calculation of the cost of equity using the CAPM was the market-risk premium, or the difference in the expected rate of return on all equity securities and the rate of return on the 10-year U.S. Treasury bond. After a bit of research she decided that the risk premium should be based on a 12 percent expected rate of return for the market portfolio and the 5.5 percent rate on the Treasury bond.

What is your estimate of the cost of common stock for Mayze using the CAPM?
(The solution can be found on page 345.)

Remember Your Principles

The capital asset pricing model, or CAPM, is a formal representation of **Principle 1: The Risk–Return Trade-Off—We Won't Take On Additional Risk Unless We Expect to Be Compensated with Additional Return**. By "formal" we mean that the specific method of calculating the additional returns needed to compensate for additional risk is specified in the form of an equation—the CAPM. The CAPM's recognition of systematic, or nondiversifiable, risk as the source of risk that is rewarded in the capital market is a reflection of **Principle 9: All Risk Is Not Equal—Some Risk Can Be Diversified Away and Some Can Not**.

market-risk premium is not fixed. It varies through time with the general business cycle. In addition, it appears that using a market-risk premium somewhere between 5 percent and 7 percent is reasonable when estimating the cost of capital using the capital asset pricing model.

Did You Get It?

1. Define the cost of debt, preferred equity, and common equity financing.
2. The cost of common equity financing is more difficult to estimate than the costs of debt and preferred equity. Explain why.
3. What is the dividend growth model, and how is it used to estimate the cost of common equity financing?
4. Describe the capital asset pricing model and how it can be used to estimate the cost of common equity financing.
5. What practical problems are encountered in using the CAPM to estimate common equity capital cost?

Finance at Work

IPOS: SHOULD A FIRM GO PUBLIC?

When a privately owned company decides to distribute its shares to the general public, it goes through a process known as an initial public offering (IPO). There are a number of advantages to having a firm's shares traded in the public equity market, including the following:

- **New capital is raised.** When the firm sells its shares to the public, it acquires new capital that can be invested in the firm.
- **The firm's owners gain liquidity of their share holdings.** Publicly traded shares are more easily bought and sold, so the owners can more easily liquidate all or part of their investment in the firm.
- **The firm gains future access to the public capital market.** Once a firm has raised capital in the public markets, it is easier to go back a second and third time.
- **Being a publicly traded firm can benefit the firm's business.** Public firms tend to enjoy a higher profile than their privately held counterparts. This may make it easier to make sales and attract vendors to supply goods and services to the firm.

However, all is not rosy as a publicly held firm. There are a number of potential disadvantages, including the following:

- **Reporting requirements can be onerous.** Publicly held firms are required to file periodic reports with the Securities and Exchange Commission (SEC). This is not only onerous in terms of the time and effort required, but also some business owners feel they must reveal information to their competitors that could be potentially damaging.

- **The private equity investors now must share any new wealth with the new public investors.** Once the firm is a publicly held company, the new shareholders share on an equal footing with the company founders the good (and bad) fortune of the firm.
- **The private equity investors lose a degree of control over the organization.** Outsiders gain voting control over the firm to the extent that they own its shares.
- **An IPO is expensive.** A typical firm may spend 15 to 25 percent of the money raised on expenses directly connected to the IPO. This cost is increased further if we consider the cost of lost management time and disruption of business associated with the IPO process.
- **Exit of the company's owners is usually limited.** The company's founders may want to sell their shares through the IPO, but this is not allowed for an extended period of time following the IPO. Therefore, this is not usually a good mechanism for cashing out the company founders.
- **Everyone involved faces legal liability.** The IPO participants are jointly and severally liable for each others' actions. This means that they can be sued for any omissions from the IPO's prospectus should the market valuation fall below the IPO offering price.

Carefully weighing the financial consequences of each of these advantages and disadvantages can provide a company's owners (and managers) with some basis for answering the question of whether they want to become a public corporation.

Other Sources: Professor Ivo Welch's Web site: **welch.som.yale.edu** provides a wealth of information concerning IPOs.

Objective **3**

Calculate a firm's weighted average cost of capital.

capital structure the mix of long-term sources of funds used by the firm. This is also called the firm's capitalization. The relative total (percentage) of each type of fund is emphasized.

THE WEIGHTED AVERAGE COST OF CAPITAL

Now that we have calculated the individual costs of capital for each of the sources of financing the firm might use, we turn to the combination of these capital costs into a single weighted average cost of capital. To estimate the weighted average cost of capital, we need to know the cost of each of the sources of capital used and the capital structure mix. We use the term **capital structure** to refer to *the proportions of each source of financing used by the firm.* Although a firm's capital structure can be quite complex, we focus our examples on the three basic sources of capital: bonds, preferred stock, and common equity.

In words, we calculate the weighted average cost of capital for a firm that uses only debt and common equity using the following equation:

$$\begin{pmatrix} \text{Weighted} \\ \text{average cost} \\ \text{of capital} \end{pmatrix} = \begin{pmatrix} \text{after--tax} \\ \text{cost of} & \times & \text{proportion} \\ \text{debt} & & \text{of debt} \\ & & \text{financing} \end{pmatrix} + \begin{pmatrix} \text{cost of} & \times & \text{proportion} \\ \text{equity} & & \text{of equity} \\ & & \text{financing} \end{pmatrix} \quad (11\text{-}10)$$

For example, if a firm borrows money at 6 percent after taxes, pays 10 percent for equity, and raises its capital in equal proportions from debt and equity, its weighted average cost of capital is 8 percent—that is,

Weighted average cost of capital $= [.06 \times .5] + [.10 \times .5] = .08$ or 8%

How Did You Do?

CALCULATING THE COST OF NEW COMMON STOCK USING THE DIVIDEND GROWTH MODEL

We can estimate the cost of equity capital using the dividend growth model by substituting into the following equation:

$$\text{Cost of new common stock } (k_{cs}) = \frac{\text{expected dividend next year } (D_1)}{\text{current stock price per share } (P_{cs})} + \text{dividend growth rate } (g) = \frac{\$8.00}{\$100.00} + .06 = 14\%$$

Taking flotation costs into account, we substitute net proceeds (NP_{cs}) for the price at which the shares were sold (P_{cs}) as follows:

$$\text{Cost of new common stock } (k_{ns}) = \frac{\text{expected dividend next year } (D_1)}{\text{net proceeds per share } (NP_{cs})} + \text{dividend growth rate } (g) = \frac{\$8.00}{\$95.00} + .06 = 14.42\%$$

How Did You Do?

CALCULATING THE COST OF COMMON STOCK USING THE CAPM

The CAPM can be used to estimate the investor's required rate of return as follows:

$$\begin{array}{c}\text{Cost of}\\\text{common equity } (k_c)\end{array} = \left(\begin{array}{c}\text{risk–free}\\\text{rate of interest } (k_{rf})\end{array}\right) + \left(\begin{array}{c}\text{Mayze's beta}\\\text{coefficient } (\beta)\end{array}\right) \times \left[\begin{array}{c}\text{expected market}\\\text{rate of return } (k_m)\end{array} - \left(\begin{array}{c}\text{risk–free}\\\text{rate of interest } (k_{rf})\end{array}\right)\right]$$

Making the appropriate substitutions, we get the following estimate of the investor's required rate of return using the CAPM model:

$$\text{Cost of common equity } (k_c) = .055 + .90 \times (.12 - .055) = .1135 \text{ or } 11.35\%$$

In practice, the calculation of the cost of capital is generally more complex than this example. For one thing, firms often have multiple debt issues with different required rates of return, and they also use preferred equity as well as common equity financing. Furthermore, when new common equity capital is raised, it is sometimes the result of retaining and reinvesting the firm's earnings and, at other times, it involves a new stock offering. Of course, in the case of retained earnings, the firm does not incur the costs associated with selling new common stock. This means that equity from retained earnings is less costly than a new stock offering. In the examples that follow, we address each of these complications.

Capital Structure Weights

The reason we calculate a cost of capital is that it enables us to evaluate one or more of the firm's investment opportunities. Remember that the cost of capital should reflect the riskiness of the project being evaluated, so a firm should calculate multiple costs of capital when it makes investments in multiple divisions or business units having different risk characteristics. Thus, for the calculated cost of capital to be meaningful, it must correspond directly to the riskiness of the particular project being analyzed. That is, in theory the cost of capital should reflect the particular way in which the funds are raised (the capital structure used) and the systemic risk characteristics of the project. Consequently, the correct way to calculate capital structure weights is to use the actual dollar amounts of the various sources of capital actually used by the firm.[3]

---

[3] There are instances when we will want to calculate the cost of capital for the firm as a whole. In this case, the appropriate weights to use are based on the market value of the various capital sources used by the firm. Market values rather than book values properly reflect the sources of financing used by a firm at any particular point in time. However, when a firm is privately owned, it is not possible to get market values of its securities, and book values are often used.

TABLE 11-1	Calculating the Weighted Average Cost of Capital

PANEL A: COMMON EQUITY RAISED BY RETAINED EARNINGS

CAPITAL STRUCTURE

SOURCE OF CAPITAL	WEIGHTS	× COST OF CAPITAL	= PRODUCT
Bonds	w_d	$k_d(1 - T_c)$	$w_d \times k_d(1 - T_c)$
Preferred stock	w_{ps}	k_{ps}	$w_{ps} \times k_{ps}$
Common equity			
Retained earnings	w_{cs}	k_{cs}	$w_{cs} \times k_{cs}$
Sum =	100%	Sum =	k_{wacc}

PANEL B: COMMON EQUITY RAISED BY SELLING NEW COMMON STOCK

CAPITAL STRUCTURE

SOURCE OF CAPITAL	WEIGHTS	× COST OF CAPITAL	= PRODUCT
Bonds	w_d	$k_d(1 - T_c)$	$w_d \times k_d(1 - T_c)$
Preferred stock	w_{ps}	k_{ps}	$w_{ps} \times k_{ps}$
Common equity			
Common stock	w_{ncs}	k_{ncs}	$w_{ncs} \times k_{ncs}$
Sum =	100%	Sum =	k_{wacc}

In practice, *the mixture of financing sources used by a firm will vary from year to year*. For this reason, many firms find it expedient to use target capital structure proportions when calculating the firm's weighted average cost of capital. For example, a firm might use its target mix of 40 percent debt and 60 percent equity to calculate its weighted average cost of capital even though, in that particular year, it raised the majority of its financing requirements by borrowing. Similarly, it would continue to use the target proportions in the subsequent year, when it might raise the majority of its financing needs by reinvesting earnings or issuing new stock.

Calculating the Weighted Average Cost of Capital

The weighted average cost of capital, k_{wacc}, is simply a weighted average of all the capital costs incurred by the firm. Table 11-1 illustrates the procedure used to estimate k_{wacc} for a firm that has debt, preferred stock, and common equity in its target capital structure mix. Two possible scenarios are described in the two panels. First, in Panel A the firm is able to finance all of its target capital structure requirements for common equity using retained earnings. Second, in Panel B the firm must use a new equity offering to raise the equity capital it requires. For example, if the firm has set a 75 percent target for equity financing and has current earnings of $750,000, then it can raise up to $750,000/.75 = $1,000,000 in new financing before it has to sell new equity. For $1,000,000 or less in capital spending, the firm's weighted average cost of capital would be calculated using the cost of equity from retained earnings (following Panel A of Table 11-1). For more than $1,000,000 in new capital, the cost of capital would rise to reflect the impact of the higher cost of using new common stock (following Panel B of Table 11-1).

➤ EXAMPLE

Ash Inc.'s capital structure and estimated capital costs are found in Table 11-2. Note that the sum of the capital structure weights must equal 100 percent if we have properly accounted for all sources of financing and in the correct amounts. For example, Ash plans to invest a total of $3 million in common equity to fund a $5 million investment. Because Ash has earnings equal to the $3,000,000 it needs in new equity financing, the entire amount of new equity will be raised by retaining earnings.

We calculate the weighted average cost of capital following the procedure described in Panel A of Table 11-1 and using the information found in Table 11-2. The resulting calculations are found in Panel A of Table 11-3, in which Ash Inc.'s weighted average cost of capital for up to $5,000,000 in new financing is found to be 12.7 percent.

TABLE 11-2   Capital Structure and Capital Costs for Ash Inc.

SOURCE OF CAPITAL	AMOUNT OF FUNDS RAISED ($)	PERCENTAGE OF TOTAL	AFTER-TAX COST OF CAPITAL
Bonds	1,750,000	35%	7%
Preferred stock	250,000	5%	13%
Common equity	3,000,000	60%	16%
Retained earnings	5,000,000	100%	

TABLE 11-3   The Weighted Average Cost of Capital for Ash Inc.

PANEL A: COST OF CAPITAL FOR $0 TO $5,000,000 IN NEW CAPITAL

SOURCE OF CAPITAL	CAPITAL STRUCTURE WEIGHTS	COST OF CAPITAL	PRODUCT
Bonds	35%	7%	2.45%
Preferred stock	5%	13%	0.65%
Common equity	60%	16%	9.60%
Retained earnings	100%	$k_{wacc} =$	12.70%

PANEL B: COST OF CAPITAL FOR MORE THAN $5,000,000

SOURCE OF CAPITAL	CAPITAL STRUCTURE WEIGHTS	COST OF CAPITAL	PRODUCT
Bonds	35%	7%	2.45%
Preferred stock	5%	13%	0.65%
Common equity	60%	18%	10.80%
Common stock	100%	$k_{wacc} =$	13.90%

If Ash needs more than $5,000,000, it will not have any retained earnings to provide the additional equity capital. Thus, to maintain its desired 60 percent equity financing proportion, Ash will now have to issue new equity that costs 18 percent.

Panel B of Table 11-3 contains the calculation of Ash's weighted average cost of capital for more than $5,000,000. The resulting cost is 13.9 percent.

In practice, many firms calculate only one cost of capital, using a cost of equity capital that ignores the transaction costs associated with raising new equity capital. In essence, they would use the capital cost calculated for Ash in Panel A of Table 11-3, regardless of the level of new financing for the year. Although this is technically incorrect, it is an understandable practice given the inexactness of the estimates of equity capital cost and the relatively small differences that result from the adjustment.[4]

Did You Get It?

1. A firm's capital structure and its target capital structure proportions are important determinants of a firm's weighted average cost of capital. Explain.

2. Explain in words the calculation of a firm's weighted average cost of capital. What exactly are we averaging and what do the weights represent?

CALCULATING DIVISIONAL COSTS OF CAPITAL: PEPSICO INC.

If a firm operates in multiple industries, each with its own particular risk characteristics, should it use different capital costs for each division? **Principle 1** suggests that the financial manager should recognize these risk differences in estimating the cost of capital to use in

Objective **4**

Describe the procedure used by PepsiCo to estimate the cost of capital for a multidivisional firm.

[4] For a discussion of the imprecise nature of equity capital cost estimates, see Eugene F. Fama and Kenneth R. French, "Industry Costs of Equity," *Journal of Financial Economics* 43 (1997), pp. 153–193.

Can You Do It?

CALCULATING THE WEIGHTED AVERAGE COST OF CAPITAL

In the fall of 2007, Grey Manufacturing was considering a major expansion of its manufacturing operations. The firm has sufficient land to accommodate the doubling of its operations, which will cost $200 million. To raise the needed funds Grey's management has decided to simply mimic the firm's present capital structure as follows:

SOURCE OF CAPITAL	AMOUNT OF FUNDS RAISED ($)	PERCENTAGE OF TOTAL	AFTER-TAX COST OF CAPITAL*
Debt	$80,000,000	40%	5.20%
Common stock	120,000,000	60%	14.50%
	$200,000,000		

What is your estimate of Grey's weighted average cost of capital?

*You may assume that these after-tax costs of capital have been appropriately adjusted for any transaction costs incurred when raising the funds.

(The solution can be found on page 350.)

each division. This is exactly what PepsiCo did before February 1997, when it was operating in three basic industries.

PepsiCo went to great lengths to estimate the cost of capital for each of its three major operating divisions (restaurants, snack foods, and beverages).[5] We briefly summarize the basic elements of the calculations involved in these estimates, including the cost of debt financing, the cost of common equity, the target capital structure weights, and the weighted average cost of capital.

Table 11-4 contains the estimates of the after-tax cost of debt for each of PepsiCo's three divisions. Table 11-5 contains the estimates of the cost of equity capital for each of PepsiCo's three operating divisions using the CAPM. We will not explain the intricacies of their method for estimating divisional betas, except to say that they make use of beta estimates for a number of competitor firms from each of the operating divisions, which involves making appropriate adjustments for differences in the use of financial leverage across the competitor firms used in the analysis.[6]

TABLE 11-4 Estimating PepsiCo's Cost of Debt

	PRETAX COST OF DEBT	×	(1 − TAX RATE)	=	AFTER-TAX COST OF DEBT
Restaurants	8.93%	×	0.62	=	5.54%
Snack foods	8.43%	×	0.62	=	5.23%
Beverages	8.51%	×	0.62	=	5.28%

TABLE 11-5 The Cost of Equity Capital for PepsiCo's Operating Divisions

	RISK-FREE RATE	+	BETA	×	(EXPECTED MARKET RETURN − RISK-FREE RATE)	=	COST OF EQUITY
Restaurants	7.28%	+	1.17	×	(11.48% − 7.28%)	=	12.19%
Snack foods	7.28%	+	1.02	×	(11.48% − 7.28%)	=	11.56%
Beverages	7.28%	+	1.07	×	(11.48% − 7.28%)	=	11.77%

[5] PepsiCo spun off its restaurants division in February 1997. However, the example used here was based on the company before the spin-off.

[6] This method of using betas from comparable firms is sometimes referred to as the pure play method, because the analyst seeks independent beta estimates for firms engaged in only one business (i.e., restaurants or beverages). The betas for these pure play companies are then used to estimate the beta for a business or division.

Finance at Work

THE PILLSBURY COMPANY ADOPTS EVA WITH A GRASSROOTS EDUCATION PROGRAM

A key determinant of the success of any incentive-based program is employee buy-in. If employees simply view a new performance measurement and reward system as "just another" reporting requirement, the program will have little impact on their behavior and, consequently, little effect on the firm's operating performance. In addition, if a firm's employees do not understand the measurement system, it is very likely that it will be distrusted and may even have counterproductive effects on the firm's performance.

So how do you instill in your employees the notion that your performance measurement and reward system does indeed lead to the desired result? Pillsbury took a unique approach to the problem by using a simulation exercise in which the value of applying the principles of Economic Value Added (EVA®) could be learned by simulating the operations of a hypothetical factory. Employees used the simulation to follow the value-creation process from the factory's revenue, to net operating profit after taxes, to the weighted average cost of capital. The results were gratifying. One Pillsbury manager noted, "you saw the lights go on in people's eyes" as employees realized, "Oh, this really does impact my work environment."

Briggs and Stratton used a similar training program to instill the basic principles of EVA in its employees. Its business-simulation example was even more basic than the Pillsbury factory. Briggs and Stratton used a convenience store's operations to teach line workers the importance of controlling waste, utilizing assets fully, and managing profit margins. Stern Stewart and Company, which coined the term *EVA*, has also developed a training tool, the EVA Training Tutor.™ The EVA Training Tutor addresses four basic issues using CD-ROM technology:

- Why is creating shareholder wealth an important corporate and investor goal?
- What is the best way to measure wealth and business success?
- Which business strategies have created wealth, and which have failed?
- What can you do to create wealth and increase the stock price of your company?

The educational programs described briefly here are examples of how major corporations are seeing the need to improve the financial literacy of their employees to make the most of their human and capital resources.

Sources: Adapted from George Donnelly, "Grassroots EVA," CFO.com (May 1, 2000), **www.cfo.com** and The EVA Training Tutor™ (Stern Stewart and Company).

TABLE 11-6 PepsiCo's Weighted Average Cost of Capital for Each of Its Operating Divisions

	COST OF EQUITY TIMES THE TARGET EQUITY RATIO	+	AFTER-TAX COST OF DEBT TIMES THE TARGET DEBT RATIO	=	WEIGHTED AVERAGE COST OF CAPITAL
Restaurants	(12.19%)(0.70)	+	(5.54%)(0.30)	=	10.20%
Snack foods	(11.56%)(0.80)	+	(5.23%)(0.20)	=	10.29%
Beverages	(11.77%)(0.74)	+	(5.28%)(0.26)	=	10.08%

The weighted average cost of capital for each of the divisions is estimated in Table 11-6 using the capital costs estimated in Tables 11-4 and 11-5 and using PepsiCo's target capital structure weights for each operating division. Note that the weighted average costs of capital for all three divisions fall within a very narrow range, between 10.08 percent and 10.29 percent.

Did You Get It?

1. Why should firms that own and operate multiple businesses with very different risk characteristics use business-specific or divisional costs of capital?
2. Describe the process used to estimate the divisional costs of capital for PepsiCo.

Table 11-7 contains a summary of the formulas you need to estimate the weighted average cost of capital. If divisional costs of capital are to be estimated, then we must apply these formulas individually to each division because the opportunity costs of capital sources and the financing mix (proportions) used can differ, as we have just seen in the PepsiCo example.

How Did You Do?

CALCULATING THE WEIGHTED AVERAGE COST OF CAPITAL

The WACC for Grey Manufacturing can be calculated using the following table:

SOURCE OF CAPITAL	PERCENTAGE OF TOTAL CAPITAL	AFTER-TAX COST OF CAPITAL	PRODUCT
Debt	40%	5.20%	2.0800%
Common stock	60%	14.50%	8.7000%
		WACC =	10.7800%

Consequently, we estimate Grey's WACC to be 10.78%.

TABLE 11-7 A Summary of Cost of Capital Formulas

1. The After-Tax Cost of Debt, $k_d (1 - T_c)$
   a) Calculate the before-tax cost of debt, k_d, as follows:

$$\text{Net proceeds } (NP_d) = \frac{\$I_1}{(1 + \text{cost of debt capital } (k_d))^1} + \frac{\$I_2}{(1 + k_d)^2} + \frac{\$I_3 + \$M}{(1 + k_d)^3} \tag{11-2a}$$

   where NP_d is the net proceeds received by the firm from the sale of each bond; $\$I_t$ is the dollar amount of interest paid to the investor in period t for each bond, $\$M$ is the maturity value of each bond paid in period n; k_d is the before-tax cost of debt to the firm; and n is the number of periods to maturity.
   b) Calculate the after-tax cost of debt as follows:
   after-tax cost of debt = $k_d (1 - T_c)$
   where T_c is the corporate tax rate.

2. The Cost of Preferred Stock, k_{ps}

$$k_{ps} = \frac{\text{preferred stock dividend}}{NP_{ps}} \tag{11-5}$$

   where NP_{ps} is the net proceeds per share of new preferred stock sold after flotation costs.

3. The Cost of Common Equity
   a) Method 1: dividend growth model
   Calculate the cost of internal common equity (retained earnings), k_{cs}, as follows:

$$k_{cs} = \frac{D_1}{P_{cs}} + g \tag{11-7}$$

   where D_1 is the expected dividend for the next year, P_{cs} is the current price of the firm's common stock, and g is the rate of growth in dividends per year.
   Calculate the cost of external common equity (new stock offering), k_{ncs}, as follows:

$$k_{ncs} = \frac{D_1}{NP_{cs}} + g \tag{11-8}$$

   where NP_{cs} is the net proceeds to the firm after flotation costs per share of stock sold.
   b) Method 2: capital asset pricing model, k_c

$$k_c = k_{rf} + \beta(k_m - k_{rf}) \tag{11-9}$$

   where the risk-free rate is k_{rf}; the systemic risk of the common stock's returns relative to the market as a whole, or the stock's beta coefficient, is β; and the market-risk premium, which is equal to the difference in the expected rate of return for the market as a whole (i.e., the expected rate of return for the "average security") minus the risk-free rate, is $k_m - k_{rf}$.

4. The Weighted Average Cost of Capital

$$\begin{pmatrix}\text{Weighted} \\ \text{average cost} \\ \text{of capital}\end{pmatrix} = \begin{pmatrix}\text{after–tax} \\ \text{cost of} \\ \text{debt}\end{pmatrix} \times \begin{pmatrix}\text{proportion} \\ \text{of debt} \\ \text{financing}\end{pmatrix} + \begin{pmatrix}\text{cost of} \\ \text{equity}\end{pmatrix} \times \begin{pmatrix}\text{proportion} \\ \text{of equity} \\ \text{financing}\end{pmatrix} \tag{11-10}$$

Note that we are simply calculating a weighted average of the costs of each of the firm's sources of capital where the weights reflect the firm's relative use of each source.

Finance at Work

WEIGHTED AVERAGE COSTS OF CAPITAL ESTIMATES: 1988–2003

The value-based management consulting firm Stern Stewart estimates the WACC for the 1,000 largest U.S. firms each year as part of its analysis of their performance. In the 2004 performance review (based on 2003 data) the average WACC across all 1,000 firms was 7.5%, and the median was 7.4%. The maximum WACC was 14% compared to a minimum of only 4.2%. The following list contains the WACC estimates for a sample of well-known firms for 5-year intervals spanning 1988–2003:

COMPANY NAME	2003	1998	1993	1988
Wal-Mart Stores	6.2%	6.6%	7.5%	9.8%
Coca-Cola Co.	6.4%	6.6%	7.6%	9.8%
ExxonMobil Corp.	7.0%	7.3%	8.0%	10.1%
General Electric Co.	7.3%	7.7%	8.6%	10.5%
American Express	8.0%	8.4%	9.5%	NA
Procter & Gamble Co.	7.4%	8.2%	9.1%	10.8%
United Parcel Service Inc.	7.8%	8.1%	9.2%	11.9%
Johnson & Johnson	8.2%	8.4%	9.3%	11.5%
Lilly (Eli) & Co.	8.0%	8.4%	9.5%	11.8%
Merck & Co.	8.0%	8.5%	9.6%	11.9%
Amgen Inc.	10.0%	10.4%	11.4%	13.8%
Dell Computer Corp.	10.8%	11.1%	11.9%	14.4%
Hewlett Packed	10.8%	11.4%	12.1%	14.6%
International Business Machines Corp.	11.3%	11.7%	12.8%	15.1%
Cisco Systems Inc.	12.2%	13.0%	14.0%	NA
Microsoft Corp.	11.8%	12.5%	13.6%	15.3%
Intel Corp.	13.7%	14.0%	14.8%	16.4%
Average	9.1%	9.5%	10.5%	12.5%
Aaa Corporate Bond Yield	5.63%	6.23%	7.00%	9.61%
Average WACC - Aaa Bond Yield	3.48%	3.31%	3.50%	2.91%

The average WACC across this sample of firms declines over the period from 12.5 percent down to 9.1 percent. This decline is attributable to the general decline in interest rates (note that the Aaa corporate bond yield declined from 9.61 percent in 1988 down to 5.63 in 2003 such that the spread of WACC over the Aaa bond yield is relatively flat).

In addition, the WACC estimates are consistent across the period, with Wal-Mart exhibiting the lowest WACC and Intel Corp. the highest.

Source: WACC estimates were taken from the Stern Stewart Annual Performance Ranking for 2004.

USING A FIRM'S COST OF CAPITAL TO EVALUATE NEW CAPITAL INVESTMENTS

Objective **5**

Use the cost of capital to evaluate new investment opportunities.

If a firm has traditionally used a single cost of capital for all projects undertaken within each of several operating divisions (or companies) with very different risk characteristics, then the company will likely encounter resistance from the high-risk divisions if it changes to a divisional cost of capital structure. Consider the case of the hypothetical firm Global Energy, whose divisional costs of capital are illustrated in Figure 11-1. Global Energy is an integrated oil company that engages in a wide range of hydrocarbon-related businesses, including exploration and development, pipelines, and refining. Each of these businesses has its unique set of risks. In Figure 11-1 we see that the overall, or enterprise-wide, cost of capital for Global Energy is 11 percent, reflecting an average of the firm's divisional costs of capital, ranging from a low of 8 percent for pipelines up to 18 percent for exploration and development.

FIGURE 11-1 Global Energy Divisional Costs of Capital
Using a company-wide cost of capital for a multidivisional firm results in systematic overinvestment in high-risk projects and underinvestment in low-risk projects.

Remember Your Principles

The firm's weighted average cost of capital provides the appropriate discount rate for evaluating new projects only when the projects offer the same riskiness as the firm as a whole. This limitation of the usefulness of the firm's weighted average cost of capital is a direct extension of **Principle 1: The Risk–Return Trade-Off—We Won't Take On Additional Risk Unless We Expect to Be Compensated with Additional Return.** If project risk differs from that of the firm, then the firm's cost of capital (which reflects the risk of the firm's investment portfolio) is no longer the appropriate cost of capital for the project. For this reason, firms that invest in multiple divisions or business units that have different risk characteristics should calculate a different cost of capital for each division. In theory, each individual investment opportunity has its own unique risk attributes and, correspondingly, should have a unique cost of capital. However, given the impreciseness with which we estimate the cost of capital, we generally calculate the cost of capital for each operating division of the firm, not each project.

At present Global Energy is using a cost of capital of 11 percent to evaluate its new investment proposals from all three operating divisions. This means that exploration and development projects earning as little as 11 percent are being accepted even though the capital market dictates that projects of this risk should earn 18 percent. Thus, Global Energy overinvests in high-risk projects. Similarly, the company will underinvest in its two lower-risk divisions, where the company-wide cost of capital is used.

Now consider the prospect of moving to division costs of capital and the implications this might have for the three divisions. Specifically, the managers of the exploration and development division are likely to see this as an adverse move for them because it will surely cut the level of new investment capital flowing into their operations. In contrast, the managers of the remaining two divisions will see the change as good news because, under the company-wide cost of capital system, they have been rejecting projects earning more than their market-based costs of capital (8 percent and 10 percent for pipelines and refining, respectively) but less than the company's 11 percent cost of capital.

Did You Get It?

1. What are the implications for a firm's capital investment decisions of using a company-wide cost of capital when the firm has multiple operating divisions that each have unique risk attributes and capital costs?

2. If a firm has decided to move from a situation in which it uses a company-wide cost of capital to divisional costs of capital, what problems is it likely to encounter?

Can You Do It?

USING DIVISIONAL COSTS OF CAPITAL TO EVALUATE NEW INVESTMENTS

Arizona Instruments Inc. (AII) is an electronics manufacturing firm that develops and sells a variety of products to the computer and telecommunications industries. The firm has two operating divisions that operate in very different markets. The first is consumer electronics, which includes a variety of products that are aimed at individual consumers, and the second is its defense business. The consumer division depends on the R&D that takes place in the defense business as a source of new products, and because these products are often low-tech in nature and are sold in a very broad market, AII requires a relatively modest 10 percent return on new investments in this business. However, the defense business is much more risky, so AII requires a 15 percent return on any new projects undertaken in this business.

The company's managers consider capital requests to fund new investment projects in the spring of each year during the firm's annual budget-planning cycle. This year the firm has received the following set of requests. "(C)" refers project requests for to the consumer division, and "(D)" refers to requests from the defense division:

PROJECT NUMBER AND DIVISION (C OR D)	FUNDING REQUESTED	ESTIMATED RATE OF RETURN (*IRR*)
Project #1 (D)	$5 million	22%
Project #2 (C)	12 million	18%
Project #3 (C)	8 million	15%
Project #4 (D)	25 million	15%
Project #5 (D)	100 million	10%
Project #6 (C)	20 million	10%

If there is no limit on the dollars spent on projects in either of the firm's divisions, which of the investments listed should be funded?

(The solution can be found on page 355.)

SHAREHOLDER VALUE-BASED MANAGEMENT

Objective **6**

Compute the economic profit earned by the firm and use this quantity to calculate incentive-based compensation.

How do you know whether a firm is creating or destroying shareholder value? Moreover, how can you tell how *much* wealth a firm has created for its shareholders? In recent years a whole host of systems have been developed that purport to answer these questions and help managers make decisions that are expected to have the greatest positive impact on shareholder wealth. We refer to this cadre of methods as shareholder value–based management, or simply value–based management tools. We focus on one very popular method in our discussion—one that is based on the concept of economic profit.

How Much Value Has a Firm Created for Its Owners?

H&L Manufacturing is trying to come to grips with why its stock price is not growing as rapidly as its competitors'. In essence, H&L needs to know whether it is creating or destroying shareholder wealth. How can we tell? The answer is **market value added (*MVA*)**. *MVA* is a very simple concept. It represents *the difference in the current market value of the firm and the sum of all the funds that are invested in the firm*. If the market value of the firm exceeds the investment made in the firm, then the firm has created shareholder wealth. *MVA* is calculated as follows:

market value added (*MVA*)
MVA is the difference in the market value of a firm's total assets and their book value.

$$MVA = \text{total market value of the firm} - \text{invested capital} \qquad (11\text{-}11a)$$

The total market value of the firm is equal to the value of all the claims, or securities, the firm has issued; that is,

$$\begin{array}{ccccccc} \text{Market value} \\ \text{of the} & = & \text{market value} \\ \text{firm} & & \text{of the firm's} & + & \text{market value} \\ & & \text{outstanding debt} & & \text{of the firm's} & + & \text{market value} \\ & & & & \text{preferred stock} & & \text{of the firm's} \quad (11\text{-}11b) \\ & & & & & & \text{common stock} \end{array}$$

TABLE 11-8 The Top and Bottom Five Firms in the 2005 Stern Stewart Performance 1,000

RANK IN 2005	RANK IN 2004	RANK IN 2000	COMPANY	MVA (IN $ MILLIONS)	EVA (IN $ MILLIONS)	INVESTED CAPITAL (IN $ MILLIONS)	RETURN ON INVESTED CAPITAL	COST OF CAPITAL
1	1	1	General Electric Co.	$282,545	$6,709	$124,960	12.2%	6.9%
2	3	3	Microsoft Corp.	229,031	8,247	28,159	40.9%	11.7%
3	7	7	Procter & Gamble Co.	172,734	4,131	50,270	15.8%	7.2%
4	2	9	ExxonMobil Corp.	167,560	28,580	229,608	18.9%	6.1%
5	4	2	Wal-Mart Stores	140,705	5,199	109,393	10.8%	5.8%
1027	1023	13	Pfizer Inc.	(19,427)	(3,838)	209,293	5.8%	7.6%
1028	1032	1021	Time Warner Inc.	(23,195)	(5,153)	132,985	3.8%	7.8%
1029	1038	1026	AT&T Corp.	(29,393)	(10,095)	192,158	3.1%	8.8%
1030	1035	1023	Lucent Technologies Inc.	(36,566)	(6,279)	61,987	−0.7%	9.6%
1031	1037	1025	JDS Uniphase Corp.	(40,610)	(5,971)	47,506	−0.8%	11.8%

For firms whose debt and equity securities are traded in public markets, we can calculate the market value of each type of security by simply multiplying the number of bonds or shares of stock by the most recent market price. It should be noted that most firms' debt is not publicly traded, so it is common practice to approximate the market value of the debt by using its book value. Invested capital is basically the sum total of the money invested in the firm to date. Invested capital is estimated by adjusting the firm's book value of total assets for things such as R&D expense and allowances for doubtful accounts receivable, which are not included in the total assets of the firm but, nonetheless, represent dollars that have been invested in the firm.[7]

In essence, *MVA* is the *NPV* of all the firm's investments.[8] A firm that is using its investments to produce what investors perceive to be positive *NPV*s will have a positive *MVA*. Similarly, a firm that is using its invested capital in ways that investors feel destroy value will have a negative *MVA*. Note that because the market value of the firm's securities is based on expected future cash flows, *MVA* is a reflection of the expected *NPV*. Because *MVA* is not a measure of historical performance but instead reflects anticipated future performance, it can change dramatically as a firm's fortunes change. For example, in 1988, IBM's *MVA* was the largest of any U.S. company. By 1990, the fortunes of IBM had changed dramatically as the personal computer became the computer of the future. In 1991, IBM ranked 31st, and by 1993 its rank slipped to 1,000th. However, changes in the perceived fortunes of the company in 1997 resulted in a dramatic turnaround in investors' perceptions of IBM's future and raised its rank to 16th. By 2004 the company ranked 11th! Not every firm experiences this degree of volatility from year to year. The sources of the volatility in *MVA* are the market value of the firm's equity and adjustments the firm makes to its invested capital through acquisitions and sales of assets.

Table 11-8 contains the top and bottom 5 firms in terms of *MVA* for 2005. All the top 5 wealth creators were ranked in the top 10 in 2000, which suggests that there is some stability among the top performers. Furthermore, of the bottom 5 performers only Pfizer was not in the bottom 10 in 2000.

Did the Firm Create Shareholder Value This Year?

MVA measures the wealth created by a firm at a particular point in time. However, the financial manager needs to evaluate the performance of the firm over a specific interval of time, say, 1 year. For this purpose, we calculate the firm's **economic profit**. (Recall that you

economic profit differs from accounting profit in that it incorporates explicit consideration for opportunity cost of equity financing, as well as debt financing.

---

[7] We will not go into the adjustments that are made to a firm's book assets to measure invested capital. The adjustments add equity-equivalent reserves to capital and periodic changes in those reserves to after-tax operating profits. For example, equivalent reserves include such items as the deferred income tax reserve, LIFO reserve, cumulative amortization of goodwill, capitalized intangibles (including R&D), allowance for doubtful accounts, and warranty claim reserves.

[8] Technically, *MVA* overstates a firm's total wealth creation because it fails to incorporate an opportunity cost of the funds the firm invested in prior periods. As a consequence, our analogy to *NPV* is truly accurate only for the case of a start-up firm in which the firm's total invested capital is equal to total assets at the beginning of the period for which *MVA* is being measured. However, for our purposes *MVA* serves as a very useful and simple approximation to the wealth a firm has created for its investors.

How Did You Do?

USING DIVISIONAL COSTS OF CAPITAL TO EVALUATE NEW INVESTMENTS

AII's investment allocation decision criteria is different for the consumer and defense divisions, with the former requiring a 10 percent rate of return (WACC) and the latter requiring a 15 percent WACC. A quick review of the six projects reveals that only projects #1 and #4 meet the "D" division's cost of capital requirement. The "C" division projects #2, #3, and #6 all meet the 10 percent capital cost hurdle. Note that projects that return their division's cost of capital are acceptable because they earn at least the cost of raising debt capital plus the cost of the equity capital invested in the project.

first encountered the concept of economic profit in Chapter 4.) Economic profit is defined as follows:

$$\text{Economic profit} = \begin{pmatrix} \text{net operating} \\ \text{profit after tax} \\ (NOPAT) \end{pmatrix} - \begin{pmatrix} \text{invested} \\ \text{captial} \end{pmatrix} \times \begin{pmatrix} \text{cost of} \\ \text{capital} \end{pmatrix} \qquad (11\text{-}12)$$

Note that the distinction between economic and accounting profit (net operating profit) is the deduction for a return on the firm's invested capital. The product of the firm's invested capital (the total dollar investment made in the firm by its creditors and owners) and the cost of capital constitutes a capital charge. This capital charge is not a recognized accounting expense, but it is a very real expense from the perspective of the firm's bondholders and stockholders. Thus, economic profit is simply accounting profit (net operating profit or income) less a charge for the use of capital.

So how does the use of economic profit help the financial manager? The answer is surprisingly simple. Most firms manage to earn positive profits. However, earning positive profits is no assurance that the firm is creating shareholder wealth, because profits fail to incorporate any opportunity cost for the dollars that investors have tied up in the business. Economic profit, on the other hand, includes an explicit charge in the form of the capital charge, which recognizes the size of the investment made in the firm and the opportunity cost of that investment.

Consider the case of Kmart, which ranked 990th in the *MVA* rankings. Kmart's economic profit for 1999 can be calculated as follows:

Economic profit = *NOPAT* − (invested capital × cost of capital)

($568.979 M) = $950 M − ($19,727 M × .0770)

How can this be? Kmart earned a positive *NOPAT* of $950 million. The answer lies in the size of Kmart's *NOPAT* relative to its investment in assets. Compared with the firm's $19,727 million invested capital, its *NOPAT* represents a meager return of only 4.82 percent, which is less than the firm's 7.70 percent cost of capital. As long as Kmart continues to earn a return on its invested capital that is lower than its cost of capital, it will continue to destroy shareholder value no matter how large its profits are. In fact, Kmart declared bankruptcy in January 2002.

How Can the Firm Increase Its Economic Profits?

What can a firm do to improve its performance so it creates more shareholder value for its owners? The answer can be found by reviewing the variables that are found on the right-hand side of equation (11-12). These variables include the level of *NOPAT*, the cost of capital, and the amount of invested capital (often referred to as *value drivers*). One way to create additional value is by finding ways to increase *NOPAT* without a corresponding increase in the firm's invested capital. This can be accomplished by increasing revenues and/or driving down expenses. There are a number of ways that a firm might reduce costs and increase profits without the need to spend additional capital. For example, the Domtar Corporation (a forest management company that deals in paper, pulp, and wood products) adopted an

Finance at Work

TWO FIRMS EXPLAIN THEIR GOALS AND OBJECTIVES IN ADOPTING EVA

The following excerpts taken from company annual reports document the rationale underlying the adoption of EVA. These companies recognized the need to place top priority on shareholders' interests by considering the impact of all the firm's decisions on share value. In addition, we see the importance of tying compensation to EVA so that value creation is reinforced and rewarded.

METRO Group (METRO AG Schlüterstrasse 1, 40235 Düsseldorf, Germany)

The METRO Group is dedicated to value-oriented business management based on economic value added (EVA). EVA is an internationally proven management and control instrument that enables companies to assess and position all strategic, operative, and investment activities and decisions in terms of their contribution to enterprise value. The groupwide introduction of this key figure at the METRO Group took place in 2000.

The METRO Group's performance potential is reflected by its ability to continuously increase its enterprise value by successfully employing its working capital.

Positive EVA is achieved when the net operating profit exceeds the cost of capital needed to finance working capital. *NOPAT* is defined as operating profit before financing costs, but after income taxes. The cost of capital represents the expected compensation of the investors for the capital they provide and for their investment risk. It is calculated by multiplying the working capital with the weighted average cost of capital (*WACC*). In 2005, the weighted average cost of capital of the METRO Group was unchanged from the previous year at 6.5 percent.

(Excerpted from 2005 annual report, URL: **www.metrogroup.de/multimedia/IGB/2005/PDF/GB2005-en.pdf**)

ThyssenKrupp (August-Thyssen-Str. 1, 40211 Düsseldorf, Germany)

The ThyssenKrupp Group is managed and controlled on the basis of an Economic Value Added ("EVA") management system. The key goal of this system is to maintain continuous increases in corporate value by focusing on business segments that—with respect to their performance—are among the best worldwide. To achieve this objective, an integrated controlling concept is applied. It allows for goal-driven controlling and coordination of activities of all segments, supports decentralized responsibility, and promotes overall transparency.

By taking timely appropriate actions, the integrated controlling concept realizes the increase of corporate value by bridging operating and strategic gaps between the actual and target situation. The prerequisite for this concept is the existence of high-quality operational and strategic reporting systems for the accounting of actual and budgeted results as well as internal and external reporting. The values determined under U.S. GAAP for each and every reporting unit form the basis for our reporting system.

In the ThyssenKrupp controlling concept, strategic and operational elements are linked to timely reporting, which is accompanied by regular pro-active communication. The concrete elements of this strategy are: economic value added performance measures and active portfolio management.

(Excerpted from 2004–2005 annual report, URL: **www.thyssenkrupp.com/fr/04_05/en/index.html**)

economic profit–based system and notes the following ways in which it can improve its economic profit by identifying operating efficiencies:

- Cutting down on waste and damaged products
- Operating machinery and equipment more efficiently
- Improving the product mix, and devising methods to save on the purchase of raw materials
- Improving the firm's health and safety performance, and attracting and retaining customers
- Making better use of time in the office and plant, and implementing or improving preventative maintenance programs
- Developing links with suppliers

A second way to improve economic profit is by growing the firm's investments in projects that earn returns in excess of the firm's cost of capital. For example, the firm might introduce new marketing plans that improve customer satisfaction and sales and profits, expand existing businesses that offer the potential to earn positive *NPV*s, or introduce new information systems to better trace customer buying habits and, correspondingly, increase sales.

The third and final approach to improving economic profits involves reducing the firm's capital charge (cost of capital × invested capital). This can be accomplished in either of two ways. If the firm is not using its minimum cost of capital financing mix, then restructuring

CHAPTER 11 THE COST OF CAPITAL

Can You Do It?

CALCULATING A FIRM'S EVA

Cameron Inc. is an oil and gas exploration and production company that operates in southeastern Oklahoma, eastern Texas, and southern Louisiana. In 2007 the firm's total invested capital was equal to $400 million and it estimated that its weighted average cost of capital was 14 percent. During 2007 the firm earned $80 million in earnings before interest and taxes and expected to have to pay income taxes at a rate of 25 percent.

What was Cameron's net operating profit after taxes (*NOPAT*) for 2007? What is the firm's EVA?
(The solution can be found on page 358.)

its financing sources might lead to a lowering of the firm's cost of capital and a corresponding decrease in the firm's dollar cost of capital. Alternatively, the firm might consider withdrawing capital from its operations through the sale of underutilized assets (for example, excess plant capacity, underperforming operating units, or real estate).

How Can a Firm Link Pay for Performance to Reinforce Wealth Creation?

Economic profit has become an important tool for aligning the interests of shareholders and managers. This is accomplished by basing managers' incentive compensation on economic profit. A very simple version of such a compensation system scheme is illustrated in equation (11-13).

$$\text{Incentive compensation} = \text{base pay} \times \frac{\text{percent incentive compensation}}{} \times \frac{\text{actual economic profit}}{\text{target economic profit}} \quad (11\text{-}13)$$

For example, consider the case of the assistant treasurer for NewCo Oil Inc. The assistant treasurer's base pay is $80,000 a year, and 20 percent of the total compensation for this position is designated by the company to be incentive based. If in a particular year NewCo set a target economic profit of $1 million and earned $1.2 million, then the assistant treasurer's incentive compensation would be calculated as following using equation (11-13):

$$\text{Incentive compensation} = \text{base pay} \times \frac{\text{percent incentive compensation}}{} \times \frac{\text{actual economic profits}}{\text{target economic profit}}$$

$$= \$80,000 \times 0.20 \times (\$1.2 \text{ million}/\$1 \text{ million})$$

$$= \$19,200$$

In this case, the assistant treasurer's total annual compensation would be $99,200 ($80,000 + $19,200). If NewCo earned only $800,000 in economic profit, then the incentive compensation paid to the assistant treasurer would be $12,800 [$80,000 × .20 × ($800,000/$1,000,000)].

Clearly, with this type of incentive compensation plan, the firm's managers will strive to increase net operating profits while holding down the firm's invested capital and maintaining the lowest possible cost of capital. If they do this, they will maximize the contribution to shareholder wealth and also maximize their own year-end bonuses.

Did You Get It?

1. What is market value added (*MVA*)?
2. Define economic profit and its determinants.
3. How is economic profit related to *MVA*?

How Did You Do?

CALCULATING A FIRM'S EVA

We calculate EVA for Cameron Inc. as follows:

$$EVA = NOPAT - k_{WACC} \times \text{invested capital}$$

where *NOPAT* is net operating profits after tax or EBIT $(1 - \text{tax rate})$. Thus, for Cameron we substitute as follows:

$$EVA = \$80 \text{ million} (1 - .25) - .14 \times \$400 \text{ million} = \$60 \text{ million} - \$56 \text{ million} = \$4 \text{ million}$$

Finance at Work

TYING INCENTIVE COMPENSATION TO ECONOMIC VALUE ADDED

In the following excerpts from company press releases, annual reports, proxy statements, and publications, we see evidence of the age-old adage, "What you measure and reward gets done." Specifically, these companies explicitly tie company incentive compensation to the creation of shareholder value as measured by EVA. Note that because EVA is a single-period-of-performance metric, many firms do not pay out the full EVA bonus in a single payment, but rather pay it into a bonus bank that gets paid out over several years. This payment practice is designed to encourage long-term value creation and to discourage schemes by managers that would increase one year's EVA at the expense of future years' EVA.

SPX Corporation (700 Terrace Point Drive, Muskegon, MI 49443)

In an EVA incentive compensation plan, managers and shareholders face similar risks. With EVA, compensation is tied to meeting investor expectations, not to meeting plan or budget. By disconnecting incentive compensation from planning and budgeting, and connecting it to investor expectations, managers focus on creating value, and not on negotiating performance targets.

Our EVA incentive compensation plan rewards managers only for continuous permanent improvement in EVA; failure to do so inflicts a cost. Meeting the EVA improvement target equates to meeting investor expectations and results in a competitive bonus. Exceeding the EVA improvement target results in a higher-than-competitive bonus. And falling short of the EVA improvement target produces a bonus that is less than

competitive and can even be negative. Two-thirds of all bonuses above target are set aside in a "bonus bank," which is carried forward, payable only upon achieving EVA targets in subsequent years. Managers must earn back any negative bonuses accumulated in the bank before any bonus payment can be made.

The EVA incentive system simulates long-term ownership by tying bonuses to improvements in EVA over time. EVA improvement targets have been set for the next 4 years to provide strong incentives for management to increase long-term investor value.

The strong correlation between changes in EVA and in market value also means that the EVA compensation system is effectively "self-financing." That is, managers win only when the shareholders are winning. (*1995 SPX Annual Report*, p. 5)

Ball Corporation (345 South High Street, P.O. Box 2407, Muncie, IN 47307-0407)

Effective January 1, 1992, the Corporation has established a new incentive compensation plan, entitled the "Ball Corporation 1992 Economic Value Added Incentive Compensation Plan for Key Members of Management." Referred to as the EVA Plan, it applies to all officers and key employees. The EVA Plan establishes a direct link between incentive compensation and the return earned on capital relative to a minimum required rate of return and historical actual performance. The EVA Plan establishes a specific target incentive amount for each participant based on a percentage of salary. (Ball Corporation *Notice of Annual Meeting and Proxy Statement*, 1992)

Objective **7**

Calculate equivalent interest rates for different countries.

FINANCE AND THE MULTINATIONAL FIRM: WHY DO INTEREST RATES DIFFER BETWEEN COUNTRIES?[9]

If borrowers and lenders can freely obtain money in one country and invest it in another, why are interest rates not the same the world over? Stated somewhat differently, if capital markets are fully integrated and money flows to the highest rate of interest, it would seem

[9] This section is from W. Carl Kester and Timothy A. Luehrman, "What Makes You Think U.S. Capital Is So Expensive?" *Journal of Applied Corporate Finance* (Summer 1992): pp. 29–41. Reprinted with permission.

Can You Do It?

EVALUATING INTEREST RATE PARITY ACROSS COUNTRIES

The rate of interest on a 1-year Treasury bill was 5 percent at the end of 2007, and the corresponding rate of interest on a 1-year note issued by the Brazilian government was 18 percent. The international Fisher effect states that the real rate of interest is the same in both countries.

   If the real rate is equal to 2 percent, what are the rates of inflation in the two countries? What is the ratio of 1 plus the nominal rates of interest in the two countries? What is the corresponding ratio of 1 plus the rate of inflation in the two countries?

   (The solution can be found on page 360.)

that the forces of competition would make interest rates the same for a borrower with a given amount of risk.

   Let's consider a hypothetical example to see how this might work. Assume that a U.S. firm can borrow 1,000 yen in Japan for 5 percent interest, paying back 1,050 yen in 1 year. Alternatively, the U.S. firm can borrow an equivalent amount in the United States and pay 15.5 percent interest. Why the big difference? Is capital 10.5 percent cheaper in Japan, and if so, why don't U.S. firms simply switch to the Japanese capital market for their funds? The answer, as we will now illustrate, lies in the differences in the anticipated rates of inflation for Japan versus the United States.

   Although it was not obvious in the preceding example, we assumed a zero rate of inflation for the Japanese economy and a 10 percent rate of inflation for the U.S. economy. With a zero anticipated rate of inflation, the nominal rate of interest in Japan (the rate we see quoted in the financial press) is equal to the real rate of 5 percent.[10] Under these assumptions, the nominal rate in the United States can be calculated using the Fisher model as follows:

$$\text{U.S. nominal rate of interest} = (1 + \text{real rate, U.S.})(1 + \text{inflation rate, U.S.}) - 1$$
$$= (1.05)(1.10) - 1 = .155, \text{ or } 15.5\%$$

To understand the reason for the different interest rates in Japan and the United States, we must extend the Fisher model to its international counterpart.

   Rearranging terms, we get the following relationship between nominal interest rates in the domestic and foreign country and the differences in anticipated inflation in the two countries:

$$r_{n,b} - r_{n,f} = i_b - i_f \tag{11-14}$$

Economists have formalized the relationship between interest rates of different countries in the interest rate parity theorem. This theorem is as follows:

$$\frac{(1 + r_{n,b})}{(1 + r_{n,f})} = \frac{E_1}{E_0} \tag{11-15}$$

where $r_{n,b}$ is the domestic one-period rate of interest, $r_{n,f}$ is the corresponding rate of interest in a foreign country, E_0 and E_1 are the exchange rates corresponding to the current period (i.e., the spot exchange rate) and one period hence (i.e., the one-period forward exchange rate).

   Thus, differences in observed nominal rates of interest should equal differences in the expected rates of inflation between the two countries. This means that when we compare the interest rates for similar loans in two countries and they are not the same, we should immediately suspect that the expected rates of inflation for the two economies differ by an amount roughly equal to the interest rate differential.

---

[10] The real rate of interest is simply the rate of interest that is earned where the expected rate of inflation is zero.

How Did You Do?

EVALUATING INTEREST RATE PARITY ACROSS COUNTRIES

The international Fisher theory of interest rate parity states that the real rate of interest should be the same across countries but nominal rates across countries will differ as a result of differential rates of anticipated inflation. Thus, for the U.S.–Brazil example, we estimate the ratio of 1 plus the nominal rates of interest as follows (where the U.S. is in the numerator):

$$\frac{(1 + .05)}{(1 + .18)} = .8898$$

Using the Fisher model to estimate the rates of inflation impounded in the nominal rates of interest for the United States and Brazil, and where the real rate is assumed to be 2 percent in both countries, we get estimated inflation for the United States equal to 2.94 percent and 15.69 percent for Brazil. The ratio of 1 plus these two rates of inflation then equals:

$$\frac{(1 + .0294)}{(1 + .1569)} = .8898$$

To illustrate, let's consider the previous example, in which the domestic one-period interest rate $(r_{n,b})$ is 15.5 percent, the Japanese rate of interest $(r_{n,f})$ is 5 percent, the spot exchange ratio (E_0) is \$1 to 1 yen, and the forward exchange rate (E_1) is \$1.10 to 1 yen. Substituting into equation (11-15) produces the following result:

$$\frac{(1 + .155)}{(1 + .05)} = \frac{1.1}{1} = 1.10$$

The key thing to note here is that nominal interest rates are tied to exchange rates, and, as we learned earlier, differences in nominal rates of interest are tied to expected rates of inflation.

Why would we expect the interest rate parity relationship to hold? The answer lies in the fact that there are investors who stand ready to engage in arbitrage (trading) to enforce this relationship (within the bounds of transaction costs). Formally, we rely on the fundamental dictum of an efficient market (the law of one price). Very simply, the exchange-adjusted prices of identical loans must be within transaction costs of equality or the opportunity exists for traders to buy the low-cost loan and sell the higher-priced loan for a profit.

Summary

Objective 1

Describe the concepts underlying the firm's cost of capital (technically, its weighted average cost of capital) and the purpose for its calculation.

In Chapter 9, we learned that the proper way to evaluate whether to undertake the investment involves calculating its net present value (*NPV*). To calculate *NPV*, we must estimate both project cash flows and an appropriate discount rate. In this chapter, we have learned that the proper discount rate is a weighted average of the after-tax costs of all the firm's sources of financing. In addition, we have learned that the cost of capital for any source of financing is estimated by first calculating the investor's required rate of return, then making appropriate adjustments for flotation costs and corporate taxes (when appropriate).

To calculate the after-tax cost of debt capital, we must first calculate the before-tax cost of debt capital using the following formula:

Objective 2

Calculate the after-tax cost of debt, preferred stock, and common equity.

$$NP_d = \sum_{t=1}^{n} \frac{\$I_t}{(1 + k_d)^t} + \frac{\$M}{(1 + k_d)^n}$$

where NP_d = the net proceeds received by the firm from the sale of each bond
$\$I_t$ = the dollar amount of interest paid to the investor in period t for each bond
$\$M$ = the maturity value of each bond paid in period n
k_d = the before-tax cost of debt to the firm
n = the number of periods to maturity

Next, we adjust for the effects of corporate taxes because the bond interest is deducted from the firm's taxable income.

$$\text{After-tax cost of debt} = k_d (1 - \text{corporate tax rate})$$

The cost of preferred stock is relatively easy to calculate. We calculate the dividend yield on the preferred issue using net proceeds from the sale of each new share as follows:

$$\text{Cost of preferred stock} = k_{ps} = \frac{\text{preferred stock dividend}}{\text{net proceeds per preferred share}} \qquad (11\text{-}5)$$

Note that no adjustment is made for corporate taxes because preferred stock dividends, unlike bond interest, are paid with after-tax earnings (i.e., preferred dividends are not tax deductible).

Common equity can be obtained by the firm in one of two ways. First, the firm can retain a portion of its net income after paying common dividends. The retention of earnings constitutes a means of raising common-equity financing internally—that is, no capital market issuance of securities is involved. Second, the firm can also raise equity capital through the sale of a new issue of common stock.

We discussed two methods for estimating the cost of common equity. The first involved using the dividend growth model:

$$k_{cs} = \frac{D_1}{P_{cs}} + g \qquad (11\text{-}7)$$

where g is the rate at which dividends are expected to grow forever, k_{cs} is the investor's required rate of return, and P_{cs} is the current price of a share of common stock. When a new issue of common shares is issued, the firm incurs flotation costs. These costs reduce the amount of funds the firm receives per share. Consequently, the cost of external common equity using the dividend growth model requires that we substitute the net proceeds per share, NP_{cs}, for share price:

$$k_{ns} = \frac{D}{NP_{cs}} + g \qquad (11\text{-}8)$$

The second method for estimating the cost of common equity involves the use of the capital asset pricing model (CAPM), which we first discussed in Chapter 9. There we learned that the CAPM provides a basis for evaluating investors' required rates of return on common equity, k_m, using three variables:

1. The risk-free rate, k_{rf}
2. The systematic risk of the common stock's returns relative to the market as a whole, or the stock's beta coefficient, β
3. The market-risk premium, which is equal to the difference in the expected rate of return for the market as a whole—that is, the expected rate of return for the "average security" minus the risk-free rate, $k_m - k_{rf}$

The CAPM is written as follows:

$$k_c = k_{rf} + \beta(k_m - k_{rf}) \qquad (11\text{-}9)$$

We found that all of the variables on the right side of equation (11-9) could be obtained from public sources for larger, publicly traded firms. However, for privately held firms, the CAPM is more difficult to apply in the estimation of investor-required rates of return.

The firm's weighted average cost of capital, k_{wacc}, can be defined as follows:

$$k_{wacc} = w_d k_d (1 - T_c) + w_{ps} k_{ps} + w_{cs} k_{cs} + w_{ncs} k_{ncs} \qquad (11\text{-}10)$$

Objective 3

Calculate a firm's weighted average cost of capital.

where the w terms represent the market value weights associated with the firm's use of each of its sources of financing. Note that we are simply calculating a weighted average of the costs of each of the firm's sources of capital where the weights reflect the firm's relative use of each source.

The weights used to calculate k_{wacc} should theoretically reflect the market values of each capital source as a fraction of the total market value of all capital sources (i.e., the market value of the firm). However, the analyst frequently finds the use of market value weights is impractical, either because the firm's securities are not publicly traded or because all capital sources are not used in proportion to their makeup of the firm's target capital structure in every financing episode. In these instances, we found that the weights should be the firm's long-term target financial mix.

The firm's weighted average cost of capital will reflect the operating or business risk of the firm's present set of investments and the financial risk attendant upon the way in which those assets are financed. Therefore, this cost of capital estimate is useful only for evaluating new investment opportunities that have similar business and financial risks. Remember that the primary determinant of the cost of capital for a particular investment is the risk of the investment itself, not the source of the capital. Multidivisional firms such as PepsiCo resolve this problem by calculating a different cost of capital for each of their major operating divisions.

How can we tell whether a firm's management is creating or destroying wealth? We found that a very commonsense measure known as market value added, or *MVA*, can be used for this purpose. *MVA* is simply the difference in the market value of the firm's securities (debt and equity) and the sum total of the funds that have been invested in the firm since its creation. If the market value of the firm's investments exceeds the total capital invested in the firm, then shareholder wealth has been created to the extent of this difference. Likewise, when the difference is negative, shareholder wealth has been destroyed.

MVA measures the total shareholder wealth created by the firm at a particular point in time. How do we know whether shareholder wealth was created last year or last month? The answer is found in calculating the firm's economic profit, which is defined as follows:

$$\text{Economic profit} = \left(\begin{array}{c}\text{net operating}\\\text{profit after tax}\\(NOPAT)\end{array}\right) - \left(\begin{array}{c}\text{invested}\\\text{capital}\end{array} \times \begin{array}{c}\text{cost of}\\\text{capital}\end{array}\right) \tag{11-12}$$

Thus, a firm's management has successfully created shareholder wealth when its after-tax net operating profits are sufficient to cover the opportunity cost of its invested capital.

Firms are increasingly using the concept of economic profit to link employee compensation to shareholder interests. The following general model can be used for this purpose:

$$\begin{array}{c}\text{Incentive}\\\text{compensation}\end{array} = \text{base pay} \times \begin{array}{c}\text{percent}\\\text{incentive}\\\text{compensation}\end{array} \times \frac{\text{actual economic profit}}{\text{target economic profit}} \tag{11-13}$$

If the firm manages to earn higher economic profits than were targeted for the period, then employee incentive compensation rises. Similarly, higher economic profits lead to greater shareholder value being created.

If borrowers and lenders can freely choose where they borrow and lend money, why aren't interest rates the same all over the world? The answer lies in differences in the anticipated rates of inflation between countries. In fact, the international Fisher effect states that the differences in the rates of interest charged for the same loan in two different countries is equal to the difference in the anticipated rates of inflation in the countries. So, rates of interest are equal around the world only after we account for differences in rates of inflation between countries. Of course, the international Fisher effect does not hold exactly due to political and other risk considerations that can serve to restrict capital flow between countries. However, the Fisher effect does provide a useful starting point for understanding why there are differences in interest rates throughout the world.

Key Terms

Capital structure 344	**Market value added (*MVA*)** 353
Economic profit 354	**Weighted average cost of capital** 335
Financial policy 334	

Review Questions

11-1. Define the term *cost of capital*.

11-2. Why do we calculate a firm's weighted average cost of capital?

11-3. In computing the cost of capital, which sources of capital do we consider?

11-4. How does a firm's tax rate affect its cost of capital? What is the effect of the flotation costs associated with a new security issue?

11-5. a. Distinguish between internal common equity and new common stock.

    b. Why is a cost associated with internal common equity?

    c. Describe the two approaches that could be used in computing the cost of common equity.

11-6. What might we expect to see in practice in the relative costs of different sources of capital?

Self–Test Problems

(The solutions to the following problems are provided at the end of the chapter.)

ST-1. (*Individual or component costs of capital*) Compute the cost for the following sources of financing:

    a. A $1,000 par value bond with a market price of $970 and a coupon interest rate of 10 percent. Flotation costs for a new issue would be approximately 5 percent. The bonds mature in 10 years and the corporate tax rate is 34 percent.

    b. A preferred stock selling for $100 with an annual dividend payment of $8. The flotation cost will be $9 per share. The company's marginal tax rate is 30 percent.

    c. Internally generated common stock totaling $4.8 million. The price of the common stock is $75 per share, and the dividend per share was $9.80 last year. The dividend is not expected to change in the future.

    d. New common stock when the most recent dividend was $2.80. The company's dividends per share should continue to increase at an 8 percent growth rate into the indefinite future. The market price of the stock is currently $53; however, flotation costs of $6 per share are expected if the new stock is issued.

ST-2. (*Weighted average cost of capital*) The capital structure for the Carion Corporation is provided here. The company plans to maintain its debt structure in the future. If the firm has a 5.5 percent after-tax cost of debt, a 13.5 percent cost of preferred stock, and an 18 percent cost of common stock, what is the firm's weighted average cost of capital?

CAPITAL STRUCTURE ($000)	
Bonds	$1,083
Preferred stock	268
Common stock	3,681
	$5,032

ST-3. (*Weighted average cost of capital*) ABBC Inc. operates a very successful chain of yogurt and coffee shops spread across the southwestern part of the United States and needs to raise funds for its planned expansion into the Northwest. The firm's balance sheet at the close of 2007 appeared as follows:

Cash	$2,010,000		
Accounts receivable	4,580,000		
Inventories	1,540,000	Long-term debt	$ 8,141,000
Net property, plant, and equipment	32,575,000	Common equity	32,564,000
Total assets	$40,705,000	Total debt and equity	$40,705,000

At present the firm's common stock is selling for a price equal to its book value, and the firm's bonds are selling at par. The company's management estimates that the market requires an 18 percent return on its common stock, the firm's bonds command a yield to maturity of 8 percent, and the firm faces a tax rate of 35 percent. At the end of the previous year ABBC's common stock was selling for a price of 2.5 times its book value, and its bonds were trading near their par value.

    a. What does ABBC's capital structure look like?

    b. What is ABBC's weighted average cost of capital?

    c. If ABBC's stock price were to rise such that it sold at 3.5 times book value and the cost of equity fell to 15 percent, what would the firm's weighted average cost of capital be (assuming the cost of debt and tax rate do not change)?

ST-4. (*Divisional costs of capital and investment decisions*) Belton Oil and Gas Inc. is a Houston-based independent oil and gas firm. In the past Belton's managers have used a single firmwide cost of capital of 13 percent to evaluate new investments. However, the firm has long recognized that its exploration and production division is significantly more risky than the pipeline and transportation division. In fact, comparable firms to Belton's E&P division have equity betas of about 1.7, whereas distribution companies typically have equity betas of only .8. Given the importance of getting the cost of capital estimate as close to correct as possible, the firm's chief financial officer has asked you to prepare cost of capital estimates for each of the two divisions. The requisite information needed to accomplish your task is contained here:

- The cost of debt financing is 7 percent before taxes of 35 percent. However, if the E&P division were to borrow based on its projects alone, the cost of debt would probably be 9 percent, and the pipeline division could borrow at 5.5 percent. You may assume these costs of debt are after any flotation costs the firm might incur.
- The risk-free rate of interest on long-term U.S. Treasury bonds is currently 4.8 percent, and the market-risk premium has averaged 7.3 percent over the past several years.
- The E&P division adheres to a target debt ratio of 10 percent, whereas the pipeline division utilizes 40 percent borrowed funds.
- The firm has sufficient internally generated funds such that no new stock will have to be sold to raise equity financing.
  a. Estimate the divisional costs of capital for the E&P and pipeline divisions.
  b. What are the implications of using a company-wide cost of capital to evaluate new investment proposals in light of the differences in the costs of capital you estimated previously?

Study Problems

11-1. (*Individual or component costs of capital*) Compute the cost of the following:

a. A bond that has $1,000 par value (face value) and a contract or coupon interest rate of 11 percent. A new issue would have a flotation cost of 5 percent of the $1,125 market value. The bonds mature in 10 years. The firm's average tax rate is 30 percent and its marginal tax rate is 34 percent.

b. A new common stock issue that paid a $1.80 dividend last year. The par value of the stock is $15, and earnings per share have grown at a rate of 7 percent per year. This growth rate is expected to continue into the foreseeable future. The company maintains a constant dividend–earnings ratio of 30 percent. The price of this stock is now $27.50, but 5 percent flotation costs are anticipated.

c. Internal common equity when the current market price of the common stock is $43. The expected dividend this coming year should be $3.50, increasing thereafter at a 7 percent annual growth rate. The corporation's tax rate is 34 percent.

d. A preferred stock paying a 9 percent dividend on a $150 par value. If a new issue is offered, flotation costs will be 12 percent of the current price of $175.

e. A bond selling to yield 12 percent after flotation costs, but before adjusting for the marginal corporate tax rate of 34 percent. In other words, 12 percent is the rate that equates the net proceeds from the bond with the present value of the future cash flows (principal and interest).

11-2. (*Individual or component costs of capital*) Compute the cost of the following:

a. A bond selling to yield 7 percent after flotation costs, but before adjusting for the marginal corporate tax rate of 34 percent. In other words, 7 percent is the rate that equates the net proceeds from the bond with the present value of the future cash flows (principal and interest).

b. A new common stock issue that paid a $1.05 dividend last year. The par value of the stock is $2, and the earnings per share have grown at a rate of 4 percent per year. This growth rate is expected to continue into the foreseeable future. The company maintains a constant dividend–earnings ratio of 40 percent. The price of this stock is now $30, but 9 percent flotation costs are anticipated.

c. A bond that has a $1,000 par value and a contract, or coupon, interest rate of 12 percent. A new issue would net the company 90 percent of the $1,150 market value. The bonds mature in 15 years, the firm's average tax rate is 30 percent, and its marginal tax rate is 34 percent.

d. A preferred stock paying a 6 percent dividend on a $100 par value. If a new issue is offered, the company can expect to net $85 per share.

e. Internal common equity when the current market price of the common stock is $35. The expected dividend this coming year should be $4, increasing thereafter at a 4 percent annual growth rate. The corporation's tax rate is 34 percent.

11-3. (*Cost of equity*) Salte Corporation is issuing new common stock at a market price of $27. Dividends last year were $1.45 and are expected to grow at an annual rate of 6 percent forever. Flotation costs will be 6 percent of market price. What is Salte's cost of equity?

11-4. (*Cost of debt*) Belton is issuing a $1,000 par value bond that pays 7 percent annual interest and matures in 15 years. Investors are willing to pay $958 for the bond. Flotation costs will be 11 percent of market value. The company is in an 18 percent tax bracket. What will be the firm's after-tax cost of debt on the bond?

11-5. (*Cost of preferred stock*) The preferred stock of Julian Industries sells for $36 and pays $3.00 in dividends. The net price of the security after issuance costs is $32.50. What is the cost of capital for the preferred stock?

11-6. (*Cost of debt*) The Zephyr Corporation is contemplating a new investment to be financed 33 percent from debt. The firm could sell new $1,000 par value bonds at a net price of $945. The coupon interest rate is 12 percent, and the bonds would mature in 15 years. If the company is in a 34 percent tax bracket, what is the after-tax cost of capital to Zephyr for bonds?

11-7. (*Cost of preferred stock*) Your firm is planning to issue preferred stock. The stock sells for $115; however, if new stock is issued, the company would receive only $98. The par value of the stock is $100, and the dividend rate is 14 percent. What is the cost of capital for the stock to your firm?

11-8. (*Cost of internal equity*) Pathos Co.'s common stock is currently selling for $23.80. Dividends paid last year were $0.70. Flotation costs on issuing stock will be 10 percent of market price. The dividends and earnings per share are projected to have an annual growth rate of 15 percent. What is the cost of internal common equity for Pathos?

11-9. (*Cost of equity*) The common stock for the Bestsold Corporation sells for $58. If a new issue is sold, the flotation costs are estimated to be 8 percent. The company pays 50 percent of its earnings in dividends, and a $4 dividend was recently paid. Earnings per share 5 years ago were $5. Earnings are expected to continue to grow at the same annual rate in the future as during the past 5 years. The firm's marginal tax rate is 34 percent. Calculate the cost of (a) internal common equity and (b) external common equity.

11-10. (*Cost of debt*) Sincere Stationery Corporation needs to raise $500,000 to improve its manufacturing plant. It has decided to issue a $1,000 par value bond with a 14 percent annual coupon rate and a 10-year maturity. The investors require a 9 percent rate of return.

    a. Compute the market value of the bonds.
    b. What will the net price be if flotation costs are 10.5 percent of the market price?
    c. How many bonds will the firm have to issue to receive the needed funds?
    d. What is the firm's after-tax cost of debt if its average tax rate is 25 percent and its marginal tax rate is 34 percent?

11-11. (*Cost of debt*)

    a. Rework problem 11-10 as follows: Assume an 8 percent coupon rate. What effect does changing the coupon rate have on the firm's after-tax cost of capital?
    b. Why is there a change?

11-12. (*Economic profit*) The following table contains the firm market value (sum of debt and equity), invested capital, cost of capital, and return on invested capital for three prominent firms measured at year-end 1999:

A	B	C	D	E
	TOTAL MARKET VALUE ($ MILLIONS)	INVESTED CAPITAL ($ MILLIONS)	NET OPERATING PROFIT AFTER TAX (*NOPAT*) ($ MILLIONS)	COST OF CAPITAL (k_{wacc})(%)
Wal-Mart Stores	$336,668	$54,013	$7,729.26	10.99%
Yahoo!	137,595	8,847	(235.33)	15.99%
Motorola	100,431	29,890	2,196.92	11.65%

    a. Based on the data presented here, which of these firms created value for its stockholders during 1999, based on their economic profit?
    b. What is the *MVA* for each of these firms, and what does it tell you about each firm's success or failure to create wealth for its stockholders?

11-13. (*Incentive compensation*) The Navasar Manufacturing Company is implementing a new incentive compensation program for its top four executives that puts a portion of each executive's compensation "at risk" as an incentive to improve performance on the job. The chief financial officer is now estimating the total compensation (base pay plus the incentive portion) for each of these executives in an effort to determine whether the total is reasonable given the historical compensation paid to them. The following table contains the necessary information for evaluating compensation under the proposed plan, as well as the total compensation paid to each executive during the past calendar year:

EMPLOYEE TITLE	PREVIOUS YEAR'S COMPENSATION	% INCENTIVE PAY	PROPOSED TARGET PERFORMANCE	BASE COMPENSATION
Chief Executive Officer	$750,000	90%	$5,000,000	$175,000
Chief Operating Officer	500,000	80%	5,000,000	100,000
Chief Financial Officer	425,000	50%	5,000,000	212,500
Controller	275,000	30%	5,000,000	192,500

a. Calculate incentive and total compensation that will be paid to each of these officers of the firm when actual firm performance is 80%, 100%, and 120% of targeted performance. To calculate incentive pay, use the following relationship:

$$\text{Incentive compensation} = \text{base pay} \times \left(\begin{array}{c} \text{percent} \\ \text{incentive} \\ \text{compensation} \end{array} \right) \times \left(\frac{\text{actual performance}}{\text{target performance}} \right)$$

b. The chief financial officer is also considering a recommendation that incentive compensation be capped based on the firm's performance. For example, incentive pay would begin only when the firm's actual performance reaches 60 percent of target performance, and no additional incentive compensation would be paid once actual performance passed 150 percent of target performance. Under this plan, what are the minimum and maximum compensations that would be paid to each of the officers?

11-14. (*Divisional costs of capital*) LPT Inc. is an integrated oil company headquartered in Dallas, Texas. The company has three operating divisions: oil exploration and production (commonly referred to as E&P), pipelines, and refining. Historically, LPT did not spend a great deal of time thinking about the opportunity costs of capital for each of its divisions and used a company-wide weighted average cost of capital of 14 percent for all new capital investment projects. Recent changes in its businesses have made it abundantly clear to LPT's management that this is not a reasonable approach. For example, investors demand a much higher expected rate of return for exploration and production ventures than for pipeline investments. Although LPT's management agrees, in principle at least, that different operating divisions should face an opportunity cost of capital that reflects their individual risk characteristics, they are not in agreement about whether a move toward divisional costs of capital is a good idea based on practical considerations.

a. Pete Jennings is the chief operating officer for the E&P division, and he is concerned that going to a system of divisional costs of capital may restrain his ability to undertake very promising exploration opportunities. He argues that the firm really should be concerned about finding those opportunities that offer the highest possible rate of return on invested capital. Pete contends that using the firm's scarce capital to take on the most promising projects would lead to the greatest increase in shareholder value. Do you agree with Pete? Why or why not?

b. The pipeline division manager, Donna Selma, has long argued that charging her division the company-wide cost of capital of 14 percent severely penalizes her opportunities to increase shareholder value. Do you agree with Donna? Explain.

c. "There is also the matter of the firm's EVA-based incentive compensation system," remarks Bill Simon, the firm's CEO. "If we move to divisional opportunity costs of capital, it seems to me that we should also define the divisional EVAs using a different cost of capital for each operating division." This, Bill contends, might make it seem as if the managers in the less-risky divisions (those that carry a lower cost of capital) would have an easier time earning EVA-based bonuses. Is Bill correct in his contention that the firm will have to move toward the use of multiple EVA formulas in which the cost of capital varies across divisions?

11-15. (*Weighted average cost of capital*) Crawford Enterprises is a publicly held company located in Arnold, Kansas. The firm began as a small tool and die shop but grew over its 35-year life to become a leading supplier of metal fabrication equipment used in the farm tractor industry. At the close of 2004 the firm's balance sheet appeared as follows:

Cash	$ 540,000		
Accounts receivable	4,580,000		
Inventories	7,400,000	Long-term debt	$12,590,000
Net property, plant, and equipment	18,955,000	Common equity	18,885,000
Total assets	$31,475,000	Total debt and equity	$31,475,000

At present the firm's common stock is selling for a price equal to its book value, and the firm's bonds are selling at par. Crawford's managers estimate that the market requires a 15 percent return on its common stock, the firm's bonds command a yield to maturity of 8 percent, and the firm faces a tax rate of 34 percent.

a. What is Crawford's weighted average cost of capital?

b. If Crawford's stock price were to rise such that it sold at 1.5 times book value, causing the cost of equity to fall to 13 percent, what would the firm's cost of capital be (assuming the cost of debt and tax rate do not change)?

11-16. (*Divisional costs of capital and investment decisions*) In May of this year Newcastle Mfg. Company's capital investment review committee received two major investment proposals. One of the proposals was put forth by the firm's domestic manufacturing division, and the other came from the firm's distribution company. Both proposals promise internal rates of return equal to approximately 12 percent. In the past Newcastle has used a single firmwide cost of capital to evaluate new investments. However, managers have long recognized that the manufacturing division is significantly more risky than the distribution division. In fact, comparable firms in the manufacturing division have equity betas of about 1.6, whereas distribution companies typically have equity betas of only 1.1. Given the size of the two proposals, Newcastle's management feels it can undertake only one, so it wants to be sure that it is taking on the more promising investment. Given the importance of getting the cost of capital estimate as close to correct as possible, the firm's chief financial officer has asked you to prepare cost of capital estimates for each of the two divisions. The requisite information needed to accomplish your task is contained here:

- The cost of debt financing is 8 percent before taxes of 35 percent. You may assume this cost of debt is after any flotation costs the firm might incur.
- The risk-free rate of interest on long-term U.S. Treasury bonds is currently 4.8 percent, and the market-risk premium has averaged 7.3 percent over the past several years.
- Both divisions adhere to target debt ratios of 40 percent.
- The firm has sufficient internally generated funds such that no new stock will have to be sold to raise equity financing.

a. Estimate the divisional costs of capital for the manufacturing and distribution divisions.

b. Which of the two projects should the firm undertake (assuming it cannot do both due to labor and other nonfinancial restraints)? Discuss.

11-17. (*Calculating EVA*) Vasalik Trading Company operates out of Fort Meyer, Florida, and is engaged in the export-import business with companies located primarily in Southeast Asia. The firm carries extensive inventories to support its business and is concerned that the growth in size of its inventory is such that the firm is no longer creating value for its owners. The firm's CFO recently attended an information session in which she learned about EVA and decided to assess her own firm's performance over the past 5 years using this performance measure. The information required to calculate the firm's EVA is found in the following table:

	2001	2002	2003	2004	2005	2006
Net operating income		$142,500	$162,200	$ 158,000	$ 168,200	$187,100
Invested capital	$750,250	780,220	842,000	1,050,100	1,420,200	
Tax rate	35%					
Cost of capital	10%					

a. Calculate the firm's EVA for 2002 through 2006 using the information provided (note that the invested capital for 2002 is the firm's invested capital at the end of 2001).

b. Based on your answer to part a, are the CFO's concerns about the build-up in inventories reason for concern?

Web Works

Barnes & Noble (B&N) is a leading retailer of new books, combining the power of traditional bricks-and-mortar storefronts throughout the nation with a state-of-the-art Internet marketing program. Use your answers to the following exercises to think about what the firm's cost of capital should be.

11-WW1. (*Defining B&N's capital structure*) Your first exercise is to assess B&N's capital structure. Begin by going to **www.sec.gov** to obtain the firm's most recent annual report (for example, the firm's 10K). You may assume that the firm's liabilities are trading for prices that are reflected in their book values. Remember, however, that the only liabilities you want to include in the capital structure are permanent, or long-term, indebtedness, the current portion of the firm's long-term debt, and any short-term, interest-bearing notes payable. For the equity component of the capital structure you will need to determine the market value of B&N shares. To do this, you can multiply the ratio of price to book value of common equity (which can be found at **www.yahoo.com**) by the current book value of the firm's equity. For example, if the price-to-book ratio were 1.5 times, and the book value of the firm's equity were $10 million, then the market value of the firm's common equity would be 1.5 times $10 million, or $15 million.

11-WW2. (*Cost of debt*) Assuming that B&N's credit rating is AA, what is the current yield required on new debt with this rating? (See the Treasury Management Web site for current yield information—**www.tmpages.com/tmp55.htm**.)

11-WW3. (*Cost of equity*) Use the capital asset pricing model to estimate the cost of equity capital for B&N. You can assume an equity market risk premium of 7 percent. Use **www.yahoo.com** to get an equity beta for B&N, and use the current yield for 20-year Treasury bonds to estimate the risk-free rate of interest (see the Treasury Management Web site for current yield information—**www.tmpages.com/tmp55.htm**).

11-WW4. (*Weighted average cost of capital*) If B&N's marginal tax rate is 35 percent, what is its weighted average cost of capital based on your answers to the preceding questions?

Mini Case

The balance sheet that follows indicates the capital structure for Nealon Inc. Flotation costs are (a) 15 percent of market value for a new bond issue, and (b) $2.01 per share for preferred stock. The dividends for common stock were $2.50 last year and are projected to have an annual growth rate of 6 percent. The firm is in a 34 percent tax bracket. What is the weighted average cost of capital if the firm's finances are in the following proportions?

TYPE OF FINANCING	PERCENTAGE OF FUTURE FINANCING
Bonds (8%, $1,000 par, 16-year maturity)	38%
Preferred stock (5,000 shares outstanding,	
$50 par, $1.50 dividend)	15%
Common equity	47%
Total	100%

a. Market prices are $1,035 for bonds, $19 for preferred stock, and $35 for common stock. There will be sufficient internal common equity funding (i.e., retained earnings) available such that the firm does not plan to issue new common stock. Calculate the firm's weighted average cost of capital.

b. In part a we assumed that Nealon would have sufficient retained earnings such that it would not need to sell additional common stock to finance its new investments. Consider the situation now, when Nealon's retained earnings anticipated for the coming year are expected to fall short of the equity requirement of 47 percent of new capital raised. Consequently, the firm foresees the possibility that new common shares will have to be issued. To facilitate the sale of shares, Nealon's investment banker has advised management that they should expect a price discount of approximately 7 percent, or $2.45 per share. Under these terms, the new shares should provide net proceeds of about $32.55. What is Nealon's cost of equity capital when new shares are sold, and what is the weighted average cost of the added funds involved in the issuance of new shares?

Self-Test Solutions

The following notations are used in this group of problems:

k_d = the before-tax cost of debt

k_{ps} = the cost of preferred stock

k_{cs} = the cost of internal common stock

k_{ncs} = the cost of new common stock

T_c = the marginal tax rate

D_t = the dollar dividend per share, where D_0 is the most recently paid dividend and D_1 is the forthcoming dividend

P_0 = the value (present value) of a security

NP_0 = the value of security less any flotation costs incurred in issuing the security

SS-1.

a. $\$921.50 = \sum_{t=1}^{n} \dfrac{\$100}{(1 + k_d)^t} + \dfrac{\$1,000}{(1 + k_d)^{10}}$

RATE	VALUE		
11%	$940.90		
k_d%	$921.50	$19.40	
			$53.90
12%	$887.00		

$$k_d = 0.11 + \left(\dfrac{\$19.40}{\$53.90}\right)0.01 = 0.1136 = 11.36\%$$

$$k_{d(1-t)} = 11.36\%(1 - 0.34) = 7.50\%$$

b.

$$k_{ps} = \dfrac{D}{NP_0}$$

$$k_{ps} = \dfrac{\$8}{\$100 - \$9} = 0.0879 = 8.79\%$$

c.

$$k_{cs} = \dfrac{D_1}{P_0} + g$$

$$k_{cs} = \dfrac{\$9.80}{\$75} + 0\% = 0.1307 = 13.07\%$$

d.

$$k_{ncs} = \dfrac{D_1}{NP_0} + g$$

$$k_{ncs} = \dfrac{\$2.80(1 + 0.08)}{\$53 - \$6} + 0.08 = 0.1443 = 14.43\%$$

SS-2.

Carion Corporation—Weighted Cost of Capital

	CAPITAL STRUCTURE	WEIGHTS	INDIVIDUAL COSTS	WEIGHTED COSTS
Bonds	$1,083	0.2152	5.5%	1.18%
Preferred stock	268	0.0533	13.5%	0.72%
Common stock	3,681	0.7315	18.0%	13.17%
	$5,032	1.0000		15.07%

SS-3. Given:

Cash	$ 2,010,000		
Accounts receivable	4,580,000		
Inventories	1,540,000	Long-term debt	$ 8,141,000
Net property, plant, and equipment	32,575,000	Common equity	32,564,000
Total assets	$40,705,000	Total debt and equity	$40,705,000
Cost of debt financing	8%		
Cost of equity	18%		
Tax rate	35%		
Market-to-book ratio	2.50		

a. *What does ABBC's capital structure look like?* Note that because the market-to-book ratio (market value of equity to book value of equity) is 2.5, the market value of the firm's equity is 2.5 × $32,564,000, or $81,410,000. The market value of debt is assumed to equal its book value. Thus,

COMPONENT	MARKET VALUE BALANCE SHEET	PROPORTION	AFTER-TAX COST	PRODUCT
Long-term debt	$ 8,141,000	9%	4.88%	0.44%
Common equity	81,410,000	91%	18.00%	16.38%
	$89,551,000			16.82%

b. *What is ABBC's weighted average cost of capital?* Based on the above calculations, the answer is 16.8 percent.

c. *If ABBC's stock price were to rise such that it sold at 3.5 times book value and the cost of equity fell to 15 percent, what would the firm's weighted average cost of capital be (assuming the cost of debt and tax rate do not change)?*

Cost of debt financing	8%
Cost of equity	15%
Tax rate	35%
Market-to-book ratio	3.50

COMPONENT	MARKET VALUE BALANCE SHEET	PROPORTION	AFTER-TAX COST	PRODUCT
Long-term debt	$ 8,141,000	7%	5.20%	0.36%
Common equity	113,974,000	93%	15.00%	13.95%
	$122,115,000			14.31%

SS-4. Given:

	E&P DIVISION	PIPELINE DIVISION
Equity beta	1.7	0.8
Tax rate	35.0%	35.0%
Cost of debt	9.0%	5.5%
Debt ratio	10.0%	40.0%
Risk-free rate	4.8%	
Market-risk premium	7.3%	

a.

EXPLORATION AND DEVELOPMENT DIVISION			
COMPONENT	PROPORTION	AFTER-TAX COST	PRODUCT
Debt	10.0%	5.9%	0.6%
Equity	90.0%	17.2%	15.5%
			16.1%

PIPELINE DIVISION			
COMPONENT	PROPORTION	AFTER-TAX COST	PRODUCT
Debt	40.0%	3.6%	1.4%
Equity	60.0%	10.6%	6.4%
			7.8%

b. The very dramatic differences in the two divisional cost of capital estimates underscore the importance of carefully analyzing the capital costs that correspond as closely as possible to the riskiness of the use for which the funds are being requested. For example, using a 13 percent cost of capital for the firm as a whole leads to accepting E&P projects that fall well below the true cost of raising funds for these types of investments (16.1 percent). Similarly, using the 13 percent company-wide cost of capital will result in the rejection of value-enhancing investments that earn in excess of the 7.8 percent cost of capital that is appropriate to the pipeline division.

PART 4

Capital Structure and Dividend Policy

➤ G. Bennett Stewart III is a senior partner with Stern Stewart & Co. (NY). (See the opener for Part 1 for more information on Stewart and this company.) We asked Bennett some questions about the firm's decisions regarding its capital structure and dividend policy, and this is what he said:

Can you make some general comments on the significance of capital structure and dividend policy decisions to a firm's success?

Let me begin by saying that decisions management makes regarding what assets to buy and the businesses in which it plans to compete are the primary drivers of value creation. However, the financial side of the business is critically important, too. From a financing perspective it is management's responsibility to make sure that the cost of raising capital is as cheap as possible, and the choice of the mix of debt and equity is an important determinant of a firm's cost of capital.

However, there is more to the firm's financial strategy than determining the mix of securities to use when financing the firm's investments. Specifically, the firm's financial strategy also includes the selection of the firm's dividend policy (the firm's strategy for returning cash to investors), the firm's overall risk management policy, its pension-planning policy, and the policy it follows with respect to the use of surplus cash. In total, these policies can be described as the corporate financial strategy of the firm.

I would also like to point out that the determination of each of these policies is inextricably linked to minimizing taxes and transaction costs. In addition, a firm's financing policies include decisions regarding opportunities for employees to own part of the equity in the firm as a managerial strategy for improving firm performance. Consequently, setting a firm's financial policies provides crucial decision opportunities for the executive who wants proactively to seek out value creation opportunities.

Good companies are proactive about their financing decisions. They don't tend to let the cash flow of the business passively dictate their capital structure. Instead they think about the mix of debt and equity that will balance the tax and incentive benefits of debt financing against the need to preserve financial flexibility. In addition, the proactive manager thoughtfully examines the best way the firm will provide a return to its stockholders via cash distributions through dividends and share repurchases.

Can you give an example of a firm that is really good at managing capital structure and make a comment or two as to why you believe that to be so?

I think a good example of a company that has approached this very thoughtfully over the years is the Coca-Cola Company. In the 1970s Coca-Cola was very passively financed. They had a AAA rating on their debt, what little debt they had, and they were an aggressive payer of dividends. When Robertô Goizueta came in as CEO in the early 1980s, he decided to stir up a more potent business model that emphasized global growth and product-line extensions. At the same time, he was a great believer in using debt financing much more aggressively to minimize the cost of capital. So the Coca-Cola Company began to borrow money and use the proceeds to repurchase the firm's common shares. This changed the firm's mix of debt and equity such that the firm lost its AAA bond rating. However, by raising the firm's use of debt, the firm reduced the overall cost of its capital. I think this is a crystal clear example of a company shifting from a passive to a proactive financial strategy.

CHAPTER 12
DETERMINING THE
FINANCING MIX

CHAPTER 13
DIVIDEND POLICY AND
INTERNAL FINANCING

After reading this chapter, you should be able to:

1. Understand the difference between business risk and financial risk.

2. Use the technique of break-even analysis in a variety of analytical settings.

3. Distinguish among the financial concepts of operating leverage, financial leverage, and combined leverage.

4. Calculate the firm's degree of operating leverage, financial leverage, and combined leverage.

5. Understand the concept of an optimal capital structure.

6. Explain the main underpinnings of capital structure theory.

7. Understand and be able to graph the moderate position on capital structure importance.

8. Incorporate the concepts of agency costs and free cash flow into a discussion on capital structure management.

9. Use the basic tools of capital structure management.

10. Understand how business risk and global sales impact the multinational firm.

CHAPTER 12

Determining the Financing Mix

When a firm needs funds to support its investment plans, it typically raises them internally by reinvesting all or part of its earnings. This process of reinvesting firm earnings is tantamount to increasing the investment of the firm's common shareholders in the firm because the earnings represent what is left for the common stockholders after everyone else has been paid. However, occasionally firms find that they need to raise funds externally from the capital markets either because they do not have sufficient earnings to reinvest or they want to rebalance their capital structures. Historically, when firms tried to raise external sources of funds, they had to go to the public capital market where they sold bonds or stocks with the help of investment bankers to a diverse group of investors.

However, external financing is no longer limited to public capital markets. Today, private equity firms raise billions of dollars through the sale of limited partnership interests and then use the proceeds to invest in other firms. In fact, the total amount of private equity now exceeds $180 billion. Private equity funds are not for everyone, however. They tend to focus their investments in turnaround situations, in which the promised returns are very high and the need for funds is brief. Nonetheless, there's a new kid on the block when it comes to raising money externally.

FIGURE 12-1 The Cost of Capital as a Link between a Firm's Asset Structure and Financial Structure

Earlier chapters allowed us to develop an understanding of how financial assets are valued in the marketplace. Drawing on the tenets of valuation theory, we presented various approaches to measuring the cost of funds to the business organization. This chapter presents concepts that relate to the valuation process and the cost of capital; it also discusses the crucial problem of planning the firm's financing mix.

The cost of capital provides a direct link between the formulation of the firm's asset structure and its financial structure. This is illustrated in Figure 12-1. Recall that the cost of capital is a basic input to the time-adjusted, capital-budgeting models. Therefore, it affects the capital-budgeting, or asset-selection, process. The cost of capital is affected, in turn, by the composition of the right-hand side of the firm's balance sheet—that is, its financial structure.

This chapter examines tools that can be useful aids to the financial manager in determining the firm's proper financial structure. First, we review the notion of risk from the perspective of the firm's shareholders as it relates to the potential volatility in shareholder earnings. Corporate CEOs and boards of directors are very sensitive to the earnings numbers they report to Wall Street, so it behooves the financial manager to understand fully how the firm's capital structure affects the variability of earnings. The sources of this variability can be decomposed into three components.

Next, we turn to a discussion of capital structure theory and the basic tools of capital structure management. Actual capital structure practices are also placed in perspective. We close with a discussion involving the multinational firm and its relationship to both the business-risk concept and global sales opportunities.

What is it about the nature of business that causes changes in sales revenues to translate into larger variations in net income and, finally, the earnings available to the common shareholders? It would be a good planning tool for management to be able to decompose such fluctuations into those policies associated with the operating side of the business and those policies associated with the financing side of the business.

This chapter shows you how to do just that—and more. The United States was recession free from April 1991 until March 2001, when the 10th post–World War II recession officially commenced. This was the longest expansion (120 months) in the history of credible business-cycle record keeping in the United States, dating back to 1853. It took until

July 17, 2003, for the National Bureau of Economic Research to announce that a "trough in business activity occurred in the U.S. economy in November 2001." A trough means a recession has ended. Note that this announcement happened a full 21 months after the recession was said to have ended. (Business-cycle "dating" is an art subject to considerable debate among financial economists and executives.) Even though this recession was officially over, the nation's labor markets continued to languish into July 2003, marked by very slow growth in payroll jobs. This postrecession adjustment period was a challenging one for many U.S. businesses that had loaded their balance sheets with debt over the "good times" of the 120-month expansion.

Financial executives had to delicately manage cash flows to service existing debt contracts or face bankruptcy. These same executives had to give considerable thought to how to finance their next (that is, incremental) capital projects.

Harley-Davidson Inc. has had a rather moderate exposure to financial risk in the management of its funds' sources. Harley has about 8,500 employees and sales revenues of $3.36 billion and, for reporting year 2001, ranked 466th among the *Fortune* 500. Even though the overall economy was slow, Harley improved to a ranking of 392nd for 2002 within this same set of 500 companies. For 2001, Harley generated $698.2 million in earnings before interest and taxes (EBIT) and incurred an interest expense of $24.8 million. This put its times interest-earned ratio at 28.2 times ($698.2 million/$24.8 million) for 2001. So in an adverse economic year, Harley's EBIT could slip to about 1/28th of its 2001 amount and the firm would still be able to pay its contractual debt obligations. This is a very safe interest coverage ratio. By the way, the times-interest-earned ratio is defined as earnings before interest and taxes divided by interest expense (refer to the glossary at the back of this text).

If you understand the material and analytical processes in this chapter, you will be able to make positive contributions to company strategies that deal with the firm's financing mix. You will be able to formulate a defensible answer to the question, Should we finance our next capital project with a new issue of bonds or a new issue of common stock? You can also help a lot of firms avoid making serious financial errors, the consequences of which can last for several years.

BUSINESS AND FINANCIAL RISK

If investors are surprised by lower-than-expected corporate earnings, this can lead to a downward revision in their expectations of the firm's future prospects and, consequently, reduce the firm's common stock price. Thus, corporate executives and their boards of directors pay close attention to the earnings that they report to Wall Street. For this reason the financial analyst needs to understand the sources of volatility in firm earnings per share.

In this section we separate the variation in the firm's income stream into one of three sources:

1. **Choice of business line**—the variation in firm earnings that arises out of the natural volatility in revenues attributable to the industry in which it operates. For example, if the firm operates in a highly volatile industry in which revenues fluctuate with the business cycle, then the firm's earnings will be more volatile than another firm that operates in an industry that is less sensitive to the business cycle. We will refer to this source of variation in firm earnings as **business risk**.
2. **Choice of an operating cost structure**—the volatility in the firm's operating earnings that results from the firm's cost structure.[1] That is, the mix of fixed and variable operating costs the firm pays to do business. Greater fixed operating costs (versus variable costs) increase the variability in operating earnings in response to changes in revenues. The firm's mixture of fixed versus variable operating costs is largely determined by the industry in which the firm operates. For example, automobile manufacturing requires that large investments be made in plant and equipment. This results in high

Objective **1**

Understand the difference between business risk and financial risk.

business risk the relative dispersion or variability in the firm's expected earnings before interest and taxes (EBIT). The nature of the firm's operations causes its business risk. This type of risk is affected by the firm's cost structure, product demand characteristics, and intra-industry competitive position. In capital structure theory, business risk is distinguished from financial risk. Compare **Financial Risk**.

---

[1] Recall that the term EBIT is the acronym for earnings before interest and taxes. If what accountants call *other income* and *other expenses* are equal to zero, then EBIT is equal to net operating income. For our purposes we use these two terms interchangeably.

fixed operating costs regardless of the level of plant operations. We will refer to this source of variation in the firm earnings as operating risk.

3. **Choice of a capital structure**—the source of variation in the firm's earnings that results from its use of sources of financing that require a fixed return, such as debt financing. We will refer to this source of variation in earnings as financial risk.

We now spend some time developing an understanding of all three of these sources of volatility in firm earnings.

Did You Get It? ....

1. Why do managers care about the volatility of their firms' earnings?
2. What are the three determinants of the volatility of a firm's earnings?

Business Risk

The amount of business risk the firm decides to take on is most critical at the time the business is started. However, because business risk can affect the volatility of a firm's revenues, it can affect the firm's earnings per share. Thus, it behooves us to spend a little time discussing the sources of business risk. We identify four basic determinants of a firm's business risk:

1. **The stability of the domestic economy.** Firms that operate in more volatile economies, such as those of developing nations, are subject to swings in revenues that are much more severe than those that operate within developed countries. For example, a chain of clothing stores operating within the United States faces a less volatile revenue stream than, say, a chain located in Nigeria or even Brazil.
2. **The exposure to, and stability of, foreign economies.** In today's global economy more and more firms produce and sell their products in multiple countries. This means that it is not only the natural volatility of the firm's home country that drives the volatility of the firm's revenues but also that of the countries in which its goods and services are produced and sold.
3. **Sensitivity to the business cycle.** Some industries are more sensitive to the business cycle than others. For example, the sales of consumer durable goods such as automobiles, housing, and appliances tend to be more sensitive to swings in the business cycle than necessities such as food and clothing.
4. **Competitive pressures in the firm's industry.** Here we refer to the forces of other firms within the firm's marketplace that provide the same (or close substitute) products and services. Greater competive pressures will force the firm to make price concessions sooner and deeper than would otherwise be the case.

Although business risk is obviously a critical determinant of earnings volatility, for the balance of this chapter we will assume that the firm's business risk is fixed, or given. This will allow us to focus on operating and financial risks, over which managers have more control.

Operating Risk

Operating risk increases when the firm incurs more fixed versus variable costs. Fixed costs do not vary with the firm's revenues, but variable costs, as the name implies, do rise and fall with revenues. A key tool for evaluating operating risk is break-even analysis. Therefore, we open our discussion of operating risk by defining the break-even chart.

BREAK-EVEN ANALYSIS

Objective **2**

Use the technique of break-even analysis in a variety of analytical settings.

Both small and large organizations utilize the break-even analysis tool for two reasons: It is based on straightforward assumptions, and companies have found that the information gained from the break-even model is beneficial in decision-making situations. A break-even analysis is used to determine the "break-even" quantity of the firm's output. What is meant by the break-

Across the Hall

ACCOUNTING—COST STRUCTURE, FORECASTING, AND INVESTMENT

Comments by Mr. Eric Gerstemeier

Mr. Eric Gerstemeier is a senior financial analyst at Harcourt Education, a global education company providing print, assessment, and development programs to students, teachers, and adults worldwide. Harcourt's corporate structure is composed of approximately a dozen primary divisions located across the United States and Canada, each division being responsible for its daily investment and operational decisions. Mr. Gerstemeier works for a 'shared services' division, a group providing a multitude of operational and financial services to each of the operating divisions. His responsibilities span a host of tasks ranging from budgeting and forecasting to process improvement, Sarbanes-Oxley compliance, and the valuation of acquisition prospects. Mr. Gerstemeier received his bachelor's degree in finance and an MBA from the University of Central Florida. He has worked in similar roles in both the technology and publishing industries.

A knowledge of cost structure, including fixed, variable, and semifixed costs is crucial to Mr. Gerstemeier's work. This base is also important to forecasting and capital-investing decisions. His comments on these areas follow.

> Many decisions regarding the direction and funding of the ongoing business at Harcourt are made during the annual budget process and include the consideration of variables such as market conditions, risk assessments, and the firm's operating cost structure. Similarly, the health of the company can be assessed and problem areas targeted through the analysis of such data. Indicative of the manufacturing industry, Harcourt's cost structure includes costs to produce the product (typically variable), costs to bring the product to

market (variable and fixed), and infrastructure costs to support the business as a whole (generally fixed).

Furthermore, many cost drivers exhibit relationships with revenue, volumes shipped, or capital invested, whereas others, typically those supporting the overall business, have fixed thresholds; that is, a fixed number of IT professionals are needed to support the general ledger system and its peripheral applications. Through quantification of these relationships, ratios and thresholds may be defined and Harcourt is able to create forward-looking income, cash flow, and balance sheet statements by which Harcourt manages the business (the budget). Some relationships (ratios) that Harcourt finds particularly valuable are as follows:

- Product investment needed to maintain or capture a given level of revenue (growth)
- Product investment and amortization
- Cost of goods sold and revenue (variable)
  - paper, print, and binding
  - freight
- Sales costs and revenue (fixed and variable)
  - commissions (variable)
  - general labor costs (fixed/semifixed)
- General and administrative (fixed/semifixed)

Based on management's knowledge of these and other cost variables and coupled with an intimate knowledge of current and future market conditions, "pro-forma" statements of financial performance can be constructed. This provides the groundwork regarding where, when, and how much investment needs to take place in the near future. It also provides key metrics by which Harcourt can identify problem areas and justify the implementation of cost control and/or process improvement initiatives.

---

even quantity of output? It is that quantity of output, denominated in units, that results in an EBIT equal to zero. In other words, a break-even analysis enables the financial officer (1) to determine the quantity of output that must be sold to cover all operating costs, as distinct from financial costs, and (2) to calculate the EBIT that will be achieved at various output levels.

Essential Elements of the Break-Even Model

To implement the break-even model, we must separate the production costs of the company into two mutually exclusive categories: fixed costs and variable costs. You will recall from your study of basic economics that in the long run all costs are variable. The break-even analysis, therefore, is a short-run concept.

Fixed Costs

Fixed costs, also referred to as **indirect costs**, *do not vary with either the firm's sales or output.* As the production volume increases, the fixed cost *per unit* of product falls, because the firm's total fixed costs are spread over larger and larger quantities of output. Figure 12-2 graphs the behavior of total fixed costs with respect to the company's relevant range of output. This total is shown to be unaffected by the quantity of product that is manufactured and sold. Over some other relevant output range, the amount of total fixed costs might be higher or lower for the same company.

fixed costs costs that do not vary in total dollar amount as sales volume or quantity of output changes. Also called indirect costs.

indirect costs see **Fixed Costs**.

FIGURE 12-2 The Behavior of Total, Fixed, and Variable Costs over a Relevant Range of Output

In a manufacturing setting, some specific examples of fixed costs are

1. Administrative salaries
2. Depreciation
3. Insurance
4. Lump sums spent on intermittent advertising programs
5. Property taxes
6. Rent

Variable Costs

variable costs costs that are fixed per unit of output but vary in total as output changes. Also called **Direct Costs**.

direct costs see **Variable Costs**.

Variable costs are sometimes referred to as **direct costs**. Variable costs *per unit vary as output changes*. Total variable costs are computed by taking the variable cost per unit and multiplying it by the total quantity produced and sold. The break-even model assumes proportionality between total variable costs and sales. Thus, if sales rise by 10 percent, it is assumed that variable costs will rise by 10 percent. Notice that if zero units of the product are manufactured, then variable costs are zero, but fixed costs are greater than zero. This implies that some contribution to the coverage of fixed costs occurs as long as the selling price per unit exceeds the variable costs per unit. This helps explain why some firms will operate a plant even when sales are temporarily depressed—that is, to try to cover fixed costs.

Some examples of variable costs include

1. Direct labor
2. Direct materials
3. Energy costs (fuel, electricity, natural gas) associated with production
4. Freight costs for products leaving the plant
5. Packaging
6. Sales commissions

Figure 12-2 also graphs total costs with respect to the company's relevant range of output. Total cost is a function of the firm's fixed and variable costs.

More on the Behavior of Costs

No one really believes that *all* costs behave as neatly as we have illustrated the fixed and variable costs in Figure 12-2. Nor does any law or accounting principle dictate that a certain element of the firm's total costs always will be classified as fixed or variable. This depends on each firm's specific circumstances. In one firm, energy costs may be predominantly fixed, whereas in another they may vary with output.[2]

---

[2] In a greenhouse operation, in which plants are grown (manufactured) under strictly controlled temperatures, heat costs will tend to be fixed whether the building is full or only half- full of seedlings. In a metal stamping operation, in which levers are being produced, there is no need to heat the plant to as high a temperature when the machines are stopped and the workers are not there. In this latter case, the heat costs will tend to be variable.

FIGURE 12-3 Semivariable–Cost Behavior over a Relevant Range of Output

Furthermore, some costs may be fixed for a while, then rise sharply to a higher level as a higher output is reached, remain fixed, and then rise again with further increases in production. Such costs may be termed either *semivariable* or *semifixed*. The label is your choice because both are used in practice. An example might be the salaries paid to production supervisors. Should output be cut back by 15 percent for a short period, the organization is not likely to lay off 15 percent of its supervisors. Similarly, the percentage commissions paid to salespeople are often incrementally stepped up the more they sell. This sort of cost behavior is shown in Figure 12-3.

To implement the break-even model and deal with such a complex cost structure, the financial manager must (1) identify the most relevant output range for planning purposes and then (2) approximate the cost effect of semivariable items over this range by segregating a portion of them to fixed costs and a portion to variable costs. In the actual business setting this procedure is not fun. It is not unusual for the analyst who deals with the figures to spend considerably more time allocating costs to fixed and variable categories than doing the actual break-even calculations.

Total Revenue and Volume of Output

Besides fixed and variable costs, the essential elements of the break-even model include total revenue from sales and volume of output. **Total revenue** means *total sales dollars* and is equal to the selling price per unit multiplied by the quantity sold. The **volume of output** refers to the *firm's level of operations* and may be *indicated either as a unit quantity or as sales dollars*.

total revenue total sales dollars.

volume of output a firm's level of operations expressed either in sales dollars or as units of output.

Finding the Break-Even Point

Finding the break-even point in terms of units of production can be accomplished in several ways. All approaches require the essential elements of the break-even model just described. The break-even model is a simple adaptation of the firm's income statement expressed in the following analytical format:

$$\text{Sales} - (\text{total variable cost} + \text{total fixed cost}) = \text{profit} \tag{12-1}$$

On a units-of-production basis, it is necessary to introduce (1) the price at which each unit is sold and (2) the variable cost per unit of output. Because the profit item studied in a break-even analysis is EBIT, we use this acronym instead of the word *profit*. In terms of units, the income statement shown in equation (12-1) becomes the break-even model by setting EBIT equal to zero:

$$\left(\begin{array}{c}\text{Sales price}\\\text{per unit}\end{array}\right) \times \left(\begin{array}{c}\text{units}\\\text{sold}\end{array}\right) - \left[\left(\begin{array}{c}\text{variable cost}\\\text{per unit}\end{array}\right) \times \left(\begin{array}{c}\text{units}\\\text{sold}\end{array}\right) + \left(\begin{array}{c}\text{total fixed}\\\text{cost}\end{array}\right)\right] = \text{EBIT} = \$0 \tag{12-2}$$

Our task now becomes finding the number of units that must be produced and sold in order to satisfy equation (12-2)—that is, to arrive at EBIT = $0. This can be done by simply solving equation (12-2) for the number of units sold that make EBIT = 0.

Specifically, the break-even number of units sold is found to equal:

$$\begin{array}{c}\text{Break-even}\\\text{level of}\\\text{units}\end{array} = \frac{\text{total fixed cost}}{\left(\begin{array}{c}\text{sales price}\\\text{per unit}\end{array} - \begin{array}{c}\text{variable cost}\\\text{per unit}\end{array}\right)} \tag{12-3}$$

> **EXAMPLE**

Even though Pierce Grain Company manufactures several different products, it has observed over a lengthy period that its product mix is rather constant. This allows management to conduct its financial planning by using a "normal" sales price per unit and a "normal" variable cost per unit. The "normal" sales price and variable cost per unit are calculated from the constant product mix. It is like assuming that the product mix is one big product. The selling price is $10 and the variable cost is $6. Total fixed costs for the firm are $100,000 per year. What is the break-even point in units produced and sold for the company during the coming year?

Substituting into equation (12-3), we calculate Pierce's break-even quantity as follows:

$$\text{Break-even level of units} = \frac{\$100,000}{(\$10.00 - \$6.00)} = 25,000 \text{ units}$$

Thus, Pierce Grain must sell 25,000 units in the coming year just to cover its fixed costs. At this point, its EBIT will be equal to zero.

The Break-Even Point in Sales Dollars

For the multiproduct firm, it is convenient to compute the break-even point in terms of sales dollars rather than units sold. Sales, in effect, become a common denominator associated with a particular product mix. Furthermore, an outside analyst might not have access to internal unit cost data. He or she may, however, be able to obtain annual reports for the firm. If the analyst can separate the firm's total costs as identified from its annual reports into their fixed and variable components, he or she can calculate a general break-even point in sales dollars.

We illustrate this procedure using Pierce Grain Company's cost structure. Suppose that the reported financial information is arranged in the format shown in Table 12-1. We refer to this type of financial statement as an *analytical income statement*. This distinguishes it from audited income statements published, for example, in the annual reports of public corporations. If we are aware of the simple mathematical relationships on which cost-volume-profit analysis is based, we can use Table 12-1 to find the break-even point in sales dollars for Pierce Grain Company.

We can solve for the break-even level of revenues (as opposed to units sold) using equation (12-4) as follows:

$$\text{Break-even level of revenues} = \frac{\text{Total fixed costs}}{\left(1 - \dfrac{\text{variable costs}}{\text{revenues}}\right)} \tag{12-4}$$

In the Pierce Grain Company example the ratio of the firm's variable costs ($180,000) to revenues ($300,000) is $180,000/$300,000, or .60, and is assumed to be constant for all revenue levels. Consequently, we can use equation (12-4) to solve for Pierce's break-even level of revenues as follows:

$$\text{Break-even level of revenues} = \frac{\$100,000}{\left(1 - \dfrac{\$180,000}{\$300,000}\right)} = \$250,000$$

TABLE 12-1 Analytical Income Statement for Pierce Grain Company

Sales	$300,000
Less: Total variable costs	180,000
Revenue before fixed costs	$120,000
Less: Total fixed costs	100,000
EBIT	$ 20,000

Can You Do It?

ANALYZING THE BREAK-EVEN SALES LEVEL

Creighton Manufacturing Company assembles brake controllers used to upgrade the brake systems of vintage automobiles that are being restored. The firm's revenues for the past year were $20 million, on which the firm had earnings before interest and taxes (EBIT) of $10 million. Fixed expenses were $2 million. Variable costs were of $8 million, or 40 percent of the firm's revenues. What do you estimate the firms break-even level of revenues to be based on its current cost structure?

(The solution can be found on page 384.)

Did You Get It?

1. Distinguish among fixed costs, variable costs, and semivariable costs.
2. When is it useful or sometimes necessary to compute the break-even point in terms of sales dollars rather than units of output?

OPERATING LEVERAGE

Operating leverage refers to when a firm has fixed operating costs, then it is subject to the effects of operating leverage. Moreover, the operating leverage increases the sensitivity of the firm's operating income to changes in sales.

For example, highly leveraged firms will see their incomes rise sharply when their sales rise. By contrast, firms with less leverage will see less-sharp rises in their incomes when their sales rise. To illustrate how this works, consider the Pierce Grain Company example. The firm's current sales are equal to $300,000, as found in Table 12-2. If Pierce's sales were to rise by 20 percent, up to $360,000, we calculate that the firm's EBIT would rise from $20,000 to $44,000. Note in the last column of Table 12-2 that we calculate the percent change in both revenues and EBIT. Revenues increase by just 20 percent, but the EBIT increases by a whopping 120 percent. The reason for this difference is the effect of operating leverage. If Pierce had no operating leverage (that is, all of its operating costs were variable), then the increase in EBIT would have been 20 percent, just like revenues. Note also that if Pierce had experienced a 20 percent decline in revenues, it would have experienced a whopping 120 percent decline in EBIT, as the numbers in Table 12-3 illustrate. Clearly, a higher operating leverage means higher volatility in EBIT!

So, what does this all mean for the management team at Pierce Grain? Is there something they can or should do in response to having high operating leverage? Yes, there is. Recognizing that firm operating earnings will be very sensitive to changes in firm revenues should make management vary wary about using lots of financial leverage that carries with it fixed principal and interest payments. Moreover, with highly variable operating earnings, Pierce's management will probably want to hold a safety net of cash and marketable securities to help the firm weather any periods when revenues falls below the break-even level.

Objective **3**

Distinguish among the financial concepts of operating leverage, financial leverage, and combined leverage.

operating leverage the incurring of fixed operating costs in a firm's income stream.

TABLE 12-2 How Operating Leverage Affects EBIT: An Increase in Pierce Grain Company's Sales

ITEM	BASE SALES LEVEL, t	FORECAST SALES LEVEL, $t+1$	PERCENTAGE CHANGE IN EARNINGS PER SHARE
Sales	$300,000	$360,000	+20%
Less: Total variable costs	180,000	216,000	
Revenue before fixed costs	$120,000	$144,000	
Less: Total fixed costs	100,000	100,000	
EBIT	$ 20,000	$ 44,000	+120%

How Did You Do?

ANALYZING THE BREAK-EVEN SALES LEVEL

Creighton Manufacturing Company has fixed operating costs of $2 million and pays variable costs equal to $8 million/$20 million = 40 percent. Therefore, using equation (12-4), we can solve for the firm's break-even sales level as follows:

$$\text{Break-even level of revenues} = \frac{\$2,000,000}{\left(1 - \dfrac{\$8,000,000}{\$20,000,000}\right)} = \$3,333,333$$

Can You Do It?

ANALYZING THE EFFECTS OF OPERATING LEVERAGE

JGC Electronics operates in a very cyclical business environment such that it is not uncommon for the firm's sales to increase or decrease by 20 percent or more from year to year. Moreover, the firm has made a substantial investment in plant and equipment. The company's high fixed operating expenses associated with the plant and equipment make the firm's earnings before interest and taxes (EBIT) very sensitive to changes in revenues. In fact, if revenues were to rise by 20 percent, the firm's managers estimate that EBIT would rise by 40 percent. If JGC's revenues were to fall by 20 percent from their current level of $10 million, what percentage decline in EBIT would you anticipate for the firm?

(The solution can be found on page 385.)

TABLE 12-3	How Operating Leverage Affects EBIT: A Decrease in Pierce Grain Company's Sales		
ITEM	BASE SALES LEVEL, *t*	FORECAST SALES LEVEL, *t* + 1	PERCENTAGE CHANGE IN EARNINGS PER SHARE
Sales	$300,000	$240,000	−20%
Less: Total variable costs	180,000	144,000	
Revenue before fixed costs	$120,000	$ 96,000	
Less: Total fixed costs	100,000	100,000	
EBIT	$ 20,000	$ −4,000	−120%

Before we complete this discussion of operating leverage and move on to the subject of financial leverage, ask yourself, "Which type of leverage is more under the control of management?" You will probably (and correctly) come to the conclusion that the firm's managers have less control over the operating cost structure and almost complete control over its financial structure. What the firm actually produces, for example, will determine to a significant degree the division between fixed and variable costs. However, there is more room for substitution among the various sources of financial capital than there is among the labor and real capital inputs that enable the firm to meet its production requirements. Thus, you can anticipate more arguments over the choice of the firm's financial structure than operating structure.

Did You Get It?

1. When is operating leverage present in the firm's cost structure? What condition is necessary for operating leverage not to be present in the firm's cost structure?
2. What is the effect of operating leverage on the volatility of a firm's EBIT?

How Did You Do?

ANALYZING THE EFFECTS OF OPERATING LEVERAGE

At its current level of sales, JGC anticipates that any percentage change in revenues will result in double that percentage change in EBIT. Thus, a decline in revenues by 20 percent would be expected to result in a decline in EBIT of 40 percent. Recall, however, that this relationship between percentage changes in revenues and EBIT changes as the level of revenue changes.

Can You Do It?

ANALYZING THE EFFECTS OF FINANCIAL LEVERAGE

JGC Electronics currently uses no financial leverage in its capital structure. Should the firm's earnings before interest and taxes (EBIT) increase by 20 percent, what percentage change would you expect in JGCs earnings per share?

(The solution can be found on page 386.)

FINANCIAL LEVERAGE

Financial leverage means *financing a portion of the firm's assets with securities bearing a fixed (limited) rate of return* in hopes of increasing the ultimate return to the common stockholders. The decision to use debt or preferred stock in the financial structure of the corporation means that those who own the common shares of the firm are exposed to financial risk. Any given level of variability in EBIT is magnified by the firm's use of financial leverage, and such additional variability is embodied in the variability of earnings available to the common stockholder and earnings per share.

Let's now focus on the responsiveness of the company's earnings per share to changes in its EBIT. (We are *not* saying that earnings per share is the appropriate criterion for all financing decisions. In fact, the weakness of such a contention is examined later. Rather, the use of financial leverage produces a certain type of *effect* on earnings per shares).

Let us assume that Pierce Grain Company is in the process of getting started as a going concern. The firm's potential owners have estimated that $200,000 is needed to purchase the necessary assets to conduct the business. Three possible financing plans have been identified for raising the $200,000; they are presented in Table 12-4. In plan A no financial

financial leverage the use of securities bearing a fixed (limited) rate of return to finance a portion of a firm's assets. Financial leverage can arise from the use of either debt or preferred stock financing. The use of financial leverage exposes the firm to financial risk.

TABLE 12-4	Possible Capital Structures for Pierce Grain Company		
	PLAN A: 0% DEBT		
		Total debt	$ 0
		Common equity	200,000ᵃ
Total assets	$200,000	Total liabilities and equity	$200,000
	PLAN B: 25% DEBT AT 8% INTEREST RATE		
		Total debt	$ 50,000
		Common equity	150,000ᵇ
Total assets	$200,000	Total liabilities and equity	$200,000
	PLAN C: 40% DEBT AT 8% INTEREST RATE		
		Total debt	$ 80,000
		Common equity	120,000ᶜ
Total assets	$200,000	Total liabilities and equity	$200,000

ᵃ2,000 common shares outstanding. ᵇ1,500 common shares outstanding. ᶜ1,200 common shares outstanding.

How Did You Do?

ANALYZING THE EFFECTS OF FINANCIAL LEVERAGE

Because JGC uses no financial leverage, there is *no* magnification effect of the percent change in EBIT on earnings per share. Therefore, a 20 percent increase in EBIT would lead to an equal 20 percent increase in the firm's earnings per share.

risk is assumed: The entire $200,000 is raised by selling 2,000 common shares for $100 per share. In plan B a moderate amount of financial risk is assumed: 25 percent of the assets are financed with a debt issue that carries an 8 percent annual interest rate. Plan C would use the most financial leverage: 40 percent of the assets would be financed with a debt issue costing 8 percent.

Table 12-5 presents the impact of financial leverage on earnings per share associated with each fund-raising alternative. If EBIT should increase from $20,000 to $40,000, then earnings per share would rise by 100 percent under plan A. The same change in EBIT would result in an earnings-per-share rise of 125 percent under plan B, and 147 percent under plan C. In plans B and C, the 100 percent increase in EBIT (from $20,000 to $40,000) is magnified to a greater-than-100-percent increase in earnings per share. The firm is employing financial leverage and exposing its owners to financial risk when the following situation exists:

$$\frac{\text{Percentage change in earnings per share}}{\text{percentage change in EBIT}} > 1.00$$

As we have illustrated using the Pierce Grain Company example, the greater the firm's use of financial leverage, the greater will be the ratio of the percent change in earnings per share divided by the corresponding percent change in EBIT. To reiterate, this means that

TABLE 12-5   An Analysis of Financial Leverage at Different EBIT Levels: Pierce Grain Company

(1)	(2)	(3) = (1) − (2)	(4) = (3) × .5	(5) = (3) − (4)	(6)	
EBIT	INTEREST	EBT	TAXES	NET INCOME TO COMMON SHAREHOLDERS	EARNINGS PER SHARE	
PLAN A: 0% DEBT; $200,000 COMMON EQUITY; 2,000 SHARES						
$ 0	$ 0	$ 0	$ 0	$ 0	$ 0	
20,000	0	20,000	10,000	10,000	5.00	} 100%
40,000	0	40,000	20,000	20,000	10.00	
60,000	0	60,000	30,000	30,000	15.00	
80,000	0	80,000	40,000	40,000	20.00	
PLAN B: 25% DEBT; 8% INTEREST RATE; $150,000 COMMON EQUITY; 1,500 SHARES						
$ 0	$4,000	$(4,000)	$(2,000)[a]	$(2,000)	$(1.33)	
20,000	4,000	16,000	8,000	8,000	5.33	} 125%
40,000	4,000	36,000	18,000	18,000	12.00	
60,000	4,000	56,000	28,000	28,000	18.67	
80,000	4,000	76,000	38,000	38,000	25.33	
PLAN C: 40% DEBT; 8% INTEREST RATE; $120,000 COMMON EQUITY; 1,200 SHARES						
$ 0	$6,400	$(6,400)	$(3,200)[a]	$(3,200)	$(2.67)	
20,000	6,400	13,600	6,800	6,800	5.67	} 147%
40,000	6,400	33,600	16,800	16,800	14.00	
60,000	6,400	53,600	26,800	26,800	22.33	
80,000	6,400	73,600	36,800	36,800	30.67	

[a]The negative tax bill recognizes the credit arising from the carryback and carryforward provision of the tax code.

Can You Do It?

ANALYZING THE COMBINED EFFECTS OF OPERATING AND FINANCIAL LEVERAGE

Peterson Timber Company operates saw mills throughout the redwood areas of the Pacific Northwest. The firm's current level of revenues, EBIT, and earnings per share are $10 million, $4 million, and $1.00 per share, respectively. Peterson's CFO recently fore-casted the firm's revenues and profits for next year and estimated that total revenues will grow to $12 million, EBIT will rise to $5.2 million, and earnings per share will be $1.60 a share. Analyze the effects of operating, financial, and combined leverage for Peterson.

(The solution can be found on page 388.)

the use of financial leverage *magnifies* the effect of changes in EBIT on earnings per share. If, for example, the aforementioned ratio were 2, then a 20 percent change in EBIT (either positive or negative) would lead to a 40 percent change in earnings per share. For a firm that had even more financial leverage in its capital structure, the ratio might be 3, such that a 20 percent change in EBIT would lead to a 60 percent change in earnings per share.

Did You Get It?

1. What creates financial leverage in a firm's capital structure?
2. How does financial leverage affect the volatility of firm earnings in response to changes in EBIT?
3. If the ratio of the percent change in earnings per share to the corresponding percent change in EBIT were 2, what percent change in earnings would you expect to follow a 15 percent decline in EBIT?

COMBINING OPERATING AND FINANCIAL LEVERAGE

Objective **4**

Calculate the firm's degree of operating leverage, financial leverage, and combined leverage.

Operating leverage causes changes in sales revenues to lead to even greater changes in EBIT. Additionally, changes in EBIT due to financial leverage translate into larger variations in both earnings per share (EPS) and the net income available to the common shareholders (NI), if the firm chooses to use financial leverage. It should be no surprise, then, to find out that combining operating and financial leverage causes rather large variations in earnings per share. This entire process is visually displayed in Figure 12-4.

Because the risk associated with possible earnings per share is affected by the use of combined, or total, leverage, it is useful to quantify the effect. To illustrate, we refer once more to Pierce Grain Company. The cost structure identified for Pierce Grain in our discussion of break-even analysis still holds. Furthermore, assume that plan B, which carried a 25 percent debt ratio, was chosen to finance the company's assets. Turn your attention to Table 12-6 to see how the effects of operating and financial leverage are combined.

FIGURE 12-4 Leverage and Earnings Fluctuations

How Did You Do?

ANALYZING THE COMBINED EFFECTS OF OPERATING AND FINANCIAL LEVERAGE

Peterson's CFO estimates that firm's revenues will increase by 20 percent, EBIT will increase by 30 percent, and earnings per share will rise 60 percent. Consequently, Peterson's operating leverage produces an increase in EBIT that is 1.5 times the 20 percent increase in sales, and earnings per share increase by 60 percent, which is twice the percent change in EBIT that is 30 percent. Once again, we see that operating and financial leverage interact in a multiplicative fashion. That is, the percent increase in earnings per share is 2 times the increase in EBIT, which is 1.5 times the increase in sales. The net result is that the percent increase in earnings per share is equal to $1.5 \times 2 = 3$ times the percent increase in sales. Consequently, the 20 percent increase in sales results in a 3×20 percent $= 60$ percent increase in earnings per share.

In Table 12-6 an increase in output for Pierce Grain from 30,000 to 36,000 units is analyzed. This increase represents a 20 percent rise in sales revenues. From our earlier discussion of operating leverage and the data in Table 12-6, we can see that this 20 percent increase in sales is magnified into a 120 percent rise in EBIT. Moreover, the 120 percent rise in EBIT induces a change in earnings per share and earnings available to the common shareholders of 150 percent. The upshot of the analysis is that the modest 20 percent rise in sales has been magnified to produce a 150 percent change in earnings per share.

Pierce Grain's use of both operating and financial leverage will cause any percentage change in sales (from the specific base level) to be magnified by a factor of 7.50 when the effect on earnings per share is computed. A 10 percent change in sales, for example, will result in a 75 percent change in earnings per share.

The total risk exposure the firm assumes can be managed by combining operating and financial leverage in different degrees. Knowing the various leverage measures will help you determine the proper level of overall risk that should be accepted. For example, if a high degree of business risk is inherent in the specific line of commercial activity, then a low amount of financial risk will minimize additional earnings fluctuations stemming from changes in the firm's sales. Conversely, the firm that by its very nature incurs a low level of fixed operating costs might choose to use a high degree of financial leverage in the hope of increasing earnings per share and the rate of return on its common equity.

TABLE 12-6   The Combined–Leverage Effect on Pierce Grain Company's Earnings per Share

ITEM	BASE SALES LEVEL, t	FORECAST SALES LEVEL, $t + 1$	PERCENTAGE CHANGE IN EARNINGS PER SHARE
Sales	$300,000	$360,000	+20%
Less: Total variable costs	180,000	216,000	
Revenue before fixed costs	$120,000	$144,000	
Less: Total fixed costs	100,000	100,000	
EBIT	$ 20,000	$ 44,000	+120%
Less: Interest expense	4,000	4,000	
Earnings before taxes (EBT)	$ 16,000	$ 40,000	
Less: Taxes at 50%	8,000	20,000	
Net income	$ 8,000	$ 20,000	+150%
Less: Preferred dividends	0	0	
Earnings available to common shareholders (EAC)	$ 8,000	$ 20,000	+150%
Number of common shares	1,500	1,500	
Earnings per share (EPS)	$ 5.33	$ 13.33	+150%

Finance at Work

THE ENRON LESSONS: LEVERAGE

The bankruptcy and failure of the Enron Corporation on December 2, 2001, shook the investment community to its very core and resulted in congressional hearings that led to new regulations with far-reaching implications. Enron's failure provides a sober warning to employees and investors and a valuable set of lessons for students of business. The lesson we offer here reaches far beyond corporate finance and touches on fundamental principles that have always been true but are sometimes forgotten.

Lesson: Even Good Firms Can Fail If They Use Too Much Leverage

Combine bad investments with too much debt and you have a recipe for financial disaster. Enron essentially superleveraged its assets by using off-balance-sheet debt in partnerships called special purpose entities (SPEs). These assets and liabilities (many of which were guaranteed by Enron) of the SPEs were not reported to the investment community, nor was the fact that Enron executives were running some of them. When Enron was forced to reveal its obligations to the SPEs when they became insolvent, it became insolvent and filed for bankruptcy.

Did You Get It?

1. How do operating and financial leverage interact to affect the volatility of a firm's earnings per share?

2. If a firm's operating and financial leverage are such that a 10 percent change in sales revenue produced a 20 percent change in EBIT, and a 10 percent change in EBIT led to a 20 percent change in earnings per share, what percentage change in earnings would you expect should revenues decline by 25 percent?

PLANNING THE FINANCING MIX

Given our understanding of both operating and financial leverage, we now direct our attention to the determination of an appropriate financing mix for the firm. First, we must distinguish between financial structure and capital structure. **Financial structure** is the *mix of all items that appear on the right-hand side of the company's balance sheet.* **Capital structure** is the *mix of the long-term sources of funds used by the firm.* The relationship between financial and capital structures can be expressed in equation form:

$$\text{(Financial structure)} - \text{(current liabilities)} = \text{capital structure} \tag{12-5}$$

To design a prudent financial structure, you need to answer these two questions:

1. What should the maturity composition of the firm's sources of fund be? In other words, how should a firm best divide its total fund sources between short- and long-term components?
2. In what proportions relative to the total should the various forms of permanent financing be utilized?

The major influence on the maturity structure of the financing plans is the nature of the assets owned by the firm. A company heavily committed to real capital investment, represented primarily by fixed assets on its balance sheet, should finance those assets with permanent (long-term) types of financial capital. Furthermore, the permanent portion of the firm's investment in current assets should likewise be financed with permanent capital. By contrast, assets held on a temporary basis should be financed with temporary sources. The present discussion assumes that the bulk of the company's current liabilities consists of temporary capital. Technically, that part of the firm's current liabilities that consists of the

Objective 5

Understand the concept of an optimal capital structure.

financial structure the mix of all funds sources that appears on the right-hand side of the balance sheet.

capital structure the mix of long-term sources of funds used by the firm. This is also called the firm's capitalization. The relative total (percentage) of each type of fund is emphasized.

TABLE 12-7 Balance Sheet

---

current portion of the firm's long-term debt plus any interest-bearing short-term debt should be part of the firm's capital structure. To simplify our discussion we will assume that there is no interest-bearing debt (e.g., bank loans on current portion of long-term debt).

Accordingly, our focus in this chapter is on answering the second of the two questions noted previously—this process is usually called *capital structure management*.

A firm's capital structure should mix the permanent sources of funds used by the firm in a manner that will maximize the company's common stock price, or, put differently, *minimize the firm's composite cost of capital*. We can call this proper mix of fund sources the **optimal capital structure**.

optimal capital structure
the capital structure that minimizes the firm's composite cost of capital (maximizes the common stock price) for raising a given amount of funds.

Table 12-7 looks at equation (12-5) in terms of a balance sheet. It helps us visualize the overriding problem of capital structure management. The sources of funds that give rise to financing fixed costs (long-term debt and preferred equity) must be combined with common equity in the proportions most suitable to the investment marketplace. If that mix can be found, then holding all other factors constant, the firm's common stock price will be maximized.

Obviously, taking on excessive financial risk can put the firm into bankruptcy proceedings. But using too little financial leverage results in an undervaluation of the firm's shares. The financial manager must know how to find the area of optimum financial leverage use—this will enhance share value, all other considerations held constant.

The rest of this chapter covers three main areas. First, we briefly discuss the theory of capital structure. Second, we examine the basic tools of capital structure management. We conclude with a real-world look at actual capital structure management.

Did You Get It?

1. What is the objective of capital structure management?
2. What is the key attribute that defines a firm's optimal capital structure?

Objective

Explain the main underpinnings of capital structure theory.

A QUICK LOOK AT CAPITAL STRUCTURE THEORY

An enduring controversy surrounds *capital structure theory* that relates to the effect financial leverage has on the overall cost of capital to the enterprise. The heart of the argument may be stated in the form of a question:

Can the Firm Affect Its Overall Cost of Funds, Either Favorably or Unfavorably, by Varying the Mixture of Financing Sources Used?

This controversy has taken many elegant forms in the finance literature and tends to appeal more to academics than financial practitioners. To emphasize the ingredients of capital structure theory that have practical applications for business financial management, we will pursue an intuitive, or nonmathematical, approach to reach a better understanding of the underpinnings of this cost of capital, or capital structure, argument.

The Importance of Capital Structure

It makes economic sense for the firm to strive to minimize the cost of using financial capital. Both capital costs and other costs, such as manufacturing costs, share a common characteristic in that they potentially reduce the size of the cash dividend that could be paid to common stockholders. Now, hold constant all factors that can affect share price except capital costs. If these capital costs can be kept at a minimum, the dividend stream flowing to the common stockholders will be maximized. This, in turn, will maximize the firm's common stock price.

The Analytical Setting

The essentials of the capital structure controversy are best highlighted within a framework that economists would call a "partial equilibrium analysis." In a partial equilibrium analysis, changes that do occur in several factors and have an impact on a certain key item are ignored to study the effect of changes in a main factor on that same item of interest. Here, two items are simultaneously of interest: (1) K_0, the firm's composite cost of capital, and (2) P_0, the market price of the firm's common stock. The firm's use of financial leverage is the main factor that is allowed to vary in the analysis. This means that important financial decisions, such as the firm's investing policy and dividend policy, are held constant throughout the discussion. We are concerned only with the effect changes in the financing mix have on the share price and capital costs.

Consider a rarified world in which the following conditions apply.

1. Corporate income is not subject to taxation.
2. Capital structures consist only of stocks and bonds.
3. Investors make homogeneous forecasts of net operating income (what we earlier called EBIT).
4. Securities are traded in perfect or efficient markets.

In this market setting, the direct answer to our question, "Can the firm affect its overall cost of funds, either favorably or unfavorably, by varying the mixture of financing sources used?" would be no. This view of capital structure importance was put into rather elegant form back in 1958 by two well-known financial economists, Franco Modigliani and Merton Miller, both of whom have been awarded the Nobel Prize in economics.

The Modigliani and Miller hypothesis, or the MM view, puts forth that within the perfect economic world previously described, the total market value of the firm's outstanding securities will be *unaffected* by the manner in which the right-hand side of the balance sheet is arranged. This means the sum of the market value of outstanding common stock plus outstanding debt will always be the same regardless of how much or little debt is actually used by the company. This MM view is sometimes called the *independence hypothesis*, as firm value is independent of capital structure design.[3]

The crux of this position on financing choice is illustrated in Figure 12-5. Here the firm's asset mix (the left-hand side of the balance sheet) is held constant. All that is different is the way the assets are financed. Under financing mix A, the firm funds 30 percent of its assets with common stock and the other 70 percent with bonds. Under financing mix B, the firm reverses this mix and funds 70 percent of the assets with common stock and only 30 percent with bonds. From our earlier discussions we know that financing mix A is the more heavily leveraged plan.

---

[3] See Franco Modigliani and Merton H. Miller, "The Cost of Capital, Corporation Finance, and the Theory of Investment," *American Economic Review* 48 (June 1958), pp. 261–97; Modigliani and Miller, "Corporate Income Taxes and the Cost of Capital: A Correction," *American Economic Review* 53 (June 1963), pp. 433–43; and Merton H. Miller, "Debt and Taxes," *Journal of Finance* 32 (May 1977), pp. 261–75. The Modigliani–Miller capital structure theories and positions are put into a longer and broader perspective in Merton H. Miller, "The Modigliani–Miller Propositions after Thirty Years," in Joel Stern and Donald Chew, eds., *The Revolution in Corporate Finance*, 3rd ed. (Malden, MA: Blackwell Publishers, 1998), pp. 99–110. A most readable review of the Modigliani–Miller propositions is provided by D. Gifford, Jr., "After the Revolution," *CFO*, Vol. 14, No. 7 (July 1998), pp. 75–79. This source is widely followed by practicing financial professionals.

FIGURE 12-5 Firm Value and Capital Structure Design

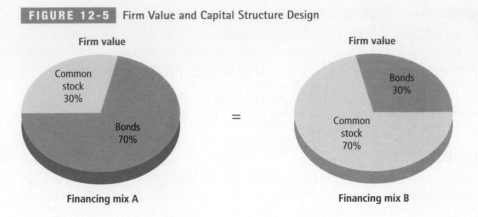

Remember Your Principles

The suggestion from capital structure theory that one capital structure is just as good as any other within a perfect ("pure") market framework relies directly on **Principle 1: The Risk–Return Trade-Off—We Won't Take On Added Risk Unless We Expect to Be Compensated with Additional Return**. This means that using more debt in the capital structure will not be ignored by investors in the financial markets. These rational investors will require a higher return on common stock investments in the firm that uses more leverage (rather than less) to compensate for the increased uncertainty stemming from the addition of the debt securities in the capital structure.

Notice, however, that the size of the "pies" in Figure 12-5 are exactly the same. The pie represents firm value—the total market value of the firm's outstanding securities. Thus, the total firm value associated with financing mix A equals that associated with financing mix B. Firm value is *independent* of the actual financing mix that has been chosen.

This implication is taken further in Figure 12-6 where we see that the firm's overall cost of capital, k_{wacc}, is unaffected by an increased use of financial leverage. If more debt is used with a cost of k_d in the capital structure, the cost of common equity, k_c, will rise at the same rate additional earnings are generated. This will keep the composite cost of capital to the corporation unchanged. Furthermore, because the overall cost of capital does not change with leverage use, neither will the firm's common stock price.

The lesson of this view on financing choices is that debt financing is not as cheap as it first appears to be because the composite cost of funds is constant over the full range of financial leverage use. The stark implication for financial officers is that one capital structure is just as good as any other.

FIGURE 12-6 Capital Costs and Financial Leverage: No Taxes—Independence Hypothesis

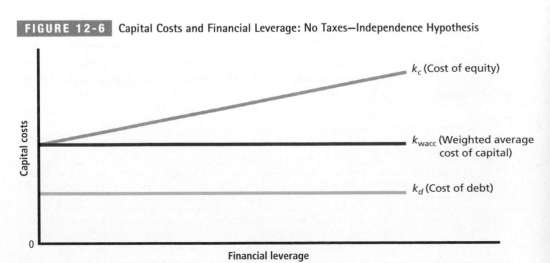

Recall, though, the strict economic world in which this viewpoint was developed. We next turn to a market and legal environment that relaxes the extreme assumptions.

The Moderate Position: Corporate Income Is Taxed and Firms May Fail

We turn now to a description of the cost of capital–capital structure relationship that has wide appeal to both business practitioners and academics. This moderate view (1) admits to the fact that interest expense is tax deductible and (2) acknowledges that the likelihood of bankruptcy and its costs are directly related to the company's use of financial leverage.

This portion of the analysis recognizes that corporate income is subject to taxation and interest expense is tax deductible for purposes of computing the firm's tax bill. In this environment, the use of debt financing can result in a higher total market value for the firm's outstanding securities. We see why subsequently.

Table 12-8 illustrates this important element of the U.S. system of corporate taxation. We assume that Skip's Camper Manufacturing Company has an expected level of earnings before interest and taxes (EBIT) of $2 million and faces a corporate tax rate (made simple for example purposes) of 50 percent. Two financing plans are analyzed. The first is an unleveraged capital structure. The other assumes that Skip's Camper has $8 million of bonds outstanding that carry an interest rate of 6 percent per year.

Notice that if corporate income were *not* taxed, then earnings before taxes of $2 million per year could be paid to shareholders in the form of cash dividends or to bond investors in the form of interest payments, or any combination of the two. This means that the *sum* of the cash flows that Skip's Camper could pay to its contributors of debt or equity is *not* affected by its financing mix.

When corporate income is taxed by the government, however, the sum of the cash flows made to all contributors of financial capital *is* affected by the firm's financing mix. Table 12-8 illustrates this point.

If Skip's Camper chooses the leveraged capital structure, the total payments to equity and debt holders will be $240,000 *greater* than under the all-common-equity capitalization. Where does this $240,000 come from? The answer is that the government's take, through taxes collected, is lower by that amount. This *difference, which flows to Skip's Camper security holders*, is called the **tax shield** on debt. In general, it may be calculated by equation (12-6), where r_d is the interest rate paid or interest tax savings on the debt, M is the principal amount of the debt, and T_c is the firm's marginal tax rate:

$$\text{Tax shield} = r_d(M)(T_c) \qquad (12\text{-}6)$$

The moderate position on the importance of capital structure presumes that the tax shield must have value in the marketplace. Accordingly, this tax benefit will increase the total market value of the firm's outstanding securities relative to the all-equity financing mix. Note that in this case financial leverage does affect firm value. Because the cost of capital is just the other side of the valuation coin, financial leverage also affects the firm's composite cost of capital. Can the firm increase firm value indefinitely and lower its cost of capital continuously by using more and more financial leverage? Common sense would tell us no! So would most financial managers and academicians. The acknowledgment of bankruptcy costs provides one possible rationale.

tax shield the element from the federal tax code that permits interest costs to be deductible when computing a firm's tax bill. The dollar difference (the shield) flows to the firm's security holders.

TABLE 12-8 Skip's Camper Cash Flows to All Investors—The Case of Taxes

	UNLEVERAGED CAPITAL STRUCTURE	LEVERAGED CAPITAL STRUCTURE
Expected level of net operating income	$2,000,000	$2,000,000
Less: Interest expense	0	480,000
Earnings before taxes	$2,000,000	$1,520,000
Less: Taxes at 50%	1,000,000	760,000
Earnings available to common stockholders	$1,000,000	$ 760,000
Expected payments to *all* security holders	$1,000,000	$1,240,000

> **Remember Your Principles**
>
> The preceding section on the tax deductibility of interest expense is a compelling example of **Principle 8: Taxes Bias Business Decisions**. We have just seen that corporations have an important incentive provided by the tax code to finance projects with debt securities rather than new issues of common stock. The interest expense on the debt issue is tax deductible. The common stock dividends are not tax deductible. So firms can indeed increase their total after-tax cash flows available to all investors in their securities by using financial leverage. This element of the U.S. tax code should also remind you of **Principle 3: Cash—Not Profits—Is King**.

The Likelihood of Firm Failure

The probability that the firm will be unable to meet the financial obligations identified in its debt contracts increases as more debt is employed. The highest costs would be incurred if the firm actually went into bankruptcy proceedings. Here, assets would be liquidated and often at distressed sale prices. If these assets do sell for something less than their perceived market values, both equity investors and debt holders could suffer losses. Other problems accompany bankruptcy proceedings. Lawyers and accountants have to be hired and paid. Managers must spend time preparing lengthy reports for those involved in the legal action. Moreover, all this distracts the firm's management from the efficient running of the business, and this causes missed opportunities and lost value.

Milder forms of financial distress also have their costs, as we have discussed. As the firm's financial condition weakens, creditors may take action to restrict normal business activity. Suppliers may not deliver materials on credit. Profitable capital investments may have to be forgone, and dividend payments may even be interrupted. At some point the expected cost of default will be large enough to outweigh the tax shield advantage of debt financing. The firm will turn to other sources of financing, mainly common equity (retained earnings).

Objective **7**

Understand and be able to graph the moderate position on capital structure importance.

THE MODERATE VIEW: THE SAUCER-SHAPED COST-OF-CAPITAL CURVE

This moderate view of the relationship between financing mix and the firm's cost of capital is depicted in Figure 12-7. The result is a saucer-shaped (or U-shaped) weighted-average-cost-of-capital curve, k_{wacc}. The firm's average cost of equity, k_c, is seen to rise over all posi-

FIGURE 12-7 Capital Costs and Financial Leverage: The Moderate View, Considering Taxes and Financial Distress

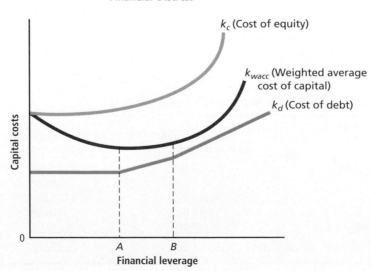

tive degrees of financial leverage use. For a while the firm can borrow funds at a relatively low after-tax cost of debt, k_d. Even though the cost of equity is rising, it does not rise at a fast enough rate to offset the use of the less-expensive debt financing. Thus, between points 0 and A on the financial-leverage axis, the average cost of capital declines, and stock price rises.

Eventually, however, the threat of financial distress causes the cost of debt to rise. In Figure 12-7 this increase in the cost of debt shows up in the after-tax average-cost-of-debt curve, k_d, at point A. Between points A and B, mixing debt and equity funds produces an average cost of capital that is (relatively) flat. The firm's **optimal range of financial leverage** lies between points A and B. *All capital structures between these two points are optimal because they produce the lowest composite cost of capital.* As we said earlier in this chapter, finding this optimal range of financing mixes is the objective of capital structure management.

Point B signifies the firm's debt capacity. **Debt capacity** is the *maximum proportion of debt the firm can include in its capital structure and still maintain its lowest composite cost of capital.* Beyond point B, additional fixed-charge capital can be attracted only at very costly interest rates. At the same time, this excessive use of financial leverage would cause the firm's cost of equity to rise at a faster rate than it did previously. The composite cost of capital would then rise quite rapidly, and the firm's stock price would decline.

FIRM VALUE AND AGENCY COSTS

In Chapter 1 we mentioned the notion of agency problems. Recall that agency problems give rise to agency costs, which tend to occur in business organizations because the owners of the firm do not run the business, managers do. Thus, the firm's managers can properly be thought of as agents of the firm's stockholders.[4] To ensure that agent-managers act in the stockholders' best interests requires that (1) they have proper incentives to do so and (2) their decisions are monitored. The incentives usually take the form of executive compensation plans and perquisites (or "perks"). The perquisites, though, might be a bloated support staff, country club memberships, luxurious corporate planes, or other amenities. Monitoring this requires that certain costs be borne by the stockholders, such as (1) bonding the managers, (2) auditing financial statements, (3) structuring the organization in unique ways that limit managerial decisions, and (4) reviewing the costs and benefits of management perquisites. This list is indicative, not exhaustive. The main point is that monitoring costs are ultimately covered by the owners of the company—its common stockholders.

Capital structure management also gives rise to agency costs. Agency problems stem from conflicts of interest, and capital structure management encompasses a natural conflict between stockholders and bondholders. Acting in the stockholders' best interests might cause managers to invest in extremely risky projects. Existing investors in the firm's bonds could logically take a dim view of such an investment policy. A change in the risk structure of the firm's assets would change the business-risk exposure of the firm. This could lead to a downward revision of the bond rating the firm currently enjoys. A lowered bond rating, in turn, would lower the current market value of the firm's bonds. Clearly, bondholders would be unhappy with this result.

To reduce this conflict of interest, the creditors (bond investors) and stockholders may agree to include several protective covenants in the bond contract. These bond covenants were discussed in more detail in Chapter 7, but essentially they may be thought of as restrictions on managerial decision making. Typical covenants restrict the payment of cash dividends on common stock, limit the acquisition or sale of assets, or limit further debt financing. To make sure managers comply with the protective covenants means that monitoring costs

---

optimal range of financial leverage the range of various capital structure combinations that yield the lowest overall cost of capital for the firm.

debt capacity the maximum proportion of debt that the firm can include in its capital structure and still maintain its lowest composite cost of capital.

Objective

Incorporate the concepts of agency costs and free cash flow into a discussion on capital structure management.

---

[4] Economists have studied the problems associated with control of the corporation for decades. An early, classic work on this topic was A. A. Berle, Jr., and G. C. Means, *The Modern Corporation and Private Property* (New York: Macmillan, 1932). The recent emphasis in corporate finance and financial economics stems from the important contribution of Michael C. Jensen and William H. Meckling, "Theory of the Firm: Managerial Behavior, Agency Costs, and Ownership Structure," *Journal of Financial Economics* 3 (October 1976), pp. 305–60. Professors Jensen and Smith have analyzed the bondholder–stockholder conflict in a very clear style. See Michael C. Jensen and Clifford W. Smith, Jr., "Stockholder, Manager, and Creditor Interests: Applications of Agency Theory," in Edward I. Altman and Marti G. Subrahmanyam, eds., *Recent Advances in Corporate Finance* (Homewood, IL: Irwin, 1985), pp. 93–131.

FIGURE 12-8 The Agency Costs of Debt: Trade-Offs

No protective bond covenants	Many protective bond covenants
High interest rates	Low interest rates
Low monitoring costs	High monitoring costs
No lost operating efficiencies	Many lost operating efficiencies

are incurred. Like all monitoring costs, they are borne by common stockholders. Furthermore, like many costs, they involve the analysis of an important trade-off.

Figure 12-8 displays some of the trade-offs involved with the use of protective bond covenants. Note (in the left panel of Figure 12-8) that the firm might be able to sell bonds that carry no protective covenants only by incurring very high interest rates. With no protective covenants, there are no associated monitoring costs. Also, there are no lost operating efficiencies, such as being able to move quickly to acquire a particular company in the acquisitions market. Conversely, restrictive covenants could reduce the explicit cost of the debt contract, but this would involve incurring significant monitoring costs and losing some operating efficiencies (which also translates into higher costs). When the debt issue is first sold, then a trade-off will be made.

Next, we have to consider the presence of monitoring costs at low and higher levels of leverage. When the firm operates at a low debt-to-equity ratio, there is little need for creditors to insist on a long list of bond covenants. The financial risk is just not there to require that type of activity. The firm will likewise benefit from low explicit interest rates when leverage is low. When the debt-to-equity ratio is high, however, it is logical for creditors to demand a great deal of monitoring. This increase in agency costs will raise the implicit cost (the true total cost) of debt financing. It seems logical, then, to suggest that monitoring costs will rise as the firm's use of financial leverage increases. Just as the likelihood of firm failure (financial distress) raises a company's overall cost of capital (k_{wacc}), so do agency costs. On the other side of the coin, this means that total firm value (the total market value of the firm's securities) will be *lower* because of agency costs. Taken together, the agency costs and the costs associated with financial distress argue in favor of the concept of an *optimal* capital structure for the individual firm.

This discussion can be summarized by introducing equation (12-7) for the market value of the leveraged firm.

$$\begin{matrix} \text{Market value of} \\ \text{leveraged firm} \end{matrix} = \begin{matrix} \text{market value of} \\ \text{unleveraged firm} \end{matrix} + \begin{matrix} \text{present value} \\ \text{of tax shields} \end{matrix} - \left(\begin{matrix} \text{present value} \\ \text{of financial} \\ \text{distress costs} \end{matrix} + \begin{matrix} \text{present value} \\ \text{of agency} \\ \text{costs} \end{matrix} \right) \quad (12\text{-}7)$$

The relationship expressed in equation (12-7) is presented graphically in Figure 12-9. There we see that the tax shield effect is dominant until point A is reached. After point A, the rising costs due to the likelihood of the firm's failure (financial distress) and agency costs cause the market value of the leveraged firm to decline. The objective for the financial manager here is to find point B by using all of his or her analytical skill; this must also include a good dose of seasoned judgment. At point B the actual market value of the leveraged firm is maximized, and its composite cost of capital (k_{wacc}) is at a minimum. The implementation problem is that the precise costs of financial distress and monitoring can be estimated only by subjective means; a definite mathematical solution is not available. Thus, planning the firm's financing mix always requires good decision making and management judgment.

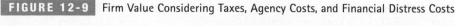

FIGURE 12-9 Firm Value Considering Taxes, Agency Costs, and Financial Distress Costs

Agency Costs, Free Cash Flow, and Capital Structure

In 1986, Professor Michael C. Jensen further extended the concept of agency costs into the area of capital structure management. The contribution revolves around a concept that Jensen labels "free cash flow," which he defines as follows:

> Free cash flow is cash flow in excess of that required to fund all projects that have positive net present values when discounted at the relevant cost of capital.[5]

Jensen then proposed that substantial free cash flow can lead to misbehavior by managers and poor decisions that are not in the best interests of the firm's common stockholders. In other words, managers have an incentive to hold onto the free cash flow and have "fun" with it, rather than "disgorge" it, say, in the form of higher cash dividend payments.

But all is not lost. This leads to what Jensen calls his "control hypothesis" for using debt. This means that by leveraging up (taking on debt), the firm's shareholders will enjoy increased control over their management team. For example, if the firm issues new debt and uses the proceeds to retire outstanding common stock, then managers are obligated to pay out cash to service the debt—this simultaneously reduces the amount of free cash flow available to them to have fun with.

Remember Your Principles

The discussions on agency costs, free cash flow, and the control hypothesis for debt creation return us to **Principle 7: The Agency Problem—Managers Won't Work for the Firm's Owners Unless It's in Their Best Interest**. The control hypothesis put forth by Jensen suggests that managers will work harder for shareholder interests when they have to "sweat it out" to meet contractual interest payments on debt securities. But we also learned that managers and bond investors can have a conflict that leads to agency costs associated with using debt capital. Thus, the theoretical benefits that flow from minimizing the agency costs of free cash flow by using more debt will cease when the rising agency costs of debt exactly offset those benefits. You can see how very difficult it is, then, for financial managers to identify precisely their true optimal capital structure.

[5] Michael C. Jensen, "Agency Costs of Free Cash Flow, Corporate Finance, and Takeovers," *American Economic Review* 76 (May 1986), pp. 323–29.

We can also refer to this motive for financial leverage use as the "threat hypothesis." Managers work under the threat of financial failure; therefore, according to the "free cash flow theory of capital structure," they work more efficiently. This is supposed to reduce the agency costs of free cash flow, which will in turn be recognized by the marketplace in the form of greater returns on the common stock.

Note that the free cash flow theory of capital structure does not give a theoretical solution to the question of just how much financial leverage is enough. Nor does it suggest how much leverage is too much. It is a way of thinking about why shareholders and their boards of directors might use more debt to control managerial behavior and decisions. The basic decision tools of capital structure management still have to be utilized. They are presented later in this chapter.

Managerial Implications

Where does our examination of capital structure theory leave us? The upshot is that determining the firm's financing mix is centrally important to the financial manager because the firm's stockholders are affected by capital structure decisions. At the very least, and before bankruptcy costs and agency costs become detrimental, the tax shield effect will cause the shares of a leveraged firm to sell at a higher price than they would if the company had avoided debt financing. Because both the risk of failure and agency costs accompany the excessive use of leverage, the financial manager must exercise caution in the use of fixed-charge capital. This problem of searching for the optimal range of financial leverage is our next task.[6]

You have now developed a workable knowledge of capital structure theory. This makes you better equipped to search for your firm's optimal capital structure. Several tools are available to help you in this search process and simultaneously help you make prudent financing choices. These tools are decision oriented. They help us answer the question, "The next time we need $20 million, should we issue common stock or sell long-term bonds?"

Did You Get It?

1. What is the basic controversy surrounding capital structure theory?
2. Who are MM and what did they have to say about capital structure?
3. Explain the independence hypothesis as it relates to capital structure management.
4. Explain the moderate view of the relationship between a firm's financing mix and its average cost of capital.
5. How do agency costs and free cash flow relate to capital structure management?

Objective **9**

Use the basic tools of capital structure management.

THE BASIC TOOLS OF CAPITAL STRUCTURE MANAGEMENT

We will review two basic tools that are commonly used in the evaluation of capital structure decisions. The first is the EBIT-EPS chart, which provides a way to visualize the effects of alternative capital structures on both the level and volatility of the firm's earnings per share (EPS). The second tool we review entails the analysis of the capital structures of comparable firms through the use of financial leverage ratios. Here we use ratios to standardize capital structure information as we did when we discussed financial ratios in Chapter 3 so that we can compare the capital structures of similar firms.

---

[6] The relationship between capital structure and enterprise valuation by the marketplace continues to stimulate considerable research output. The complexity of the topic is reviewed in Stewart C. Myers, "The Capital Structure Puzzle," *Journal of Finance* 39 (July 1984), pp. 575–92. Ten useful papers are contained in Benjamin M. Friedman, ed., *Corporate Capital Structures in the United States* (Chicago: National Bureau of Economic Research and University of Chicago Press, 1985). A more recent treatment is Stewart C. Myers, "Still Searching for Optimal Capital Structure," in Joel Stern and Donald Chew, eds., *The Revolution in Corporate Finance*, 3rd ed. (Malden, MA: Blackwell Publishers, 1998), pp. 120–30.

EBIT-EPS Analysis

➤ EXAMPLE

Assume that plan B presented earlier in Table 12-4 is the existing capital structure for the Pierce Grain Company. Furthermore, the asset structure of the firm is such that EBIT is expected to be $20,000 per year for a very long time. A capital investment is available to Pierce Grain that will cost $50,000. Acquisition of this asset is expected to raise the projected EBIT level to $30,000 permanently. The firm can raise the needed cash by (1) selling 500 shares of common stock at $100 each or (2) selling new bonds that will net the firm $50,000 and carry an interest rate of 8.5 percent. These capital structures and corresponding EPS amounts are summarized in Table 12-9.

At the projected EBIT level of $30,000, the EPS for the common stock and debt alternatives are $6.50 and $7.25, respectively. Both are considerably above the $5.33 that would occur if the new project were rejected and the additional financial capital were not raised. Based on a criterion of selecting the financing plan that will provide the highest EPS, the bond alternative is favored. But what if the basic business risk to which the firm is exposed causes the EBIT level to vary over a considerable range? Can we be sure that the bond alternative will *always* have the higher EPS associated with it? The answer, of course, is no. When the EBIT level is subject to uncertainty, a graphic analysis of the proposed financing plans can provide useful information to the financial manager.

Before we launch into an analysis of the relationship between earnings per share (EPS) and EBIT for alternative capital structures, we need to remind ourselves as to why this is important. Specifically, in light of our discussions of capital structure theory you might ask, "Why should the firm's owners care about the effects of the capital structure on earnings per share (EPS)?" One possible response to this question is that corporate CEOs and boards of directors are very sensitive to the earnings numbers they report to Wall Street. The reason we offered earlier for this sensitivity relates to the perception of investors that the level of a

TABLE 12-9 Analyzing Pierce Grain Company's Financing Choices

PART A: CAPITAL STRUCTURES

EXISTING CAPITAL STRUCTURE		WITH NEW COMMON STOCK FINANCING		WITH NEW DEBT FINANCING	
Long-term debt at 8%	$ 50,000	Long-term debt at 8%	$ 50,000	Long-term debt at 8%	$ 50,000
Common stock	150,000	Common stock	200,000	Long-term debt at 8.5%	50,000
				Common stock	150,000
Total liabilities and equity	$200,000	Total liabilities and equity	$250,000	Total liabilities and equity	$250,000
Common shares outstanding	1,500	Common shares outstanding	2,000	Common shares outstanding	1,500

PART B: PROJECTED EPS LEVELS

	EXISTING CAPITAL STRUCTURE	WITH NEW COMMON STOCK FINANCING	WITH NEW DEBT FINANCING
EBIT	$20,000	$30,000	$30,000
Less: Interest expense	4,000	4,000	8,250
Earnings before taxes (EBT)	$16,000	$26,000	$21,750
Less: Taxes at 50%	8,000	13,000	10,875
Net income	$ 8,000	$13,000	$10,875
Less: Preferred dividends	0	0	0
Earnings available to common shareholders	$ 8,000	$13,000	$10,875
EPS	$ 5.33	$ 6.50	$ 7.25

firm's reported EPS signals important information about the firm's future prospects. For example, when a firm announces that its earnings will fall short of analyst expectations, this often triggers a revision in investor expectations regarding the future earnings prospects for the firm. This downward revision, in turn, results in a drop in the firm's stock price. Thus, corporate executives are very aware of the importance investors attach to earnings and take this information into account when considering the design of the firm's capital structure.

Graphic Analysis

The EBIT-EPS analysis chart allows the decision maker to visualize the impact of different financing plans on EPS over a range of EBIT levels. The relationship between EPS and EBIT is linear. All we need, therefore, to construct the chart is two points for each alternative. Part B of Table 12-9 already provides us with one of these points. The answer to the following question for each choice gives us the second point: At what EBIT level will the EPS for the plan be exactly zero? If the EBIT level *just covers* the plan's financing costs (on a before-tax basis), then EPS will be zero. For the stock plan, an EPS of zero is associated with an EBIT of $4,000. The $4,000 is the interest expense incurred under the existing capital structure. If the bond plan is elected, the interest costs will be the present $4,000 plus $4,250 per year arising from the new debt issue. An EBIT level of $8,250, then, is necessary to provide a zero EPS with the bond plan.

The EBIT-EPS analysis chart representing the financing choices available to the Pierce Grain Company is shown as Figure 12-10. EBIT is charted on the horizontal axis and EPS on the vertical axis. The intercepts on the horizontal axis represent the before-tax equivalent financing charges related to each plan. The straight lines for each plan tell us the EPS amounts that will occur at different EBIT amounts.

Notice that the bond-plan line has a *steeper slope* than the stock-plan line. This ensures that the lines for each financing choice will *intersect*. Above the intersection point, the EPS for the plan with greater leverage will exceed that for the plan with lesser leverage. The intersection point, circled in Figure 12-10, occurs at an EBIT level of $21,000 and produces EPS of $4.25 for each plan. When EBIT is $30,000, notice that the bond plan produces EPS of $7.25, and the stock plan, $6.50. Below the intersection point, the EPS with the stock plan will *exceed* that of the more highly leveraged bond plan. The steeper slope of the bond-plan line indicates that with greater leverage, EPS is more sensitive to EBIT changes.

FIGURE 12-10   EBIT–EPS Analysis Chart for Pierce Grain Company

Computing Indifference Points

The point of intersection in Figure 12-10 is called the **EBIT-EPS indifference point**. It identifies the *EBIT level at which the EPS will be the same regardless of the financing plan chosen by the financial manager*. This indifference point, sometimes called the break-even point, has major implications for financial planning. At EBIT amounts in excess of the EBIT indifference level, the more heavily leveraged financing plan will generate a higher EPS. At EBIT amounts below the EBIT indifference level, the financing plan involving less leverage will generate a higher EPS. It is important, then, to know the EBIT indifference level.

We can find it graphically, as in Figure 12-10. At times it may be more efficient, though, to calculate the indifference point directly. This can be done by using the following equation:

EBIT-EPS indifference point the level of earnings before interest and taxes (EBIT) that will equate earnings per share (EPS) between two different financing plans.

$$\underbrace{\frac{(\text{EBIT} - I)(1 - T_c) - P}{S_s}}_{\text{EPS: STOCK PLAN}} = \underbrace{\frac{(\text{EBIT} - I)(1 - T_c) - P}{S_b}}_{\text{EPS: BOND PLAN}} \tag{12-8}$$

where S_s and S_b are the number of common shares outstanding under the stock and bond plans, respectively; I is interest expense; T_c is the firm's income tax rate; and P is preferred dividends paid. In the present case, P is zero because there is no preferred stock outstanding. If preferred stock is associated with one of the financing alternatives, keep in mind that the preferred dividends, P, are not tax deductible. Equation (12-8) does take this fact into consideration.

For the present example, we calculate the indifference level of EBIT as

$$\frac{(\text{EBIT} - \$4,000)(1 - 0.5) - 0}{2,000} = \frac{(\text{EBIT} - \$8,250)(1 - 0.5) - 0}{1,500}$$

When the expression above is solved for EBIT, we obtain $21,000. If EBIT turns out to be $21,000, then EPS will be $4.25 under both plans.

A Word of Caution

Ok, now we know that using more financial leverage *may* provide higher firm earnings if EBIT is above the break-even point. But this is not all that we need to take away from this analysis. For example, assume that EBIT is expected to be above the break-even point 99.9 percent of the time for two alternative capital structure policies. Does this mean that we should automatically select the higher leverage option? The answer, as you might have suspected, is no, and here's the logic for this answer. The higher the firm's use of financial leverage, the steeper the slope of the EBIT-EPS line, which means the firm will experience larger swings in EPS for any given change in EBIT. CEOs and corporate boards care about these swings for the reason we noted earlier. That is, if the firm fails to meet its earnings expectations, investors may revise their expectations for the firm's future earnings prospects downward, at which point the share price might suffer. So, higher financial leverage increases the likelihood that an unanticipated swing in the firm's EBIT might have a very detrimental effect on the reported EPS, and this is a real source of concern.

How then are we to interpret and use the EBIT-EPS chart to analyze capital structure design issues? The answer, like many tools of financial analysis, entails the use of managerial judgment. The EBIT-EPS chart is simply a tool that can be used to learn about the consequences of using more or less financial leverage. The decision as to whether to use more or less financial leverage must be made after weighing all the factors that impinge on a firm's capital structure decision. For example, in the next section we look at the use of comparative financial ratios, which indicate the degree of similarity of the firm's capital structure to others in its same industry, or peer group.

Comparative Leverage Ratios

In Chapter 4 we explored the overall usefulness of financial ratio analysis. Leverage ratios, one of the categories of financial ratios, are identified in that chapter. We emphasize here that the computation of leverage ratios is one of the basic tools of capital structure management.

Finance at Work

THE WALT DISNEY COMPANY ON CAPITAL COSTS AND CAPITAL STRUCTURE

At the end of fiscal year 1998, the Walt Disney Company had a total market capitalization of $65 billion; this placed it among the 40 largest corporations in the United States, whereas its sales revenues of $23.0 billion placed it 53rd on the 1999 *Fortune* 500 list. This multinational giant with 117,000 employees provides several real examples of the capital structure concepts presented in this chapter.

In the following discussion from Disney management, notice how the firm (1) relates capital costs to shareholder value; (2) believes in the "prudent degree of leverage" concept; (3) is concerned with its interest coverage ratio—measured as earnings before net interest, taxes, depreciation, and amortization, or EBITDA, divided by net interest expense; and (4) strives to maintain a minimum desired or target bond rating. Within the accompanying graph you see that Disney's coverage ratio for fiscal year 1998 of EBITDA to net interest expense is 8.1 times (that is, $5,019 million/$622 million).

Disney's solid balance sheet allows the company to borrow at attractive rates, helping to reduce the overall cost of capital and thereby creating value for shareholders. As of year-end, Disney maintained total borrowings of approximately $12 billion and a debt-to-total-capital ratio of 38%. The company believes that this level of debt represents a prudent degree of leverage, which provides for substantial financial flexibility to borrow should sound business opportunities present themselves. As measured by the ratio of earnings before net interest, taxes, depreciation,

and amortization (EBITDA) to net interest expense, the company covered its interest costs by a factor of more than eight times for the year ended September 30.

The company monitors its cash flow, interest coverage, and its debt-to-total-capital ratio with the long-term goal of maintaining a strong single-A or better credit rating.

Source: The Walt Disney Company, *1998 Annual Report*, p. 12.

Two types of leverage ratios must be computed when a financing decision faces the firm. We call these *balance-sheet leverage ratios* and *coverage ratios*. The firm's balance sheet supplies inputs for computing the balance-sheet leverage ratios. In various forms these balance-sheet metrics compare the firm's use of funds supplied by creditors with those supplied by owners.

Inputs to the coverage ratios generally come from the firm's income statement. At times the external analyst may have to refer to balance-sheet information to construct some of these needed estimates. On a privately placed debt issue, for example, some fraction of the current portion of the firm's long-term debt might have to be used as an estimate of that issue's sinking fund. Coverage ratios provide estimates of the firm's ability to service its financing contracts. High coverage ratios, compared with a standard, imply unused debt capacity.

In reality, we know that EBIT might be expected to vary over a considerable range of outcomes. For this reason the coverage ratios should be calculated several times, each at a different level of EBIT. If this is accomplished over all possible values of EBIT, a probability distribution for each coverage ratio can be constructed. This provides the financial manager with much more information than simply calculating the coverage ratios based on the expected value of EBIT.

Industry Norms

The comparative leverage ratios have utility only if they can be compared with some standard. Generally, corporate financial analysts, investment bankers, commercial bank loan officers, and bond-rating agencies rely on industry classes to compute "normal" ratios. Although industry groupings may actually contain firms whose basic business-risk exposure differs widely, the practice is entrenched in American business behavior. At the very least, then, the financial officer must be interested in industry standards because almost everybody else is.

Several published studies indicate that capital structure ratios vary in a significant manner among industry classes.[7] For example, random samplings of the common equity ratios of large retail firms seem to differ statistically from those of major steel producers. The major steel producers use financial leverage to a lesser degree then do the large retail organizations. On the whole, firms operating in the *same* industry tend to exhibit capital structure ratios that cluster around a central value that we call a norm. The degree of business risk varies from industry to industry as well. As a consequence, the capital structure norms vary from industry to industry.

This is not to say that all companies in the industry will maintain leverage ratios "close" to the norm. For instance, firms that are very profitable might display high coverage ratios and high balance-sheet leverage ratios. The moderately profitable firm, though, might find such a posture unduly risky. Here the usefulness of industry-normal leverage ratios is clear. If the firm chooses to deviate substantially from the accepted values for the key ratios, it must have a sound reason.

Did You Get It?

1. Explain the meaning of the EBIT-EPS indifference point.
2. How are various leverage ratios and industry norms used in capital structure management?

A GLANCE AT ACTUAL CAPITAL STRUCTURE MANAGEMENT

We now examine some opinions and practices of financial executives that reinforce the importance of capital structure management.

Figure 12-11 reports a portion of the results of a survey of 392 corporate executives about the factors they considered to be either important or very important in deciding whether to use debt in their firm's capital structure. Specifically, we report the top 10 factors that the corporate executives as a group felt were most important factors influencing the decision to issue debt.

These 10 factors provide some practical guidance to the financial manager who is wrestling with capital structure design and management issues. Let's briefly consider each factor to see why it is relevant.

Financial Flexibility   When a firm needs to raise additional funds, its bargaining position is better if it has options or choices. For example, firms that have used very little debt in the past will find it easier to borrow or sell new shares of stock than firms that have borrowed heavily.

Credit Rating   Dropping a notch in the rating system leads to an increase in the firm's borrowing costs, so managers like to avoid this if at all possible.[8] Moreover, sometimes firms have contractual provisions inserted into some of their other debt agreements that require the firm to maintain a particular credit rating. For example, Enron's bankruptcy was triggered by the firm dropping one credit rating, which put the firm below investment-grade status. The firm had billions of dollars in outstanding debt that contained a covenant requiring them to maintain a BBB or higher rating.

Insufficient Internal Funds   It has long been known that firms tend to follow a priority list when raising new funds that has been referred to as a "pecking order."[9] The

---

[7] See, for example, Eli Schwartz and J. Richard Aronson, "Some Surrogate Evidence in Support of the Concept of Optimal Financial Structure," *Journal of Finance* 22 (March 1967), pp. 10–18; David F. Scott, Jr., "Evidence on the Importance of Financial Structure," *Financial Management* 1 (Summer 1972), pp. 45–50; and David F. Scott, Jr., and John D. Martin, "Industry Influence on Financial Structure," *Financial Management* 4 (Spring 1975), pp. 67–73.

[8] We discussed bond ratings in Chapter 7.

[9] S. C. Myers and N. S. Majluf, "Corporate financing and investment decisions when firms have information that investors do not have," *Journal of Financial Economics* 35 (1994), 99–122.

FIGURE 12-11   Factors That Affect the Decision to Issue Debt

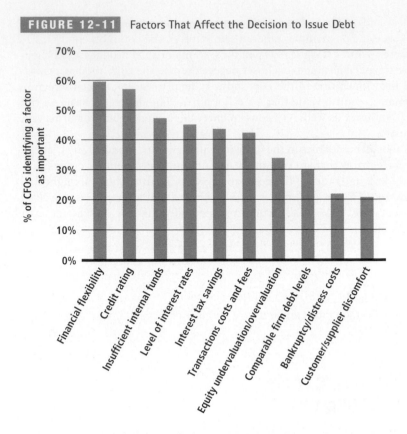

Source: John Graham and Campbell Harvey, "How do CFOs make capital budgeting and capital structure decisions?," *Journal of Applied Corporate Finance*, Volume 15, Number 1, Spring 2002, 8–23. (Used with permission)

order in which firms typically finance their operations begins with internally generated profits, followed by debt financing, and, finally, by issuing new equity.

Level of Interest Rates   Other things being the same, firms prefer to borrow when they feel interest rates are low relative to their expectations. For example, when interest rates are historically very low, a CFO may feel more inclined to enter into long-term debt agreements. However, there is little evidence that a CFO, or anyone for that matter, has any talent for knowing when rates are low and about to rise, or high and about to fall. Nonetheless, all that is required for this factor to be considered important is a strong opinion about the future path of interest rates.

Interest Tax Savings   Interest expense, unlike dividends paid to shareholders, is a tax-deductible expense. This tax-savings feature serves as a subsidy to corporate borrowing and makes debt appear cheap relative to alternative sources of financing.

Transaction Costs and Fees   When a firm chooses between debt and equity, it faces very different costs of issuing the two types of securities. For example, debt holders receive interest and principal payments as prescribed in the debt contract (indenture). This type of security is relatively straightforward, and its value hinges on the creditworthiness of the firm. However, when a firm issues equity, there are no rules prescribing how much will be paid back to the buyers of the stock. This means that it can be much more costly to entice an investor to become a stockholder than to entice them to loan money to the firm. Thus, the differentially higher costs of issuing equity make it less attractive as a source of financing.

Equity Undervaluation/Overvaluation   Earlier we mentioned that CFOs often try to time their debt offerings to take advantage of abnormally low interest rates. The same holds true for equity offerings. For example, if the CFO thinks that the firm's shares of stock are undervalued, he or she will want to borrow money rather than sell new shares and risk the price of the shares falling further. Once again, there is no evidence that corporate executives are any better at forecasting their own share prices than they are at predicting the future of interest rates, but they only have to think they are good at it to believe it is an important factor.

Comparable Firm Debt Levels   Firms in similar businesses tend to have similar capital structures. This is made doubly important by virtue of the fact that lenders and credit-rating agencies often compare a firm's debt ratios to that of comparable firms when deciding credit terms and ratings.

Bankruptcy/Distress Costs   The more debt a firm has used in the past, the higher is the likelihood that the firm will at some point face financial distress and possibly fail. This risk forms the basis for the firm's credit rating.

Customer/Supplier Discomfort   An important source of financial distress brought on by the use of debt financing comes in the form of pressures from both the firm's customers (who fear that financial distress may interrupt their source of supply) and the firm's suppliers (who fear that financial distress may interrupt an important source of demand for their goods and services). The latter is compounded further if the supplier has provided the firm with trade credit, which is at risk if the firm fails.

After reading through the discussion of each of the 10 factors, you are probably beginning to think that capital structure management is more art than science. In other words, there simply is no magic formula that you can use to solve for the optimal capital structure. However, you should be gaining an appreciation for the basic considerations that go into the judgment call that the CFOs ultimately must make and that drives the capital structure of firms

Selected comments from financial executives point to the widespread use of target debt ratios.

Did You Get It?

1. Identify several factors that influence the decision to issue debt.
2. Why is capital structure design both an art and a science?

FINANCE AND THE MULTINATIONAL FIRM: BUSINESS RISK AND GLOBAL SALES

Objective **10**

Understand how business risk and global sales impact the multinational firm.

Early in this chapter we defined business risk as the relative dispersion (variability) in the firm's expected earnings before interest and taxes (EBIT). And when we discussed operating leverage, we learned that changes or shocks to the firm's overall sales level will cause a greater percentage change in EBIT if the company has fixed operating costs. Thus, any event that causes sales to fluctuate will impact a firm's business risk and its resulting EBIT.

Business risk is both multidimensional and international. It is directly affected by several factors, including (1) the sensitivity of the firm's product demand to general economic conditions, (2) the degree of competition to which the firm is exposed, (3) product diversification, (4) growth prospects, and (5) global sales volume and production output. The latter factor is especially important to the multinational firm, and some seek to take advantage of it in an aggressive manner.

Consider the Coca-Cola Company. In his statement to shareholders published in 1998, Mr. M. Douglas Ivester, CEO and chairman of Coke's board, commented on the firm's commercial strategy in both China and Russia.[10] He said, "In China, the world's largest market, our volume soared another 30 percent in 1997. But the average resident of China still drinks just six of our products a year—certainly a business in its infancy." Notice that although Coke's presence in China increases its total business-risk exposure, Mr. Ivester views this exposure as a commercial opportunity for the firm.

In his discussion of the Russian market, Mr. Ivester offered, "In Russia, where we took the lead over our largest competitor in 1996, we widened that lead to 3-to-1 in 1997; we

[10] The Coca-Cola Company, *Annual Report*, 1997, pp. 5–6.

opened four more plants there on October 1, bringing our system's Russian investment to $650 million and pointing to strong future growth." Here we see that Coke is both cultivating the Russian consumer and simultaneously investing in plant and equipment there. Thus, Coke's broad commercial strategy, which impacts business risk, also encompasses the capital budgeting decision discussed earlier in this text.

Did You Get It?

1. Identify several factors that directly affect a firm's business risk.
2. How might a firm's commercial strategy be influenced by its presence in foreign markets?

Summary

Objective **1**

Understand the difference between business risk and financial risk.

In this chapter we studied the process of arriving at an appropriate financial structure for the firm, and we examined tools that can assist the financial manager in this task. We are concerned with assessing the variability in the firm's residual earnings stream (either earnings per share or earnings available to the common shareholders) as a result of the use of operating and financial leverage. This assessment builds on the tenets of break-even analysis.

We then dealt with the design of the firm's financing mix, emphasizing the management of the firm's permanent sources of funds—that is, its capital structure. The objective of capital structure management is to arrange the company's sources of funds so that its common stock price is maximized.

Objective **2**

Use the technique of break-even analysis in a variety of analytical settings.

A break-even analysis permits the financial manager to determine the quantity of output or the level of sales that will result in an EBIT level of zero. This means the firm has neither a profit nor a loss before any tax considerations. The effect of price changes, cost structure changes, or volume changes on profits (EBIT) can be studied. But to do so it is necessary to first classify the firm's costs as fixed or variable. Not all costs fit neatly into one of these two categories. Over short planning horizons, though, the preponderance of costs can be assigned to either the fixed or variable classification. Once the cost structure has been identified, the break-even point can be found.

Objective **3**

Distinguish among the financial concepts of operating leverage, financial leverage, and combined leverage.

Operating leverage is the responsiveness of the firm's EBIT to changes in sales revenues. It arises from the firm's use of fixed operating costs. When fixed operating costs are present in the company's cost structure, increases in sales are magnified into even greater changes in EBIT. But leverage is a two-edged sword. For example, when sales decrease by some percentage, the negative impact on EBIT is again even larger.

A firm employs financial leverage when it finances a portion of its assets with securities bearing a fixed rate of return. The presence of debt and/or preferred stock in the company's financial structure means that it is using financial leverage. When financial leverage is used, changes in EBIT translate into larger changes in earnings per share. Very simply, the firm's use of financial leverage makes its earnings per share more sensitive to changes in EBIT higher. All other things equal, the more fixed-charge securities the firm employs in its financial structure, the greater its financial leverage. Clearly, EBIT can rise or fall. If it falls, and financial leverage is used, the firm's shareholders endure negative changes in earnings per share that are larger than the relative decline in EBIT. Again, leverage is a two-edged sword.

Objective **4**

Calculate the firm's degree of operating leverage, financial leverage, and combined leverage.

Firms use operating and financial leverage in various degrees. The joint use of operating and financial leverage is reflected in the percentage change in earnings per share divided by the percentage change in sales. This measure indicates the combined effects of financial leverage on top of operating leverage.

Objective **5**

Understand the concept of an optimal capital structure.

Can the firm affect its composite cost of capital by altering its financing mix? Attempts to answer this question have surrounded capital structure theory for over 3 decades. Those taking extreme positions say that the firm's stock price is either unaffected or continually affected as the firm infinitely increases its reliance on leverage. However, in the real world, interest expense is tax deductible, and market imperfections operate to restrict the amount of fixed-income obligations a firm can issue. Consequently, most financial officers and financial academics subscribe to the concept of an optimal capital structure. The optimal capital structure minimizes the firm's composite cost of capital. Searching for a proper range of financial leverage, then, is an important financial management activity.

Objective **6**

Explain the main underpinnings of capital structure theory.

Complicating the manager's search for an optimal capital structure are conflicts that lead to agency costs. A natural conflict exists between stockholders and bondholders (the agency costs of debt). To reduce excessive risk taking by managers on behalf of stockholders, it may be necessary to include several protective covenants in bond contracts that serve to restrict managerial decision making.

Another type of agency cost is related to "free cash flow." Managers, for example, have an incentive to hold onto free cash flow and enjoy it, rather than pay it out in the form of higher cash dividend payments. This conflict between managers and stockholders leads to the concept of the *free cash flow theory of capital structure*. This same theory is also known as the *control hypothesis* and the *threat hypothesis*. The ultimate resolution of these agency costs affects the specific form of the firm's capital structure.

The decision to use debt financing in the firm's capital structure causes two types of financial-leverage effects. The first is the added variability in the earnings-per-share stream that accompanies the use of fixed-charge securities. The second financial-leverage effect relates to the level of earnings per share (EPS) at a given EBIT under a specific capital structure. Via an EBIT-EPS analysis, the decision maker can inspect the impact of alternative financing plans on EPS over a full range of EBIT levels.

A second tool of capital structure management is the calculation of comparative leverage ratios. Comparing these ratios with industry standards enables the financial officer to determine if the firm's key ratios are in line with accepted practice.

CFO indicate that several factors influence the decision to issue debt. The top two are the firm's financial flexibility and its credit rating. If the firm has the flexibility to choose either debt or equity, then it is in a better financial position. Maintaining the firm's credit rating reflects the CFO's recognition that interest costs vary inversely with the firm's credit rating. If the firm has AA credit, then dropping to A or lower will drive up the firm's cost of borrowing.

Business risk is both multidimensional and international. It is directly affected by several factors, including (1) the sensitivity of the firm's product demand to general economic conditions, (2) the degree of competition to which the firm is exposed, (3) product diversification, (4) growth prospects, and (5) global sales. On the last factor, we explored how the Coca-Cola Company related the firm's commercial strategy to include sales prospects in the huge markets of China and Russia.

Objective **7**

Understand and be able to graph the moderate position on capital structure importance.

Objective **8**

Incorporate the concepts of agency costs and free cash flow into a discussion on capital structure management.

Objective **9**

Use the basic tools of capital structure management.

Objective **10**

Understand how business risk and global sales impact the multinational firm.

Key Terms

Business risk   377

Capital structure   389

Debt capacity   395

Direct costs (see variable costs)   380

EBIT-EPS indifference point   401

Financial leverage   385

Financial structure   389

Fixed costs   379

Indirect costs (see fixed costs)   379

Operating leverage   383

Optimal capital structure   390

Optimal range of financial leverage   395

Tax shield   393

Total revenue   381

Variable costs   380

Volume of output   381

Review Questions

12-1. Distinguish between business risk and financial risk. What gives rise to, or causes, each type of risk?

12-2. Define the term *financial leverage*. Does the firm use financial leverage if preferred stock is present in its capital structure?

12-3. Define the term *operating leverage*. What type of effect occurs when the firm uses operating leverage?

12-4. A manager in your firm decides to employ a break-even analysis. Of what shortcomings should this manager be aware?

12-5. A break-even analysis assumes linear revenue and cost functions. In reality, these linear functions deviate over large output and sales levels. Why?

12-6. Define the following terms:

    a. Financial structure

    b. Capital structure

    c. Optimal capital structure

    d. Debt capacity

12-7. What is the primary weakness of using EBIT-EPS analysis as a financing decision tool?

12-8. What is the objective of capital structure management?

12-9. Why might firms whose sales levels change drastically over time choose to use debt only sparingly in their capital structures?

12-10. What does the term *independence hypothesis* mean as it applies to capital structure theory?

12-11. Many CFOs believe that the firm's composite cost of capital is saucer-shaped or U-shaped. What does this mean?

12-12. Define the EBIT-EPS indifference point.

12-13. Explain how industry norms might be used by the financial manager in the design of the company's financing mix.

12-14. Define the term *free cash flow*.

12-15. What is meant by the *free cash flow theory of capital structure*?

12-16. In almost every instance, what funds source do managers use first?

Self-Test Problem

(The solution to the following problem is provided at the end of the chapter.)

ST-1. (*Fixed costs and the break-even point*) Bonaventure Manufacturing expects to earn $210,000 next year after taxes. Sales will be $4 million. The firm's single plant is located on the outskirts of Olean, New York. The firm manufactures a combined bookshelf and desk unit used extensively in college dormitories. These units sell for $200 each and have a variable cost per unit of $150. Bonaventure experiences a 30 percent tax rate.

    a. What are the firm's fixed costs expected to be next year?
    b. Calculate the firm's break-even point in both units and dollars.

Study Problems

12-1. (*Leverage analysis*) You have developed the following income statement for the Hugo Boss Corporation. It represents the most recent year's operations, which ended yesterday.

Sales	$ 50,439,375
Variable costs	(25,137,000)
Revenue before fixed costs	$ 25,302,375
Fixed costs	(10,143,000)
EBIT	$ 15,159,375
Interest expense	(1,488,375)
Earnings before taxes	$ 13,671,000
Taxes at 50%	(6,835,500)
Net income	$ 6,835,500

Your supervisor in the controller's office has just handed you a memorandum asking for written responses to the following questions:

    a. What is the firm's break-even point in sales dollars?
    b. If sales should increase by 30 percent, by what percent would earnings before taxes (and net income) increase?

12-2. (*EBIT-EPS analysis*) Two inventive entrepreneurs have interested a group of venture capitalists in backing a new business project. The proposed plan would consist of a series of international retail outlets to distribute and service a full line of ingenious home garden tools. The stores would be located in high-traffic cities in Latin America such as Panama City, Bogotá, São Paulo, and Buenos Aires. Two financing plans have been proposed by the entrepreneurs. Plan A is an all-common-equity structure. Five million dollars would be raised by selling 160,000 shares of common stock. Plan B would involve the use of long-term debt financing. Three million dollars would be raised by marketing bonds with an effective interest rate of 14 percent. Under the alternative, another $2 million would be raised by selling 64,000 shares of common stock. With both plans, $5 million is needed to launch the new firm's operations. The debt funds raised under plan B are considered to have no fixed maturity date, because this portion of financial leverage is thought to be a permanent part of the company's capital structure. The two promising entrepreneurs have decided to use a 35 percent tax rate in their analysis, and they have hired you on a consulting basis to do the following:

    a. Find the EBIT indifference level associated with the two financing proposals.

    b. Prepare income statements for the two plans that proves EPS will be the same regardless of the plan chosen at the EBIT level found in part a.

12-3. (*EBIT-EPS analysis*) Four recent liberal arts graduates have interested a group of venture capitalists in backing a new business enterprise. The proposed operation would consist of a series of retail outlets to distribute and service a full line of vacuum cleaners and accessories. These stores would be located in Dallas, Houston, and San Antonio. Two financing plans have been proposed by the graduates. Plan A is an all-common-equity structure. Two million dollars would be raised by selling 100,000 shares of common stock. Plan B would involve the use of long-term debt financing. One million dollars would be raised by marketing bonds with an effective interest rate of 8 percent. Under this alternative, another $1 million would be raised by selling 50,000 shares of common stock. With both plans, then, $2 million is needed to launch the new firm's operations. The debt funds raised under plan B are considered to have no fixed maturity date, in that this portion of financial leverage is thought to be a permanent part of the company's capital structure. The fledgling executives have decided to use a 30 percent tax rate in their analysis, and they have hired you on a consulting basis to do the following:

    a. Find the EBIT indifference level associated with the two financing proposals.

    b. Prepare an income statement that proves EPS will be the same regardless of the plan chosen at the EBIT level found in part a.

12-4. (*Leverage analysis*) You have developed the following income statement for your corporation. It represents the most recent year's operations, which ended yesterday.

Sales	$45,750,000
Variable costs	22,800,000
Revenue before fixed costs	$22,950,000
Fixed costs	9,200,000
EBIT	$13,750,000
Interest expense	1,350,000
Earnings before taxes	$12,400,000
Taxes at 50%	6,200,000
Net income	$ 6,200,000

Your supervisor in the controller's office has just handed you a memorandum asking for written responses to the following questions:

    a. What is the firm's break-even point in sales dollars?

    b. If sales should increase by 25 percent, by what percent would earnings before taxes (and net income) increase?

12-5. (*Break-even point and operating leverage*) Footwear Inc. manufactures a complete line of men's and women's dress shoes for independent merchants. The average selling price of its finished product is $85 per pair. The variable cost for this same pair of shoes is $58. Footwear Inc. incurs fixed costs of $170,000 per year.

    a. What is the break-even point in pairs of shoes for the company?

    b. What is the dollar sales volume the firm must achieve to reach the break-even point?

    c. What would be the firm's profit or loss at the following units of production sold: 7,000 pairs of shoes? 9,000 pairs of shoes? 15,000 pairs of shoes?

12-6. (*Leverage analysis*) You have developed the following analytical income statement for your corporation. It represents the most recent year's operations, which ended yesterday.

Sales	$30,000,000
Variable costs	13,500,000
Revenue before fixed costs	$16,500,000
Fixed costs	8,000,000
EBIT	$ 8,500,000
Interest expense	1,000,000
Earnings before taxes	$ 7,500,000
Taxes at 50%	3,750,000
Net income	$ 3,750,000

Your supervisor in the controller's office has just handed you a memorandum asking for written responses to the following questions:

    a. What is the firm's break-even point in sales dollars?

    b. If sales should increase by 25 percent, by what percent would earnings before taxes (and net income) increase?

12-7. (*Break-even point and selling price*) Parks Castings Inc. will manufacture and sell 200,000 units next year. Fixed costs will total $300,000, and variable costs will be 60 percent of sales.

    a. The firm wants to achieve a level of earnings before interest and taxes of $250,000. What selling price per unit is necessary to achieve this result?

    b. Set up an analytical income statement to verify your solution to part a.

12-8. (*Operating leverage*) Rocky Mount Metals Company manufactures an assortment of wood-burning stoves. The average selling price for the various units is $500. The associated variable cost is $350 per unit. Fixed costs for the firm average $180,000 annually.

    a. What is the break-even point in units for the company?

    b. What is the dollar sales volume the firm must achieve to reach the break-even point?

    c. What is the degree of operating leverage for a production and sales level of 5,000 units for the firm? (Calculate to three decimal places.)

    d. What will be the projected effect on earnings before interest and taxes if the firm's sales level should increase by 20 percent from the volume noted in part c?

12-9. (*EBIT-EPS analysis*) A group of retired college professors has decided to form a small manufacturing corporation. The company will produce a full line of traditional office furniture. Two financing plans have been proposed by the investors. Plan A is an all-common-equity alternative. Under this agreement, 1 million common shares will be sold to net the firm $20 per share. Plan B involves the use of financial leverage. A debt issue with a 20-year maturity period will be privately placed. The debt issue will carry an interest rate of 10 percent, and the principal borrowed will amount to $6 million. The corporate tax rate is 50 percent.

    a. Find the EBIT indifference level associated with the two financing proposals.

    b. Prepare an analytical income statement that proves EPS will be the same regardless of the plan chosen at the EBIT level found in part a.

    c. Prepare an EBIT-EPS analysis chart for this situation.

    d. If a detailed financial analysis projects that long-term EBIT will always be close to $2.4 million annually, which plan will provide for the higher EPS?

12-10. (*EBIT-EPS analysis*) Four recent liberal arts graduates have interested a group of venture capitalists in backing a new business enterprise. The proposed operation would consist of a series of retail outlets to distribute and service a full line of vacuum cleaners and accessories. These stores would be located in Dallas, Houston, and San Antonio. Two financing plans have been proposed by the graduates. Plan A is an all-common-equity structure. Two million dollars would be raised by selling 80,000 shares of common stock. Plan B would involve the use of long-term debt financing. One million dollars would be raised by marketing bonds with an effective interest rate of 12 percent. Under the alternative, another $1 million would be raised by selling 40,000 shares of common stock. With both plans, then, $2 million is needed to launch the new firm's operations. The debt funds raised under plan B are considered to have no fixed maturity date, in that this portion of financial leverage is thought to be a permanent part of the company's capital structure. The fledgling executives have decided to use a 40 percent tax rate in their analysis, and they have hired you on a consulting basis to do the following:

    a. Find the EBIT indifference level associated with the two financing proposals.

    b. Prepare an analytical income statement that proves EPS will be the same regardless of the plan chosen at the EBIT level found in part a.

12-11. (*Assessing leverage use*) Some financial data for three corporations are displayed here.

MEASURE	FIRM A	FIRM B	FIRM C	INDUSTRY NORM
Debt ratio	20%	25%	40%	20%
Times interest covered	8 times	10 times	7 times	9 times
Price–earnings ratio	9 times	11 times	6 times	10 times

    a. Which firm appears to be excessively leveraged?

    b. Which firm appears to be employing financial leverage to the most appropriate degree?

    c. What explanation can you provide for the higher price–earnings ratio enjoyed by firm B as compared with firm A?

Web Works

12-WW1. The Coca-Cola Company consistently publishes an outstanding and useful annual report. It can be found at **www.coca-cola.com** or accessed through **www.reportgallery.com.** Coca-Cola is one of the few firms of which we are aware that actually includes a "glossary" in its annual report. Many of the entries in its glossary are of a financial nature. Check out (a) dividend payout ratio, (b) economic profit, (c) operating margin, and (d) return on common equity. Then see how its listings stack up against those noted in the glossary to this text. You will notice that the resulting definitions are very close in each case. **Key Points:** As you can see, we don't make up this stuff. Such concepts drive the decision making of financial executives. Thus, you want to make these concepts a part of your everyday vocabulary.

12-WW2. This exercise focuses on capital structure management and its direct relationship to corporate capital costs. We will work with actual relationships from the Coca-Cola Company (ticker symbol KO). Find the 10K report for Coke at **www.reportgallery.com.** There you will find that Coke's long-term debt was rated Baa by Moody's and BBB by Standard & Poor's as of December 28, 2003. One year earlier, by the way, Coke's debt by Moody's was actually higher at Aa. Next go to **www.federalreserve.com** to ascertain recent yield levels for Aaa-rated long-term bonds. Recall that you want to access the Fed's H.15 report on "Selected Interest Rates." Finally, go to **www.cnnfn.com** and click on "markets." The latter site will allow you to do some bond research of your own and find out what the current yield is on bonds rated Aa. **Then answer:** How many basis points (a basis point is one one-hundredth of 1 percent) would Coke financial management gain if its bonds were rated Aaa rather than Aa? Then, using the sources noted previously, how many basis points would the firm give up if its long-term debt rating were lowered to Baa? **The Point:** You now understand the importance of bond ratings to corporate costs of capital.

12-WW3. The Federal Reserve Bank of St. Louis maintains an outstanding Web site at **www.stlouisfed.org.** It is a fertile source for financial and economic time series data. Go to the St. Louis Fed site and click on "Economic Research." Once you get there, click on "Economic-Data-FRED II." The latter acronym stands for "Federal Reserve economic data." Once you have pulled up FRED II, under "categories" click on the category labeled "Business/Fiscal." This will enable you to find the S&P 500 Composite Total Return (calculated by assuming monthly reinvestment of dividends). Inspect the direction of the index from August 2000 through December 2002. **The question:** Over the 2001–2002 time period, do you think nonfinancial corporate businesses raised more cash by issuing new corporate bonds or by issuing new corporate equities? **Hint:** You can verify your answer by going to any Federal Reserve Web site and searching for the statistical release Z.1, "Flow of Funds Accounts of the United States."

Mini Case

1. Imagine that you were hired recently as a financial analyst for a relatively new, highly leveraged ski manufacturer located in the foothills of Colorado's Rocky Mountains. Your firm manufactures only one product, a state-of-the-art snow ski. The company has been operating up to this point without much quantitative knowledge of the business and financial risks it faces.

Ski season just ended, however, so the president of the company has started to focus more on the financial aspects of managing the business. He has set up a meeting for next week with the CFO, Maria Sanchez, to discuss matters such as the business and financial risks faced by the company. Accordingly, Maria has asked you to prepare an analysis to assist her in her discussions with the president.

As a first step in your work, you compiled the following information regarding the cost structure of the company:

Output level	80,000 units
Operating assets	$4,000,000
Operating asset turnover	8 times
Return on operating assets	32%
Degree of operating leverage	6 times
Interest expense	$600,000
Tax rate	35%

As the next step, you need to determine the break-even point in units of output for the company. One of your strong points has been that you always prepare supporting work papers, which show how you arrived at your conclusions. You know Maria would like to see these work papers to facilitate her review of your work. Therefore, you will have the information you require to prepare an analytical income statement for the company. You are sure that Maria would also like to see this statement. In addition, you know that you need it to be able to answer the following questions. You also know Maria expects you to prepare, in a format that is presentable to the president, answers to the following questions to serve as a basis for her discussions with the president.

    a. What is the firm's break-even point in sales dollars?

    b. If sales should increase by 30 percent (as the president expects), by what percentage would EBT (earnings before taxes) and net income increase?

    c. Prepare another income statement, this time to verify the calculations from part b.

2. Camping USA Inc. has only been operating for 2 years in the outskirts of Albuquerque, New Mexico, and is a new manufacturer of a top-of-the-line camping tent. You are starting an internship as assistant to the chief financial officer of the company, and the owner and CEO, Tom Charles, has decided that this is the right time to know more about the business and financial risks his company must deal with. For this, the CFO has asked you to prepare an analysis to support him in his next meeting with Tom Charles a week from today.

To make the required calculations, you have put together the following data regarding the cost structure of the company:

Output level	120,000 units
Operating assets	$6,000,000
Operating asset turnover	12 times
Return on operating assets	48%
Degree of operating leverage	10 times
Interest expense	$720,000
Tax rate	42%

The CFO has instructed you to first determine the break-even point in units of output for the company. He requires that you prepare supporting documents, which demonstrate how you arrived at your conclusion and can facilitate his review of your work. Accordingly, you are required to have the information needed to prepare an analytical income statement for the company to be presented to the CFO. In a format that is acceptable for a meeting discussion with the CEO, you also need to prepare answers to the following questions:

    a. What is the firm's break-even point in sales dollars?

    b. If sales should increase by 40 percent, by what percentage would EBT (earnings before taxes) and net income increase?

    c. Prepare another income statement, this time to verify the calculations from part d.

Self-Test Solution

ST-1.

a. $[(P \cdot Q) - [(V \cdot Q) + F]](1 - .3) = \$210,000$

$[(\$4,000,000) - (\$3,000,000) - F](.7) = \$210,000$

$(\$1,000,000 - F)(.7) = \$210,000$

$\$700,000 - .7F = \$210,000$

$.7F = \$490,000$

$F = \underline{\underline{\$700,000}}$

Fixed costs next year, then, are expected to be $700,000.

b. $Q_B = \dfrac{F}{P - V} = \dfrac{\$700,000}{\$50} = \underline{\underline{14,000}} \text{ units}$

$S^* = \dfrac{F}{1 - \dfrac{VC}{S}} = \dfrac{\$700,000}{1 - 0.75} = \dfrac{\$700,000}{0.25} = \underline{\underline{\$2,800,000}}$

The firm will break even (EBIT = 0) when it sells 14,000 units. With a selling price of $200 per unit, the break-even sales level is $2,800,000.

After reading this chapter, you should be able to:

1. Describe the trade-off between paying dividends and retaining the profits within the company.

2. Explain the relationship between a corporation's dividend policy and the market price of its common stock.

3. Describe practical considerations that may be important to the firm's dividend policy.

4. Distinguish among the types of dividend policies corporations frequently use.

5. Specify the procedures a company follows in administering the dividend payment.

6. Describe why and how a firm might pay noncash dividends (stock dividends and stock splits) instead of cash dividends.

7. Explain the purpose and procedures related to stock repurchases.

8. Understand the relationship between a policy of low dividend payments and international capital budgeting opportunities that confront the multinational firm.

CHAPTER 13

Dividend Policy and Internal Financing

Corporate stock repurchases are rapidly replacing dividend payments as the preferred method for companies to return cash to their stockholders. Microsoft, General Electric, and American Greetings Corporation have all recently announced big stock buyback programs, and they are not alone. For example, in 2004, Microsoft announced that its board of directors approved a plan to buy back up to $30 billion of the company's stock over the course of 4 years and to pay a special one-time dividend of $3 per share. CEO Steve Balmer described his thinking on the decision in the following way:

"We are confident in our long-term ability to grow revenue, profits, and shareholder value through our innovation and execution. We have been successful in addressing a significant portion of our ongoing legal exposure, and all seven of our businesses are growing. We will continue to make major investments across all our businesses and maintain our position as a leading innovator in the industry, but we can now also provide up to $75 billion in total value to shareholders over the next 4 years."[1]

In addition to the share-repurchasing plan and one-time dividend of $3 per share, Microsoft essentially doubled its annual dividend of $0.16 per share by raising the quarterly dividend to $0.08 per share. Under the plan, the shareholders reap up to $75 billion over 4 years, assuming that quarterly dividends continue to be paid at the new $0.08 level.

[1] Press Release, Microsoft Corp., July 20, 2004.

Because the goal of a firm should be to maximize the value, or price, of the firm's common stock, the success or failure of managerial decisions can be evaluated only in light of their impact on the price. We observed that the company's investment (Chapters 9 and 10) and financing decisions (Chapter 12) can increase the value of the firm. As we look at the firm's policies regarding dividends and internal financing (how much of the company's financing comes from cash flows generated internally), we return to the same basic question: Can managers influence the price of the firm's stock, in this case through its dividend policies? After addressing this important question, we then look at the practical side of the question: What practices do managers commonly follow when making decisions about paying or not paying a dividend to the firm's stockholders? We conclude with a discussion of the multinational firm that chooses to follow a policy of low dividend payments but is confronted, then, with the prospect of exploring international markets for high net present value projects.

Objective **1**

Describe the trade-off between paying dividends and retaining the profits within the company.

dividend payout ratio the amount of dividends relative to the company's net income or earnings per share.

KEY TERMS

Before taking up the particular issues relating to dividend policy, we must understand several key terms and interrelationships.

A firm's dividend policy includes two basic components. First, the **dividend payout ratio** indicates the *amount of dividends paid relative to the company's earnings*. For instance, if the dividend per share is $2, and the earnings per share are $4, the payout ratio is 50 percent ($2/$4). The second component is the stability of the dividends over time. As you will learn later in the chapter, dividend stability can be almost as important to the investor as the amount of dividends received.

In formulating a dividend policy, the financial manager faces trade-offs. Assuming that management has already decided how much to invest and has chosen its debt–equity mix for financing the firm's investments, the decision to pay a large dividend means simultaneously deciding to retain less of the firms profits; this in turn results in a greater reliance on external equity financing. Conversely, given the firm's investment and financing decisions, a small dividend payment corresponds to high profit retention, making it less necessary to generate funds externally. These trade-offs, which are fundamental to our discussion, are illustrated in Figure 13-1.

Did You Get It?

1. Provide a financial executive a useful definition of the term *dividend payout ratio*.
2. How does the firm's actual dividend policy affect its need for externally generated financial capital?

FIGURE 13-1   Dividend-versus-Retention Trade-Offs

DOES A FIRM'S DIVIDEND POLICY AFFECT THE COMPANY'S STOCK PRICE?[2]

Objective **2**

Explain the relationship between a corporation's dividend policy and the market price of its common stock.

What is a sound rationale or motivation for dividend payments? Put another way, given the firm's capital-budgeting and borrowing decisions, what is the effect of the firm's dividend policies on the stock price? *Does a high dividend payment decrease a stock's value, increase it, or make no real difference?*

At first glance, we might reasonably conclude that a firm's dividend policy is important. We have already (in Chapter 8) pointed out that the value of a stock is equal to the present value of its future dividends. Why else do so many companies pay dividends, and why else is a page in the *Wall Street Journal* devoted to dividend announcements? How can we not conclude that dividend policies are important? You might be surprised to learn that the dividend question has been a controversial issue for more than 3 decades. Economist Fischer Black, some 30 years ago, called it the "dividend puzzle." In his words:

> Why do corporations pay dividends? Why do investors pay attention to dividends? Perhaps the answers to these questions are obvious. Perhaps the answers are not so obvious. I claim the answers to these questions are not obvious at all. The harder we look at the dividend picture, the more it seems like a puzzle, with pieces that just don't fit together. What should the individual investor do about dividends in his portfolio? We don't know. What should the corporation do about dividend policy? We don't know.[3]

Twenty years later, in 1996, economist Peter Bernstein reexamined the "puzzle that fascinated Fischer Black."[4] Bernstein concluded the role of dividend policy in creating shareholder value is still very much a puzzle.

Three Basic Views

Some would argue that the amount of a dividend is irrelevant and any time spent on the decision is a waste of energy. Others contend that a high dividend results in a high stock price. Still others take the view that dividends actually hurt the value of stocks.

Before we delve into the various theories, or "views," on the dividend policy question, we need to be very careful about the conditions under which we pose the question. Specifically, we begin with the basic assumption that the firm plans to undertake all positive *NPV* investment opportunities *regardless* of whether it pays dividends or not. This is critical because if we allow the decision to pay a dividend to interfere with the firm's decision to undertake a good investment, then the policy obviously matters to the firm's stockholders. So, assuming that the firm will make the right set of investment decisions, why might the company's dividend policy matter?

View 1: A Firm's Dividend Policy Is Irrelevant

Much of the controversy about the dividend issue is based in time-honored disagreements between the academic and professional communities. Experienced practitioners tend to believe that stock prices change as a result of dividend announcements and, therefore, see dividends as important. Professors often argue that the seemingly apparent relationship between dividends and stock prices may be an illusion.[5]

The position that dividends are not important rests on two preconditions. First, we must assume that the firm's investment and borrowing decisions have already been made and that

---

[2] The concepts of this section draw heavily from Donald H. Chew, Jr., ed., "Do Dividends Matter? A Discussion of Corporate Dividend Policy," in *Six Roundtable Discussions of Corporate Finance with Joel Stern* (New York: Quorum Books, 1986), pp. 67–101; and a book of readings edited by Joel M. Stern and Donald H. Chew, Jr., *The Revolution in Corporate Finance* (New York: Basil Blackwell, 1986). A later discussion on the firm's dividend policy, but with the same conclusions as the other articles just listed, is Michael J. Barclay, Clifford W. Smith, and Ross L. Watts, "The Determinants of Corporate Leverage and Dividend Policies," *Journal of Applied Corporate Finance* 7, no. 4 (Winter 1995), pp. 4–19.

[3] Fischer Black, "The Dividend Puzzle," *Journal of Portfolio Management* 2 (Winter 1976), pp. 5–8.

[4] Peter L. Bernstein, "Dividends: The Puzzle," *Journal of Applied Corporate Finance* 9, no. 1 (Spring 1996), pp. 16–22.

[5] For an excellent presentation of this issue, see Merton Miller, "Can Management Use Dividends to Influence the Value of the Firm?" in Stern and Chew, eds., *The Revolution in Corporate Finance* (New York: Basil Blackwell, 1986), pp. 299–305.

perfect capital markets
an assumption that allows one to study the effect of dividend decisions in isolation. It assumes that (1) investors can buy and sell stocks without incurring any transaction costs, such as brokerage commissions; (2) companies can issue stocks without any cost of doing so; (3) there are no corporate or personal taxes; (4) complete information about the firm is readily available; (5) there are no conflicts of interest between management and stockholders; and (6) financial distress and bankruptcy costs are nonexistent.

these decisions will not be altered by the amount of any dividend payments. Second, **perfect capital markets** must exist, which means that *(1) investors can buy and sell stocks without incurring any transaction costs, such as brokerage commissions; (2) companies can issue stocks without any cost of doing so; (3) there are no corporate or personal taxes; (4) complete information about the firm is readily available; (5) there are no conflicts of interest between managers and stockholders; and (6) financial distress and bankruptcy costs are nonexistent.*

The first assumption—that the firm has already made its investment and financing decisions—simply keeps us from confusing the issues. We want to know the effect of dividend decisions on a stand-alone basis, without mixing in other decisions. The second assumption, that of perfect markets, also allows us to study the effect of dividend decisions in isolation, much as a physicist studies motion in a vacuum to avoid the influence of friction.

Given these assumptions, the effect of a dividend decision on share price may be stated unequivocally: *There is no relationship between dividend policy and stock value.* One dividend policy is as good as another. In the aggregate, investors are concerned only with *total* returns from investment decisions; they are indifferent to whether these returns come from capital gains or dividend income. They also recognize that the dividend decision is really a choice of financing strategy. That is, to finance growth, the firm (a) may choose to issue stock, allowing internally generated funds (profits) to be used to pay dividends, or (b) may use internally generated funds to finance its growth, paying less in dividends but not having to issue stock. In the first case, shareholders receive dividend income; in the second case, the value of their stocks should increase. Thus, the nature of the return is the only difference; total returns should be about the same.

View 2: High Dividends Increase Stock Values

The belief that a firm's dividend policy is unimportant implicitly assumes that an investor is indifferent about whether the increased income comes through capital gains (stock price increase) or comes through dividends. However, dividends are more predictable than capital gains. Managers can control dividends, but they cannot dictate the price of the stock. Investors are less certain of receiving income from capital gains than from dividends. The incremental risk associated with capital gains relative to dividend income implies a higher required rate for discounting a dollar of capital gains than for discounting a dollar of dividends. In other words, we would value a dollar of expected dividends more highly than a dollar of expected capital gains. We might, for example, require a 14 percent rate of return for a stock that pays its entire return from dividends, but a 20 percent return for a high-growth stock that pays no dividends. This view, which says *dividends are more certain than capital gains*, has been called the **bird-in-the-hand dividend theory**.

bird-in-the-hand dividend theory
the view that dividends are more certain than capital gains.

The position that dividends are less risky than capital gains, and should, therefore, be valued differently, is not without its critics. If we hold to our basic decision not to let the firm's dividend policy influence its investment and capital-mix decisions, the company's operating cash flows, in both expected amount and variability, are unaffected by its dividend policy. Because the dividend policy has no impact on the volatility of the company's overall cash flows, it has no impact on the riskiness of the firm.

Increasing a firm's dividend does not reduce the basic riskiness of the stock; rather, if a dividend payment requires managers to issue new stock, it only transfers risk *and* ownership from the current owners to new owners. We would have to acknowledge that the current investors who receive the dividend trade an uncertain capital gain for a "safe" asset (the cash dividend). However, if risk reduction is the only goal, the investor could have kept the money in the bank and not bought the stock in the first place.

We might find fault with this bird-in-the-hand dividend theory, but there is still a strong perception among many investors and professional investment advisers that dividends are important. They frequently argue their case based on their own personal experience, as expressed by one investment adviser:

> In advising companies on dividend policy, we're absolutely sure on one side that the investors in companies like the utilities and the suburban banks want dividends. We're absolutely sure on the other side that . . . the high-technology companies should have no dividends. For the high earners—the ones that have a high rate of return like 20 percent or more than their cost

Remember Your Principles

The previous discussion specifying the "bird-in-the-hand" theory between the relationship of stock price and the firm's dividend policy relates directly to **Principle 2: The Time Value of Money—A Dollar Received Today Is Worth More Than a Dollar Received in the Future**. This theory suggests that because the dollar of dividends is received today it should be valued more highly than an uncertain capital gain that might be received in the future. The fundamental premise of this position is that the cash dividend in your hand (placed there today by the firm's payout policy) is more certain (less risky) than a possible capital gain. Many practitioners adhere to this theory; but many also adhere to the theory that is advanced in the next section. If nothing else, because it is controversial, a dividend policy is important to the firm and its stockholders. And, in reality, many companies do pay cash dividends. Cash dividends are ubiquitous, so they are discussed in depth.

of capital—we think they should have a low payout ratio. We think a typical industrial company which earns its cost of capital—just earns its cost of capital—probably should be in the average [dividend payout] range of 40 to 50 percent.[6]

View 3: Low Dividends Increase Stock Values

The third view of how dividends affect stock price argues that dividends actually hurt the investors. This belief has largely been based on the difference in the tax treatment of dividends versus capital gains. Contrary to the perfect-markets assumption of no taxes, most investors do pay income taxes. For these taxpayers, the objective is to maximize the *after-tax* return on an investment relative to the risk assumed. This is done by *minimizing* the effective tax rate on the income and, whenever possible, by *deferring* the payment of taxes.

Like most tax code complexities, Congress over the years has changed whether capital gains are taxed at a lower or similar rate to "earned income." Think of a water faucet being randomly turned on and then off. From 1987 through 1992, no federal tax advantage was provided for capital gains income relative to dividend income. A revision in the tax code that took effect beginning in 1993 did provide a preference for capital gains income. Then the Taxpayer Relief Act of 1997 made the difference (preference) even more favorable for capital gains as opposed to cash dividend income. For some taxpayers, if a minimum holding period had been reached, the tax rate applied to capital gains was reduced to 20 percent from the previous level of 28 percent. But wait: Then in 2003, Congress again felt the need to change the tax code as it pertained to both dividend income and capital gains income. On May 28, President Bush signed into law the Jobs and Growth Tax Relief Reconciliation Act. Part of the impetus for this act was the recession that commenced in 2001 and the slow rate of job creation that followed that recession.

In a nutshell, this 2003 act lowered the top tax rate on dividend income to 15 percent from a previous top rate of 38.6 percent and also lowered the top rate paid on realized long-term capital gains to the same 15 percent from a previous 20 percent. Thus, you can see that the so-called investment playing field was (mostly) leveled for dividend income relative to qualifying capital gains. This rather dramatic change in the tax code will immediately remind you of **Principle 8: Taxes Bias Business Decisions**. In effect, a major portion of the previous bias against paying cash dividends to investors was mitigated. But not all of it, as is pointed out next.

Actually, a different benefit exists for capital gains returns relative to dividend income. Taxes on dividend income are paid when the dividend is received, whereas taxes on price appreciation (capital gains) are deferred until the stock is actually sold. Thus, when it comes to tax considerations, many investors prefer the retention of a firm's earnings—in expectation of a later capital gain—as opposed to the near-term payment of cash dividends. Again, if earnings are retained within the firm, hopefully the stock price increases, but the increase is not taxed until the stock is sold.

Although the majority of investors are subject to taxes, certain investment companies, trusts, and pension plans are not when it comes to their dividend income. Also, for tax purposes,

[6] From a discussion by John Childs, an investment adviser at Kidder Peabody, in Chew, ed., "Do Dividends Matter?" in *Six Roundtable Discussions of Corporate Finance with Joel Stern* (New York: Quorum Books, 1986), pp. 83–84.

a corporation can generally exclude 70 percent of the dividend income it receives from another corporation. In these cases, investors will prefer dividends over capital gains.

To summarize, when it comes to taxes, we want to maximize our *after*-tax return, as opposed to our *before*-tax return. Investors try to defer taxes whenever possible. Stocks that allow tax deferral (low dividends–high capital gains) will possibly sell at a premium relative to stocks that require current taxation (high dividends–low capital gains). This suggests that a policy of paying low or no dividends will result in a higher stock price. That is, high dividends hurt investors, whereas low dividends and high retention help investors. This is the logic of the advocates of the low-dividend policy. It does presume that the firm's management has a roster of positive net present value projects that will put the dollars retained to productive use. However, as pointed out, the 2003 act lowered the taxes on dividends to such a great extent that this logic can now be reasonably questioned.

Improving Our Thinking

We have now looked at three views on dividend policy. Which is right? The argument that dividends are irrelevant is difficult to refute, given the perfect-market assumptions. However, in the real world, it is not always easy to feel comfortable with such an argument. Conversely, the high-dividend philosophy, which measures risk by how we split the firm's cash flows between dividends and retained earnings, is not particularly appealing when studied carefully. The third view, which is essentially a tax argument against high dividends, is persuasive. Even today, although the preferential tax rate for capital gains is limited, the "deferral advantage" of capital gains is still alive and well. However, if low dividends are so advantageous and generous dividends are so hurtful, why do companies continue to pay dividends? It is difficult to believe that managers would forgo such an easy opportunity to benefit their stockholders. What are we missing?

The need to find the missing elements in our "dividend puzzle" has not been ignored. When we need to better understand an issue or phenomenon, we can either improve our thinking or gather more evidence about the topic. Scholars and practitioners have taken both approaches. Although no single definitive answer has yet been found that is acceptable to all, several plausible explanations have been developed. Some of the more popular explanations include (1) the residual dividend theory, (2) the clientele effect, (3) the information effect, (4) agency costs, and (5) the expectations theory.

The Residual Dividend Theory

In perfect markets, we assume there is no cost to the firm when it issues new securities. However, in reality the process is quite expensive, and the flotation costs associated with a new offering may be as much as 20 percent of the dollar issue size. Thus, if managers choose to issue stock rather than retain profits to finance new investments, a larger amount of securities is required to finance the investment. For example, if $300,000 is needed to finance the investment, more than $300,000 will have to be issued to offset the flotation costs. This means, very simply, that new equity capital raised through the sale of common stock will be more expensive than capital raised via retained earnings.

In effect, flotation costs eliminate our indifference between financing by using internal capital versus issuing new common stock. Given these costs, *dividends should be paid only if the firm's profits are not completely used for investment purposes.* That is, only "residual earnings" should be paid out. This policy is called the **residual dividend theory**.[7]

residual dividend theory a theory that a company's dividend payment should equal the cash left after financing all the investments that have positive net present values.

Given the existence of flotation costs, the firm's dividend policy should therefore be as follows:

1. Accept an investment if the *NPV* is positive; that is, if the expected rate of return exceeds the cost of capital.

---

[7] The residual dividend theory is consistent with the "pecking order" theory of finance as described by Stewart Myers, "The Capital Structure Puzzle," *Journal of Finance* (July 1984), pp. 575–92.

2. Finance the equity portion of new investments *first* by using internally generated funds. Only after this capital is fully utilized should the firm issue new common shares.

3. If any internally generated funds still remain after making all acceptable investments, pay dividends to the investors. However, if all of the internal capital is needed to finance acceptable investments, pay no dividends.

Thus, dividend policy is influenced by (1) the company's investment opportunities and (2) the availability of internally generated capital. Dividends are then paid *only* after all acceptable investments have been financed. According to this concept, a dividend policy is totally passive in nature and can't affect the market price of the common stock.

Now, let us consider a dose of corporate reality.

The Clientele Effect

What if the investors do not like the dividend policy chosen by managers? In perfect markets, in which we incur no costs buying or selling stock, there is no problem. Investors can simply satisfy their personal income preferences by purchasing or selling securities when the dividends they receive do not satisfy their current needs. In other words, if an investor does not view the dividends received in any given year to be sufficient, he or she can simply sell a portion of stock, thereby "creating a dividend." In addition, if the dividend is larger than the investor desired, he or she can simply purchase stock with the "excess cash" created by the dividend.

However, once we remove the assumption of perfect markets, we find that buying or selling stock is not cost free. Brokerage fees are incurred, ranging approximately from 1 percent to 10 percent. Even more costly is that the investor who buys the stock with cash received from a dividend will have to pay taxes before reinvesting the cash. And when a stock is bought or sold, it must first be reevaluated. This can be time consuming and costly for investors. Finally, some institutional investors, such as investors in university endowment funds, are precluded from selling stock.

As a result of these considerations, investors may not be too inclined to buy stocks that require them to "create" a dividend stream more suitable to their purposes. Rather, if investors do in fact have a preference between dividends and capital gains, we could expect them to invest in firms that have a dividend policy consistent with these preferences. They would, in essence, "sort themselves out" by buying stocks that satisfy their preferences for dividends and capital gains. For example, individuals and institutions that need current income would be drawn to companies that have high dividend payouts. Other investors, such as wealthy individuals, would much prefer to avoid taxes by holding securities that offer no or small dividend income but large capital gains. In other words, there would be a **clientele effect**: *Firms draw a given clientele, depending upon their stated dividend policy.*

The possibility that clienteles of investors exist might lead us to believe that the firm's dividend policy matters. However, unless there is a greater aggregate demand for a particular policy than the market can satisfy, one policy is as good as the other. The clientele effect only warns firms to avoid making capricious changes in their dividend policy. Moreover, given that the firm's investment decisions are already made, the level of the dividend is still unimportant. The change in the policy matters only when it requires clientele to shift to another company.

The Information Effect

An investor in a world of perfect markets would argue with considerable persuasion that a firm's value is determined strictly by its investment and financing decisions and that its dividend policy has no impact on value. Yet we know from experience that a large, unexpected change in dividends can have a significant impact on the stock price. For instance, in November 1990, Occidental Petroleum cut its dividend from $2 to $1. In response, the firm's stock price went from about $32 to $17. How can we suggest that dividend policy matters little, when we can cite numerous such examples?

clientele effect the belief that individuals and institutions that need current income will invest in companies that have high dividend payouts. Other investors prefer to avoid taxes by holding securities that offer only small dividend income but large capital gains. Thus, we have a "clientele" of investors.

Despite such "evidence," some experts claim we are not looking at the real cause and effect. It may be that investors use a change in dividend policy as a *signal* about the firm's financial condition, especially its earning power. Thus, a dividend increase that is larger than expected might signal to investors that managers expect significantly higher earnings in the future. Conversely, a dividend decrease, or even a less-than-expected increase, might signal that managers are forecasting less-favorable future earnings.

Likewise, some claim that managers frequently have inside information about the firm that cannot be made available to investors. This *difference in accessibility to information*, called **information asymmetry**, *they believe, can result in a lower or higher stock price than would otherwise occur.*

Dividends may, therefore, be important as a communication tool because managers may have no other credible way to inform investors about future earnings, or at least no convincing way that is less costly.

Agency Costs

As you can see, conflicts often exist between owners and their managers. As a result, the stock price of a company owned by investors who are separate from management may be less than the stock price of a closely held firm. This potential difference in price is the *cost of the conflict to the owners*, which has come to be called **agency costs**.[8]

Recognizing the possible problem, managers, acting independently or at the insistence of the firm's board of directors, frequently take action to minimize agency costs. Such action, which in itself is costly, includes auditing by independent accountants, assigning supervisory functions to the company's board of directors, creating covenants in lending agreements that restrict managerial powers, and providing incentive compensation plans for managers that help "bond" them with the owners.

A firm's dividend policy may be perceived by owners as a tool to minimize agency costs. Assuming that the payment of a dividend requires managers to issue stock to finance new investments, new investors will be attracted to the company only if they are convinced that the capital will be used profitably. Thus, the payment of dividends indirectly results in a closer monitoring of management's investment activities. In this case, dividends may make a meaningful contribution to the value of the firm.

The Expectations Theory[9]

A common thread through much of our discussion of dividend policy, particularly as it relates to information effects, is the word *expected*. We should not overlook the significance of this word when we are making any financial decision within the firm. *No matter what the decision area, how the market price responds to a firm's actions is not determined entirely by the action itself; it is also affected by investors' expectations about the ultimate decision to be made by management.* This concept or idea is called the **expectations theory**.

information asymmetry
the difference in accessibility to information between managers and investors, which may result in a lower stock price than would be true in conditions of certainty.

agency costs the costs, such as a reduced stock price, associated with potential conflict between managers and investors when these two groups are not the same.

expectations theory the concept that, no matter what the decision area, how the market price responds to management's actions is not determined entirely by the action itself; it is also affected by investors' expectations about the ultimate decision to be made by management.

Remember Your Principles

Principle 7 warned us there may be a conflict between management and owners, especially in large firms in which managers and owners have different incentives. That is, **Managers Won't Work for the Owners Unless It Is in Their Best Interest** to do so. As we shall see in this section, the dividend policy may be one way to reduce this problem.

---

[8] See M. C. Jensen and W. H. Meckling, "Theory of the Firm: Managerial Behavior, Agency Costs, and Ownership Structure," *Journal of Financial Economics* (October 1976), pp. 305–60.
[9] Much of the thinking in this section came from Miller, "Can Management Use Dividends to Influence the Value of the Firm?" in Stern and Chew, eds., *The Revolution in Corporate Finance* (New York: Basil Blackwell, 1986), pp. 299–303.

For example, as the time approaches for managers to announce the amount of the firm's next dividend, investors form expectations about how much that dividend will be. These expectations are based on several factors related to the firm, such as past dividend decisions, current and expected earnings, investment strategies, and financing decisions. Investors also consider such things as the condition of the general economy, the strength or weakness of the industry at the time, and possible changes in government policies.

When the actual dividend decision is announced, the investor compares the actual decision with the expected decision. If the amount of the dividend is as expected, even if it represents an increase from prior years, the market price of the stock will remain unchanged. However, if the dividend is higher or lower than expected, investors will reassess their perceptions of the firm. In short, an actual decision about the firm's dividend policy is not likely to be terribly significant unless it departs from investors' expectations. But if there is a difference between actual and expected dividends, we will more than likely see a movement in the stock price.

What Are We to Conclude?

A firm must develop a dividend policy regardless, so here are some of the things we have learned about the relevance of a firm's dividend policy.

1. As a firm's investment opportunities increase, its dividend payout ratio should decrease. In other words, an inverse relationship should exist between the amount of money a firm invests with expected rates of return that exceed the cost of capital (positive *NPV*s) and the dividends it remits investors. Because of flotation costs, internally generated equity financing is preferable to selling stock (in terms of the wealth of the current common shareholders).

2. The firm's dividend policy appears to be important; however, appearances can be deceptive. The real issue is the firm's *expected* earning power, and investors will use the dividend payment as a source of information about these earnings. The dividend may carry greater weight than a statement by management that earnings will be increasing or decreasing. (Actions speak louder than words.)

3. If dividends influence the stock price, this is probably based on the investor's desire to minimize or defer taxes and on the fact that dividends can minimize agency costs.

4. If the expectations theory has merit, which we believe it does, the firm should avoid surprising investors when it comes to its dividend decision.

5. The firm's dividend policy should effectively be treated as a *long-term residual*. Rather than project investment requirements for a single year, managers should anticipate financing needs for several years. If internal funds remain after the firm has undertaken all acceptable investments, dividends should be paid. Conversely, if over the long term the entire amount of internally generated capital is needed for reinvestment in the company, then no dividend should be paid.

In setting a firm's dividend policy, financial managers must work in the messy world of reality. This means that our theories do not provide an equation that perfectly explains the key relationships. However, they give us a more complete view of the world, which can only help us make better decisions.

Did You Get It?

1. Summarize the position that a dividend policy may be irrelevant with regard to the firm's stock price.
2. What is meant by the bird-in-the-hand dividend theory?
3. Why are cash dividend payments thought to be more certain than prospective capital gains?
4. How might personal taxes affect both the firm's dividend policy and its share price?
5. Distinguish between the residual dividend theory and the clientele effect.

Objective **3**

Describe practical considerations that may be important to the firm's dividend policy.

THE DIVIDEND DECISION IN PRACTICE

There are a number of practical considerations that will have an impact on a firm's decision to pay dividends. Some of the more obvious ones include the following.

Legal Restrictions

Certain legal restrictions can limit the amount of dividends a firm may pay. These legal constraints fall into two categories. First, *statutory restrictions* may prevent a company from paying dividends. Although the specific limitations vary by state, generally a corporation may not pay a dividend (1) if the firm's liabilities exceed its assets, (2) if the amount of the dividend exceeds the firm's accumulated profits (retained earnings), and (3) if the dividend is being paid from capital invested in the firm.

The second type of legal restriction is unique to each firm and results from the restrictions in debt and preferred stock contracts. To minimize their risk, investors frequently impose restrictive provisions on managers as a condition to their investment in the company. These constraints might include the provision that dividends may not be declared before the debt is repaid. Also, the corporation might be required to maintain a given amount of working capital. Preferred stockholders might stipulate that common dividends may not be paid when any preferred dividends are delinquent.

Liquidity Constraints

Contrary to common opinion, the mere fact that a company shows a large amount of retained earnings in its balance sheet does not indicate that cash is available for the payment of dividends. The firm's liquid assets, including its cash, are basically independent of its retained earnings account. Generally, retained earnings are either reinvested in the company within a short period or are used to pay maturing debt. Thus, a firm can be extremely profitable and still be *cash poor*. Because dividends are paid with cash, *and not with retained earnings*, the firm must have cash available for the dividends to be paid. Hence, the firm's liquidity position has a direct bearing on its ability to pay dividends.

Earnings Predictability

A company's dividend payout ratio depends to some extent on the predictability of a firm's profits over time. If its earnings fluctuate significantly, the firm's managers know they cannot necessarily rely on internally generated funds to meet its future needs. As a result, when profits *are* realized, the firm is likely to retain larger amounts to ensure that money is available when needed. Conversely, a firm with a stable earnings trend will typically pay out a larger portion of its earnings in dividends. This company has less concern about the availability of profits to meet its future capital requirements.

Maintaining Ownership Control

For many large corporations, control through the ownership of common stock is not an important issue. However, for many small and medium-sized companies, maintaining voting control is a high priority. If the current common stockholders are unable to participate in a new offering, issuing new stock is unattractive, in that the control of the current stockholder is diluted. The owners might prefer that managers finance new investments with debt and retained earnings rather than issue new common stock. This firm's growth is then constrained by the amount of debt capital available to it and by the company's ability to generate profits.

Objective **4**

Distinguish among the types of dividend policies corporations frequently use.

ALTERNATIVE DIVIDEND POLICIES

Regardless of a firm's long-term dividend policy, most firms choose one of several year-to-year dividend payment patterns.

1. A **constant dividend payout ratio**. Under this policy, the *percentage of earnings paid out in dividends is held constant*. Although the dividend-to-earnings ratio is stable, the dollar amount of the dividend naturally fluctuates from year to year as profits vary.

2. A **stable dollar dividend per share**. This policy *maintains a relatively stable dollar dividend over time*. An increase in the dollar dividend usually does not occur until management is convinced that the higher dividend level can be maintained in the future. Conversely, a lower dollar dividend will not be paid until the evidence clearly indicates that a continuation of the current dividend cannot be supported.

3. A **small, regular dividend plus a year-end extra**. A corporation following this policy *pays a small, regular dollar dividend plus a year-end extra dividend in prosperous years*. The extra dividend is declared toward the end of the fiscal year after the company's profits for the period can be estimated. The objective is *to avoid the connotation of a permanent dividend being paid*. However, this purpose may be defeated if *recurring* extra dividends come to be expected by investors.

constant dividend payout ratio a dividend payment policy in which the percentage of earnings paid out in dividends is held constant. The dollar amount fluctuates from year to year as profits vary.

stable dollar dividend per share a dividend policy that maintains a relatively stable dollar dividend per share over time.

small, regular dividend plus a year-end extra a corporate policy of paying a small regular dollar dividend plus a year-end extra dividend in prosperous years to avoid the connotation of a permanent dividend.

Did You Get It? ....

1. Identify some practical considerations that affect a firm's payout policy.
2. Identify and explain three different dividend policies. *Hint:* One of these is a constant dividend payout ratio.

DIVIDEND PAYMENT PROCEDURES

Objective **5**

Specify the procedures a company follows in administering the dividend payment.

After the firm's dividend policy has been structured, several procedural details must be arranged. For instance, how frequently are dividend payments to be made? If a stockholder sells the shares during the year, who is entitled to the dividend? To answer these questions, we need to understand dividend payment procedures.

Generally, companies pay dividends on a quarterly basis. To illustrate, General Electric pays $6.72 per share in annual dividends. However, the firm actually issues a $1.68 quarterly dividend for a total yearly dividend of $6.72 ($1.68 × 4 quarters).

The final approval of a dividend payment comes from a firm's board of directors. As an example, Emerson Electric on February 7, 2006, announced that holders of record as of February 17 would receive a $0.44 dividend. The dividend payment was to be made on March 10. February 7 is the **declaration date**—the *date when the dividend is formally declared by the board of directors*. The **date of record**, February 17, designates *when the stock transfer books are to be closed*. Investors shown to own the stock on this date receive the dividend. If a notification of a transfer is recorded subsequent to February 17, the new owner is not entitled to the dividend. However, a problem could develop if the stock were sold on February 16, one day prior to the record date. Time would not permit the sale to be reflected on the stockholder list by the February 17 date of record. To avoid this problem, *stock brokerage companies have uniformly terminated the right of ownership to the dividend 2 working days before the date of record*. This prior date is the **ex-dividend date**. Therefore, any acquirer of Emerson Electric stock on February 15 or thereafter does not receive the dividend. Finally, the *company mails the dividend check to each investor* on March 10, the **payment date**. These events may be diagrammed as follows:

declaration date the date upon which a dividend is formally declared by the board of directors.

date of record date at which the stock transfer books are to be closed for determining the investor to receive the next dividend payment.

ex-dividend date the date upon which stock brokerage companies have uniformly decided to terminate the right of ownership to the dividend, which is two days prior to the date of record.

payment date the date on which the company mails a dividend check to each investor of record.

Source: Franklin/Templeton Group Hypothetical Illustration Program.

Did You Get It? ....

1. What is the typical frequency with which cash dividends are paid to investors?

2. Distinguish among the (a) declaration date, (b) date of record, and (c) ex-dividend date.

<table>
<tr><td>*Objective* </td></tr>
</table>

Describe why and how a firm might pay noncash dividends (stock dividends and stock splits) instead of cash dividends.

stock split a stock dividend exceeding 25 percent of the number of shares currently outstanding.

stock dividend a distribution of shares of up to 25 percent of the number of shares currently outstanding, issued on a pro rata basis to the current stockholders.

STOCK DIVIDENDS AND STOCK SPLITS

A stock dividend entails the distribution of additional shares of stock in lieu of a cash payment. A stock split involves exchanging more (or less in the case of a "reverse" split) shares of stock for the firm's outstanding shares. In both cases the number of common shares outstanding changes but the firm's investments and future earnings prospects do not. In essence, the ownership pie is simply cut into more pieces (or less pieces in the case of a reverse split).

The only difference between a stock dividend and a stock split relates to their respective accounting treatments. Both represent a proportionate distribution of additional shares to the current stockholders. However, *for accounting purposes* the **stock split** has been defined as a *stock dividend exceeding 25 percent*. Thus, a **stock dividend** is conventionally defined as a *distribution of shares up to 25 percent of the number of shares currently outstanding.*

Although stock dividends and splits occur far less frequently than cash dividends, a significant number of companies choose to use these share distributions either with or in lieu of cash dividends. The extent of stock splits and stock dividends over the years can be made clear by a little price comparison. In 1926, a ticket to the movies cost 25¢—and even much less in the rural communities. At the same time, the average share price on the New York Stock Exchange was $35. Today, if we want to go to a new movie, we pay $7 or more. However, the average share price is still about $35. The relatively constant share price is the result of the shares being split over and over again. We can only conclude that investors apparently like it that way. But why do they, if no economic benefit results to the investor from doing so?

Proponents of stock dividends and splits frequently maintain that stockholders receive a key benefit because the price of the stock will not fall precisely in proportion to the share increase. For a two-for-one split, the price of the stock might not decrease a full 50 percent, so the stockholder is left with a higher total value. There are two reasons for this disequilibrium. First, many financial executives believe that an optimal price range exists. Within this range, the total market value of the common stockholders is thought to be maximized. As the price exceeds this range, fewer investors can purchase the stock, thereby restraining demand for the shares. Consequently, downward pressure is placed on its price. For instance, Apple Computer Corporation announced a two-for-one split of its stock in February 2005. This was the third time that Apple had used a two-for-one split (the others were in 1987 and 2000). If Apple had not used the three splits, its stock price on November 15, 2006, would have been four times $85.54, or $342.16.

The second explanation relates to the *informational content* of the dividend-split announcement. Stock dividends and splits have generally been associated with companies with growing earnings. The announcement of a stock dividend or split has therefore been perceived as favorable news. The empirical evidence, however, fails to verify these conclusions. Most studies indicate that investors are perceptive in identifying the true meaning of such a distribution. If the stock dividend or split is not accompanied by a positive trend in earnings and increases in cash dividends, price increases surrounding the stock dividend or split are insignificant.[10] Therefore, we should be suspicious of the assertion that a stock dividend or split can help increase investors' net worth.

A second reason for stock dividends or splits is the conservation of corporate cash. If a company is encountering cash problems, it may substitute a stock dividend for a cash divi-

---

[10] See James A. Millar and Bruce D. Fielitz, "Stock-Split and Stock-Dividend Decisions," *Financial Management* 2 (Winter 1973), pp. 35–45; and Eugene Fama, Lawrence Fisher, Michael Jensen, and Richard Roll, "The Adjustment of Stock Prices to New Information," *International Economic Review* (February 1969), pp. 1–21.

dend. However, as before, investors will probably look beyond the dividend to ascertain the underlying reason for conserving cash. If the stock dividend is an effort to conserve cash for attractive investment opportunities, shareholders might bid up the stock price. If the move to conserve cash relates to financial difficulties within the firm, the market price will most likely react adversely.

Did You Get It?

1. What is the difference between a stock split and a stock dividend?
2. What managerial logic might lie behind a stock split or a stock dividend?

STOCK REPURCHASES

A **stock repurchase (stock buyback)** occurs when a *firm repurchases its own stock. This results in a reduction in the number of shares outstanding*. For well over 3 decades, corporations have been actively repurchasing their own equity securities. For example, the Ford Motor Company on September 14, 2000, announced in a press release that it planned to buy back up to a full $5 billion of its stock. Immediately after the public announcement of this plan, shares of Ford common stock rose by 2.2 percent in the financial markets. Now, a key word in such announcements is the word *plan*. Companies give themselves room across time to execute these buybacks. And, Ford, at the time, was mired in a major-league tire-quality problem on some of its best-selling vehicles, so not all financial analysts and market watchers were sure when the actual repurchases would commence.

The Walt Disney Company provides another actual example of a firm seeking to increase shareholder returns by repurchasing stock. In its 2001 annual report, Disney management said, "In 2001, the company invested a total of $1.1 billion to purchase 63.9 million shares of Disney common stock at an average price of $16.62 per share. Since 1983, the company has repurchased nearly 549 million shares at a total cost of just under $4.4 billion. At the November 30 (2001) stock price, these shares represent a market value of more than $11 billion."[11] Clearly, Disney management is proud of its financial policy in this regard.

Also, if you were to look at the balance sheet of a firm such as the McDonald's Corporation, you would see that the firm's treasury stock—the amount paid for repurchasing its own stock—is severalfold the total amount originally invested by the stockholders. This situation is not unusual for many large companies. Several reasons have been given for stock repurchases. The benefits include:

1. A means for providing an internal investment opportunity
2. An approach for modifying the firm's capital structure
3. A favorable impact on earnings per share
4. The elimination of a minority ownership group of stockholders
5. The minimization of the dilution in earnings per share associated with mergers
6. The reduction in the firm's costs associated with servicing small stockholders

Also, from the shareholders' perspective, a stock repurchase, as opposed to a cash dividend, has a potential tax advantage.

A Share Repurchase as a Dividend Decision

Clearly, the payment of a common stock dividend is the conventional method for distributing a firm's profits to its owners. However, it need not be the only way. Another approach is to repurchase the firm's stock. The concept may best be explained by an example.

Objective **7**

Explain the purpose and procedures related to stock repurchases.

stock repurchase (stock buyback) the repurchase of common stock by the issuing firm for any of a variety of reasons, resulting in reduction of shares outstanding. Also called **Stock Buyback.**

[11] The Walt Disney Company, *Annual Report* 2001, p. 12.

> ➤ **EXAMPLE**

Telink Inc. is planning to pay $4 million ($4 per share) in dividends to its common stock-holders. The following earnings and market price information is provided for Telink:

Net income	$7,500,000
Number of shares	1,000,000
Earnings per share	$7.50
Price–earnings ratio	8
Expected market price per share after dividend payment	$60

In a recent meeting, several board members, who are also major stockholders, question the need for a dividend payment. They maintain that they do not need the income, so why not allow the firm to retain the funds for future investments? In response, managers contend that the available investments are not sufficiently profitable to justify retention of the income. That is, the investors' required rates of return exceed the expected rates of return that could be earned with the additional $4 million in investments.

Because managers oppose the idea of retaining the profits for investment purposes, one of the firm's directors has suggested that the $4 million be used to repurchase the company's stock. In this way, the value of the stock should increase. This result can be demonstrated as follows:

1. Assume that shares are repurchased by the firm at the $60 market price (ex-dividend price) plus the contemplated $4 dividend per share, or for $64 per share.
2. Given a $64 price, 62,500 shares would be repurchased ($4 million ÷ $64 price).
3. If net income is not reduced but the number of shares declines as a result of the share repurchase, earnings per share would increase from $7.50 to $8, computed as follows:

$$\text{Earnings per share} = \text{net income/outstanding shares}$$
$$\text{(before repurchase)} = \$7,500,000/1,000,000$$
$$= \$7.50$$
$$\text{(after repurchase)} = \$7,500,000/(1,000,000 - 62,500)$$
$$= \$8$$

4. Assuming that the price–earnings ratio remains at 8, the new price after the repurchase would be $64, up from $60, where the increase exactly equals the amount of the forgone dividend.

In this example, Telink's stockholders are essentially provided the same value, whether a dividend is paid or stock is repurchased. If managers pay a dividend, the investor will have a stock valued at $60 plus $4 received from the dividend. Conversely, if stock is re-purchased in lieu of the dividend, the stock will be worth $64. These results were based on assuming (1) the stock is being repurchased at the exact $64 price, (2) the $7,500,000 net income is unaffected by the repurchase, and (3) the price–earnings ratio of 8 does not change after the repurchase. Given these assumptions, however, the stock repurchase serves as a perfect substitute for the dividend payment to the stockholders.

The Investor's Choice

Given the choice between a stock repurchase and a dividend payment, which should an investor prefer? If there are no taxes, no commissions when buying and selling stock, and no informational content assigned to a dividend, the investor should be indifferent with regard to the choices. For example, if the investor wants cash flow and the stock he owns does not pay a dividend, he can create a dividend by simply selling a portion of his shares. Note that these sales will not necessarily deplete the value of his investment as the value of the firm's shares should be growing because the firm's earnings are not being paid in dividends but are being reinvested.

Finance at Work

COMPANIES INCREASINGLY USE SHARE REPURCHASES TO DISTRIBUTE CASH TO THEIR STOCKHOLDERS

There has been a fundamental shift away from paying dividends and toward the buyback of company shares of stock. This change is at least partially due to changes in the U.S. tax code, which charges an additional 15% tax on dividends paid out to shareholders (before the Bush administration, this tax was as high as the graduated income tax—in some cases exceeding 35% on the federal level alone).

Evidence supporting the growth in share repurchases is found in the fact that the firms in the Standard & Poor's 500 repurchased $349 billion of their shares in 2005 alone. In fact, firms spent 73% more on buybacks than they did on dividends. On average, stock repurchases represented 61% of company earnings and dividends were only 32%. Clearly, there is a strong preference for share repurchases.*

Obviously firms are finding share repurchases a preferred way to distribute cash, but is this always best for the investor? Asked somewhat differently, are there reasons to prefer dividends over share repurchases? The answer is yes. For example, investors who need cash from their investments to live on may prefer dividends rather than being forced to sell shares and incur broker-age fees. Also, there's something comforting about receiving a regular check in the mail and not having to worry so much about fluctuations in the value of your shares from day to day.

Some companies now recognize the varied interests of their stockholders and attempt to blend share repurchases with cash dividends. For example, Home Depot has paid out about 65% of its earnings in a mix of share repurchases and dividend payments. For example, for the year ended January 29, 2006, the firm reported total net income of $5.838 billion, paid $0.857 billion in dividends and repurchased $2.626 billion in company shares. This represents a total distribution of 59.7% of company earnings with 45% being distributed via share repurchase and 14.7% via dividends.**

*Matt Krantz, "More companies go for stock buybacks," *USA Today* (March 23, 2006).
**http://finance.yahoo.com/q/cf?s=HD&annual.
Source: Leslie Schism, "Many Companies Use Excess Cash to Repurchase Their Shares," September 2, 1993, the *Wall Street Journal*, Eastern edition. Copyright by Dow Jones & Co. Inc. Reproduced with permission of Dow Jones & Co. Inc.

There are certainly drawbacks related to repurchasing stock that investors should care about. First, the firm may have to pay too high a price for the repurchased stock, which is to the detriment of the remaining stockholders. If a relatively large number of shares are being bought, the price may be bid up too high, only to fall after the repurchase operation. Second, as a result of the repurchase, the market may perceive the riskiness of the corporation as increasing, which would lower the price–earnings ratio and the value of the stock.

A Financing or Investment Decision?

Repurchasing stock when the firm has excess cash can be regarded as a dividend decision. However, a stock repurchase can also be viewed as a financing decision. By issuing debt and then repurchasing stock, a firm can immediately alter its debt–equity mix toward a higher proportion of debt. Essentially, rather than choose how to distribute cash to the stockholders, managers are using stock repurchases as a means to change the corporation's capital structure.

In addition to dividend and financing decisions, many managers consider a stock repurchase to be an investment decision. When equity prices are depressed in the marketplace, they may view the firm's own stock as being materially undervalued and therefore a good investment opportunity. Although this may be a wise move, the decision cannot and should not be viewed in the context of an investment decision. Buying its own stock cannot provide expected returns as other investments do. No company can survive, much less prosper, by investing only in its own stock.

Practical Considerations—The Stock Repurchase Procedure

If management intends to repurchase a block of the firm's outstanding shares, it should make this information public. All investors should be given the opportunity to work with complete information. They should be told the purpose of the repurchase, as well as the method to be used to acquire the stock.

Three methods for stock repurchase are available. First, the shares can be bought in the open market. Here the firm acquires the stock through a stockbroker at the going market price. This approach can put upward pressure on the stock price. Also, commissions must be paid to the stockbrokers as a fee for their services.

tender offer a formal offer by the company to buy a specified number of shares at a predetermined and stated price. The tender price is set above the current market price in order to attract sellers.

The second method is to make a tender offer to the firm's shareholders. A **tender offer** is a *formal offer by the company to buy a specified number of shares at a predetermined and stated price. The tender price is set above the current market price in order to attract sellers.* A tender offer is best when a relatively large number of shares are to be bought because the company's intentions are clearly known and each shareholder has the opportunity to sell the stock at the tendered price.

The third and final method for repurchasing stock entails the purchase of the stock from one or more major stockholders. These purchases are made on a negotiated basis. Care should be taken to ensure a fair and equitable price. Otherwise, the remaining stockholders may be hurt as a result of the sale.

Did You Get It?

1. Identify three reasons why a firm might buy back its own common stock shares.
2. What financial relationships must hold for a stock repurchase to be a perfect substitute for a cash dividend payment to stockholders?
3. Within the context of a stock repurchase, what is meant by a tender offer?

Objective

Understand the relationship between a policy of low dividend payments and international capital budgeting opportunities that confront the multinational firm.

FINANCE AND THE MULTINATIONAL FIRM: THE CASE OF LOW DIVIDEND PAYMENTS; SO WHERE DO WE INVEST?

During late 2000 through March 2001, the U.S. economy continued an outstanding period of aggregate expansion that ultimately made it the longest in domestic business cycle history. When such periods of relative prosperity occur, financially strong firms tend to focus their business strategies on growth. As a direct result, corporate dividend yields (i.e., cash dividends divided by common stock prices) tend to decline. Firms retain more cash dollars for internal investment opportunities and disgorge less cash to investors. This might properly remind you of what we called the *residual dividend theory* earlier in this chapter.

During general economic prosperity, the multinational firm logically looks to international markets for prospective high-*NPV* projects. There are at least two solid reasons for such investing behavior: (1) to spread or dilute country-related economic risks by diversifying geographically and (2) to achieve a cost advantage over one's competitors. These two reasons for U.S. direct investment abroad should remind you of **Principle 9: All Risk Is Not Equal—Some Risk Can Be Diversified Away and Some Can Not**; and **Principle 5: The Curse of Competitive Markets—Why It's Hard to Find Exceptionally Profitable Projects**.

Did You Get It?

1. Identify two reasons why multinational firms might turn to international markets in search of high-*NPV* projects.

Objective **1**

Describe the trade-off between paying dividends and retaining the profits within the company.

Objective **2**

Explain the relationship between a corporation's dividend policy and the market price of its common stock.

Summary

A company's dividend decision has an immediate impact on the firm's financial mix. If the dividend payment is increased, fewer funds are available internally for financing investments. Consequently, if additional equity capital is needed, the company has to issue new common stock.

In perfect markets, the choice between paying or not paying a dividend does not matter. However, when we realize that in the real world there are costs of issuing stock, we have a preference to use internal equity to finance our investment opportunities. Here the dividend decision is simply a residual factor, in which the dividend payment should equal the remaining internal capital after the firm finances all of its investments.

Other market imperfections that may cause a company's dividend policy to affect the firm's stock price include (1) the deferred tax benefit of capital gains, (2) agency costs, (3) the clientele effect, and (4) the informational content of a given policy.

Other practical considerations that may affect a firm's dividend payment decision include

- Legal restrictions
- The firm's liquidity position
- The company's accessibility to capital markets
- The stability of the firm's earnings
- The desire of investors to maintain control of the company

In practice, managers have generally followed one of three dividend policies:

- A constant dividend payout ratio, whereby the percentage of dividends to earnings is held constant
- A stable dollar dividend per share, whereby a relatively stable dollar dividend is maintained over time
- A small, regular dividend plus a year-end extra, whereby the firm pays a small, regular dollar dividend plus a year-end extra dividend in prosperous years

Of the three dividend policies, the stable dollar dividend is by far the most common. The Jobs and Growth Tax Relief Reconciliation Act of 2003 reduced the top tax rate on dividend income to 15 percent and placed the top tax rate on realized long-term capital gains at this same 15 percent rate. This helped level the investment landscape for dividend income relative to qualifying capital gains. Taxes paid on capital gains, however, are still deferred until realized, but dividend income is taxed in the year that it is received by the investing taxpayer.

Generally, companies pay dividends on a quarterly basis. The final approval of a dividend payment comes from the board of directors. The critical dates in this process are as follows:

- Declaration date—the date when the dividend is formally declared by the board of directors
- Date of record—the date when the stock-transfer books are closed to determine who owns the stock
- Ex-dividend date—two working days before the date of record, after which the right to receive the dividend no longer goes with the stock
- Payment date—the date the dividend check is mailed to the stockholders

Stock dividends and stock splits have been used by corporations either in lieu of or to supplement cash dividends. At present, no empirical evidence identifies a relationship between stock dividends and splits and the market price of the stock. Yet a stock dividend or split could conceivably be used to keep the stock price within an optimal trading range. Also, if investors perceive that the stock dividend contains favorable information about the firm's operations, the price of the stock could increase.

As an alternative to paying a dividend, the firm can repurchase stock. In perfect markets, an investor would be indifferent between receiving a dividend or a share repurchase. The investor could simply create a dividend stream by selling stock when income is needed. If, however, market imperfections exist, the investor may have a preference for one of the two methods of distributing the corporate income.

A stock repurchase can also be viewed as a financing decision. By issuing debt and then repurchasing stock, a firm can immediately alter its debt–equity mix toward a higher proportion of debt. Also, many managers consider a stock repurchase an investment decision— buying the stock when they believe it to be undervalued.

During periods of general economic prosperity, financially strong firms tend to focus their business strategies on growth. As a result, dividend yields and cash dividend payments can decline. With internally generated cash to invest, the multinational firm will look to international markets for prospective high-*NPV* projects. This may allow the firm to (1) spread country-related economic risks by diversifying geographically and (2) achieve a cost advantage over competitors.

Objective

Describe practical considerations that may be important to the firm's dividend policy.

Objective 4

Distinguish among the types of dividend policies corporations frequently use.

Objective 5

Specify the procedures a company follows in administering the dividend payment.

Objective 6

Describe why and how a firm might pay noncash dividends (stock dividends and stock splits) instead of cash dividends.

Objective 7

Explain the purpose and procedures related to stock repurchases.

Objective

Understand the relationship between a policy of low dividend payments and international capital budgeting opportunities that confront the multinational firm.

Key Terms

Agency costs   422

Bird-in-the-hand dividend theory   418

Clientele effect   421

Constant dividend payout ratio   425

Date of record   425

Declaration date   425

Dividend payout ratio   416

Ex-dividend date   425

Expectations theory   423

Information asymmetry   422

Payment date   425

Perfect capital markets   418

Review Questions

13-1. What is meant by the term *dividend payout ratio*?

13-2. Explain the trade-off between retaining internally generated funds and paying cash dividends.

13-3. a. What are the assumptions of a perfect market?

    b. What effect does a dividend policy have on the share price in a perfect market?

13-4. What is the impact of flotation costs on the financing decision?

13-5. a. What is the *residual dividend theory*?

    b. Why is this theory operational only in the long term?

13-6. Why might investors prefer capital gains to the same amount of dividend income?

13-7. What legal restrictions may limit the amount of dividends to be paid?

13-8. How does a firm's liquidity position affect the payment of dividends?

13-9. How can ownership control constrain the growth of a firm?

13-10. a. Why is a stable dollar dividend policy popular from the viewpoint of the corporation?

    b. Is it also popular with investors? Why?

13-11. Explain what a dividend's declaration date, date of record, and ex-dividend date are.

13-12. What are the advantages of a stock split or dividend over a cash dividend?

13-13. Why would a firm repurchase its own stock?

Self-Test Problems

(Solutions to these problems are found at the end of the chapter.)

ST-1. (*Dividend growth rate*) Schulz Inc. maintains a constant dividend payout ratio of 35 percent. Earnings per share last year were $8.20 and are expected to grow indefinitely at a rate of 12 percent. What will be the dividend per share this year? In 5 years?

ST-2. (*Stock split*) The debt and equity section of the Robson Corporation balance sheet is shown here. The current market price of the common shares is $20. Reconstruct the financial statement assuming that (a) a 15 percent stock dividend is issued and (b) a two-for-one stock split is declared.

Debt	$1,800,000
Common equity	
Par ($2; 100,000 shares)	200,000
Paid-in capital	400,000
Retained earnings	900,000
	$3,300,000

Study Problems

13-1. (*Dividend policies*) Final earnings estimates for Chilean Health Spa & Fitness Center have been prepared for the CFO of the company and are shown in the following table. The firm has 7,500,000 shares of common stock outstanding. As assistant to the CFO, you are asked to determine the yearly dividend per share to be paid depending on the following possible policies:

a. A stable dollar dividend targeted at 40 percent of earnings over a 5-year period
b. A small, regular dividend of $0.60 per share plus a year-end extra when the profits in any
year exceed $20,000,000. The year-end extra dividend will equal 50 percent of profits
exceeding $20,000,000.
c. A constant dividend payout ratio of 40 percent

YEAR	PROFITS AFTER TAXES
1	$18,000,000
2	21,000,000
3	19,000,000
4	23,000,000
5	25,000,000

13-2. (*Flotation costs and issue size*) Your firm needs to raise $10 million. Assuming that flotation costs are expected to be $15 per share, and that the market price of the stock is $120, how many shares would have to be issued? What is the dollar size of the issue?

13-3. (*Flotation costs and issue size*) If the flotation costs for a common stock issue are 18 percent, how large must the issue be so that the firm will net $5,800,000? If the stock sells for $85 per share, how many shares must be issued?

13-4. (*Dividend policies*) The earnings for Crystal Cargo Inc. have been predicted for the next 5 years and are as follows. There are 1 million shares outstanding. Determine the yearly dividend per share to be paid if the following policies are enacted:

a. A constant dividend payout ratio of 50 percent
b. A stable dollar dividend targeted at 50 percent of the earnings over the 5-year period
c. A small, regular dividend of $0.50 per share plus a year-end extra when the profits in any year exceed $1,500,000. The year-end extra dividend will equal 50 percent of profits exceeding $1,500,000.

YEAR	PROFITS AFTER TAXES
1	$1,400,000
2	2,000,000
3	1,860,000
4	900,000
5	2,800,000

13-5. (*Repurchase of stock*) The Dunn Corporation is planning to pay dividends of $500,000. There are 250,000 shares outstanding, and earnings per share are $5. The stock should sell for $50 after the ex-dividend date. If, instead of paying a dividend, the firm decides to repurchase stock,

a. What should be the repurchase price?
b. How many shares should be repurchased?
c. What if the repurchase price is set below or above your suggested price in part a?
d. If you own 100 shares, would you prefer that the company pay the dividend or repurchase stock?

13-6. (*Flotation costs and issue size*) D. Butler Inc. needs to raise $14 million. Assuming that the market price of the firm's stock is $95, and flotation costs are 10 percent of the market price, how many shares would have to be issued? What is the dollar size of the issue?

Web Works

13-WW1. Stock repurchase plans, as discussed in this chapter, have become a rather common financial activity in corporate America. IBM is one well-known firm that has had a vigorous repurchase program. You can review a discussion of the IBM repurchase plan at **www.IBM.com** and find out how much IBM spent on common stock repurchases in the 2005 fourth quarter and how many fewer shares were left outstanding over the year due to the repurchase program.

13-WW2. Let us continue with a further look at IBM and its dividend policy. Visit the same Web site and this time look up the annual report for fiscal year 2005. Locate the "management discussion" section. How much did IBM return to shareholders via dividend and share repurchases over each of the 5 years ended 2005?

Mini Case

The following article appeared in the July 2, 1995, issue of the *Dallas Morning News*. In the article, Scott Burns, the author, makes the case for the importance of dividends.

Let us now praise the lowly dividend.

Insignificant to some. Small potatoes to others. An irksome sign of tax liability to many. However characterized, dividends are experiencing yet another round of defamation on Wall Street.

Why pay out dividends, the current argument goes, when a dollar of dividend can be retained as a dollar of book value that the market will value at two, three, or four dollars? With the average stock now selling at more than three times book value, investors should prefer companies that retain earnings rather than pay them out, even if they do nothing more with the money than repurchase shares.

The New Wisdom

Instead, the New Wisdom says, the investor should go for companies that retain earnings, reinvest them, and try to maximize shareholder value. Dividends should be avoided in the pursuit of long-term capital gains.

The only problem with this reasoning is that we've heard it before. And always at market tops.
- We heard it in the late 1960s as stock prices soared and dividend yields fell.
- We heard it again in the early 1970s as investors fixated on the "Nifty Fifty" and analysts calmly projected that with growth companies yielding 1 percent or less, the most important part of the return was the certainty of 20 percent annual earnings growth.
- And we're hearing it now, with stock prices hitting new highs each day. The Standard & Poor's 500 Index, for instance, is up 19.7 percent since December 31, the equivalent of more than 7 years of dividends at the current yield of 2.6 percent.

Tilting the Yield

Significantly, we didn't hear that dividends were irrelevant in the late 1970s, as stock valuations moved to new lows. At that time, portfolio managers talked about "yield tilt"—running a portfolio with a bias toward dividend return to offset some of the risk of continuing stock market decline. Indeed, many of the best performing funds in the late 1970s were equity-income funds, the funds that seek above-average dividend income.

You can understand how much dividends contribute to long-term returns by taking a look at the performance of a major index, with and without dividend reinvestment. If you had invested $10,000 in the S&P's 500 Index in January 1982 and taken all dividends in cash, your original investment would have grown to $37,475 by the end of 1994.

It doesn't get much better than that.

The gain clocks a compound annual return of 10.7 percent, and a total gain of $27,475. During the same period you would have collected an additional $14,244 in dividends.

Not a trivial sum, either.

In other words, during one of the biggest bull markets in history, unreinvested dividend income accounted for more than one-third of your total return.

If you had reinvested those dividends in additional stock, the final score would be even better: $60,303. The appreciation of your original investment would have been $27,475, and the growth from reinvested dividends would have been $22,828. Nearly half—45 percent—of your total return came from reinvested dividends. And this happened during a stellar period of rising stock prices.

Now consider the same investment during a period of misery. If you had invested $10,000 in the S&P's 500 Index stocks in January 1968, your investment would have grown to only $14,073 over the next 13 years, a gain of only $4,073. During much of that time, the value of your original investment would have been less than $10,000. Dividends during the period would have totaled $7,088—substantially more than stock appreciation. Reinvested, the same dividends would have grown to $9,705, helping your original investment grow to $23,778.

In a period of major ups and downs that many investors don't like to remember, dividends accounted for 70 percent of total return (see the accompanying table).

We could fiddle with these figures any number of ways. We could reduce the value of dividends by calculating income taxes. We could raise it by starting with the Dow Jones industrial average stocks, which tend to have higher dividends. But the point here is very simple:

Whether you spend them or reinvest them, dividends are always an important part of the return on common stock.

Source: Scott Burns, "Those Lowly Dividends," *Dallas Morning News*, July 2, 1995, p. 1H. Reprinted with permission of the *Dallas Morning Star*.

A Close Look at Dividends in Two Markets

ANATOMY OF THE BULL MARKET, 1982 TO 1994		
Original investment		$10,000
Gain on original investment		$27,475
Total dividends	$14,244	
Gain on reinvested dividends	$ 8,584	
Total gain from dividends		$22,828
Total		$60,303
Compound annualized return equals 14.8%; 45% from dividends.		

ANATOMY OF A BEAR MARKET, 1968 TO 1980		
Original investment		$10,000
Gain on original investment		$ 4,073
Total dividends	$ 7,088	
Gain on reinvested dividends	$ 2,617	
Total gain from dividends		$ 9,705
Total		$23,778
Compound annualized return equals 6.9%; 70% from dividends		

Source: Franklin/Templeton Group Hypothetical Illustration Program.

Based on your reading of this chapter, evaluate what Burns is saying. Do you agree or disagree with him? Why?

Self-Test Solutions

SS-1.

$$\text{Dividend per share} = 35\% \times \$8.20$$
$$= \$2.87$$

Dividends:

$$1 \text{ year} = \$2.87(1 + 0.12)$$
$$= \$3.21$$
$$5 \text{ years} = \$2.87(1 + 0.12)^5$$
$$= \$2.87(1.762)$$
$$= \$5.06$$

SS-2.

a. If a 15 percent stock dividend is issued, the financial statement would appear as follows:

Debt	$1,800,000
Common equity	
Par ($2 par; 115,000 shares)	230,000
Paid-in capital	670,000
Retained earnings	600,000
	$3,300,000

b. A two-for-one split would result in a 100 percent increase in the number of shares. Because the total par value remains at $200,000, the new par value per share is $1 ($200,000/200,000 shares). The new financial statement would be as follows:

Debt	$1,800,000
Common equity	
Par ($1 par; 200,000 shares)	200,000
Paid-in capital	400,000
Retained earnings	900,000
	$3,300,000

Working-Capital Management and International Business Finance

➤ Milwaukee-based Harley-Davidson Corporation has a state-of-the-art Parts and Accessories division, and the people that work there take tremendous pride of ownership for what happens in *their* part of the business. They simply feel they are the best. But it was not always this way.

In the early 1990s Harley-Davidson was experiencing tremendous growth in all segments of the business, including Parts and Accessories. Having come through a turnaround in the 1980s, the distribution and logistics functions in support of this business growth were strained and in need of change. In mid-1994 a team was formed to develop and implement a new strategy.

The issues at the time were significant. Their distribution center was a seven-level facility that was 84 years old and looked more like an old red brick school building than a modern warehouse. The facility was served by two freight elevators and limited technology support. In addition, the facility contained slightly over half the inventory, requiring off-site storage with daily shuttle runs to replenish stock.

Symptoms of Harley-Davidson's inventory problems included inventory turnover rates that were less than two turns per year; inventory accuracy levels in the 75% to 80% range; order cycle times from receipt of order to shipment in the 3- to 10-day range; lost inventory; inventory write-offs in the millions of dollars; and extremely low productivity.

The new strategy centered on designing a facility with appropriate storage, automation, and technology for each class of inventory. This would create optimum performance against a comprehensive set of metrics for cost, quality, and timing goals. In addition, a new relationship with employees called "partnering" was being instituted throughout the firm. The partnering program empowered employees and capitalized on their individual and collective knowledge and skills.

Brian Smith, general manager for Parts and Accessories with Harley-Davidson, describes the improvements as follows:

This project was implemented in 1997, and the results have been excellent. Inventory accuracy and fill rates have improved dramatically, and recovery time on stock-outs has been substantially improved. Turnover rates have more than doubled and are approaching world class. Slow moving and obsolete inventories have been reduced by over 60%. Order cycle times to customers have become top-notch. The majority of orders are shipped the same day as they are received, with very high levels of reliability.

Based on our experience, employees are typically the masters of the universe in which they work. They know more about the issues and possible solutions than anyone else. The creation of a culture where employees [are] encouraged to contribute their ideas for improving the work processes and systems and where resources are made available for them to bring their ideas to fruition may be the most important part of the solution.

CHAPTER 14
SHORT-TERM
FINANCIAL PLANNING

CHAPTER 15
WORKING-CAPITAL
MANAGEMENT

CHAPTER 16
CURRENT ASSET
MANAGEMENT

CHAPTER 17
INTERNATIONAL
BUSINESS FINANCE

Short-Term Financial Planning

Forecasting is an integral part of the planning process, yet there are countless examples when our ability to predict the future is not very good.

After the first energy crisis of the 1970s when the price of crude oil rose from $2.00 to more than $20.00 per barrel and many thought that the oil price would rise above $50.00. Then in 1986 the price dropped to only $10.00 per barrel and the $50.00 price looked like a foolish dream. Then in 2006 the price of a barrel of oil rose to over $70.00. What's next, will the price continue to rise or will it drop again as it did in an earlier crisis?

If forecasting the future is so difficult and plans are built on forecasts, why do firms engage in planning efforts? Obviously, they do, but why? The answer, oddly enough, does not lie in the accuracy of the firm's projections, for planning offers its greatest value when the future is the most uncertain. The value of planning is derived out of the process itself. That is, by thinking about what the future might be like, the firm builds contingency plans that can improve its ability to respond to adverse events and take advantage of opportunities that arise.

Chapter 14 has two primary objectives: First, it will help you gain an appreciation for the role forecasting plays in the firm's financial planning process. Basically, forecasts of future sales revenues and their associated expenses give the firm the information it needs to project its future financing needs. Second, this chapter provides an overview of the firm's cash budget, its pro forma (planned) income statement, and its pro forma balance sheet. Pro forma financial statements give us a useful tool for analyzing the effects of the firm's forecasts and planned activities on its financial performance, as well as its needs for financing. In addition, pro forma statements can be used as a benchmark or standard to compare against actual operating results. Used in this way, pro forma statements are an instrument for monitoring and controlling the firm's progress throughout the planning period. For example, after the first energy crisis of the 1970s, the price of crude oil rose from $2.00 to more than $20.00 per barrel. Many thought that the price would rise above $50.00. Then in 1986, the price dropped to only $10.00 per barrel, and the $50.00 price looked like a foolish dream. However, in 2006, the price of a barrel of oil rose to over $70.00. What's next, will the price continue to rise or will it drop again as it did in an earlier crisis?

Objective **1**

Use the percent of sales method to forecast the financing requirements of a firm.

FINANCIAL FORECASTING

Financial forecasting is the process of attempting to estimate a firm's future financing requirements. The basic steps involved in predicting those financing needs are the following:

Step 1. Project the firm's sales revenues and expenses over the planning period.
Step 2. Estimate the levels of investment in current and fixed assets that are needed to support the projected sales.
Step 3. Determine the firm's financing needs throughout the planning period.

The Sales Forecast

The key ingredient in the firm's planning process is the sales forecast. This projection is generally derived using information from a number of sources. At a minimum, the sales forecast for the coming year reflects (1) any past trend in sales that is expected to carry through into the new year and (2) the influence of any anticipated events that might materially affect that trend.[1] An example of the latter is the initiation of a major advertising campaign or a change in the firm's pricing policy.

Forecasting Financial Variables

Traditional financial forecasting takes the sales forecast as a given and projects its impact on the firm's various expenses, assets, and liabilities. The most commonly used method for making these projections is the percent of sales method.

The Percent of Sales Method of Financial Forecasting

percent of sales method a method of financial forecasting that involves estimating the level of an expense, asset, or liability for a future period as a percent of the sales forecast.

The **percent of sales method** involves *estimating the level of an expense, asset, or liability for a future period as a percentage of the sales forecast*. The percentage used can come from the most recent financial statement item as a percentage of current sales, from an average computed over several years, from the judgment of the analyst, or from some combination of these sources.

---

[1] A complete discussion of forecast methodologies is outside the scope of this book. The interested reader will find the following reference helpful: Paul Newbold and Theodore Bos, *Introductory Business Forecasting*, 2nd ed., (Cincinnati: Southwestern, 1994).

TABLE 14-1 Using the Percent of Sales Method to Forecast Drew Inc.'s Financing Requirements for 2008

	A	B	C	D	E	F	G	H	I	J
1	Drew Inc.						Drew Inc.			
2	Income Statement for 2007						Pro forma Income Statement for 2008			
3					% of 2007 Sales			Calculation		
4							Sales growth rate =	20%		
5	Sales		$ 10,000,000				Sales	$10 million x (1+.20) =	$ 12,000,000	
6	Net Income		$ 500,000	[$500,000 /$10,000,000 =	5.0%		Net Income	$12 million x .05 =	$ 600,000	
7										
8										
9										
10	Drew Inc.						Drew Inc.			
11	Balance Sheet for 2007						Pro forma Balance Sheet for 2008			
12					% of 2007 Sales			Calculation		
13										
14	Current assets		$ 2,000,000	[$2m / $10m] =	20.0%		Current assets	.20 x$12m =	$ 2,400,000	
15	Net fixed assets		4,000,000	[$4m / $10m] =	40.0%		Net fixed assets	.40 x$12m =	$ 4,800,000	
16	Total		$ 6,000,000				Total		$ 7,200,000	
17										
18	Accounts payable		$ 1,000,000	[$1m /$10 m] =	10.0%		Accounts payable	.10 x$12m =	$ 1,200,000	
19	Accrued expenses		1,000,000	[$1m /$10m] =	10.0%		Accrued expenses	.10 x$12m =	1,200,000	
20	Notes payable		500,000		NA*		Notes payable	No change	500,000	
21	Current Liabilities		$ 2,500,000				Current Liabilities		$ 2,900,000	
22	Long-term debt		2,000,000		NA*		Long-term debt	No change	$ 2,000,000	
23	Total Liabilities		$ 4,500,000				Total Liabilities		$ 4,900,000	
24	Common stock (par)		100,000		NA*		Common stock (par)	No change	100,000	
25	Paid-in-capital		200,000		NA*		Paid-in-capital	No change	200,000	
26	Retained earnings		1,200,000				Retained earnings	Calculation*	1,500,000	
27	Common Equity		$ 1,500,000				Common Equity		1,800,000	
28	Total		$ 6,000,000				Total Financing Provided		$ 6,700,000	
29							Discretionary Financing Needed (Plug)*		$ 500,000	
30							Total Financing Needed = Total Assets		$ 7,200,000	
31										
32	*Not applicable. These account balances do not vary with sales.									
33	*Projected retained earnings for 2008 equals $1,500,000 which is equal to the 2007 level of retained earnings of $1,200,000 plus net income of $600,000 less common dividends									
34	equal to 50% of projected net income or $300,000 .									
35	*Discretionary financing needed (DFN) for 2008 is a "plug figure" that equals the difference in the firm's projected total financing requirements or total assets equal to $7,200,000									
36	and total financing provided which is $6,700,000. In this scenario DFN is $500,000.									
37										
38										

Table 14-1 presents a complete example that uses the percent of sales method of financial forecasting for Drew Inc. In this example each item in the firm's balance sheet that varies with sales is converted to a percentage of 2007 sales, which was $10 million. The forecast of the new balance for each item is then calculated by multiplying this percentage times the $12 million in projected sales for the 2008 planning period. This method offers a relatively low-cost and easy-to-use way to estimate the firm's future financing needs.

Note that in the example in Table 14-1, both current and fixed assets are assumed to vary with the level of sales. This means that the firm does not have sufficient productive capacity to absorb a projected increase in sales. Thus, if sales were to rise by $1, fixed assets would rise by $0.40, or 40 percent of the projected increase in sales. If instead the fixed assets the firm currently owns are sufficient to support the projected level of sales, then the assets will not be converted to a percentage of sales and will be projected to remain unchanged for the period being forecast.

Also, note that accounts payable and accrued expenses are the only liabilities allowed to vary with sales. Both these liability accounts might reasonably be expected to rise and fall with the level of firm sales, hence, the use of the percent of sales forecast. Because these two categories of current liabilities normally vary directly with the level of sales, they are often referred to as sources of **spontaneous financing**. Included in spontaneous financing are *trade credit and other accounts payable that arise spontaneously in the firm's day-to-day operations*. Chapter 15, which discusses working-capital management, has more to say about these forms of financing. Notes payable, long-term debt, common stock, and paid-in capital are not assumed to vary directly with the level of firm sales. These sources of financing are termed **discretionary financing**, *which requires an explicit decision on the part of the firm's management every time funds are raised. An example is a bank note that requires that negotiations be undertaken and an agreement signed setting*

spontaneous financing the trade credit and other accounts payable that arise "spontaneously" in the firm's day-to-day operations.

discretionary financing sources of financing that require an explicit decision on the part of the firm's management every time funds are raised. An example is a bank note that requires that negotiations be undertaken and an agreement signed setting forth the terms and conditions of the financing.

forth the terms and conditions for the financing. Finally, note that the level of retained earnings does vary with estimated sales. The predicted change in the level of retained earnings equals the estimated after-tax profits (projected net income) equal to 5 percent of sales, or $600,000, less the common stock dividends of $300,000.

In the Drew Inc. example found in Table 14-1, we estimate that firm sales will increase from $10 million to $12 million, which will cause the firm's need for total assets to rise to $7.2 million. These assets will then be financed by $4.9 million in existing liabilities plus spontaneous liabilities; $1.8 million in owner funds, including an additional $300,000 in retained earnings from next year's sales; and finally, $500,000 in discretionary financing, which can be raised by issuing notes payable, selling bonds, offering an issue of stock, or some combination of these sources.

In summary, we can estimate the firm's discretionary financing needs (*DFN*), using the percent of sales method of financial forecasting, by following a four-step procedure:

Step 1. Convert each asset and liability account that varies directly with firm sales to a percentage of the current year's sales.

> ### ► EXAMPLE: EXPRESSING CURRENT ASSETS AS A PERCENTAGE OF SALES

$$\frac{\text{Current assets}}{\text{sales}} = \frac{\$2M}{\$10M} = .2 \text{ or } 20\%$$

Step 2. Project the level of each asset and liability account in the balance sheet using its percentage of sales multiplied by projected sales or by leaving the account balance unchanged when the account does not vary with the level of sales.

> ### ► EXAMPLE: PREDICTING CURRENT ASSETS

$$\text{Projected current assets} = \text{projected sales} \times \frac{\text{current assets}}{\text{sales}} = \$12M \times .2 = \$2.4M$$

Step 3. Project the addition to retained earnings available to help finance the firm's operations. This equals projected net income for the period less planned common stock dividends.

> ### ► EXAMPLE: PREDICTING ADDITIONAL RETAINED EARNINGS

$$\begin{array}{l}\text{Projected addition} \\ \text{to retained earnings}\end{array} = \text{projected sales} \times \frac{\text{net income}}{\text{sales}} \times \left(1 - \frac{\text{cash dividends}}{\text{net income}}\right) = \$12M \times .05 \times (1 - .5) = \$300,000$$

Step 4. Project the firm's *DFN* as the projected level of total assets less projected liabilities and owners' equity.

> ### ► EXAMPLE: PREDICTING DISCRETIONARY FINANCING NEEDS

$$\begin{array}{l}\text{Discretionary financing needed} = \text{projected total assets} - \text{projected total liabilities} - \text{projected owner's equity} \\ = \$7.2M - \$4.9M - \$1.8M = \$500,000\end{array}$$

Analyzing the Effects of Profitability and Dividend Policy on *DFN*

Projecting discretionary financing needed, we can quickly and easily evaluate the sensitivity of our projected financing requirements to changes in key variables. For example, using the information from the preceding example, we evaluate the effect of net profit margins (*NPMs*) equal to 1 percent, 5 percent, and 10 percent in combination with dividend payout ratios of 30 percent, 50 percent, and 70 percent, as follows:

Discretionary Financing Needed for Various Net Profit Margins and Dividend Payout Ratios

| NET PROFIT MARGIN | DIVIDEND PAYOUT RATIOS = DIVIDENDS ÷ NET INCOME | | |
	30%	50%	70%
1%	$716,000	$740,000	$764,000
5%	380,000	500,000	620,000
10%	(40,000)	200,000	440,000

If these *NPMs* are reasonable estimates of the possible ranges of values the firm might experience, and if the firm is considering dividend payouts ranging from 30 percent to 70 percent, then we estimate that the firm's financing requirements will range from ($40,000), which represents a surplus of $40,000, to a situation in which it would need to acquire $764,000. Lower *NPMs* mean higher funding requirements. Also, higher dividend payout percentages, other things remaining constant, lead to a need for more discretionary financing. This is a direct result of the fact that a high-dividend-paying firm retains less of its earnings.

Analyzing the Effects of Sales Growth on a Firm's *DFN*

In Figure 14-1 we analyzed the *DFN* for Drew Inc., whose sales were expected to grow from $10 million to $12 million during the coming year. Recall that the 20 percent expected increase in sales led to an increase in the firm's needs for financing in the amount of $500,000. We referred to this added financing requirement as the firm's *DFN* because all these funds must be raised from sources, such as bank borrowing or a new equity issue, that require that management exercise its discretion in selecting the source. In this section we want to investigate how a firm's *DFN* varies with different rates of anticipated sales growth.

Table 14-2 expands on the financial forecast found in Table 14-1. Specifically, we use the same assumptions and prediction methods that underlie Table 14-1 but apply them to sales

FIGURE 14-1 Sales Growth and the Discretionary Financing Needs of the Firm

Sales growth rate

Can You Do It?

PERCENT OF SALES FORECASTING

The CFO for Madrigal Plumbing Supplies Inc. is developing financial plans for next year when he estimates that his sales will reach $10 million. During the 4 years the firm has been in business, its inventories have represented approximately 15% of its revenues. What would you estimate the firm's needs for inventories to be next year (using the percent of sales forecast method)? If Madrigal has economies of scale, would you expect its inventory needs to be more than, the same, or less than the percent of sales forecast?

(The solution can be found on page 445.)

growth rates of 0 percent, 20 percent, and 40 percent. The *DFN* for these sales growth rates ranges from ($250,000) to $1,250,000. When *DFN* is negative, this means that the firm has more money than it needs to finance the assets used to generate the projected sales. Alternatively, when *DFN* is positive, this means that the firm must raise additional funds in this amount, by either borrowing or issuing stock. We can calculate *DFN* using the following relationship:

$$DFN = \frac{\text{predicted change}}{\text{in total assets}} - \frac{\text{predicted change}}{\text{in spontaneous liabilities}} - \frac{\text{predicted change}}{\text{in retained earnings}} \quad (14\text{-}1)$$

Notice that in defining *DFN* we consider only changes in spontaneous liabilities, which you will recall are those liabilities that arise more or less automatically in the course of doing

TABLE 14-2   Discretionary Financing Needs (*DFN*) and the Growth Rate in Sales

	A	B	C	D	E	F	G	H	I	J	K
1	Drew Inc.						Drew Inc.				
2	Income Statement for 2007						Pro forma Income Statement for 2008				
3					% of 2007 Sales						
4								Alternative Growth Rates in Sales	0%	20%	40%
5	Sales		$ 10,000,000				Sales		$ 10,000,000	$ 12,000,000	$ 14,000,000
6	Net Income		$ 500,000	[$500,000 /$10,000,000 =]	5.0%		Net Income		$ 500,000	$ 600,000	$ 700,000
7											
8											
9	Drew Inc.						Drew Inc.				
10	Balance Sheet for 2007						Pro forma Balance Sheet for 2008				
11					% of 2007 Sales			Calculation			
12											
13	Current assets		$ 2,000,000	[$2m /$10m] =	20.0%		Current assets	.20 x$12m =	$ 2,000,000	$ 2,400,000	$ 2,800,000
14	Net fixed assets		4,000,000	[$4m /$10m] =	40.0%		Net fixed assets	.40 x$12m =	4,000,000	$ 4,800,000	$ 5,600,000
15	Total		$ 6,000,000				Total		$ 6,000,000	$ 7,200,000	$ 8,400,000
16											
17	Accounts payable		$ 1,000,000	[$1m /$10m] =	10.0%		Accounts payable	.10 x$12m =	$ 1,000,000	$ 1,200,000	$ 1,400,000
18	Accrued expenses		1,000,000	[$1m /$10m] =	10.0%		Accrued expenses	.10 x$12m =	1,000,000	1,200,000	1,400,000
19	Notes payable		500,000		NA*		Notes payable	No change	500,000	500,000	500,000
20	Current Liabilities		$ 2,500,000				Current Liabilities		$ 2,500,000	$ 2,900,000	$ 3,300,000
21	Long-term debt		2,000,000		NA*		Long-term debt	No change	2,000,000	2,000,000	2,000,000
22	Total Liabilities		$ 4,500,000				Total Liabilities		$ 4,500,000	$ 4,900,000	$ 5,300,000
23	Common stock (par)		100,000		NA*		Common stock (par)	No change	$ 100,000	$ 100,000	$ 100,000
24	Paid-in-capital		200,000		NA*		Paid-in-capital	No change	200,000	200,000	200,000
25	Retained earnings		1,200,000				Retained earnings	Calculation*	1,450,000	1,500,000	1,550,000
26	Common Equity		$ 1,500,000				Common Equity		$ 1,750,000	$ 1,800,000	$ 1,850,000
27	Total		$ 6,000,000				Total Financing Provided		$ 6,250,000	$ 6,700,000	$ 7,150,000
28							Discretionary Financing Needed (Plug)*		$ (250,000)	$ 500,000	$ 1,250,000
29							Total Financing Needed = Total Assets		$ 6,000,000	$ 7,200,000	$ 8,400,000
30											
31											
32	*Not applicable. These account balances do not vary with sales.										
33	bProjected retained earnings for 2008 based on the 20% growth rate scenario is $1,500,000 and is calculated as follows: The 2007 retained earnings of $1,200,000 added to 2008 projected net										
34	income of $600,000 less common dividends of $300,000. Note that dividends are assumed to be 50% or net income, so dividends vary across the three scenarios.										
35	cDiscretionary financing needed (DFN) for 2008 and the 20% growth rate scenario is a "plug figure" that equals the difference in the firm's projected total financing requirements or total assets of										
36	$7,200,000 and total financing provided of $6,700,000. In this scenario DFN is $500,000.										
37											
38											

How Did You Do?

PERCENT OF SALES FORECASTING

Madrigal projects that its inventories will be 15% of revenues such that its projected inventory needs for next year will be the following:

$$.15 \times \$10 \text{ million} = \$1,500,000$$

If Madrigal faces economies of scale, then its inventory needs will be less than the $1,500,000 predicted using the percent of sales method. When economies of scale are present, the firm's inventory needs do not increase proportionately with sales (nor do they decrease proportionately).

business (examples include accrued expenses and accounts payable). In Table 14-1 the only liabilities that are allowed to change with sales are spontaneous liabilities, so we can calculate the change in spontaneous liabilities simply by comparing total liabilities at the current sales level with total liabilities for the predicted sales level.

Equation (14-1) can be used to estimate the *DFN* numbers found in Table 14-2. For example, when sales are expected to grow at a rate of 10 percent (that is, *g* equals 10 percent), *DFN* can be calculated as follows:

$$DFN(g = 10\%) = (\$6,600,000 - \$6,000,000) - (\$4,700,000 - \$4,500,000) - (\$1,475,000 - \$1,200,000) = \$125,000$$

Sometimes analysts prefer to calculate a firm's **external financing needs (*EFN*)**, which include *all the firm's needs for financing beyond the funds provided internally through the retention of earnings*. Thus,

$$EFN = \text{predicted change in total assets} - \text{change in retained earnings} \qquad (14\text{-}2)$$

external financing needs
that portion of a firm's requirements for financing that exceeds its sources of internal financing (i.e., the retention of earnings) plus spontaneous sources of financing (e.g., trade credit).

For an anticipated growth in sales of 10 percent, *EFN* equals $325,000. The difference between *EFN* and *DFN* equals the $200,000 in added spontaneous financing that the firm anticipates receiving when its sales rise from $10 million to $11 million. We prefer to use the *DFN* concept because it focuses the analyst's attention on the amount of funds that the firm must actively seek to meet the firm's financing requirements.

Figure 14-1 contains a graphic representation of the relationship between growth rates for sales and *DFN*. The straight line in the graph depicts the level of *DFN* for each of the different rates of growth in firm sales. For example, if sales grow by 20 percent, then the firm projects a *DFN* of $500,000, which must be raised externally by borrowing or a new equity offering. Note that when sales grow at 6.667 percent, the firm's *DFN* will be exactly zero. For firms that have limited sources of external financing or choose to grow through internal financing plus spontaneous financing, it is important that they be able to estimate the sales growth rate that they can "afford," which in this case is 6.667 percent.

Did You Get It?

1. If we cannot predict the future perfectly, then why do firms engage in financial forecasting?
2. Why are sales forecasts so important to developing a firm's financial plans?
3. What is the percent of sales method of financial forecasting?
4. What are some examples of spontaneous and discretionary sources of financing?
5. What is the distinction between discretionary financing needs (*DFN*) and external financing needs (*EFN*)?

Objective 2

Describe the limitations of the percent of sales forecast method.

LIMITATIONS OF THE PERCENT OF SALES FORECASTING METHOD

The percent of sales method of financial forecasting provides reasonable estimates of a firm's financing requirements only when asset requirements and financing sources can be accurately forecast as a constant percent of sales. For example, predicting inventories for 2008 using the percent of sales method involves the following equation.

$$\text{Predicted inventories for 2008} = \left(\frac{\text{inventories for 2007}}{\text{sales for 2007}} \right) \times \text{predicted sales for 2008}$$

Figure 14-2a depicts this predictive relationship. Note that the percent of sales predictive model is simply a straight line that passes through the origin (that is, has a zero intercept). There are some fairly common instances in which this type of relationship fails to describe the relationship between an asset category and sales. Two such examples involve assets for which there are scale economies and assets that must be purchased in discrete quantities ("lumpy assets").

Economies of scale are sometimes realized from investing in certain types of assets. For example, a new computer system is likely to support a firm's operations over a wide range of firm sales. This means that these assets do not increase in direct proportion to sales. Figure 14-2b reflects one instance in which the firm realizes economies of scale from its investment in inventory. Note that inventories as a percentage of sales decline from 120 percent of sales, or $120 when sales are $100, to 30 percent of sales, or $300 when sales equal $1,000. This reflects the fact that there is a fixed component of inventories (in this case $100) that the firm must have on hand regardless of the level of sales, plus a variable component (20 percent of sales). In this instance the predictive equation for inventories is as follows:

$$\text{Inventories}_t = a + b\,\text{sales}_t$$

In this example, a (the intercept[2] of the inventories equation) is equal to 100 and b (the slope in the equation) is .20.

Figure 14-2c is an example of *lumpy assets*, that is, assets that must be purchased in large, nondivisible components. For example, if the firm spends $500 on plant and equipment, it can produce up to $100 in sales per year. If it spends another $500 (for a total of $1,000), then it can support sales of $200 to $300 per year, and so forth. Note that when a block of assets is purchased, it creates excess capacity until sales grow to the point at which the capacity is fully used. The result is a step function like the one depicted in Figure 14-2c. Thus, if the firm does not expect sales to exceed the current capacity of its plant and equipment, there would be no projected need for added plant and equipment capacity.

FIGURE 14-2A   Percent of Sales Forecast

---

[2] Economies of scale are evidenced by the nonzero intercept value. However, scale economies can also result in nonlinear relationships between sales and a particular asset category. Later, when we discuss cash management, we will find that one popular cash management model predicts a nonlinear relationship between the optimal cash balance and the level of cash transactions.

FIGURE 14-2B Economics of Scales

Inventories = 100 + .2 × sales

Note that a fixed amount of inventory ($100) is required to do business. However, as sales grow, the need for inventory does not grow as fast as in Figure 14-2a.

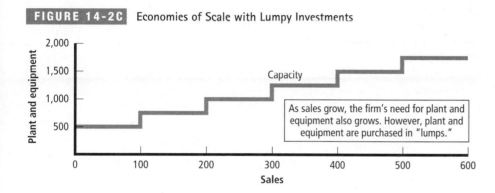

FIGURE 14-2C Economies of Scale with Lumpy Investments

Capacity

As sales grow, the firm's need for plant and equipment also grows. However, plant and equipment are purchased in "lumps."

CONSTRUCTING AND USING A CASH BUDGET

Objective **3**

Prepare a cash budget and use it to evaluate the amount and timing of a firm's financing needs.

As we noted earlier, the principal virtue of the percent of sales method of financial forecasting is its simplicity. To obtain a more precise estimate of the amount and timing of the firm's future financing needs, we require a cash budget. The percent of sales method of financial forecasting provides a very useful, low-cost forerunner to the development of the more detailed cash budget, which the firm will ultimately use to estimate its financing needs.

Budget Functions

A **budget** is simply *a forecast of future events*. For example, students preparing for final exams make use of time budgets to help them allocate their limited preparation time among their courses. Students also must budget their financial resources among competing uses, such as books, tuition, food, rent, clothes, and extracurricular activities.

budget an itemized forecast of a company's expected revenues and expenses for a future period.

   Budgets perform three basic functions for a firm.

- First, they indicate the amount and timing of the firm's needs for future financing.
- Second, they provide the basis for taking corrective action in the event budgeted figures do not match actual or realized figures.

Remember Your Principles

Budgets have many important uses; however, their use as a tool of managerial control is critically important and often overlooked in the study of financial management. **Principle 7: The Agency Problem—Managers Won't Work for the Firm's Owners Unless It's in Their Best Interest** speaks to the root source of the problem, and budgets provide one tool for attempting to deal with it. Specifically, budgets provide management with a tool for evaluating performance and, consequently, maintaining a degree of control over employee actions.

Ethics in Financial Management

TO BRIBE OR NOT TO BRIBE

The pressure to "get the forecast right" can be tremendous, and these pressures can lead managers to engage in practices (especially in underdeveloped countries) of offering bribes and payoffs to public officials because they are considered the norm in business transactions. This raises a perplexing ethical question. If paying bribes is not considered unethical in a foreign country, should you consider it unethical to make these payments?

This situation provides an example of an ethical issue that gave rise to legislation. The Foreign Corrupt Practices Act of 1977 (as amended in the Omnibus Trade and Competitiveness Act of 1988) established criminal penalties for making payments to foreign officials, political parties, or candidates in order to obtain or retain business. Ethical problems are fre-

quently areas just outside the boundaries of current legislation and often lead to the passage of new legislation.

Consider the following question: If you were involved in negotiating an important business deal in a foreign country and the success or failure of the deal hinged on whether you paid a local government official to help you consummate the deal, would you authorize the payment? Assume that the form of the payment is such that you do not expect to be caught and punished; for example, your company agrees to purchase supplies from a family member of the government official at a price slightly above the competitive price. Can you see any pitfalls related to such a deal?

- Third, budgets provide the basis for performance evaluation and control. Plans are carried out by people, and budgets provide benchmarks that management can use to evaluate the performance of those responsible for carrying out those plans and, in turn, to control their actions.

Did You Get It?

1. What, in words, is the fundamental relationship (equation) used in making percent of sales forecasts?
2. Under what circumstances does a firm violate the basic relationship underlying the percent of sales forecast method?

The Cash Budget

cash budget a detailed plan of future cash flows. This budget is composed of four elements: cash receipts, cash disbursements, net change in cash for the period, and new financing needed.

The **cash budget** represents a *detailed plan of future cash flows* and is composed of four elements: cash receipts, cash disbursements, net change in cash for the period, and new financing needed.

➤ EXAMPLE: CONSTRUCTING A CASH BUDGET

To demonstrate the construction and use of the cash budget, consider Salco Furniture Company Inc., a regional distributor of household furniture. Sales is in the process of preparing a monthly cash budget for the upcoming 6 months (January through June 2008). The company's sales are highly seasonal, peaking in the months of March through May. Roughly 30 percent of Salco's sales are collected 1 month after the sale, 50 percent 2 months after the sale, and the remainder during the third month following the sale.

Salco attempts to pace its purchases with its forecast of future sales. Purchases generally equal 75 percent of sales and are made 2 months in advance of anticipated sales. Payments are made in the month following purchases. For example, June sales are estimated at $100,000; thus, April purchases are .75 × $100,000 = $75,000. Correspondingly, payments for purchases in May equal $75,000. Wages, salaries, rent, and other cash expenses are recorded in Table 14-3, which shows Salco's cash budget for the 6-month period ended in June 2008. Additional expenditures are recorded in the cash budget related to the purchase of equipment in the amount of $14,000 during February and the repayment of a $12,000 loan in May. In June, Salco will pay $7,500 interest on its $150,000 in long-

Ethics in Financial Management

BEING HONEST ABOUT THE UNCERTAINTY OF THE FUTURE

Put yourself in the shoes of Ben Tolbert, who is the CFO of Bonajet Enterprises. Ben's CEO is scheduled to meet with a group of outside analysts tomorrow to discuss the firm's financial forecast for the last quarter of the year. Ben's analysis suggests that there is a very real prospect that the coming quarter's results could be very disappointing. How would you handle Ben's dilemma?

As Ben looks over a draft of the report he must submit to the company CEO, he becomes increasingly concerned. Although the forecast is below initial expectations, this is not what worries Ben. The problem is that some of the basic assumptions underlying his prediction might not come true. If this is the case, then the company's performance for the last quarter of the

year will be dramatically below its annual forecast. The result would be a potentially severe reaction in the investment community, causing a downward adjustment of unknown proportions in the firm's stock price.

Bonajet's CEO is a no-nonsense guy who really doesn't like to see his CFO hedge his predictions, so Ben is under pressure to decide whether to ignore the downside prospects or make them known to his CEO. Complicating matters is the fact that the worst-case scenario would probably give rise to a reorganization of Bonajet that would lead to substantial layoffs of its workforce. Here is Ben's dilemma: What should he tell the CEO in their meeting tomorrow morning?

---

term debt for the period of January to June 2008. Interest on the $12,000 short-term note repaid in May for the period January through May equals $600 and is paid in May.

Salco currently has a cash balance of $20,000 and wants to maintain a minimum balance of $10,000. Additional borrowing necessary to maintain that minimum balance is estimated in the final section of Table 14-3. Borrowing takes place at the beginning of the month in which the funds are needed. Interest on the borrowed funds equals 12 percent per annum, or 1 percent per month, and is paid in the month following the one in which funds are borrowed. Thus, interest on funds borrowed in January will be paid in February equal to 1 percent of the loan amount outstanding during January.

The financing-needed line in Salco's cash budget determines that the firm's cumulative short-term borrowing will be $36,350 in February, $65,874 in March, $86,633 in April, and $97,599 in May. In June the firm will be able to reduce its borrowing to $79,875. Note that the cash budget indicates not only the amount of financing needed during the period but also when the funds will be needed.

TABLE 14-3 Salco Furniture Co. Inc. Cash Budget for the 6 Months Ended June 30, 2008

	A	B	C	D	E	F	G	H	I	J	K	L
1		October	November	December	January	February	March	April	May	June	July	August
2	Worksheet											
3	Sales (forecasted)	55,000	62,000	50,000	60,000	75,000	88,000	100,000	110,000	100,000	80,000	75,000
4	Purchases (75% of sales in 2 months)			56,250	66,000	75,000	82,500	75,000	60,000	56,250		
5												
6	Cash Receipts											
7	Collections:											
8	First Month after sale (30%)				15,000	18,000	22,500	26,400	30,000	33,000		
9	Second Month after sale (50%)				31,000	25,000	30,000	37,500	44,000	50,000		
10	Third Month after sale (20%)				11,000	12,400	10,000	12,000	15,000	17,600		
11	Total Cash Receipts				57,000	55,400	62,500	75,900	89,000	100,600		
12												
13	Cash Disbursements											
14	Payments (one-month lag of purchases from row 4)				56,250	66,000	75,000	82,500	75,000	60,000		
15	Wages and Salaries				3,000	10,000	7,000	8,000	6,000	4,000		
16	Rent				4,000	4,000	4,000	4,000	4,000	4,000		
17	Other Expenses				1,000	500	1,200	1,500	1,500	1,200		
18	Interest expense on existing debt[a]								600	7,500		
19	Taxes						4,460			5,200		
20	Purchase of Equipment					14,000						
21	Loan Repayment[b]								12,000			
22	Total Cash Disbursements				64,250	94,500	91,660	96,000	99,100	81,900		
23												
24	Net Change in Cash for the Period				(7,250)	(39,100)	(29,160)	(20,100)	(10,100)	18,700		
25	Plus: Beginning cash balance				20,000	12,750	10,000	10,000	10,000	10,000		
26	Less: Interest on short-term borrowing				0	0	(364)	(659)	(866)	(976)		
27	Equals: Ending cash balance before short-term borrowing				12,750	(26,350)	(19,524)	(10,759)	(966)	27,724		
28												
29	New Financing Needed[c]				0	36,350	29,524	20,759	10,966	(17,724) [d]		
30	Ending cash balance				12,750	10,000	10,000	10,000	10,000	10,000		
31	Cumulative borrowing				0	36,350	65,874	86,633	97,599	79,875		
32												
33												
34	[a]An interest payment of $600 on the $12,000 loan is due in May, and an interest payment of $7500 on the $150,000 long-term debt is due in June.											
35	[b]The principal amount of the $12,000 loan is also due in May.											
36	[c]The amount of financing that is required to raise the firm's ending cash balance up to its $10,000 desired cash balance.											
37	[d]Negative financing needed simply means the firm has excess cash that can be used to retire a part of its short-term borrowing from prior months.											
38												

Did You Get It? ....

1. What is a cash budget?
2. How is a cash budget used in financial planning?

Summary

Objective **1**

Use the percent of sales method to forecast the financing requirements of a firm.

This chapter developed the role of forecasting within the context of the firm's financial-planning activities. Forecasts of the firm's sales revenues and related expenses provide the basis for projecting future financing needs. The most popular method for forecasting financial variables is the percent of sales method.

Objective **2**

Describe the limitations of the percent of sales forecast method.

The percent of sales method presumes that the asset or liability being forecast is a constant percent of sales for all future levels of sales. There are instances when this assumption is not reasonable and, consequently, the percent of sales method does not provide reasonable predictions. One such instance arises when there are economies of scale in the use of the asset being forecast. For example, the firm may need at least $10 million in inventories to open its doors and operate even for sales as low as $100 million per year. If sales double to $200 million, inventories may only increase to $15 million. Thus, inventories do not increase with sales in a constant proportion. A second situation in which the percent of sales method fails to work properly is when asset purchases are lumpy. That is, if plant capacity must be purchased in, say, $50 million increments, then plant and equipment will not remain a constant percentage of sales.

How serious are these possible problems and should we use the percent of sales method? Even in the face of these problems, the percent of sales method works reasonably well when predicted sales levels do not differ drastically from the level used to calculate the percentage of sales. For example, if the current sales level used in calculating the percentage of sales for inventories is $40 million, then we can feel more comfortable forecasting the level of inventories corresponding to a new sales level of $42 million than when sales are predicted to rise to $60 million.

Objective **3**

Prepare a cash budget and use it to evaluate the amount and timing of a firm's financing needs.

The cash budget is the primary tool of financial forecasting and planning. It contains a detailed plan of the firm's future cash flow estimates and consists of four elements or segments: cash receipts, cash disbursements, net change in cash for the period, and new financing needed. Once prepared, the cash budget also serves as a tool for monitoring and controlling the firm's operations. By comparing actual cash receipts and disbursements to those in the cash budget, the financial manager can gain an appreciation of how well the firm is performing. In addition, deviations from the plan can serve as an early warning system to signal the onset of financial difficulties ahead.

Key Terms

Budget   447

Cash budget   448

Discretionary financing   441

External financing needs   445

Percent of sales method   440

Spontaneous financing   441

Review Questions

14-1. Discuss the shortcomings of the percent of sales method of financial forecasting.

14-2. What would be the probable effect on a firm's cash position of the following events?

    a. Rapidly rising sales

    b. A delay in the payment of payables

    c. A more liberal credit policy on sales (to the firm's customers)

    d. Holding larger inventories

14-3. A cash budget is usually thought of as a means of planning for future financing needs. Why would a cash budget also be important for a firm that has excess cash on hand?

14-4. Explain why a cash budget would be of particular importance to a firm that experiences seasonal fluctuations in its sales.

Self-Test Problems

(Solutions to these problems are found at the end of the chapter.)

ST-1. (*Financial forecasting*) Use the percent of sales method to prepare a pro forma income statement for Calico Sales Co. Inc. Projected sales for next year equal $4 million. Cost of goods sold equals 70 percent of sales, administrative expense equals $500,000, and depreciation expense is $300,000. Interest expense equals $50,000, and income is taxed at a rate of 40 percent. The firm plans to spend $200,000 during the period to renovate its office facility and will retire $150,000 in notes payable. Finally, selling expense equals 5 percent of sales.

ST-2. (*Cash budget*) Stauffer Inc. has estimated its sales and purchase requirements for the last half of the coming year. Past experience indicates that it will collect 20 percent of its sales in the month of the sale, 50 percent of the remainder 1 month after the sale, and the balance in the second month following the sale. Stauffer prefers to pay for half its purchases in the month of the purchase and the other half in the following month. The labor expense for each month is expected to equal 5 percent of that month's sales, with cash payment being made in the month in which the expense is incurred.

Depreciation expense is $5,000 per month; miscellaneous cash expenses are $4,000 per month and are paid in the month incurred. General and administrative expenses of $50,000 are recognized and paid monthly. A $60,000 truck is to be purchased in August and is to be depreciated on a straight-line basis over 10 years with no expected salvage value. The company also plans to pay a $9,000 cash dividend to its stockholders in July. The company feels that a minimum cash balance of $30,000 should be maintained. Any borrowing will cost 12 percent annually, with interest paid in the month following the month in which the funds are borrowed. Borrowing takes place at the beginning of the month in which the need for funds arises. For example, if during the month of July the firm should need to borrow $24,000 to maintain its $30,000 desired minimum balance, then $24,000 will be taken out on July 1 with interest owed for the entire month of July. Interest for the month of July would then be paid on August 1. Sales and purchase estimates are shown here. Prepare a cash budget for the months of July and August (cash on hand June 30 was $30,000, sales for May and June were $100,000, and purchases were $60,000 for each of these months).

MONTH	SALES	PURCHASES
July	$120,000	$50,000
August	150,000	40,000
September	110,000	30,000

ST-3. (*Forecasting net income*) The chief financial officer of Clairmont Manufacturing Inc. prepares a forecast of net income for the coming year as a starting point for developing financial plans. At the close of 2008, the firm's income statement appeared as follows (in $000):

Income Statement ($000)

FOR THE YEAR ENDED 2008	
Sales	$25,000
Cost of goods sold	(16,250)
Gross profit	8,750
Operating costs	(4,500)
Depreciation expense	(150)
Net operating profit	4,100
Interest expense	(1,580)
Earnings before taxes	2,520
Taxes	(882)
Net income	$ 1,638
Dividends	$ 1,500
Addition to retained earnings	$ 138

The CFO normally uses the most recent income statement to guide her estimate of what the future will bring. For example, she has made the following assumptions and estimates for 2009:

Sales growth rate	15%
COGS/sales	65%
Operating expenses/sales	18%
Depreciation expense ($000)	$ 150
Interest expense ($000)	$1,580
Tax rate	35%
Dividends ($000)	$1,500

Note that these estimates are derived from the 2008 income statement, reflecting the fact that the CFO believes the only real change for the coming year is the level of sales, which she estimates to be 15 percent higher. Of course, cost of goods sold and operating expenses will rise in proportion to the increase in sales following the percent of sales noted earlier.

What do you estimate net income for the firm to be in 2009? If the firm retains its $1,500,000 dividend payment, how much do you estimate the firm will be able to retain in 2009?

Study Problems

14-1. (*Financial forecasting*) Zapatera Enterprises is evaluating its financing requirements for the coming year. The firm has been in business for only 1 year, but its CFO predicts that the firm's operating expenses, current assets, net fixed assets, and current liabilities will remain at their current proportion of sales.

Last year Zapatera had $12 million in sales, and net income of $1.2 million. The firm anticipates that next year's sales will reach $15 million, with net income rising to $2 million. Given its present high rate of growth, the firm retains all its earnings to help defray the cost of new investments.

The firm's balance sheet for the year just ended is found here:

Zapatera Enterprises Inc.

BALANCE SHEET		
	12/31/2008	**% OF SALES**
Current assets	$3,000,000	25%
Net fixed assets	6,000,000	50%
Total	$9,000,000	
LIABILITIES AND OWNERS' EQUITY		
Accounts payable	$3,000,000	25%
Long-term debt	2,000,000	NA[a]
Total liabilities	$5,000,000	
Common stock	1,000,000	NA
Paid-in capital	1,800,000	NA
Retained earnings	1,200,000	
Common equity	4,000,000	
Total	$9,000,000	

[a] Not applicable. This figure does not vary directly with sales and is assumed to remain constant for purposes of making next year's forecast of financing requirements.

Estimate Zapatera's financing requirements (i.e., total assets) for 2008 and its discretionary financing needs (*DFN*).

14-2. (*Pro forma accounts receivable balance calculation*) On March 31, 2007, Mike's Bike Shop had outstanding accounts receivable of $17,500. Mike's sales are roughly evenly split between credit and cash sales, with the credit sales collected half in the month after the sale and the remainder 2 months after the sale. Historical and projected sales for the bike shop are given here:

MONTH	SALES	MONTH	SALES
January	$15,000	March	$25,000
February	20,000	April (projected)	30,000

   a. Under these circumstances, what should the balance in accounts receivable be at the end of April?
   b. How much cash did Mike's realize during April from sales and collections?

14-3. (*Financial forecasting*) Sambonoza Enterprises projects its sales next year to be $4 million and expects to earn 5 percent of that amount after taxes. The firm is currently in the process of projecting its financing needs and has made the following assumptions (projections):
   1. Current assets will equal 20 percent of sales, and fixed assets will remain at their current level of $1 million.

2. Common equity is currently $0.8 million, and the firm pays out half its after-tax earnings in dividends.

3. The firm has short-term payables and trade credit that normally equal 10 percent of sales, and it has no long-term debt outstanding.

What are Sambonoza's financing needs for the coming year?

14-4. (*Financial forecasting—percent of sales*) Tulley Appliances Inc. projects next year's sales to be $20 million. Current sales are $15 million, based on current assets of $5 million and fixed assets of $5 million. The firm's net profit margin is 5 percent after taxes. Tulley forecasts that its current assets will rise in direct proportion to the increase in sales, but that its fixed assets will increase by only $100,000. Currently, Tulley has $1.5 million in accounts payable (which vary directly with sales), $2 million in long-term debt (due in 10 years), and common equity (including $4 million in retained earnings) totaling $6.5 million. Tulley plans to pay $500,000 in common stock dividends next year.

   a. What are Tulley's total financing needs (i.e., total assets) for the coming year?
   b. Given the firm's projections and dividend payments plans, what are its discretionary financing needs?
   c. Based on your projections, and assuming that the $100,000 expansion in fixed assets will occur, what is the largest increase in sales the firm can support without having to resort to the use of discretionary sources of financing?

14-5. (*Pro forma balance sheet construction*) Use the following industry-average ratios to construct a pro forma balance sheet for Phoebe's Cat Foods Inc.

Total asset turnover	1.5 times
Average collection period (assume 365-day year)	15 days
Fixed asset turnover	5 times
Inventory turnover (based on cost of goods sold)	3 times
Current ratio	2 times
Sales (all on credit)	$3.0 million
Cost of goods sold	75% of sales
Debt ratio	50%

		Current liabilities	
Cash		Long-term debt	
Accounts receivable	_____	Common stock plus	_____
Net fixed assets	$ _____	Retained earnings	$ _____

14-6. (*Cash budget*) The Sharpe Corporation's projected sales for the first 8 months of 2008 are as follows:

January	$190,000	May	$300,000
February	120,000	June	270,000
March	135,000	July	225,000
April	240,000	August	150,000

Of Sharpe's sales, 10 percent is for cash, another 60 percent is collected in the month following the sales, and 30 percent is collected in the second month following sales. November and December sales for 2005 were $220,000 and $175,000, respectively.

Sharpe purchases its raw materials 2 months in advance of its sales. The purchases are equal to 60 percent of the final sales price of Sharpe's products. The supplier is paid 1 month after it makes a delivery. For example, purchases for April sales are made in February, and payment is made in March.

In addition, Sharpe pays $10,000 per month for rent and $20,000 each month for other expenditures. Tax prepayments of $22,500 are made each quarter, beginning in March.

The company's cash balance on December 31, 2007, was $22,000. This is the minimum balance the firm wants to maintain. Any borrowing that is needed to maintain this minimum is paid off in the subsequent month if there is sufficient cash. Interest on short-term loans (12 percent) is paid monthly. Borrowing to meet estimated monthly cash needs takes place at the beginning of the month. Thus, if in the month of April the firm expects to have a need for an additional $60,500, these funds would be borrowed at the beginning of April with interest of $605 (.12 × 1/12 × $60,500) owed for April and paid at the beginning of May.

    a. Prepare a cash budget for Sharpe covering the first 7 months of 2008.

    b. Sharpe has $200,000 in notes payable due in July that must be repaid or renegotiated for an extension. Will the firm have ample cash to repay the notes?

14-7. (*Percent of sales forecasting*) Which of the following accounts would most likely vary directly with the level of a firm's sales? Discuss each briefly.

	YES	NO		YES	NO
Cash	___	___	Notes payable	___	___
Marketable securities	___	___	Plant and equipment	___	___
Accounts payable	___	___	Inventories	___	___

14-8. (*Financial forecasting—percent of sales*) The balance sheet of the Boyd Trucking Company (BTC) follows:

Boyd Trucking Company Balance Sheet, December 31, 2007 ($ Millions)

Current assets	$10	Accounts payable	$ 5
Net fixed assets	15	Notes payable	0
Total	$25	Bonds payable	10
		Common equity	10
		Total	$25

BTC had sales for the year ended December 31, 2007, of $25 million. The firm follows a policy of paying all net earnings out to its common stockholders in cash dividends. Thus, BTC generates no funds from its earnings that can be used to expand its operations. (Assume that depreciation expense is just equal to the cost of replacing worn-out assets.)

    a. If BTC anticipates sales of $40 million during the coming year, develop a pro forma balance sheet for the firm on December 31, 2008. Assume that current assets vary as a percent of sales, net fixed assets remain unchanged, and accounts payable vary as a percent of sales. Use notes payable as a balancing entry.

    b. How much "new" financing will BTC need next year?

    c. What limitations does the percent of sales forecast method suffer from? Discuss briefly.

14-9. (*Financial forecasting—discretionary financing needs*) The most recent balance sheet for the Armadillo Dog Biscuit Co. Inc. is shown in the following table. The company is about to embark on an advertising campaign, which is expected to raise sales from the current level of $5 million to $7 million by the end of next year. The firm is currently operating at full capacity and will have to increase its investment in both current and fixed assets to support the projected level of new sales. In fact, the firm estimates that both categories of assets will rise in direct proportion to the projected increase in sales.

Armadillo Dog Biscuit Co. Inc. ($ Millions)

	PRESENT LEVEL	PERCENT OF SALES	PROJECTED LEVEL
Current assets	$2.0		
Net fixed assets	3.0		
Total	$5.0		
Accounts payable	$0.5		
Accrued expense	0.5		
Notes payable	—		
Current liabilities	$1.0		
Long-term debt	$2.0		
Common stock	0.5		
Retained earnings	1.5		
Common equity	$2.0		
Total	$5.0		

The firm's net profits were 6 percent of the current year's sales but are expected to rise to 7 percent of next year's sales. To help support its anticipated growth in asset needs next year, the firm has suspended plans to pay cash dividends to its stockholders. In past years a $1.50-per-share dividend has been paid annually. Armadillo's accounts payable and accrued expenses are expected to vary directly with sales. In addition, notes payable will be used to supply the funds needed to finance next year's operations that are not forthcoming from other sources.

  a. Fill in the table and project the firm's needs for discretionary financing. Use notes payable as the balancing entry for future discretionary financing needs.
  b. Compare Armadillo's current ratio and debt ratio (total liabilities ÷ total assets) before the growth in sales and after. What was the effect of the expanded sales on these two dimensions of Armadillo's financial condition?
  c. What difference, if any, would have resulted if Armadillo's sales had risen to $6 million in 1 year and $7 million only after 2 years? Discuss only; no calculations are required.

14-10. (*Forecasting discretionary financing needs*) Fishing Charter Inc. estimates that it invests $0.30 in assets for each dollar of new sales. However, $0.05 in profits are produced by each dollar of additional sales, of which $0.01 can be reinvested in the firm. If sales rise by $500,000 next year from their current level of $5 million, and the ratio of spontaneous liabilities to sales is 15 percent, what will be the firm's need for discretionary financing? (*Hint:* In this situation you do not know what the firm's existing level of assets is, nor do you know how those assets have been financed. Thus, you must estimate the change in financing needs and match this change with the expected changes in spontaneous liabilities, retained earnings, and other sources of discretionary financing.)

14-11. (*Preparation of a cash budget*) Lewis Printing has projected its sales for the first 8 months of 2008 as follows:

January	$100,000	April	$300,000	July	$200,000
February	120,000	May	275,000	August	180,000
March	150,000	June	200,000		

Lewis collects 20 percent of its sales in the month of the sale, 50 percent in the month following the sale, and the remaining 30 percent 2 months following the sale. During November and December of 2007, Lewis's sales were $220,000 and $175,000, respectively.

Lewis purchases raw materials 2 months in advance of its sales. These purchases are equal to 65 percent of its final sales. The supplier is paid 1 month after delivery. Thus, purchases for April sales are made in February and payment is made in March.

In addition, Lewis pays $10,000 per month for rent and $20,000 each month for other expenditures. Tax prepayments of $22,500 are made each quarter beginning in March. The company's cash balance as of December 31, 2007, was $28,000; a minimum balance of $25,000 must be maintained at all times to satisfy the firm's bank line of credit agreement. Lewis has arranged with its bank for short-term credit at an interest rate of 12 percent per annum (1 percent per month) to be paid monthly. Borrowing to meet estimated monthly cash needs takes place at the end of the month, and interest is not paid until the end of the following month. Consequently, if the firm needed to borrow $50,000 during April, then it would pay $500 (= .01 × $50,000) in interest during May. Finally, Lewis follows a policy of repaying its outstanding short-term debt in any month in which its cash balance exceeds the minimum desired balance of $25,000.

  a. Lewis needs to know what its cash requirements will be for the next 6 months so that it can renegotiate the terms of its short-term credit agreement with its bank, if necessary. To evaluate this problem, the firm plans to evaluate the impact of a ±20 percent variation in its monthly sales efforts. Prepare a 6-month cash budget for Lewis and use it to evaluate the firm's cash needs.
  b. Lewis has a $20,000 note due in June. Will the firm have sufficient cash to repay the loan?

14-12. (*Forecasting inventories*) Findlay Instruments produces a complete line of medical instruments used by plastic surgeons and has experienced rapid growth over the past 5 years. In an effort to make more accurate predictions of its financing requirements, Findlay is currently attempting to construct a financial-planning model based on the percent of sales forecasting method. However, the firm's chief financial analyst (Sarah Macias) is concerned that the projections for inventories will be seriously in error. She recognizes that the firm has begun to accrue substantial economies of scale in its inventory investment and has documented this fact in the following data and calculations:

YEAR	SALES ($000)	INVENTORY ($000)	% OF SALES
2004	$15,000	$1,150	7.67%
2005	18,000	1,180	6.56%
2006	17,500	1,175	6.71%
2007	20,000	1,200	6.00%
2008	25,000	1,250	5.00%
			Average 6.39%

a. Plot Findlay's sales and inventories for the past 5 years. What is the relationship between these two variables?

b. Estimate firm inventories for 2009, when firm sales are projected to reach $30 million. Use the average percentage of sales for the past 5 years, the most recent percentage of sales, and your evaluation of the true relationship between the sales and inventories from part a to make three predictions.

14-13. (*Forecasting net income*) In November of each year the CFO of Barker Electronics begins the financial forecasting process to determine the firm's projected needs for new financing during the coming year. Barker is a small electronics manufacturing company located in Moline, Illinois, which is best known as the home of the John Deere Company. The CFO begins the process with the most recent year's income statement, projects sales growth for the coming year, and then estimates net income and finally the additional earnings he can expect to retain and reinvest in the firm. The firm's income statement for 2007 follows (in $000):

Income Statement ($000)

	YEAR ENDED DECEMBER 31, 2007
Sales	$ 1,500
Cost of goods sold	(1,050)
Gross profit	$ 450
Operating costs	(225)
Depreciation expense	(50)
Net operating profit	$ 175
Interest expense	(10)
Earnings before taxes	$ 165
Taxes	(58)
Net income	$ 107
Dividends	$ 20
Addition to retained earnings	$ 87

The electronics business has been growing rapidly over the past 18 months as the economy recovers, and the CFO estimates that sales will expand by 20 percent in the next year. In addition, he estimates the following relationships between each of the income statement expense items and sales:

COGS/sales	70%
Operating expenses/sales	15%
Depreciation expense ($000)	$50
Interest expense ($000)	$10
Tax rate	35%

Note that for the coming year both depreciation expense and interest expense are projected to remain the same as in 2007.

a. Estimate Barker's net income for 2008 and its addition to retained earnings under the assumption that the firm leaves its dividends paid at the 2007 level.

b. Reevaluate Barker's net income and addition to retained earnings where sales grow at 40 percent over the coming year. However, this scenario requires the addition of new plant and equipment in the amount of $100,000, which increases annual depreciation to $58,000 per year, and interest expense rises to $15,000.

Web Works

14-WW1. Look up the most recent income statement and balance sheet for Starbucks (**www.starbucks.com**), Home Depot (**www.homedepot.com**), and Wal-Mart (**www.walmart.com**). For each firm calculate the ratio of current assets to sales for each of the past 3 years. If you projected that sales for each firm are anticipated to increase by 35 percent in the coming year, what would the percent of sales method of financial forecasting predict next year's current assets to be for each of the firms?

14-WW2. Assume that each of the firms analyzed in the preceding question retains its current dividend payout ratio and that the firm's net profit margin remains constant. How much should each firm expect to be able to reinvest out of next year's earnings?

Mini Case

Phillips Petroleum is an integrated oil and gas company with headquarters in Bartlesville, Oklahoma, where it was founded in 1917. The company engages in petroleum exploration and production worldwide. In addition, it engages in natural gas gathering and processing, as well as petroleum refining and marketing primarily in the United States. The company has three operating groups: Exploration and Production, Gas and Gas Liquids, and Downstream Operations, which encompasses Petroleum Products and Chemicals.

In the mid-1980s, Phillips engaged in a major restructuring following two failed takeover attempts, one led by T. Boone Pickins and the other by Carl Ichan.[3] The restructuring resulted in a $4.5 billion plan to exchange a package of cash and debt securities for roughly half the company's shares and to sell $2 billion worth of assets. Phillips's long-term debt increased from $3.4 billion in late 1984 to a peak of $8.6 billion in April 1985.

During 1992, Phillips was able to strengthen its financial structure dramatically. Its subsidiary Phillips Gas Company completed an offering of $345 million of Series A 9.32% cumulative preferred stock. As a result of this action and prior years' debt reductions, the company lowered its long-term debt-to-capital ratio over the past 5 years from 75 percent to 55 percent. In addition, the firm refinanced over a billion dollars of its debt at reduced rates. A company spokesman said, "Our debt-to-capital ratio is still on the high side, and we'll keep working to bring it down. But the cost of debt is manageable, and we're beyond the point where debt overshadows everything else we do."[4]

Summary Financial Information for Phillips Petroleum Corporation:
1986 to 1992 (in Millions of Dollars Except for per Share Figures)

	1986	1987	1988	1989	1990	1991	1992
Sales	$10,018.00	$10,917.00	$11,490.00	$12,492.00	$13,975.00	$13,259.00	$12,140.00
Net income	228.00	35.00	650.00	219.00	541.00	98.00	270.00
EPS	0.89	0.06	2.72	0.90	2.18	0.38	1.04
Current assets	2,802.00	2,855.00	3,062.00	2,876.00	3,322.00	2,459.00	2,349.00
Total assets	12,403.00	12,111.00	11,968.00	11,256.00	12,130.00	11,473.00	11,468.00
Current liabilities	2,234.00	2,402.00	2,468.00	2,706.00	2,910.00	2,503.00	2,517.00
Long-term debt	8,175.00	7,887.00	7,387.00	6,418.00	6,505.00	6,113.00	5,894.00
Total liabilities	10,409.00	10,289.00	9,855.00	9,124.00	9,411.00	8,716.00	8,411.00
Preferred stock	270.00	205.00	0.00	0.00	0.00	0.00	359.00
Common equity	1,724.00	1,617.00	2,113.00	2,132.00	2,719.00	2,757.00	2,698.00
Dividends per share	2.02	1.73	1.34	0.00	1.03	1.12	1.12

Source: Phillips annual reports for 1986 to 1992.

Highlights of Phillips's financial condition from 1986 to 1992 are found in the accompanying table. These data reflect the company's financial restructuring following the downsizing and reorganization of Phillips's operations begun in the mid-1980s.

Phillips's managers are currently developing its financial plans for the next 5 years and want to develop a forecast of its financing requirements. As a first approximation, they have asked you to develop a model that can be used to make "ballpark" estimates of the firm's financing needs under the proviso that existing relationships found in the firm's financial statements remain the same over the

[3] This discussion is based on a story in the *New York Times*, January 7, 1986.

[4] From *SEC Online*, 1992.

period. Of particular interest is whether Phillips will be able to further reduce its reliance on debt financing. You may assume that Phillips's projected sales (in millions) for 1993 through 1997 are as follows: $13,000; $13,500; $14,000; $14,500; and $15,500.

    a. Project net income for 1993 to 1997 using the percent of sales method based on an average of this ratio for 1986 to 1992.

    b. Project total assets and current liabilities for 1993 to 1997 using the percent of sales method and your sales projections from part a.

    c. Assuming that common equity increases only as a result of the retention of earnings and holding long-term debt and preferred stock equal to its 1992 balances, project Phillips's discretionary financing needs for 1993 to 1997. (*Hint:* Assume that total assets and current liabilities vary as a percentage of sales as per your answers to part b. In addition, assume that Phillips plans to continue to pay its dividends of $1.12 per share in each of the next 5 years.)

Self-Test Solutions

SS-1.

Calico Sales Co. Inc. Pro Forma Income Statement

Sales		$4,000,000
Cost of goods sold (70%)		(2,800,000)
Gross profit		1,200,000
Operating expense		
Selling expense (5%)	$200,000	
Administrative expense	500,000	
Depreciation expense	300,000	(1,000,000)
Net operating income		200,000
Interest expense		(50,000)
Earnings before taxes		150,000)
Taxes (40%)		(60,000)
Net income		$ 90,000

Although the office-renovation expenditure and debt retirement are surely cash outflows, they do not enter the income statement directly. These expenditures affect expenses for the period's income statement only through their effect on depreciation and interest expense. A cash budget would indicate the full cash impact of the renovation and debt-retirement expenditures.

SS-2.

	MAY	JUNE	JULY	AUGUST
Sales	$100,000	$100,000	$ 120,000	$ 150,000
Purchases	60,000	60,000	50,000	40,000
Cash receipts:				
Collections from month of sale (20%)	20,000	20,000	24,000	30,000
1 month later (50% of uncollected amount)		40,000	40,000	48,000
2 months later (balance)			40,000	40,000
Total receipts			$ 104,000	$ 118,000
Cash disbursements:				
Payments for purchases—				
From 1 month earlier			$ 30,000	$ 25,000
From current month			$ 25,000	20,000
Total			$ 55,000	$ 45,000
Miscellaneous cash expenses			4,000	4,000
Labor expense (5% of sales)			6,000	7,500
General and administrative expense				
($50,000 per month)			50,000	50,000
Truck purchase			0	60,000
Cash dividends			9,000	–
Total disbursements			$(124,000)	$(166,500)
Net change in cash			(20,000)	(48,500)
Plus: Beginning cash balance			30,000	30,000
Less: Interest on short-term borrowing (1% prior month's borrowing)				(200)
Equals: Ending cash balance—without borrowing			10,000	(18,700)
Financing needed to reach target cash balance			20,000	48,700
Cumulative borrowing			$ 120,000	$ 168,700

SS-3. The projected net income for 2008 is found by first estimating firm sales. For 2009 the CFO anticipates 2008 sales of $25,000,000 will grow by 15 percent to $28,750,000. Deducting cost of goods sold and operating expenses as a proportion of sales, as well as taxes, and the fixed amounts we estimate for depreciation and interest expense, we estimate net income for 2009 to be $2,052,000. Details are provided in the pro forma income statement for 2009 that follows:

Income Statement ($000)

	2008	2009		2008	2009
Sales	$25,000	$28,750	Interest expense	(1,580)	(1,580)
Cost of goods sold	(16,250)	(18,688)	Earnings before taxes	2,520	3,157
Gross profit	8,750	10,062	Taxes	(882)	(1,105)
Operating costs	(4,500)	(5,175)	Net income	$ 1,638	$ 2,052
Depreciation expense	(150)	(150)	Dividends	$ 1,500	$ 1,500
Net operating profit	4,100	4,737	Addition to retained earnings	$ 138	$ 552

Assuming that the firm's dividend payment remains constant at $1,500,000, we estimate that retained earnings will rise by $552,000 in 2009.

After reading this chapter, you should be able to:

1. Describe the risk–return trade-off involved in managing a firm's working capital.

2. Explain the determinants of net working capital.

3. Calculate a firm's cash conversion cycle and interpret its determinants.

4. Calculate the effective cost of short-term credit.

5. List and describe the basic sources of short-term credit.

6. Describe the special problems encountered by multinational firms in managing working capital.

CHAPTER 15

Working-Capital Management

In 1994, Dell Computer Corporation's sales plummeted and the firm faced a serious cash shortfall. At the same time, the company realized that it had to accelerate its growth in order to move from the list of declining, second-tier manufacturers to the list of prospering, top-tier producers, and this required even more cash. The new Dell business model that emerged was designed to better manage the firm's working capital. Specifically, the model sought to lower inventory by 50 percent, improve lead time by 50 percent, reduce assembly costs by 30 percent, and reduce obsolete inventory by 75 percent.

The net result was that inventory dropped because Dell was aligning its inventory with sales and not holding inventories in anticipation of future sales. Furthermore, as its inventory disappeared, the company's profitability grew disproportionately because Dell avoided not only the carrying costs of holding inventories but also the losses associated with obsolete stock. Moreover, Dell was able to save money on purchasing components because the component prices were dropping 3 percent per month.

Because the firm's capital requirements to support its rapidly growing sales did not increase proportionately with sales, the companys' financial needs were reduced. All this was brought about by better working-capital management!

working capital a concept traditionally defined as a firm's investment in current assets. Compare **Net Working Capital**.

nct working capital the difference between the firm's current assets and its current liabilities.

Chapter 15 addresses two related topics: It introduces the principles involved in managing a firm's investment in working capital, and it presents a discussion of short-term financing. Traditionally, **working capital** is defined as the *firm's total investment in current assets*. **Net working capital**, on the other hand, is the *difference between the firm's current assets and its current liabilities*.

$$\text{Net working capital} = \text{current assets} - \text{current liabilities} \qquad (15\text{-}1)$$

Throughout this chapter, the term *working capital* refers to net working capital. In managing the firm's net working capital, we are concerned with *managing the firm's liquidity*. This entails managing two related aspects of the firm's operations: (1) its investment in current assets, and (2) its use of short-term or current liabilities.

Short-term sources of financing include all forms of financing that have maturities of 1 year or less—that is, current liabilities. There are two major issues involved in analyzing a firm's use of short-term financing: (1) How much short-term financing should the firm use? and (2) What specific sources of short-term financing should the firm select? We use the hedging principle of working-capital management to address the first of these questions. We then address the second issue by considering three basic factors: (1) the effective cost of credit, (2) the availability of credit in the amount needed and for the period that financing is required, and (3) the influence of the use of a particular credit source on the cost and availability of other sources of financing.

Objective **1**

Describe the risk–return trade-off involved in managing a firm's working capital.

MANAGING CURRENT ASSETS AND LIABILITIES

A firm's current assets consist of cash and marketable securities, accounts receivable, inventories, and other assets that the firm's managers expect to be converted to cash within a period of a year or less. Consequently, firms that choose to hold more current assets are, in general, more liquid than firms that do not.

The Risk–Return Trade-Off

Actually firms that want to reduce their risk of illiquidity by holding more current assets do so by investing in larger cash and marketable securities balances. Holding larger cash and marketable securities balances has an unfortunate consequence, however. Because investments in cash and marketable securities earn relatively modest returns when compared with the firm's other investments, the firm that holds larger investments in these assets will reduce its overall rate of return. Thus, the increased liquidity must be traded off against the firm's reduction in return on investment. Managing this trade-off is an important theme of working-capital management.

The firm's use of current versus long-term debt also involves a risk–return trade-off. *Other things remaining the same, the greater the firm's reliance on short-term debt or current liabilities in financing its assets, the greater the risk of illiquidity.* However, the use of current liabilities offers some very real advantages in that they can be less costly than long-term financing, and they provide the firm with a flexible means of financing its fluctuating needs for assets. However, if for some reason the firm has problems raising short-term funds or it should need funds for longer than expected, it can get into real trouble. Thus, a firm can reduce its risk of illiquidity through the use of long-term debt at the expense of a reduction in its return on invested funds. Once again we see that the risk–return trade-off involves an increased risk of illiquidity versus increased profitability.

▓ *Remember Your Principles*

Many of the working-capital decisions made by financial managers involve risk–return trade-offs between liquidity and profitability. The principles that guide these decisions are the same ones set out in **Principle 1: The Risk–Return Trade-Off—We Won't Take On Additional Risk Unless We Expect to Be Compensated with Additional Return**. The more current assets held and the more long-term financing used, the less the risk and the less the return.

The Advantages of Current Liabilities: Return

Flexibility

Current liabilities offer the firm a flexible source of financing. They can be used to match the timing of a firm's needs for short-term financing. If, for example, a firm needs funds for a 3-month period during each year to finance a seasonal expansion in inventories, then a 3-month loan can provide substantial cost savings over a long-term loan (even if the interest rate on short-term financing should be higher). The use of long-term debt in this situation involves borrowing for the entire year rather than for the period when the funds are needed, which increases the amount of interest the firm must pay. This brings us to the second advantage generally associated with the use of short-term financing.

Interest Cost

In general, interest rates on short-term debt are lower than on long-term debt for a given borrower. This relationship was introduced in Chapter 2 and is referred to as the term structure of interest rates. For a given firm, the term structure might appear as follows.

LOAN MATURITY	INTEREST RATE
3 months	4.00%
6 months	4.60
1 year	5.30
3 years	5.90
5 years	6.75
10 years	7.50
30 years	8.25

Note that this term structure reflects the rates of interest applicable to a given borrower at a particular time. It would not, for example, describe the rates of interest available to another borrower or even those applicable to the same borrower at a different time.

The Disadvantages of Current Liabilities: Risk

The use of current liabilities, or short-term debt, as opposed to long-term debt subjects the firm to a greater risk of illiquidity for two reasons. First, short-term debt, because of its very nature, must be repaid or rolled over more often, so it increases the possibility that the firm's financial condition might deteriorate to a point at which the needed funds might not be available.[1]

A second disadvantage of short-term debt is the uncertainty of interest costs from year to year. For example, a firm borrowing during a 6-month period each year to finance a seasonal expansion in current assets might incur a different rate of interest each year. This rate reflects the current rate of interest at the time of the loan, as well as the lender's perception of the firm's riskiness. If fixed-rate, long-term debt were used, the interest cost would be stable for the entire period of the loan agreement.

Did You Get It?

1. How does investing more heavily in current assets while not increasing the firm's current liabilities decrease both the firm's risk and its expected return on its investment?

2. How does the use of current liabilities enhance profitability and also increase the firm's risk of default on its financial obligations?

---

[1] The dangers of such a policy are readily apparent in the experiences of firms that have been forced into bankruptcy. Penn Central, for example, went bankrupt when it had $80 million in short-term debt that it was unable to finance (roll over).

Objective 2

Explain the determinants of net working capital.

THE APPROPRIATE LEVEL OF WORKING CAPITAL

Managing the firm's net working capital (its liquidity) involves interrelated decisions regarding its investments in current assets and use of current liabilities. Fortunately, a guiding principle exists that can be used as a benchmark for the firm's working-capital policies: the hedging principle, or principle of self-liquidating debt. This principle provides a guide to the maintenance of a level of liquidity sufficient for the firm to meet its maturing obligations on time.[2]

In Chapter 12 we discussed the firm's financing decision in terms of the choice between debt and equity sources of financing. There is, however, yet another critical dimension of the firm's financing decision. This relates to the maturity structure of the firm's debt. How should the decision be made about whether to use short-term (current debt) or longer-maturity debt? This is one of the fundamental questions addressed in this chapter and one that is critically important to the financial success of the firm.

The Hedging Principles

hedging principle (principle of self-liquidating debt) a working-capital management policy which states that the cash flow–generating characteristics of a firm's investments should be matched with the cash flow requirements of the firm's sources of financing. Very simply, short-lived assets should be financed with short-term sources of financing while long-lived assets should be financed with long-term sources of financing.

Very simply, the **hedging principle**, or **principle of self-liquidating debt**, involves *matching the cash-flow-generating characteristics of an asset with the maturity of the source of financing used to fund its acquisition*. For example, a seasonal expansion in inventories, according to the hedging principle, should be financed with a short-term loan or current liability. The rationale underlying the rule is straightforward. The funds are needed for a limited period, and when that time has passed, the cash needed to repay the loan will be generated by the sale of the extra inventory items. Obtaining the needed funds from a long-term source (longer than 1 year) would mean that the firm would still have the funds after the inventories they helped finance had been sold. In this case the firm would have "excess" liquidity, which it would either hold in cash or invest in low-yield marketable securities until the seasonal increase in inventories occurs again and the funds are needed. The result of all this would be lower profits.

Consider an example in which a firm purchases a new conveyor belt system, which is expected to produce cash savings to the firm by eliminating the need for two employees and, consequently, their salaries. This amounts to an annual savings of $24,000. The conveyor belt costs $250,000 to install and will last 20 years. If the firm chooses to finance this asset with a 1-year note, then it will not be able to repay the loan from the $24,000 cash flow generated by the asset. In accordance with the hedging principle, the firm should finance the asset with a source of financing that more nearly matches the expected life and cash-flow-generating characteristics of the asset. In this case, a 15- to 20-year loan would be more appropriate.

Permanent and Temporary Assets

permanent investments an investment that the firm expects to hold longer than one year. The firm makes permanent investments in fixed and current assets.

temporary investments a firm's investments in current assets that will be liquidated and not replaced within a period of one year or less. Examples include seasonal expansions in inventories and accounts receivable.

The notion of maturity matching in the hedging principle can be most easily understood when we think in terms of the distinction between permanent and temporary investments in assets, as opposed to the more traditional fixed and current asset categories. **Permanent investments** in an asset are *investments that the firm expects to hold for a period longer than 1 year*. Note that we are referring to the period the firm plans to hold an investment, not the useful life of the asset. For example, permanent investments are made in the firm's minimum level of current assets, as well as in its fixed assets. **Temporary investments**, by contrast, consist of *current assets that will be liquidated and not replaced within the current year*. Thus, some part of the firm's current assets is permanent and the remainder is temporary. For example, a seasonal increase in level of inventories is a temporary investment: the buildup in inventories that will be eliminated when no longer needed. In contrast, the buildup in inventories to meet a long-term increasing sales trend is a permanent investment.

---

[2] A value-maximizing approach to the management of the firm's liquidity involves assessing the value of the benefits derived from increasing the firm's investment in liquid assets and weighing them against the added costs to the firm's owners resulting from investing in low-yield current assets. Unfortunately, the benefits derived from increased liquidity relate to the expected costs of bankruptcy to the firm's owners, and these costs are very difficult to measure. Thus, a "valuation" approach to liquidity management exists only in the theoretical realm.

Temporary, Permanent, and Spontaneous Sources of Financing

Because total assets must always equal the sum of temporary, permanent, and spontaneous sources of financing, the hedging approach provides the financial manager with the basis for determining the sources of financing to use at any point.

What constitutes a temporary, permanent, or spontaneous source of financing? Temporary sources of financing consist of current liabilities. Short-term notes payable are the most common example of a temporary source of financing. Examples of notes payable include unsecured bank loans, commercial paper, and loans secured by accounts receivable and inventories. Permanent sources of financing include intermediate-term loans, long-term debt, preferred stock, and common equity.

Spontaneous sources of financing consist of trade credit and other accounts payable that arise *spontaneously* in the firm's day-to-day operations. For example, as the firm acquires materials for its inventories, **trade credit** is often *made available spontaneously or on demand from the firm's suppliers when it orders its supplies or more inventory of products to sell. Trade credit appears on the firm's balance sheet as accounts payable*, and the size of the accounts-payable balance varies directly with the firm's purchases of inventory items. In turn, inventory purchases are related to anticipated sales. Thus, part of the financing needed by the firm is spontaneously provided in the form of trade credit.

In addition to trade credit, wages and salaries payable, accrued interest, and accrued taxes also provide valuable sources of spontaneous financing. These expenses accrue throughout the period until they are paid. For example, if a firm has a wage expense of $10,000 a week and pays its employees monthly, then its employees effectively provide financing equal to $10,000 by the end of the first week following a payday, $20,000 by the end of the second week, and so forth, until the workers are paid. Because these expenses generally arise in direct conjunction with the firm's ongoing operations, they, too, are referred to as spontaneous.

trade credit credit made available by a firm's suppliers in conjunction with the acquisition of materials. Trade credit appears on the balance sheet as accounts payable.

The Hedging Principle: A Graphic Illustration

The hedging principle can now be stated very succinctly: *Asset needs of the firm not financed by spontaneous sources should be financed in accordance with this rule: Permanent-asset investments are financed with permanent sources, and temporary investments are financed with temporary sources.*

The hedging principle is depicted in Figure 15-1 and described in Table 15.1. Total assets are broken down into temporary- and permanent-asset investment categories. The firm's permanent investment in assets is financed by the use of permanent sources of financing (intermediate- and long-term debt, preferred stock, and common equity) or

FIGURE 15-1 The Hedging Principle Illustrated

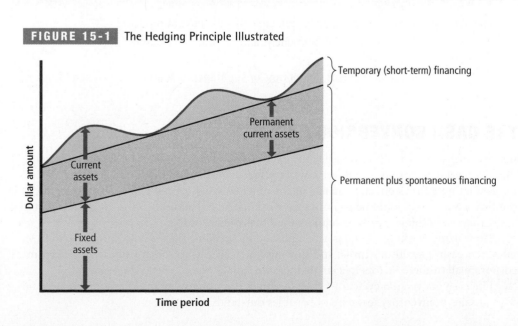

TABLE 15-1   The Hedging Principle Applied to Working-Capital Management

A firm's asset needs that are not financed by spontaneous sources of financing should be financed in accordance with the following "matching rule"—permanent-asset investments are financed with permanent sources, and temporary-asset investments are financed with temporary sources of financing.

CLASSIFICATION OF A FIRM'S INVESTMENTS IN ASSETS	DEFINITIONS AND EXAMPLES	CLASSIFICATION OF A FIRM'S SOURCES OF FINANCING	DEFINITIONS AND EXAMPLES
Temporary investments	*Definition*: Current assets that will be liquidated and not replaced within the year. *Examples*: Seasonal expansions in inventories and accounts receivable.	Spontaneous financing	*Definition*: Financing that arises more or less automatically in response to the purchase of an asset. *Examples*: Trade credit that accompanies the purchase of inventories and other types of accounts payables created by the purchase of services (for example, wages payable).
		Temporary financing	*Definition*: Current liabilities other than spontaneous sources of financing. *Examples*: Notes payable and revolving credit agreements that must be repaid in a period less than 1 year.
Permanent investments	*Definition*: Current and long-term asset investments that the firm expects to hold for a period longer than 1 year. *Examples*: Minimum levels of inventory and accounts receivable the firm maintains throughout the year as well as its investments in plant and equipment.	Permanent financing	*Definition*: Long-term liabilities not due and payable within the year and equity financing. *Examples*: Term loans, notes, and bonds as well as preferred and common equity.

spontaneous sources (trade credit and other accounts payable). For illustration purposes, spontaneous sources of financing are treated as if their amount were fixed. In practice, of course, spontaneous sources of financing fluctuate with the firm's purchases and its expenditures for wages, salaries, taxes, and other items that are paid on a delayed basis. Its temporary investment in assets is financed with temporary (short-term) debt.

Did You Get It?

1. What is the hedging principle or principle of self-liquidating debt?
2. What are some examples of permanent and temporary investments in current assets?
3. Is trade credit a permanent, temporary, or spontaneous source of financing? Explain.

Objective **3**

Calculate a firm's cash conversion cycle and interpret its determinants.

THE CASH CONVERSION CYCLE

Because firms vary widely with respect to their ability to manage their new working capital, there exists a need for an overall measure of effectiveness. An increasingly popular method for evaluating a firm's effective management of its working capital takes the approach that the firm's objective should be to minimize working capital subject to the constraint that it has sufficient working capital to support the firm's operations.

Minimizing working capital is accomplished by speeding up the collection of cash from sales, increasing inventory turns, and slowing down the disbursement of cash. We can incorporate all of these factors in a single measure called the *cash conversion cycle*.

The cash conversion cycle, or CCC, is simply the sum of days of sales outstanding and days of sales in inventory less days of payables outstanding:

$$\begin{array}{cccc} \text{Cash} & \text{days of} & \text{days of} & \text{days of} \\ \text{conversion} = & \text{sales} & + & \text{sales in} & - & \text{payables} \\ \text{cycle (CCC)} & \text{outstanding (DSO)} & \text{inventory (DSI)} & \text{outstanding (DPO)} \end{array}$$

We calculate days of sales outstanding as follows:

$$\begin{array}{c} \text{Days of} \\ \text{sales} \\ \text{outstanding (DSO)} \end{array} = \frac{\text{accounts receivable}}{\text{sales}/365} \qquad (15\text{-}2)$$

Recall from Chapter 4 that DSO can also be thought of as the average age of the firm's accounts receivable or the average collection period.

Days of sales in inventory is defined as follows:

$$\begin{array}{c} \text{Days of} \\ \text{sales} \\ \text{in inventory (DSI)} \end{array} = \frac{\text{inventories}}{\text{cost of goods sold}/365} \qquad (15\text{-}3)$$

Note that DSI can also be thought of as the average age of the firm's inventory; that is, the average number of days that a dollar of inventory is held by the firm.

Days of payables outstanding is defined as follows:

$$\begin{array}{c} \text{Days of} \\ \text{payables} \\ \text{outstanding (DPO)} \end{array} = \frac{\text{accounts payable}}{\text{cost of goods sold}/365} \qquad (15\text{-}4)$$

This ratio indicates the average age, in days, of the firm's accounts payable.

To illustrate the use of the CCC metric, consider Dell Computer Corporation. In 1989 Dell was a fledgling start-up whose CCC was 121.88 days. By 1998, Dell had reduced this number to – 5.6 days. (See Table 15-2.) How, you might ask, does a firm reduce its CCC below zero? The answer is through very aggressive management of its working capital. As Table 15-2 indicates, Dell achieved this phenomenal reduction in CCC primarily through very effective management of inventories (days of sales in inventories dropped from 37.36 in 1995 to 4.65 in 2005) and more favorable trade credit payment practices (days of payables outstanding increased from 40.58 in 1995 to 81.46 in 2004). Specifically, Dell, a direct marketer of personal computers, does not build a computer until an order is received. It purchases its supplies using trade credit. This business model results in minimal investment in inventories. Dell has obviously improved its working-capital management practices, as evidenced in Figure 15-2, where we compare Dell with Apple. Obviously both firms follow similar strategies and have been very successful in managing their cash conversion cycle in recent years.

Did You Get It?

1. What three actions can a firm take to minimize its net working capital?
2. Define *days of sales outstanding, days of sales in inventory,* and *days of payables outstanding.*

TABLE 15-2 The Determinants of Dell Computer Corporation's Cash Conversion Cycle for 1995–2005

Cash conversion cycle (CCC) = days of sales outstanding (DSO) + days of sales in inventory (DSI) − days of payables outstanding (DPO)

	1995	1996	1997	1998	1999	2000	2001	2002	2003	2004	2005
Days of sales outstanding (DSO)	50.04	42.48	44.00	49.64	38.69	33.14	26.57	26.66	32.01	32.74	35.59
Days of sales in inventory (DSI)	37.36	15.15	8.92	7.10	7.17	5.79	3.99	9.22	7.75	4.20	4.65
Days of payables outstanding (DPO)	40.58	62.79	62.87	62.34	64.92	62.07	72.87	75.79	79.41	81.46	79.41
Cash conversion cycle (CCC)	46.81	(5.15)	(9.96)	(5.60)	(19.06)	(23.14)	(42.30)	(39.90)	(39.64)	(44.51)	(39.17)

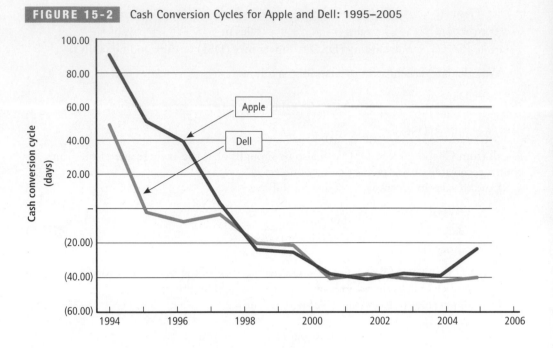

FIGURE 15-2   Cash Conversion Cycles for Apple and Dell: 1995–2005

ESTIMATING THE COST OF SHORT-TERM CREDIT USING THE APPROXIMATE COST-OF-CREDIT FORMULA

In Chapter 5 when we introduced the time value of money we first introduced the principles that underlie the computation of the cost of credit. However, we repeat much of that discussion in this chapter because it is critical to gaining an understanding of how to estimate the cost of short-term credit.

The procedure for estimating the cost of short-term credit is a very simple one and relies on the basic interest equation:

$$\text{Interest} = \text{principal} \times \text{rate} \times \text{time} \tag{15-5}$$

where *interest* is the dollar amount of interest on a *principal* that is borrowed at some annual *rate* for a fraction of a year (represented by *time*). For example, a 6-month loan for $1,000 at 8 percent interest would require an interest payment of $40.

$$\text{Interest} = \$1,000 \times .08 \times \frac{1}{2} = \$40$$

We use this basic relationship to solve for the cost of a source of short-term financing or the annual percentage rate (*APR*) when the interest amount, the principal sum, and the time period for financing are known. Thus, solving the basic interest equation for *APR* produces[3]

$$APR = \frac{\text{interest}}{\text{principal} \times \text{time}} \tag{15-6}$$

or

$$APR = \frac{\text{interest}}{\text{principal}} \times \frac{1}{\text{time}} \tag{15-7}$$

---

[3] For ease of computation, we assume a 30-day month and 360-day year in this chapter.

Can You Do It?

THE APPROXIMATE COST OF SHORT-TERM CREDIT

Hempstead Electric buys its wiring materials in bulk directly from Hamilton Wire and Cable Company. Hamilton offers credit terms that involve a cash discount of 3 percent if payment is received in 30 days. Otherwise, the full amount is due in 90 days. What is the approximate cost of credit to Hempstead if it exceeds 30 days and passes up the cash discount?

(The solution can be found on page 471.)

This equation, called the *APR* calculation, is clarified by the following example.

> **EXAMPLE**

The SKC Corporation plans to borrow $1,000 for a 90-day period. At maturity the firm will repay the $1,000 principal amount plus $30 interest. The effective annual rate of interest for the loan can be estimated using the *APR* equation, as follows:

$$APR = \frac{\$30}{\$1,000} \times \frac{1}{90/360}$$

$$= .03 \times \frac{360}{90} = .12 = 12\%$$

The effective annual cost of funds provided by the loan is, therefore, 12 percent.

The simple *APR* calculation does not consider compound interest. To account for the influence of compounding, we can use the following equation:

$$APY = \left(1 + \frac{i}{m}\right)^{m} - 1 \tag{15-8}$$

where *APY* is the annual percentage yield, *i* is the nominal rate of interest per year (12 percent in the previous example), and *m* is the number of compounding periods within a year [$m = 1/\text{time} = 1/(90/360) = 4$ in the preceding example]. Thus, the effective rate of interest on the loan in the example problem, considering compounding, is

$$APY = \left(1 + \frac{.12}{4}\right)^{4} - 1 = .126 = 12.6\%$$

Compounding effectively raises the cost of short-term credit. Because the differences between *APR* and *APY* are usually small, we use the simple interest values of *APR* to compute the cost of short-term credit.

Did You Get It?

1. What is the fundamental interest equation that underlies the calculation of the approximate cost-of-credit formula?
2. What is the annual percentage yield (*APY*) and how does it differ from the annual percentage rate (*APR*)?

Objective **5**

List and describe the basic sources of short-term credit.

SOURCES OF SHORT-TERM CREDIT

Short-term credit sources can be classified into two basic groups: unsecured and secured. **Unsecured loans** include all those *sources that have as their security only the lender's faith in the ability of the borrower to repay the funds when due.* The major sources of unsecured short-term

unsecured loans all sources of credit that have as their security only the lender's faith in the borrower's ability to repay the funds when due.

Finance at Work

MANAGING WORKING CAPITAL BY TRIMMING RECEIVABLES

LaFarge Corporation is located in Reston, Virginia, and operates in the building materials industry. Last year LaFarge was able to dramatically improve its management of accounts receivable. This improvement is reflected in a decrease in the days of sales outstanding ratio (DSO); that is,

$$DSO = \frac{\text{accounts receivable}}{\text{sales}/365}$$

After reviewing this formula, you may recall that we referred to DSO in Chapter 4 as the average collection period. The company's success is due in large part to the fact that it ties incentive pay to the return on net assets (RONA) as defined here:

$$RONA = \frac{\text{earnings before interest and taxes}}{\text{net assets}}$$

Note that improvements in accounts receivable management that result in a decrease in DSO also lead to a reduction in the firm's net assets and a corresponding increase in RONA. Of course, this presumes that the reduction in DSO does not have an adverse impact on the firm's revenues and, consequently, earnings.

How Did They Do It?

Pete Sacripanti, vice president and controller of LaFarge's Calgary-based construction materials business, credits the firm's improved collections to 12 fundamental steps:[a]

1. **Focusing on customers and collections,** which involves all layers of management and is not just a finance responsibility.
2. **Building a base of preferred customers** that confers a competitive advantage.
3. **Delineating clear ownership of customer accounts** among the sales staff, which prevents passing the buck on delinquent accounts.
4. **Fixing clear guidelines** that govern LaFarge's commitments and responsibilities to customers.
5. **Articulating standard sales terms and conditions,** stipulating terms that are negotiable and those that are never negotiable.
6. **Establishing monthly collection targets by salesperson and division,** with collection targets based on the prior month's sales plus past-due accounts.

7. **Training salespeople on customer profitability,** with particular attention to (1) the link between past-due accounts and increased risk of bad debt write-offs, (2) the volume of business required to recover the cost of bad debts, and (3) higher borrowing costs for the company.
8. **Engaging in regular (weekly) credit and collection meetings** with the sales team, the credit manager, and the general manager.
9. **Encouraging constant "in-your-face" executive management,** featuring weekly status updates of collections by salespeople, including key account information.
10. **Facilitating collections through advance phone calls** to establish expected payment amount and availability and to provide a courier to pick up the payments.
11. **Developing collection skills,** including partial holdback releases; offsetting balances owed for services or equipment; use of construction liens, guarantees, letters of credit, and payment bonds; negotiation techniques for securing extras in lieu of write-offs; and better knowledge of the company's products, its industry, and its customers.
12. **Developing unique value** by building stronger relationships with customers, such as air-miles loyalty programs, engineered solutions, quality assurance, and new-product development.

The key thing to note in this list is that each item represents a managerial action aimed at improving the firm's success in collecting its receivables. The DSO metric captures the success of these actions, but it is these 12 steps that actually brought about the improvements.

Measuring Success

LaFarge engaged in a 3-year program aimed at reducing its investment in working capital. The success of the program is most clearly evident in the company's western Canadian construction-materials operation based in Calgary. This unit slashed its working capital by 38 percent to around $36 million while increasing sales by 10 percent to $425 million. The effect on RONA was dramatic because the firm simultaneously increased earnings (the numerator of the ratio) and decreased net assets (the denominator).

[a]From S. L. Mintz, "The 1999 Working Capital Survey: Dollars in the Details," *CFO Magazine* (July 1999), p. 58. Used by permission.

---

secured loan sources of credit that require security in the form of pledged assets. In the event the borrower defaults in payment of principal or interest, the lender can seize the pledged assets and sell them to settle the debt

credit include accrued wages and taxes, trade credit, unsecured bank loans, and commercial paper. A **secured loan** involves the *pledge of specific assets as collateral in the event the borrower defaults in payment of principal or interest*. Commercial banks, finance companies, and factors are the primary suppliers of secured credit. The principal sources of collateral include accounts receivable and inventories.

How Did You Do?

THE APPROXIMATE COST OF SHORT-TERM CREDIT

If Hempstead chooses to pass up the cash discount, then the cost of credit will reflect the loss of the 3 percent discount so that the firm can use the principal amount of the purchases (that is, 97 percent of each dollar of wire purchased) for a period of 60 days (the difference in the discount period of 30 days and the end of the credit period of 90 days). The *APR* is calculated as follows using equation (15-6):

$$APR = \frac{interest}{principal \times time} = \frac{.03}{.97 \times \frac{60}{360}} = .1856, \text{ or } 18.56\%$$

Unsecured Sources: Accrued Wages and Taxes

Because most businesses pay their employees only periodically (weekly, biweekly, or monthly), firms accrue a wages payable account that is, in essence, a loan from their employees. For example, if the wage expense for the Appleton Manufacturing Company is $450,000 per week and it pays its employees monthly, then by the end of a 4-week month the firm will owe its employees $1.8 million in wages for services they have already performed during the month. Consequently, the employees finance their own efforts by waiting a full month for payment.

Similarly, firms generally make quarterly income tax payments for their estimated quarterly tax liability. This means that the firm has the use of the tax money it owes based on its quarterly profits through the end of the quarter. In addition, the firm pays sales taxes and withholding (income) taxes for its employees on a deferred basis. The longer the period that the firm holds the tax payments, the greater the amount of financing they provide for the firm.

Note that these sources of financing *rise and fall spontaneously* with the level of the firm's sales. That is, as the firm's sales increase, so do its labor expenses, sales taxes collected, and income tax. Consequently, these accrued expense items provide the firm with automatic, or spontaneous, sources of financing.

Unsecured Sources: Trade Credit

Trade credit provides one of the most flexible sources of short-term financing available to the firm. We previously noted that trade credit is a primary source of spontaneous, or on-demand, financing. That is, trade credit arises spontaneously with the firm's purchases. To arrange for credit, the firm need only place an order with one of its suppliers. The supplier checks the firm's credit and, if it is good, sends the merchandise. The purchasing firm then pays for the goods in accordance with the supplier's credit terms.

Credit Terms and Cash Discounts

Very often the credit terms offered with trade credit involve a cash discount for early payment. For example, a supplier might offer terms of 2/10, net 30, which means that a 2 percent discount is offered if payment is made within 10 days or the full amount is due in 30 days. Thus, a 2 percent penalty is involved for not paying within 10 days, or for delaying payment from the tenth to the thirtieth day (that is, for 20 days). The effective annual cost of not taking the cash discount can be quite severe. Using a $1 invoice amount, the effective cost of passing up the discount period using the preceding credit terms and our *APR* equation can be estimated.

$$APR = \frac{\$.02}{\$.98} \times \frac{1}{20/360} = .3673 = 36.73\%$$

Can You Do It?

THE COST OF SHORT-TERM CREDIT (CONSIDERING COMPOUNDING EFFECTS)

Re-evaluate the cost of short-term credit for Hempstead using the annual percentage yield (*APY*), which incorporates compound interest.

(The solution can be found on page 473.)

Note that the 2 percent cash discount is the *interest* cost of extending the payment period an *additional* 20 days. Note also that the principal amount of the credit is $0.98. This amount constitutes the full principal amount as of the tenth day of the credit period, after which time the cash discount is lost. The effective cost of passing up the 2 percent discount for 20 days is quite expensive: 36.73 percent. Furthermore, once the discount period has passed, there is no reason to pay before the final due date (the thirtieth day). Table 15-3 lists the effective annual cost of a number of alternative credit terms. Note that the cost of trade credit varies directly with the size of the cash discount and inversely with the length of time between the end of the discount period and the final due date.

The Stretching of Trade Credit

Some firms that use trade credit engage in a practice called *stretching of trade accounts*. This practice involves delaying payments beyond the prescribed credit period. For example, a firm might purchase materials under credit terms of 3/10, net 60; however, when faced with a shortage of cash, the firm might delay payment until the eightieth day. Continued violation of trade terms can eventually lead to a loss of credit. However, for short periods, and at infrequent intervals, stretching offers the firm an emergency source of short-term credit.

The Advantages of Trade Credit

As a source of short-term financing, trade credit has a number of advantages. First, trade credit is conveniently obtained as a normal part of the firm's operations. Second, no formal agreements are generally involved in extending credit. Furthermore, the amount of credit extended expands and contracts with the needs of the firm; this is why it is classified as a spontaneous, or on-demand, source of financing.

line of credit generally an informal agreement or understanding between a borrower and a bank as to the maximum amount of credit the bank will provide the borrower at any one time. Under this type of agreement there is no "legal" commitment on the part of the bank to provide the stated credit.

revolving credit agreement an understanding between the borrower and the bank as to the amount of credit the bank will be legally obligated to provide the borrower.

Unsecured Sources: Bank Credit

Commercial banks provide unsecured short-term credit in two basic forms: lines of credit and transaction loans (notes payable). Maturities of both types of loans are usually 1 year or less, with rates of interest depending on the creditworthiness of the borrower and the level of interest rates in the economy as a whole.

Line of Credit

A **line of credit** is *generally an informal agreement or understanding between the borrower and the bank about the maximum amount of credit that the bank will provide the borrower at any one time.* Under this type of agreement there is *no legal commitment on the part of the bank to provide the credit.* In a **revolving credit agreement**, which is a variant of this form of financing,

TABLE 15-3	The Effective Rates of Interest on Selected Trade Credit Terms
CREDIT TERMS	**EFFECTIVE RATES**
2/10, net 60	14.69%
2/10, net 90	9.18
3/20, net 60	27.84
6/10, net 90	28.72

How Did You Do?

THE COST OF SHORT-TERM CREDIT (CONSIDERING COMPOUNDING EFFECTS)

Using equation (15-8) we can estimate the cost of short-term credit to Hempstead as follows:

$$APY = \left(1 + \frac{i}{m}\right)^m - 1 = \left(1 + \frac{.18}{6}\right)^6 - 1 = .1941, \text{ or } 19.41\%$$

where i is the nominal annual rate of interest. That is, the cash discount is 3 percent and this gets Hempstead an added 60 days or 1/6th of a year. Therefore, the nominal rate of interest for a year is $6 \times .03$, or 18 percent. Considering the effects of compound interest, the cost of short-term credit from deferring payment to Hamilton for wiring until the end of the 90-day credit period is 19.41 percent

---

a *legal obligation is involved.* The line of credit agreement generally covers a period of 1 year corresponding to the borrower's *fiscal* year. Thus, if the borrower is on a July 31 fiscal year, its lines of credit are based on the same annual period.

Lines of credit generally do not involve fixed rates of interest; instead they state that credit will be extended at $\frac{1}{2}$ *percent over prime* or some other spread over the bank's prime rate.[4] Furthermore, the agreement usually does not spell out the specific use that will be made of the funds beyond a general statement, such as *for working-capital purposes.*

Lines of credit usually require that the borrower maintain a *minimum balance in the bank throughout the loan period,* called a **compensating balance**. This required balance (which can be stated as a percentage of the line of credit or the loan amount) increases the effective cost of the loan to the borrower unless a deposit balance equal to or greater than this balance requirement is maintained in the bank.

The effective cost of short-term bank credit can be estimated using the *APR* equation. Consider the following example.

compensating balance a balance of a given amount that the firm maintains in its demand deposit account. It may be required by either a formal or informal agreement with the firm's commercial bank. Such balances are usually required by the bank (1) on the unused portion of a loan commitment, (2) on the unpaid portion of an outstanding loan, or (3) in exchange for certain services provided by the bank, such as check-clearing or credit information. These balances raise the effective rate of interest paid on borrowed funds.

➤ EXAMPLE

M&M Beverage Company has a $300,000 line of credit that requires a compensating balance equal to 20 percent of the loan amount. The rate paid on the loan is 10 percent per annum, $200,000 is borrowed for a 6-month period, and the firm does not currently have a deposit with the lending bank. The dollar cost of the loan includes the interest expense and the opportunity cost of maintaining an idle cash balance equal to the 20 percent compensating balance. To accommodate the cost of the compensating-balance requirement, assume that the added funds will have to be borrowed and simply left idle in the firm's checking accounts. Thus, the amount actually borrowed (B) will be larger than the $200,000 needed. In fact, the needed $200,000 will constitute 80 percent of the total borrowed funds because of the 20 percent compensating-balance requirement; hence, $.80B = \$200,000$, such that $B = \$250,000$. Thus, interest is paid on a $250,000 loan ($\$250,000 \times .10 \times \frac{1}{2} = \$12,500$), of which only $200,000 is available for use by the firm.[5] The effective annual cost of credit, therefore, is

$$APR = \frac{\$12,500}{\$200,000} \times \frac{1}{180/360} = .125 = 12.5\%$$

---

[4] The *prime rate of interest* is the rate that a bank charges its most creditworthy borrowers.

[5] The same answer would have been obtained by assuming a total loan of $200,000, of which only 80 percent, or $160,000, was available for use by the firm; that is,

$$APR = \frac{\$10,000}{\$160,000} \times \frac{1}{180/360} = 12.5\%$$

Interest is now calculated on the $200,000 loan amount ($\$10,000 = \$200,000 \times .10 \times \frac{1}{2}$).

In the M&M Beverage Company example, the loan required the payment of principal ($250,000) plus interest ($12,500) at the end of the 6-month loan period. Frequently, bank loans will be made on a discount basis. That is, the loan interest will be deducted from the loan amount before the funds are transferred to the borrower. Extending the M&M Beverage Company example to consider discounted interest involves reducing the loan proceeds ($200,000) in the previous example by the amount of interest for the full 6 months ($12,500). The effective rate of interest on the loan is now

$$APR = \frac{\$12,500}{\$200,000 - \$12,500} \times \frac{1}{180/360}$$
$$= .1333 = 13.33\%$$

The effect of discounting interest was to raise the cost of the loan from 12.5 percent to 13.33 percent. This results from the fact that the firm pays interest on the same amount of funds as before ($250,000); however, this time it gets the use of $12,500 less, or $200,000 - $12,500 = $187,500.[6]

Transaction Loans

transaction loan a loan where the proceeds are designated for a specific purpose—for example, a bank loan used to finance the acquisition of a piece of equipment.

Still another form of unsecured short-term bank credit can be obtained in the form of a **transaction loan**. Here the loan is *made for a specific purpose*. This is the type of loan that most individuals associate with bank credit and is obtained by signing a promissory note.

An unsecured transaction loan is very similar to a line of credit with regard to its cost, term to maturity, and compensating-balance requirements. In both instances commercial banks often require that the borrower *clean up* its short-term loans for a 30- to 45-day period during the year. This means, very simply, that the borrower must be free of any bank debt for the stated period. The purpose of such a requirement is to ensure that the borrower is not using short-term bank credit to finance a part of its permanent needs for funds.

Unsecured Sources: Commercial Paper

commercial paper short-term unsecured promissory notes sold by large businesses in order to raise cash. Unlike most other money-market instruments, commercial paper has no developed secondary market.

Only the largest and most creditworthy companies are able to use **commercial paper**, which is simply a *short-term promise to pay that is sold in the market for short-term debt securities*.

The maturity of the credit source is generally 6 months or less, although some issues carry 270-day maturities. The interest rate on commercial paper is generally slightly lower ($\frac{1}{2}$ to 1 percent) than the prime rate on commercial bank loans. Also, the interest is usually discounted, although sometimes interest-bearing commercial paper is available.

New issues of commercial paper are either directly placed (sold by the issuing firm directly to the investing public) or dealer placed. A dealer placement involves the use of a commercial paper dealer, who sells the issue for the issuing firm. Many major finance companies, such as General Motors Acceptance Corporation, place their commercial paper directly. The volume of direct versus dealer placements is roughly 4 to 1 in favor of direct placements. Dealers are used primarily by industrial firms that either make only infrequent use of the commercial paper market or, owing to their small size, would have difficulty placing the issue without the help of a dealer.

---

[6] If M&M needs the use of a full $200,000, then it will have to borrow more than $250,000 to cover both the compensating-balance requirement *and* the discounted interest. In fact, the firm will have to borrow some amount B such that

$$B - .2B - \left(.10 \times \tfrac{1}{2}\right)B = \$200,000$$
$$.75B = \$200,000$$
$$B = \frac{\$200,000}{.75} = \$266,667$$

The cost of credit remains the same at 13.33 percent, as we see here:

$$APR = \frac{\$13,333}{\$266,667 - \$53,333 - \$13,333} \times \frac{1}{180/360}$$
$$= .1333 = 13.33\%$$

Commercial Paper as a Source of Short-Term Credit

Several advantages accrue to the user of commercial paper.

1. **Interest rate.**   Commercial paper rates are generally lower than rates on bank loans and comparable sources of short-term financing.
2. **Compensating-balance requirement.**   No minimum balance requirements are associated with commercial paper. However, issuing firms usually find it desirable to maintain line-of-credit agreements sufficient to back up their short-term financing needs in the event that a new issue of commercial paper cannot be sold or an outstanding issue cannot be repaid when due.
3. **Amount of credit.**   Commercial paper offers the firm with very large credit needs a single source for all its short-term financing. Because of loan amount restrictions placed on the banks by the regulatory authorities, obtaining the necessary funds from a commercial bank might require borrowing from a number of institutions.[7]
4. **Prestige.**   Because it is widely recognized that only the most creditworthy borrowers have access to the commercial paper market, its use signifies a firm's credit status.

Using commercial paper for short-term financing, however, involves a very important risk. The commercial paper market is highly impersonal and denies even the most creditworthy borrower any flexibility in terms of repayment. When bank credit is used, the borrower has someone with whom he or she can work out any temporary difficulties that might be encountered in meeting a loan deadline. This flexibility simply does not exist for the user of commercial paper.

Estimating the Cost of Using Commercial Paper

The cost of commercial paper can be estimated using the simple, effective cost-of-credit equation (*APR*). The key points to remember are that commercial paper interest is usually discounted and that if a dealer is used to place the issue, a fee is charged. Even if a dealer is not used, the issuing firm will incur costs associated with preparing and placing the issue, and these costs must be included in estimating the cost of this credit.

➤ **EXAMPLE**

The EPG Manufacturing Company uses commercial paper regularly to support its needs for short-term financing. The firm plans to sell $100 million in 270-day-maturity paper, on which it expects to pay discounted interest at a rate of 12 percent per annum ($9 million). In addition, EPG expects to incur a cost of approximately $100,000 in dealer placement fees and other expenses of issuing the paper. The effective cost of credit to EPG can be calculated as follows:

$$APR = \frac{\$9{,}000{,}000 + \$100{,}000}{\$100{,}000{,}000 - \$100{,}000 - \$9{,}000{,}000} \times \frac{1}{270/360}$$

$$= .1335 = 13.35\%$$

where the interest cost is calculated as $100,000,000 × .12 × (270/360) = $9,000,000 plus the $100,000 dealer placement fee. Thus, the effective cost of credit to EPG is 13.35 percent.

Secured Sources: Accounts-Receivable Loans

Secured sources of short-term credit have certain assets of the firm pledged as collateral to secure the loan. Upon default of the loan agreement, the lender has first claim to the pledged assets in addition to its claim as a general creditor of the firm. Hence, the secured credit agreement offers an added margin of safety to the lender.

---

[7] Member banks of the Federal Reserve System are limited to 10 percent of their total capital, surplus, and undivided profits when making loans to a single borrower. Thus, when a corporate borrower's needs for financing are very large, it may have to deal with a group of participating banks to raise the needed funds.

Generally, a firm's receivables are among its most liquid assets. For this reason they are considered by many lenders to be prime collateral for a secured loan. Two basic procedures can be used in arranging for financing based on receivables: pledging and factoring.

Pledging Accounts Receivable

pledging accounts receivable
a loan the firm obtains from a commercial bank or a finance company using its accounts receivable as collateral.

Under the **pledging accounts receivable** arrangement, the *borrower simply pledges accounts receivable as collateral for a loan obtained from either a commercial bank or a finance company*. The amount of the loan is stated as a percentage of the face value of the receivables pledged. If the firm provides the lender with a *general line* on its receivables, then all of the borrower's accounts are pledged as security for the loan. This method of pledging is simple and inexpensive. However, because the lender has no control over the quality of the receivables being pledged, it will set the maximum loan at a relatively low percentage of the total face value of the accounts, generally ranging downward from a maximum of around 75 percent.

Still another approach to pledging involves the borrower presenting specific invoices to the lender as collateral for a loan. This method is somewhat more expensive because the lender must assess the creditworthiness of each individual account pledged; however, given this added knowledge, the lender should be willing to increase the loan as a percentage of the face value of the invoices. In this case the loan might reach as high as 85 or 90 percent of the face value of the pledged receivables.

Credit Terms   Accounts receivable loans generally carry an interest rate that is 2 to 5 percent higher than the bank's prime lending rate. Finance companies charge an even higher rate. In addition, the lender usually charges a handling fee stated as a percentage of the face value of the receivables processed, which may be as much as 1 to 2 percent of the face value.

➤ EXAMPLE

The A. B. Good Company sells electrical supplies to building contractors on terms of net 60. The firm's average monthly sales are $100,000; thus, given the firm's 2-month credit terms, its average receivables balance is $200,000. The firm pledges all of its receivables to a local bank, which in turn advances up to 70 percent of the face value of the receivables at 3 percent over prime and charges a 1 percent processing fee on *all* receivables pledged. A. B. Good follows a practice of borrowing the maximum amount possible, and the current prime rate is 10 percent.

The *APR* of using this source of financing for a full year is computed as follows:

$$APR = \frac{\$18,200 + \$12,000}{\$140,000} \times \frac{1}{360/360} = .2157 = 21.57\%$$

where the total dollar cost of the loan consists of both the annual interest expense (.13 × .70 × $200,000 = $18,200) and the annual processing fee (.01 × $100,000 × 12 months = $12,000). The amount of credit extended is .70 × $200,000 = $140,000. Note that the processing charge applies to *all* receivables pledged. Thus, the A. B. Good Company pledges $100,000 each month, or $1,200,000 during the year, on which a 1 percent fee must be paid, for a total annual charge of $12,000.

One more point: The lender, in addition to making advances or loans, may be providing certain credit services to the borrower. For example, the lender may provide billing and collection services. The value of these services should be considered in computing the cost of credit. In the preceding example, A. B. Good Company may *save* $10,000 per year in credit department expenses by pledging all of its accounts and letting the lender provide those services. In this case, the cost of short-term credit is only

$$APR = \frac{\$18,200 + \$12,000 - \$10,000}{\$140,000} \times \frac{1}{360/360} = .1443 = 14.43\%$$

The Advantages and Disadvantages of Pledging   The primary advantage of pledging as a source of short-term credit is the flexibility it provides the borrower. Financing is available on a continuous basis. The new accounts created through credit sales provide the collateral for the financing of new production. Furthermore, the lender may provide credit services that eliminate or at least reduce the need for similar services within the firm. The primary disadvantage associated with this method of financing is its cost, which can be relatively high compared with other sources of short-term credit, owing to the level of the interest rate charged on loans and the processing fee on pledged accounts.

Factoring Accounts Receivable

Factoring accounts receivable involves the *outright sale of a firm's accounts to a financial institution called a factor*. A **factor** is *a firm that acquires the receivables of other firms*. The factoring institution might be a commercial finance company that engages solely in the factoring of receivables (known as an *old-line factor*) or it might be a commercial bank. The factor, in turn, bears the risk of collection and, for a fee, services the accounts. The fee is stated as a percentage of the face value of all receivables factored (usually 1 to 3 percent).

> **factoring accounts receivable** the outright sale of a firm's accounts receivable to another party (the factor) without recourse. The factor, in turn, bears the risk of collection.

The factor firm typically does *not* make payment for factored accounts until the accounts have been collected or the credit terms have been met. Should the firm wish to receive immediate payment for its factored accounts, it can borrow from the factor, using the factored accounts as collateral. The maximum loan the firm can obtain is equal to the face value of its factored accounts less the factor's fee (1 to 3 percent) less a reserve (6 to 10 percent) less the interest on the loan. For example, if $100,000 in receivables is factored, carrying 60-day credit terms, a 2 percent factor's fee, a 6 percent reserve, and interest at 1 percent per month on advances, then the maximum loan or advance the firm can receive is computed as follows:

> **factor** a firm that, in acquiring the receivables of other firms, bears the risk of collection and, for a fee, services the accounts.

Face amount of receivables factored	$100,000
Less: Fee (.02 × $100,000)	(2,000)
Reserve (.06 × $100,000)	(6,000)
Interest (.01 × $92,000 × 2 months)	(1,840)
Maximum advance	$90,160

Note that interest is discounted and calculated based on a maximum amount of funds available for advance ($92,000 = $100,000 − $2,000 − $6,000). Thus, the effective cost of credit can be calculated as follows:

$$APR = \frac{\$1,840 + \$2,000}{\$90,160} \times \frac{1}{60/360}$$
$$= .2555 = 25.55\%$$

Secured Sources: Inventory Loans

Inventory loans, or *loans secured by inventories*, provide a second source of security for short-term credit. The amount of the loan that can be obtained depends on both the marketability and perishability of the inventory. Some items, such as raw materials (grains, oil, lumber, and chemicals), are excellent sources of collateral, because they can easily be liquidated. Other items, such as work-in-process inventories, provide very poor collateral because of their lack of marketability.

> **inventory loans** loans secured by inventories. Examples include floating or blanket lien agreements, chattel mortgage agreements, field-warehouse receipt loans, and terminal-warehouse receipt loans.

There are several methods by which inventory can be used to secure short-term financing. These include a floating, or blanket, lien, a chattel mortgage, a field warehouse receipt, and a terminal warehouse receipt.

Under a **floating lien agreement**, *the borrower gives the lender a lien against all of its inventories*. This provides the simplest but least secure form of inventory collateral. The borrowing firm maintains full control of the inventories and continues to sell and replace them as it sees fit. Obviously, this lack of control over the collateral greatly dilutes the value of this type of security to the lender.

> **floating lien agreement** an agreement, generally associated with a loan, whereby the borrower gives the lender a lien against all its inventory.

chattel mortgage agreement
a loan agreement in which the lender can increase his or her security interest by having specific items of inventory identified in the loan agreement. The borrower retains title to the inventory but cannot sell the items without the lender's consent.

field warehouse agreement
a security agreement in which inventories pledged as collateral are physically separated from the firm's other inventories and placed under the control of a third-party field-warehousing firm.

terminal warehouse agreement
a security agreement in which the inventories pledged as collateral are transported to a public warehouse that is physically removed from the borrower's premises. This is the safest (though costly) form of financing secured by inventory.

Under a **chattel mortgage agreement**, *the inventory is identified (by serial number or otherwise) in the security agreement, and the borrower retains title to the inventory but cannot sell the items without the lender's consent.*

Under a **field warehouse agreement**, *inventories used as collateral are physically separated from the firm's other inventories and are placed under the control of a third-party field-warehousing firm.*

A **terminal warehouse agreement** differs from a field warehouse agreement in only one respect. Here *the inventories pledged as collateral are transported to a public warehouse that is physically removed from the borrower's premises.* The lender has an added degree of safety or security because the inventory is totally removed from the borrower's control. Once again the cost of this type of arrangement is increased because the warehouse firm must be paid by the borrower; in addition, the inventory must be transported to and, eventually, from the public warehouse.

Did You Get It?

1. What are some examples of unsecured and secured sources of short-term credit?
2. What is the difference between a line of credit and a revolving credit agreement?
3. What are the types of credit agreements a firm can get that are secured by its accounts receivable as collateral?
4. What are some examples of loans secured by a firm's inventories?

Objective **6**

Describe the special problems encountered by multinational firms in managing working capital.

MULTINATIONAL WORKING-CAPITAL MANAGEMENT

The basic principles of working-capital management are the same for multinational and domestic firms. However, because multinationals spend and receive money in different countries, the exchange rate between the firm's home country and each of the countries in which it does business poses an added source of concern when managing working capital.

Multinational firms, by definition, have assets that are denominated or valued in foreign currencies. This means that the multinational will lose value if that foreign currency declines in value vis-à-vis that of the home currency. Technically, the foreign assets of the firm are exposed to exchange-rate risk, the risk that tomorrow's exchange rate will differ from today's rate. However, this risk can be offset by the decline in value of any liability that is also denominated in terms of that foreign currency. Thus, a firm would normally be interested in its net exposed position (exposed assets – exposed liabilities) for each period and in each currency to which the firm has exposure.

If a firm is to manage its foreign-exchange-risk exposure, it needs good measures. There are three popular measures of foreign-exchange risk that can be used: translation exposure, transaction exposure, and economic exposure. *Translation exposure* arises because the foreign operations of multinational corporations have financial accounting statements denominated in the local currency of the country in which the operation is located. For U.S. multinational corporations, the reporting currency for their consolidated financial statements is the dollar, so the assets, liabilities, revenues, and expenses of the foreign operations must be translated into dollars. Furthermore, international transactions often require a payment to be made or received in a foreign currency in the future, so these transactions are exposed to exchange-rate risk, or *transaction risk*. *Economic exposure* exists over the long term because the value of the future cash flows in the reporting currency (that is, the dollar) from foreign operations is exposed to exchange-rate risk. Indeed, the whole stream of future cash flows is exposed. We will discuss these three types of exposures in more detail in Chapter 17.

Objective **1**

Describe the risk–return trade-off involved in managing a firm's working capital.

Summary

Working-capital management involves managing the firm's liquidity, which in turn involves managing (1) the firm's investment in current assets and (2) its use of current liabilities. Each of these problems involves risk–return trade-offs. Investing in current assets reduces the firm's risk of illiquidity at the expense of lowering its overall rate of return on its investment in assets. By contrast, the use of long-term sources of financing enhances the firm's liquidity while reducing its rate of return on assets.

The hedging principle, or principle of self-liquidating debt, is a benchmark for working-capital decisions. Basically, this principle involves matching the cash-flow-generating characteristics of an asset with the maturity of the source of financing used to acquire it.

The cash conversion cycle is a key measure of how efficient the firm is in managing its working capital. Specifically, it equals the number of days it takes to collect on credit sales plus the number of days items are in inventory less the number of days that payables are outstanding. The importance of the length of the conversion cycle is that this is the number of days that the firm has its cash tied up in inventories and accounts receivable for which it must provide financing.

The key consideration in selecting a source of short-term financing is the effective cost of credit.

The various sources of short-term credit can be categorized into two groups: unsecured and secured. Unsecured credit offers no specific assets as security for the loan agreement. The primary sources include trade credit, lines of credit, unsecured transaction loans from commercial banks, and commercial paper. Secured credit is generally provided to business firms by commercial banks, finance companies, and factors. The most popular sources of security involve the use of accounts receivable and inventories. Loans secured by accounts receivable include pledging agreements, in which a firm pledges its receivables as security for a loan, and factoring agreements, in which the firm sells the receivables to a factor. In a pledging arrangement, the lender retains the right of recourse in the event of default, whereas in factoring, a lender is generally without recourse.

Loans secured by inventories can be made using one of several types of security arrangements. Among the most widely used are the floating lien, chattel mortgage, field warehouse agreement, and terminal warehouse agreement. The form of agreement used depends on the type of inventories pledged as collateral and the degree of control the lender wishes to exercise over the collateral.

The problems of working-capital management are fundamentally the same for multinational firms as they are for domestic firms, with some complications. The primary source of complication comes from the fact that the multinational receives and makes payment with foreign currencies. This means that the multinational firm must be concerned not only with having sufficient liquidity but also with the value of its cash and marketable securities in terms of the value of the currencies of the countries in which it does business. Specifically, the multinational firm faces three types of currency exposure risk: translation exposure, transaction exposure, and economic exposure. All three types of currency risk must be managed by the multinational, in addition to the traditional risks of illiquidity.

Objective **2**

Explain the determinants of net working capital.

Objective **3**

Calculate a firm's cash conversion cycle and interpret its determinants.

Objective **4**

Calculate the effective cost of short-term credit.

Objective **5**

List and describe the basic sources of short-term credit.

Objective **6**

Describe the special problems encountered by multinational firms in managing working capital.

Key Terms

Chattel mortgage agreement   478

Commercial paper   474

Compensating balance   473

Factor   477

Factoring accounts receivable   477

Field warehouse agreement   478

Floating lien agreement   477

Hedging principle   464

Inventory loans   477

Line of credit   472

Net working capital   462

Permanent investments   464

Pledging accounts receivable   476

Principle of self-liquidating debt (see hedging principle)   464

Revolving credit agreement   472

Secured loan   470

Temporary investments   464

Terminal warehouse agreement   478

Trade credit   465

Transaction loan   474

Unsecured loans   469

Working capital   462

Review Questions

15-1. Define and contrast the terms *working capital* and *net working capital*.

15-2. Discuss the risk–return relationship involved in the firm's asset-investment decisions as that relationship pertains to its working-capital management.

15-3. What advantages and disadvantages are generally associated with the use of short-term debt? Discuss.

15-4. Explain what is meant by the statement "The use of current liabilities as opposed to long-term debt subjects the firm to a greater risk of illiquidity."

15-5. Define the hedging principle. How can this principle be used in the management of working capital?

15-6. Define the following terms:
   a. Permanent asset investments
   b. Temporary asset investments
   c. Permanent sources of financing
   d. Temporary sources of financing
   e. Spontaneous sources of financing

15-7. What distinguishes short-term, intermediate-term, and long-term debt?

15-8. What criteria should be used to select a source of short-term credit? Discuss each.

15-9. How can the formula "interest = principle × rate × time" be used to estimate the effective cost of short-term credit?

15-10. How can we accommodate the effects of compounding in our calculation of the effective cost of short-term credit?

15-11. There are three major sources of unsecured short-term credit other than accrued wages and taxes. List and discuss the distinguishing characteristics of each.

15-12. What is meant by the following trade credit terms: 2/10, net 30? 4/20, net 60? 3/15, net 45?

15-13. Define the following:
   a. Line of credit
   b. Commercial paper
   c. Compensating balance
   d. Prime rate

15-14. List and discuss four advantages of the use of commercial paper.

15-15. What risk is involved in the firm's use of commercial paper as a source of short-term credit? Discuss.

15-16. List and discuss the distinguishing features of the principal sources of secured credit based on a firm's accounts receivable.

Self-Test Problems

(Solutions to these problems are found at the end of the chapter.)

ST-1. (*Analyzing the cost of a commercial paper offering*) The Marilyn Sales Company is a wholesale machine tool broker that has gone through a recent expansion of its activities, resulting in the doubling of its sales. The company has determined that it needs an additional $200 million in short-term funds to finance its peak-season sales during roughly 6 months of the year. Marilyn's treasurer has recommended that the firm use a commercial paper offering to raise the needed funds. Specifically, he has determined that a $200 million offering would require 10 percent interest (paid in advance or discounted) plus a $125,000 placement fee. The paper would carry a 6-month (180-day) maturity. What is the effective cost of credit?

ST-2. (*Analyzing the cost of short-term credit*) The treasurer of the Lights-a-Lot Manufacturing Company is faced with three alternative bank loans. The firm wishes to select the one that minimizes its cost of credit on a $200,000 note that it plans to issue in the next 10 days. Relevant information for the three 1-year loan configurations includes:

   a. An 18 percent rate of interest with interest paid at year-end and no compensating-balance requirement.
   b. A 16 percent rate of interest but carrying a 20 percent compensating-balance requirement. This loan also calls for interest to be paid at year-end.
   c. A 14 percent rate of interest that is discounted, plus a 20 percent compensating-balance requirement.

Analyze the cost of each of these alternatives. You can assume the firm would not normally maintain a bank balance that might be used to meet the 20 percent compensating-balance requirements of alternatives b and c.

ST-3. (*Analyzing the cost of a transaction loan*) The Ace Compost Company of Mart, Texas, has been in the business of converting feedlot manure into garden compost since 1984. The firm has approached the First State Bank of Mart about a short-term loan to help finance the firm's seasonal working-capital needs. Ace's management estimates that it will need a total of $100,000 for a period of 6 months during the coming year. The bank agreed to provide the financing under the following terms: Interest of 10 percent per annum will be paid along with the full principal amount of the loan at maturity. Furthermore, the bank has requested that Ace maintain a 15 percent compensating balance with the bank. Ace has kept an average account balance with the bank of $5,000 over the past year and plans to continue to do so. Consequently, Ace is $10,000 short of the mandatory compensating balance so it will have to borrow an additional $10,000 more than its $100,000 loan needed. What is the effective cost of credit for Ace if it accepts the bank's terms?

Study Problems

15-1. (*Estimating the cost of bank credit*) Paymaster Enterprises has arranged to finance its seasonal working-capital needs with a short-term bank loan. The loan will carry a rate of 12 percent per annum with interest paid in advance (discounted). In addition, Paymaster must maintain a minimum demand deposit with the bank of 10 percent of the loan balance throughout the term of the loan. If Paymaster plans to borrow $100,000 for a period of 3 months, what is the effective cost of the bank loan?

15-2. (*Estimating the cost of commercial paper*) On February 3, 2003, the Burlington Western Company plans a commercial paper issue of $20 million. The firm has never used commercial paper before but has been assured by the firm placing the issue that it will have no difficulty raising the funds. The commercial paper will carry a 270-day maturity and require interest based on a rate of 11 percent per annum. In addition, the firm will have to pay fees totaling $200,000 to bring the issue to market and place it. What is the effective cost of the commercial paper to Burlington Western?

15-3. (*Cost of trade credit*) Calculate the effective cost of the following trade credit terms when payment is made on the net due date.

    a. 2/10, net 30
    b. 3/15, net 30
    c. 3/15, net 45
    d. 2/15, net 60

15-4. (*Annual percentage yield*) Compute the cost of the trade credit terms in problem 15-3 using the compounding formula, or annual percentage yield.

15-5. (*Cost of short-term financing*) The R. Morin Construction Company needs to borrow $100,000 to help finance the cost of a new $150,000 hydraulic crane used in the firm's commercial construction business. The crane will pay for itself in 1 year, and the firm is considering the following alternatives for financing its purchase:

    Alternative A—The firm's bank has agreed to lend the $100,000 at a rate of 14 percent. Interest would be discounted, and a 15 percent compensating balance would be required. However, the compensating-balance requirement would not be binding on R. Morin because the firm normally maintains a minimum demand deposit (checking account) balance of $25,000 in the bank.

    Alternative B—The equipment dealer has agreed to finance the equipment with a 1-year loan. The $100,000 loan would require payment of principal and interest totaling $116,300.

    a. Which alternative should R. Morin select?
    b. If the bank's compensating-balance requirement were to necessitate idle demand deposits equal to 15 percent of the loan, what effect would this have on the cost of the bank loan alternative?

15-6. (*Cost of short-term bank loan*) On July 1, 2003, the Southwest Forging Corporation arranged for a line of credit with the First National Bank of Dallas. The terms of the agreement call for a $100,000 maximum loan with interest set at 1 percent over prime. In addition, the firm has to maintain a 20 percent compensating balance in its demand deposit account throughout the year. The prime rate is currently 12 percent.

    a. If Southwest normally maintains a $20,000 to $30,000 balance in its checking account with FNB of Dallas, what is the effective cost of credit under the line-of-credit agreement when the maximum loan amount is used for a full year?

    b. Recompute the effective cost of credit if the firm borrows the compensating balance and the maximum possible amount under the loan agreement. Again, assume the full amount of the loan is outstanding for a whole year.

15-7. (*Cost of commercial paper*) Tri-State Enterprises plans to issue commercial paper for the first time in the firm's 35-year history. The firm plans to issue $500,000 in 180-day maturity notes. The paper will carry a 10½ percent rate with discounted interest and will cost Tri-State $12,000 (paid in advance) to issue.

    a. What is the effective cost of credit to Tri-State?

    b. What other factors should the company consider in analyzing whether to issue the commercial paper?

15-8. (*Cost of accounts receivable*) Johnson Enterprises Inc. is involved in the manufacture and sale of electronic components used in small AM/FM radios. The firm needs $300,000 to finance an anticipated expansion in receivables due to increased sales. Johnson's credit terms are net 60, and its average monthly credit sales are $200,000. In general, the firm's customers pay within the credit period; thus, the firm's average accounts receivable balance is $400,000. Chuck Idol, Johnson's comptroller, approached the firm's bank with a request for a loan for the $300,000 using the firm's accounts receivable as collateral. The bank offered to make a loan at a rate of 2 percent over prime plus a 1 percent processing charge on all receivables pledged ($200,000 per month). Furthermore, the bank agreed to lend up to 75 percent of the face value of the receivables pledged.

    a. Estimate the cost of the receivables loan to Johnson when the firm borrows the $300,000. The prime rate is currently 11 percent.

    b. Idol also requested a line of credit for $300,000 from the bank. The bank agreed to grant the necessary line of credit at a rate of 3 percent over prime and required a 15 percent compensating balance. Johnson currently maintains an average demand deposit of $80,000. Estimate the cost of the line of credit to Johnson.

    c. Which source of credit should Johnson select? Why?

15-9. (*Cost of factoring*) MDM Inc. is considering factoring its receivables. The firm has credit sales of $400,000 per month and has an average receivables balance of $800,000 with 60-day credit terms. The factor has offered to extend credit equal to 90 percent of the receivables factored less interest on the loan at a rate of 1½ percent per month. The 10 percent difference in the advance and the face value of all receivables factored consists of a 1 percent factoring fee plus a 9 percent reserve, which the factor maintains. In addition, if MDM Inc. decides to factor its receivables, it will sell them all, so that it can reduce its credit department costs by $1,500 a month.

    a. What is the cost of borrowing the maximum amount of credit available to MDM Inc. through the factoring agreement?

    b. What considerations other than cost should be accounted for by MDM Inc. in determining whether to enter the factoring agreement?

15-10. (*Cost of secured short-term credit*) The Sean-Janeow Import Co. needs $500,000 for the 3-month period ending September 30, 2008. The firm has explored two possible sources of credit.

1. S-J has arranged with its bank for a $500,000 loan secured by its accounts receivable. The bank has agreed to advance S-J 80 percent of the value of its pledged receivables at a rate of 11 percent plus a 1 percent fee based on all receivables pledged. S-J's receivables average a total of $1 million year-round.

2. An insurance company has agreed to lend the $500,000 at a rate of 9 percent per annum, using a loan secured by S-J's inventory of salad oil. A field warehouse agreement would be used, which would cost S-J $2,000 a month.

Which source of credit should S-J select? Explain.

15-11. (*Cost of short-term financing*) You plan to borrow $20,000 from the bank to pay for inventories for a gift shop you have just opened. The bank offers to lend you the money at 10 percent annual interest for the 6 months the funds will be needed.

    a. Calculate the effective rate of interest on the loan.

    b. In addition, the bank requires you to maintain a 15 percent compensating balance in the bank. Because you are just opening your business, you do not have a demand deposit account at the bank that can be used to meet the compensating-balance requirement. This means that you will have to put up 15 percent of the loan amount from your own personal money (which you had planned to use to help finance the business) in a checking account. What is the cost of the loan now?

    c. In addition to the compensating-balance requirement in part b, you are told that interest will be discounted. What is the effective rate of interest on the loan now?

15-12. (*Cost of factoring*) A factor has agreed to lend the JVC Corporation working capital on the following terms: JVC's receivables average $100,000 per month and have a 90-day average collection period. (Note that JVC's credit terms call for payment in 90 days, and accounts receivable average $300,000 because of the 90-day average collection period.) The factor will charge 12 percent interest on any advance (1 percent per month paid in advance) and a 2 percent processing fee on all receivables factored and will maintain a 20 percent reserve. If JVC undertakes the loan, it will reduce its own credit department expenses by $2,000 per month. What is the annual effective rate of interest to JVC on the factoring arrangement? Assume that the maximum advance is taken.

15-13. (*Cost of a short-term bank loan*) Jimmy Hale is the owner and operator of the grain elevator in Brownfield, Texas, where he has lived for most of his 62 years. The rains during the spring have been the best in a decade, and Mr. Hale is expecting a bumper wheat crop. This prompted him to rethink his current financing sources. He now believes he will need an additional $240,000 for the 3-month period ending with the close of the harvest season. After meeting with his banker, Mr. Hale is puzzling over what the additional financing will actually cost. The banker quoted him a rate of 1 percent over prime (which is currently 7 percent) and also requested that the firm increase its current bank balance of $4,000 up to 20 percent of the loan.

    a. If interest and principal are all repaid at the end of the 3-month loan term, what is the annual percentage rate on the loan offer made by Mr. Hale's bank?

    b. If the bank were to offer to lower the rate to prime if interest is discounted, should Mr. Hale accept this alternative?

15-14. (*Cash conversion cycle*) Sims Electric Corp. has been striving for the last five years to improve its management of working capital. Historical data for the firm's sales, accounts receivable, inventories, and accounts payable follow:

	JAN-03	JAN-04	JAN-05	JAN-06	JAN-07
Sales-Net	2,873	3,475	5,296	7,759	12,327
Receivables-Total	411	538	726	903	1,486
Accounts Payable	283	447	466	1,040	1,643
Inventories-Total	220	293	429	251	233

    a. Calculate Sims' days of sales outstanding and days of sales in inventory for each of the five years. What has Sims accomplished in its attempts to better manage its investments in accounts receivable and inventory?

    b. Calculate Sims' cash conversion cycle for each of the five years. Evaluate Sims' overall management of its working capital.

Web Works

15-WW1. Assume that you are the owner of an import business that specializes in the sale of floor tiles from around the world. Your business has grown dramatically over the 2 years since its founding, and you are looking for a way to convert your accounts receivable to cash more quickly than the 90 days it presently takes to collect them. Search the Internet for sources of factoring services. What types of information do factors typically ask for before initiating client services?

15-WW2. When Jaime Classwell arrived at work, he found a note on his cubicle asking him to come by his supervisor's office as soon as possible. When he arrived at her office, she asked him to look into inventory loans. She explained that the firm's rapid rate of growth was putting pressure on its ability to continue to finance its growth. Use the Internet to search out a list of sources of inventory loans. Prepare a brief report for Jaime's supervisor that describes the nature of the sources of financing that are available and any other information you feel should be included in such a preliminary analysis.

15-WW3. The Adirondack Furniture Company of Bentonville, Arkansas, makes and sells a line of lawn furniture throughout the United States. In May the company completed its annual planning process and realized that the firm would have to increase its sources of financing if it was to be able to continue to expand its operations to meet the rapidly growing demand for its products. After some deliberation, the firm decided that an increase in its line of bank credit was an important component of its financing plans. The problem was that the firm had already reached the maximum loan it could obtain from its longtime local bank. Thus, a broader search of credit sources and terms was needed. Assume that you have been asked to survey bank rates for a prime borrower. Use the Internet to establish current rates of interest being charged for short-term (less than 1 year) prime credit borrowers.

Self-Test Solutions

SS-1. The discounted interest cost of the commercial paper issue is calculated as follows:

Interest expense $= .10 \times \$200,000,000 \times 180/360 = \$10,000,000$

The effective cost of credit can now be calculated as follows:

$$APR = \frac{\$10,000,000 + \$125,000}{\$200,000,000 - \$125,000 - \$10,000,000} \times \frac{1}{180/360}$$
$$= .1066 = 10.66\%$$

SS-2.

a.

$$APR = \frac{.18 \times \$200,000}{\$200,000} \times \frac{1}{1}$$
$$= .18 = 18\%$$

b.

$$APR = \frac{.16 \times \$200,000}{\$200,000 - (.20 \times \$200,000)} \times \frac{1}{1}$$
$$= .20 = 20\%$$

c.

$$APR = \frac{.14 \times \$200,000}{\$200,000 - (.14 \times \$200,000) - (.20 \times \$200,000)} \times \frac{1}{1}$$
$$= .2121 = 21.21\%$$

Alternative "a" offers the lowest-cost service of financing, although it carries the highest stated rate of interest. The reason for this is that there is no compensating-balance requirement, nor is interest discounted for this alternative.

SS-3. Ace needs $100,000 to finance its seasonal inventory needs for a period of 6 months during the coming year. However, the bank requires a minimum compensating balance of 15 percent of the loan, or $15,000. This is $10,000 larger than Ace's average minimum balance over the past year, so the firm will have to borrow $110,000 to get the funds it needs plus cover the minimum balance requirement. The *APR* for the loan can be calculated as follows:

$$APR = \frac{.10 \times (\$100,000 + \$10,000) \times .5}{\$100,000} \times \frac{1}{.5} = .11, \text{ or } 11\%$$

After reading this chapter, you should be able to:

1. Understand why a firm holds cash.

2. Explain various cash management objectives and decisions.

3. Describe and analyze the different mechanisms for managing the firm's cash collection and disbursement procedures.

4. Be able to quantitatively evaluate the expected costs and benefits of cash management services.

5. Determine a prudent composition for the firm's marketable-securities portfolio.

6. Discuss the determinants of the firm's investment in accounts receivable and learn how decisions regarding changes in credit policy are determined.

7. Discuss the reasons for carrying inventory and how inventory management decisions are made.

CHAPTER 16

Current Asset Management

At the end of fiscal year 2005, the Walt Disney Company held 3.2 percent of its total assets of approximately $53.0 billion in the form of cash and short-term marketable securities. During 2005, Disney generated sales revenues of $31,944 billion. Based on a 365-day year, this means Disney "produced" $87,517,808 in sales revenues each day.

If Disney could have freed up only 1 day's worth of sales and invested it in 3-month U.S. Treasury bills yielding 2.21 percent, the firm's before-tax profits would have jumped by $1,934,144. That is a significant sum, and it demonstrates why firms like to have efficient treasury management departments in place. Shareholders enjoy the added profits that should, in turn, increase the market value of their common stock holdings.

Now, if Disney's managers felt it could bear just a tad more risk, then the freed-up cash might be invested in bank certificates of deposit (CDs) of a similar maturity yielding 2.39 percent to in-

vestors. That difference of a mere 18 basis points (2.39 − 2.21) may not seem like much, but when you put it to work on an investment of over $87 million, it produces a tidy income. Thus, by investing the excess cash in CDs rather than in Treasury bills, Disney's before-tax profits would be $157,531 greater ($2,091,675 − $1,934,144). This might be enough for the firm to hire a new business school graduate or two—just like you.

Managing the cash and the marketable-securities portfolio are important tasks for the financial executive. This chapter teaches you about sophisticated cash management systems and about prudent places to "park" the firm's excess cash balances so they earn a positive rate of return and are liquid at the same time. We also explore sound management techniques that relate to the other asset components of the firm's working capital—accounts receivable and inventory.

Chapter 15 provided an introduction and overview of the concept of working-capital management. In this chapter, we explore the management of the asset components of the working-capital equation. Accordingly, we focus on the alternatives available to managers for increasing shareholder wealth with respect to the most important types of current assets: (1) cash, (2) marketable securities, (3) accounts receivable, and (4) inventory. These are listed in order of declining liquidity.

Such alternatives include (1) techniques available to management for favorably influencing cash receipt and disbursement patterns, (2) investments that allow a firm to employ excess cash balances productively, (3) critical decision formulas for determining the appropriate amount of investment in accounts receivable, and (4) methods, such as those pertaining to order quantity and order point issues, for evaluating the most suitable levels of inventory.

These issues are important to the financial manager for several reasons. For example, judicious management of cash and near-cash assets allows the firm to hold the minimum amount of cash necessary to meet the firm's obligations in a timely manner. As a result, the firm is able to take advantage of the opportunity to earn a return on its liquid assets and increase its profitability.

With this in mind, we begin the study of current asset management by exploring the various aspects of the management of cash and marketable securities. Afterward, we analyze the important issues related to the management of accounts receivable and inventory.

Before proceeding to our discussion of cash management, it will be helpful to distinguish among several terms. **Cash** is the *currency and coin the firm has on hand in petty cash drawers, in cash registers, or in checking accounts (demand deposit accounts) at various commercial banks.* **Marketable securities**, also called near cash or near-cash assets, are *security investments that the firm can quickly convert into cash balances.* Generally, firms hold marketable securities with very short maturity periods—less than 1 year. Together, cash and marketable securities constitute the most liquid assets of a firm.

cash currency and coins plus demand deposit accounts.

marketable securities security investments (financial assets) the firm can quickly convert to cash balances. Also known as near cash or near-cash assets.

Objective **1**

Understand why a firm holds cash.

WHY A COMPANY HOLDS CASH

A thorough understanding of why and how a firm holds cash requires an accurate look at how cash flows into and through the enterprise. Figure 16-1 depicts the process of cash generation and disposition in a typical manufacturing setting. The arrows designate the direction of the flow—that is, whether the cash balance increases or decreases.

FIGURE 16-1   The Cash Generation and Disposition Process

The Cash Flow Process

The irregular increases in the firm's cash holdings can come from several external sources. Funds can be obtained in the financial markets from the sale of securities such as bonds, preferred stock, and common stock, or the firm can enter into nonmarketable-debt contracts with lenders such as commercial banks. These irregular cash inflows do not occur on a daily basis. The reason is that external financing contracts, or arrangements, usually involve huge sums of money stemming from a major need identified by the company's management, and these needs do not occur every day. For example, a new product might be in the launching process, or a plant expansion might be required to provide added productive capacity.

In most organizations the financial officer responsible for cash management also controls the transactions that affect the firm's investment in marketable securities. As excess cash becomes temporarily available, marketable securities are purchased. By contrast, when cash is in short supply, a portion of the marketable-securities portfolio is liquidated.

Whereas the irregular cash inflows are from external sources, the other main sources of cash arise from internal operations and occur on a more regular basis. Over long periods, the largest receipts come from accounts-receivable collections and, to a lesser extent, from direct cash sales of finished goods. Many manufacturing concerns also generate cash on a regular basis through the liquidation of scrap or obsolete inventory. At various times fixed assets may also be sold, thereby generating some cash inflow.

Apart from the investment of excess cash in near-cash assets, the cash balance experiences reductions for three key reasons. First, on an irregular basis, withdrawals are made to (1) pay cash dividends on preferred and common stock shares, (2) meet interest requirements on debt contracts, (3) repay the principal borrowed from creditors, (4) buy the firm's own shares in the financial markets for use in executive compensation plans or as an alternative to paying a cash dividend, and (5) pay tax bills. Again, by an *irregular basis*, we mean items *not* occurring on a daily or frequent schedule. Second, the company's capital expenditure program designates that fixed assets be acquired at various intervals. Third, inventories are purchased on a regular basis to ensure a steady flow of finished goods rolls off the production line. Note that the arrow linking the investment in fixed assets with the inventory account is labeled *depreciation*. This indicates that a portion of the cost of fixed assets is charged against the products coming off the assembly line. This cost is subsequently recovered through the sale of the finished-goods inventory. This is because the product's selling price will be set by managers to cover all of the costs of production, including depreciation.

Motives for Holding Cash

The influences that affect the firm's cash balance can be classified in terms of the three motives put forth by economist John Maynard Keynes: (1) the transactions motive, (2) the precautionary motive, and (3) the speculative motive.[1]

The Transactions Motive

Balances held for transaction purposes allow the firm to meet its cash needs that arise in the ordinary course of doing business. In Figure 16-1, cash would be used to meet the irregular outflows as well as the planned acquisition of fixed assets and inventories. The relative amount of cash needed to satisfy transaction requirements is affected by a number of factors, including the industry in which the firm operates. It is well known that utilities can forecast cash receipts quite accurately because of stable demand for their services. Computer software firms, however, have a more difficult time predicting their cash flows. In this industry, new products are brought to market at a rapid pace, thereby making it difficult to project cash flows and balances precisely.

---

[1] John Maynard Keynes, *The General Theory of Employment, Interest, and Money* (New York: Harcourt Brace Jovanovich, 1936).

The Precautionary Motive

Precautionary balances serve as a buffer. This motive for holding cash relates to the maintenance of balances used to satisfy possible, but as yet unknown, needs.

The cash flow predictability of the firm has a material influence on this precautionary motive. The airline industry provides a typical illustration. Air passenger carriers are plagued with a high degree of cash flow uncertainty. The weather, rising fuel costs, and continual strikes by operating personnel make cash forecasting difficult for any airline. The upshot of this problem is that because of all of the things that *might* happen, the minimum cash balances desired by air carriers tend to be large.

In actual business practice, the precautionary motive is met to a large extent by the holding of a portfolio of *liquid assets*, not just cash. Notice in Figure 16-1 the two-way flow of funds between the company's holdings of cash and marketable securities. In large corporate organizations, funds may flow either into or out of the marketable-securities portfolio on a daily basis.

The Speculative Motive

Cash is held for speculative purposes in order to take advantage of potential profit-making situations. Construction firms that build private dwellings will, at times, accumulate cash in anticipation of a significant drop in lumber costs. If the price of building supplies does drop, the companies that built up their cash balances stand to profit by purchasing materials in large quantities. This will reduce their cost of goods sold and increase their net profit margins. Generally, the speculative motive is the least important component of a firm's preference for liquidity. The transactions and precautionary motives account for most of the reasons why a company holds cash balances.

Did You Get It?

1. Describe the typical cash flow cycle for a firm.
2. What are the three motives for holding cash?

Objective **2**

Explain various cash management objectives and decisions.

insolvency the inability to meet interest payments or to repay debt at maturity.

CASH MANAGEMENT OBJECTIVES AND DECISIONS

The Risk–Return Trade-Off

A company-wide cash management program must be concerned with minimizing the firm's risk of insolvency. In the context of cash management, the term **insolvency** describes the *situation in which the firm is unable to meet its maturing liabilities on time*. In such a case the company is *technically insolvent* in that it lacks the necessary liquidity to make prompt payment on its current debt obligations. A firm could avoid this problem by carrying large cash balances to pay the bills that come due.

The financial manager must strike an acceptable balance between holding too much cash and too little cash. This is the focal point of the risk–return trade-off. A large cash investment minimizes the chances of insolvency, but it penalizes the company's profitability. A small cash investment frees up excess balances for investment in both marketable securities and longer-lived assets; this enhances profitability and the value of the firm's common shares, but it also increases the chances of the firm running out of cash.

▌ *Remember Your Principles*

The dilemma faced by the financial manager is a clear application of **Principle 1: The Risk–Return Trade-Off—We Won't Take On Additional Risk Unless We Expect to Be Compensated with Additional Return.** To accept the risk of not having sufficient cash on hand, the firm must be compensated with a return on the cash that is invested. Moreover, the greater the risk of the investment in which the cash is placed, the greater the return the firm demands.

Objectives

The risk–return trade-off can be reduced to two prime objectives for the firm's cash management system.

1. Enough cash must be on hand to meet the disbursal needs that arise in the course of doing business.
2. Investment in idle cash balances must be reduced to a minimum.

Evaluating these objectives and meeting them gives rise to the need for some typical cash management decisions.

Decisions

Two conditions or ideals would allow the firm to operate for extended periods with cash balances near or at zero: (1) a completely accurate forecast of its net cash flows over the planning horizon and (2) perfect synchronization of its cash receipts and disbursements.

Cash flow forecasting is the initial step in any effective cash management program. Given that the firm will, as a matter of necessity, invest in some cash balances, certain types of decisions related to the size of those balances dominate the cash management process. These include decisions that answer the following questions:

1. What can be done to speed up cash collections and slow down or better control cash outflows?
2. What should be the composition of the firm's marketable-securities portfolio?

Did You Get It?

1. Describe the relationship between the firm's cash management program and the firm's risk of insolvency.
2. What are the fundamental decisions that the financial manager must make with respect to cash management?

COLLECTION AND DISBURSEMENT PROCEDURES

The efficiency of the firm's cash management program can be improved by (1) accelerating cash receipts and (2) improving the methods used to disburse cash. In simple terms the firm improves its cash management system by speeding up collections and slowing down disbursements.

Managing the Cash Inflow—Speeding Up Collections

Figure 16-2 illustrates the cash collection system for a firm that does not utilize any advanced methods to enhance the speed of its collections. Note that there are three key events that delay the time it takes the firm to actually get the customer's money. These delays are referred to as **float**.

- First, the customer sends the payment to the firm through the mail. The time required to receive the check is called *mail float*.
- Second, the firm processes the check internally to record the account to which the payment belongs and then sends the check on to the firm's bank to begin the process of transferring funds from the customer to the company. The time required to process the check by the company is called *processing float*.
- Finally, the company's bank sends the check through the check-clearing system used by banks to actually transfer funds from the customer's account to the firm's account. The time required to accomplish this is referred to as *transit float*.

Speeding up the firm's collection process simply involves reducing the float that enters into the collection process in each of these three ways. The "lockbox" arrangement described

Objective 3

Describe and analyze the different mechanisms for managing the firm's cash collection and disbursement procedures.

float the length of time from when a check is written until the actual recipient can draw upon or use the "good funds."

FIGURE 16-2 Ordinary Cash Collection System

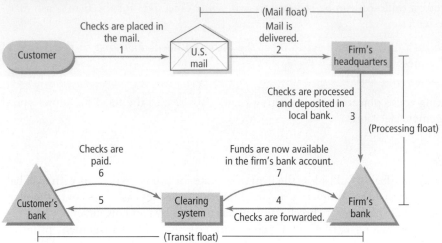

shortly is probably the most widely used tool for speeding up the collection process and thereby reducing the float.

➤ EXAMPLE

The positive operating-profit effects that stem from a float reduction can be dramatic when large total revenues are involved. Suppose that we want to estimate the value of a 1-day float reduction for Starbucks Corporation. Starbucks' 2004 sales revenues were reported at $5.294 billion. Let's assume that prudent investment in money-market securities will earn 4 percent annually. We ask, What is the estimated value of a 1-day float reduction to Starbucks? We can calculate this as follows:

$$\frac{\text{Annual revenues}}{\text{days in year}} = \text{1-day float reduction}$$

which for Starbucks in 2004 was

$$\frac{\$5.294 \text{ billion}}{365} = \$14,504,110$$

Thus, 1 day's freed-up balances for Starbucks will be $14,504,110. Then we find the annual (before-tax) value of the float reduction is

(Sales per day) × (assumed yield) = $14,504,110 × .04 = $580,164

Profits like these make it worthwhile for the firm and its treasury manager to closely evaluate the cash management services offered by commercial banks—even when the bank fees can also be quite costly. We learn how to make decisions of this nature later in the chapter.

The Lockbox Arrangement

The lockbox system is the most widely used commercial banking service for expediting cash gathering. Banks have offered this service since 1946. Such a system speeds up the conversion of receipts into usable funds by reducing both the mail and processing float of payments. In addition, it is possible to reduce transit float if lockboxes are located near Federal Reserve Banks and their branches. For large corporations that receive checks from all parts of the country, float reductions of 2 to 4 days are not unusual.

FIGURE 16-3 Simple Lockbox System

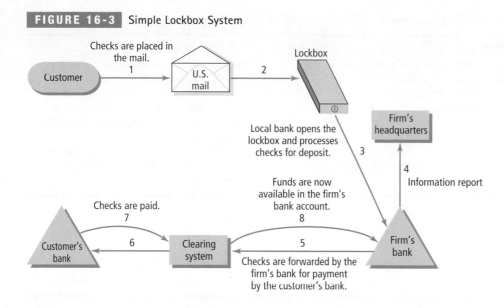

The lockbox arrangement in Figure 16-3 is based on a simple procedure. The firm's customers are instructed to mail their remittance checks not to company headquarters or regional offices, but to a numbered post office box. The bank that is providing the lockbox service is authorized to open the box, collect the mail, process the checks, and deposit the checks directly into the company's account.

In the introduction to this chapter we calculated the 2005 sales per day for Disney to be in excess of $87 million and assumed the firm could invest its excess cash in marketable securities to yield 2.21 percent annually. If Disney could speed up its cash collections by 4 days, it would be to the firm's advantage. Specifically, the gross annual savings to Disney (apart from operating the lockbox system) would amount to $7.737 million as follows:

(Sales per day) × (days of float reduction) × (assumed yield) = gross annual savings
($87,517,808) ×   (4)   ×   (.0221)   = $7,736,574

As you might guess, the prospects for generating revenues of this magnitude are important not only to the firms involved but also to commercial banks that offer lockbox services.

Lockbox services are not free, however. Usually, the bank levies a charge for each check processed through the system. The benefits derived from the acceleration of receipts must exceed the incremental costs of the lockbox system or the firm would be better off without it. Later in this chapter, a straightforward method for assessing the desirability of a specific cash management service, such as the lockbox arrangement, is illustrated.

Managing the Cash Outflow—Slowing Down Disbursements

The objective of managing cash outflows is to increase the company's float by slowing down the disbursement process. This is exactly the opposite of our objective of managing cash collections. There are several tools at the disposal of the cash manager for accomplishing this end, and we describe two here. These are the use of (1) zero balance accounts and (2) payable-through drafts. (See Table 16-1.)

Zero Balance Accounts

Large corporations that operate multiple branches, divisions, or subsidiaries often maintain numerous bank accounts (in different banks) for the purpose of making timely operating disbursements. It does make good business sense for payments for purchased parts that go into, say, an automobile transmission to be made by the Transmission and Chassis Division of the auto manufacturer rather than its central office.

TABLE 16-1   Selected Cash Disbursal Techniques: A Summary

TECHNIQUE	OBJECTIVE	HOW ACCOMPLISHED
Zero balance accounts	(1) Achieve better control over cash payments, (2) reduce excess cash balances held in regional banks, and possibly (3) increase disbursing float.	Establish zero balance accounts for all of the firm's disbursing units. These accounts are all in the same concentration bank. Checks are drawn against these accounts, with the balance in each account never exceeding $0. Divisional disbursing authority is thereby maintained at the local level of management.
Payable-through drafts	Achieve effective central-office control over field-authorized payments.	Field office issues drafts rather than checks to settle up payables.

zero balance accounts (ZBA)
a cash management tool that permits centralized control over cash outflow while maintaining divisional disbursing authority. Objectives are (1) to achieve better control over cash payments; (2) to reduce excess cash balances held in regional banks for disbursing purposes; and (3) to increase disbursing float.

Zero balance accounts (ZBA) *permit centralized control (at the headquarters level) over the firm's cash outflows while maintaining divisional disbursing authority.* Under this system the firm's authorized employees, representing their various divisions, continue to write checks on their individual accounts. Note that the numerous individual disbursing accounts are now *all* located in the same "concentration" bank. Actually these separate accounts contain no funds at all, thus the label, "zero balance."

The firm's authorized agents write their payment checks as usual against their specific accounts. These checks clear through the banking system in the usual way. On a daily basis the checks are presented to the firm's concentration bank (the drawee bank) for payment. As the checks are paid by the bank, negative (debit) balances build up in the proper disbursing accounts. At the end of each day the negative balances are restored to a zero level by means of credits to the ZBAs; a corresponding reduction of funds is then made against the firm's concentration (master) demand deposit account.

Payable-Through Drafts

payable-through drafts (PTD)
a legal instrument that has the physical appearance of an ordinary check but is not drawn on a bank. A payable-through draft is drawn on and paid by the issuing firm. The bank serves as a collection point and passes the draft on to the firm.

Payable-through drafts (PTD) *are legal instruments that have the physical appearance of ordinary checks but are not drawn on a bank. Instead, payable-through drafts are drawn on and payment is authorized by the issuing firm against its demand deposit account.*

Like checks, the drafts are cleared through the banking system and are presented to the issuing firm's bank. The bank serves as a collection point and passes the drafts on to the firm. The corporate issuer usually has to return by the following business day all drafts it does not wish to cover (pay). Those documents not returned to the bank are automatically paid. The firm inspects the drafts for validity by checking signatures, amounts, and dates. Stop-payment orders can be initiated by the company on any drafts considered inappropriate.

The main purpose of using a payable-through draft system is *to provide for effective control over field payments.* The firm's central office can control payments begun by the regional units because the drafts are reviewed in advance of their final payment. Payable-through drafts, for example, are used extensively in the insurance industry. The claims agent does not typically have check-signing authority against a corporate disbursement account. This agent can issue a draft, however, for quick settlement of a claim.

Remember Your Principles

These collection and disbursement procedures are an illustration of **Principle 2: The Time Value of Money—A Dollar Received Today Is Worth More Than a Dollar Received in the Future**. The faster the firm can take possession of the money to which it is entitled, the sooner the firm can put that money to work generating a return. Similarly, the longer the firm can hold on to the liquid assets in its possession, the greater the return the firm can receive on these funds.

Did You Get It?

1. Define *float* and its origins in the cash management process (i.e., mail, processing and transit).
2. What is a lockbox arrangement and how does its use reduce a firm's float?
3. Describe the following methods for managing cash outflow: zero balance accounts and payable-through drafts.

EVALUATING THE COSTS OF CASH MANAGEMENT SERVICES

Objective **4**

Be able to quantitatively evaluate the expected costs and benefits of cash management services.

A form of break-even analysis can help the financial officer decide whether a particular collection or disbursement service will provide an economic benefit to the firm. The evaluation process involves a very basic relationship in microeconomics:

$$\text{Added costs} = \text{added benefits} \tag{16-1}$$

If equation (16-1) holds exactly, then the firm is no better or worse off for having adopted the given service. We will illustrate this procedure in terms of the desirability of installing an additional lockbox. Equation (16-1) can be restated on a per unit basis as follows:

$$P = (D)(S)(i) \tag{16-2}$$

where P = increases in per check processing cost if the new system is adopted
D = days saved in the collection process (float reduction)
S = average check size in dollars
i = the daily, before-tax opportunity cost (rate of return) of carrying cash

Assume that check processing cost P will rise by $0.18 per check if the lockbox is used. The firm has determined that the average check size, S, that will be mailed to the lockbox location will be $900. If funds are freed up by use of the lockbox, they will be invested in marketable securities yielding an *annual* before-tax return of 6 percent. With these data, it is possible to determine the reduction in check collection time D required to justify the use of the lockbox. That level of D is found to be

$$\$0.18 = (D)(\$900)\left(\frac{.06}{365}\right)$$

$$1.217 \text{ days} = D$$

Thus, the lockbox is justified if the firm can speed up its collections by *more* than 1.217 days. This same style of analysis can be adapted to analyze the other tools of cash management.

Did You Get It?

1. Describe the use of the break-even concept with respect to the management of cash.
2. How would you estimate the financial benefits of using a lockbox system?

THE COMPOSITION OF A MARKETABLE-SECURITIES PORTFOLIO

Objective **5**

Determine a prudent composition for the firm's marketable-securities portfolio.

Earlier we described two fundamental decision problems related to cash management. The first related to managing the firm's cash collections and disbursements procedures. The second involved managing the firm's portfolio of marketable securities, which serve as an important source of liquidity for the firm.

General Selection Criteria

Certain criteria can provide a financial manager with a useful framework for selecting a proper marketable-securities mix. These considerations include evaluating the (1) financial risk, (2) interest rate risk, (3) liquidity, (4) taxability, and (5) yields among different financial assets. The following sections briefly delineate these criteria from the investor's viewpoint.

Financial Risk

Financial risk here refers to the uncertainty of expected returns from a security attributable to possible changes in the financial capacity of the security issuer to make future payments to the security owner. If the chance of default on the terms of the instrument is high (or low), then the financial risk is said to be high (or low).

Interest Rate Risk

Interest rate risk, of course, refers to the uncertainty of expected returns from a financial instrument attributable to changes in interest rates. Of particular concern to the corporate treasurer is the price volatility associated with instruments that have long, as opposed to short, terms to maturity. An illustration can help clarify this point.

Suppose the financial officer is weighing the merits of investing temporarily available corporate cash in a new offering of U.S. Treasury obligations that will mature in either 3 years or 20 years from the date of issue. The purchase prices of the 3-year notes or 20- year bonds are at their par values of $1,000 per security. The maturity value of either class of security is equal to par, $1,000, and the coupon rate (stated interest rate) is set at 7 percent, compounded annually.

If after 1 year from the date of purchase, prevailing interest rates rise to 9 percent, the market prices of these currently outstanding Treasury securities will fall to bring their yields to maturity in line with what investors could obtain by buying a new issue of a given instrument. The market prices of *both* the 3-year and 20-year obligations will therefore decline. The price of the 20-year instrument will decline by a greater dollar amount, however, than that of the 3-year instrument.

One year from the date of issue, the price obtainable in the marketplace for the original 20-year instrument, which now has 19 years to go to maturity, can be found by computing P as follows:

$$P = \sum_{t=1}^{19} \frac{\$70}{(1 + .09)^t} + \frac{\$1,000}{(1 + .09)^{19}} = \$821.10$$

Where t is the year in which the particular return, either interest or principal amount, is received; $70 is the annual interest payment; and $1,000 is the contractual maturity value of the bond. The rise in interest rates has forced the market price of the bond down to $821.01.

What will happen to the price of the note that has 2 years remaining to maturity? In a similar manner, we can compute its price, P:

$$P = \sum_{t=1}^{2} \frac{\$70}{(1 + .09)^t} + \frac{\$1,000}{(1 + .09)^2} = \$964.82$$

The market price of the shorter-term note will decline to $964.84. Table 16-2 shows that the market value of the shorter-term security was penalized much less by the given rise in the general level of interest rates.

TABLE 16-2   Market Price Effect of Rise in Interest Rates

ITEM	THREE-YEAR INSTRUMENT	TWENTY-YEAR INSTRUMENT
Original price	$1,000.00	$1,000.00
Price after 1 year	964.82	821.10
Decline in price	$ 35.18	$ 178.90

If we extended the illustration, we would see that, in terms of market price, a 1-year security would be affected less than a 2-year security, a 91-day security less than a 182-day security, and so on. Equity securities would exhibit the largest price changes because of their infinite maturity periods. To hedge against the price volatility caused by interest rate risk, the firm's marketable-securities portfolio will tend to be composed of instruments that mature over short periods.

Liquidity

In the present context of managing the marketable-securities portfolio, *liquidity* refers to the ability to transform a security into cash. Should an unforeseen event require that a significant amount of cash be immediately available, then a sizable portion of the portfolio might have to be sold. The financial manager will want the cash quickly and will not want to accept a large price concession in order to convert the securities. Thus, when choosing the securities for the firm's portfolio, the manager must consider (1) the period needed to sell the security and (2) the likelihood that the security can be sold at or near its prevailing market price.

Taxability

The tax treatment of the income a firm receives from its security investments does not affect the ultimate mix of the marketable-securities portfolio as much as the criteria mentioned earlier. This is because the interest income from most instruments suitable for inclusion in the portfolio is taxable at the federal level. Still, some corporate treasurers seriously evaluate the taxability of interest income and capital gains.

The interest income from only one class of securities escapes the federal income tax. That class of securities is generally referred to as *municipal obligations*, or more simply as *municipals*. Because of the tax-exempt feature of interest income from state and local government securities, municipals sell at lower yields to maturity in the market than securities that pay taxable interest. The after-tax yield on a municipal obligation, however, could be higher than the yield from a non-tax-exempt security. This would depend mainly on the purchasing firm's tax situation.

Consider Table 16-3. A firm is assumed to be analyzing whether to invest in a 1-year tax-free debt issue yielding 6 percent on a $1,000 outlay or a 1-year taxable issue that yields 8 percent on a $1,000 outlay. The firm pays federal taxes at the rate of 34 percent. The yields quoted in the financial press and in the prospectuses that describe debt issues are *before-tax*

TABLE 16-3   Comparing After-Tax Yields

	TAX-EXEMPT DEBT ISSUE (6% COUPON)	TAXABLE DEBT ISSUE (8% COUPON)
Interest income	$ 60.00	$ 80.00
Income tax (.34)	0.00	27.20
After-tax interest income	$ 60.00	$ 52.80
After-tax yield	$ 60.00 = 6%	$ 52.80 = 5.28%
	$1,000.00	$1,000.00

Derivation of the equivalent before-tax yield on a taxable debt issue:

$$r = \frac{r^*}{1 - T} = \frac{.06}{1 - .34} = 9.091\%$$

where r = the eqivalent before-tax yield
r^* = the after-tax yield on the tax-exempt security
T = the firm's marginal income tax rate

Proof: Interest income ($1,000 × .09091)		$ 90.91
Income tax (.34)		$ 30.91
After-tax interest income		$ 60.00

FIGURE 16-4 Designing the Marketable–Securities Portfolio

Considerations $\longrightarrow$	Influence $\longrightarrow$	Focus upon $\longrightarrow$	Determine
Financial risk Interest rate risk Liquidity Taxabillty	Yields	Risk vs. return preferences	Marketable- securities mix

returns. The actual *after-tax* return enjoyed by the investor depends on his or her tax bracket. Notice that the actual after-tax yield received by the firm is only 5.28 percent on the taxable issue versus 6 percent on the tax-exempt obligation. The lower portion of Table 16-3 shows that the fully taxed bond must yield 9.091 percent to make it comparable with the tax-exempt issue.

Yields

The final selection criterion that we mention is a significant one—the yields that are available on the different financial assets suitable for inclusion in the near-cash portfolio. By now it is probably obvious that the factors of (1) financial risk, (2) interest rate risk, (3) liquidity, and (4) taxability all influence the available yields on financial instruments. The yield criterion involves an evaluation of the risks and benefits inherent in all of these factors. For example, if a given risk is assumed, such as lack of liquidity, a higher yield will be expected on the nonliquid instrument.

Figure 16-4 summarizes our framework for designing the firm's marketable-securities portfolio. The four basic considerations are shown to influence the yields available on securities. The financial manager must focus on the risk–return trade-offs. Coming to grips with these trade-offs will enable the financial manager to determine the proper marketable-securities mix for the company. Let us look now at the marketable securities prominent in firms' near-cash portfolios.

Marketable-Security Alternatives

Money-market securities generally have short-term maturity and are highly marketable. Consequently, they can be quickly liquidated if the firm needs the cash. Table 16-4 summarizes the characteristics of the most widely used money-market securities in terms of five key attributes: (1) the denominations in which securities are available; (2) the maturities that are offered; (3) the basis used (for example, whether the security is sold at a discount or offers coupon interest payments); (4) the liquidity of the instrument, which relates principally to the availability of a secondary market for the security; and (5) taxability of the investment returns.

What type of return can the financial manager expect on a marketable-securities portfolio? This is a reasonable question. Some insight can be obtained by looking at the past, although we must realize that future returns are not guided by past experience. It is also useful to have some understanding of how the returns on one type of instrument stack up against another. The behavior of yields on short-term debt instruments over the 1980 to 2006 period is shown in Table 16-5.

Did You Get It?

1. What are financial risk and interest rate risk?
2. What is meant by the yield structure of marketable securities?

TABLE 16-4 Features of Selected Money-Market Instruments

INSTRUMENTS	DENOMINATIONS	MATURITIES	BASIS	LIQUIDITY	TAXABILITY
U.S. Treasury bills— direct obligations of the U.S. government	$1,000 and increments of $1,000	91 days, 182 days, and 4 weeks	Discount	Excellent secondary market	Exempt from state and local income taxes
Federal agency securities—obligations of corporations and agencies created to effect the federal government's lending programs	Wide variation; from $1,000 to $1 million	5 days (Farm Credit consolidated discound notes) to more than 10 years	Discount or coupon; usually on coupon	Good for issues of "big five" agencies	Generally exempt at local level; FNMA issues are not exempt
Bankers' acceptance— drafts accepted for future payment by commercial banks	No set size; typically range from $25,000 to $1 million	Predominantly from 30 to 180 days	Discount	Good for acceptances of large "money-market" banks	Taxed at all levels of government
Negotiable certificates of deposit—marketable receipts for funds deposited in a bank for a fixed time period	$25,000 to $10 million	1 to 18 months	Accrued interest	Fair to good	Taxed at all levels of government
Commercial paper— short-term unsecured promissory notes	$5,000 to $5 million; $1,000 and $5,000 multiples above the initial offering size are sometimes available.	3 to 270 days	Discount	Poor; no active secondary market in usual sense	Taxed at all levels of government
Repurchase agreements—legal contracts between a borrower (security seller) and lender (security buyer). The borrower will repurchase at the contract price plus an interest charge.	Typical sizes are $500,000 or more.	According to terms of contract	Not applicable	Fixed by the agreement; that is, borrower will repurchase	Taxed at all levels of government
Money-market mutual funds—holders of diversified portfolios of short-term, high-grade debt instruments	Some require an initial investment as small as $1,000.	Shares can be sold at any time.	Net asset value	Good; provided by the fund itself	Taxed at all levels of government

ACCOUNTS-RECEIVABLE MANAGEMENT

We now turn from the most liquid of the firm's current assets (cash and marketable securities) to those that are less liquid—accounts receivable and inventories. All firms by their very nature are involved in selling either goods or services. Although some of these sales will be for cash, a large portion will involve credit. Whenever a sale is made on credit, it increases the firm's accounts receivable. Thus, the importance of how a firm manages its accounts receivable depends on the degree to which the firm sells on credit.

Accounts receivable typically comprise more than 25 percent of a firm's assets. In effect, when we discuss the management of accounts receivable, we are discussing the management of one-quarter of the firm's assets. Moreover, because the cash flows from a sale cannot be

Objective 6

Discuss the determinants of the firm's investment in accounts receivable and learn how decisions regarding changes in credit policy are determined.

TABLE 16-5   Annual Yields (Percent) on Selected Three-Month Marketable Securities

YEAR	T-BILLS	COMMERCIAL PAPER	CDS
1980	11.51%	12.66%	13.07%
1985	7.48%	7.95%	8.05%
1990	7.51%	8.06%	8.15%
1995	5.51%	5.93%	5.92%
1996	5.01%	5.42%	5.39%
1997	5.06%	5.60%	5.62%
1998	4.78%	5.37%	5.47%
1999	4.64%	5.22%	5.33%
2000	5.82%	6.33%	6.46%
2001	3.40%	3.65%	3.71%
2002	1.61%	1.69%	1.73%
2003	1.01%	1.11%	1.15%
2004	1.03%	1.41%	1.57%
2005	3.15%	3.42%	3.51%
2006 (Mar)	4.51%	4.76%	4.88%

Source: *Federal Reserve Statistical Release* G.13 (415), various issues, and *Statistical Supplement to the Federal Reserve Bulletin*, November 2006, p. 23.

invested until the account is collected, the control of receivables takes on added importance in that it affects both the profitability and liquidity of the firm.

The size of the investment in accounts receivable is determined by several factors. First, the percentage of the firm's credit sales to total sales affects the level of accounts receivable held. Although this factor certainly plays a major role in determining a firm's investment in accounts receivable, it generally is not within the control of the financial manager. The nature of the business tends to determine the blend between credit sales and cash sales. A large grocery store tends to sell exclusively on a cash basis, whereas most construction-lumber supply firms make their sales primarily on credit.

The level of sales is also a factor in determining the size of the investment in accounts receivable. Very simply, the more sales, the greater the accounts receivable. It is not a decision variable for the financial manager, however.

The final determinants of the level of investment in accounts receivable are the firm's credit and collection policies—more specifically, the terms of sale, the quality of the customer, and the collection efforts. These policies *are* under the control of the financial manager. The terms of sale specify both the time period during which the customer must pay and the terms, such as penalties for late payments or discounts for early payments. The type of credit customer also affects the level of investment in accounts receivable. For example, the acceptance of poorer-credit-risk customers and their subsequent delinquent payments may lead to an increase in accounts receivable. The strength and timing of the collection efforts can affect the period for which past-due accounts remain delinquent, which in turn affects the level of accounts receivable. Collection and credit policy decisions can further affect the level of investment in accounts receivable by causing changes in the sales level and the ratio of credit sales to total sales. The factors that determine the level of investment in accounts receivable are displayed in Figure 16-5.

The Terms of Sale—A Decision Variable

Using the annual percentage rate (*APR*), in Chapter 15 we analyzed the approximate cost of short-term credit from the perspective of the firm that pays for the credit. Likewise we can utilize the *APR* to solve for the rate of return realized on the credit offered by the firm to its own customers.

The **terms of sale** *identify the possible discount for early payment, the discount period, and the total credit period.* They are generally stated in the form *a/b,* net *c,* indicating that the customer can deduct *a* percent if the account is paid within *b* days; otherwise, the account must be paid

terms of sale the credit terms identifying the possible discount for early payment.

FIGURE 16-5 Determinants of Investment in Accounts Receivable

within c days. Thus, for example, trade credit terms of 2/10, net 30, indicate that a 2 percent discount can be taken if the account is paid within 10 days; otherwise it must be paid within 30 days. Failing to take the discount represents a cost to the customer. For instance, if the terms are 2/10, net 30, the annualized opportunity cost of passing up this 2 percent discount in order to withhold payment for an additional 20 days is 36.73 percent. This is determined as follows:

$$\text{Annualized opportunity cost of forgoing the discount} = \frac{a}{1-a} \times \frac{360}{c-b} \qquad (16\text{-}3)$$

Substituting the values from the example, we get

$$36.73\% = \frac{.02}{1-.02} \times \frac{360}{30-10}$$

Typically the discount ranges anywhere from 1/2 to 10 percent, whereas the discount period is generally 10 days and the total credit period varies from 30 to 90 days. Although the terms of credit vary radically from industry to industry, they tend to remain relatively uniform within any particular industry. Moreover, the terms tend to remain relatively constant over time, and they do not appear to be used frequently as a decision variable.

The Type of Customer—A Decision Variable

A second decision variable involves determining the *type of customer* who qualifies for trade credit. Several costs are always associated with extending credit to less-creditworthy customers. First, it is important that the firm be able to identify which of its customers is a poor risk. However, when more time is spent investigating the less-creditworthy customer, the costs of credit investigation increase.

Default costs also vary directly with the quality of the customer. As the customer's credit rating declines, the chance that the account will not be paid on time increases. In the extreme case, payment never occurs. Thus, taking on less-creditworthy customers results in increases in default costs.

Collection costs also increase as the quality of the customer declines. More delinquent accounts force the firm to spend more time and money collecting them. Overall, the decline in customer quality results in increased costs of credit investigation, collection, and default.

In determining whether to grant credit to an individual customer, we are primarily interested in the customer's short-run financial well-being. Thus, its liquidity ratios, other obligations, and overall profitability are the focal point in this analysis. Credit-rating services, such as Dun & Bradstreet, provide information on the financial status, operations, and payment history for most firms. Other possible sources of information include credit bureaus, trade associations, chambers of commerce, competitors, bank references, public financial statements, and, of course, the firm's past relationship with the customer.

credit scoring the numerical evaluation of credit applicants where the score is evaluated relative to a predetermined standard.

One way in which both individuals and firms are often evaluated as credit risks is through the use of credit scoring. **Credit scoring** involves the *numerical evaluation of each applicant*. An applicant receives a score based on his or her answers to a simple set of questions. This score is then evaluated according to a predetermined standard to determine whether credit should be extended. The major advantage of credit scoring is that it is inexpensive and easy to perform. For example, once the standards are set, a computer or clerical worker without any specialized training can easily evaluate any applicant.

The techniques used for constructing credit-scoring indexes range from simply adding up the default rates associated with the answers given to each question, to sophisticated evaluations using multiple discriminate analysis (MDA). MDA is a statistical technique for calculating the appropriate importance to assign each question used in evaluating the applicant.

Finance professor Edward Altman used multiple discriminant analysis to identify businesses that might go bankrupt. In his landmark study, Altman used financial ratios to develop the following index:

$$Z = 3.3\left(\frac{\text{EBIT}}{\text{total assets}}\right) + 1.0\left(\frac{\text{sales}}{\text{total assets}}\right) + .06\left(\frac{\text{market value of equity}}{\text{book value of debt}}\right)$$
$$+ 1.4\left(\frac{\text{retained earnings}}{\text{total assets}}\right) + 1.2\left(\frac{\text{working capital}}{\text{total assets}}\right) \quad (16\text{-}4)$$

Thus, to use the Altman Z-score model to predict a firm's likelihood of bankruptcy, we substitute the firm's values for each of the predictor variables on the right-hand side of equation (16-4). Altman found that firms that went bankrupt within a year's time tended to have a Z-score below 2.7, whereas firms that did not go bankrupt had Z-scores larger than 2.7.

➤ EXAMPLE

To see how the credit-scoring model is used, let's consider the credit application of Jamison Electric Corporation. Column D contains the products of the credit-scoring model coefficients found in column B and Jamison's financial attributes found in column C. Adding up all the individual product terms produces a credit score of 2.00. Because this credit score is less than 2.7, we would anticipate that there is a high likelihood that Jamison will become bankrupt sometime during the coming year.[2]

	A	B	C	D
1	Variable	Coefficient	Firm Value	Product
2	EBIT/total assets	3.30	0.10	0.33
3	sales/total assets	1.00	0.85	0.85
4	market value of equity/book value of debt	0.06	4.00	0.24
5	retained earnings/total assets	1.40	0.20	0.28
6	Working capital/total assets	1.20	0.25	0.30
7			Z =	2.00
8				

The Collection Effort—A Decision Variable

The key to maintaining control over the collection of accounts receivable is the fact that the probability of default increases with the age of the account. Thus, eliminating past-due receivables is key. One common way of evaluating the situation is with *ratio analysis*. The financial manager can determine whether accounts receivable are under control by examining the average collection period, the ratio of receivables to assets, the ratio of credit sales to receivables (called the accounts-receivable turnover ratio), and the amount of bad debts rela-

---

[2] We should caution the user that the Z-score model is not a perfect predictor (although it was quite good). For example, of 100 firms that actually did go bankrupt over the period of 1 year, Altman found that the model correctly classified 94 firms. Similarly, of 100 firms that did not go bankrupt, the model correctly classified 97 as nonbankrupt.

tive to sales over time. In addition, the manager can perform what is called an aging of accounts receivable to provide a breakdown in both dollars and percentages of the proportion of receivables that are past due. Comparing the current aging of receivables with past data offers even more control.

Once the delinquent accounts have been identified, the firm's accounts-receivable group makes an effort to collect them. For example, a past-due letter, called a *dunning letter*, is sent if payment is not received on time, followed by an additional dunning letter in a more serious tone if the account becomes 3 weeks past due, followed after 6 weeks by a telephone call. Finally, if the account becomes 12 weeks past due, it might be turned over to a collection agency. Again, a direct trade-off exists between collection expenses and lost goodwill on one hand and noncollection of accounts on the other. This trade-off is always part of making the decision.

INVENTORY MANAGEMENT

Objective **7**

Inventory management involves the *control of the assets that are produced to be sold in the normal course of the firm's operations*. The general categories of inventory include raw-materials inventory, work-in-process inventory, and finished-goods inventory. The importance of inventory management to the firm depends on the extent of its inventory investment. For an average firm, approximately 4.88 percent of all assets are in the form of inventory. However, the percentage varies widely from industry to industry. Thus, the importance of inventory management and control varies from industry to industry also. For example, this activity is much more important in the automotive dealer and service station trade, in which inventories make up 49.72 percent of total assets, than in the hotel business, in which the average investment in inventory is only 1.56 percent of total assets.

Discuss the reasons for carrying inventory and how inventory management decisions are made.

inventory management the control of assets used in the production process or produced to be sold in the normal course of the firm's operations.

Types of Inventory

The purpose of carrying inventories is to uncouple the operations of the firm—that is, to make each function of the business independent of each other function—so that delays or shutdowns in one area do not affect the production and sale of the final product. Because production shutdowns result in increased costs, and because delays in delivery can lose customers, the management and control of inventory are important duties of the financial manager.

Decision making about inventory levels involves a basic trade-off between risk and return. The risk is that if the level of inventory is too low, the various functions of business do not operate independently, and delays in product and customer delivery can result. But a lower level of inventory can also save the firm money and increase returns. Moreover, as the size of inventory increases, storage and handling costs as well as the required return on capital invested in the inventory rise. In short, as the inventory a firm holds is increased, the risk of running out of inventory is lessened, but inventory expenses rise.

Raw-Materials Inventory

Raw-materials inventory consists of *basic materials purchased from other firms to be used in the firm's production operations*. These goods may include steel, lumber, petroleum, or manufactured items such as wire, ball bearings, or tires that the firm does not produce itself. Regardless of the specific form of the raw-materials inventory, all manufacturing firms by definition maintain a raw-materials inventory. The purpose is to uncouple the production function from the purchasing function—that is, to make these two functions independent of each other—so delays in the shipment of raw materials do not cause production delays. In the event of a delay, the firm can satisfy its need for raw materials by liquidating its inventory.

raw-materials inventory the basic materials purchased from other firms to be used in the firm's production operations.

Work-in-Process Inventory

Work-in-process inventory consists of *partially finished goods requiring additional work before they become finished goods*. The more complex and lengthy the production process, the larger the investment in work-in-process inventory. The purpose of work-in-process inventory is to

work-in-process inventory partially finished goods requiring additional work before they become finished goods.

uncouple the various operations in the production process so that machine failures and work stoppages in one operation will not affect other operations. Assume, for example, there are 10 different production operations, each one involving the piece of work produced in the previous operation. If the machine performing the first production operation breaks down, a firm with no work-in-process inventory will have to shut down all 10 production operations. But if a firm has work-in-process inventory, all remaining 9 operations can continue by drawing the input for the second operation from inventory.

Finished-Goods Inventory

finished-goods inventory
goods on which the production has been completed but that are not yet sold.

Finished-goods inventory consists of *goods on which production has been completed but that are not yet sold.* The purpose of a finished-goods inventory is to uncouple the production and sales functions so that it is not necessary to produce the goods before a sale can occur—sales can be made directly out of inventory. In the auto industry, for example, a person would not buy from a dealer who made them wait weeks or months when another dealer could fill the order immediately.

Stock of Cash

Although we have already discussed cash management at some length, it is worthwhile to mention cash again in the light of inventory management. This is because the *stock of cash* carried by a firm is simply a special type of inventory. In terms of uncoupling the various operations of the firm, the purpose of holding a stock of cash is to make the payment of bills independent of the collection of accounts due. When cash is kept on hand, bills can be paid without prior collection of accounts.

Inventory Management Techniques

As we explained, the importance of effective inventory management is directly related to the size of the investment in inventory. The effective management of these assets is essential to the goal of maximizing shareholder wealth. To control the investment in inventory, managers must solve two problems: the order quantity problem and the order point problem.

The Order Quantity Problem

order quantity problem
determining the optimal order size for an inventory item given its usage, carrying costs, and ordering costs.

The **order quantity problem** involves *determining the optimal order size for an inventory item given its expected usage, carrying costs, and ordering costs.*

The economic order quantity (*EOQ*) model attempts to determine the order size that will minimize total inventory costs. It assumes that

$$\frac{\text{Total}}{\text{inventory costs}} = \frac{\text{total}}{\text{carrying costs}} + \frac{\text{total}}{\text{ordering costs}} \qquad (16\text{-}5)$$

Assuming the inventory is allowed to fall to zero and then is immediately replenished (this assumption will be lifted when we discuss the order point problem), the average inventory becomes $Q/2$, where Q is inventory order size in units. This can be seen graphically in Figure 16-6.

If the average inventory is $Q/2$ and the carrying cost per unit is C, then carrying costs become

$$\frac{\text{Total}}{\text{carrying costs}} = \left(\frac{\text{number}}{\text{of orders}}\right)\left(\frac{\text{carrying cost}}{\text{per order}}\right)$$

$$= \left(\frac{Q}{2}\right)C \qquad (16\text{-}6)$$

where Q = the inventory order size in units
C = the carrying cost per unit

The carrying costs on inventory include the required rate of return on investment in inventory, in addition to warehouse or storage costs, wages for those who operate the warehouse, and costs associated with having too little inventory on hand. Thus, carrying costs include both real cash flows and the opportunity costs associated with having funds tied up in inventory.

FIGURE 16-6 Inventory Level and the Replenishment Cycle

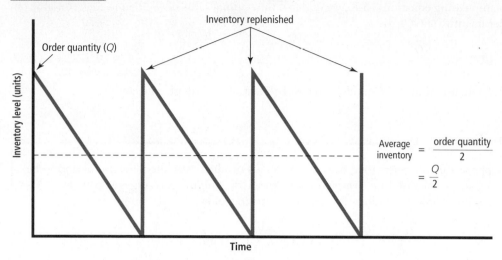

The ordering costs incurred are equal to the ordering costs per order times the number of orders. If we assume total demand over the planning period is S, and we order in lot sizes of Q, then S/Q represents the number of orders over the planning period. If the ordering cost per order is O, then

$$\text{Total ordering costs} = \left(\begin{array}{c}\text{number}\\\text{of orders}\end{array}\right)\left(\begin{array}{c}\text{ordering cost}\\\text{per order}\end{array}\right) \qquad (16\text{-}7)$$

$$= \left(\frac{S}{Q}\right)O \qquad (16\text{-}7a)$$

where S = total demand in units over the planning period
$\quad\ O$ = ordering cost per order

Thus, total costs in equation (16-5) become

$$\text{Total costs} = \left(\frac{Q}{2}\right)C + \left(\frac{S}{Q}\right)O \qquad (16\text{-}8)$$

Figure 16-7 illustrates this equation graphically.

FIGURE 16-7 Total Costs and *EOQ* Determination

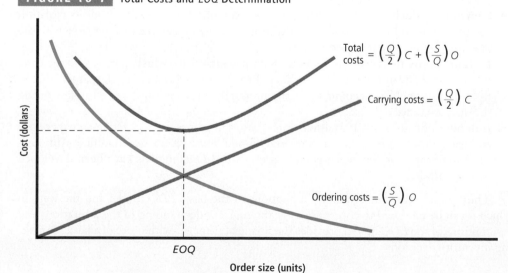

What we are looking for is the order size Q^* that provides the minimum total costs. By manipulating equation (16-8), we find that the optimal value of Q—that is, the economic order quantity (EOQ)—is

$$Q^* = \sqrt{\frac{2SO}{C}} \qquad\qquad (16\text{-}9)$$

The use of the EOQ model can best be illustrated through an example.

> ## EXAMPLE

Suppose a firm expects total demand (S) for its product over the planning period to be 5,000 units, the ordering cost per order (O) is $200, and the carrying cost per unit (C) is $2. Substituting these values into equation (16-9) yields

$$Q^* = \sqrt{\frac{2 \cdot 5,000 \cdot \$200}{\$2}} = \sqrt{1,000,000} = 1,000 \text{ units}$$

Thus, if this firm orders in 1,000-unit lot sizes, it will minimize its total inventory costs.

Assumptions of the EOQ Model

Despite the fact that the EOQ model tends to yield quite good results, there are weaknesses associated with several of its assumptions. However, when its assumptions have been dramatically violated, the EOQ model can generally be modified to accommodate the situation. The model's assumptions are as follows:

1. **Constant, or uniform, demand.**   Although the EOQ model assumes constant demand, demand may vary from day to day. If demand is stochastic—that is, not known in advance—the model must be modified through the inclusion of a safety stock.
2. **A constant unit price.**   The inclusion of variable prices resulting from quantity discounts can be handled quite easily through a modification of the original EOQ model, and then redefining total costs and solving for the optimum order quantity.
3. **Constant carrying costs.**   Unit carrying costs can vary substantially as the size of the inventory rises, perhaps decreasing because of economies of scale or storage efficiencies or increasing as storage space runs out and new warehouses have to be rented. This situation can be handled through a modification in the original model similar to the one used for variable unit price.
4. **Constant ordering costs.**   Although this assumption is generally valid, its violation can be accommodated by modifying the original EOQ model in a manner similar to the one used for variable unit prices.
5. **Instantaneous delivery.**   If delivery is not instantaneous, which is generally the case, the original EOQ model must be modified through the inclusion of a safety stock, that is, the inventory held to accommodate any unusually large and unexpected usage during the delivery time.
6. **Independent orders.**   If multiple orders result in cost savings by reducing paperwork and transportation cost, the original EOQ model must be further modified. Although this modification is somewhat complicated, special EOQ models have been developed to deal with it.

These assumptions illustrate the limitations of the basic EOQ model and the ways in which it can be modified to compensate for them. An understanding of the limitations and assumptions of the EOQ model provides the financial manager with more of a base for making inventory decisions.

FIGURE 16-8 Order Point Determination

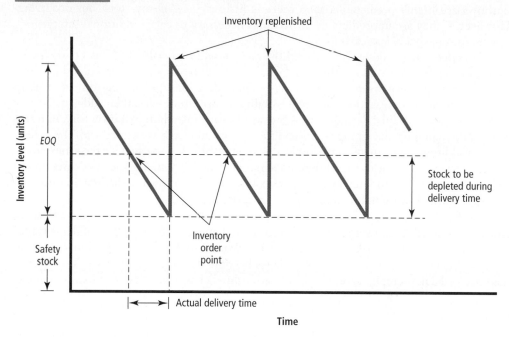

The Order Point Problem

The two most limiting assumptions—those of constant or uniform demand and instantaneous delivery—are dealt with through the inclusion of **safety stock**, which is the *inventory held to accommodate any unusually large and unexpected usage during delivery time*. The *decision about how much safety stock to hold* is generally referred to as the **order point problem**; that is, how low should inventory be depleted before it is reordered?

Two factors that go into the determination of the appropriate order point: (1) the procurement or delivery-time stock and (2) the safety stock desired. Figure 16-8 graphs the process involved in order point determination. We observe that the order point problem can be decomposed into its two components, the **delivery-time stock**—that is, the *inventory needed between the order date and the receipt of the inventory ordered*—and the safety stock. Thus, the order point is reached when inventory falls to a level equal to the delivery-time stock plus the safety stock.

$$
\begin{array}{l}\text{Inventory order point}\\ \text{(order new inventory}\\ \text{when the level of inventory}\\ \text{falls to the level)}\end{array} = \begin{array}{l}\text{delivery–time}\\ \text{stock}\end{array} + \begin{array}{l}\text{safety}\\ \text{stock}\end{array} \qquad (16\text{-}10)
$$

As a result of constantly carrying safety stock, the average level of inventory increases. Whereas before the inclusion of safety stock the average level of inventory was equal to $EOQ/2$, now it will be

$$
\text{Average inventory} = \frac{EOQ}{2} + \text{safety stock} \qquad (16\text{-}11)
$$

In general, several factors simultaneously determine how much delivery-time stock and safety stock should be held. First, the efficiency of the replenishment system affects how much delivery-time stock is needed. Because the delivery-time stock is the expected inventory usage between ordering and receiving inventory, the efficient replenishment of inventory would reduce the need for delivery-time stock.

The uncertainty surrounding both the delivery time and the demand for the product affects the level of safety stock needed. The more certain the patterns of these inflows and

safety stock inventory held to accommodate any unusually large and unexpected usage during delivery time.

order point problem determining how low inventory should be depleted before it is reordered.

delivery-time stock the inventory needed between the order date and the receipt of the inventory ordered.

outflows from the inventory, the less safety stock required. In effect, if these inflows and outflows are highly predictable, then there is little chance of any stock-out occurring. However, if they are unpredictable, it becomes necessary to carry additional safety stock to prevent unexpected stock-outs.

The safety margin desired also affects the level of safety stock held. If it is a costly experience to run out of inventory, the safety stock held will be larger than it would be otherwise. If running out of inventory and the subsequent delay in supplying customers result in strong customer dissatisfaction and the possibility of lost future sales, then additional safety stock is necessary. A final determinant is the cost of carrying additional inventory, in terms of both the handling and storage costs and the opportunity cost associated with the investment in additional inventory. Very simply, the greater the costs, the smaller the safety stock.

just-in-time inventory control system a production and management system in which inventory is cut down to a minimum through adjustments to the time and physical distance between the various production operations. Under this system the firm keeps a minimum level of inventory on hand, relying upon suppliers to furnish parts "just in time" for them to be assembled.

Over the past decade or so, a different technique aimed at reducing the firm's investment in inventory has been adopted by numerous companies. It is known as the **just-in-time inventory control system.** The aim is to operate with the *lowest average level of inventory possible*. Within the *EOQ* model, the basics are to reduce (1) ordering costs and (2) safety stocks. This is achieved by attempting to receive an almost continuous flow of deliveries of component parts. The result is to actually have about 2 to 4 hours worth of inventory on hand. In effect, trucks, railroads, and airplanes become the firm's warehouses. This system has spawned a new emphasis on the dual relationship between the firm and its suppliers.

Inflation and *EOQ*

anticipatory buying
buying in anticipation of a price increase to secure goods at a lower cost.

Inflation affects the *EOQ* model in two major ways. First, although the *EOQ* model can be modified to assume constant price increases, often major price increases occur only once or twice a year and are announced ahead of time. If this is the case, the *EOQ* model may lose its predictability and may be replaced with **anticipatory buying**—that is, *buying in anticipation of a price increase to secure the goods at a lower cost*. Of course, as with most decisions, there are trade-offs. The costs are the added carrying costs associated with the inventory. The benefits, of course, come from buying at a lower price. The second way inflation affects the *EOQ* model is through increased carrying costs. As inflation pushes interest rates up, the cost of carrying inventory increases. In our *EOQ* model this means that *C* increases, which results in a decline in Q^*, the optimal economic order quantity.

$$\downarrow Q^* = \sqrt{\frac{2SO}{C \uparrow}} \tag{16-12}$$

Did You Get It?

1. Describe the types of inventory that firms have.
2. What is the fundamental objective of the economic order quantity (*EOQ*) formula?
3. What assumptions underlie the *EOQ* formula?

Summary

Objective **1**

Understand why a firm holds cash.

As you recall, several of the fundamental principles of financial management relate to the importance of cash and cash flows. In this chapter, we have developed many of the tools that a financial manager needs to manage the firm's cash and other current assets with the overall objective of ensuring that the firm has an appropriate level of liquidity, or net working capital, to carry out the goal of maximizing shareholder wealth.

Objective **2**

Explain various cash management objectives and decisions.

The firm experiences both regular and irregular cash flows. Once cash is obtained, the firm has three motives for holding cash rather than investing it: to satisfy transactions, precautionary, and speculative liquidity needs. To a certain extent, such needs can be satisfied by holding readily marketable securities rather than cash. A significant challenge of cash management, then, is dealing with the trade-off between the firm's need to have cash on hand to pay liabilities that arise in the course of doing business and the objective of maximizing wealth by minimizing idle cash balances that earn no return.

Various procedures exist to improve the efficiency of a firm's cash management. Such procedures focus on accelerating the firm's cash receipts and improving the methods for disbursing cash. To accelerate cash receipts, significant effort is made to reduce the mail, processing, and transit elements of the float.

On the cash disbursements side, firms try to prolong the time cash stays in their own accounts by increasing the disbursement float through the use of zero balance accounts and payable-through drafts. These methods offer much better central-office control over disbursements. Before any collection or disbursement procedure is introduced, however, a careful analysis should be performed to ensure that expected benefits outweigh the expected costs of such procedures.

Because idle cash earns no return, a financial manager looks for opportunities to invest it until it is required in the operations of the company. A variety of different readily marketable securities, described in the chapter, are available in the market today. The yields on such securities vary depending on four factors: the (1) financial risk, (2) interest rate risk, (3) liquidity, and (4) taxability of the security. By simultaneously taking into account these factors and the desired rate of return, the financial manager is able to determine the most suitable mix of cash and marketable securities for the firm.

When we consider that accounts receivable constitute approximately 25 percent of total assets for the typical firm, the importance of accounts-receivable management becomes even more apparent. The size of a firm's investment in accounts receivable depends on three factors: the percentage of credit sales to total sales, the level of sales, and the credit and collection policies of the firm. The financial manager, however, generally has control only over the terms of the sale, the quality of the customer, and the collection efforts.

Although the level of investment in inventories by the typical firm is less than the investment in accounts receivable, inventory management and control remains an important function of the financial manager because inventories play a significant role in the operations of the firm. The purpose of holding inventory is to make each function of the business independent of the other functions. The primary issues related to inventory management are: (1) How much inventory should be ordered? and (2) When should the order be placed? The *EOQ* model is used to answer the first of these questions. The order point model, which depends on the desired levels of delivery-time stock and safety stock, is applied to answer the second question. The relatively new just-in-time approach to inventory control is growing in popularity as an attempt to obtain additional cost savings by reducing the level of inventory a firm needs to have on hand. Instead of depending solely on its own inventories, the firm relies on its vendors to furnish supplies "just in time" to satisfy the firm's production requirements.

Objective **3**

Describe and analyze the different mechanisms for managing the firm's cash collection and disbursement procedures.

Objective **4**

Be able to quantitatively evaluate the expected costs and benefits of cash management services.

Objective **5**

Determine a prudent composition for the firm's marketable-securities portfolio.

Objective **6**

Discuss the determinants of the firm's investment in accounts receivable and learn how decisions regarding changes in credit policy are determined.

Objective **7**

Discuss the reasons for carrying inventory and how inventory management decisions are made.

Key Terms

Anticipatory buying   508

Cash   488

Credit scoring   502

Delivery-time stock   507

Finished-goods inventory   504

Float   491

Insolvency   490

Inventory management   503

Just-in-time inventory control system   508

Marketable securities   488

Order point problem   507

Order quantity problem   504

Payable-through drafts (PTD)   494

Raw-materials inventory   503

Safety stock   507

Terms of sale   500

Work-in-process inventory   503

Zero balance accounts (ZBA)   494

Review Questions

16-1. What is meant by the cash flow process?

16-2. Identify the principal motives for holding cash and near-cash assets. Explain the purpose of each motive.

16-3. What are the two major objectives of the firm's cash management system?

16-4. What decisions dominate the cash management process?

16-5. Within the context of cash management, what are the key elements of (total) float? Briefly define each element.

16-6. Distinguish between *financial risk* and *interest rate risk* as these terms are commonly used in discussions of cash management.

16-7. What factors determine the size of the investment a firm has in its accounts receivable? Which of these factors are under the control of the financial manager?

16-8. If a credit manager experienced no bad-debt losses over the past year, would this be an indication of proper credit management? Why or why not?

16-9. What are the risk–return trade-offs associated with adopting a more liberal trade credit policy?

16-10. What is the purpose of holding inventory? Name several types of inventory and describe their purpose.

16-11. What are the major assumptions made by the *EOQ* model?

Self-Test Problems

(Solutions to these problems are found at the end of the chapter.)

ST-1. (*Buying and selling marketable securities*) Mountaineer Outfitters has $2 million in excess cash to invest in marketable securities. To buy and sell the securities, however, the firm must pay a transaction fee of $45,000.

    a. Would you recommend purchasing the securities if they yield 12 percent annually and are held for
      1. One month?
      2. Two months?
      3. Three months?
      4. Six months?
      5. One year?
    b. What minimum required yield would the securities have to return for the firm to hold them for 3 months? (What is the break-even yield for a 3-month holding period?)

ST-2. (*EOQ calculations*) Consider the following inventory information and relationships for the F. Beamer Corporation:

1. Orders can be placed only in multiples of 100 units.
2. Annual unit usage is 300,000. (Assume a 50-week year in your calculations.)
3. The carrying cost is 30 percent of the purchase price of the goods.
4. The purchase price is $10 per unit.
5. The ordering cost is $50 per order.
6. The desired safety stock is 1,000 units. (This does not include delivery-time stock.)
7. Delivery time is 2 weeks.

Given this information

    a. What is the optimal *EOQ* level?
    b. How many orders will be placed annually?
    c. At what inventory level should a reorder be made?

Study Problems

16-1. (*Buying and selling marketable securities*) Pearl Islands Tour Operator, located in the Pacific Ocean near Panama City, has effectively collected $1,500,000 in excess cash that it plans to invest in marketable securities. The firm will have to pay total transaction costs of $30,000 to buy and sell the securities.

    a. Would you recommend purchasing the securities if they yield 8.25 percent annually and are held for
      1. One month?
      2. Two months?
      3. Three months?
      4. Six months?
      5. One year?
    b. What minimum required yield would the securities have to return for the firm to hold them for 3 months? (What is the break-even yield for a 3-month holding period?)

16-2. (*Cost of services*) As CFO of Portobello Scuba Diving Inc. you are asked to look into the possibility of adopting a lockbox system to expedite cash receipts from clients. Portobello receives check remittances totaling $24 million in a year. The firm records and processes 10,000 checks in the same period. The National Bank of Brazil has informed you that it could provide the service of expediting checks and associated documents through the lockbox system for a unit cost of $0.25 per check. After conducting an analysis, you project that the cash freed up by the adoption of the system can be invested in a portfolio of near-cash assets that will yield an annual before-tax return of 8 percent. The company usually uses a 365-day year in its procedures.

    a. What reduction in check collection time is necessary for Portobello to be neither better nor worse off for having adopted the lockbox system?

    b. How would your solution to part a be affected if Portobello could invest the freed-up balances at an expected annual return of only 4 percent?

    c. What is the logical explanation for the differences in your answers to part a and part b?

16-3. (*Concentration banking*) Byron Sporting Goods operates in Miami, Florida. The firm produces and distributes a full line of athletic equipment on a nationwide basis. The firm currently uses a centralized billing system. Byron Sporting Goods has annual credit sales of $438 million. Austin National Bank has presented an offer to operate a concentration-banking system for the company. Byron already has an established line of credit with Austin. Austin says it will operate the system on a flat-fee basis of $200,000 per year. The analysis done by the bank's cash management services division suggests that 3 days in mail float and 1 day in processing float can be eliminated.

Because Byron borrows almost continuously from Austin National, the value of the float reduction would be applied against the line of credit. The borrowing rate on the line of credit is set at an annual rate of 8 percent. Furthermore, because of the reduction in clerical help, the new system will save the firm $66,000 in processing costs. Byron uses a 365-day year in analyses of this sort. Should Byron accept the bank's offer to install the new system?

16-4. (*Concentration banking*) Treemont Shops operates in Naples, Florida. The firm distributes specialty gardening supplies nationwide. The firm currently uses a centralized billing system.

Treemont has annual credit sales of $362 million. Lasdon National Bank has presented an offer to operate a concentration-banking system for the company. Treemont already has an established line of credit with Lasdon. The bank says it will operate the system on a flat-fee basis of $175,000 per year. The analysis done by the bank's cash management services division suggests that 3 days in mail float and 1 day in processing float can be eliminated. Because Treemont borrows almost continuously, the value of the float reduction would be applied against the line of credit. The borrowing rate on the line of credit is set at an annual rate of 7 percent. Furthermore, because of the reduction in clerical help, the new system will save the firm $57,500 in processing costs. Treemont uses a 365-day year in analyses of this sort. Should Treemont's management accept the bank's offer to install the new system?

16-5. (*Buying and selling marketable securities*) Miami Dice & Card Company has generated $800,000 in excess cash that it could invest in marketable securities. In order to buy and sell the securities, the firm will pay total transaction fees of $20,000.

    a. Would you recommend purchasing the securities if they yield 10.5 percent annually and are held for

        1. One month?

        2. Two months?

        3. Three months?

        4. Six months?

        5. One year?

    b. What minimum required yield would the securities have to return for the firm to hold them for 2 months? (What is the break-even yield for a 2-month holding period?

16-6. (*Costs of services*) Mustang Ski-Wear Inc. is investigating the possibility of adopting a lockbox system as a cash receipts acceleration device. In a typical year this firm receives remittances totaling $12 million by check. The firm will record and process 6,000 checks over this same period. The Colorado Springs Second National Bank has informed the management of Mustang that it will expedite checks and associated documents through the lockbox system for a unit cost of $0.20 per check. Mustang's financial manager has projected that cash freed up by adoption of the system can be invested in a portfolio of near-cash assets that will yield an annual before-tax return of 7 percent. Mustang financial analysts use a 365-day year in their procedures.

    a. What reduction in check collection time is necessary for Mustang to be neither better nor worse off for having adopted the proposed system?

    b. How would your solution to part a be affected if Mustang could invest the freed-up balances at an expected annual return of only 4.5 percent?

    c. What is the logical explanation for the difference in your answers to part a and part b?

16-7. (*Lockbox system*) Penn Steelworks is a distributor of cold-rolled steel products to the automobile industry. All of its sales are on a credit basis, net 30 days. Sales are evenly distributed over its 10 sales regions throughout the United States. Delinquent accounts are no problem. The company has recently undertaken an analysis aimed at improving its cash management procedures. Penn determined that it takes an average of 3.2 days for customers' payments to reach the head office in Pittsburgh from the time they are mailed. It takes another full day in processing time prior to depositing the checks with a local bank. Annual sales average $4.8 million for each regional office. Reasonable investment opportunities can be found that yield 7 percent per year. To alleviate the float problem confronting the firm, the use of a lockbox system in each of the 10 regions is being considered. This would reduce mail float by 1.2 days. One day in processing float would also be eliminated, plus a full day in transit float. The lockbox arrangement would cost each region $250 per month.

    a. What is the opportunity cost to Penn Steelworks of the funds tied up in mailing and processing? Use a 365-day year.

    b. What would the net cost or savings be from use of the proposed cash acceleration technique? Should Penn adopt the system?

16-8. (*Cash receipts acceleration system*) Peggy Pierce Designs Inc. is a vertically integrated, national manufacturer and retailer of women's clothing. Currently, the firm has no coordinated cash management system. A proposal, however, from the First Pennsylvania Bank aimed at speeding up cash collections is being examined by several of Pierce's corporate executives.

The firm currently uses a centralized billing procedure, which requires that all checks be mailed to the Philadelphia head office for processing and eventual deposit. Under this arrangement all the customers' remittance checks take an average of 5 business days to reach the head office. Once in Philadelphia, another 2 days are required to process the checks for ultimate deposit at the First Pennsylvania Bank.

The firm's daily remittances average $1 million. The average check size is $2,000. Pierce Designs currently earns 6 percent annually on its marketable-securities portfolio.

The cash acceleration plan proposed by officers of First Pennsylvania involves both a lockbox system and concentration banking. First Pennsylvania would be the firm's only concentration bank. Lockboxes would be established in (1) San Francisco, (2) Dallas, (3) Chicago, and (4) Philadelphia. This would reduce funds tied up by mail float to 3 days, and processing float will be eliminated. Funds would then be transferred twice each business day by means of automated depository transfer checks from local banks in San Francisco, Dallas, and Chicago to the First Pennsylvania Bank. Each DTC costs $15. These transfers will occur all 270 business days of the year. Each check processed through the lockbox system will cost $0.18.

    a. What amount of cash balances will be freed up if Peggy Pierce Designs Inc. adopts the system suggested by First Pennsylvania?

    b. What is the opportunity cost of maintaining the current banking setup?

    c. What is the projected annual cost of operating the proposed system?

    d. Should Pierce adopt the new system? Compute the net annual gain or loss associated with adopting the system.

16-9. (*Marketable-securities portfolio*) The Alex Daniel Shoe Manufacturing Company currently pays its employees on a weekly basis. The weekly wage bill is $500,000. This means that on average the firm has accrued wages payable of ($500,000 + $0)/2 = $250,000.

Alex Daniel Jr. works as the firm's senior financial analyst and reports directly to his father, who owns all of the firm's common stock. Alex Daniel Jr. wants to move to a monthly wage-payment system. Employees would be paid at the end of every fourth week. The younger Daniel is fully aware that the labor union representing the company's workers will not permit the monthly payments system to take effect unless the workers are given some type of fringe benefit compensation. A plan has been worked out whereby the firm will make a contribution to the cost of life insurance coverage for each employee. This will cost the firm $35,000 annually. Alex Daniel Jr. expects the firm to earn 7 percent annually on its marketable-securities portfolio.

    a. Based on the projected information, should Daniel Shoe Manufacturing move to the monthly wage-payment system?

    b. What annual rate of return on the marketable-securities portfolio would enable the firm to just break even on this proposal?

16-10. (*Valuing float reduction*) The Cowboy Bottling Company will generate $12 million in credit sales next year. Collection of these credit sales will occur evenly over this period. The firm's employees work 270 days a year. Currently, the firm's processing system ties up 4 days' worth of remittance checks. A recent report from a financial consultant indicated procedures that will enable Cowboy Bottling to reduce processing float by 2 full days. If Cowboy invests the released funds to earn 6 percent, what will be the annual savings?

16-11. (*Accounts-payable policy and cash management*) Bradford Construction Supply Company is suffering from a prolonged decline in new construction in its sales area. In an attempt to improve its cash position, the firm is considering changes in its accounts-payable policy. After careful study, it has determined that the only alternative available is to slow disbursements. Purchases for the coming year are expected to be $37.5 million. Sales will be $65 million, which represents about a 20 percent drop from the current year. Currently, Bradford discounts approximately 25 percent of its payments at 3 percent, 10 days, net 30, and the balance of accounts is paid in 30 days. If Bradford adopts a policy of payment in 45 days or 60 days, how much can the firm gain if the annual opportunity cost of investment is 12 percent? What will be the result if this action causes Bradford Construction suppliers to increase their prices to the company by $\frac{1}{2}$ percent to compensate for the 60-day extended term of payment? In your calculations, use a 365-day year and ignore any compounding effects related to the expected returns.

16-12. (*Interest rate risk*) Two years ago your corporate treasurer purchased for the firm a 20-year bond at its par value of $1,000. The coupon rate on this security is 8 percent. Interest payments are made to bondholders once a year. Currently, bonds of this particular risk class are yielding investors 9 percent. A cash shortage has forced you to instruct your treasurer to liquidate the bond.

    a. At what price will your bond be sold? Assume annual compounding.

    b. What will be the amount of your gain or loss over the original purchase price?

    c. What would be the amount of your gain or loss had the treasurer originally purchased a bond with a 4-year rather than a 20-year maturity? (Assume all characteristics of the bonds are identical except their maturity periods.)

    d. What do we call this type of risk assumed by your corporate treasurer?

16-13. (*Comparison of after-tax yields*) The corporate treasurer of Aggieland Fireworks is considering the purchase of a BBB-rated bond that carries a 9 percent coupon. The BBB-rated security is taxable, and the firm is in the 46 percent marginal tax bracket. The face value of this bond is $1,000.

A financial analyst who reports to the corporate treasurer has alerted him to the fact that a municipal obligation is coming to the market with a $5\frac{1}{2}$ percent coupon. The par value of this security is also $1,000.

    a. Which one of the two securities do you recommend the firm purchase? Why?

    b. What must the fully taxed bond yield before tax to make it comparable with the municipal offering?

16-14. (*Trade credit discounts*) Determine the effective annualized cost of forgoing the trade credit discount on the following terms:

    a. 1/10, net 20

    b. 2/10, net 30

    c. 3/10, net 30

    d. 3/10, net 60

    e. 3/10, net 90

    f. 5/10, net 60

16-15. (*Altman model*) The following ratios were supplied by six loan applicants. Given this information and the credit-scoring model developed by Altman (equation [16-4]), which loans have a high probability of defaulting next year?

	EBIT ÷ TOTAL ASSETS	SALES ÷ TOTAL ASSETS	MARKET VALUE OF EQUITY ÷ BOOK VALUE OF DEBT	RETAINED EARNINGS ÷ TOTAL ASSETS	WORKING CAPITAL ÷ TOTAL ASSETS
Applicant 1	.2	.2	1.2	.3	.5
Applicant 2	.2	.8	1.0	.3	.8
Applicant 3	.2	.7	.6	.3	.4
Applicant 4	.1	.4	1.2	.4	.4
Applicant 5	.3	.7	.5	.4	.7
Applicant 6	.2	.5	.5	.4	.4

16-16. (*Ratio analysis*) Assuming a 360-day year, calculate what the average investment in inventory would be for a firm, given the following information in each case.

   a. The firm has sales of $600,000, a gross profit margin of 10 percent, and an inventory turnover ratio of 6.
   b. The firm has a cost-of-goods-sold figure of $480,000 and an average age of inventory of 40 days.
   c. The firm has a cost-of-goods-sold figure of $1.15 million and an inventory turnover rate of 5.
   d. The firm has a sales figure of $25 million, a gross profit margin of 14 percent, and an average age of inventory of 45 days.

16-17. (*EOQ calculations*) A downtown bookstore is trying to determine the optimal order quantity for a popular novel just printed in paperback. The store feels that the book will sell at four times its hardback figures. It would, therefore, sell approximately 3,000 copies in the next year at a price of $1.50. The store buys the book at a wholesale figure of $1. Costs for carrying the book are estimated at $0.10 a copy per year, and it costs $10 to order more books.

   a. Determine the *EOQ*.
   b. What would be the total costs for ordering the books 1, 4, 5, 10, and 15 times a year?
   c. What questionable assumptions are being made by the *EOQ* model?

16-18. (*Comprehensive EOQ calculations*) Knutson Products Inc. is involved in the production of airplane parts and has the following inventory, carrying, and storage costs:
   1. Orders must be placed in round lots of 100 units.
   2. Annual unit usage is 250,000. (Assume a 50-week year in your calculations.)
   3. The carrying cost is 10 percent of the purchase price.
   4. The purchase price is $10 per unit.
   5. The ordering cost is $100 per order.
   6. The desired safety stock is 5,000 units. (This does not include delivery-time stock.)
   7. The delivery time is 1 week.

Given the foregoing information:
   a. Determine the optimal *EOQ* level.
   b. How many orders will be placed annually?

c. What is the inventory order point? (That is, at what level of inventory should a new order be placed?)

d. What is the average inventory level?

e. What would happen to the *EOQ* if annual unit sales doubled (all other unit costs and safety stocks remaining constant)? What is the elasticity of *EOQ* with respect to sales? (That is, what is the percentage change in *EOQ* divided by the percentage change in sales?)

f. If carrying costs double, what will happen to the *EOQ* level? (Assume the original sales level of 250,000 units.) What is the elasticity of *EOQ* with respect to carrying costs?

g. If the ordering costs double, what will happen to the level of *EOQ*? (Again assume original levels of sales and carrying costs.) What is the elasticity of *EOQ* with respect to ordering costs?

h. If the selling price doubles, what will happen to *EOQ*? What is the elasticity of *EOQ* with respect to selling price?

Web Works

16-WW1. Visit **www.federalreserve.gov** and click on "Research and Data." Find the H.15 (519) report on "Selected Interest Rates." This report is updated and published each week, with the last data entry being for Friday of that week. Here you can check both the available yields on different marketable securities that comprise the firm's short-term portfolio and the yield structure across different investment instruments within the portfolio. Interest rate data are available on commercial paper, certificates of deposit, and U.S. Treasury securities of varying maturities. It is a very useful weekly report.

16-WW2. The Procter & Gamble Company (P&G) is a major producer and distributor of a wide range of consumer goods. Familiar products include Tide, Bounty, Pringles, and Folgers. Find the firm's 2005 Annual Report at **www.pg.com/investing** or at **www.reportgallery.com.** Check out P&G's consolidated balance sheets for 2004 and 2005. Now answer these questions dealing with current asset management: (1) What percentage of total current assets was represented by cash and cash equivalents in 2004 and 2005? (2) Was the amount invested in cash and cash equivalents more or less than the amount invested in accounts receivable? (3) Of the following three categories, cash and cash equivalents, accounts receivable, and inventories, which represented the largest investment for P&G each year?

16-WW3. Now call up the 2005 Annual Report for the Walt Disney Company at **www.disney.com/investors**. Find Disney's consolidated balance sheets for 2004 and 2005. We will focus on 2005. Of all the different current asset accounts, which single one dominated the others in terms of total dollars invested? Is it the same category that dominated P&G's current assets (from question 2)?

Mini Case

New Wave Surfing Stuff Inc. is a manufacturer of surfboards and related gear that sells to exclusive surf shops located in several Atlantic and Pacific mainland coastal towns as well as several Hawaiian locations. The company's headquarters are located in Carlsbad, California, a small southern California coastal town. True to form, the company's officers, all veteran surfers, have been somewhat laid back about various critical areas of financial management. With an economic downturn in California adversely affecting their business, however, the officers of the company have decided to focus intently on ways to improve New Wave's cash flows. The CFO, Willy Bonik, has been requested to forgo any more daytime surfing jaunts until he has wrapped up a plan to accelerate New Wave's cash flows.

In an effort to ensure his quick return to the surf, Willy has decided to focus on what he believes is one of the easiest methods of improving New Wave's cash collections, namely, the adoption of a cash receipts acceleration system that includes a lockbox system and concentration banking. Willy is well aware that New Wave's current system leaves much room for improvement. The company's accounts receivable system currently requires that remittances from customers be mailed to the headquarters office for processing and then deposited in the local branch of the Bank of the U.S. Such an arrangement takes a considerable amount of time. The checks take an average of 5 days to reach the Carlsbad headquarters. Then, depending on the surf conditions, processing within the company takes anywhere from 2 to 4 days, with the average from the day of receipt by the company to the day of deposit at the bank being 3 days.

Willy feels pretty certain that such delays are costly. After all, New Wave's average daily collections are $150,000. The average remittance size is $750. If Willy could get these funds into his marketable-securities account more quickly, he could earn an annual rate of 5 percent on them. In addition, if he could arrange for someone else to do the processing, Willy could save $55,000 per year in costs related to clerical staffing.

New Wave's banker was pleased to provide Willy with a proposal for a combination of a lockbox system and a concentration-banking system. Bank of the U.S. would be New Wave's concentration bank. Lockboxes would be established in Honolulu, Newport Beach, and Daytona Beach. Each check processed through the lockbox system would cost New Wave $0.30. This arrangement, however, would reduce mail float by an average 2.5 days. The funds so collected would be transferred twice each day, 270 days a year, from each of the local lockbox banks to Bank of the U.S. Each transfer would cost $0.35. The combination of lockbox system and concentration banking would eliminate the time it takes the company to process cash collections, thereby making the funds available for short-term investment.

   a. What would be the average amount of cash made available if New Wave were to adopt the system proposed by Bank of the U.S.?
   b. What is the annual opportunity cost of maintaining the current cash collection and deposit system?
   c. What is the expected annual cost of the complete system proposed by Bank of the U.S.?
   d. What is the net gain or loss that is expected to result from the proposed new system? Should New Wave adopt the new system?

Self-Test Solutions

SS-1.

a. Here we must calculate the dollar value of the estimated return for each holding period and compare it with the transaction fee to determine if a gain can be made by investing in the securities. Those calculations and the resultant recommendations follow.

			RECOMMENDATION
1. $2,000,000 (.12)($\frac{1}{12}$)	= $ 20,000	<$45,000	No
2. $2,000,000 (.12)($\frac{2}{12}$)	= $ 40,000	<$45,000	No
3. $2,000,000 (.12)($\frac{3}{12}$)	= $ 60,000	>$45,000	Yes
4. $2,000,000 (.12)($\frac{6}{12}$)	= $120,000	>$45,000	Yes
5. $2,000,000 (.12)($\frac{12}{12}$)	= $240,000	>$45,000	Yes

b. Let (%) be the required yield. With $2 million to invest for 3 months, we have

$$\$2,000,000(\%)(3/12) = \$45,000$$
$$\$2,000,000(\%) = \$180,000$$
$$= \$180,000/\$2,000,000 = 9\%$$

The break-even yield, therefore, is 9 percent.

SS-2.

a. $EOQ = \sqrt{\dfrac{2SO}{C}}$

$\qquad = \sqrt{\dfrac{2(300,000)(\$50)}{\$3}}$

$\qquad = 3,162$ units, but because orders must be placed in 100-unit lots, the effective *EOQ* becomes 3,200 units

b. $\dfrac{\text{total usage}}{EOQ} = \dfrac{300,000}{3,200} = 93.75$ orders per year

c. Inventory order point = delivery-time stock + safety stock

$\qquad\qquad\qquad = \dfrac{2}{50} \times 300,000 + 1,000$

$\qquad\qquad\qquad = 12,000 + 1,000$

$\qquad\qquad\qquad = 13,000$ units

<LEARNING OBJECTIVES >

LEARNING OBJECTIVES

After reading this chapter, you should be able to:

1. Discuss the internationalization of business.

2. Explain why foreign exchange rates in two different countries must be in line with each other.

3. Discuss the concept of interest rate parity.

4. Explain the purchasing-power parity theory and the law of one price.

5. Explain what exchange rate risk is and how it can be controlled.

6. Identify working-capital management techniques that are useful for international businesses to reduce

exchange rate risk and potentially increase profits.

7. Explain how the financing sources available to multinational corporations differ from those available to domestic firms.

8. Discuss the risks involved in direct foreign investment.

CHAPTER 17

International Business Finance

Finding new projects doesn't necessarily mean coming up with a new product; it may mean taking an existing product and introducing it to a new market. That's certainly been the direction that McDonald's has taken in recent years. Today, McDonald's operates more than 29,000 restaurants in over 119 countries. The busiest McDonald's restaurant in the world is not in America but thousands of miles away in Pushkin Square in Moscow, Russia. The store serves 30,000 customers a day, as many as on its opening day, January 31, 1990. The menu is essentially the same as in the United States, with the addition of cabbage pie, among other traditional Russian food items.

Was this an expensive venture? It certainly was. In fact, the food plants that McDonald's built to supply burgers, fries, and everything else sold there cost more than $60 million. In addition to the costs, there are a number of other factors that make opening an outlet outside of the United States both different and challenging. First, in order to keep the quality consistent with what is served at any McDonald's anywhere in the world, McDonald's spent 6 years putting together a supply chain that would provide the necessary raw materials McDonald's demands. On top of that, there are risks associated with the Russian economy and its currency that are well beyond the scope of what is experienced in the United States.

These risks all materialized in 1998, when the Russian economy, along with its currency, the ruble, went in the tank. In an attempt to shore up the economy, the Russian government cut the exchange rate from 6,000 rubles for each U.S. dollar to a new rate of 6 rubles per U.S. dollar—in effect, the government cut off three zeros. Unfortunately, that didn't solve the problems the Russian economy faced. In May 1998, the first Russian bank crashed, and the value of the ruble started to drop. That summer, the Russian economy spun out of control, and in August the entire banking system failed.

When it was all over by the end of 1998, the exchange rate had fallen to 23 rubles per dollar, a change of more than 280 percent. Because McDonald's sells its burgers for rubles, when it came time to trade the rubles for U.S. dollars, McDonald's wasn't worth nearly as much as it was the year before. In spite of all this, the Moscow McDonald's has proven to be enormously successful since it opened. In fact, by 2006, McDonald's had 127 stores in 22 Russian cities, and it has plans for 75 more by 2007. It all goes to show that not all capital-budgeting projects have to be new products; they can be existing domestic products that are introduced into international markets.

This chapter highlights the complications that an international business faces when it deals in multiple currencies. Effective strategies for reducing foreign exchange risk are discussed. Working-capital management and capital structure decisions in the international context are also covered.

THE GLOBALIZATION OF PRODUCT AND FINANCIAL MARKETS

Objective 1

Discuss the internationalization of business.

To say the least, the market for most products crosses many borders. In fact, some industries and states are highly dependent on the international economy. For example, the electronic consumer products and automobile industries are widely considered to be global industries. Ohio ranks fourth in terms of manufactured exports, and more than half of Ohio workers are employed by firms that depend to some extent on exports.

There has also been a rise in the global level of international portfolio and direct investment. Both direct and portfolio investments in the United States have been increasing faster than U.S. investment overseas. *Direct foreign investment* (DFI) occurs when the **multinational corporation (MNC)**, *a corporation with holdings and/or operations in more than one country*, has control over the investment, such as when it builds an offshore manufacturing facility. *Portfolio investment* involves financial assets with maturities greater than 1 year, such as the purchase of foreign stocks and bonds. Total foreign investment in the United States now exceeds such U.S. investment overseas.

multinational corporation (MNC) a corporation with holdings and/or operations in more than one country.

A major reason for direct foreign investment by U.S. companies is the high rates of return obtainable from these investments. And the amount of U.S. direct foreign investment (DFI) a broad is large and growing. Significant amounts of the total assets, sales, and profits of American MNCs are attributable to foreign investments and foreign operations. Direct foreign investment is not limited to American firms. Many European and Japanese firms have operations abroad, too. During the past decade, these firms have been increasing their sales and setting up production facilities abroad, especially in the United States.

Capital flows (portfolio investment) between countries have also been increasing. Many firms, investment companies, and individuals invest in the capital markets in foreign countries. The motivation is twofold: to obtain returns higher than those obtainable in the domestic capital markets, and to reduce portfolio risk through international diversification. The increase in world trade and investment activity is reflected in the recent globalization of financial markets. The Eurodollar market is now larger than any domestic financial market, and U.S. companies are increasingly turning to this market for funds. Even companies and public entities that have no overseas presence are beginning to rely on this market for financing.

In addition, most national financial markets are becoming more integrated with global markets because of the rapid increase in the volume of interest rate and currency swaps. (We will discuss currency swaps later in the chapter.) Because of the widespread availability of these swaps, the currency denomination and the source country of financing for many globally integrated companies are dictated by accessibility and relative-cost considerations, regardless of the currency ultimately needed by the firm. Even a *purely domestic firm* that buys all its inputs and sells all its output in its home country is not immune to foreign competition, nor can it totally ignore the workings of the international financial markets.

Did You Get It? ....

1. Why do U.S. companies invest overseas?

Objective 2

Explain why foreign exchange rates in two different countries must be in line with each other.

EXCHANGE RATES

Floating Exchange Rates

floating-rate international currency system a system in which the exchange rates of different currencies are allowed to fluctuate with supply and demand conditions.

Since 1973, a **floating-rate international currency system**, *a system in which exchange rates between different national currencies are allowed to fluctuate with supply and demand conditions*, has been operating. For most currencies, there are no "parity rates" and no "bands" within which the currencies fluctuate.[1] Most major currencies, including the U.S. dollar, fluctuate freely, depending on their values as perceived by the traders in foreign exchange markets. A country's relative economic strengths, its level of exports and imports, the level of monetary activity, and the deficits or surpluses in its balance of payments (BOP) are all important factors that determine exchange rates.[2] Short-term, day-to-day fluctuations in exchange rates are caused by changing supply and demand conditions for different currencies.

The Euro: The New Currency of Europe

Since 2002, 11 countries in the European Union have begun using a new, single currency, the euro, and phasing out their old currencies. These countries, often referred to as Euroland, are Germany, France, Italy, Spain, Portugal, Belgium, the Netherlands, Luxembourg, Ireland, Finland, and Austria. Without question, Germany and France are the big players, accounting for over 50 percent of Euroland's output.

Why did the European Union go to a single currency? For several reasons: First, it makes it easier for goods, people, and services to travel across national borders. A common currency eliminates the exchange costs that occur when you have to trade your German marks for French francs. It also eliminates the uncertainty associated with exchange rate fluctuations. It should also help eliminate cost differences for goods in different countries. For example, before the single European currency, "The Classics" Swatch watch was selling for an equivalent of 39.2 euros ($45.97) in Belgium and only 25.7 euros ($30.14) in Italy. With the introduction of the euro, it made it easier to compare prices and reduce the discrepancies. As a result, the economies of the European Union are flourishing.

What does all this mean for the United States? First, it means the competition from abroad will be stronger. It also makes the exchange rate between the euro and the U.S. dollar a very important exchange rate. If the euro is strong, it helps U.S. exports by making them cheaper. On the other hand, if the euro is weak, U.S. exports suffer. Fortunately, many U.S. multinational firms appear to be in good shape to cash in on any economic surge that may hit Euroland. For example, look at Wal-Mart, which has 21 stores in Germany. In Germany, Wal-Mart is doing just what it does here in the United States—it is wiping out the competition. For the Germans, this is their first sight of wide aisles—(bigger than some of the local streets)—and discount shopping. The euro has allowed Wal-Mart both to offer even more bargains from all over Euroland and to provide a much more diverse selection of goods. That's because in Europe, with all the exchange rate uncertainties, most goods are regional in nature. That's the bottom line: The euro has led greater choice and greater competition—both good for the consumer.

The Foreign Exchange Market

The foreign exchange market provides a mechanism for the transfer of purchasing power from one currency to another. This market is not a physical entity like the New York Stock Exchange; it is a network of telephone and computer connections among banks, foreign exchange dealers, and brokers. The market operates simultaneously at three levels. At the first level, customers buy and sell foreign exchange (foreign currency) through their banks. At the second level, banks buy and sell foreign exchange from other banks in the same commercial center. At the last level, banks buy and sell foreign exchange from banks in commercial centers in other countries. Some important commercial centers for foreign exchange trading are New York, London, Zurich, Frankfurt, Hong Kong, Singapore, and Tokyo.

An example illustrates this multilevel trading. A trader in Texas may buy foreign exchange (pounds) from a bank in Houston for payment to a British supplier against some purchase made. The Houston bank, in turn, may purchase the foreign currency (pounds) from a New York bank. The New York bank may buy the pounds from another bank in New York or from a bank in London.

Because this market provides transactions in a continuous manner for a very large volume of sales and purchases, the currency markets are efficient: In other words, it is difficult

---

[1] The system of floating rates is referred to as the "floating-rate regime."
[2] The balance of payments for the United States reflects the difference between the import and export of goods (the trade balance) and services. Capital inflows and outflows are tabulated in the capital account.

to make a profit by shopping around from one bank to another. Minute differences in the quotes from different banks are quickly eliminated. Because of constant trading, simultaneous quotes to different buyers in London and New York are likely to be the same.

Two major types of transactions are carried out in the foreign exchange markets: spot transactions and forward transactions, which we explain next.

Spot Exchange Rates

spot transaction a transaction made immediately in the marketplace at the market price.

exchange rate the price of a foreign currency stated in terms of the domestic or home currency.

forward transaction an agreement today to deliver a specified number of units of a currency on a future date in return for a specified number of units of another currency.

direct quote the exchange rate that indicates the number of units of the home currency required to buy one unit of foreign currency.

indirect quote the exchange rate that expresses the number of units of a foreign currency that can be bought for one unit of the home currency.

In a typical **spot transaction** *one currency is traded for another currency today.* For example, an American firm might buy foreign currency from its bank and pay for it in dollars. Another type of spot transaction is when an American firm receives foreign currency from abroad and sells the foreign currency to its bank for dollars. *The price of foreign currency in terms of the domestic currency* is the **exchange rate**. The actual exchange rate quotes are expressed in several different ways, as discussed later. To allow time for the transfer of funds, the *value date* when the currencies are actually exchanged is two days after the spot transaction occurs. Four banks could easily be involved in the transactions: the local banks of the buyer and seller of the foreign exchange, and the money-center banks that handle the purchase and sale. Perhaps the buyer or seller will have to move the funds from one of its local banks to another, bringing even more banks into the transaction. A **forward transaction** (as apposed to a spot transaction) entails an agreement today to deliver a specified number of units of a currency on a *future* date in return for a specified number of units of another currency.

In the spot exchange market, contrasted with the over-the-counter market, the quoted exchange rate is typically called a direct quote. A **direct quote** *indicates the number of units of the home currency required to buy one unit of the foreign currency.* That is, in New York the typical exchange rate quote indicates the number of dollars needed to buy one unit of a foreign currency: dollars per pound, dollars per euro, and so on. The spot rates in column 1 of Table 17-1 are the direct exchange quotes taken from the *Wall Street Journal*. Thus, according to Table 17-1, to buy 1 British pound (£1), $1.8720 was needed. To buy Swiss francs and euros, $.8212 and $1.2795 were needed, respectively.

An **indirect quote** *indicates the number of units of a foreign currency that can be bought for one unit of the home currency.* This reads as pounds per dollar, euros per dollar, and so forth. An indirect quote is the general method used in the over-the-counter market. Exceptions to this rule include British pounds, Irish punts, Australian dollars, and New Zealand dollars, which are quoted via direct quotes for historical reasons. Indirect quotes are given in the last column of Table 17-1.

In summary, a direct quote is the dollar/foreign currency rate ($/FC), and an indirect quote is the foreign currency/dollar (FC/$) rate. Therefore, an indirect quote is the reciprocal of a direct quote and vice versa. The following example illustrates the computation of an indirect quote from a given direct quote.

➤ EXAMPLE

Suppose you want to compute the indirect quote from the direct quote of the spot rate for pounds given in column 1 of Table 17-1. The direct quote for the U.K. pound is $1.8720. The related indirect quote is calculated as the *reciprocal* of the direct quote as follows:

$$\text{Indirect quote} = \frac{1}{\text{direct quote}}$$

Thus,

$$\frac{1}{\$1.8720} = £.5342$$

Notice that the previous direct quote and indirect quote are identical to those shown in Table 17-1.

Direct and indirect quotes are useful in conducting international transactions, as the following examples show.

TABLE 17-1   Foreign Exchange Rates Reported May 25, 2006

KEY CURRENCY CROSS RATES

			LATE NEW YORK TRADING THURSDAY, MAY 25, 2006				
	DOLLAR	**EURO**	**POUND**	**SFRANC**	**PESO**	**YEN**	**CDNDLR**
Canada	1.1067	1.4160	2.0717	0.9088	.09934	.00990	...
Japan	111.78	143.02	209.26	91.795	10.034	...	101.006
Mexico	11.1408	14.2547	20.856	9.1488	...	0.9967	10.0668
Switzerland	1.2177	1.5581	2.2796	...	.10930	.01089	1.1003
U.K.	.53420	.6835	...	.4387	.4795	.00478	.48269
Euro	.78160	...	1.4631	.64181	.07015	.00699	.70621
U.S.	...	1.2795	1.8720	.82120	.08976	.00895	.90360

Source: Reuters

EXCHANGE RATES   May 25, 2006

The foreign exchange midrange rates below apply to trading among banks in amounts of $1 million and more, as quoted at 4 p.m. Eastern time by Reuters and other sources. Retail transactions provide fewer units of foreign currency per dollar.

Country	U.S. $ EQUIVALENT	CURRENCY PER U.S. $	Country	U.S. $ EQUIVALENT	CURRENCY PER U.S. $
Argentina (Peso)-y	.3244	3.0826	New Zealand (Dollar)	.6400	1.5625
Australia (Dollar)	.7607	1.3146	Norway (Krone)	.1636	6.1125
Bahrain (Dinar)	2.6526	.3770	Pakistan (Rupee)	.01662	60.169
Brazil (Real)	.4377	2.2847	Peru (new Sol)	.3064	3.2637
Canada (Dollar)	.9036	1.1067	Philippines (Peso)	.01890	52.910
1-month forward	.9042	1.1060	Poland (Zloty)	.3253	3.0741
3-months forward	.9058	1.1040	Russia (Ruble)-a	.03698	27.042
6-months forward	.9082	1.1011	Saudi Arabia (Riyal)	.2666	3.7509
Chile (Peso)	.001900	526.32	Singapore (Dollar)	.6335	1.5785
China (Renminbi)	.1246	8.0250	Slovak Rep. (Koruna)	.03383	29.560
Colombia (Peso)	.0003999	2500.63	South Africa (Rand)	.1533	6.5232
Czech, Rep. (Koruna)					
Commercial rate	.04544	22.007	South Korea (Won)	.0010536	949.13
Denmark (Krone)	.1715	5.8309	Sweden (Krona)	.1374	7.2780
Ecuador (US Dollar)	1.0000	1.0000	Switzerland (Franc)	.8212	1.2177
Egypt (Pound)-y	.1734	5.7663	1-month forward	.8238	1.2139
Hong Kong (Dollar)	.1289	7.7564	3-months forward	.8291	1.2061
Hungary (Forint)	.004897	204.21	6-months forward	.8368	1.1950
India (Rupee)	.02185	45.767	Taiwan (Dollar)	.03115	32.103
Indonesia (Rupiah)	.0001068	9363	Thailand (Baht)	.02613	38.270
Israel (Shekel)	.2215	4.5147	Turkey (New Lira)-d	.6525	1.5325
Japan (Yen)	.008946	111.78	U.K. (Pound)	1.8720	.5342
1-month forward	.008984	111.31	1-month forward	1.8728	.5340
3-months forward	.009059	110.39	3-months forward	1.8748	.5334
6-months forward	.009171	109.04	6-months forward	1.8777	.5326
Jordan (Dinar)	1.4110	.7087	United Arab (Dirham)	.2724	3.6711
Kuwait (Dinar)	3.4581	.2892	Uruguay (Peso)		
Lebanon (Pound)	.0006634	1507.39	Financial	.04180	23.923
Malaysia (Ringgit)-b	.2742	3.6470	Venezuela (Bolivar)	.000466	2145.92
Malta (Lira)	2.9798	.3356	SDR	1.4883	.6719
Mexico (Peso) Floating rate	.0898	11.1408	Euro	1.2795	.7816

Special Drawing Rights (SDR) are based on exchange rates for the U.S., British, and Japanese currencies. Source: International Monetary Fund.

a-Russian Central Bank rate. b-Government rate. d-Rebased as of Jan. 1, 2005. y-Floating rate.

Source: *Wall Street Journal*, May 24, 2006, p. B6.

> **EXAMPLE**

An American business must pay 1,000 euros to a German firm on May 25, 2006. How many dollars will be required for this transaction?

$$\$1.2795/€ \times €1,000 = \$1,279.50$$

> **EXAMPLE**

An American business must pay \$2,000 to a U.K. resident on May 25, 2006. How many pounds will the U.K. resident receive?

$$£.5342/\$ \times \$2,000 = £1,068.40$$

Exchange Rates and Arbitrage

The foreign exchange quotes in two different countries must be in line with each other. If the exchange rate quotations between the London and New York spot exchange markets were *out of line*, then an *enterprising trader could make a profit by buying in the market where the currency was cheaper and selling it in the other*. Such a buy-and-sell strategy would involve a zero net investment of funds and no risk bearing, yet it would provide a sure profit. Such a person is called an **arbitrageur**, and the process of buying and selling in more than one market to make a riskless profit is called arbitrage. Spot exchange markets are efficient in the sense that arbitrage opportunities do not persist for any length of time. That is, the exchange rates between two different markets are quickly brought *in line*, aided by the arbitrage process. **Simple arbitrage** *eliminates exchange rate differentials across the markets for a single currency*, as in the preceding example for the New York and London quotes. **Triangular arbitrage** does the *same across the markets for all currencies*. **Covered-interest arbitrage** *eliminates differentials across currency* and *interest rate markets*.

Suppose that London quotes £.5500/\$ instead of £.5342/\$. If you simultaneously bought a pound in London for £.5500/\$ and sold a pound in New York for £.5342/\$, you would have (1) taken a zero net investment position because you bought £1 and sold £1, (2) locked in a sure profit of £.0158/\$ *no matter which way* the pound subsequently moves, and (3) set in motion the forces that will eliminate the different quotes in New York and London. As others in the marketplace learn of your transaction, they will attempt to make the same transaction. The increased demand to buy pounds in London will lead to a higher quote there, and the increased supply of pounds will lead to a lower quote in New York. The workings of the market will produce a new spot rate that lies between £.5342/\$ and £.5500/\$ and is the same in New York and in London.

Asked and Bid Rates

Two types of rates are quoted in the spot exchange market: the asked and the bid rates. The **asked rate** is the *rate the bank or the foreign exchange trader "asks" the customer to pay in home currency for foreign currency when the bank is selling and the customer is buying*. The asked rate is also known as the **selling rate** or the *offer rate*. The **bid rate** is *the rate at which the bank buys the foreign currency from the customer by paying in home currency*. The bid rate is also known as the **buying rate**. Note that Table 17-1 contains only the selling, offer, or asked rates, not the buying rate.

The banks sells a unit of foreign currency for more than it pays for it. Therefore, the direct asked quote (\$/FC) is greater than the direct bid quote. *The difference between the asked quote and the bid quote* is known as the **bid-asked spread**. When there is a large volume of transactions and the trading is continuous, the spread is small and can be less than 1 percent (.01) for the major currencies. The spread is much higher for infrequently traded currencies. The spread exists to compensate the banks for holding the risky foreign currency and for providing the service of converting currencies.

---

arbitrageur an individual involved in the process of buying and selling in more than one market to make a riskless profit.

simple arbitrage trading to eliminate exchange rate differentials across the markets for a single currency.

triangular arbitrage arbitrage across three markets for three currencies.

covered-interest arbitrage designed to eliminate differentials across currency and interest rate markets.

asked rate the rate the bank or the foreign exchange trader "asks" the customer to pay in home currency for foreign currency when the bank is selling and the customer is buying. The asked rate is also known as the selling rate or the offer rate.

selling rate the rate the bank or the foreign exchange trader "asks" the customer to pay in home currency for foreign currency when the bank is selling and the customer is buying. The selling rate is also known as the asked rate or the offer rate.

bid rate the rate at which the bank buys the foreign currency from the customer by paying in home currency. The bid rate is also known as the buying rate.

buying rate the rate at which the bank buys the foreign currency from the customer by paying in home currency. The buying rate is also known as the bid rate.

bid-asked spread the difference between the asked quote and the bid quote.

Can You Do It?

USING THE SPOT RATE TO CALCULATE A FOREIGN CURRENCY PAYMENT

An American business must pay the equivalent of $10,000 in shekels to an Israeli firm on May 25, 2006. Using the information in Table 17-1, how many shekels will the Israeli citizen receive?

(The solution can be found on page 526.)

Cross Rates

A **cross rate** is *the computation of an exchange rate for a currency from the exchange rates of two other currencies*. These are given at the top of Table 17-1. The following example illustrates how this works.

cross rate the computation of an exchange rate for a currency from the exchange rates of two other currencies.

> ### ➤ EXAMPLE
>
> Taking the dollar/pound and the euro/dollar rates from columns 1 and 2 of Table 17-1, determine the euro/pound and pound/euro exchange rates. We see that
>
> $$(\$/\pounds) \times (€/\$) = (€/\pounds)$$
>
> or
>
> $$1.8720 \times .7816 = €1.46316/\pounds$$
>
> Thus, the pound/euro exchange rate is
>
> $$1/1.46316 = \pounds.68345/€$$
>
> You'll notice that, other than the number of decimal places, these rates are the same as those given in the top portion of Table 17-1 under Key Currency Cross Rates.

Cross-rate computations make it possible to use quotations in New York to compute the exchange rate between pounds, euros, and other currencies. Arbitrage conditions hold in cross rates, too. For example, the pound exchange rate in euros (the direct quote euros/pound) must be €1.4631/£. The euro exchange rate in London must be £.6835/€. If the rates were different from the computed cross rates, using quotes from New York, a trader could use three different currencies to lock in arbitrage profits through triangular arbitrage.

Forward Exchange Rates

A **forward exchange contract** *requires delivery, at a specified future date, of one currency for a specified amount of another currency*. The exchange rate for the forward transaction is agreed on today; the actual payment of one currency and the receipt of another currency take place at the future date. For example, a 30-day contract agreed upon March 1 will be delivered March 31. Note that the forward rate is not the same as the spot rate that will prevail in the future. The actual spot rate that will prevail is not known today; only the forward rate is known. The actual spot rate will depend on the market conditions at that time; it may be more or less than today's forward rate. **Exchange rate risk** is the *risk that tomorrow's exchange rate will differ from today's rate*.

As indicated earlier, it is extremely unlikely that the future spot rate will be exactly the same as the forward rate quoted today. Assume that you are going to receive a payment denominated in pounds from a British customer in 30 days. If you wait for 30 days

forward exchange contract a forward contract that requires delivery, at a specified future date, of one currency for a specified amount of another currency.

exchange rate risk the risk that tomorrow's exchange rate will differ from today's rate.

How Did You Do?

USING THE SPOT RATE TO CALCULATE A FOREIGN CURRENCY PAYMENT

On the previous page you were asked to determine how much an American firm had to pay an Israeli firm if the Israeli firm was to receive an equivalent of $10,000 in Israeli shekels.

4.5147 shekels/$ × $10,000 = 45,147 shekels

and exchange the pounds at the spot rate, you will receive a dollar amount reflecting the exchange rate 30 days hence (that is, the future spot rate). As of today, you have no way of knowing the exact dollar value of your future pound receipts. Consequently, you cannot make precise plans about the use of these dollars. If, conversely, you buy a futures contract, then you know the exact dollar value of your future receipts, and you can make precise plans concerning their use. The forward contract, therefore, can reduce your uncertainty about the future. In fact, the major advantage of the forward market is that of risk reduction.

Forward contracts are usually quoted for periods of 30, 90, and 180 days. A contract for any intermediate date can be obtained, usually with the payment of a small premium. Forward contracts for periods longer than 180 days can be obtained by special negotiations with banks. Contracts for periods greater than 1 year can be costly.

Forward rates, like spot rates, are quoted in both direct and indirect form. The direct quotes for the 30-day, 90-day, and 180-day forward contracts on pounds, Swiss francs, Canadian dollars, and Japanese yen are given in the lower half of Table 17-1. The indirect quotes are also indicated. The direct quotes are the dollar/foreign currency rate, and the indirect quotes are the foreign currency/dollar rate similar to the spot exchange quotes.

In Table 17-1 the 1-month forward quote for pounds is $1.8728 per pound. This means that the bank is contractually bound to deliver £1 at this price, and the buyer of the contract is legally obligated to buy it at this price in 30 days. Therefore, this is the price the customer must pay regardless of the actual spot rate prevailing in 30 days. If the spot price of the pound is less than $1.8728, then the customer pays *more* than the spot price. If the spot price is greater than $1.8728, then the customer pays *less* than the spot price.

The forward rate is often quoted at a premium or a discount from the existing spot rate. For example, the 30-day forward rate for the pound may be quoted as a .0008 premium (1.8728 forward rate −1.8720 spot rate). If the British pound is more expensive in the future than it is today, it is said to be selling at a premium relative to the dollar, and the dollar is said to be selling at a discount to the British pound. This premium or discount is also called the **forward-spot differential**.

forward-spot differential
the premium or discount between forward and spot currency exchange rates.

Notationally, the relationship may be written

$$F - S \text{ premium } (F > S) \text{ or discount } (S > F) \tag{17-1}$$

where F = the forward rate, direct quote
S = the spot rate, direct quote

The premium or discount can also be expressed as an annual percentage rate, computed as follows:

$$\frac{F - S}{S} \times \frac{12}{n} \times 100 = \text{annualized percentage}$$

premium (F > S) or discount (S > F) (17-2)

where n = the number of months of the forward contract.

Can You Do It?

COMPUTING A PERCENT-PER-ANNUM PREMIUM

Using the information in Table 17-1, compute the percent-per-annum premium on the 90-day (3 month) yen.
(The solution can be found on page 529.)

> ## EXAMPLE

Compute the percent-per-annum premium on the 30-day pound.

Step 1. Identify F, S, and n.

$$F = 1.8728, S = 1.8720, n = 1 \text{ month}$$

Step 2. Because F is greater than S, we compute the annualized percentage premium:

$$= \frac{1.8728 - 1.8720}{1.8720} \times \frac{12 \text{ months}}{1 \text{ month}} \times 100$$
$$= 0.5128\%$$

The percent-per-annum premium on the 30-day pound is 0.5128 percent.

Exchange Rate Risk

The concept of exchange rate risk applies to all types of international business. The measurement of these risks, and the type of risk, differ among businesses. Let us see how exchange rate risk affects international trade contracts, international portfolio investments, and direct foreign investments.

Exchange Rate Risk in International Trade Contracts

The idea of exchange rate risk in trade contracts is illustrated in the following situations.

Case I   An American automobile distributor agrees to buy a car from the manufacturer in Detroit. The distributor agrees to pay $25,000 on delivery of the car, which is expected to be 30 days from today. The car is delivered on the 30th day and the distributor pays $25,000. Notice that from the day this contract was written until the day the car was delivered, the buyer knew the *exact dollar amount* of the liability. There was, in other words, *no uncertainty* about the value of the contract.

Case II   An American automobile distributor enters into a contract with a British supplier to buy a car from Britain for £13,500. The amount is payable upon the delivery of the car, 30 days from today. Unfortunately, the exchange rate between British pounds and U.S. dollars may change in the next 30 days. In effect, the American firm is not certain what its future dollar outflow will be 30 days hence. That is, the *dollar value of the contract is uncertain*.

These two examples help illustrate the idea of foreign exchange risk in international trade contracts. In the domestic trade contract (Case I), the exact dollar amount of the future dollar payment is known today with certainty. In the case of the international trade contract (Case II), in which the *contract is written in the foreign currency*, the exact dollar amount of the contract is not known. The variability of the exchange rate causes variability in the future cash flow of the firm.

Exchange rate risk exists when the contract is written in terms of the foreign currency, or *denominated* in foreign currency. There is no direct exchange rate risk if the international trade contract is written in terms of the domestic currency. That is, in Case II, if the contract were written in dollars, the American importer would face *no* direct exchange rate risk. With

Across the Hall

MARKETING

When reaching out to global markets, you not only need a good product, but you also need one that fits the culture of the market. As a result, although some products that are successful in the United States can be successfully introduced in global markets, others need to be adapted to the culture into which they are being introduced. For example, McDonald's has found great success globally, but it has done so by adapting its product line to fit the culture of the country it is entering. Understanding this is important because, whereas a new project will generally be evaluated using capital-budgeting techniques by the people in finance, determining how a product should be culturally adapted is the job of marketers. Their ability to modify and price the product so that it appeals abroad will go a long way toward determining whether or not a new capital-budgeting approach succeeds.

For this reason, as a marketing student, you must understand exchange rates so you can price the new product in a way that creates wealth for the corporation. You also need to understand how the product must be culturally adapted for the new market. For example, although a Big Mac may taste pretty good to most people in the United States, that may not be the case around the world. As a result, McDonald's marketing staff many times offers alternative items that fit the cultural eating habits of different countries. For example, in Thailand McDonald's sells the McPork Burger with Thai Basil, in Japan it offers the Tatsuta Burger, and in India it offers the Maharaja Mac, which has two all-mutton patties, special sauce, lettuce, cheese, pickles, onions on a sesame seed bun—kinda sounds familiar, doesn't it? Similarly, when Gerber entered the baby food market in Japan, rather than strained peas and blueberry delight, it introduced sardines ground up in white radish sauce, cod roe spaghetti, and mug-wort casserole.

Moreover, a good product can fail abroad because of translation problems in its advertising campaign. A classic example is the Coors beer advertising slogan, "get loose with Coors," which translates in Spanish to "get the runs with Coors." The bottom line here is that in the international arena, marketing can take a good idea for a new product and help turn it into a success or a failure.

---

the contract written in dollars, the British exporter would bear *all* of the exchange rate risk because the British exporter's future pound receipts would be uncertain. That is, the British exporter would receive payment in dollars, which would have to be converted into pounds at an unknown (as of today) pound/dollar exchange rate. In international trade contracts of this type, at least one of the two parties to the contract *always* bears the exchange rate risk.

Certain types of international trade contracts are denominated in a third currency that is different from either the importer's or the exporter's domestic currency. In Case II, the contract might have been denominated in, say, the Hong Kong dollar. With a Hong Kong dollar contract, both the importer and exporter would be subject to exchange rate risk.

Exchange rate risk is not limited to the two-party trade contracts; it exists also in foreign portfolio investments and direct foreign investments.

Exchange Rate Risk in Foreign Portfolio Investments

Let us look at an example of exchange rate risk in the context of portfolio investments. An American investor buys a Hong Kong security. The exact return on the investment in the security is unknown. Thus, the security is a risky investment. The investment return in the holding period of, say, 3 months stated in HK$ could be anything from −2 to +8 percent. In addition, the U.S. dollar/HK$ exchange rate may depreciate by, say, 4 percent or appreciate by 6 percent during in the 3-month period. The return to the American investor in U.S. dollars will, therefore, be in the range of −6 to +14 percent. Hence, the exchange rate fluctuations may increase the riskiness of the investments.

Exchange Rate Risk in Direct Foreign Investment

The exchange rate risk of a direct foreign investment (DFI) is more complicated. In a DFI, the parent company invests in assets denominated in a foreign currency. That is, the balance sheet and the income statement of the subsidiary are written in terms of the foreign currency. The parent company, if based in the United States, receives the repatriated (or converted) profit stream from the subsidiary in dollars. Thus, the exchange rate risk concept applies to fluctuations in the dollar value of the assets located abroad as well as to the fluctuations in the home currency–denominated profit stream. Moreover, exchange risk not only affects immediate profits, but it may also affect the future profit stream as well.

How Did You Do?

COMPUTING A PERCENT-PER-ANNUM PREMIUM

Compute the percent-per-annum premium on the 90-day yen.

Step 1: Identify F, S, and n.

$F = \$0.009059/\yen$, $S = \$0.008946/\yen$, and $n = 3$ months

Step 2: Because F is greater than S, we compute the annualized percentage premium:

$$\frac{0.009059 - 0.008946}{0.008946} \times \frac{12 \text{ months}}{3 \text{ months}} \times 100 = 5.0525\%$$

The percent-per-annum discount on the 90-day yen is 5.0525 percent.

Remember Your Principles

In international transactions, just as in domestic transactions, the key to value is the timing and amounts of cash flow spent and received. However, economic transactions across international borders add an element of risk because cash flows are denominated in the currency of the country in which business is being transacted. Consequently, the dollar value of the cash flows will depend on the exchange rate that exists at the time the cash changes hands. The fact remains, however, that it's cash spent and received that matters. This is the point of **Principle 3: Cash—Not Profits—Is King**.

Although exchange rate risk can be a serious complication in international business activity, remember the principle of the risk–return trade-off: Traders and corporations find numerous reasons why the returns from international transactions outweigh the risks.

Did You Get It?

1. What is a spot transaction? What is a direct quote? An indirect quote?
2. Who is an arbitrageur? How does an arbitrageur make money?
3. What is a forward exchange rate?
4. Describe exchange rate risk in direct foreign investment.

INTEREST RATE PARITY THEORY

Objective **3**

Discuss the concept of interest rate parity.

Forward rates generally entail a premium or a discount relative to current spot rates. However, these forward premiums and discounts can differ between currencies and maturities. These differences depend solely on the difference in the level of interest rates between the two countries, called the *interest rate differential*. The value of the premium or discount can be theoretically computed from the **interest rate parity (IRP) theory**. This theory states that *(except for the effects of small transaction costs) the forward premium or discount should be equal and opposite in size to the difference in the national interest rates for securities of the same maturity*.

Stated very simply, what does all this mean? It means that because of arbitrage, the interest rate differential between two countries must be equal to the difference between the forward and spot exchange rates. If this were not true, arbitrageurs would buy in the forward market and sell in the spot market (or vice versa) until prices were back in line and there were no profits left to be made. For example, if prices in the forward market were too

interest rate parity (IRP) theory a theory that states that (except for the effects of small transaction costs) the forward premium or discount should be equal and opposite in size to the difference in the national interest rates for securities of the same maturity.

low, arbitrageurs would enter the market, increase the demand for the forward foreign currency, and drive up the prices in the forward market until those prices obeyed the interest rate parity theory.

Did You Get It?

1. In simple terms, what does the interest rate parity theory mean?

Objective | **4**

Explain the purchasing-power parity theory and the law of one price.

purchasing-power parity (PPP) theory a theory that states that, in the long run, exchange rates adjust so that the purchasing power of each currency tends to be the same. Thus, exchange rate changes tend to reflect international differences in inflation rates.

PURCHASING-POWER PARITY THEORY

Long-run changes in exchange rates are influenced by international differences in inflation rates and the purchasing power of each nation's currency. According to the **purchasing-power parity (PPP) theory**, *in the long run, exchange rates adjust so that the purchasing power of each currency tends to be the same. Thus, exchange rate changes tend to reflect international differences in inflation rates. Countries with high rates of inflation tend to experience declines in the value of their currencies.* Thus, if Britain experiences a 10 percent rate of inflation in a year that Japan experiences only a 6 percent rate, the U.K. currency (the pound) will be expected to decline in value approximately by 3.77 percent [(1.10/1.06) − 1] against the Japanese currency (the yen). More accurately, according to the PPP theory,

Expected spot rate = current spot rate × expected difference in inflation rate

$$
\begin{array}{c} \text{Expected spot rate} \\ \text{domestic currency} \\ \text{per unit of foreign} \\ \text{currency} \end{array} = \begin{array}{c} \text{current spot rate} \\ \text{domestic currency} \\ \text{per unit of foreign} \\ \text{currency} \end{array} \times \begin{array}{c} 1 + \text{expected domestic} \\ \text{inflation rate} \\ \hline 1 + \text{expected foreign} \\ \text{inflation rate} \end{array} \qquad (17\text{-}3)
$$

Thus, if the beginning value of the Japanese yen were £.00478, with a 6 percent inflation rate in Japan and a 10 percent inflation rate in Britain, according to the PPP, the expected value of the Japanese yen at the end of that year will be £.00478 × [1.10/1.06], or £.00496.

Again, stated very simply, what does this mean? It means that a dollar should have the same purchasing power anywhere in the world—well, at least on average. Obviously, this is not quite true. However, what the PPP theory tells us is that we should expect, on average, that differences in inflation rates between two countries should be reflected in changes in the exchange rates. In effect, the best forecast of the difference in inflation rates between two countries should also be the best forecast of the change in the spot rate of exchange.

The Law of One Price

law of one price a proposition that in competitive markets in which there are no transportation costs or barriers to trade, the same goods sold in different countries sell for the same price if all the different prices are expressed in terms of the same currency.

Underlying the PPP relationship is the **law of one price**. This law is actually *a proposition that in competitive markets in which there are no transportation costs or barriers to trade, the same goods sold in different countries should sell for the same price if all of the different prices are expressed in terms of the same currency.* The idea is that the worth of a good does not depend on where it is bought or sold. Because inflation will erode the purchasing power of any currency, its exchange rate must adhere to the PPP relationship if the law of one price is to hold over time.

There are enough obvious exceptions to the concept of purchasing-power parity that it may, at first glance, seem difficult to accept. For example, recently a Big Mac cost $2.36 in the United States, and given the then-existing exchange rates, it cost an equivalent of $2.02 in Mexico, $2.70 in Japan, and $3.22 in Germany. On the surface this might appear to violate the PPP theory and the law of one price; however, we must remember that this theory is based on the concept of arbitrage. In the case of a Big Mac, it's pretty hard to imagine buying Big Macs in Mexico for $2.02, shipping them to Germany, and reselling them for $3.22. But for commodities such as gold and other items that are relatively inexpensive to ship and do not have to be consumed immediately, the law of one price holds much better.

The International Fisher Effect

According to the domestic Fisher effect (FE), nominal interest rates reflect the expected inflation rate, a real rate of interest and the product of the real rate of interest and the inflation rate. In other words,

$$
\begin{array}{l}
\text{Nominal} \\
\text{interest rate}
\end{array}
=
\begin{array}{l}
\text{expected} \\
\text{inflation rate}
\end{array}
+
\begin{array}{l}
\text{real rate} \\
\text{of interest}
\end{array}
+
\left(
\begin{array}{l}
\text{expected} \\
\text{inflation rate}
\end{array}
\times
\begin{array}{l}
\text{real rate} \\
\text{of interest}
\end{array}
\right)
\qquad \text{(17-4)}
$$

Although there is mixed empirical support for the international Fisher effect (IFE), it is widely thought that, for the major industrial countries, the real rate of interest is about 3 percent when a long-term period is considered. In such a case, with the previous assumption regarding inflation rates, interest rates in Britain and Japan would be (.10 + .03 + .003) or 13.3 percent and (.06 + .03 + .0018) or 9.18 percent, respectively.

In effect, the IFE states that the real interest rate should be the same all over the world, with the difference in nominal or stated interest rates simply resulting from the differences in expected inflation rates. As we look at interest rates around the world, this tells us that we should not necessarily send our money to a bank account in the country with the highest interest rates. That course of action might only result in sending our money to a bank in the country with the highest expected level of inflation.

Did You Get It?

1. What does the law of one price say?
2. What is the international Fisher effect?

EXPOSURE TO EXCHANGE RATE RISK

An asset denominated or valued in terms of foreign-currency cash flows will lose value if that foreign currency declines in value. It can be said that such an asset is exposed to exchange rate risk. However, this possible decline in asset value may be offset by the decline in value of any liability that is also denominated or valued in terms of that foreign currency. Thus, a firm would normally be interested in its *net exposed position* (exposed assets – exposed liabilities) for each period in each currency.

Although expected changes in exchange rates can often be included in the cost–benefit analysis relating to such transactions, in most cases there is an unexpected component in exchange rate changes, and often the cost–benefit analysis for such transactions does not fully capture even the expected change in the exchange rate. For example, price increases for the foreign operations of many MNCs often have to be less than those necessary to fully offset exchange rate changes, owing to the competitive pressures generated by local businesses.

Recall from Chapter 15 that three measures of foreign exchange exposure are translation exposure, transaction exposure, and economic exposure. The three measures of exposure now are examined more closely.

Translation Exposure

Translation exposure arises because the foreign operations of MNCs have financial statements denominated in the local currency of the country in which the operation is located. But for U.S. MNCs, the *reporting currency* for its consolidated financial statements is the dollar, so the assets, liabilities, revenues, and expenses of the foreign operations must be translated into dollars.

Foreign currency assets and liabilities are considered exposed if their foreign currency value for accounting purposes has to be translated into the domestic currency using the currency exchange rate—the exchange rate in effect on the balance sheet date. Other assets and liabilities and equity amounts that are translated at the historic exchange rate—the rate in effect when these items were first recognized in the company's books—are not considered

translation exposure risk that arises because the foreign operations of MNCs have financial statements denominated in the local currencies of the countries in which the operation are located. These denominations must be translated into the MNCs home currency at the prevailing exchange rate.

to be exposed. The rate (current or historic) used to translate various accounts depends on the translation procedure used.

Whereas transaction exposure can result in exchange rate change–related losses and gains that are realized and have an impact on both reported and taxable income, translation exposure results in exchange rate losses and gains that are reflected in the company's accounting books but are unrealized and have little or no impact on taxable income. Theoretically, then, a firm should not have to waste real resources hedging against possible paper losses caused by translation exposure. After all, it's the firm's stock price that really matters. However, there are times a firm may indeed find it economical to hedge against translation losses or gains.

Transaction Exposure

transaction exposure
risk associated with transaction exposure, that is, risk associated with contracts on which the monetary value is fixed at a time different from when the transaction is actually completed and will be impacted by exchange rate changes.

Receivables, payables, and fixed-price sales or purchase contracts are examples of foreign currency transactions whose monetary values are fixed at a time different from the time when these transactions are actually completed. **Transaction exposure** is a term that *describes the net contracted foreign currency transactions for which the settlement amounts are subject to changing exchange rates*. A company normally must set up an additional reporting system to track transaction exposure because several of these amounts are not recognized in the accounting books of the firm.

Exchange rate risk can be neutralized, or hedged, by a change in the firm's asset and liability position in the foreign currency. For example, an exposed asset position (such as an account receivable) can be hedged, or covered, by creating a liability of the same amount and maturity denominated in the foreign currency (such as a forward contract to sell the foreign currency). An exposed liability position (such as an account payable) can be covered by acquiring assets of the same amount and maturity in the foreign currency (such as a forward contract to buy the foreign currency). The objective is to have a zero net asset position in the foreign currency. This eliminates exchange rate risk because the loss (gain) in the liability (asset) is exactly offset by the gain (loss) in the value of the asset (liability) when the foreign currency appreciates (depreciates). Two popular forms of hedges are the money-market hedge and the exchange-market, or forward-market, hedge. In both types of hedge, the amount and the duration of the asset (liability) positions are matched. Note as you read the next two subsections how IRP theory ensures that each hedge provides the same cover.

Money-Market Hedge

In a money-market hedge, the exposed position in a foreign currency is offset by borrowing or lending in the money market. Consider the case of the American firm with a net liability position of £3,000. The firm knows the exact amount of its pound liability in 30 days, but it does not know the liability in dollars. Assume that the 30-day money-market rates in both the United States and Britain are, respectively, 1 percent for lending and 1.5 percent for borrowing. The American business can take the following steps:

Step 1. Calculate the present value of the foreign currency liability (£3,000) that is due in 30 days. Use the money-market rate applicable for the foreign country (1 percent in the United Kingdom). The present value of £3,000 is £2,970.30, computed as follows: £3,000/(1 + .01).

Step 2. Exchange dollars on today's spot market to obtain the £2,970.30. The dollar amount needed today is $5,560.40 (£2,970.30 × 1.8720).

Step 3. Invest £2,970.30 in a United Kingdom 1-month, money-market instrument. This investment will compound to exactly £3,000 in 1 month. The future liability of £3,000 is therefore covered by the £2,970.30 investment.[3]

Note: If the American business does not own this amount today, it can borrow $5,560.40 from the U.S. money market at the going rate of 1.5 percent. In 30 days the American business will need to repay $5,643.81 [$5,560.40 × (1 + .015).

Assuming that the American business borrows the money, it may base its calculations on the knowledge that the British goods, upon delivery in 30 days, will cost it $5,643.81. The

---

[3] Observe that £2,970.30 × (1 + .01) = £3,000.

British business will receive £3,000. The American business need not wait for the future spot exchange rate to be revealed because the future dollar payment of the contract is known with certainty. This certainty helps the American business make its pricing and financing decisions.

Many businesses hedge in the money market. The firm needs to borrow (creating a liability) in one market, lend or invest in the other money market, and use the spot exchange market on today's date. The mechanics of hedging a net asset position in the foreign currency are the exact reverse of the mechanics of hedging the liability position. With a net asset position in pounds: Borrow in the U.K. money market in pounds, convert it to dollars on the spot exchange market, and invest it in the U.S. money market. When the net assets are converted into pounds (that is, when the firm receives what it is owed), pay off the loan and the interest. The cost of hedging in the money market is the cost of doing business in three different markets. Information about the three markets is needed, and analytical calculations of the type indicated here must be made.

Many small and infrequent traders find the cost of the money-market hedge prohibitive, especially because of the need for information about the market. These traders use the exchange-market, or forward-market, hedge, which has very similar hedging benefits.

The Forward-Market Hedge

The forward market provides a second possible hedging mechanism. It works as follows: A net asset (or liability) position is covered by a liability (or asset) in the forward market. Consider again the case of the American firm with a liability of £3,000 that must be paid in 30 days. The firm can take the following steps to cover its liability position:

Step 1. Buy a forward contract today to purchase £3,000 in 30 days. The 30-day forward rate is $1.8728/£.

Step 2. On the 30th day pay the banker $5,618.40 (£3,000 × $1.8728) and collect £3,000. Pay these pounds to the British supplier.

By using the forward contract, the American business knows the exact worth of the future payment in dollars ($5,618.40). The exchange rate risk in pounds is totally eliminated by the net asset position in the forward pounds. In the case of a net asset exposure, the steps open to the American firm are the exact opposite: Sell the pounds forward and on the future day receive and deliver the pounds to collect the agreed-on dollar amount.

The use of the forward market as a hedge against exchange rate risk is simple and direct—that is, match the liability or asset position against an offsetting position in the forward market. The forward-market hedge is relatively easy to implement. The firm directs its banker that it needs to buy or sell a foreign currency on a future date, and the banker gives the firm a forward quote.

The forward-market hedge and the money-market hedge result in an identical future dollar payment (or receipt) if the forward contracts are priced according to the interest rate parity theory. The alert student may have noticed that the dollar payments in the money-market hedge and the forward-market hedge examples were, respectively, $5,560.40 and $5,618.40. Recall from our previous discussions that in efficient markets, the forward contracts do indeed conform to IRP theory. However, the numbers in our example are not identical because the forward rate used in the forward-market hedge is not exactly equal to the interest rates in the money-market hedge.

Currency-Futures Contracts and Options

The forward-market hedge is not adequate for some types of exposure. If the foreign currency asset or liability position occurs on a date for which forward quotes are not available, the forward-market hedge cannot be accomplished. In certain cases the forward-market hedge may cost more than the money-market hedge. In these cases, a corporation with a large amount of exposure may prefer the money-market hedge. In addition to forward-market and money-market hedges, a company can also hedge its exposure by buying (or selling) some relatively new instruments—foreign currency-futures contracts and foreign currency options. Although futures contracts are similar to forward contracts in that they provide fixed prices for the delivery of foreign currency in the future, foreign currency options permit fixed-price deliverily to be made anytime *before* maturity.

Both futures contracts and options differ from forward contracts in that, unlike forward contracts, which have customized amounts and maturity dates, futures and options are traded in standard amounts with standard maturity dates. In addition, although forward contracts are written by banks, futures and options are traded on organized exchanges, and individual traders deal with the exchange-based clearing organization rather than with each other.

Economic Exposure

economic exposure the impact of exchange rate changes on the value of the firm including both the strategic impact of comparative relationships arising from exchange rate change and the economic impact of transaction exposure.

The economic value of a company can vary in response to exchange rate changes. This change in value may be caused by a rate change–induced decline in the level of expected cash flows and/or by an increase in the riskiness of these cash flows. **Economic exposure** refers to the overall impact of exchange rate changes on the value of the firm and includes not only the strategic impact of changes in competitive relationships that arise from exchange rate changes but also the economic impact of transaction exposure and, if any, translation exposure.

Economic exposure to exchange rate changes depends on the competitive structure of the markets for a firm's inputs and outputs and how these markets are influenced by changes in exchange rates. This influence, in turn, depends on several economic factors, including price elasticities of the products, the degree of competition from foreign markets, and the direct (through prices) and indirect (through incomes) impact of exchange rate changes on these markets. Assessing the economic exposure faced by a particular firm, thus, depends on your ability to understand and model the structure of the markets for the firm's major inputs (purchases) and outputs (sales).

However, a company need not engage in any cross-border business activity to be exposed to exchange rate changes because product and financial markets in most countries are related and influenced to a large extent by the same global forces. The output of a company engaged in business activity only within one country may be competing with imported products, or it may be competing for its inputs with other domestic and foreign purchasers. For example, a Canadian chemical company that did no cross-border business nevertheless found that its profit margin depended directly on the U.S. dollar/Japanese yen exchange rate. The company used coal as an input in its production process, and the Canadian price of coal was heavily influenced by the extent to which the Japanese bought U.S. coal, which in turn depended on the dollar/yen exchange rate.

Although translation exposure need not be managed, it might be useful for a firm to manage its transaction and economic exposures because they affect firm value directly. In most companies, transaction exposure is generally tracked and managed by the office of the corporate treasurer. Economic exposure is difficult to define in operating terms, and very few companies manage it actively. In most companies, economic exposure is generally considered part of the strategic planning process, rather than a treasurer's or finance function.

Did You Get It?

1. Give a simple explanation of translation exposure.
2. Give a simple explanation of transaction exposure.
3. Give a simple explanation of economic exposure.

Objective **6**

Identify working-capital management techniques that are useful for international businesses to reduce exchange rate risk and potentially increase profits.

MULTINATIONAL WORKING-CAPITAL MANAGEMENT

The basic principles of working-capital management for a multinational corporation are similar to those for a domestic firm. However, tax and exchange rate factors are additional considerations for the MNC. For the MNC with subsidiaries in many countries, the optimal decisions in the management of working capital are made by considering the market as a whole. The global, or centralized, financial decisions for the MNC are superior to the set of independent optimal decisions for the subsidiaries. This is the control problem of the

MNC. If the individual subsidiaries make decisions that are best for them individually, the consolidation of these decisions may not be best for the MNC as a whole. To achieve global management, sophisticated computerized models incorporating many variables for each subsidiary are utilized to provide the best overall decision for the MNC.

Before considering the components of working-capital management, we examine two techniques that are useful in the management of a wide variety of working-capital components.

Leading and Lagging Strategies

Two important risk-reduction techniques for many working-capital problems are called "leading" and "lagging." Often forward-market and money-market hedges are not available to eliminate exchange risk. Under such circumstances, leading and lagging may be used to reduce exchange risk.

Recall that holding a net asset (long) position is not desirable in a weak or potentially depreciating currency. If a firm has a net asset position in such a currency, it should expedite the disposal of the asset. The firm should get rid of the asset earlier than it otherwise would have, or *lead*, and convert the funds into assets in a relatively stronger currency. By the same reasoning, the firm should *lag*, or delay the collection against a net asset position in a strong currency. Likewise, if the firm has a net liability (short) position in the weak currency, then it should delay the payment against the liability, or lag, until the currency depreciates. In the case of an appreciating or strong foreign currency and a net liability position, the firm should lead the payments—that is, reduce the liabilities earlier than it would have otherwise.

These principles are useful in the management of working capital of an MNC. They cannot, however, eliminate the foreign exchange risk. When exchange rates change continuously, it is almost impossible to guess whether or when the currency will depreciate or appreciate. This is why the risk of exchange rate changes cannot be eliminated. Nevertheless, the reduction of risk, or the increased gain from exchange rate changes via the lead and lag, is useful for cash management, accounts-receivable management, and short-term liability management.

Cash Management and the Positioning of Funds

The positioning of funds takes on an added importance in the international context. For example, an MNC can move funds from a subsidiary in one country to a subsidiary in another country so foreign exchange exposure and the tax liability of the MNC as a whole are minimized.

The transfer of funds among subsidiaries and the parent company is done via royalties, fees, and transfer pricing. A **transfer price** is the *price a subsidiary or a parent company charges other companies that are part of the MNC for its goods or services.* For example, a parent that wishes to transfer funds from a subsidiary in a depreciating-currency country might charge a higher price on the goods and services sold to this subsidiary by the parent or by subsidiaries in strong-currency countries.

> **transfer price** the price a subsidiary or a parent company charges other companies that are part of the MNC for its goods or services.

Did You Get It? ....

1. Describe the risk-reduction techniques of leading and lagging.
2. How can a parent company use transfer pricing to move funds from a subsidiary in a depreciating-currency country to a strong-currency country?

INTERNATIONAL FINANCING AND CAPITAL STRUCTURE DECISIONS

Objective **7**

Explain how the financing sources available to multinational corporations differ from those available to domestic firms.

An MNC has access to many more financing sources than a domestic firm. It can tap not only the financing sources in its home country that are available to its domestic counterparts but also sources in the foreign countries in which it operates. Host countries often provide access to low-cost subsidized financing to attract foreign investment. In addition, the MNC

currency swaps the exchange of principal and interest in one currency for the same in another currency for an agreed period of time.

may enjoy preferential credit standards because of its size and investors' preferences for its home currency. For financing purposes, the MNC may be able to access third-country capital markets—countries in which it does not operate but that may have large, well-functioning capital markets. Finally, an MNC can also access external currency markets: Eurodollar, Eurocurrency, or Asian dollar markets. These external markets are unregulated, and because of their lower spreads, can offer very attractive rates for financing *and* for investments. With the increasing availability of interest rate and **currency swaps**, a firm can raise funds in the lowest-cost maturities and currencies and "swap" them into funds with the maturity and currency denomination it requires. Because of its ability to tap a larger number of financial markets, the MNC may have a lower cost of capital; and because it may be better able to avoid the problems or limitations of any one financial market, it may have more continuous access to external financing compared with a domestic company.

Access to national financial markets is regulated by governments. For example, in the United States, access to capital markets is governed by SEC regulations. Access to Japanese capital markets is governed by regulations issued by the Ministry of Finance. Some countries have extensive regulations; other countries have relatively open markets. These regulations can differ depending on the legal residency of the company raising funds. A company that cannot use a local subsidiary to raise funds in a given market will be treated as foreign. In order to increase their visibility in a foreign capital market, a number of MNCs are now listing their equities on the stock exchanges of many of these countries.

The external currency markets are predominantly centered in Europe, but about 80 percent of their value is denominated in terms of the U.S. dollar. Thus, most external currency markets can be characterized as Eurodollar markets. Such markets consist of an active short-term money market and an intermediate-term capital market with maturities ranging up to 15 years and averaging about 7 to 9 years. The intermediate-term market consists of the Eurobond and the Syndicated Eurocredit markets. Recall from Chapter 7 that Eurobonds are usually issued as unregistered bearer bonds and generally tend to have higher flotation costs but lower coupon rates compared with similar bonds issued in the United States. A *Syndicated Eurocredit* loan is simply a large-term loan that involves contributions by a number of lending banks.

In arriving at its capital structure decisions, an MNC has to consider a number of factors. First, the capital structure of its local affiliates is influenced by local norms regarding that industry and in that country. Local norms for companies in the same industry can differ considerably from country to country too. Second, the local-affiliate capital structure must also reflect corporate attitudes toward exchange rate and political risks in that country. Third, the local-affiliate capital structure must reflect home-country requirements with regard to the company's consolidated capital structure. Finally, the optimal MNC capital structure should reflect its wider access to financial markets, its ability to diversify its economic and political risks, and its other advantages over domestic companies.

Did You Get It?

1. What factors might an MNC consider in making a capital structure decision?

Objective **8**

Discuss the risks involved in direct foreign investment.

DIRECT FOREIGN INVESTMENT

An MNC often makes direct foreign investments abroad in the form of plants and equipment. The decision process for this type of investment is very similar to the capital-budgeting decision in the domestic context—with some additional twists. Most real-world capital-budgeting

Remember Your Principles

Investment across international boundaries gives rise to special risks not encountered when investing domestically. Specifically, political risks and exchange rate risk are unique to international investing. Once again, **Principle 1: The Risk–Return Trade-Off—We Won't Take On Additional Risk Unless We Expect to Be Compensated with Additional Return** provides a rationale for evaluating these considerations. Where added risks are present, added rewards are necessary to induce investment.

decisions are made with uncertain future outcomes. Recall that a capital-budgeting decision has three major components: the estimation of the future cash flows (including the initial cost of the proposed investment), the estimation of the risk in these cash flows, and the choice of the proper discount rate. We will assume that the *NPV* criterion is appropriate as we examine (1) the risks associated with direct foreign investment and (2) factors to be considered in making the investment decision that may be unique to the international scene.

Risks in domestic capital budgeting arise from two sources: business risk and financial risk. The international capital-budgeting problem incorporates these risks as well as political risk and exchange risk.

Business Risk and Financial Risk

International business risk is due to the response of a business to economic conditions in the foreign country. Thus, the U.S. MNC needs to be aware of the business climate in both the United States and the foreign country. Additional business risk is due to competition from other MNCs, local businesses, and imported goods. Financial risk refers to the risks introduced in the profit stream by the firm's financial structure. The financial risks of foreign operations are not very different from those of domestic operations.

Political Risk

Political risk arises because the foreign subsidiary conducts its business in a political system different from that of the home country. Many foreign governments, especially those in the third world, are less stable than the U.S. government. A change in a country's political setup frequently brings a change in policies with respect to businesses—and especially with respect to foreign businesses. An extreme change in policy might involve nationalization or even outright expropriation (government seizure) of certain businesses. These are the political risks of conducting business abroad. A business with no investment in plant and equipment is less susceptible to these risks. Some examples of political risk are listed here:

1. Expropriation of plant and equipment without compensation.
2. Expropriation with minimal compensation that is below actual market value.
3. Nonconvertibility of the subsidiary's foreign earnings into the parent's currency—the problem of *blocked funds*.
4. Substantial changes in the laws governing taxation.
5. Governmental controls in the foreign country regarding the sale price of certain products, wages and compensation paid to personnel, the hiring of personnel, transfer payments made to the parent, and local borrowing.
6. Some governments require certain amounts of local ownership in the business.

All these controls and governmental actions put the cash flows of the investment to the parent company at risk. Thus, these risks must be considered before making the foreign investment decision. For example, the MNC might decide against investing in countries with risks of types 1 and 2. Whereas other risks can be borne—provided that the returns from the foreign investments are high enough to compensate for them. In fact, insurance against some types of political risks can be purchased from private insurance companies or from the U.S. Government Overseas Private Investment Corporation. It should be noted that although an MNC cannot protect itself against all foreign political risks, political risks are also present in domestic business.

Exchange Rate Risk

The exposure of the firm's fixed assets is best measured by exchange rate changes that affect the firm's future earnings stream: that being economic exposure rather than translation exposure. For instance, changes in the exchange rate can adversely affect sales by making competing imported goods cheaper. Changes in the cost of goods sold can result if some components are imported and their foreign currency prices change. The thrust of these examples is that the effect of exchange rate changes on income statement items should be properly measured to evaluate exchange rate risk. Finally, exchange rate risk affects the dollar-denominated profit stream of the parent company, whether or not it affects the firm's foreign-operations profits.

Did You Get It?

1. What are some of the risks associated with direct foreign investments?

Summary

The growth of our global economy, the increasing number of multinational corporations, and the increase in foreign trade itself underscore the importance of the study of international finance.

Under floating systems, exchange rates between currencies vary depending upon supply and demand conditions in the exchange market. Important economic factors affecting the level of exchange rates include the relative economic strengths of the countries involved, the balance-of-payments mechanism, and the countries' monetary policies and interest rates. Several important exchange rate terms are introduced. These include the asked and the bid rates, which represent the selling and buying rates of currencies. The direct quote is the units of home currency per unit of foreign currency, and the indirect quote is the reciprocal of the direct quote. Cross-rate computations reflect the exchange rate between two foreign currencies.

The forward exchange market provides a valuable service by quoting rates for the delivery of foreign currencies in the future. The foreign currency is said to sell at a discount relative to the spot rate when the forward rate is lower than the spot rate. It is said to sell at a premium relative to the spot rate when the forward rate is higher than the spot rate. According to the interest rate parity theory, these premiums and discounts depend solely on the differences in the level of the interest rates of countries.

According to the purchasing-power parity (PPP) theory, in the long run, exchange rates adjust so that the purchasing power of each currency tends to be the same. Thus, exchange rate changes tend to reflect international differences in inflation rates. As a result, countries with high rates of inflation tend to experience declines in the value of their currency. Underlying the PPP relationship is the law of one price. This law is actually a proposition that in competitive markets in which there are no transportation costs or barriers to trade, the same goods sold in different countries sell for the same price if all of the different prices are expressed in terms of the same currency.

An MNC faces three types of exchange rate risk: Transaction exposure, translation exposure, and economic exposure. The company can offset its exposure using various tools including: by setting up an offsetting asset or liability of the same amount as the foreign-currency asset or liability; by using money-market and forward-market hedges, futures-market contracts and options, and currency swaps.

With regard to working-capital management in an international environment, we find leading and lagging techniques useful in minimizing exchange rate risk and increasing profitability. In addition, positioning funds is a useful tool for reducing exchange rate risk exposure.

The MNC may have a lower cost of capital because it has access to a larger set of financial markets than a domestic company. In addition to the home, host, and third-country financial markets, the MNC can tap the rapidly growing external currency markets. In making capital structure decisions, the MNC must consider political and exchange rate risks and host- and home-country capital structure norms.

The complexities encountered in the direct foreign investment decision include the usual sources of risk—business and financial—and the additional risks associated with fluctuating exchange rates and political factors. Political risk is due to differences in political climates, institutions, and processes between the home country and abroad. This makes estimating future cash flows and choosing the proper discount rates more complicated than for the domestic investment situation.

Key Terms

Arbitrageur 524	**Covered-interest arbitrage** 524
Asked rate 524	**Cross rate** 525
Bid-asked spread 524	**Currency swaps** 536
Bid rate 524	**Direct quote** 522
Buying rate 524	**Economic exposure** 534

Review Questions

17-1. What additional factors are encountered in international as compared with domestic financial management? Discuss each briefly.

17-2. What different types of businesses operate in the international environment? Why are the techniques and strategies available to these firms different?

17-3. What is meant by arbitrage profits?

17-4. What are the markets and mechanics involved in generating (a) simple arbitrage profits and (b) triangular arbitrage profits?

17-5. How do purchasing-power parity, interest rate parity, and the Fisher effect explain the relationships among the current spot rate, the future spot rate, and the forward rate?

17-6. What is meant by (a) exchange risk and (b) political risk?

17-7. How can exchange risk be measured?

17-8. What are the differences among transaction, translation, and economic exposures? Should all of them be ideally reduced to zero?

17-9. What steps can a firm take to reduce exchange risk? Indicate at least two different techniques.

17-10. How are forward-market and the money-market hedges used? What are the major differences between these two types of hedges?

17-11. In the New York exchange market, the forward rate for the Indian currency, the rupee, is not quoted. If you were exposed to exchange risk in rupees, how could you hedge your position?

17-12. Compare and contrast the use of forward contracts, futures contracts, and futures options to reduce foreign exchange exposure. When is each instrument most appropriate?

17-13. Indicate two working-capital management techniques that are useful for international businesses to reduce exchange risk and potentially increase profits.

17-14. How do the financing sources available to an MNC differ from those available to a domestic firm? What do these differences mean for the company's cost of capital?

17-15. What risks are associated with direct foreign investment? How do these risks differ from those encountered in domestic investment?

17-16. How is the direct foreign investment decision made? What are the inputs to this decision process? Are the inputs more complicated than those to the domestic investment problem? If so, why?

17-17. A corporation wants to enter a particular foreign market, but a DFI analysis indicates that putting a plant in the foreign country will not profitable. What other course of action can the company take to enter the foreign market? What are the important considerations?

Self-Test Problem

(The solution to this problem is found at the end of the chapter.)
The data for Self-Test Problem ST-1 are given in the following table:

COUNTRY	CONTRACT	$/FOREIGN CURRENCY
New Zealand—dollar	Spot	.3893
	30-day	.3910
	90-day	.3958

ST-1. You own $10,000. The U.S. dollar rate on the New Zealand dollar is 2.5823 NZ$/US$. The New Zealand dollar rate is given in the accompanying table. Are arbitrage profits possible? Set up an arbitrage scheme with your capital. What is the gain (loss) in dollars?

Study Problems

The data for Study Problems 17-1 through 17-6 are given in the following table:

COUNTRY	CONTRACT	$/FOREIGN CURRENCY
Canada—dollar	Spot	.8437
	30-day	.8417
	90-day	.8395
Japan—yen	Spot	.004684
	30-day	.004717
	90-day	.004781
Switzerland—franc	Spot	.5139
	30-day	.5169
	90-day	.5315

17-1. (*Spot exchange rates*) An American business needs to pay (a) 10,000 Canadian dollars, (b) 2 million yen, and (c) 50,000 Swiss francs to businesses abroad. What are the dollar payments to the respective countries?

17-2. (*Spot exchange rates*) An American business pays $10,000, $15,000, and $20,000 to suppliers in, respectively, Japan, Switzerland, and Canada. How much, in local currencies, do the suppliers receive?

17-3. (*Indirect quotes*) Compute the indirect quote for the spot and forward Canadian dollar, yen, and Swiss franc contracts.

17-4. (*Exchange rates*) The spreads on the contracts as a percentage of the asked rates are 2 percent for yen, 3 percent for Canadian dollars, and 5 percent for Swiss francs. Show, in a table similar to the preceding one, the bid rates for the different spot and forward rates.

17-5. (*Exchange rate arbitrage*) You own $10,000. The dollar rate in Tokyo is 216.6743. The yen rate in New York is given in the preceding table. Are arbitrage profits possible? Set up an arbitrage scheme with your capital. What is the gain (loss) in dollars?

17-6. (*Cross rates*) Compute the Canadian dollar/yen and the yen/Swiss franc spot rate from the data in the preceding table.

Web Works

If you ever need to convert money from one currency to another, the Web is the place to go. There are a number of different currency converters available that are easy to use.

17-WW1. Take a look at the FX Converter (**www.oanda.com/convert/classic**). Use it to convert 100 Fiji dollars to U.S. dollars. How much are the 100 Fiji dollars worth in U.S. dollars?

17-WW2. Use the Bank of Canada currency converter (**www.bankofcanada.ca/en/exchform.htm**) to convert 100 Croatian kunas to U.S. dollars. How much are they worth?

17-WW3. Try the Yahoo! Finance currency calculator (**finance.yahoo.com/m3?u**) to convert 100 U.S. dollars into euros. How many euros would you get for $100?

17-WW4. Now use whatever currency calculator you'd like and move 100 U.S. dollars to euros. Convert those euros to Japanese yen and then convert those Japanese yen into U.S. dollars. How many U.S. dollars do you have?

Mini Case

For your job as the business reporter for a local newspaper, you are asked to put together a series of articles on multinational finance and the international currency markets for your readers. Much recent local press coverage has been given to losses in the foreign exchange markets by JGAR, a local firm that is the subsidiary of Daedlufetarg, a large German manufacturing firm.

Your editor would like you to address several specific questions dealing with multinational finance. Prepare a response to the following memorandum from your editor:

To: Business Reporter
From: Perry White, Editor, *Daily Planet*
Re: Upcoming Series on Multinational Finance

In your upcoming series on multinational finance, I would like to make sure you cover several specific points. Before you begin this assignment, I want to make sure we are all reading from the same script because accuracy has always been the cornerstone of the *Daily Planet*. I'd like a response to the following questions before we proceed:

a. What new problems and factors are encountered in international, as opposed to domestic, financial management?
b. What does the term *arbitrage profits* mean?
c. What can a firm do to reduce exchange risk?
d. What are the differences among a forward contract, a futures contract, and options?

Use the following data in your responses to the remaining questions:

Selling Quotes for Foreign Currencies in New York

COUNTRY—CURRENCY	CONTRACT	$/FOREIGN
Canada—dollar	Spot	.8450
	30-day	.8415
	90-day	.8390
Japan—yen	Spot	.004700
	30-day	.004750
	90-day	.004820
Switzerland—franc	Spot	.5150
	30-day	.5182
	90-day	.5328

e. An American business needs to pay (a) 15,000 Canadian dollars, (b) 1.5 million yen, and (c) 55,000 Swiss francs to businesses abroad. What are the dollar payments to the respective countries?
f. An American business pays $20,000, $5,000, and $15,000 to suppliers in, respectively, Japan, Switzerland, and Canada. How much, in local currencies, do the suppliers receive?
g. Compute the indirect quote for the spot and forward Canadian dollar contract.
h. You own $10,000. The dollar rate in Tokyo is 216.6752. The yen rate in New York is given in the preceding table. Are arbitrage profits possible? Set up an arbitrage scheme with your capital. What is the gain (loss) in dollars?
i. Compute the Canadian dollar/yen spot rate from the data in the preceding table.

Self-Test Solution

SS-1. The New Zealand rate is 2.5823 NZ$/$1, and the (indirect) New York rate is 1/.3893 = 2.5687 NZ$/US$.

Assuming no transaction costs, the rates between New Zealand and New York are out of line. Thus, arbitrage profits are possible.

Step 1. Because the New Zealand dollar is cheaper in New Zealand, buy $10,000 worth of New Zealand dollars in New Zealand. The number of New Zealand dollars purchased would be $10,000 × 2.5823 = 25,823 New Zealand dollars.

Step 2. Simultaneously, sell the New Zealand dollars in New York at the prevailing rate. The amount received upon the sale of the New Zealand dollars would be:

25,823 NZ$ × $.3893/NZ$ = $10,052.89

The net gain is $10,052.89 − $10,000 = $52.89.

APPENDIX A

USING A CALCULATOR

As you prepare for a career in business, the ability to use a financial calculator is essential, whether you are in the finance division or the marketing department. For most positions, it will be assumed that you can use a calculator in making computations that at one time were simply not possible without extensive time and effort. The following examples let us see what is possible, but they represent only the beginning of using the calculator in finance.

With just a little time and effort, you will be surprised at how much you can do with the calculator, such as calculating a stock's beta, or determining the value of a bond on a specific day given the exact date of maturity, or finding net present values and internal rates of return, or calculating the standard deviation. The list is almost endless.

In demonstrating how calculators may make our work easier, we must first decide which calculator to use. The options are numerous and largely depend on personal preference. We have chosen the Texas Instruments BA II Plus and the Hewlett-Packard 10bII.

We will limit our discussion to the following issues:

 I. Introductory Comments
 II. An Important Starting Point
 III. Calculating Table Values for:
  A. Appendix B (Compound sum of $1)
  B. Appendix C (Present value of $1)
  C. Appendix D (Sum of an annuity of $1 for *n* periods)
  D. Appendix E (Present value of an annuity of $1 for *n* periods)
 IV. Calculating Present Values
 V. Calculating Future Values (Compound sum)
 VI. Calculating the Number of Payments or Receipts
 VII. Calculating the Payment Amount
 VIII. Calculating the Interest Rate
 IX. Bond Valuation
  A. Computing the value of a bond
  B. Calculating the yield to maturity of a bond
 X. Computing the Net Present Value and Internal Rate of Return
  A. Where future cash flows are equal amounts in each period (annuity)
  B. Where future cash flows are unequal amounts in each period

I. Introductory Comments

In the examples that follow, you are told (1) which keystrokes to use, (2) the resulting appearance of the calculator display, and (3) a supporting explanation.

The keystrokes column tells you which keys to press. The keystrokes shown in a white box tell you to use one of the calculator's dedicated or "hard" keys. For example, if +/− is shown in the keystrokes instruction column, press that key on the keyboard of the calculator. With the Texas Instruments BA II Plus, to use a function printed in a shaded box above a dedicated key, always press the shaded key 2nd first, then the function key. The HP 10bII has two shift keys, one purple (PRP) and one orange (ORG). To use the functions printed in purple (stats) on the keypad press the purple button first. To use the functions printed in orange (shift) on the keypad, press the orange button first.

II. AN IMPORTANT STARTING POINT - TEXAS INSTRUMENTS BA II PLUS

Example: You want to display four numbers to the right of the decimal.

Keystrokes	Display	Explanation
2nd		
FORMAT	DEC =	
4 ENTER	DEC = 4.0000	Sets display to show four numbers to the right of the decimal
CE/C CE/C	0.0000	Clears display

Example: You want to display two payments per year to be paid at the end of each period.

Keystrokes	Display	Explanation
2nd		
P/Y	P/Y =	
2 ENTER	P/Y = 2.0000	Sets number of payments per year at 2
2nd		
BGN	END	Sets timing of payment at the end of each period
CE/C CE/C	0.0000	Clears display

II. AN IMPORTANT STARTING POINT - HEWLETT-PACKARD 10BII

Example: You want to display four numbers to the right of the decimal. Note that ORG refers to the orange key, which is a "shifted" function used to access the functions printed in orange. There is also a purple shift key that gives you access to the statistical functions in purple.

Keystrokes	Display	Explanation
ORG, C ALL	0.00	Clears registers
ORG, Disp, 4	0.0000	Displays 4 decimal places

Example: You want to display two payments per year to be paid at the end of the period.

Keystrokes	Display	Explanation
ORG, C ALL	0.0000	Clears registers
2, ORG, P/YR	2.0000	Sets payments per year
ORG, BEG/END	2.0000	Sets END mode unless BEGIN enunciator on

III. CALCULATING TABLE VALUES - TEXAS INSTRUMENTS BA II PLUS

A. The compound sum of $1 (Appendix B)

Example: What is the table value for the compound sum of $1 for 5 years at a 12 percent annual interest rate?

Keystrokes	Display	Explanation
2nd		
P/Y	P/Y =	
1 ENTER	P/Y = 1.0000	Sets number of payments per year at 1
2nd		
BGN	END	Sets timing of payment at the end of each period
CE/C CE/C	0.0000	Clears display
2nd		
CLR TVM	0.0000	Clears TVM variables
1 +/−	PV = −1.0000	Stores initial $1 as a negative present value.
PV		Otherwise the answer will appear as negative.
5 N	N = 5.0000	Stores number of periods
12 I/Y	I/Y = 12.0000	Stores interest rate
CPT FV	FV = 1.7623	Table value

B. The present value of $1 (Appendix C)

Example: What is the table value for the present value of $1 for 8 years at a 10 percent annual interest rate?

Keystrokes	Display	Explanation
2nd		
P/Y	P/Y =	
1 ENTER	P/Y = 1.0000	Sets number of payments per year at 1
2nd		
BGN	END	Sets timing of payment at the end of each period
CE/C CE/C	0.0000	Clears display
2nd		
CLR TVM	0.0000	Clears TVM variables
1 +/−	FV = −1.0000	Stores future amount as negative value
FV		
8 N	N = 8.0000	Stores number of periods
10 I/Y	I/Y = 10.0000	Stores interest rate
CPT PV	PV = 0.4665	Table value

C. The sum of an annuity of $1 for *n* periods (Appendix D)

Example: What is the table value for the compound sum of an annuity of $1 for 6 years at a 14 percent annual interest rate?

Keystrokes	Display	Explanation
2nd		
P/Y	P/Y =	
1 ENTER	P/Y = 1.0000	Sets number of payments per year at 1
2nd		
BGN	END	Sets timing of payment at the end of each period
CE/C CE/C	0.0000	Clears display
2nd		
CLR TVM	0.0000	Clears TVM variables
1 +/−	PMT = −1.0000	Stores annual payment (annuity) as a negative number.
PMT		Otherwise the answer will appear as a negative.
6 N	N = 6.0000	Stores number of periods
14 I/Y	I/Y = 14.0000	Stores interest rate
CPT FV	FV = 8.5355	Table value

D. The present value of an annuity of $1 for *n* periods (Appendix E)

Example: What is the table value for the present value of an annuity of $1 for 12 years at a 9 percent annual interest rate?

Keystrokes	Display	Explanation
2nd		
P/Y	P/Y =	
1 ENTER	P/Y = 1.0000	Sets number of payments per year at 1
2nd		
BGN	END	Sets timing of payment at the end of each period
CE/C CE/C	0.0000	Clears display
2nd		
CLR TVM	0.0000	Clears TVM variables
1 +/−	PMT = −1.0000	Stores annual payment (annuity) as a negative number.
PMT		Otherwise the answer will appear as a negative.
12 N	N = 12.0000	Stores number of periods
9 I/Y	I/Y = 9.0000	Stores interest rate
CPT PV	PV = 7.1607	Table value

III. CALCULATING TABLE VALUES - HEWLETT-PACKARD 10BII

A. The compound sum of $1 (Appendix B)

Example: What is the table value for the compound sum of $1 for 5 years at 12 percent annual interest rate?

Keystrokes	Display	Explanation
ORG, C ALL	0.0000	Clears registers
1, ORG, P/YR	1.0000	Sets number of payments per year at 1
ORG, BEG/END	1.0000	Sets timing of payment at the end of each period
		(If BEGIN shows then press ORG, BEG/END again)
1, +/−, PV	−1.0000	Stores initial $1 as a negative present value.
		Otherwise the answer will appear as a negative.
5, N	5.0000	Stores number of periods
12, I/YR	12.0000	Stores interest rate
FV	1.7623	Table value

B. The Present Value of $1 (Appendix C)

Example: What is the table value for the present value of $1 for 8 years at a 10 percent annual interest rate?

Keystrokes	Display	Explanation
ORG, C ALL	0.0000	Clears registers
1, ORG, P/YR	1.0000	Sets number of payments per year at 1
ORG, BEG/END	1.0000	Sets timing of payment at the end of each period
		(If BEGIN shows press ORG, BEG/END again)
1, +/−, FV	−1.0000	Stores future amount as negative value
8, N	8.0000	Stores number of periods
10, I/YR	10.0000	Stores interest rate
PV	0.4665	Table value

C. The sum of an annuity of $1 for *n* periods (Appendix D)

Example: What is the table value for the compound sum of an annuity of $1 for 6 years at a 14 percent annual interest rate?

Keystrokes	Display	Explanation
ORG, C ALL	0.0000	Clears registers
1, ORG, P/YR	1.0000	Sets number of payments per year at 1
ORG, BEG/END	1.0000	Sets timing of payment at the end of each period
		(If BEGIN shows press ORG, BEG/END again)
1, +/−, PMT	−1.0000	Stores the annual payment (annuity) as a negative number. Otherwise the
		answer will appear as a negative.
6, N	6.0000	Stores the number of periods
14, I/YR	14.0000	Stores interest rate
FV	8.5355	Table value

D. The present value of an annuity of $1 for *n* periods (Appendix E)

Example: What is the table value for the present value of an annuity of $1 for 12 years at a 9 percent annual interest rate?

Keystrokes	Display	Explanation
ORG, C ALL	0.0000	Clears registers
1, ORG, P/YR	1.0000	Sets number of payments per year at 1
ORG, BEG/END	1.0000	Sets timing of payment at the end of each period
		(If BEGIN shows press ORG, BEG/END again)
1, +/−, PMT	−1.0000	Stores the annual payment (annuity) as a negative number.
		Otherwise the answer will appear as a negative.
12, N	12.0000	Stores number of periods
9, I/Y	9.0000	Stores interest rate
PV	7.1607	Table value

IV. CALCULATING PRESENT VALUES - TEXAS INSTRUMENTS BA II PLUS

Example: You are considering the purchase of a franchise of quick oil-change locations, which you believe will provide an annual cash flow of $50,000. At the end of 10 years, you believe that you will be able to sell the franchise for an estimated $900,000. Calculate the maximum amount you should pay for the franchise (present value) in order to realize at least an 18 percent annual yield.

Keystrokes	Display	Explanation
2nd		
BGN	END	Sets timing of payment at the end of each period
CE/C CE/C	0.0000	Clears display
2nd		
CLR TVM	0.0000	Clears TVM variables
10 N	N = 10.0000	Stores *n*, the holding period
18 I/Y	I/Y = 18.0000	Stores *i*, the required rate of return
50,000 PMT	PMT = 50,000.0000	Stores *PMT*, the annual cash flow to be received
900,000 FV	FV = 900,000.0000	Stores *FV*, the cash flow to be received at the end of the project
CPT PV	PV = −396,662.3350	The present value, given a required rate of return of 18 percent. (Note: The present value is displayed with a minus sign since it represents cash paid out.)

IV. CALCULATING PRESENT VALUES - HEWLETT-PACKARD 10BII

Example: You are considering the purchase of a franchise of quick oil-change locations, which you believe will provide an annual cash flow of $50,000. At the end of 10 years, you believe that you will be able to sell the franchise for an estimated $900,000. Calculate the maximum amount you should pay for the franchise (present value) in order to realize at least an 18 percent annual yield.

Keystrokes	Display	Explanation
ORG, C ALL	0.0000	Clears registers
ORG, BEG/END	0.0000	Sets timing of payment at the end of each period (If BEGIN shows press ORG, BEG/END again)
10, N	10.0000	Stores *n*, the holding period
18, I/Y	18.0000	Stores *i*, the required rate of return
50,000, PMT	50,000.0000	Stores PMT, the annual cash flow to be received
900,000, FV	900,000.0000	Stores FV, the cash flow to be received at the end of the project
PV	−396,662.3350	The present value, given a required rate of return of 18 percent. (Note: The present value is displayed with a minus sign since it represents cash paid out.)

V. CALCULATING FUTURE VALUES (COMPOUND SUM) - TEXAS INSTRUMENTS BA II PLUS

Example: If you deposit $300 a month (at the beginning of each month) into a new account that pays 6.25 percent annual interest compounded monthly, how much will you have in the account after 5 years?

Keystrokes	Display	Explanation
2nd		
BGN	END	Sets timing of payment at the end of each period
2nd		
SET	BGN	Sets timing of payments to beginning of each period
2nd		
P/Y	P/Y =	
12 ENTER	P/Y = 12.0000	Sets 12 payments per year
CE/C CE/C	0.0000	Clears display

(continues on next page)

Keystrokes	Display	Explanation
2nd		
CLR TVM	0.0000	Clears TVM variables
60 N	N = 60.0000	Stores n, the number of months for the investment
6.25 I/Y	I/Y = 6.2500	Stores i, the annual rate
300 +/– PMT	PMT = –300.0000	Stores PMT, the monthly amount invested (with a minus sign for cash paid out)
CPT FV	FV = 21,175.7613	The future value after 5 years

V. CALCULATING FUTURE VALUES (COMPOUND SUM) - HEWLETT-PACKARD 10BII

Example: If you deposit $300 a month (at the beginning of each month) into a new account that pays 6.25 percent annual interest compounded monthly, how much will you have in the account after 5 years?

Keystrokes	Display	Explanation
ORG, C ALL	0.0000	Clears registers
ORG, BEG/END	0.0000(BEGIN)	Sets timing of payments to beginning of each period
12, ORG, P/YR	12.0000	Sets 12 payments per year
60, N	60.0000	Stores n, the number of months for the investment
6.25, I/Y	6.2500	Stores I, the annual rate
300, +/–, PMT	–300.0000	Stores PMT, the monthly amount invested (with a minus sign for cash paid out)
FV	21,175.7613	The future value after 5 years

VI. CALCULATING THE NUMBER OF PAYMENTS OR RECEIPTS - TEXAS INSTRUMENTS BA II PLUS

Example: If you wish to retire with $500,000 saved, and can only afford payments of $500 at the beginning of each month, how long will you have to contribute toward your retirement if you can earn a 10 percent return on your contributions?

Keystrokes	Display	Explanation
2nd		
BGN	BGN	Verifies timing of payment at the beginning of each period
2nd		
P/Y	P/Y = 12.0000	
12 ENTER	P/Y = 12.0000	Sets 12 payments per year
CE/C CE/C	0.0000	Clears display
2nd		
CLR TVM	0.0000	Clears TVM variables
10 I/Y	I/Y = 10.0000	Stores i, the interest rate
500 +/– PMT	PMT = –500.0000	Stores PMT, the monthly amount invested (with a minus sign for cash paid out)
500,000 FV	FV = 500,000.0000	The value we want to achieve
CPT N	N = 268.2539	Number of months (since we considered monthly payments) required to achieve our goal

VI. CALCULATING THE NUMBER OF PAYMENTS OR RECEIPTS - HEWLETT-PACKARD 10BII

Example: If you wish to retire with $500,000 saved and can only afford payments of $500 at the beginning of each month, how long will you have to contribute toward your retirement if you can earn a 10 percent return on your contributions?

Keystrokes	Display	Explanation
ORG, C ALL	0.0000	Clears registers
ORG, BEG/END	0.0000(BEGIN)	Sets timing of payments to beginning of each period

12, ORG, P/YR	12.0000	Sets 12 payments per year
10, I/YR	10.0000	Stores *I*, the interest rate
500, +/−, PMT	500.0000	Stores PMT, the monthly amount invested (with a minus sign for cash paid out)
500,000, FV	500,000.0000	The value we want to achieve
N	268.2539	Number of months (since we considered monthly payments) required to achieve our goal

VII. CALCULATING THE PAYMENT AMOUNT - TEXAS INSTRUMENTS BA II PLUS

Example: Suppose your retirement needs were $750,000. If you are currently 25 years old and plan to retire at age 65, how much will you have to contribute at the beginning of each month for retirement if you can earn 12.5 percent on your savings?

Keystrokes	Display	Explanation
2nd		
BGN	BGN	Verifies timing of payment at the beginning of each period
2nd		
P/Y	P/Y = 12.0000	
12 ENTER	P/Y = 12.0000	Sets 12 payments per year
CE/C CE/C	0.0000	Clears display
2nd		
CLR TVM	0.0000	Clears TVM variables
12.5 I/Y	I/Y = 12.5000	Stores *i*, the interest rate
480 N	N = 480.0000	Stores *n*, the number of periods until we stop contributing (40 years × 12 months/year = 480 months)
750,000 FV	FV = 750,000.0000	The value we want to achieve
CPT PMT	PMT = −53.8347	Monthly contribution required to achieve our ultimate goal (shown as negative since it represents cash paid out)

VII. CALCULATING THE PAYMENT AMOUNT - HEWLETT-PACKARD 10BII

Example: Suppose your retirement needs are $750,000. If you are currently 25 years old and plan to retire at age 65, how much will you have to contribute at the beginning of each month for retirement if you can earn 12.5 percent on your savings?

Keystrokes	Display	Explanation
ORG, C ALL	0.0000	Clears registers
ORG, BEG/END	0.0000(BEGIN)	Sets timing of payments to the beginning of each period
12, ORG, P/YR	12.0000	Sets 12 payments per year
12.5, I/YR	12.5000	Stores *I*, the interest rate
480 N	N = 480.0000	Stores *n*, the number of periods until we stop contributing (40 years × 12 months/year = 480 months)
750,000, FV	750,000.0000	The value we want to achieve
PMT	−53.8347	Monthly contribution required to achieve our ultimate goal (shown as a negative since it represents cash paid out)

VIII. CALCULATING THE INTEREST RATE - TEXAS INSTRUMENTS BA II PLUS

Example: If you invest $300 at the end of each month for 6 years (72 months) for a promised $30,000 return at the end, what interest rate are you earning on your investment?

Keystrokes	Display	Explanation
2nd		
BGN	BGN	Sets timing of payments to beginning of each period

Keystrokes	Display	Explanation
2nd		
SET	END	Sets timing of payments to end of each period
2nd		
P/Y	P/Y = 12.0000	
12 ENTER	P/Y = 12.0000	Sets 12 payments per year
CE/C CE/C	0.0000	Clears display
2nd		
CLR TVM	0.0000	Clears TVM variables
72 N	N = 72.0000	Stores *n*, the number of deposits (investments)
300 +/− PMT	PMT = −300.0000	Stores *PMT*, the monthly amount invested (with a minus sign for cash paid out)
30,000 FV	FV = 30,000.0000	Stores the future value to be received in 6 years
CPT I/Y	I/Y = 10.5892	The annual interest rate earned on the investment

VIII. CALCULATING THE INTEREST RATE - HEWLETT-PACKARD 10BII

Example: If you invest $300 at the end of each month for 6 years (72 months) for a promised $30,000 return at the end, what interest rate are you earning on your investment?

Keystrokes	Display	Explanation
ORG, C ALL	0.0000	Clears registers
ORG, BEG/END	0.0000	Sets timing of payments to the end of each period
72, N	72.000	Stores *n*, the number of deposits (investments)
300, +/−, PMT	−300.0000	Stores PMT, the monthly amount invested (with a minus sign for cash paid out)
30,000, FV	30,000.0000	Stores the future value to be received in 6 years
I/YR	10.5892	The annual interest rate earned on the investment

IX. BOND VALUATION - TEXAS INSTRUMENTS BA II PLUS

A. Computing the value of a bond

Example: Assume the current date is January 1, 2006, and that you want to know the value of a bond that matures in 10 years and has a coupon rate of 9 percent (4.5 percent semiannually). Your required rate of return is 12 percent.

Keystrokes	Display	Explanation
2nd		
BGN	END	Verifies timing of payments to end of each period
2nd		
P/Y	P/Y = 12.0000	
2 ENTER	P/Y = 2.0000	Sets 2 payments per year; end mode (END) assumes cash flows are at the end of each 6-month period
CE/C CE/C	0.0000	Clears display
2nd		
CLR TVM	0.0000	Clears TVM variables
20 N	N = 20.0000	Stores the number of semiannual periods (10 years × 2)
12 I/Y	I/Y = 12.0000	Stores annual rate of return
45 PMT	PMT = 45.0000	Stores the semiannual interest payment
1,000 FV	FV = 1,000.0000	Stores the bond's maturity or par value
CPT PV	PV = −827.9512	Value of the bond, expressed as a negative number

SOLUTION Using the Bond Feature:

CE/C CE/C	0.0000	Clears display
2nd		
BOND	SDT = 1-01-1970	(This will be the last date entered)

Keystrokes	Display	Explanation
2nd		
CLR WORK	SDT = 1-01-1970	Clears BOND variables
1.01.06 ENTER	SDT = 1-01-2006	Stores the current date (month, date, year)
↓	CPN = 0.0000	
9 ENTER	CPN = 9.0000	Stores the coupon interest rate
↓	RDT = 12-31-1990	(This will be the last date entered)
1.01.16 ENTER	RDT = 1-01-2016	Stores the maturity date in 10 years
↓	RV = 100.0000	Verifies bond maturity or par value
↓	ACT	
2nd		
SET	360	Sets calculations to be based on 360-day year
↓	2/Y	Verifies semiannual compounding rate
↓	YLD = 0.0000	
12 ENTER	YLD = 12.0000	Stores the investor's required rate of return
↓	PRI = 0.0000	
CPT	PRI = 82.7951	Value of bond as a percent of par value; i.e., value of bond is $827.95

B. Computing the yield to maturity of a bond

Example: Assume the current date is January 1, 2006, and that you want to know your yield to maturity on a bond that matures in 8 years and has a coupon rate of 12 percent (6 percent semiannually). The bond is selling for $1,100.

Keystrokes	Display	Explanation
2nd		
BGN	END	Verifies timing of payments to end of each period
2nd		
P/Y	P/Y = 12.0000	
2 ENTER	P/Y = 2.0000	Sets 2 payments per year; end mode (END) assumes cash flows are at the end of each 6-month period
CE/C CE/C	0.0000	Clears display
2nd		
CLR TVM	0.0000	Clears TVM variables
16 N	N = 16.0000	Stores the number of semiannual periods (8 years × 2)
1100 +/−	PV = −1,100.0000	Value of the bond, expressed as a negative number
PV		
60 PMT	PMT = 60.0000	Stores the semiannual interest payments
1,000 FV	FV = 1,000.0000	Stores the bond's maturity or par value
CPT I/Y	I/Y = 10.1451	The yield to maturity, expressed on an annual basis

SOLUTION Using the Bond Feature:

Keystrokes	Display	Explanation
CE/C CE/C	0.0000	Clears display
2nd		
Bond	SDT = 1-01-1993	(This will be the last date entered)
2nd		
CLR WORK	SDT = 1-01-1993	Clears BOND variables
1.01.06 ENTER	SDT = 1-01-2006	Stores the current date (month, date, year)
↓	CPN = 0.0000	
12 ENTER	CPN = 12.0000	Stores the coupon interest rate
↓	RDT = 1-01-2003	(This will be the last date entered)
1.01.14 ENTER	RDT = 1-01-2014	Stores the maturity date in 8 years
↓	RV = 100.0000	Verifies bond's maturity or par value
↓	360	
2nd		

(continues on next page)

Keystrokes	Display	Explanation
SET	ACT	Sets calculations to be based on 360-day year
		Verifies semiannual compounding rate
↓	2/Y	
↓	YLD = 0.0000	
↓	PRI = 0.0000	
110 ENTER	PRI = 110.0000	Stores the bond value as a percentage of par value
↑	YLD = 0.0000	
CPT	YLD = 10.1451	Bond's yield to maturity

IX. BOND VALUATION - HEWLETT-PACKARD 10BII

A. Computing the value of a bond

Example: Assume the current date is January 1, 2006, and that you want to know the value of a bond that matures in 10 years and has a coupon rate of 9 percent (4.5 percent semiannually). Your required rate of return is 12 percent.

Keystrokes	Display	Explanation
ORG, C ALL	0.0000	Clears registers
2, ORG, P/YR	2.0000	Sets payments at 2 per year END mode
20, N	20.0000	Stores the number of semiannual periods
12, I/YR	12.0000	Stores annual rate of return
45, PMT	45.0000	Stores the semiannual interest payments
1000, FV	1,000.0000	Stores the bond's maturity or par value
PV	−827.9512	Value of the bond, expressed as a negative number

B. Computing the yield to maturity of a bond

Example: Assume the current date is January 1, 2006, and that you want to know your yield to maturity on a bond that matures in 8 years and has a coupon rate of 12 percent (6 percent semiannually). The bond is selling for $1,100.

Keystrokes	Display	Explanation
ORG, C ALL	0.0000	Clears registers
2, ORG, P/YR	2.0000	Sets payments at 2 per year END mode
16, N	16.0000	Stores the number of semiannual periods (8 years × 2)
1100, +/−, PV	−1,100.0000	Value of the bond expressed as a negative number
60, PMT	60.0000	Stores the semiannual interest payments
1000, FV	1,000.0000	Stores the bond's maturity or par value
I/YR	10.1451	The yield to maturity expressed on an annual basis

X. COMPUTING THE NET PRESENT VALUE AND INTERNAL RATE OF RETURN - TEXAS INSTRUMENTS BA II PLUS

A. Where future cash flows are equal amounts in each period (annuity)

Example: The firm is considering a capital project that would cost $80,000. The firm's cost of capital is 12 percent. The project life is 10 years, during which time the firm expects to receive $15,000 per year. Calculate the *NPV* and *IRR*.

Keystrokes	Display	Explanation
2nd		
BGN	END	Verifies timing of payments to end of each period
2nd		
P/Y	P/Y = 12.0000	
1 ENTER	P/Y = 1.0000	Sets 1 payment per year; end mode (END) assumes cash flows are at the end of each year
CE/C CE/C	0.0000	Clears display

2nd		
CLR TVM	0.0000	Clears TVM variables
15,000 PMT	PMT = 15.0000	Stores the annual cash flows of $15,000
10 N	N = 10.0000	Stores the life of the project
12 I/Y	I/Y = 12.0000	Stores the cost of capital
CPT PV	PV = −84,753.3454	Calculates present value
+/−	84,753.3454	Changes *PV* to positive
−80,000 =	4,753.3454	Calculates net present value by subtracting the cost of the project
80,000 +/−	−80,000.0000	
PV	PV = −80,000.0000	
CPT I/Y	I/Y = 13.4344	Calculates the *IRR*

B. Where future cash flows are unequal amounts in each period

Example: The firm is considering a capital project that would cost $110,000. The firm's cost of capital is 15 percent. The project life is 5 years, with the following expected cash flows: $–25,000, $50,000, $60,000, $60,000 and $70,000. In addition, you expect to receive $30,000 in the last year from the salvage value of the equipment. Calculate the NPV and IRR.

Keystrokes	Display	Explanation
CE/C CE/C	0.0000	Clears display
CF	CF$_0$ = 0.0000	
2nd		
CLR WORK	CF$_0$ = 0.0000	Clears cash flow variables
110,000 +/−	CF$_0$ = −110,000.0000	Stores CF$_0$, the initial investment (with a minus sign for a negative cash flow)
ENTER		
↓	CO1 = 0.0000	Stores CF$_1$, the first year's cash flow (with a minus sign for a negative cash flow)
25,000 +/−	CO1 = −25,000.0000	
ENTER		
↓	FO1 = 1.0000	Stores the number of years CF$_1$ is repeated (in this case, 1 year only)
ENTER		
↓	CO2 = 0.0000	
50,000	CO2 = 50,000.0000	Stores CF$_2$
ENTER		
↓	FO2 = 1.0000	
ENTER	FO2 = 1.0000	Stores the number of years CF$_2$ is repeated
↓	CO3 = 0.0000	
60,000	CO3 = 60,000.0000	Stores CF$_3$
ENTER		
↓	FO3 = 2.0000	Stores the number of years CF$_3$ is repeated
2 ENTER		(here, 2 years, so our response is 2 to the FO$_3$ prompt)
↓	CO4 = 0.0000	
100,000	CO4 = 100,000.0000	Stores CF$_4$, $70,000 plus expected $30,000
ENTER		
↓	FO4 = 1.0000	Stores the number CF$_4$
ENTER		
2nd		
QUIT	0.0000	Ends storage of individual cash flows
NPV	I = 0.0000	
15 ENTER	I = 15.0000	Stores interest rate

(continues on next page)

Keystrokes	Display	Explanation
↓	NPV = 0.0000	
CPT	NPV = 29,541.8951	Calculates the project's *NPV* at the stated interest rate
IRR	IRR = 0.0000	
CPT	IRR = 22.0633	Calculates the project's *IRR*

X. COMPUTING THE NET PRESENT VALUE AND INTERNAL RATE OF RETURN - HEWLETT-PACKARD 10BII

A. Where future cash flows are equal amounts in each period (annuity)

Example: The firm is considering a capital project that would cost $80,000. The firm's cost of capital is 12 percent. The project life is 10 years, during which time the firm expects to receive $15,000 per year. Calculate the *NPV* and *IRR*.

Keystrokes	Display	Explanation
ORG, C ALL	0.0000	Clears registers
ORG, BEG/END	0.0000	Verifies timing of payments to end of each period
1, ORG, P/YR	1.0000	Sets 1 payment per year; end mode (END); assumes cash flows are at the end of each year
15,000, PMT	15,000.0000	Stores annual cash flows of $15,000
10, N	10.0000	Stores the life of the project
12, I/YR	12.0000	Stores the cost of capital
PV	−84,753.3454	Calculates present value
+/−	84,753.3454	Changes *PV* to positive
−80,000, =	4753.3454	Calculates net present value by subtracting the cost of the project
80,000, +/−	−80,000.0000	
PV	−80,000.0000	
I/YR	13.4344	Calculates the *IRR*

B. Where future cash flows are unequal amounts in each period

Example: The firm is considering a capital project that would cost $110,000. The firm's cost of capital is 15 percent. The project life is 5 years, with the following expected cash flows: −$25,000, $50,000, $60,000, $60,000, and $70,000. In addition, you expect to receive $30,000 in the last year from the salvage value of the equipment. Calculate the *NPV* and *IRR*.

Keystrokes	Display	Explanation
ORG, C ALL	0.0000	Clears registers
1, ORG, P/YR	1.0000	Sets 1 payment per year END mode
110,000, +/−, CFj	−110,000.0000	Stores CF0, the initial investment (with a minus sign for negative cash flow)
25,000, +/−, CFJ	−25,000.0000	Stores CF1, the first year's cash flow (with a minus sign for negative cash flow)
50,000, CFj	50,000.0000	Stores CF2
60,000, CFj	60,000.0000	Stores CF3
2, ORG, Nj	2.0000	Stores the number of years CF3 is repeated
100,000, CFj	100,000.0000	Stores CF4, $70,000 plus expected $30,000
15, I/YR	15.0000	Stores interest rate
ORG, NPV	29,541.8951	Calculates the project's *NPV* at the stated interest rate
ORG, IRR/YR	22.0633	Calculates the project's *IRR*

COMPOUND SUM OF $1 – $FVIF_{i\%,n}$ years

n	1%	2%	3%	4%	5%	6%	7%	8%	9%	10%
1	1.010	1.020	1.030	1.040	1.050	1.060	1.070	1.080	1.090	1.100
2	1.020	1.040	1.061	1.082	1.102	1.124	1.145	1.166	1.188	1.210
3	1.030	1.061	1.093	1.125	1.158	1.191	1.225	1.260	1.295	1.331
4	1.041	1.082	1.126	1.170	1.216	1.262	1.311	1.360	1.412	1.464
5	1.051	1.104	1.159	1.217	1.276	1.338	1.403	1.469	1.539	1.611
6	1.062	1.126	1.194	1.265	1.340	1.419	1.501	1.587	1.677	1.772
7	1.072	1.149	1.230	1.316	1.407	1.504	1.606	1.714	1.828	1.949
8	1.083	1.172	1.267	1.369	1.477	1.594	1.718	1.851	1.993	2.144
9	1.094	1.195	1.305	1.423	1.551	1.689	1.838	1.999	2.172	2.358
10	1.105	1.219	1.344	1.480	1.629	1.791	1.967	2.159	2.367	2.594
11	1.116	1.243	1.384	1.539	1.710	1.898	2.105	2.332	2.580	2.853
12	1.127	1.268	1.426	1.601	1.796	2.012	2.252	2.518	2.813	3.138
13	1.138	1.294	1.469	1.665	1.886	2.133	2.410	2.720	3.066	3.452
14	1.149	1.319	1.513	1.732	1.980	2.261	2.579	2.937	3.342	3.797
15	1.161	1.346	1.558	1.801	2.079	2.397	2.759	3.172	3.642	4.177
16	1.173	1.373	1.605	1.873	2.183	2.540	2.952	3.426	3.970	4.595
17	1.184	1.400	1.653	1.948	2.292	2.693	3.159	3.700	4.328	5.054
18	1.196	1.428	1.702	2.026	2.407	2.854	3.380	3.996	4.717	5.560
19	1.208	1.457	1.753	2.107	2.527	3.026	3.616	4.316	5.142	6.116
20	1.220	1.486	1.806	2.191	2.653	3.207	3.870	4.661	5.604	6.727
21	1.232	1.516	1.860	2.279	2.786	3.399	4.140	5.034	6.109	7.400
22	1.245	1.546	1.916	2.370	2.925	3.603	4.430	5.436	6.658	8.140
23	1.257	1.577	1.974	2.465	3.071	3.820	4.740	5.871	7.258	8.954
24	1.270	1.608	2.033	2.563	3.225	4.049	5.072	6.341	7.911	9.850
25	1.282	1.641	2.094	2.666	3.386	4.292	5.427	6.848	8.623	10.834
30	1.348	1.811	2.427	3.243	4.322	5.743	7.612	10.062	13.267	17.449
40	1.489	2.208	3.262	4.801	7.040	10.285	14.974	21.724	31.408	45.258
50	1.645	2.691	4.384	7.106	11.467	18.419	29.456	46.900	74.354	117.386

n	11%	12%	13%	14%	15%	16%	17%	18%	19%	20%
1	1.110	1.120	1.130	1.140	1.150	1.160	1.170	1.180	1.190	1.200
2	1.232	1.254	1.277	1.300	1.322	1.346	1.369	1.392	1.416	1.440
3	1.368	1.405	1.443	1.482	1.521	1.561	1.602	1.643	1.685	1.728
4	1.518	1.574	1.630	1.689	1.749	1.811	1.874	1.939	2.005	2.074
5	1.685	1.762	1.842	1.925	2.011	2.100	2.192	2.288	2.386	2.488
6	1.870	1.974	2.082	2.195	2.313	2.436	2.565	2.700	2.840	2.986
7	2.076	2.211	2.353	2.502	2.660	2.826	3.001	3.185	3.379	3.583
8	2.305	2.476	2.658	2.853	3.059	3.278	3.511	3.759	4.021	4.300
9	2.558	2.773	3.004	3.252	3.518	3.803	4.108	4.435	4.785	5.160
10	2.839	3.106	3.395	3.707	4.046	4.411	4.807	5.234	5.695	6.192
11	3.152	3.479	3.836	4.226	4.652	5.117	5.624	6.176	6.777	7.430
12	3.498	3.896	4.334	4.818	5.350	5.936	6.580	7.288	8.064	8.916
13	3.883	4.363	4.898	5.492	6.153	6.886	7.699	8.599	9.596	10.699
14	4.310	4.887	5.535	6.261	7.076	7.987	9.007	10.147	11.420	12.839
15	4.785	5.474	6.254	7.138	8.137	9.265	10.539	11.974	13.589	15.407
16	5.311	6.130	7.067	8.137	9.358	10.748	12.330	14.129	16.171	18.488
17	5.895	6.866	7.986	9.276	10.761	12.468	14.426	16.672	19.244	22.186
18	6.543	7.690	9.024	10.575	12.375	14.462	16.879	19.673	22.900	26.623
19	7.263	8.613	10.197	12.055	14.232	16.776	19.748	23.214	27.251	31.948
20	8.062	9.646	11.523	13.743	16.366	19.461	23.105	27.393	32.429	38.337
21	8.949	10.804	13.021	15.667	18.821	22.574	27.033	32.323	38.591	46.005
22	9.933	12.100	14.713	17.861	21.644	26.186	31.629	38.141	45.923	55.205
23	11.026	13.552	16.626	20.361	24.891	30.376	37.005	45.007	54.648	66.247
24	12.239	15.178	18.788	23.212	28.625	35.236	43.296	53.108	65.031	79.496
25	13.585	17.000	21.230	26.461	32.918	40.874	50.656	62.667	77.387	95.395
30	22.892	29.960	39.115	50.949	66.210	85.849	111.061	143.367	184.672	237.373
40	64.999	93.049	132.776	188.876	267.856	378.715	533.846	750.353	1051.642	1469.740
50	184.559	288.996	450.711	700.197	1083.619	1670.669	2566.080	3927.189	5988.730	9100.191

n	21%	22%	23%	24%	25%	26%	27%	28%	29%	30%
1	1.210	1.220	1.230	1.240	1.250	1.260	1.270	1.280	1.290	1.300
2	1.464	1.488	1.513	1.538	1.562	1.588	1.613	1.638	1.664	1.690
3	1.772	1.816	1.861	1.907	1.953	2.000	2.048	2.097	2.147	2.197
4	2.144	2.215	2.289	2.364	2.441	2.520	2.601	2.684	2.769	2.856
5	2.594	2.703	2.815	2.932	3.052	3.176	3.304	3.436	3.572	3.713
6	3.138	3.297	3.463	3.635	3.815	4.001	4.196	4.398	4.608	4.827
7	3.797	4.023	4.259	4.508	4.768	5.042	5.329	5.629	5.945	6.275
8	4.595	4.908	5.239	5.589	5.960	6.353	6.767	7.206	7.669	8.157
9	5.560	5.987	6.444	6.931	7.451	8.004	8.595	9.223	9.893	10.604
10	6.727	7.305	7.926	8.594	9.313	10.086	10.915	11.806	12.761	13.786
11	8.140	8.912	9.749	10.657	11.642	12.708	13.862	15.112	16.462	17.921
12	9.850	10.872	11.991	13.215	14.552	16.012	17.605	19.343	21.236	23.298
13	11.918	13.264	14.749	16.386	18.190	20.175	22.359	24.759	27.395	30.287
14	14.421	16.182	18.141	20.319	22.737	25.420	28.395	31.691	35.339	39.373
15	17.449	19.742	22.314	25.195	28.422	32.030	36.062	40.565	45.587	51.185
16	21.113	24.085	27.446	31.242	35.527	40.357	45.799	51.923	58.808	66.541
17	25.547	29.384	33.758	38.740	44.409	50.850	58.165	66.461	75.862	86.503
18	30.912	35.848	41.523	48.038	55.511	64.071	73.869	85.070	97.862	112.454
19	37.404	43.735	51.073	59.567	69.389	80.730	93.813	108.890	126.242	146.190
20	45.258	53.357	62.820	73.863	86.736	101.720	119.143	139.379	162.852	190.047
21	54.762	65.095	77.268	91.591	108.420	128.167	151.312	178.405	210.079	247.061
22	66.262	79.416	95.040	113.572	135.525	161.490	192.165	228.358	271.002	321.178
23	80.178	96.887	116.899	140.829	169.407	203.477	244.050	292.298	349.592	417.531
24	97.015	118.203	143.786	174.628	211.758	256.381	309.943	374.141	450.974	542.791
25	117.388	144.207	176.857	216.539	264.698	323.040	393.628	478.901	581.756	705.627
30	304.471	389.748	497.904	634.810	807.793	1025.904	1300.477	1645.488	2078.208	2619.936
40	2048.309	2846.941	3946.340	5455.797	7523.156	10346.879	14195.051	19426.418	26520.723	36117.754
50	13779.844	20795.680	31278.301	46889.207	70064.812	104354.562	154942.687	229345.875	338440.000	497910.125

n	31%	32%	33%	34%	35%	36%	37%	38%	39%	40%
1	1.310	1.320	1.330	1.340	1.350	1.360	1.370	1.380	1.390	1.400
2	1.716	1.742	1.769	1.796	1.822	1.850	1.877	1.904	1.932	1.960
3	2.248	2.300	2.353	2.406	2.460	2.515	2.571	2.628	2.686	2.744
4	2.945	3.036	3.129	3.224	3.321	3.421	3.523	3.627	3.733	3.842
5	3.858	4.007	4.162	4.320	4.484	4.653	4.826	5.005	5.189	5.378
6	5.054	5.290	5.535	5.789	6.053	6.328	6.612	6.907	7.213	7.530
7	6.621	6.983	7.361	7.758	8.172	8.605	9.058	9.531	10.025	10.541
8	8.673	9.217	9.791	10.395	11.032	11.703	12.410	13.153	13.935	14.758
9	11.362	12.166	13.022	13.930	14.894	15.917	17.001	18.151	19.370	20.661
10	14.884	16.060	17.319	18.666	20.106	21.646	23.292	25.049	26.924	28.925
11	19.498	21.199	23.034	25.012	27.144	29.439	31.910	34.567	37.425	40.495
12	25.542	27.982	30.635	33.516	36.644	40.037	43.716	47.703	52.020	56.694
13	33.460	36.937	40.745	44.912	49.469	54.451	59.892	65.830	72.308	79.371
14	43.832	49.756	54.190	60.181	66.784	74.053	82.051	90.845	100.509	111.190
15	57.420	64.358	72.073	80.643	90.158	100.712	112.410	125.366	139.707	155.567
16	75.220	84.953	95.857	108.061	121.713	136.968	154.002	173.005	194.192	217.793
17	98.539	112.138	127.490	144.802	164.312	186.277	210.983	238.747	269.927	304.911
18	129.086	148.022	169.561	194.035	221.822	253.337	289.046	329.471	375.198	426.875
19	169.102	195.389	225.517	260.006	299.459	344.537	395.993	454.669	521.525	597.625
20	221.523	257.913	299.937	348.408	404.270	468.571	542.511	627.443	724.919	836.674
21	290.196	340.446	398.916	466.867	545.764	637.256	743.240	865.871	1007.637	1171.343
22	380.156	449.388	530.558	625.601	736.781	865.668	1018.238	1194.900	1400.615	1639.878
23	498.004	593.192	705.642	838.305	994.653	1178.668	1394.986	1648.961	1946.854	2295.829
24	652.385	783.013	938.504	1123.328	1342.781	1602.988	1911.129	2275.564	2706.125	3214.158
25	854.623	1033.577	1248.210	1505.258	1812.754	2180.063	2618.245	3140.275	3761.511	4499.816
30	3297.081	4142.008	5194.516	6503.285	8128.426	10142.914	12636.086	15716.703	19517.969	24201.043
40	49072.621	66519.313	89962.188	121388.437	163433.875	219558.625	294317.937	393684.687	525508.312	700022.688

PRESENT VALUE OF $1 – $PVIF_{i\%,\,n\text{ years}}$

n	1%	2%	3%	4%	5%	6%	7%	8%	9%	10%
1	.990	.980	.971	.962	.952	.943	.935	.926	.917	.909
2	.980	.961	.943	.925	.907	.890	.873	.857	.842	.826
3	.971	.942	.915	.889	.864	.840	.816	.794	.772	.751
4	.961	.924	.888	.855	.823	.792	.763	.735	.708	.683
5	.951	.906	.863	.822	.784	.747	.713	.681	.650	.621
6	.942	.888	.837	.790	.746	.705	.666	.630	.596	.564
7	.933	.871	.813	.760	.711	.665	.623	.583	.547	.513
8	.923	.853	.789	.731	.677	.627	.582	.540	.502	.467
9	.914	.837	.766	.703	.645	.592	.544	.500	.460	.424
10	.905	.820	.744	.676	.614	.558	.508	.463	.422	.386
11	.896	.804	.722	.650	.585	.527	.475	.429	.388	.350
12	.887	.789	.701	.625	.557	.497	.444	.397	.356	.319
13	.879	.773	.681	.601	.530	.469	.415	.368	.326	.290
14	.870	.758	.661	.577	.505	.442	.388	.340	.299	.263
15	.861	.743	.642	.555	.481	.417	.362	.315	.275	.239
16	.853	.728	.623	.534	.458	.394	.339	.292	.252	.218
17	.844	.714	.605	.513	.436	.371	.317	.270	.231	.198
18	.836	.700	.587	.494	.416	.350	.296	.250	.212	.180
19	.828	.686	.570	.475	.396	.331	.277	.232	.194	.164
20	.820	.673	.554	.456	.377	.312	.258	.215	.178	.149
21	.811	.660	.538	.439	.359	.294	.242	.199	.164	.135
22	.803	.647	.522	.422	.342	.278	.226	.184	.150	.123
23	.795	.634	.507	.406	.326	.262	.211	.170	.138	.112
24	.788	.622	.492	.390	.310	.247	.197	.158	.126	.102
25	.780	.610	.478	.375	.295	.233	.184	.146	.116	.092
30	.742	.552	.412	.308	.231	.174	.131	.099	.075	.057
40	.672	.453	.307	.208	.142	.097	.067	.046	.032	.022
50	.608	.372	.228	.141	.087	.054	.034	.021	.013	.009

n	11%	12%	13%	14%	15%	16%	17%	18%	19%	20%
1	.901	.893	.885	.877	.870	.862	.855	.847	.840	.833
2	.812	.797	.783	.769	.756	.743	.731	.718	.706	.694
3	.731	.712	.693	.675	.658	.641	.624	.609	.593	.579
4	.659	.636	.613	.592	.572	.552	.534	.516	.499	.482
5	.593	.567	.543	.519	.497	.476	.456	.437	.419	.402
6	.535	.507	.480	.456	.432	.410	.390	.370	.352	.335
7	.482	.452	.425	.400	.376	.354	.333	.314	.296	.279
8	.434	.404	.376	.351	.327	.305	.285	.266	.249	.233
9	.391	.361	.333	.308	.284	.263	.243	.225	.209	.194
10	.352	.322	.295	.270	.247	.227	.208	.191	.176	.162
11	.317	.287	.261	.237	.215	.195	.178	.162	.148	.135
12	.286	.257	.231	.208	.187	.168	.152	.137	.124	.112
13	.258	.229	.204	.182	.163	.145	.130	.116	.104	.093
14	.232	.205	.181	.160	.141	.125	.111	.099	.088	.078
15	.209	.183	.160	.140	.123	.108	.095	.084	.074	.065
16	.188	.163	.141	.123	.107	.093	.081	.071	.062	.054
17	.170	.146	.125	.108	.093	.080	.069	.060	.052	.045
18	.153	.130	.111	.095	.081	.069	.059	.051	.044	.038
19	.138	.116	.098	.083	.070	.060	.051	.043	.037	.031
20	.124	.104	.087	.073	.061	.051	.043	.037	.031	.026
21	.112	.093	.077	.064	.053	.044	.037	.031	.026	.022
22	.101	.083	.068	.056	.046	.038	.032	.026	.022	.018
23	.091	.074	.060	.049	.040	.033	.027	.022	.018	.015
24	.082	.066	.053	.043	.035	.028	.023	.019	.015	.013
25	.074	.059	.047	.038	.030	.024	.020	.016	.013	.010
30	.044	.033	.026	.020	.015	.012	.009	.007	.005	.004
40	.015	.011	.008	.005	.004	.003	.002	.001	.001	.001
50	.005	.003	.002	.001	.001	.001	.000	.000	.000	.000

n	21%	22%	23%	24%	25%	26%	27%	28%	29%	30%
1	.826	.820	.813	.806	.800	.794	.787	.781	.775	.769
2	.683	.672	.661	.650	.640	.630	.620	.610	.601	.592
3	.564	.551	.537	.524	.512	.500	.488	.477	.466	.455
4	.467	.451	.437	.423	.410	.397	.384	.373	.361	.350
5	.386	.370	.355	.341	.328	.315	.303	.291	.280	.269
6	.319	.303	.289	.275	.262	.250	.238	.227	.217	.207
7	.263	.249	.235	.222	.210	.198	.188	.178	.168	.159
8	.218	.204	.191	.179	.168	.157	.148	.139	.130	.123
9	.180	.167	.155	.144	.134	.125	.116	.108	.101	.094
10	.149	.137	.126	.116	.107	.099	.092	.085	.078	.073
11	.123	.112	.103	.094	.086	.079	.072	.066	.061	.056
12	.102	.092	.083	.076	.069	.062	.057	.052	.047	.043
13	.084	.075	.068	.061	.055	.050	.045	.040	.037	.033
14	.069	.062	.055	.049	.044	.039	.035	.032	.028	.025
15	.057	.051	.045	.040	.035	.031	.028	.025	.022	.020
16	.047	.042	.036	.032	.028	.025	.022	.019	.017	.015
17	.039	.034	.030	.026	.023	.020	.017	.015	.013	.012
18	.032	.028	.024	.021	.018	.016	.014	.012	.010	.009
19	.027	.023	.020	.017	.014	.012	.011	.009	.008	.007
20	.022	.019	.016	.014	.012	.010	.008	.007	.006	.005
21	.018	.015	.013	.011	.009	.008	.007	.006	.005	.004
22	.015	.013	.011	.009	.007	.006	.005	.004	.004	.003
23	.012	.010	.009	.007	.006	.005	.004	.003	.003	.002
24	.010	.008	.007	.006	.005	.004	.003	.003	.002	.002
25	.009	.007	.006	.005	.004	.003	.003	.002	.002	.001
30	.003	.003	.002	.002	.001	.001	.001	.001	.001	.000
40	.000	.000	.000	.000	.000	.000	.000	.000	.000	.000
50	.000	.000	.000	.000	.000	.000	.000	.000	.000	.000

n	31%	32%	33%	34%	35%	36%	37%	38%	39%	40%
1	.763	.758	.752	.746	.741	.735	.730	.725	.719	.714
2	.583	.574	.565	.557	.549	.541	.533	.525	.518	.510
3	.445	.435	.425	.416	.406	.398	.389	.381	.372	.364
4	.340	.329	.320	.310	.301	.292	.284	.276	.268	.260
5	.259	.250	.240	.231	.223	.215	.207	.200	.193	.186
6	.198	.189	.181	.173	.165	.158	.151	.145	.139	.133
7	.151	.143	.136	.129	.122	.116	.110	.105	.100	.095
8	.115	.108	.102	.096	.091	.085	.081	.076	.072	.068
9	.088	.082	.077	.072	.067	.063	.059	.055	.052	.048
10	.067	.062	.058	.054	.050	.046	.043	.040	.037	.035
11	.051	.047	.043	.040	.037	.034	.031	.029	.027	.025
12	.039	.036	.033	.030	.027	.025	.023	.021	.019	.018
13	.030	.027	.025	.022	.020	.018	.017	.015	.014	.013
14	.023	.021	.018	.017	.015	.014	.012	.011	.010	.009
15	.017	.016	.014	.012	.011	.010	.009	.008	.007	.006
16	.013	.012	.010	.009	.008	.007	.006	.006	.005	.005
17	.010	.009	.008	.007	.006	.005	.005	.004	.004	.003
18	.008	.007	.006	.005	.005	.004	.003	.003	.003	.002
19	.006	.005	.004	.004	.003	.003	.003	.002	.002	.002
20	.005	.004	.003	.003	.002	.002	.002	.002	.001	.001
21	.003	.003	.003	.002	.002	.002	.001	.001	.001	.001
22	.003	.002	.002	.002	.001	.001	.001	.001	.001	.001
23	.002	.002	.001	.001	.001	.001	.001	.001	.001	.000
24	.002	.001	.001	.001	.001	.001	.001	.001	.000	.000
25	.001	.001	.001	.001	.001	.000	.000	.000	.000	.000
30	.000	.000	.000	.000	.000	.000	.000	.000	.000	.000
40	.000	.000	.000	.000	.000	.000	.000	.000	.000	.000

SUM OF AN ANNUITY OF $1 FOR n PERIODS – $FVIFA_{i\%,\ n\ years}$

n	1%	2%	3%	4%	5%	6%	7%	8%	9%	10%
1	1.000	1.000	1.000	1.000	1.000	1.000	1.000	1.000	1.000	1.000
2	2.010	2.020	2.030	2.040	2.050	2.060	2.070	2.080	2.090	2.100
3	3.030	3.060	3.091	3.122	3.152	3.184	3.215	3.246	3.278	3.310
4	4.060	4.122	4.184	4.246	4.310	4.375	4.440	4.506	4.573	4.641
5	5.101	5.204	5.309	5.416	5.526	5.637	5.751	5.867	5.985	6.105
6	6.152	6.308	6.468	6.633	6.802	6.975	7.153	7.336	7.523	7.716
7	7.214	7.434	7.662	7.898	8.142	8.394	8.654	8.923	9.200	9.487
8	8.286	8.583	8.892	9.214	9.549	9.897	10.260	10.637	11.028	11.436
9	9.368	9.755	10.159	10.583	11.027	11.491	11.978	12.488	13.021	13.579
10	10.462	10.950	11.464	12.006	12.578	13.181	13.816	14.487	15.193	15.937
11	11.567	12.169	12.808	13.486	14.207	14.972	15.784	16.645	17.560	18.531
12	12.682	13.412	14.192	15.026	15.917	16.870	17.888	18.977	20.141	21.384
13	13.809	14.680	15.618	16.627	17.713	18.882	20.141	21.495	22.953	24.523
14	14.947	15.974	17.086	18.292	19.598	21.015	22.550	24.215	26.019	27.975
15	16.097	17.293	18.599	20.023	21.578	23.276	25.129	27.152	29.361	31.772
16	17.258	18.639	20.157	21.824	23.657	25.672	27.888	30.324	33.003	35.949
17	18.430	20.012	21.761	23.697	25.840	28.213	30.840	33.750	36.973	40.544
18	19.614	21.412	23.414	25.645	28.132	30.905	33.999	37.450	41.301	45.599
19	20.811	22.840	25.117	27.671	30.539	33.760	37.379	41.446	46.018	51.158
20	22.019	24.297	26.870	29.778	33.066	36.785	40.995	45.762	51.159	57.274
21	23.239	25.783	28.676	31.969	35.719	39.992	44.865	50.422	56.764	64.002
22	24.471	27.299	30.536	34.248	38.505	43.392	49.005	55.456	62.872	71.402
23	25.716	28.845	32.452	36.618	41.430	46.995	53.435	60.893	69.531	79.542
24	26.973	30.421	34.426	39.082	44.501	50.815	58.176	66.764	76.789	88.496
25	28.243	32.030	36.459	41.645	47.726	54.864	63.248	73.105	84.699	98.346
30	34.784	40.567	47.575	56.084	66.438	79.057	94.459	113.282	136.305	164.491
40	48.885	60.401	75.400	95.024	120.797	154.758	199.630	295.052	337.872	442.580
50	64.461	84.577	112.794	152.664	209.341	290.325	406.516	573.756	815.051	1163.865

n	11%	12%	13%	14%	15%	16%	17%	18%	19%	20%
1	1.000	1.000	1.000	1.000	1.000	1.000	1.000	1.000	1.000	1.000
2	2.110	2.120	2.130	2.140	2.150	2.160	2.170	2.180	2.190	2.200
3	3.342	3.374	3.407	3.440	3.472	3.506	3.539	3.572	3.606	3.640
4	4.710	4.779	4.850	4.921	4.993	5.066	5.141	5.215	5.291	5.368
5	6.228	6.353	6.480	6.610	6.742	6.877	7.014	7.154	7.297	7.442
6	7.913	8.115	8.323	8.535	8.754	8.977	9.207	9.442	9.683	9.930
7	9.783	10.089	10.405	10.730	11.067	11.414	11.772	12.141	12.523	12.916
8	11.859	12.300	12.757	13.233	13.727	14.240	14.773	15.327	15.902	16.499
9	14.164	14.776	15.416	16.085	16.786	17.518	18.285	19.086	19.923	20.799
10	16.722	17.549	18.420	19.337	20.304	21.321	22.393	23.521	24.709	25.959
11	19.561	20.655	21.814	23.044	24.349	25.733	27.200	28.755	30.403	32.150
12	22.713	24.133	25.650	27.271	29.001	30.850	32.824	34.931	37.180	39.580
13	26.211	28.029	29.984	32.088	34.352	36.786	39.404	42.218	45.244	48.496
14	30.095	32.392	34.882	37.581	40.504	43.672	47.102	50.818	54.841	59.196
15	34.405	37.280	40.417	43.842	47.580	51.659	56.109	60.965	66.260	72.035
16	39.190	42.753	46.671	50.980	55.717	60.925	66.648	72.938	79.850	87.442
17	44.500	48.883	53.738	59.117	65.075	71.673	78.978	87.067	96.021	105.930
18	50.396	55.749	61.724	68.393	75.836	84.140	93.404	103.739	115.265	128.116
19	56.939	64.439	70.748	78.968	88.211	98.603	110.283	123.412	138.165	154.739
20	64.202	72.052	80.946	91.024	102.443	115.379	130.031	146.626	165.417	186.687
21	72.264	81.698	92.468	104.767	118.809	134.840	153.136	174.019	197.846	225.024
22	81.213	92.502	105.489	120.434	137.630	157.414	180.169	206.342	236.436	271.028
23	91.147	104.602	120.203	138.295	159.274	183.600	211.798	244.483	282.359	326.234
24	102.173	118.154	136.829	158.656	184.166	213.976	248.803	289.490	337.007	392.480
25	114.412	133.333	155.616	181.867	212.790	249.212	292.099	342.598	402.038	471.976
30	199.018	241.330	293.192	356.778	434.738	530.306	647.423	790.932	966.698	1181.865
40	581.812	767.080	1013.667	1341.979	1779.048	2360.724	3134.412	4163.094	5529.711	7343.715
50	1668.723	2399.975	3459.344	4994.301	7217.488	10435.449	15088.805	21812.273	31514.492	45496.094

n	21%	22%	23%	24%	25%	26%	27%	28%	29%	30%
1	1.000	1.000	1.000	1.000	1.000	1.000	1.000	1.000	1.000	1.000
2	2.210	2.220	2.230	2.240	2.250	2.260	2.270	2.280	2.290	2.300
3	3.674	3.708	3.743	3.778	3.813	3.848	3.883	3.918	3.954	3.990
4	5.446	5.524	5.604	5.684	5.766	5.848	5.931	6.016	6.101	6.187
5	7.589	7.740	7.893	8.048	8.207	8.368	8.533	8.700	8.870	9.043
6	10.183	10.442	10.708	10.980	11.259	11.544	11.837	12.136	12.442	12.756
7	13.321	13.740	14.171	14.615	15.073	15.546	16.032	16.534	17.051	17.583
8	17.119	17.762	18.430	19.123	19.842	20.588	21.361	22.163	22.995	23.858
9	21.714	22.670	23.669	24.712	25.802	26.940	28.129	29.369	30.664	32.015
10	27.274	28.657	30.113	31.643	33.253	34.945	36.723	38.592	40.556	42.619
11	34.001	35.962	38.039	40.238	42.566	45.030	47.639	50.398	53.318	56.405
12	42.141	44.873	47.787	50.895	54.208	57.738	61.501	65.510	69.780	74.326
13	51.991	55.745	59.778	64.109	68.760	73.750	79.106	84.853	91.016	97.624
14	63.909	69.009	74.528	80.496	86.949	93.925	101.465	109.611	118.411	127.912
15	78.330	85.191	92.669	100.815	109.687	119.346	129.860	141.302	153.750	167.285
16	95.779	104.933	114.983	126.010	138.109	151.375	165.922	181.867	199.337	218.470
17	116.892	129.019	142.428	157.252	173.636	191.733	211.721	233.790	258.145	285.011
18	142.439	158.403	176.187	195.993	218.045	242.583	269.885	300.250	334.006	371.514
19	173.351	194.251	217.710	244.031	273.556	306.654	343.754	385.321	431.868	483.968
20	210.755	237.986	268.783	303.598	342.945	387.384	437.568	494.210	558.110	630.157
21	256.013	291.343	331.603	377.461	429.681	489.104	556.710	633.589	720.962	820.204
22	310.775	356.438	408.871	469.052	538.101	617.270	708.022	811.993	931.040	1067.265
23	377.038	435.854	503.911	582.624	673.626	778.760	990.187	1040.351	1202.042	1388.443
24	457.215	532.741	620.810	723.453	843.032	982.237	1144.237	1332.649	1551.634	1805.975
25	554.230	650.944	764.596	898.082	1054.791	1238.617	1454.180	1706.790	2002.608	2348.765
30	1445.111	1767.044	2160.459	2640.881	3227.172	3941.953	4812.891	5873.172	7162.785	8729.805
40	9749.141	12936.141	17153.691	22728.367	30088.621	39791.957	52570.707	69376.562	91447.375	120389.375

n	31%	32%	33%	34%	35%	36%	37%	38%	39%	40%
1	1.000	1.000	1.000	1.000	1.000	1.000	1.000	1.000	1.000	1.000
2	2.310	2.320	2.330	2.340	2.350	2.360	2.370	2.380	2.390	2.400
3	4.026	4.062	4.099	4.136	4.172	4.210	4.247	4.284	4.322	4.360
4	6.274	6.362	6.452	6.542	6.633	6.725	6.818	6.912	7.008	7.104
5	9.219	9.398	9.581	9.766	9.954	10.146	10.341	10.539	10.741	10.946
6	13.077	13.406	13.742	14.086	14.438	14.799	15.167	15.544	15.930	16.324
7	18.131	18.696	19.277	19.876	20.492	21.126	21.779	22.451	23.142	23.853
8	24.752	25.678	26.638	27.633	28.664	29.732	30.837	31.982	33.167	34.395
9	33.425	34.895	36.429	38.028	39.696	41.435	43.247	45.135	47.103	49.152
10	44.786	47.062	49.451	51.958	54.590	57.351	60.248	63.287	66.473	69.813
11	59.670	63.121	66.769	70.624	74.696	78.998	83.540	88.335	93.397	98.739
12	79.167	84.320	89.803	95.636	101.840	108.437	115.450	122.903	130.822	139.234
13	104.709	112.302	120.438	129.152	138.484	148.474	159.166	170.606	182.842	195.928
14	138.169	149.239	161.183	174.063	187.953	202.925	219.058	236.435	255.151	275.299
15	182.001	197.996	215.373	234.245	254.737	276.978	301.109	327.281	355.659	386.418
16	239.421	262.354	287.446	314.888	344.895	377.690	413.520	452.647	495.366	541.985
17	314.642	347.307	383.303	422.949	466.608	514.658	567.521	625.652	689.558	759.778
18	413.180	459.445	510.792	567.751	630.920	700.935	778.504	864.399	959.485	1064.689
19	542.266	607.467	680.354	761.786	852.741	954.271	1067.551	1193.870	1334.683	1491.563
20	711.368	802.856	905.870	1021.792	1152.200	1298.809	1463.544	1648.539	1856.208	2089.188
21	932.891	1060.769	1205.807	1370.201	1556.470	1767.380	2006.055	2275.982	2581.128	2925.862
22	1223.087	1401.215	1604.724	1837.068	2102.234	2404.636	2749.294	3141.852	3588.765	4097.203
23	1603.243	1850.603	2135.282	2462.669	2839.014	3271.304	3767.532	4336.750	4989.379	5737.078
24	2101.247	2443.795	2840.924	3300.974	3833.667	4449.969	5162.516	5985.711	6936.230	8032.906
25	2753.631	3226.808	3779.428	4424.301	5176.445	6052.957	7073.645	8261.273	9642.352	11247.062
30	10632.543	12940.672	15737.945	19124.434	23221.258	28172.016	34148.906	41357.227	50043.625	60500.207

APPENDIX E

PRESENT VALUE OF AN ANNUITY OF $1 FOR *n* PERIODS – PVIFA$_{i\%, n}$ years

n	1%	2%	3%	4%	5%	6%	7%	8%	9%	10%
1	.990	.980	.971	.962	.952	.943	.935	.926	.917	.909
2	1.970	1.942	1.913	1.886	1.859	1.833	1.808	1.3783	1.759	1.736
3	2.941	2.884	2.829	2.775	2.723	2.673	2.624	2.577	2.531	2.487
4	3.902	3.808	3.717	3.630	3.546	3.465	3.387	3.312	3.240	3.170
5	4.853	4.713	4.580	4.452	4.329	4.212	4.100	3.993	3.890	3.791
6	5.795	5.601	5.417	5.242	5.076	4.917	4.767	5.623	4.486	4.355
7	6.728	6.472	6.230	6.002	5.786	5.582	5.389	5.206	5.033	4.868
8	7.652	7.326	7.020	6.733	6.463	6.210	5.971	5.747	5.535	5.335
9	8.566	8.162	7.786	7.435	7.108	6.802	6.515	6.247	5.995	5.759
10	9.471	8.983	8.530	8.111	7.722	7.360	7.024	6.710	6.418	6.145
11	10.368	9.787	9.253	8.760	8.306	7.887	7.499	7.139	6.805	6.495
12	11.255	10.575	9.954	9.385	8.863	8.384	7.943	7.536	7.161	6.814
13	12.134	11.348	10.635	9.986	9.394	8.853	8.358	7.904	7.487	7.103
14	13.004	12.106	11.296	10.563	9.899	9.295	8.746	8.244	7.786	7.367
15	13.865	12.849	11.938	11.118	10.380	9.712	9.108	8.560	8.061	7.606
16	14.718	13.578	12.561	11.652	10.838	10.106	9.447	8.851	8.313	7.824
17	15.562	14.292	13.166	12.166	11.274	10.477	9.763	9.122	8.544	8.022
18	16.398	14.992	13.754	12.659	11.690	10.828	10.059	9.372	8.756	8.201
19	17.226	15.679	14.324	13.134	12.085	11.158	10.336	9.604	8.950	8.365
20	18.046	16.352	14.878	13.590	12.462	11.470	10.594	9.818	9.129	8.514
21	18.857	17.011	15.415	14.029	12.821	11.764	10.836	10.017	9.292	8.649
22	19.661	17.658	15.937	14.451	13.163	12.042	11.061	10.201	9.442	8.772
23	20.456	18.292	16.444	14.857	13.489	12.303	11.272	10.371	9.580	8.883
24	21.244	18.914	16.936	15.247	13.799	12.550	11.469	10.529	9.707	8.985
25	22.023	19.524	17.413	15.622	14.094	12.783	11.654	10.675	9.823	9.077
30	25.808	22.397	19.601	17.292	15.373	13.765	12.409	11.258	10.274	9.427
40	32.835	27.356	23.115	19.793	17.159	15.046	13.332	11.925	10.757	9.779
50	39.197	31.424	25.730	21.482	18.256	15.762	13.801	12.234	10.962	9.915

n	11%	12%	13%	14%	15%	16%	17%	18%	19%	20%
1	.901	.893	.885	.877	.870	.862	.855	.847	.840	.833
2	1.713	1.690	1.668	1.647	1.626	1.605	1.585	1.566	1.547	1.528
3	2.444	2.402	2.361	2.322	2.283	2.246	2.210	2.174	2.140	2.106
4	3.102	3.037	2.974	2.914	2.855	2.798	2.743	2.690	2.639	2.589
5	3.696	3.605	3.517	3.433	3.352	3.274	3.199	3.127	3.058	2.991
6	4.231	4.111	3.998	3.889	3.784	3.685	3.589	3.498	3.410	3.326
7	4.712	4.564	4.423	4.288	4.160	4.039	3.922	3.812	3.706	3.605
8	5.146	4.968	4.799	4.639	4.487	4.344	4.207	4.078	3.954	3.837
9	5.537	5.328	5.132	4.946	4.772	4.607	4.451	4.303	4.163	4.031
10	5.889	5.650	5.246	5.216	5.019	4.833	4.659	4.494	4.339	4.192
11	6.207	5.938	5.687	5.453	5.234	5.029	4.836	4.656	4.487	4.327
12	6.492	6.194	5.918	5.660	5.421	5.197	4.988	4.793	4.611	4.439
13	6.750	6.424	6.122	5.842	5.583	5.342	5.118	4.910	4.715	4.533
14	6.982	6.628	6.303	6.002	5.724	5.468	5.229	5.008	4.802	4.611
15	7.191	6.811	6.462	6.142	5.847	5.575	5.324	5.092	4.876	4.675
16	7.379	6.974	6.604	6.265	5.954	5.669	5.405	5.162	4.938	4.730
17	7.549	7.120	6.729	6.373	6.047	5.749	5.475	5.222	4.990	4.775
18	7.702	7.250	6.840	6.467	6.128	5.818	5.534	5.273	5.033	4.812
19	7.839	7.366	6.938	6.550	6.198	5.877	5.585	5.316	5.070	4.843
20	7.963	7.469	7.025	6.623	6.259	5.929	5.628	5.353	5.101	4.870
21	8.075	7.562	7.102	6.687	6.312	5.973	5.665	5.384	5.127	4.891
22	8.176	7.645	7.170	6.743	6.359	6.011	5.696	5.410	5.149	4.909
23	8.266	7.718	7.230	6.792	6.399	6.044	5.723	5.432	5.167	4.925
24	8.348	7.784	7.283	6.835	6.434	6.073	5.747	5.451	5.182	4.937
25	8.422	7.843	7.330	6.873	6.464	6.097	5.766	5.467	5.195	4.948
30	8.694	8.055	7.496	7.003	6.566	6.177	5.829	5.517	5.235	4.979
40	8.951	8.244	7.634	7.105	6.642	6.233	5.871	5.548	5.258	4.997
50	9.042	8.305	7.675	7.133	6.661	6.246	5.880	5.554	5.262	4.999

n	21%	22%	23%	24%	25%	26%	27%	28%	29%	30%
1	.826	.820	.813	.806	.800	.794	.787	.781	.775	.769
2	1.509	1.492	1.474	1.457	1.440	1.424	1.407	1.392	1.376	1.361
3	2.074	2.042	2.011	1.981	1.952	1.923	1.896	1.868	1.842	1.816
4	2.540	2.494	2.448	2.404	2.362	2.320	2.280	2.241	2.203	2.166
5	2.926	2.864	2.803	2.745	2.689	2.635	2.583	2.532	2.483	2.436
6	3.245	3.167	3.092	3.020	2.951	2.885	2.821	2.759	2.700	2.643
7	3.508	3.416	3.327	3.242	3.161	3.083	3.009	2.937	2.868	2.802
8	3.726	3.619	3.518	3.421	3.329	3.241	3.156	3.076	2.999	2.925
9	3.905	3.786	3.673	3.566	3.463	3.366	3.273	3.184	3.100	3.019
10	4.054	3.923	3.799	3.682	3.570	3.465	3.364	3.269	3.178	3.092
11	4.177	4.035	3.902	3.776	3.656	3.544	3.437	3.335	3.329	3.147
12	4.278	4.127	3.985	3.851	3.725	3.606	3.493	3.387	3.286	3.190
13	4.362	4.203	4.053	3.912	3.780	3.656	3.538	3.427	3.322	3.223
14	4.432	4.265	4.108	3.962	3.824	3.695	3.573	3.459	3.351	3.249
15	4.489	4.315	4.153	4.001	3.859	3.726	3.601	3.483	3.373	3.268
16	4.536	4.357	4.189	4.003	3.887	3.751	3.623	3.503	3.390	3.283
17	4.576	4.391	4.219	4.059	3.910	3.771	3.640	3.518	3.403	3.295
18	4.608	4.419	4.243	4.080	3.928	3.786	3.654	3.529	3.413	3.304
19	4.635	4.442	4.263	4.097	3.942	3.799	3.664	3.539	3.421	3.311
20	4.657	4.460	4.279	4.110	3.954	3.808	3.673	3.546	3.427	3.316
21	4.675	4.476	4.292	4.121	3.963	3.816	3.679	3.551	3.432	3.320
22	4.690	4.488	4.302	4.130	3.970	3.822	3.684	3.556	3.436	3.323
23	4.703	4.499	4.311	4.137	3.976	3.827	3.689	3.559	3.438	3.325
24	4.713	4.507	4.318	4.143	3.981	3.831	3.692	3.562	3.441	3.327
25	4.721	4.514	4.323	4.147	3.985	3.834	3.694	3.564	3.442	3.329
30	4.746	4.534	4.339	4.160	3.995	3.842	3.701	3.569	3.447	3.332
40	4.760	4.544	4.347	4.166	3.999	3.846	3.703	3.571	3.448	3.333
50	4.762	4.545	4.348	4.167	4.000	3.846	3.704	3.571	3.448	3.333

n	31%	32%	33%	34%	35%	36%	37%	38%	39%	40%
1	.763	.758	.752	.746	.741	.735	.730	.725	.719	.714
2	1.346	1.331	1.317	1.303	1.289	1.276	1.263	1.250	1.237	1.224
3	1.791	1.766	1.742	1.719	1.696	1.673	1.652	1.630	1.609	1.589
4	2.130	2.096	2.062	2.029	1.997	1.966	1.935	1.906	1.877	1.849
5	2.390	2.345	2.302	2.260	2.220	2.181	2.143	2.106	2.070	2.035
6	2.588	2.534	2.483	2.433	2.385	2.339	2.294	2.251	2.209	2.168
7	2.739	2.677	2.619	2.562	2.508	2.455	2.404	2.355	2.308	2.263
8	2.854	2.786	2.721	2.658	2.598	2.540	2.485	2.432	2.380	2.331
9	2.942	2.868	2.798	2.730	2.665	2.603	2.544	2.487	2.432	2.379
10	3.009	2.930	2.855	2.784	2.715	2.649	2.587	2.527	2.469	2.414
11	3.060	2.978	2.899	2.824	2.752	2.683	2.618	2.555	2.496	2.438
12	3.100	3.013	2.931	2.853	2.779	2.708	2.641	2.576	2.515	2.456
13	3.129	3.040	2.956	2.876	2.799	2.727	2.658	2.592	2.529	2.469
14	3.152	3.061	2.974	2.892	2.814	2.740	2.670	2.603	2.539	2.477
15	3.170	3.076	2.988	2.905	2.825	2.750	2.679	2.611	2.546	2.484
16	3.183	3.088	2.999	2.914	2.834	2.757	2.685	2.616	2.551	2.489
17	3.193	3.097	3.007	2.921	2.840	2.763	2.690	2.621	2.555	2.492
18	3.201	3.104	3.012	2.926	2.844	2.767	2.693	2.624	2.557	2.494
19	3.207	3.109	3.017	2.930	2.848	2.770	2.696	2.626	2.559	2.496
20	3.211	3.113	3.020	2.933	2.850	2.772	2.698	2.627	2.561	2.497
21	3.215	3.116	3.023	2.935	2.852	2.773	2.699	2.629	2.562	2.498
22	3.217	3.118	3.025	2.936	2.853	2.775	2.700	2.629	2.562	2.498
23	3.219	3.120	3.026	2.938	2.854	2.775	2.701	2.630	2.563	2.499
24	3.221	3.121	3.027	2.939	2.855	2.776	2.701	2.630	2.563	2.499
25	3.222	3.122	3.028	2.939	2.856	2.776	2.702	2.631	2.563	2.499
30	3.225	3.124	3.030	2.941	2.857	2.777	2.702	2.631	2.564	2.500
40	3.226	3.125	3.030	2.941	2.857	2.778	2.703	2.632	2.564	2.500
50	3.226	3.125	3.030	2.941	2.857	2.778	2.703	2.632	2.564	2.500

APPENDIX F

CHECK FIGURES FOR SELECTED END-OF-CHAPTER STUDY PROBLEMS

CHAPTER 1

1-1. Taxable income = $526,800
Tax liability = $179,112

1-3. Taxable income = $365,000
Tax liability = $124,100

1-5. Taxable income = ($38,000)
Tax liability = $0

1-7. Taxable income = $153,600
Tax liability = $43,154

1-9. Taxable income = $370,000
Tax liability = $125,800

1-11. Taxable income = $1,813,000
Tax liability = $616,420

CHAPTER 2

2-1. Inferred real rate on Treasury bills: 0.06%
Inferred real rate on Treasury bonds: 2.51%

2-3. 11.28%

2-5. 12.35%

CHAPTER 3

3-1.

Total current assets	$32,650
Net buildings and equipment	$88,000
Total assets	$120,650
Total current liabilities	$5,400
Total liabilities	$60,400
Total equity	$60,250
Gross profits	$7,050
Operating income (EBIT)	$5,700
Net income	$3,360

3-3.

Total current assets	$491,800
Net fixed assets	$632,000
Total assets	$1,123,800
Total current liabilities	$237,900
Total liabilities	$571,900
Total equity	$551,900
Total liabilities and equity	$1,123,800
Gross profits	$276,000
Operating income (EBIT)	$131,000
Net income	$75,750

3-5.

After-tax cash flows from operations	$190
Increase in operating working capital	$135
Increase in fixed assets	$55
Free cash flows	$0

3-7.

After-tax cash flows from operations	$442
Increase in operating working capital	$50
Increase in gross fixed assets	$400
Free cash flows	($8)
Interest expense	$64
Common stock dividends	$78
Financing cash flows	$8

3-9.

After-tax cash flows from operations	$64,000
Increase in current assets	$5,000
Change in non-interest bearing current liabilities	$0
Increase in operating working capital	$5,000
Increase in fixed assets	$73,000
Interest paid to investors	$4,000
Decrease in long-term debt	$70,000
Common stock dividends	$22,000

CHAPTER 4

4-1. $429,000

4-3. a. Gross profit $288,000; operating income $158,000; net income $93,200
b. Ooperating profit margin 39.5%
c. Times interest earned 9.41

4-5. $500,000

4-7. a. Total asset turnover = 2
b. Increase in sales = $7.5m
Percentage increase = 75%
c. For last year, OROA = 20%
Projected OROA = 35%

4-9.

Current ratio	4.0x
Acid-test (quick) ratio	1.92x
Average collection period	107 days
Inventory turnover	1.36x
Operating return on assets	13.8%
Operating profit margin	24.8%
Total asset turnover	0.56x
Inventory turnover	1.36x
Fixed asset turnover	1.04x
Debt ratio	34.6%
Times interest earned	5.63x
Return on common equity	10.5%

4-11. a. Current ratio = 1.84
b. Acid-test ratio = 0.72
c. Debt ratio = 0.55
d. Times interest earned = 8
e. Inventory turnover = 5.48
f. Fixed asset turnover = 2.22
g. Return on equity = 23.4%

CHAPTER 5

5-1. a. $12,970
c. $3,019.40

5-2. a. n = 15 years

5-3. b. 5%
c. 9%

5-4. b. PV = $235.20

5-5. a. $6,289
c. $302.89

5-6. c. $1,562.96

5-7. a. FV_1 = $10,600
FV_5 = $13,380
FV_{15} = $23,970

5-9. a. $6,690
b. Semiannual: $6,720   Bimonthly: $6,740

5-11. Year 1: 18,000 books
Year 2: 21,600 books
Year 3: 25,920 books

5-13. $6,108.11

5-15. 8%

5-17. $658,197.85

5-21. b. $8,333.33

5-24. $6,509

5-26. 22%

5-27. $6,934.81

5-30. a. $1,989.73

5-33. $15,912

5-42. $2,054.81

5-45. $485.65

5-48. $18,071.11

5-50. b. 11.6123%

CHAPTER 6

6-1. $\bar{k} = 9.85\%$; $\sigma^2 = 6.99\%$; $\sigma = 2.64\%$

6-3. A: $\bar{k} = 16.7\%$; $\sigma^2 = 102.6\%$; $\sigma = 10.13\%$

B: $\bar{k} = 9.2\%$; $\sigma^2 = 12.76\%$; $\sigma = 3.57\%$

6-5. The beta is approximately 0.5.

6-7. 10.94%

6-9. a. Jazmon: For time = 4, 30%; Solomon for time = 3, 14.29%

6-11. a. 15.8%

b. 0.95

CHAPTER 7

7-1. a. 8%

b. $744.59

7-3. a. $865.80

b. 22%

7-5. a. Series A: For 5%, $1,310.21; for 8%, $1,037.68; for 12%, $783.20

Series B: For 5%, $1,033.33; for 8%, $1,004.63; for 12%, $968.75

7-7. 4.45%

7-9. 5.28%

7-11. a. $863.78

b. Market value $707.63 when required rate of return is 15%

Market value $1,171.19 when required rate of return is 8%

7-13. $547

CHAPTER 8

8-1. Stock A: Expected return = 12.86%

Stock B: Expected return = 11.81%

8-3. a. 6.33%

b. 14.96%

8-5. $116.67

8-7. a. 8.5%

b. $42.50

8-9. a. 18.9%

b. $28.57

8-11. 7.2%

8-13. $39.96

8-15. a. 10.91%

b. $36

8-17. $50

8-19.

Years	1	2	3	4	5	6
Free Cash Flows	$52	$59	$110	$120	$131	$209
Shareholder Value	$1,949					

CHAPTER 9

9-1. a. $IRR = 7\%$

b. $IRR = 17\%$

9-3. a. IRR = approximately 19%

9-5. a. payback period = 4 years

9-7. a. Project A:

Payback period = 2.5 years

9-13. b. $MIRR = 15.0749\%$

9-14. a. $NPV_A = \$136.30$

$NPV_B = \$455$

b. $PI_A = 1.2726$

$PI_B = 1.09$

c. $IRR_A = 40\%$

$IRR_B = 20\%$

CHAPTER 10

10-1. a. $6,800

b. $3,400

c. No taxes

d. $1,020

10-3. Free Cash Flow = $404,500

10-6. Operating cash flows = $1,522,000

10-9. a. $110,000

b. Free Cash Flow = $33,600

10-11. d. $NPV = \$106,477$

CHAPTER 11

11-1. a. $k_d(1 - t) = 6.53\%$

b. $k_{nc} = 14.37\%$

c. $k_c = 15.14\%$

d. $k_p = 8.77\%$

e. $k_d(1 - t) = 7.92\%$

11-3. $k_{nc} = 12.06\%$

11-5. $k_p = 9.23\%$

11-7. $k_p = 14.29\%$

11-9. a. $k_c = 17.59\%$

b. $k_{nc} = 18.25\%$

11-11. $P_0 = \$935.82$

$NP_0 = \$837.56$

Number of bonds = 597

$k_d(1 - t) = 7.08\%$

11-13. a.

	Incentive Compensation		
	80%	100%	120%
CEO	$540,000	$675,000	$810,000

b.

	60%	150%
CEO	$405,000	$1,012,500

11-15. a. 11.11%

b. 10.62%

11-17.

Years	2002	2003	2004	2005	2006
a. EVA	$17,600	27,408	18,500	4,320	-20,405

CHAPTER 12

12-1. a. $20,205,179.28

b. 55.5%

12-3. b. 45.85%

c. $479,825.52

12-7. a. $F = \$780,000$

b. $S_B = \$1,560,000$

12-9. a. $P = \$6.875$ (selling price per unit)

12-10. a. 1,200 units

b. $600,000

c. $1.316 times

d. 26.32%

12-13. a. EBIT 5 $2,000,000

b. EPS will be $1.00 for each plan

d. Plan B

CHAPTER 13

13-2. 95,238 shares; $11,428,560

13-6. 163,743 shares; $15,555,556

CHAPTER 14

14-1. Total assets = $11.75 million

14-3. Total assets = $1.8 million

Fixed assets = $1 million

14-5.

Cash	$526,712
Accounts receivable	$123,288
Current liabilities	$700,000
Net fixed assets	$600,000
Total assets	$2,000,000

14-9. a. Notes payable $1.11 million

b. Current ratio (before) 5 2 times

Current ratio (after) = 1.12 times

14-11. Cumulative borrowing (March) = $59,000

Ending cash balance (June) = $107,724

14-13. a. $117,000

b. $133,000

CHAPTER 15

15-1.   Rate = 13.79%

15-3.   a. Rate = 36.73%
         b. Rate = 74.23%

15-7.   a. Rate = 16.27%

15-11.   a. APR = 10%
         b. APR = 11.76%
         c. APR = 12.5%

15-13.   a. 9.8%
         b. Yes

CHAPTER 16

16-1.   b. Break-even yield is 8.0%.

16-3.   Yes; the company will save $250,000 annually by switching to the new concentration-banking system.

16-6.   a. Need to speed up collections by more than 0.5214 day.
         b. Cash collections would have to be accelerated by more than 0.8110 day.

16-8.   a. $4 million
         b. $240,000
         c. $48,600
         d. Yes, net annual gain = $191,400

16-12.   a. $912.44
         b. The loss will be $87.56.
         c. The capital loss here would be only $17.59.
         d. Interest rate risk. Thus leads to the maturity premium discussed in Chapter 2.

16-14.   a. 36.36%
         b. 36.73%
         c. 55.67%

16-16.   a. Average inventory = $90,000
         b. $53,333

16-18.   a. EOQ = 7,071 units, or rounded to 7,100
         b. 35.2 orders per year

CHAPTER 17

17-1.   a. $8,437
         b. $9,368
         c. $25,695

17-3.   Canada; 1.1853; 1.1881; 1.1912
         Japan: 213.4927; 211.9992; 209.1613
         Switzerland: 1.9459; 1.9346; 1.8815

17-5.   Net gain = $149.02

accounting book value the value of an asset as shown on a firm's balance sheet. It represents the historical cost of the asset rather than its current market value or replacement cost.

accounts payable (trade credit) money owed to suppliers for goods or services purchased in the ordinary course of business.

accounts receivable turnover ratio a firm's credit sales divided by its accounts receivable. This ratio expresses how often accounts receivable are "rolled over" during a year.

accounts receivable money owed by customers who purchased goods or services from the firm on credit.

accrual basis accounting a method of accounting whereby revenue is recorded when it is earned, whether or not the revenue has been received in cash. Likewise, expenses are recorded when they are incurred, even if the money has not actually been paid out.

accrued expenses expenses that have been incurred but not yet paid in cash.

accumulated depreciation the sum of all depreciation taken over the entire life of a depreciable asset.

acid-test (quick) ratio a firm's current assets and accounts receivable divided by its current liabilities. This ratio is a more stringent measure of liquidity than the current ratio in that it excludes inventories and other current assets (those that are least liquid) from current assets.

additional paid-in capital the amount a company receives from selling stock to investors above par value.

agency costs the costs, such as a reduced stock price, associated with potential conflict between managers and investors when these two groups are not the same.

agency problem problems and conflicts resulting from the separation of the management and ownership of the firm.

amortized loan a loan that is paid off in equal periodic payments.

annual percentage yield (APY) or **effective annual rate (EAR)** the annual compound rate that produces the same return as the nominal, or quoted, rate when something is compounded on a nonannual basis. In effect, the APY, or EAR, provides the true rate of return.

annuity due an annuity in which the payments occur at the beginning of each period.

annuity a series of equal dollar payments made for a specified number of years.

anticipatory buying buying in anticipation of a price increase to secure goods at a lower cost

arbitrageur an individual involved in the process of buying and selling in more than one market to make a riskless profit.

asked rate the rate the bank or the foreign exchange trader "asks" the customer to pay in home currency for foreign currency when the bank is selling and the customer is buying. The asked rate is also known as the selling rate or the offer rate.

asset allocation identifying and selecting the asset classes appropriate for a specific investment portfolio and determining the proportions of those assets within the portfolio.

asset efficiency how well a firm is managing its assets.

average collection period a firm's accounts receivable divided by the company's average daily credit sales (annual credit sales ÷ 365). This ratio expresses how rapidly the firm is collecting its credit accounts.

balance sheet a statement that shows a firm's assets, liabilities, and shareholder equity at a given point in time. It is a snapshot of the firm's financial position on a particular date.

beta the relationship between an investment's returns and the market's returns. This is a measure of the investment's nondiversifiable risk.

bid rate the rate at which the bank buys the foreign currency from the customer by paying in home currency. The bid rate is also known as the buying rate.

bid-asked spread the difference between the asked quote and the bid quote.

bird-in-the-hand dividend theory the view that dividends are more certain than capital gains.

bond a long-term (10-year or more) promissory note issued by the borrower, promising to pay the owner of the security a predetermined, fixed amount of interest each year.

book value (1) the value of an asset as shown on the firm's balance sheet. It represents the historical cost of the asset rather than its current market value or replacement cost. (2) The depreciated value of a company's assets (original cost less accumulated depreciation) less outstanding liabilities.

budget an itemized forecast of a company's expected revenues and expenses for a future period.

business risk the relative dispersion or variability in the firm's expected earnings before interest and taxes (EBIT). The nature of the firm's operations causes its business risk. This type of risk is affected by the firm's cost structure, product demand characteristics, and intra-industry competitive position. In capital structure theory, business risk is distinguished from financial risk. Compare **Financial Risk**

buying rate the rate at which the bank buys the foreign currency from the customer by paying in home currency. The buying rate is also known as the bid rate.

call protection period a prespecified time period during which a company cannot recall a bond.

call provision a provision that entitles the corporation to repurchase its preferred stock from investors at stated prices over specified periods.

callable bond (redeemable bond) an option available to a company issuing a bond whereby the issuer can call (redeem) the bond before it matures. This is usually done if interest rates decline below what the firm is paying on the bond.

capital asset pricing model (CAPM) an equation stating that the expected rate of return on a project is a function of (1) the risk-free rate, (2) the investment's systematic risk, and (3) the expected risk premium for the market portfolio of all risky securities.

capital budgeting the process of decision making with respect to investments made in fixed assets that is, should a proposed project be accepted or rejected.

capital gain (or loss) as defined by the revenue code, a gain or loss resulting from the sale or exchange of a capital asset.

capital market all institutions and procedures that facilitate transactions in long-term financial instruments.

capital rationing placing a limit on the dollar size of the capital budget.

capital structure the mix of long-term sources of funds used by the firm. This is also called the firm's capitalization. The relative total (percentage) of each type of fund is emphasized

capital structure the mix of long-term sources of funds used by the firm. This is also called the firm's capitalization. The relative total (percentage) of each type of fund is emphasized

cash budget   a detailed plan of future cash flows. This budget is composed of four elements: cash receipts, cash disbursements, net change in cash for the period, and new financing needed

cash   cash on hand, demand deposits, and short-term marketable securities that can quickly be converted into cash.

cash   currency and coins plus demand deposit accounts

characteristic line   the line of "best fit" through a series of returns for a firm's stock relative to the market's returns. The slope of the line, frequently called beta, represents the average movement of the firm's stock returns in response to a movement in the market's returns.

chattel mortgage agreement   a loan agreement in which the lender can increase his or her security interest by having specific items of inventory identified in the loan agreement. The borrower retains title to the inventory but cannot sell the items without the lender's consent

clientele effect   the belief that individuals and institutions that need current income will invest in companies that have high dividend payouts. Other investors prefer to avoid taxes by holding securities that offer only small dividend income but large capital gains. Thus, we have a "clientele" of investors.

commercial paper   short-term unsecured promissory notes sold by large businesses in order to raise cash. Unlike most other money-market instruments, commercial paper has no developed secondary market

common stock   shares that represent ownership in a corporation.

common stock   shares that represent the ownership in a corporation.

common stockholders   investors who own the firm's common stock. Common stockholders are the residual owners of the firm.

common-sized balance sheet   a balance sheet in which a firm's assets and sources of debt and equity are expressed as a percentage of its total assets.

common-sized income statement   an income statement in which a firm's expenses and profits are expressed as a percentage of its sales.

company-unique risk   see Unsystematic risk.

compensating balance   a balance of a given amount that the firm maintains in its demand deposit account. It may be required by either a formal or informal agreement with the firm's commercial bank. Such balances are usually required by the bank (1) on the unused portion of a loan commitment, (2) on the unpaid portion of an outstanding loan, or (3) in exchange for certain services provided by the bank, such as check-clearing or credit information. These balances raise the effective rate of interest paid on borrowed funds

competitive-advantage period   the number of years a firm's managers believes it can sustain a competitive advantage, given the company's present strategies.

compound annuity   depositing an equal sum of money at the end of each year for a certain number of years and allowing it to grow.

compound interest   the situation in which interest paid on an investment during the first period is added to the principal. During the second period, interest is earned on the original principal plus the interest earned during the first period.

constant dividend payout ratio   a dividend payment policy in which the percentage of earnings paid out in dividends is held constant. The dollar amount fluctuates from year to year as profits vary.

contribution-to-firm risk   the amount of risk that the project contributes to the firm as a whole; this measure considers the fact that some of the project's risk will be diversified away as the project is combined with the firm's other projects and assets, but ignores the effects of diversification of the firm's shareholders.

convertible bond   a debt security that can be converted into a firm's stock at a prespecified price.

convertible preferred stock   preferred shares that can be converted into a predetermined number of shares of common stock, if investors so choose.

corporation   an entity that legally functions separate and apart from its owners.

cost of goods sold   the cost of producing or acquiring a product or service to be sold in the ordinary course of business.

coupon interest rate   the interest rate contractually owed on a bond as a percent of its par value.

covered-interest arbitrage   designed to eliminate differentials across currency and interest rate markets.

credit scoring   the numerical evaluation of credit applicants where the score is evaluated relative to a predetermined standard

cross rate   the computation of an exchange rate for a currency from the exchange rates of two other currencies.

cumulative feature   a requirement that all past, unpaid preferred stock dividends be paid before any common stock dividends are declared.

cumulative voting   voting in which each share of stock allows the shareholder a number of votes equal to the number of directors being elected. The shareholder can then cast all of his or her votes for a single candidate or split them among the various candidates.

currency swaps   the exchange of principal and interest in one currency for the same in another currency for an agreed period of time.

current assets (gross working capital)   current assets consist primarily of cash, marketable securities, accounts receivable, inventories, and prepaid expenses.

current debt (short-term liabilities)   due to be paid within 12 months.

current ratio   a firm's current assets divided by its current liabilities. This ratio indicates the firm's degree of liquidity by comparing its current assets to its current liabilities.

current yield   the ratio of a bond's annual interest payment to its market price.

date of record   date at which the stock transfer books are to be closed for determining the investor to receive the next dividend payment.

debenture   any unsecured long-term debt.

debt capacity   the maximum proportion of debt that the firm can include in its capital structure and still maintain its lowest composite cost of capital

debt ratio   a firm's total liabilities divided by its total assets. It is a ratio that measures the extent to which a firm has been financed with debt.

debt ratio   a firm's total liabilities divided by its total assets. This ratio measures the extent to which a firm has been financed with debt.

debt   liabilities consisting of such sources as credit extended by suppliers or a loan from a bank.

declaration date   the date upon which a dividend is formally declared by the board of directors.

delivery-time stock   the inventory needed between the order date and the receipt of the inventory ordered

depreciation expense   a noncash expense to allocate the cost of depreciable assets, such as plant and equipment, over the life of the asset.

depreciation   the means by which an asset's value is expensed over its useful life for federal income tax purposes.

direct costs   see **Variable Costs**

direct quote   the exchange rate that indicates the number of units of the home currency required to buy one unit of foreign currency.

direct sale   the sale of securities by a corporation to the investing public without the services of an investment-banking firm.

discount bond   a bond that sells at a discount, or below par value.

discretionary financing   sources of financing that require an explicit decision on the part of the firm's management every time funds are raised. An example is a bank note that requires that negotiations be undertaken and an agreement signed setting forth the terms and conditions of the financing

diversifiable risk   see Unsystematic risk.

dividend payout ratio   the amount of dividends relative to the company's net income or earnings per share.

dividend-payout ratio   dividends as a percentage of earnings.

dividends per share   the amount of dividends a firm pays for each share outstanding.

Dutch auction   a method of issuing securities (common stock) where investors place bids indicating how many shares they are willing to buy and at what price. The price the stock is then sold for becomes the lowest price at which the issuing company can sell all the available shares.

earnings before taxes (taxable income) operating income minus interest expense.

earnings per share   net income on a per share basis.

EBIT-EPS indifference point   the level of earnings before interest and taxes (EBIT) that will equate earnings per share (EPS) between two different financing plans

economic exposure   the impact of exchange rate changes on the value of the firm including both the strategic impact of comparative relationships arising from exchange rate change and the economic impact of transaction exposure.

economic profit   differs from accounting profit in that it incorporates explicit consideration for opportunity cost of equity financing, as well as debt financing.

efficient market   a market in which the prices of securities at any instant in time fully reflect all publicly available information about the securities and their actual public values.

equity   stockholders' investment in the firm and the cumulative profits retained in the business up to the date of the balance sheet.

equivalent annual annuity (EAA)   an annuity cash flow that yields the same present value as the project's *NPV*.

eurobond   a bond issued in a country different from the one in which the currency of the bond is denominated; for example, a bond issued in Europe or Asia by an American company that pays interest and principal to the lender in U.S. dollars.

exchange rate risk   the risk that tomorrow's exchange rate will differ from today's rate.

exchange rate   the price of a foreign currency stated in terms of the domestic or home currency.

ex-dividend date   the date upon which stock brokerage companies have uniformly decided to terminate the right of ownership to the dividend, which is two days prior to the date of record.

expectations theory   the concept that, no matter what the decision area, how the market price responds to management's actions is not determined entirely by the action itself; it is also affected by investors' expectations about the ultimate decision to be made by management.

expected rate of return   (1) the discount rate that equates the present value of the future cash flows of a bond (interest and maturity value) with the current market price of the bond. It is the rate of return an investor will earn if the bond is held to maturity. (2) The rate of return the investor expects to receive on an investment by paying the market price of the security. (3) The arithmetic mean or average of all possible outcomes where those outcomes are weighted by the probability that each will occur.

expected rate of return   (1) the discount rate that equates the present value of the future cash flows (interest and maturity value) of a bond with its current market price. It is the rate of return an investor will earn if the bond is held to maturity. (2) The rate of return the investor expects to receive on an investment by paying the existing market price of the security.

expected rate of return   (1) the discount rate that equates the present value of the future cash flows (interest and maturity value) of a bond with the current market price of the bond. It is the rate of return an investor will earn if the bond is held to

maturity. (2) The rate of return investors expect to receive on an investment by paying the current market price of the security. (3) The arithmetic mean, or average, of all possible outcomes where those outcomes are weighted by the probability that each will occur.

external financing needs   that portion of a firm's requirements for financing that exceeds its sources of internal financing (i.e., the retention of earnings) plus spontaneous sources of financing (e.g., trade credit).

factor   a firm that, in acquiring the receivables of other firms, bears the risk of collection and, for a fee, services the accounts

factoring accounts receivable   the outright sale of a firm's accounts receivable to another party (the factor) without recourse. The factor, in turn, bears the risk of collection

fair value   the present value of an asset's expected future cash flows.

field warehouse agreement   a security agreement in which inventories pledged as collateral are physically separated from the firm's other inventories and placed under the control of a third-party field-warehousing firm

financial leverage   the use of securities bearing a fixed (limited) rate of return to finance a portion of a firm's assets. Financial leverage can arise from the use of either debt or preferred stock financing. The use of financial leverage exposes the firm to financial risk

financial policy   the firm's policies regarding the sources of financing it plans to use and the particular mix (proportions) in which they will be used

financial ratios   accounting data restated in relative terms in order to help people identify some of the financial strengths and weaknesses of a company.

financial structure   the mix of all funds sources that appears on the right-hand side of the balance sheet

financing cash flows   cash flows paid to or received from investors and lenders.

financing cost   cost incurred by a company that often includes interest expenses and preferred dividends.

finished-goods inventory   goods on which the production has been completed but that are not yet sold

fixed asset turnover   a firm's sales divided by its net fixed assets. This ratio indicates how efficiently the firm is using its fixed assets.

fixed assets   assets such as equipment, buildings, and land.

fixed costs   costs that do not vary in total dollar amount as sales volume or quantity of output changes. Also called indirect costs

float   the length of time from when a check is written until the actual recipient can draw upon or use the "good funds."

floating lien agreement   an agreement, generally associated with a loan, whereby the borrower gives the lender a lien against all its inventory

floating-rate international currency system   a system in which the exchange rates of different currencies are allowed to fluctuate with supply and demand conditions.

flotation costs   the transaction cost incurred when a firm raises funds by issuing a particular type of security.

forward exchange contract   a forward contract that requires delivery, at a specified future date, of one currency for a specified amount of another currency.

forward transactionan agreement today to deliver a specified number of units of a currency on a future date in return for a specified number of units of another currency.

forward-spot differential   the premium or discount between forward and spot currency exchange rates.

free cash flow valuation   valuing a firm as the present value of its expected future cash flows.

free cash flows   the amount of cash available from operations after the firm pays for the investments it has made in operating working capital and fixed assets. This cash is available to distribute to the firm's creditors and owners.

future-value interest factor ($FVIF_{i, n}$)   the value $(1 \ 1 \ i)^n$ used as a multiplier to calculate an amount's future value.

future-value interest factor for an annuity ($FVIFA_{i,n}$)   the value used as a multiplier to calculate the future value of an annuity.

general partnership   a partnership in which all partners are fully liable for the indebtedness incurred by the partnership.

gross fixed assets   the original cost of a firm's fixed assets.

gross income   a firm's dollar sales from its product or services less the cost of producing or acquiring them.

gross profit margin   gross profit divided by net sales. It is a ratio denoting the gross profit earned by the firm as a percentage of its net sales.

gross profit   sales or revenue minus the cost of goods sold.

hedging principle (principle of self-liquidating debt)   a working-capital management policy which states that the cash flow–generating characteristics of a firm's investments should be matched with the cash flow requirements of the firm's sources of financing. Very simply, short-lived assets should be financed with short-term sources of financing while long-lived assets should be financed with long-term sources of financing

high-yield bond   see Junk bond.

holding-period return   the return an investor would receive from holding a security for a designated period of time. For example, a monthly holding-period return would be the return for holding a security for a month.

income statement (profit and loss statement)   a basic accounting statement that measures the results of a firm's operations over a specified period, commonly 1 year. Also known as the profit and loss statement. The bottom line of the income statement shows the firm's profit or loss for the period.

incremental after-tax free cash flows   the funds that the firm receives and is able to reinvest, as opposed to accounting profits, which are shown when they are earned rather than when the money is actually in hand.

incremental cash flow   the cash flows that result from the acceptance of a project the firm takes on.

indenture   the legal agreement between the firm issuing bonds and the bond trustee who represents the bondholders, providing the specific terms of the loan agreement.

indirect costs   see **Fixed Costs**

indirect quote   the exchange rate that expresses the number of units of a foreign currency that can be bought for one unit of the home currency.

information asymmetry   the difference in accessibility to information between managers and investors, which may result in a lower stock price than would be true in conditions of certainty.

initial outlay   the immediate cash outflow necessary to purchase the asset and put it in operating order.

initial public offering, IPO   the first time a company issues its stock to the public.

insolvency   the inability to meet interest payments or to repay debt at maturity

interest rate parity (IRP) theory   a theory that states that (except for the effects of small transaction costs) the forward premium or discount should be equal and opposite in size to the difference in the national interest rates for securities of the same maturity.

interest rate risk   (1) the variability in a bond's value (risk) caused by changing interest rates. (2) The uncertainty that envelops the expected returns from a security caused by changes in interest rates. Price changes induced by interest rate changes are greater for long-term than for short-term financial instruments.

internal growth   a firm's growth rate resulting from reinvesting the company's profits rather than distributing them as dividends. The growth rate is a function of the amount retained and the return earned on the retained funds.

internal rate of return (IRR)   the rate of return that the project earns. For computational purposes, the internal rate of return is defined as the discount rate that equates the present value of the project's free cash flows with the project's initial cash outlay.

intrinsic, or economic, value   the present value of an asset's expected future cash flows. This value is the amount the investor considers to be fair value, given the amount, timing, and riskiness of future cash flows.

inventories   raw materials, work in progress, and finished goods held by the firm for eventual sale.

inventory loans   loans secured by inventories. Examples include floating or blanket lien agreements, chattel mortgage agreements, field-warehouse receipt loans, and terminal-warehouse receipt loans

inventory management   the control of assets used in the production process or produced to be sold in the normal course of the firm's operations

inventory turnover   a firm's cost of goods sold divided by its inventory. This ratio measures the number of times a firm's inventories are sold and replaced during the year, that is, the relative liquidity of the inventories.

investment banker   a financial specialist who underwrites and distributes new securities and advises corporate clients about raising new funds.

junk bond   any bond rated BB or below.

just-in-time inventory control system   aproduction and management system in which inventory is cut down to a minimum through adjustments to the time and physical distance between the various production operations. Under this system the firm keeps a minimum level of inventory on hand, relying upon suppliers to furnish parts "just in time" for them to be assembled

law of one price   a proposition that in competitive markets in which there are no transportation costs or barriers to trade, the same goods sold in different countries sell for the same price if all the different prices are expressed in terms of the same currency.

limited liability company (LLC)   a cross between a partnership and a corporation under which the owners retain limited liability but the company is run and is taxed like a partnership.

limited liability   a protective provision whereby the investor is not liable for more than the amount he or she has invested in the firm.

limited partnership   a partnership in which one or more of the partners has limited liability, restricted to the amount of capital he or she invests in the partnership.

line of credit   generally an informal agreement or understanding between a borrower and a bank as to the maximum amount of credit the bank will provide the borrower at any one time. Under this type of agreement there is no "legal" commitment on the part of the bank to provide the stated credit

liquidation value   the dollar sum that could be realized if an asset were sold.

liquidity preference theory   the theory that the shape of the term structure of interest rates is determined by an investor's additional required interest rate in compensation of additional risks.

liquidity premium   the additional return required by investors for securities that cannot be quickly converted into cash at a reasonably predictable price.

liquidity   a firm's ability to pay its bills on time. Liquidity is related to the ease and quickness with which a firm can convert its noncash assets into cash, as well as the size of the firm's investment in noncash assets relative to its short-term liabilities.

long-term debt   loans from banks or other sources that lend money for longer than 12 months.

majority voting   voting in which each share of stock allows the shareholder one vote, and each position on the board of directors is voted on separately. As a result, a

majority of shares has the power to elect the entire board of directors.

marginal tax rate   the tax rate that would be applied to the next dollar of income.

market risk   see Systematic risk.

market segmentation theory   the theory that the shape of the term structure of interest rates implies that the rate of interest for a particular maturity is determined solely by demand and supply for a given maturity. This rate is independent of the demand and supply for securities having different maturities.

market value added (MVA)   the difference in the market value of a firm's total assets and their book value.

market value   the value observed in the marketplace.

marketable securities   security investments (financial assets) the firm can quickly convert to cash balances. Also known as near cash or near-cash assets

maturity premium   the additional return required by investors in longer-term securities to compensate them for the greater risk of price fluctuations on those securities caused by interest rate changes.

maturity   the length of time until the bond issuer returns the par value to the bondholder and terminates the bond.

money market   all institutions and procedures that facilitate transactions for short-term instruments issued by borrowers with very high credit ratings.

mortgage bond   a bond secured by a lien on real property.

mortgage   a loan to finance real estate where the lender has first claim on the property in the event the borrower is unable to repay the loan.

multinational corporation (MNC)   a corporation with holdings and/or operations in more than one country.

mutually exclusive projects   projects that, if undertaken, would serve the same purpose. Thus, accepting one will necessarily mean rejecting the others.

net fixed assets   gross fixed assets minus the accumulated depreciation taken over the life of the assets.

net income (earnings available to common stockholders)   a figure representing a firm's profit or loss for the period. It also represents the earnings available to the firm's common and preferred stockholders.

net operating loss carryback and carryforward   a tax provision that permits the taxpayer first to apply a loss against the profits earned in the 2 prior years

(carryback). If the loss has not been completely absorbed by the profits in these 2 years, it may be applied to taxable profits in each of the 20 following years (carryforward).

net present value (NPV)   the present value of an investment's annual free cash flows less the investment's initial outlay.

net present value profile   a graph showing how a project's *NPV* changes as the discount rate changes.

net profit margin   net income divided by sales. A ratio that measures the net income of the firm as a percent of sales.

net working capital   the difference between a firm's current assets and its current liabilities. When the term *working capital* is used, it is frequently intended to mean net working capital.

net working capital   the difference between the firm's current assets and its current liabilities

nominal rate of interest   the interest rate paid on debt securities without an adjustment for any loss in purchasing power.

nondiversifiable risk   see Systematic risk.

non-interest-bearing current liabilities (NIBCL)   current liabilities that incur no interest expense, such as accounts payable and accrued expenses.

operating expense   marketing and selling expenses, general and administrative expenses, and depreciation expense.

operating income (earnings before interest and taxes)   sales less the cost of goods sold less operating expenses.

operating leverage   the incurring of fixed operating costs in a firm's income stream

operating profit margin   a firm's operating income (earnings before interest and taxes) divided by sales. This ratio serves as an overall measure of operating effectiveness.

operating profit margin   operating income divided by sales. This ratio serves as an overall measure of the company's operating effectiveness.

operating return on assets (OROA)   the ratio of a firm's operating income divided by its total assets. This ratio indicates the rate of return being earned on the firm's assets.

operating working capital   the firm's current assets less its *non-interest-bearing* current liabilities (rather than *all* of its current liabilities).

opportunity cost of funds   the next-best rate of return available to the investor for a given level of risk.

optimal capital structure   the capital structure that minimizes the firm's composite cost of capital (maximizes the common stock price) for raising a given amount of funds

optimal range of financial leverage   the range of various capital structure combinations that yield the lowest overall cost of capital for the firm

order point problem   determining how low inventory should be depleted before it is reordered

order quantity problem   determining the optimal order size for an inventory item given its usage, carrying costs, and ordering costs

ordinary annuity   an annuity where the cash flows occur at the end of each period.

organized security exchanges   formal organizations that facilitate the trading of securities.

over-the-counter markets   all security markets except organized exchanges. The money market is an over-the-counter market. Most corporate bonds also are traded in this market.

par value   on the face of a bond, the stated amount that the firm is to repay upon the maturity date.

par value   on the face of a bond, the stated amount that the firm is to repay upon the maturity date.

partnership   an association of two or more individuals joining together as co-owners to operate a business for profit.

payable-through drafts (PTD)   a legal instrument that has the physical appearance of an ordinary check but is not drawn on a bank. A payable-through draft is drawn on and paid by the issuing firm. The bank serves as a collection point and passes the draft on to the firm

payback period   The number of years it takes to recapture a project's initial outlay.

payment date   the date on which the company mails a dividend check to each investor of record.

percent of sales method   a method of financial forecasting that involves estimating the level of an expense, asset, or liability for a future period as a percent of the sales forecast

perfect capital markets   an assumption that allows one to study the effect of dividend decisions in isolation. It assumes that (1) investors can buy and sell stocks without incurring any transaction costs, such as brokerage commissions; (2) companies can issue stocks without any cost of doing so;

(3) there are no corporate or personal taxes; (4) complete information about the firm is readily available; (5) there are no conflicts of interest between management and stockholders; and (6) financial distress and bankruptcy costs are nonexistent.

permanent investments   an investment that the firm expects to hold longer than one year. The firm makes permanent investments in fixed and current assets

perpetuity   an annuity with an infinite life.

pledging accounts receivable   a loan the firm obtains from a commercial bank or a finance company using its accounts receivable as collateral

portfolio beta   the relationship between a portfolio's returns and the market returns. It is a measure of the portfolio's nondiversifiable risk.

preemptive right   the right entitling the common shareholder to maintain his or her proportionate share of ownership in the firm.

preferred stock   a hybrid security with characteristics of both common stock and bonds. Preferred stock is similar to common stock in that it has no fixed maturity date, the nonpayment of dividends does not bring on bankruptcy, and dividends are not deductible for tax purposes. Preferred stock is similar to bonds in that dividends are limited in amount.

preferred stockholders   stockholders who have claims on the firm's income and assets after creditors, but before common stockholders.

premium bond   a bond that is selling above its par value.

present value   the value in today's dollars of a future payment discounted back to present at the required rate of return.

present-value interest factor ($PVIF_{i,\,n}$)   the value $[1/(1 + i)^n]$ used as a multiplier to calculate an amount's present value.

present-value interest factor for an annuity ($PVIFA_{i,\,n}$)   the value used as a multiplier to calculate the present value of an annuity.

price/book ratio   the market value of a share of the firm's stock divided by the book value per share of the firm's reported equity in the balance sheet.

price/earnings ratio   the price the market places on \$1 of a firm's earnings. For example, if a firm has an earnings per share of \$2, and a stock price of \$30 per share, its price/earnings ratio is 15 (\$30 ÷ \$2).

primary market   a market in which securities are offered for the first time for sale to potential investors.

private placement   a security offering limited to a small number of potential investors.

privileged subscription   the process of marketing a new security issue to a select group of investors.

profit margins   financial ratios (sometimes simply referred to as margins) that reflect the level of the firm's profits relative to its sales. Examples include the gross profit margin (gross profit divided by sales), operating profit margin (operating earnings divided by sales), and the net profit margin (net profit divided by sales).

profitability index (PI) or benefit–cost ratio   the ratio of the present value of an investment's future free cash flows to the investment's initial outlay.

profit-retention rate   the company's percentage of profits retained.

project standing alone risk   a project's risk ignoring the fact that much of this risk will be diversified away as the project is combined with the firm's other projects and assets.

protective provisions   provisions for preferred stock that protect the investor's interest. The provisions generally allow for voting in the event of nonpayment of dividends, or they restrict the payment of common stock dividends if sinking-fund payments are not met or if the firm is in financial difficulty.

proxy fight   a battle between rival groups for proxy votes in order to control the decisions made in a stockholders' meeting.

proxy   a means of voting in which a designated party is provided with the temporary power of attorney to vote for the signee at the corporation's annual meeting.

public offering   a security offering where all investors have the opportunity to acquire a portion of the financial claims being sold.

purchasing-power parity (PPP) theory   a theory that states that, in the long run, exchange rates adjust so that the purchasing power of each currency tends to be the same. Thus, exchange rate changes tend to reflect international differences in inflation rates.

pure play method   a method for estimating a project's or division's beta that attempts to identify publicly traded firms engaged solely in the same business as the project or division.

raw-materials inventory   the basic materials purchased from other firms to be used in the firm's production operations

real rate of interest   the nominal (quoted) rate of interest less any loss in purchasing power of the dollar during the time of the investment.

required rate of return   minimum rate of return necessary to attract an investor to purchase or hold a security.

residual dividend theory   a theory that a company's dividend payment should equal the cash left after financing all the investments that have positive net present values.

residual value   the present value of a firm's post-competitive-advantage period cash flows.

retained earnings   cumulative profits retained in a business up to the date of the balance sheet.

return on equity   a firm's net income divided by its common book equity. This ratio is the accounting rate of return earned on the common stockholders' investment.

revolving credit agreement   an understanding between the borrower and the bank as to the amount of credit the bank will be legally obligated to provide the borrower

right   a certificate issued to common stockholders giving them an option to purchase a stated number of new shares at a specified price during a 2- to 10-week period.

risk premium   the additional return expected for assuming risk.

risk   potential variability in future cash flows. The likely variability associated with revenue or income streams. Risk can be measured as the standard deviation or beta.

risk-adjusted discount rate   a method of risk adjustment when the risk associated with the investment is greater than the risk involved in a typical endeavor. Using this method, the discount rate is adjusted upward to compensate for this added risk.

risk-free rate of return   the rate of return on risk-free investments. The interest rates on short-term U.S. government securities are commonly used to measure this rate.

safety stock   inventory held to accommodate any unusually large and unexpected usage during delivery time

scenario analysis   a simulation approach for gauging a project's risk under the worst, best, and most likely outcomes. The firm's management examines the distribution of the outcomes to determine the project's level of risk and then makes the appropriate adjustment.

seasoned equity offering, SEO   the sale of additional stock by a company whose shares are already publicly traded.

secondary market   a market in which currently outstanding securities are traded.

secured loan   sources of credit that require security in the form of pledged assets. In the event the borrower defaults in payment of principal or interest, the lender can seize the pledged assets and sell them to settle the debt

security market line   the return line that reflects the attitudes of investors regarding the minimum acceptable return for a given level of systematic risk associated with a security.

selling rate   the rate the bank or the foreign exchange trader "asks" the customer to pay in home currency for foreign currency when the bank is selling and the customer is buying. The selling rate is also known as the asked rate or the offer rate.

sensitivity analysis   a method for dealing with risk where the change in the distribution of possible net present values or internal rates of return for a particular project resulting from a change in one particular input variable is calculated. This is done by changing the value of one input variable while holding all other input variables constant.

short-term notes (debt)   amounts borrowed from lenders, mostly financial institutions such as banks, where the loan is to be repaid within 12 months.

simple arbitrage   trading to eliminate exchange rate differentials across the markets for a single currency.

simulation   a method for dealing with risk where the performance of the project under evaluation is estimated by randomly selecting observations from each of the distributions that affect the outcome of the project and continuing with this process until a representative record of the project's probable outcome is assembled.

sinking-fund provision   a protective provision that requires the firm periodically to set aside an amount of money for the retirement of its preferred stock. This money is then used to purchase the preferred stock in the open market or through the use of the call provision, whichever method is cheaper.

small, regular dividend plus a year-end extra   a corporate policy of paying a small regular dollar dividend plus a year-end extra dividend in prosperous years to avoid the connotation of a permanent dividend.

sole proprietorship   a business owned by a single individual.

spontaneous financing   the trade credit and other accounts payable that arise "spontaneously" in the firm's day-to-day operations

spot transaction   a transaction made immediately in the marketplace at the market price.

stable dollar dividend per share   a dividend policy that maintains a relatively stable dollar dividend per share over time.

standard deviation   a statistical measure of the spread of a probability distribution calculated by squaring the difference between each outcome and its expected value, weighting each value by its probability, summing over all possible outcomes, and taking the square root of this sum.

stock dividend   a distribution of shares of up to 25 percent of the number of shares currently outstanding, issued on a pro rata basis to the current stockholders.

stock repurchase (stock buyback)   the repurchase of common stock by the issuing firm for any of a variety of reasons, resulting in reduction of shares outstanding. Also called **Stock Buyback**.

stock split   a stock dividend exceeding 25 percent of the number of shares currently outstanding.

S-type corporation   a corporation that, because of specific qualifications, is taxed as though it were a partnership.

subordinated debenture   a debenture that is subordinated to other debentures in terms of its payments in case of insolvency.

syndicate   a group of investment bankers who contractually assist in the buying and selling of a new security issue.

systematic risk   (1) the risk related to an investment return that cannot be eliminated through diversification. Systematic risk results from factors that affect all stocks. Also called market risk or nondiversifiable risk. (2) The risk of a project from the viewpoint of a well-diversified shareholder. This measure takes into account that some of the project's risk will be diversified away as the project is combined with the firm's other projects, and, in addition, some of the remaining risk will be diversified away by shareholders as they combine this stock with other stocks in their portfolios.

systematic risk   the risk of the project from the viewpoint of a well-diversified shareholder; this measure takes into account that some of a project's risk will be diversified away as the project is combined with the firm's other projects, and, in addition, some of the remaining risk will be diversified away by shareholders as they combine this stock with other stocks in their portfolios.

tax shield   the element from the federal tax code that permits interest costs to be deductible when computing a firm's tax bill. The dollar difference (the shield) flows to the firm's security holders

taxable income   gross income from all sources, except for allowable exclusions, less any tax-deductible expenses.

temporary investments   a firm's investments in current assets that will be liquidated and not replaced within a period of one year or less. Examples include seasonal expansions in inventories and accounts receivable

tender offer   a formal offer by the company to buy a specified number of shares at a predetermined and stated price. The tender price is set above the current market price in order to attract sellers.

term structure of interest rates   the relationship between interest rates and the term to maturity, where the risk of default is held constant.

terminal warehouse agreement   a security agreement in which the inventories pledged as collateral are transported to a public warehouse that is physically removed from the borrower's premises. This is the safest (though costly) form of financing secured by inventory

terms of sale   the credit terms identifying the possible discount for early payment

times interest earned   a firm's earnings before interest and taxes (EBIT) divided by interest expense. This ratio measures a firm's ability to meet its interest payments from its annual operating earnings.

total asset turnover   a firm's sales divided by its total assets. This ratio is an overall measure of asset efficiency based on the relation between a firm's sales and the total assets.

total revenue   total sales dollars

trade credit   credit made available by a firm's suppliers in conjunction with the acquisition of materials. Trade credit appears in the accounts payable section of the balance sheet.

trade credit   credit made available by a firm's suppliers in conjunction with the

acquisition of materials. Trade credit appears on the balance sheet as accounts payable

transaction exposure   risk associated with transaction exposure, that is, risk associated with contracts on which the monetary value is fixed at a time different from when the transaction is actually completed and will be impacted by exchange rate changes.

transaction loan   a loan where the proceeds are designated for a specific purpose for example, a bank loan used to finance the acquisition of a piece of equipment

transfer price   the price a subsidiary or a parent company charges other companies that are part of the MNC for its goods or services.

translation exposure   risk that arises because the foreign operations of MNCs have financial statements denominated in the local currencies of the countries in which the operation are located. These denominations must be translated into the MNCs home currency at the prevailing exchange rate.

treasury stock   the firm's stock that has been issued and then repurchased by the firm.

triangular arbitrage   arbitrage across three markets for three currencies.

unbiased expectations theory   the theory that the shape of the term structure of interest rates is determined by an investor's expectations about future interest rates.

underwriter's spread   the difference between the price the corporation raising money gets and the public offering price of a security.

underwriting   the purchase and subsequent resale of a new security issue. The risk of selling the new issue at a satisfactory (profitable) price is assumed (underwritten) by the investment banker.

unsecured loans   all sources of credit that have as their security only the lender's faith in the borrower's ability to repay the funds when due

unsystematic risk   the risk related to an investment return that can be eliminated through diversification. Unsystematic risk is the result of factors that are unique to

the particular firm. Also called company-unique risk or diversifiable risk.

variable costs   costs that are fixed per unit of output but vary in total as output changes. Also called **Direct Costs**

venture capital   funds made available to start-up companies or companies in the early stages of business, as well as firms in "turn-around" situations. These are risky investments, generally in innovative enterprises and many times in high-technology areas.

volume of output   a firm's level of operations expressed either in sales dollars or as units of output

weighted average cost of capital   a composite of the individual costs of financing incurred by each capital source. A firm's weighted cost of capital is a function of (1) the individual costs of capital, (2) the capital structure mix, and (3) the level of financing necessary to make the investment

working capital   a concept traditionally defined as a firm's investment in current assets. Compare Net Working Capital

work-in-process inventory   partially finished goods requiring additional work before they become finished goods

yield to maturity   (1) see Term structure of interest rates. (2) The rate of return a bondholder will receive if the bond is held to maturity. (It is equivalent to the expected rate of return.)

yield to maturity   the rate of return a bondholder will receive if the bond is held to maturity.

zero and very low coupon bond   a bond issued at a substantial discount from its $1,000 face value and that pays little or no interest.

zero balance accounts (ZBA)   a cash management tool that permits centralized control over cash outflow while maintaining divisional disbursing authority. Objectives are (1)to achieve better control over cash payments; (2) to reduce excess cash balances held in regional banks for disbursing purposes; and (3) to increase disbursing float

INDEXES

SUBJECT

CORPORATE